Divine Stories

Classics of Indian Buddhism

The flourishing of Buddhism in South Asia during the first millennium of the Common Era produced many texts that deserve a place among the classics of world literature. Exploring the full extent of the human condition and the limits of language and reason, these texts have the power to edify and entertain a wide variety of readers. The *Classics of Indian Buddhism* series aims to publish widely accessible translations of important texts from the Buddhist traditions of South Asia, with special consideration given to works foundational for the Mahāyāna.

The Divyāvadāna

The *Divyāvadāna* is a large collection of Indian Buddhist stories written in Sanskrit from the early centuries of the Common Era. These stories have frequently been used in the moral education of monastics and laypeople, and they have often been considered to be the word of the Buddha himself. These stories have since spread throughout Asia, as both narrative and narrative art, leaving an indelible mark on Buddhist thought and practice. Representations of these stories can be found across Asia, from Kizil in China to Sanchi in India to Borobudur in Indonesia. It is not hyperbole to say that these are some of the most influential stories in the history of Buddhism. This volume contains the first half of the stories in the collection.

CLASSICS OF INDIAN BUDDHISM

Divine Stories

Divyāvadāna

Part 1

Translated by Andy Rotman

Wisdom Publications • Boston

Wisdom Publications, Inc.
199 Elm Street
Somerville MA 02144 USA
www.wisdompubs.org

Library of Congress Cataloging-in-Publication Data

Tripiṭaka. Sūtrapiṭaka. Avadāna. Divyāvadāna. English.
Divine stories : Divyāvadāna / translated by Andy Rotman.
p. cm.
Translated from Sanskrit.
Includes bibliographical references and index.
ISBN 0-86171-295-1 (pbk. : alk. paper)
1. Buddhist literature, Sanskrit—Translations into English. I. Rotman, Andy, 1966– II. Title.
BQ1562.E5R68 2008
294.3'823—dc22

2008016709

12 11 10 09 08
5 4 3 2 1

Cover and interior design by Gopa&Ted2, Inc. Set in Diacritical Garamond Pro 11.75/15.75.

Cover photograph of the Sanchi stūpa, North Gate, by Raja Deen Dayal, circa 1880s, is printed with permission of the Royal Ontario Museum.

Wisdom Publications' books are printed on acid-free paper and meet the guidelines for permanence and durability of the Production Guidelines for Book Longevity of the Council on Library Resources.

Printed in the United States of America.

This book was produced with environmental mindfulness. We have elected to print this title on 30% PCW recycled paper. As a result, we have saved the following resources: 26 trees, 18 million BTUs of energy, 2,327 lbs. of greenhouse gases, 9,659 gallons of water, and 1,240 lbs. of solid waste. For more information, please visit our website, www.wisdompubs.org. This paper is also FSC certified. For more information, please www.fscus.org.

To my teachers,
who have given me so much

विद्या नाम नरस्य रूपमधिकं प्रच्छन्नगुप्तं धनं
विद्या भोगकरी यशःसुखकरी विद्या गुरूणां गुरुः।
विद्या बन्धुजनो विदेशगमने विद्या परा देवता
विद्या राजसु पूज्यते न हि धनं विद्याविहीनः पशुः॥

—Bhartṛhari, *Nītiśataka*

Publisher's Acknowledgment

The publisher gratefully acknowledges the generous help of the Hershey Family Foundation in sponsoring the production of this book.

Table of Contents

Preface

> Meritorious deeds are to be performed.
> Not performing meritorious deeds brings suffering.
> Those who perform meritorious deeds
> can rejoice in this world and in the next.
>
> —The *Divyāvadāna*

IT IS MY HONOR to have this translation of the first half of the *Divyāvadāna* presented as the inaugural volume in the new *Classics of Indian Buddhism* series. I believe that the *Divyāvadāna* is an excellent choice to launch the series, for it encapsulates much of what is distinctive and inspiring about classical Indian Buddhism. Here one is introduced to various people, places, and philosophies of the Middle Country, with the Buddha and his disciples as the star performers. Traveling through the kingdoms of Kośala, Magadha, and beyond, they encounter characters from all walks of life: animal, human, divine, and demonic. In these encounters, they teach the dharma by word and deed, generating faith and new converts, as well as illustrating for the listener the merits of the Buddhist path.

The *avadānas*, or stories, in the *Divyāvadāna* have traditionally served as a means of sharing Buddhist teachings with a broad audience of both monastics and laypeople, and this, too, makes the present volume a good choice for launching the *Classics of Indian Buddhism* series. The aim of the series is to present Buddhist texts that were influential within classical India in a way that both specialists and more general readers can appreciate. To this end, translations are meant to combine accuracy with readability—a tall task indeed. I have tried to succeed on both accounts, providing readers with a glimpse of Indian Buddhism that complements and enriches the perspective gained from more contemporary works.

I first began studying the *Divyāvadāna* as a graduate student at the University of Chicago, and the critical study of the text that began as my dissertation is being published simultaneously by Oxford University Press (Rotman 2008). That book, *Thus Have I Seen: Visualizing Faith in Early Indian Buddhism,* can be read as a companion to this translation. In it I consider faith as a visual practice in Buddhism, and how seeing and faith function as part of overlapping visual and moral economies. In particular, I analyze the mental states of *śraddhā* and *prasāda*—terms rendered as "belief" and "faith" in this translation; how these relate to practices of "seeing" *(darśana)* and "giving" *(dāna);* and what this configuration of seeing, believing, and giving tells us about the power of images, the logic of pilgrimage, and the function of narratives in Buddhist India.

During the last twenty years, scholars with interests ranging from gender, ritual, and cultural studies to visual anthropology, intellectual history, and the sociology of religion have increasingly recognized and made use of the *Divyāvadāna* as an important repository of religious and cultural knowledge (e.g., Lewis 2000; Mrozik 2006; Ohnuma 2007; Rotman 2003b; Schopen 2004; Strong 1992; Tatelman 2000; Wilson 1996). Our work, however, has often been hampered by the lack of reliable translations of the stories in the collection—and in many cases, by the lack of any translation at all. Few of the stories in the *Divyāvadāna* have ever been translated into English, owing to the bias of scholars from previous centuries who favored philosophy over narrative, and owing as well to the text's complex linguistic structure and idiosyncratic vocabulary. The present volume will help remedy this situation by offering translations of the first seventeen of the thirty-eight stories in the *Divyāvadāna*. The remaining stories will be published later in this series in a second volume.

I have tried to be both colloquial and technical in my translations, for these stories are precise legal documents as well as popular tales. Whether they were legends incorporated into Buddhist scholarly discourse or Buddhist didacticism crafted into a folksy idiom, these narratives are certainly more than transcriptions of folklore. They're also fakelore—learned treatises posing as popular tales—and as such they need to be translated meticulously to capture their subtleties. In short, I have tried to refrain from translating this text into what Paul Griffiths (1981) has so poignantly referred to as "Buddhist Hybrid English." My goal has been to produce a document in English that could be studied by specialists and appreciated by nonspecialists, yet still be entertaining to both. I hope I have been successful.

Acknowledgments

So many people and institutions have helped me with this project that I am humbled as I try to catalogue all the teaching, advice, and financial assistance that I have received over the years. At the University of Chicago, I was fortunate to read portions of the *Divyāvadāna* with Sheldon Pollock and Steven Collins. I was also fortunate to learn much about the complexities of Sanskrit from Wendy Doniger, David Gitomer, Paul Griffiths, and Bruce Perry, and from A. K. Ramanujan, quite a lot about the art of translating. From my years in Chicago there are so many friends to thank for so many kindnesses: Nick Collier, Laura Desmond, William Elison, Arnika Fuhrmann, Caitrin Lynch, Erin O'Donnell, Elizabeth Pérez, and Amy Wescott, to name just a few, for kindnesses far too many to list.

In India, those who helped me can primarily be divided by region: those in and around Sarnath and those in Pune. In Sarnath, most of my work was done at the Central Institute of Higher Tibetan Studies, and I am most thankful to Samdhong Rinpoche for facilitating my stay there. During my years at the Institute, I read with K. N. Mishra, who patiently taught me the pleasures of Sanskrit narrative, and also on occasion with Ram Shankar Tripathi, whose breadth of learning in Buddhist Sanskrit was a wonderful resource. I was also fortunate to read Tibetan with many scholars at the Institute: Ramesh Negi and Pema Tenzin, who guided my work through Tibetan translations of Sanskrit avadānas, teaching me Tibetan as well as Sanskrit and Hindi, and Geshe Ngawang Samten and Lobsang Norbu Shastri, who helped me to make sense of many obscure passages, particularly those in part II of this translation, and whose hospitality never ceased to amaze me. I was also fortunate to have the help of John Dunne and Sara McClintock during part of my stay there. Both of them were enormously helpful, not just answering my questions about Tibetan grammar and linguistics, but offering me great warmth and friendship. I am also thankful to Abhaya Jain and his family for offering me food and refuge—a home away from home in Sarnath. In Varanasi, I was especially lucky in this regard, for there I was the recipient of much hospitality. Virendra Singh provided me with impromptu Hindi lessons and a role model for how to be a dedicated teacher. Ramu Pandit helped me so frequently and in so many ways, offering advice, encouragement, and always friendship. Andrea Pinkney offered me enormous kindness and counsel, all with a glorious view of the Ganga. Mat Schmalz (a.k.a. Prem Kumar) was always ready with paan and companionship, and Rabindra Goswami, with wonderful food and even better music.

My debts in Pune are also considerable. J. R. Joshi spent so many afternoons reading Sanskrit with me that I can't possibly calculate how much material we read together or how many of my mistakes he corrected. What M. G. Dhadphale gave to me is also difficult to measure. He taught me about the subtleties of Sanskrit, always answering my most difficult questions with a bravura performance. His enthusiasm for reading Sanskrit literature continues to inspire me. I would also like to thank Shrikant Bahulkar who first directed me to Pune and offered me friendship, guidance, and considerable help in Sanskrit. Others who helped me include Ramchandra Gadgil, who read various avadānas with me, Sucheta Paranjpe, who taught me spoken Sanskrit, and Mandeep Bhander, Jeffrey Brackett, Gayatri Chatterjee, Sunila Kale, Suresh Nadkarni, Christian Novetzke, Parimal Patil, and Michael Youngblood, all of whom made Pune feel like home.

I also have many institutions to thank for the financial support that I received. A Fulbright-Hays grant allowed me to begin this translation project, three years worth of funding from the Rocky Foundation allowed me to extend my tenure in India, and two summers of financial support from Smith College allowed me to travel to India and Professor Dhadphale to travel to the United States for work on final revisions.

Closer to my current home, I'd like to thank my family and friends who have given me so much support. My parents, Arline and Barry, and brothers, Dave and Al, have been incredibly patient with my progress, and their constant encouragement and unstinting confidence have been invaluable. Numerous friends have also been exceedingly generous, with their time, their help, and their comments on my work. Over the years, the Five College Buddhist Studies faculty has kept me motivated and inspired, while those at Northampton Coffee have kept me caffeinated and inspired. I would also like to thank Christian Haskett for assisting me with some difficult passages in the Tibetan, Shilpa Sumant for correcting my errant transliterations, Connie Kassor for helping me organize the index, Paul Harrison for making some great suggestions about better readings and reconstructions, and David Kittelstrom for his sage editorial advice and assistance. Laura Cunningham, Joe Evans, Tony Lulek, Tim McNeill, Rod Meade Sperry, and the rest of the folks at Wisdom Publications also deserve special recognition for their exemplary and tireless work.

Finally, I'd like to thank April Strickland for making my life so full of love and joy. Thanks everybody.

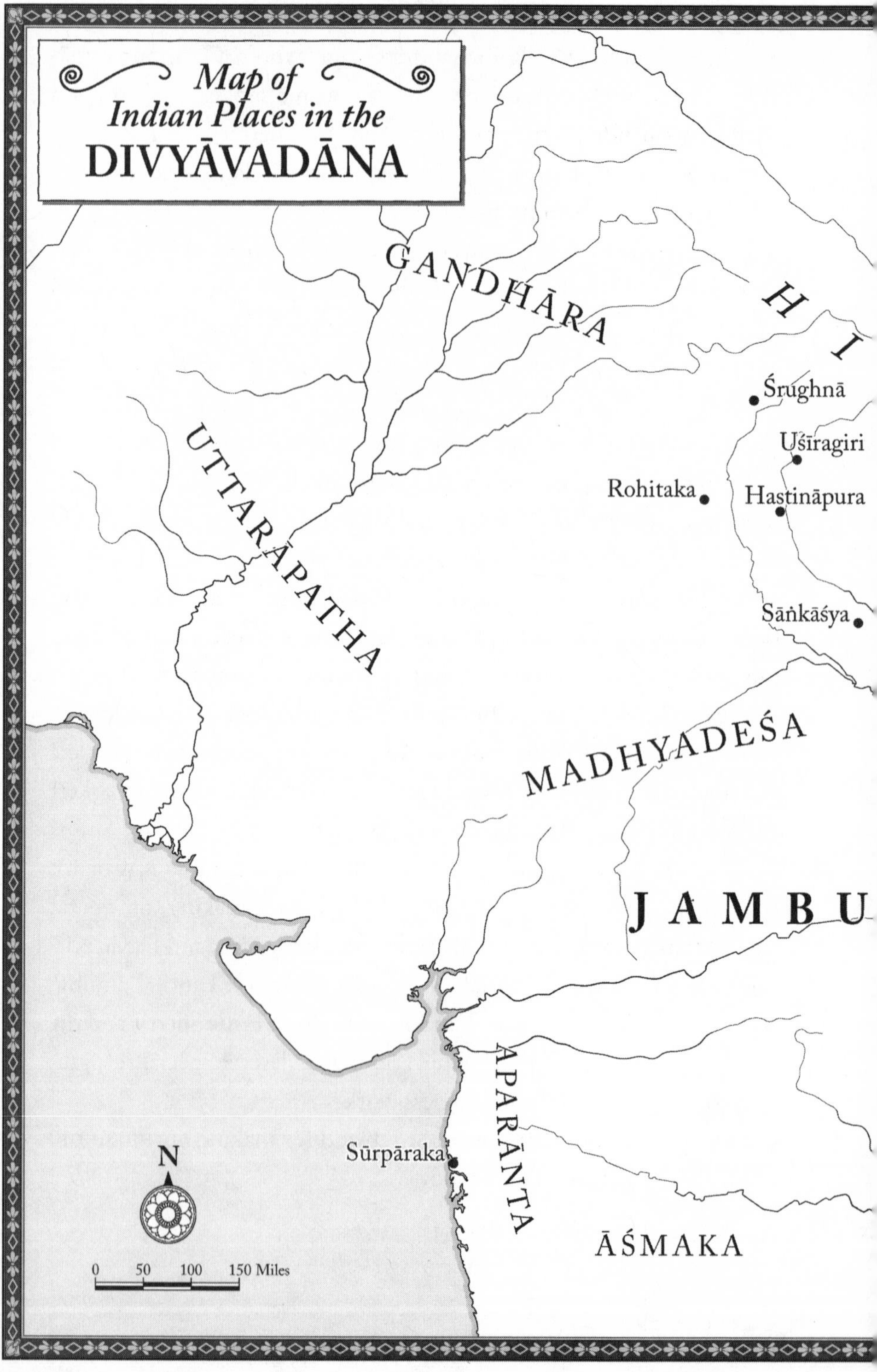

Map of
Indian Places in the
DIVYĀVADĀNA
GANDHĀRA
HI
Śrughnā
Uśīragiri
Rohitaka
Hastināpura
UTTARĀPATHA
Sāṅkāśya
MADHYADEŚA
JAMBU
APARĀNTA
Sūrpāraka
N
ĀŚMAKA
0 50 100 150 Miles

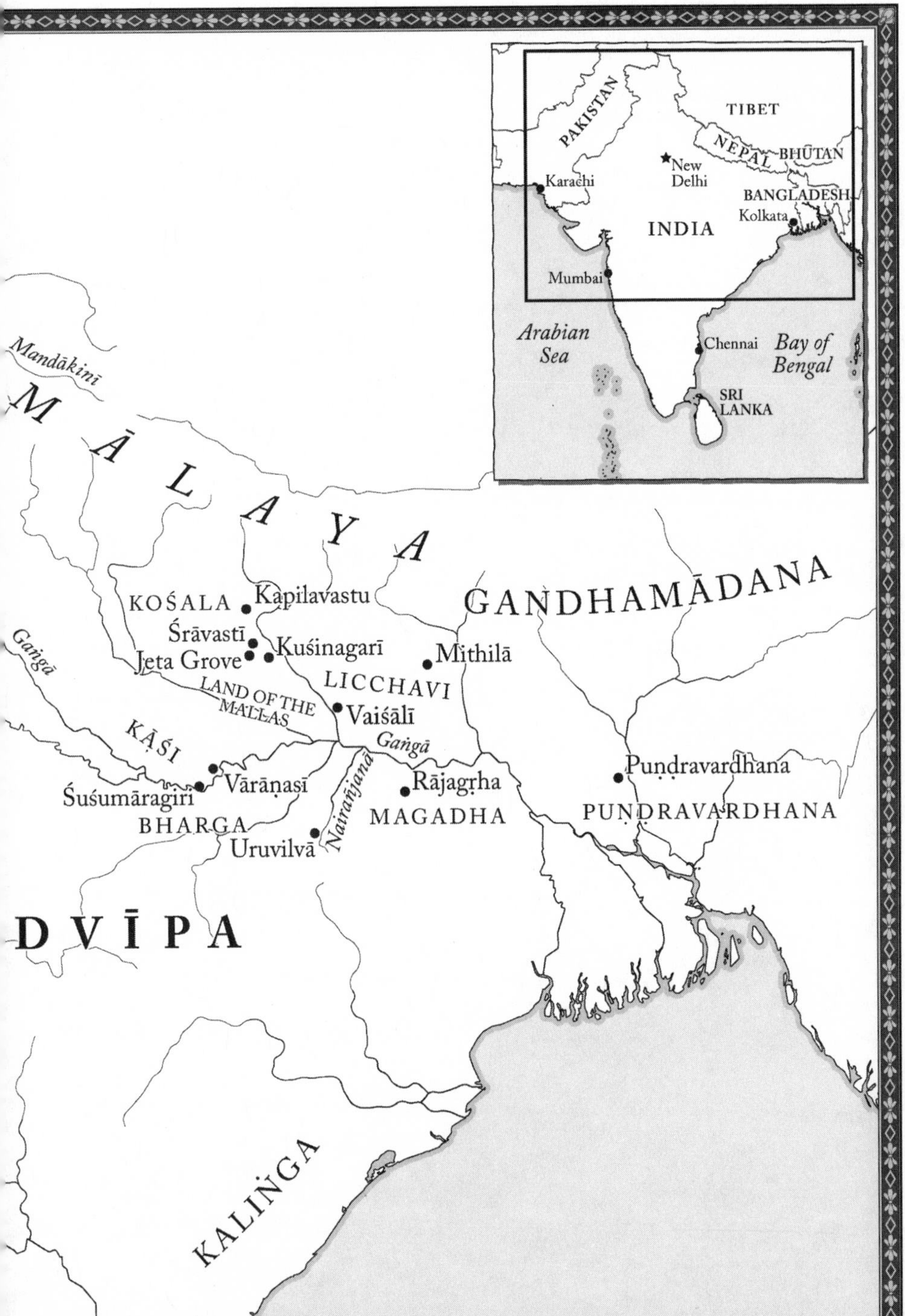

PAKISTAN
TIBET
NEPAL
BHUTAN
New Delhi
Karachi
BANGLADESH
Kolkata
INDIA
Mumbai
Arabian Sea
Chennai
Bay of Bengal
SRI LANKA
Mandākinī
M Ā L A Y A
GANDHAMĀDANA
KOŚALA
Kapilavastu
Śrāvastī
Jeta Grove
Kuśinagarī
Mithilā
LICCHAVI
Gaṅgā
LAND OF THE MALLAS
Vaiśālī
KĀŚI
Gaṅgā
Puṇḍravardhana
Vārāṇasī
Nairañjanā
Rājagṛha
Śuśumāragiri
MAGADHA
PUṆḌRAVARDHANA
BHARGA
Uruvilvā
DVĪPA
KALIṄGA

Technical Notes

Sources

THE FOLLOWING TRANSLATION is based on the Sanskrit edition of the *Divyāvadāna* compiled by E. B. Cowell and R. A. Neil in 1886 (= Divy). I also refer to the edition by P. L. Vaidya from 1959 (= Divy-V). Though for the most part Vaidya's edition just reworks Cowell and Neil's Roman-script edition into Devanāgarī, it does contain some welcome emendations as well as some unfortunate mistakes. I indicate the former in my notes and, on occasion, the latter as well. I include page numbers to Cowell and Neil's edition in square brackets within the translation. Fortunately, this pagination has been retained in the margins of Vaidya's edition. Vaidya's edition is also available online through the Göttingen Register of Electronic Texts in Indian Languages (http://www.sub.uni-goettingen.de/ebene_1/fiindolo/gretil.htm#Divyav), but there Cowell and Neil's pagination has unfortunately not been preserved. In instances when versions of the stories from the *Divyāvadāna* are also contained in the *Mūlasarvāstivāda-vinaya*—in its Tibetan recensions, as in the Derge edition of the Tripiṭaka (= D), or in the Sanskrit of the *Gilgit Manuscripts* (= GM)—I do note some of the major discrepancies and preferable readings. For most of the Tibetan variants, I rely on the work of D. R. Shackleton Bailey (1950, 1951), who has compiled a list of many preferable readings in the Tibetan as well as their Sanskrit equivalents.

In my work on this translation, I have benefited enormously from the labor of previous scholars, though my debt to them can only partially be inferred from my footnotes. Cowell and Neil as well as Vaidya provided useful addenda to their editions, such as glossaries and notes; D. R. Shackleton Bailey, whom I just mentioned, as well as J. S. Speyer (1902) published critical remarks and corrections to the *Divyāvadāna;* Eugène Burnouf (1844), Kenneth Ch'en (1945–47, 1953), Joel Tatelman (2000), and James Ware (1928) produced translations and studies of some of its stories; and Franklin Edgerton compiled a monumental dictionary of Buddhist Hybrid Sanskrit (1993) that contains many references to the text. Their work has made my work much, much easier.

Conventions

In my translation, I have tried to be consistent in following certain conventions. I try to translate prose as prose and verse as verse, though I do offset certain stereotypical passages for ease of reading. I do not translate proper names and place names, though the first time they occur in each story I include a translation in parentheses (if a translation is helpful and/or possible). Some of these names will be found in the glossary, though not the names of the heavens and hells. It would be difficult to say much of anything about many of them other than their relative positioning in the cosmos. I do include a table of the various realms of existence, however, in appendix 2.

Technical terms have been translated when possible, and when not, they have been left in the original Sanskrit and italicized. There are, however, some exceptions. Terms that have been adopted in vernacular English, such as dharma, brahman, and saṃsāra, have been left untranslated and unitalicized, as have terms that appear frequently and are part of the naturalized lexicon of the text, such as arhat, bodhisattva, and tathāgata. Conversely, some rather technical terms have been translated, such as antigod (for *asura*), celestial musician (for *gandharva*), and great snake (for *mahoraga*). Though all of these terms could be usefully glossed, I think that the vernacular understanding of the former and the translations of the latter are sufficient for the reader to understand these stories in their complexity. These technical terms, whether translated or not, can be found in the glossary.

I have added subheadings within the stories to guide the reader. These interpolations, while not part of the text itself, nonetheless appear without brackets. As I note in the introduction, these stories were meant to be recited orally; hence, I understand abbreviations such as "and so on as before" *(pūrvavat yāvat)* to be instructions to the reciter to fill in the requisite missing words. I therefore translate abbreviated passages in full. In my efforts to remain faithful to the voice of text, I have also retained the repetitions and some of the idiosyncrasies of style in the Sanskrit text in my English translation.

In the Sanskrit, Pāli, and Tibetan passages in my notes, the use of [ ] brackets indicates a gap in the text that has been filled. The use of <> brackets indicates a restoration or reconstruction based on another source.

Abbreviations

Aśokāv	*Aśokāvadāna*. See Mukhopadhyaya 1963.
BHSD	*Buddhist Hybrid Sanskrit Dictionary*. See Edgerton 1993.
CPD	*A Critical Pali Dictionary*. See Trenckner et al. 1924–.
D	Derge edition of the Tibetan Tripiṭaka.
Divy	*Divyāvadāna*. See Cowell and Neil 1886.
Divy-V	*Divyāvadāna*. See Vaidya 1959a.
DPPN	*Dictionary of Pali Proper Names*. See Malalasekera 1995.
GM	*Gilgit Manuscripts*. See Dutt 1984.
L	Lhasa edition of the Tibetan Tripiṭaka.
MPS	*Mahāparinirvāṇasūtra*. See Waldschmidt 1951.
ms.	manuscript
mss.	manuscripts
N	Narthang edition of the Tibetan Tripiṭaka.

P	Peking edition of the Tibetan Tripiṭaka.
PSED	*The Practical Sanskrit-English Dictionary*. See Apte 1986.
PTSD	*The Pali Text Society's Pali-English Dictionary*. See Rhys Davids and Stede 1986.
SED	*A Sanskrit-English Dictionary*. See Monier-Williams 1990.
Skt.	Sanskrit
trans.	translator or translated

Sanskrit Pronunciation

The vowels and consonants in Sanskrit listed below are pronounced much like the italicized letters in the English words that follow them. Note that an "h" after a consonant is not a separate letter. It signifies instead that the consonant it follows is to be aspirated. The Sanskrit letters are listed in Sanskrit alphabetical order.

Vowels

a	b*u*t
ā	f*a*ther
i	p*i*t
ī	*see*
u	f*oo*t
ū	dr*oo*l
ṛ	*ri*g
ṝ	no obvious English equivalent; lengthened *ṛ*
e	r*ay*
ai	h*i*gh
o	h*o*pe
au	r*ou*nd

Gutturals (pronounced by slightly raising the back of the tongue and closing off the throat)

k	*k*ick

kh	blo*ckh*ead
g	*g*o
gh	do*gh*ouse
ṅ	ri*ng*

Palatals (pronounced with the tongue lying on the bottom of the mouth)

c	*ch*ip
ch	mat*chh*ead
j	*j*ob
jh	he*dge*hog
ñ	i*n*jury

Retroflex (pronounced by curling the tip of the tongue to touch the roof of the mouth)

ṭ	*t*ry
ṭh	*t*art
ḍ	*d*rum
ḍh	no obvious English equivalent; strongly aspirated *ḍ*
ṇ	ti*n*t

Dentals (pronounced by placing the tip of the tongue against the back of the upper teeth)

t	s*t*ick
th	an*th*ill
d	*d*inner
dh	roun*dh*ouse
n	*n*ice

Labials (pronounced with the lips together)

p	s*p*in
ph	u*ph*eaval
b	*b*in

bh	clu*bh*ouse
m	*m*other

Semivowels, sibilants, and additional sounds

y	*y*es
r	d*r*ama
l	*l*ife
v	a sound between English *v* and *w* (e.g., between *v*ine and *w*ine)
ś	*sh*ip
ṣ	retroflex *ś*
s	*s*ip
h	*h*ope
ṃ	*anusvāra:* nasalizes the preceding vowel
ḥ	*visarga:* an aspiration with an echoing of the preceding vowel (e.g., *devaḥ* as devaha)

Introduction

Ordé's words were the truth. You could see every image,
feel every sensation he described. His metaphors (what we
thought were metaphors) took on a palpable reality that hung
in our nostrils, stuck in the back of our throats.
Halfway through any sermon I would notice that I was
no longer listening to his words but instead experiencing
the phenomena he described.

—Walter Mosley[3]

The *Divyāvadāna* ("Divine Stories") is a large compendium of Indian Buddhist narratives written in Sanskrit from the early centuries of the Common Era whose stories have since spread throughout Asia, as both narrative and narrative art, leaving an indelible mark on Buddhist thought and practice. The stories in the collection were frequently used in the education of both monastics and laity in premodern Asia, exerting a powerful influence as moral exempla and legal precedent, and considered by many to be the word of the Buddha himself. These stories were likewise canonical in their influence on Buddhist art, and representations of them can be found across Asia, from Kizil in China to Sanchi in India to Borobudur in Indonesia. For scores of generations, these stories have been repeatedly recited, reworked, painted, and sculpted. It is not hyperbole to say that these are some of the most influential stories in the history of Buddhism.

The text contains thirty-six avadānas, or stories, along with two sūtras, which chronicle the spiritual development of Buddhist devotees with special attention given to their karmic legacies. There are stories of kings and beggars, monks and prostitutes, gods and hell beings, how they came to their present circumstances, the futures they have created for themselves, and the pivotal role the Buddha and his teachings can play in their betterment.

Generally the avadānas presented here contain three elements: a story in the present tense in which characters discover the benefits of Buddhist practice and meet the Buddha;[4] a story of the past detailing the deeds done by those characters in a previous lifetime that have now come to karmic fruition; and a juncture at which time the Buddha—who is quite literally an "omniscient narrator"—identifies the characters in the story of the past with those in the story of the present.[5] Although some avadānas diverge from this tripartite structure,[6] all of them tend to exemplify the inexorability of karma. As the Buddha often explains at the end of avadānas in the *Divyāvadāna,*

> And so, monks, the result of absolutely evil actions is absolutely evil, the result of absolutely pure actions is absolutely pure, and the result of mixed actions is mixed. Therefore, monks, because of this, you should reject absolutely evil actions and mixed ones as well, and strive to perform only absolutely pure actions. It is this, monks, that you should learn to do.[7]

Yet these avadānas are much more than formulaic accounts of good and bad deeds and their repercussions. They also contain and embody rules and practices integral to a Buddhist identity; in fact, they are amalgams of rules, etiological accounts, and foretellings that function as a complex and interlinking moral code. This is not a moral code, however, that can easily be distilled into pithy maxims, such as the Buddha's observation above about the laws of karma. The moral universe embodied in these stories far exceeds such confines. Its complexity—the dexterity with which certain ideas are brought to life, then developed, nuanced, and imposed, all within a densely textured narrative—prevents such a distillation. These stories may be didactic in their intent, but along the way to their ultimate lessons they create diverse moral worlds, showing different ways of thinking and being, and portray characters interacting and commenting on their engagements with these worlds. The result is an argument—not through philosophical analysis or through poetry, but through really good stories. These are entertaining pieces of literature, with plenty of miracles and adventures across the cosmos, but they are also stories to live by, stories that demonstrate a variety of ways of living and the consequences of such behavior.

Not surprisingly these avadānas have circulated widely since their creation. Many of these stories are included in the monastic code *(vinaya)* of the branch of Buddhists known as the Mūlasarvāstivādins ("The Original Sarvāstivādins"), who flourished in the first half of the first millennium in northwest India. This legal code, which stipulates rules for personal behavior, private property, and social relations, helped regulate monastic and lay conduct in many parts of India for nearly a millennium. This text was then translated into Tibetan in the ninth century, and to this day functions as the only monastic legal code for Tibetan Buddhists, regardless of sectarian affiliation. The text was also translated into Chinese and Japanese, influencing economic policy and commercial relations in China between the fifth and tenth centuries (Gernet 1995) and guiding the revival of Buddhist monasticism in Tokugawa Japan, beginning in the seventeenth century and continuing to the present day (Clarke 2006).

Other avadānas in the text have been equally influential, though preserved in a more circuitous fashion. Versions of the *Pūrṇa-avadāna* ("The Story of Pūrṇa") exist in Pāli, Sanskrit, Tibetan, and

Chinese, and images of the story were also painted in the caves at Ajanta outside of Bombay in the fifth century and in those at Kizil in China in the sixth century.[8] Likewise, the *Śārdūlakarṇa-avadāna* ("The Story of Śārdūlakarṇa"), which will appear in *Divine Stories, Part II*, was translated into Chinese four times between the second and fourth centuries, and then translated into Tibetan in the ninth century (Mukhopadhyaya 1954: xii–xiii). The first part of this story was translated into French by Eugène Burnouf in 1844, and this in turn inspired Richard Wagner, who in 1856 sketched out an opera, *Die Sieger* ("The Victors"), based upon it. Though he abandoned this work, doctrinal elements from it can be found in his great musical drama *Parsifal*.[9] In 1882, Rajendralal Mitra (1981: 223–27) offered a summary of the work in English in his descriptive catalogue of Sanskrit manuscripts in Nepal, and some fifty years later his friend, the Nobel laureate Rabindranath Tagore, wrote a play in Bengali called *Caṇḍālikā* retelling the story.[10] Tagore later transformed the play into a ballet, for which he wrote the music, and it is still performed quite frequently. One performance took place in 1987 at Smith College where I teach and is still preserved on a video recording in our library.

Though most of the stories in the *Divyāvadāna* serve a legal function—to establish rules of ethical behavior, such as the prohibition against drinking, and to explain the etiology and importance of such rules (e.g., Divy 167–93)—the text defies simple genre classification, for the stories in the collection are eclectic. There are passages that focus on monastic regulations, practical wisdom, moral prescriptions, philosophical truth, metaphysical hypotheses, and even astrological calculations, and many such passages can be found in a single story. This hybridity of style may help account for the text's enormous popularity across place and time, among both monastics and laity, and in painting, sculpture, and theater.

Despite this hybridity, the *Divyāvadāna* offers enormous insight into Buddhist history, both subaltern and royal. Many stories in the text depict a practice of faith *(prasāda)* that allows the disenfranchised to accrue enormous reserves of merit, establishing them on the spiritual path and enabling them to leapfrog those who have been more fortunate, if not more virtuous, than they themselves have been (Rotman 2008, chaps. 3–6). This practice allows one with little material wealth, little knowledge, even little interest in Buddhism to embark on the Buddhist spiritual path with the promise of great results. One need only come into visual contact with an object that is an "agent of faith" *(prāsādika),* such as a buddha, an image of a buddha, an arhat, or a stūpa, and faith will invariably arise.

Charged with this form of faith, the downtrodden can make offerings of very little worth or utility and earn huge amounts of merit. The rich, conversely, are excluded from the practice, handicapped by their wealth and success. In the *Nagarāvalambikā-avadāna* ("The Story of a Woman Dependent on a City for Alms"), for example, a leprous beggar woman sees the venerable Mahākāśyapa, who "instills faith in her through his body and his mind,"[11] and then the woman offers him some rice gruel along with her rotten finger, which happened to fall in. From that single deed, however negligible the use-value of the gift, she earns enough merit to be reborn among the gods in Tuṣita heaven. This practice of faith, unattested in philosophical tracts and inscriptions, seems to have offered wonderful promise for the disenfranchised.

As for royalty, the second half of the text *(Divine Stories, Part II)* contains a story cycle that chronicles the life of King Aśoka (stories 26–29), the great ruler who controlled an empire in the third century B.C.E. that stretched across India and westward to present-day Afghanistan and Iran. This biographical account offers an important counter-history of Aśoka, one that complements yet complicates the Aśoka who can be gleaned from his famous edicts (Nikam and McKeon 1959). In this account, Aśoka becomes devoted to making donations to the monastic community, and though he achieves his goal of becoming the greatest giver in Buddhist history, he is "deceived by his own actions"[12] and dies imprisoned and in penury, his sovereignty lost and all his orders countermanded. This troubling story figured prominently in the Buddhist (and Indian) imaginary for millennia, testifying to the great difficulties of being a virtuous king.

The stories in the *Divyāvadāna* also offer great insight into the art-historical record. Representations from the text can be found throughout India, from Sanchi to Bharhut and Mathura, and there are particularly famous stories, such as the *Prātihārya-sūtra* ("The Miracle Sūtra"), which features a miracle competition at Śrāvasti, that are popular at Buddhist sites the world over.[13] In this way, the text functions as a wonderful tool for deciphering and interpreting much Buddhist painting and sculpture. The text's detailed descriptions of constructing stūpas (Divy 244ff.), decorating shrines (Divy 78ff.), and making Buddha images (Divy 547ff.) are all likewise enormously beneficial to art historians.

Although the stories in the *Divyāvadāna* offer significant insight into the history of early Buddhism, the history of the stories themselves is less clear. While the consensus among scholars has been that the *Divyāvadāna* was produced in northwest India between 200–350 C.E. by the Mūlasarvāstivādins,[14] the dating of the text is too complicated to make such a straightforward pronouncement. We don't really know when, where, why, or by whom the text was produced. So how does one put these stories into perspective? While these stories are compelling as literature and moral exempla, how does one make sense of them as part of Buddhism's historical record?

The Historical Value of the *Divyāvadāna*

> These legends [in the *Divyāvadāna*] scarcely contain anything of much historical value.
>
> —Moriz Winternitz[15]

Many of the avadānas in the *Divyāvadāna* seem to be intentionally naturalized and dehistoricized, repeating stock phrases in lieu of historical descriptions of people, places, actions, and events: householders are "rich, wealthy, and prosperous, with vast and extensive holdings...";[16] kingdoms are "thriving, prosperous, and safe, with plenty of food and crowds of people...";[17] young boys are "raised by eight nurses who nourish him with milk, yogurt, fresh butter, clarified butter, butter scum, and other special provisions that are very pure...";[18] and the list goes on. Since the dharma always holds true, regardless of time or place, the reliance on such tropes in these avadānas creates an aura of timeless truth—or perhaps a world of make-believe.[19]

Winternitz's observation in 1913 about the lack of historical value in the stories of the *Divyāvadāna* is not completely untrue, but the great Indologist's insight needs to be put in perspective. Scholarship on the *Divyāvadāna* has often involved attempts to extract historical data directly from its stories, with only somewhat successful results.[20] This scholarship is unfortunately marked by the positivism of its age—a tendency to read texts as unproblematically representing historical events. Even the most erudite scholars have occasionally confused narrative incident with historical fact. In discussing an avadāna from the vinaya of the Mūlasarvāstivādins in which a doctor cures a woman of her venereal disease by inserting a piece of meat into her vagina to entice and capture disease-causing worms, one scholar remarks, "The story speaks for itself regarding the beliefs about venereal diseases and the cures thereof. It reveals the morals of rich, young widows of respectable families, and certainly provides a unique insight into the scruples of a young physician in his relationship with his patients" (Jaini 1989: 220). This practice of attempting to pick out the historical elements from the nonhistorical elements in Buddhist literature—what Louis de La Vallée Poussin called the "subtraction method"—has not, in my opinion, provided an effective methodology for scholarship on the *Divyāvadāna*. It has instead yielded dubious results, proving in part Winternitz's observation.

Yet Winternitz's assessment is limited in its purview. There are more ways to engage with these avadānas than merely trying to extract what Winternitz (1993: 277n4) refers to as "a historical nucleus." History can be narrated, but it can also be embedded within narrative, even among avadānas that share the same structure and stock passages, and that claim to reveal the past and predict the future. While on the surface the avadānas in the *Divyāvadāna* display an unambiguous Buddhist moral discourse—good and bad actions always have, respectively, good and bad results for laymen, monks, and buddhas in the past, present, and future—the reasoning and representation in these stories exposes an intricate and evolving Buddhist world beneath this apparently smooth surface. It is this inscribed representation of Buddhist consciousness—this complex world with its thoughts, desires, practices, and anxieties—which is the historical prize. And the dichotomy between historical and nonhistorical elements is not a principal concern when historicizing consciousness, because everything contained within it—the miraculous and the mundane—is already historically located in time and place.[21]

Even this revised methodological pursuit, however, is thwarted by the complex history of the *Divyāvadāna*. The *Divyāvadāna* is a compendium of stories most likely produced by multiple authors at different times, whose dates and sites of production are uncertain, whose intended audience is unclear, whose expected use is unknown, and whose intertextual relations are unresolved. A review of the manuscript history of the *Divyāvadāna* demonstrates these difficulties quite clearly.

Manuscript History

> It is one thing to analyse footprints, stars, faeces (animal or human), catarrhs, corneas, pulses, snow-covered fields or dropped cigarette ash; and another to analyse writing or painting or speech.
>
> —Carlo Ginzburg[22]

In producing the first Western edition of the *Divyāvadāna* in 1886, E. B. Cowell and R. A. Neil used seven manuscripts of the text. According to Cowell and Neil's (1886: vi) account, they are:

> A. Add. 865 in the [Cambridge] Univ. Library; 258 leaves, 14–15 lines, dated 1873. Fairly written in the ordinary Nepalese character, but not very correct.
>
> B. Our own MS., 283 leaves, 12–13 lines; very incorrect.
>
> C. Our own MS., 274 leaves, 14–15 lines; correct.
>
> D. The MS. given in 1837 by Mr. Hodgson to the Asiatic Society at Paris; 337 leaves, 9 lines. This is a very correct copy, and having been made for Mr. Hodgson more than 50 years ago, it in some places preserves the old text which has since become illegible in the original. Unlike the others, it is written in ordinary Nagari characters...
>
> [-]. The authorities of the Imperial Library at St. Petersburg kindly lent us for a short time their MS. (P.—272 leaves), which is a similar copy to ABC and contains the same omissions in the 34th avadāna.[23]
>
> E. We were also similarly favored with the loan from the Bibliothèque Nationale of [Eugène] Burnouf's own MS...but as this is only like our other MSS. we made no use of it beyond collating it for the first few pages.[24]
>
> F. In Appendix C [Divy 663–70], we have given some account of another MS...in the same Library, which was also kindly lent to us for a time.

Unlike many critical editions of Sanskrit texts, however, their edition is not a piecemeal reconstruction of some would-be original; instead, it is a slightly edited version of the single best manuscript.[25] As editors, they corrected spelling mistakes and offered alternate readings for unclear words and phrases, but as their footnotes make clear, the manuscripts with which they worked were nearly uniform. As Cowell and Neil (1886: vi–vii) observe,

> All these MSS., except F, are thus only modern copies, made with more or less care from one original...Our MS. authorities

> therefore go back immediately to only one source, and our various readings are simply the result of the greater or less care of the respective transcribers.

Cowell and Neil then conclude that this one source is the *Divyāvadāna* manuscript possessed by Pandit Indrānand of Patan, Nepal.

Though Cowell and Neil never saw this original manuscript, the noted Buddhologist Cecil Bendall examined it, and he determined that the text was produced in the seventeenth century (Cowell and Neil 1886: vii). Even if Cowell and Neil had been mistaken about the genealogy of these various *Divyāvadāna* manuscripts, judging from their remarks and those of Bendall, it does seem that none of these *Divyāvadāna* manuscripts was written before the seventeenth century. Considering that there is also no mention of the *Divyāvadāna* by name in any extant Buddhist literature prior to the seventeenth century, the possibility exists that the *Divyāvadāna*, as the particular compilation of stories reproduced in these manuscripts, is not a third- or fourth-century artifact, but a seventeenth-century one.

An analysis of manuscript F, the only text not from this "single" manuscript tradition, shows that it is not simply a variant of the *Divyāvadāna* but a different text entirely. Cowell and Neil (1886: 663) write that the text is "evidently a modern transcript, very inaccurately written," which partially agrees with the other *Divyāvadāna* manuscripts, but which is "plainly a distinct compilation." According to the manuscript extracts that Cowell and Neil provide in their Appendix C, the text refers to itself throughout as the *Divyāvadānamālā* ("Garland of Divine Stories"). Four years previously, in 1882, Rajendralala Mitra (1981: 304–16) had provided an extended summary of another manuscript of the *Divyāvadānamālā,* though the two manuscripts preserve different stories. Most likely, these are examples of a medieval *avadānamālā* or "garland of avadānas"—one of the many anonymous retellings of earlier avadānas, mostly metrical in form with Mahāyāna characteristics, from some time between the fifth and eleventh centuries.[26]

Compounding this problem of the singularity and non-antiquity of *Divyāvadāna* manuscripts is the possibility that the extant *Divyāvadāna* manuscripts are incomplete—that the title "Divyāvadāna" previously referred to a collection of materials other than the one that exists in these manuscripts. The coda "this is found in the glorious *Divyāvadāna*" *(iti śrīdivyāvadāne)* is also found once in manuscript F,[27] the "distinct compilation" that generally refers to itself as the *Divyāvadānamālā,* and in the colophon to the manuscript of the *Vīrakuśāvadāna* ("The Story of Brave Kuśa") preserved in the Cambridge University Library (Add. 1538). The colophon of that text reads, "So ends *The Story of Kuśa* and *The Glorification of the Fast on the Eighth Day of the Waxing Moon,* which were selected from the glorious *Divyāvadāna.*"[28] Neither of these texts, however, occurs in any extant *Divyāvadāna* manuscripts.

In his introduction to the Devanāgarī edition of the *Divyāvadāna* in 1959, P. L. Vaidya explains that these references to the *Divyāvadāna* occur because at one time the *Divyāvadāna* was a larger text that incorporated these and perhaps other avadānas, while the present collection of avadānas in *Divyāvadāna* manuscripts is abridged. To support his hypothesis, Vaidya (1959a: ix) discusses the case of a Newari writer who translated nine of the thirty-two avadānas in the *Vicitrakarṇikāvadānamālā* ("The Garland of Stories of Vicitrakarṇikā") into a separate volume.[29] Vaidya conjectures that perhaps the *Divyāvadāna* underwent a similar phenomenon—a few choice avadānas were selected from the larger collection and codified as a separate text—but that in this case the larger collection of avadānas that existed under the name *Divyāvadāna* was lost and only the abridged collection survived.

But Vaidya could be mistaken. Perhaps these references to the *Divyāvadāna* from other manuscripts simply tell us, as Cowell and Neil (1886: viii) note, that "the name was current in Nepal." The author or scribe of the *Kuśāvadāna* may have employed the name of the *Divyāvadāna* because the text was well known or well regarded at the time, and he wanted his text to share in that acclaim. If this were the case, then the extant *Divyāvadāna* manuscripts would be complete, though representing only one of the manuscript traditions by that name. Also possible is that they are complete but somehow not *really* the *Divyāvadāna*. Although the coda "this is found in the glorious *Divyāvadāna*" occurs at the end of each avadāna and at the end of the work as a whole in the two older manuscripts, D and E, there are no references to the *Divyāvadāna* anywhere in the more recent manuscripts, A, B, and C.[30] Did the scribes of these manuscripts not know what they were copying? Nevertheless, the possibility of Vaidya's claim being correct frustrates any facile hypotheses about the completeness and ordering of the text.

There is also the possibility that the extant *Divyāvadāna* manuscripts contain accretions to what once was a core original. As Vaidya (1959: x) explains,

> The literary qualities of these avadānas vary considerably, and contain elements of old tales in Purāṇa style, tales from the sacred literature, tales modelled on classical style with considerable dramatic element as in no. 26 [the *Pāṃśupradāna-avadāna* ('The Story of a Gift of Dirt')], tales in the semi-classical style as in no. 22 [the *Candraprabhabodhisattvacaryā-avadāna* ('The Story of the Deeds of the Bodhisattva Candraprabha')], and tales in purely classical style as in no. 38 [the *Maitrakanyaka-avadāna* ('The Story of Maitrakanyaka')].[31]

The *Maitrakanyaka-avadāna* in particular appears to be a later composition that, as Michael Hahn (1992: 5) observes, then "found its way into the *Divyāvadāna,* where it does not belong at all."[32] Likewise, the *Prātihārya-sūtra* ("The Miracle Sūtra") and the *Dānādhikaraṇa-mahāyānasūtra* ("The Mahāyāna Sūtra Dealing with the Topic of Giving") are included in the *Divyāvadāna* even though, as is clear from their names, neither are avadānas. In addition, the latter is the only entry that affiliates itself by name with the Mahāyāna. While the *Prātihārya-sūtra* is at least narrative in form, the *Dānādhikaraṇa-mahāyānasūtra* is instead an enumeration of proper gifts and their results—a multiple anomaly to the collection.

Hence, not all the stories in the *Divyāvadāna* necessarily arose at the same time or in the same place or from the same hand. In addition to the possibility that the text contains accretions in the form of extraneous chapters, it is quite possible that the *Divyāvadāna* is "not an original book, but compilations from various sources" (Nariman 1923: 297). It is also possible that the text is an accumulation of narrative fragments from centuries of Indian discourse (Prakash 1970: 285), a collection of pre-Buddhist stories reworked and revised for many generations (Sarkar 1990: 163), or even a compendium of inspired derivations from an earlier canonical tradition (Lamotte 1988: 591).[33] Cowell and Neil (1886: vii, n1) make the point explicitly: "The stories evidently belong to various authors."

Yet, even if, as G. K. Nariman (1923: 293) observes, "the component parts of the...*[Divyāvadāna]* are of unequal age," this doesn't necessarily mean that the *Divyāvadāna* had an original core that was vastly augmented. If Aśvaghoṣa could write his *Buddhacarita* in classical Sanskrit in the first or second century C.E., similarly classical compositions cannot be immediately dismissed as later accretions.[34] In fact, as I will discuss shortly, there is evidence for the early existence of the *Candraprabha-bodhisattvacaryā-avadāna*. Also possible is that the *Divyāvadāna* was compiled using materials of differing antiquities, as if the stories it contains were Buddhist heirlooms from different eras put together by a diligent curator. Perhaps, then, it may be better to think of the *Divyāvadāna* as the work of an editor or compiler, not of an author.[35]

The historicity and unity of the avadānas in the *Divyāvadāna* is further problematized when one examines the occurrence of these avadānas in the Tibetan tradition. Twenty-one of the thirty-eight stories in the *Divyāvadāna* were translated from Sanskrit and are preserved within the Tibetan canon, in the vinaya section of the Kangyur.[36]

These avadānas, however, only occur separately as individual texts; they aren't grouped together, and there is no mention anywhere of a text called the *Divyāvadāna*.

As a final cautionary tale for those trying to understand the *Divyāvadāna* historically, I will offer an account of one more manuscript. In the process of creating this present volume, I was fortunate to make use of a manuscript from the National Archives Nepal, labeled 5819, A120/5–121/1, which contained 303 leaves, fourteen lines to a side. The copy I examined was preserved in microfilm at the Central Institute of Higher Tibetan Studies in Sarnath, and though I'm not able to attest to the manuscript's age, it is written reasonably clearly and accurately in Devanāgarī script. I refer to it throughout this volume as manuscript H.

First there is the question of the text that this manuscript preserves. While the title of the text doesn't occur at the end of any individual stories, at the very end of the manuscript the text identifies itself as the *Divyāvadānamālā*.[37] It does, however, contain some stories that differ from either of the texts by the same name described by Mitra or Cowell and Neil. This manuscript of the *Divyāvadānamālā* and manuscripts A, B, and C of the *Divyāvadāna* contain many nearly identical stories with nearly identical colophons, neither mentioning the name of the collection to which they belong. What differentiates these collections are the other stories that they contain and the final name appended to the manuscript.[38] It is as though the *Divyāvadānamālā* is just the *Divyāvadāna* with bonus stories.

One notable difference between manuscripts A, B, and C and this *Divyāvadānamālā* manuscript is the *treatment* of the colophons at the end of each story. Though they often bear similar inscriptions, those in the *Divyāvadānamālā* manuscript are always crossed out.[39] The one exception is the final colophon, which also includes the name of the manuscript. Since little else in the manuscript is crossed out, why cross out the names of the stories? Did the scribe who copied this manuscript have some question, hesitation, or denial about the names of the stories? And why leave the name of the manuscript intact? Was this a case of repackaging old stories with a new name? Was this an effort to create a new and improved collection?

While manuscript H does contain omissions that suggest a later provenance,[40] it also preserves certain unique and helpful readings,[41] some of which may even predate those preserved in the manuscripts of the *Divyāvadāna*.[42] Then again, maybe this text really is a *Divyāvadāna*—as opposed to *the Divyāvadāna*—regardless of what it says in the final colophon. Yutaka Iwamoto, for example, observes that, to quote Joel Tatelman (2000: 13; cf. Iwamoto 1978: 143–48), "there are only seven stories which occur in every manuscript [of the *Divyāvadāna*] and that, of these, only two, the *Koṭikarṇa-avadāna* and the *Pūrṇa-avadāna*, always occur in the same place, as the first and second stories respectively. In fact, Iwamoto defines *Divyāvadāna* as a collection of Sanskrit avadānas, the first two stories of which are *Koṭikarṇa-avadāna* and *Pūrṇa-avadāna*." By this criterion, the manuscripts of the *Divyāvadānamālā* examined by Cowell and Neil, Mitra, and myself are all versions of the *Divyāvadāna*, rendering that designation less a title than a marker of genre. Perhaps the *Divyāvadāna* was a brand name that marked its contents as valuable, a veritable bible of stories, but only delineated some of the stories that it contained.

A Story of the Stories

The entire map of the lost will be candled.

—AGHA SHAHID ALI[43]

Setting aside these doubts about the unity and historicity of the *Divyāvadāna*, other manuscript evidence exists that demonstrates that some of the avadānas in the form in which they exist in the *Divyāvadāna* date back to the Kuṣāṇa or Gupta periods. The *Śārdūlakarṇa-avadāna* was first translated into Chinese sometime circa 148–70. Furthermore, fragments from the *Svāgata-avadāna* ("The Story of Svāgata") (Divy 183.21–185.7) and the *Saṅgharakṣita-avadāna* ("The Story of Saṅgharakṣita") (Divy 336.22–339.5), which were found in Gilgit, in what is now northern Pakistan, in 1931, have been dated to approximately the sixth century (Lévi 1932: 16–20; cf. Bapat 1949). Also among the manuscript finds in Gilgit is a fragmentary avadāna collection that contains excerpts from six avadānas found in the *Divyāvadāna*. As Jens-Uwe Hartmann (1980: 251) notes, "The homogeneous script, the identical number of lines on all the folios, and—possibly—the corresponding size of the leaves all suggest that the different texts formed part of one collection." Fortunately, one manuscript folio contains both the end of the *Sahasodgata-avadāna* ("The Story of Sahasodgata") and the beginning of the *Candraprabhabodhisattvacaryā-avadāna* (Vira and Chandra 1995: f. 1487), linking these avadānas in the same order as they occur in the *Divyāvadāna* (nos. 21–22), though their date is uncertain. Less fortunately, however, as Hartmann (1980: 251) observes, "the stories, in so far as they are complete, give neither titles nor colophons, and there is no hint either as to the title of the collection, if any, or to the numbers of the preserved *avadāna*s."

In recent years, there have been additional large finds of manuscripts from Pakistan and Afghanistan that contain avadānas. The British Library Collection contains many collections of stories, dating from the first or second century C.E., "most of which," as Richard Salomon (1999: 35) notes, "are explicitly labeled in the manuscripts as 'avadānas.'" Representatives from the *Divyāvadāna* are unfortunately not among them. The Schøyen Collection, housed in Norway, which is even larger than the British Library Collection, also contains avadāna materials. In this collection, there are various fragments, perhaps from the sixth century, of all four avadānas in the Aśoka cycle (Wille 2000), as well as individual fragments from the *Dānādhikaraṇa-mahāyānasūtra* and the *Jyotiṣka-avadāna* ("The Story of Jyotiṣka") (Baums 2002).[44] Hence, although there is no complete *Divyāvadāna* manuscript from before the seventeenth century, there are significant indications that many of the stories in the *Divyāvadāna* have been circulating independently from the early centuries of the Common Era.

There is also significant linguistic and textual evidence that connects the stories in the *Divyāvadāna* with the Mūlasarvāstivādins. Most notably, more than half of the stories in the *Divyāvadāna* also occur in a similar form in the *Mūlasarvāstivāda-vinaya* (Huber 1906; Lévi 1907), an immense collection of monastic law and moral tales that is preserved partially in Sanskrit (Dutt 1984), more fully in Tibetan and Chinese translations, and was compiled perhaps as early as the first or second century C.E.[45]

Since Edouard Huber (1906) first made this observation, Sylvain Lévi (1907), Heinrich Lüders (1926), and D. R. Shackleton Bailey (1950) have all concluded with him that these stories in the *Divyāvadāna* were deliberate abridgments of their counterparts in the *Mūlasarvāstivāda-vinaya*. Though Jean Przyluski (1929) came to the opposite conclusion, suggesting as well that both might come from an earlier and no longer extant source, Satoshi Hiraoka (1998) has argued quite convincingly in the tradition of Huber that the stories in the *Divyāvadāna* that also appear in the *Mūlasarvāstivāda-vinaya* are reworked versions of the latter. With just a few exceptions, the stories in the *Divyāvadāna* even follow the same sequence as their counterparts in the *Mūlasarvāstivāda-vinaya* (Panglung 1981: xiv–xvii). In short, someone (at some time) abridged some stories from the *Mūlasarvāstivāda-vinaya* and then compiled them together with stories from other vinayas, a few sūtras, and some other favorite narratives to create a "greatest hits" compilation known as the *Divyāvadāna*.[46]

Since many of the stories in the *Divyāvadāna* have their origin in the *Mūlasarvāstivāda-vinaya,* there are, not surprisingly, references to Mūlasarvāstivādin texts,[47] strongholds,[48] and perhaps doctrines,[49] though such proprietary claims are put into doubt because of the unclear relationship between the Mūlasarvāstivādins and the Buddhist sect known as the Sarvāstivādins. In the *Śikṣāsamuccaya* ("Compendium of Training"), for example, an extract from the

Cakravartivyākṛta-avadāna ("The Story of One Foretold to Be a Wheel-Turning King"), which occurs in the *Divyāvadāna,* is introduced as a Sarvāstivādin text: "This is recited by the noble Sarvāstivādins."[50] This could signify that this story was shared by the Sarvāstivādins and the Mūlasarvāstivādins, that the Sarvāstivādins wanted to claim it for themselves, or that the author of this passage considered the Mūlasarvāstivādins to be somehow the same as the Sarvāstivādins and not a separate sect. Much has been written about the relationship between the Mūlasarvāstivādins and the Sarvāstivādins—who was in Mathurā, who was in Kashmir, who came first, etc.[51] I will nevertheless recuse myself, following Lambert Schmithausen (1987: 379), from making any definitive statements about the relationship between these two schools. As he remarks,

> I cannot enter into the controversial question whether the Mūlasarvāstivādins were, originally, a Vinaya school of the Mathurā area, completely independent of the Sarvāstivādins (as advocated by Frauwallner on the basis of a comprehensive and thorough investigation of the Vinayas) or only a comparatively late offshoot of the Sarvāstivāda school with a Vinaya that is nothing but an enlarged and remodelled version of the Vinaya of the Sarvāstivādins (as Lamotte and Iwamoto seem to think, in opposition to Bareau and Gnoli who assert that the Vinaya of the Mūlasarvāstivādins looks more archaic than that of the Sarvāstivādins).[52]

And so, considering how little is known about the Mūlasarvāstivādins outside of the contents of their voluminous monastic literature, and since the possibility still exists that the *Divyāvadāna* was constructed not by the Mūlasarvāstivādins but by some other Sarvāstivādin sect or, more doubtfully, some other Buddhist sect at some later date,[53] it is more judicious to treat the *Divyāvadāna* not as a text created exclusively within a Mūlasarvāstivādin framework, but as one created more generally within the context of early Indian Buddhist monastic culture—probably during the period of Sarvāstivādin Buddhism in Northwest India during the first half of the first millennium.[54]

This context for interpreting the *Divyāvadāna* is, unfortunately, rather vague. But there are other contexts for making sense of the text. While it may not be possible to locate the origin of the avadānas in the *Divyāvadāna* or even the compilation of the text as a whole in a historical place or moment—for most avadānas resist such efforts—it may be possible to interpret these stories within the context of their own telling. Accounts of stories being told and heard in the *Divyāvadāna* may offer insight into the sociology and mechanics of how avadānas were used.

An Avadāna of Avadānas

"Everything comes from somewhere," Haroun reasoned, "so these stories can't simply come out of thin air..."

—Salman Rushdie[55]

Although there is a degree of guesswork in determining the origin and use of the avadānas in the *Divyāvadāna,* we do know something about the status of avadānas among the Mūlasarvāstivādins. They came to identify certain stories as avadānas, constituents of a new division of Buddhist literature (Thomas 1933),[56] and they also created independent avadāna texts, such as the *Sthavirāvadāna* ("The Story of the Elders") and the *Avadānaśataka* ("The One Hundred Stories").[57] But why did the Mūlasarvāstivādins suddenly elevate the avadāna, a mode of composition long in circulation and yet not discussed in any traditional commentaries, to a new and canonical genre?

A number of possible explanations for the uses of these avadānas have been offered. They may have been used (1) to popularize Buddhism—"Aśoka's preference for the life of an ideal *upāsaka* [lay disciple] as against that of a monk may have stimulated the Buddhist monks to devise ways and means to popularize their religion, and as the result of the efforts of the monks in this direction, we have the large number of the jātakas and avadānas" (Dutt 1930: 20); (2) to inspire the laity—"As it is evident from the subject-matter of most of these stories, the avadāna purports to kindle faith and devotion in the ordinary believer by laying before him the fruits of good acts...and the bad consequences of evil acts" (Perera 1966: 397); (3) to educate the common people—"But the common people could not be made familiar with the glorious deeds of the world-famed heroes *(bodhisattvas)*; they could not understand [that] what the great hero had done they too could do. So there was a need for something humbler, i.e., the glorious deeds of some ordinary humans with whom the common folk could make identity" (Sharma 1985: 19); (4) to educate young monks—"These avadānas...[were] put together for the ease and convenience of instruction of young monks" (Vaidya 1959a: xii); or (5) to offer preliminary teachings—"One begins to teach dharma by telling *avadāna* stories" (Tatelman 2000: 12).

While these hypotheses may very well be true, recent finds of avadāna manuscripts provide additional data that suggests a more specific sociology of practice. As Richard Salomon (1999: 36) observes, the terse form of the avadānas in the British Library Collection, with their instructions to expand upon various abridgments in their own specific idiom,[58] "give the impression that the texts are merely skeletons or outlines, which were evidently meant to be filled in and expanded by the reader or reciter." This is also the case with both the *Divyāvadāna* and *Avadānaśataka*. Both contain numerous stereotypical passages that are often abridged with the expression "and so on as before" *(pūrvavat yāvat)*.[59]

Yet, as Salomon (1999: 35) also notes with regard to the British Library Collection, "an unusual feature of the texts of this genre is that nearly all of them are written in the same distinctive large hand." Salomon (1999: 36; cf. 1999: 54) concludes from this that the scribe "evidently was a specialist in this genre," lending support to the hypothesis of John Strong (1985: 869) that there was "a general class of specialists concerned with avadāna literature."[60] If this is the case, then the avadānas in the British Library Collection were for the use of avadānists, for only they could properly follow the terse instructions found in the manuscripts, and they were also copied and preserved by avadānists. Furthermore, they were also, it seems, composed by avadānists. Unlike their counterparts in the *Divyāvadāna,* which are primarily simplified narratives from the vinaya, "the specific content of these stories does not correspond to any previously known material" (Salomon 1999: 136).

This hypothesis that these manuscripts were composed, preserved, and used by avadānists is further supported by an examination of the genres represented therein. Among the fragments of the British Library Collection of Gandhāran manuscripts, there is "a total absence...of vinaya texts of any kind" (Salomon 1999: 163), and the same is true among Central Asian Sanskrit Buddhist manuscripts before the fifth century C.E. (Sander 1991: 142; cited in Salomon 1999: 163).[61] This raises the possibility that, as Salomon (1999: 163) notes,

> At this relatively early stage of the written preservation and transmission of Buddhist texts, not all texts or genres of texts had yet been set down in writing...It appears that at this point in the development of the written tradition of Buddhist texts, writing was viewed primarily as a practical matter; texts were set down in written form only when this seemed necessary or useful, as for instance when, for one reason or another, a text was not firmly set in memory or was perceived to be in danger of being forgotten.

Considering the number of specialized abbreviations in the avadānas of the British Library Collection, it seems unlikely that these avadānas were written down because they were "perceived to be in danger of being forgotten"; instead, according to Salomon (1999: 165), "the Gāndhārī avadānas seem to be more in the nature of notes of memory aids than of formal written texts. In other words, they fall somewhere between the strict division of written versus oral texts, serving, evidently, as written supplements to oral deliveries."[62] In short, these avadānas had a different mode of preservation from vinayas, indicating quite possibly a different status or function, and this difference may very well have involved oral recitation.

Yet the avadānas in the *Divyāvadāna* are not new compositions like those in the British Library Collection, and the reason for their compilation poses a different mystery. Following the traditions recorded by Kumārajīva, Seng-hu, and Hui-chiao during the fourth and fifth centuries C.E., Lamotte (1988: 174) surmises that various avadānas were excerpted from the Mūlasarvāstivādin vinaya because the latter had become unwieldy. As Strong (1985: 876) explains,

> Apparently, the vinayadharas [vinaya masters] of Upagupta's time could simply no longer handle the load; they opted to cut out the avadānas from their repertoire, but, I would argue, they did so not because they were thought to be nonessential or of dubious status canonically, but because there were other oral specialists around—the avadānists—who were already taking charge of them.

Following Salomon's notions about the orality of avadānas and Strong's hypothesis about the avadāna specialist, I would like to suggest another possibility for the creation of the *Divyāvadāna* and the use of its stories. Here the text itself is our best guide, for it describes the telling of stories in detail—who tells them and to whom, and when they are recounted and where.[63] Although I don't claim that these accounts are historically referential, they do offer traces of past beliefs from which, it seems, a number of storytelling settings and audiences can be identified.

Stories about Telling Stories

This was how she would learn about the world, in sentences at meals; other people's distillations amid her own vague pain, dumb with itself. This, for her, would be knowledge—a shifting to hear, an emptying of her arms, other people's experiences walking through the bare rooms of her brain, looking for a place to sit.

—Lorrie Moore[64]

In the stories in the *Divyāvadāna,* the Buddha, and occasionally one of his disciples: (1) tells a story to the monastic community to resolve their doubts and questions; (2) tells a story to a lay follower or audience who happens to approach him; or (3) tells a story to a lay audience in a lay disciple's home after having been invited there for a meal and consuming it. In the first instance, the stories that are told are often accounts of someone's deeds, both previous and future, that are integral to his or her karmic history. In the second instance, the stories that are told are often referred to as "discourses on the dharma."[65] And in the third instance these stories are referred to as either "discourses on the dharma"[66] or "dharma stories."[67] One suspects that Buddhist monks had a penchant for expounding, telling stories rather than giving moral directives or performing rituals. This is even parodied in the *Saṅgharakṣita-avadāna,* with Buddhist monks being shunned and chastised for being "great talkers."[68]

Now, this last scenario—a monk is invited to a layperson's home for a meal, consumes the food offered to him, and then offers some instruction in the dharma—is well represented in the *Divyāvadāna,* and examining the rules for lay and monastic behavior that are preserved in other Buddhist sources, one finds regulations that, when enacted, are in accordance with it. In the *Aṅguttara-Nikāya*, for example, among the duties prescribed for a Buddhist householder are inviting monastics to one's home for a meal (ii, 65) and listening to dharma teachings (iv, 209).[69] Considering that householders composed a large percentage of lay disciples (Dutt 1940: 166) and were the group most responsible for providing the monastic community with its material needs (Chakravarti 1987: 65–93), it is not surprising that this relationship between householders and the monastic community would be well regulated and well represented.

Intrinsic to this relationship is an exchange—laypeople offer food to monastics, and monastics in turn offer those laypeople merit. This "food for merit" exchange is made explicit in the *Sahasodgata-avadāna*. A solitary buddha who is traveling through the countryside arrives at a park on the outskirts of a town but then decides to go elsewhere. A householder sees him and says,

> Noble one, why are you turning back? You are in want of food, and I, of merit. Take up residence here in this park and I'll support you with alms without interruption.[70]

But on such occasions, with food given and merit assigned, if dharma teachings were to be given, which ones would they be? It is often said that the Buddha, after finishing a meal that had been offered to him, "instructs, incites, inspires, and delights"[71] the listener with dharma stories. This indicates that these stories were instructive and entertaining, but suggests little else with regard to their specific content.

Two passages in the *Dharmaruci-avadāna* ("The Story of Dharmaruci") offer some additional insight. Early in the story, it is said that as a baby, Dharmaruci was insatiably hungry and thirsty and could only be appeased when listening to the stories told by monastics:

> From time to time monks and nuns would enter that house for alms and tell a roundabout story. The boy would listen to that roundabout story, and at that time he wouldn't cry. He'd listen attentively and silently to their stories about lis-

> tening to the dharma. When the monks and nuns would depart, he would again experience the suffering of thirst and begin to cry.[72]

In this case, the monastics tell a "roundabout story" *(parikathā),*[73] an apparent variant of the "dharma story" *(dharmīkathā).* Though its exact meaning is unclear, it may mean "involved story," "intricate story," or even "story cycle." More clear, however, is the notion of listening to stories about listening to the dharma. This involves the mimetic act of listeners listening to stories of others doing what they themselves are already doing.

Later in the story, in response to some monks' queries about Dharmaruci's insatiable hunger, the Buddha asks them, "Do you want to hear a dharma story about the former karmic bonds of Dharmaruci?"[74] They assent, and the dharma story that the Buddha tells is a chapter in Dharmaruci's dharma history when he was a powerful fighter capable of battling a thousand men. These "karmic bonds" *(karmaploti)* are, in fact, the "connective thread" *(ploti)* that ties together one's karmic history; hence the dharma story in this instance is a dharma case study.

But what were these roundabout stories, the dharma biographies, which were presumably instructive and entertaining, that featured characters benefiting from listening to the dharma?

The most likely answer is—these avadānas themselves. The structure of avadānas, with their stories of the present, then of the past and future, all unfolding in an interactive process between teller and listener is far more roundabout than jātaka tales or stories in the sūtra literature. Furthermore, the instructive value of these stories is thematized within the stories themselves, most notably in what I referred to previously as the first scenario. On those occasions, the past and future stories that the Buddha tells are prompted by a query from some inquisitive monks who are unsure how a particular event came about or how a particular prediction will come true. As it is frequently said, "Those monks in doubt asked the Lord Buddha, the remover of all doubts..."[75] And, one presumes, since the Buddha is here introduced as "the remover of all doubts," his stories have precisely that effect. As Ānanda says to the Buddha on multiple occasions,

> O you who are resolute, an ascetic, and an excellent victor,
> you know at once with your mind the desires of your listeners.
> Destroy their doubts that have arisen, O best of sages,
> with words excellent, enduring, and virtuous.[76]

Instructive as well is the way that many avadānas exemplify the utility of making offerings to monastics, with the donor being promised great rewards in the future.[77] Listening to such stories would naturally reinforce the "food for merit" exchange, a give-and-take that is as essential for the physical survival of monastics as it is for the karmic development of the laity.

Since most avadānas also feature the "doubt removal" scenario, listening is necessarily thematized, for the very structure of these avadānas involves monks listening to stories that the Buddha tells. The above extract from the *Dharmaruci-avadāna* testifies to this experience—Dharmaruci listens to a story about others listening to the dharma. And since the Buddha can remove the doubts of his monks, shouldn't his avadānas, or even his stories within avadānas, do the same for the listener? Would one be in error if they didn't? Hence, shouldn't any doubts about the utility of the "food for merit" exchange between monastics and the laity be removed by listening to the numerous stories that exemplify the utility of making offerings to monastics, with the donor being promised great rewards in the future? Perhaps, then, the reason that the content of the dharma stories told in the "post-mealtime" scenario is never revealed is that these stories are the avadānas themselves. In short, the dharma stories alluded to are already being heard.

In most Buddhist vinaya literature, the description of a monastic rule is accompanied by a story recounting the event that necessitated the enactment of that rule, but in the *Mūlasarvāstivāda-vinaya,* far more stories are included, creating an even stronger connection between the establishment of rules and the telling of stories. In the *Divyāvadāna,* this connection between rules and stories is clarified by placing both within a larger frame-story that narrativizes the entire process. A common scenario finds the Buddha telling a story to the monastic community in order to explain a particular phenomenon and to exemplify proper behavior, but all of this is placed within a larger story depicting the process of educating the monastic community. This larger story allows the audience to view the process of rule-giving and storytelling within a more elaborate context. For example, unlike the version of the Svāgata story in the Pāli vinaya (*Vinayapiṭaka* ii, 108–10) which recounts the drunken exploits of Svāgata and the rule discerned from this story (i.e., drinking liquor is an offense requiring expiation), the *Svāgata-avadāna* includes the story of the Buddha telling that larger Svāgata story—the tale of his drunken exploits and the rule against drinking—as well as a sequence in which the monks question those actions of Svāgata. Then, in response, the Buddha tells a story about Svāgata's past life as a householder when he both abused and served a solitary buddha and the results of these actions.

In the Pāli, vinaya rules appear to be determined from stories: a story is told, a judgment is offered, a rule is established. In the *Mūlasarvāstivāda-vinaya* and in the *Divyāvadāna,* rules are also determined from stories, but then secondary stories are used to explain the phenomena and karmic connections within those primary stories. These layered stories allow one to view the process of how rules are taught, through stories of origin and stories of explanation, and to see how the intertwining of stories and rules can allow stories to embody rules and, perhaps, even supplant them. In the *Divyāvadāna,* there are examples of rules being determined from stories, as in the Svāgata story in the Pāli vinaya, and even more examples of rules and stories being intertwined, with the latter functioning as something between a complementary moral code and a contentious one, what A. K. Ramanujan

(1999: 446) referred to as a "counter-system."[78] But more often stories themselves seem to replace rules, as though the latter was the preferred form of moral guidance, in style if not in content. These stories offer moral exempla, possibilities for ethical action that, as Ramanujan (1999: 456) explains of oral literature, provide "forms, presumptions of meaning, that are filled out by later living." One wonders if this is what the reciters of avadānas had in mind when, later in the *Dharmaruci-avadāna,* the monks respond to the Buddha's offer to tell a story about Dharmaruci's former karmic bonds. As they say, "Let the Blessed One tell the monks a dharma story about Dharmaruci. Hearing such a story from the Blessed One, the monks will keep it in mind."[79]

Now if a Buddhist monk in premodern India were to tell a didactic story to educate a group of householders, what kind of story would he tell? What kind of story would he have known? A Mūlasarvāstivādin monk, for example, would presumably have known stories from his vinaya. Considering the strong connection between rules and stories in his vinaya and the critical position of the vinaya to Buddhist identity—disputes over vinaya rules were the main cause of schisms among early Buddhist sects, and differences over vinaya rules the fundamental distinction between these groups (Lamotte 1988: 290–92)—a Mūlasarvāstivādin monk would most likely have learned vinaya stories while learning the rules that defined his order.[80] Certainly one of the fundamental distinctions between the Mūlasarvāstivādins and the Sarvāstivādins was the content of their respective vinayas. Considering as well that vinaya stories contain the genealogy of problems and their solutions (do not commit such-and-such an act, which such-and-such a person previously performed), a narrativization of this process would have provided those uneducated in Buddhist monasticism with a mimicked account of the educational process itself.

All this is not to say definitively that the *Divyāvadāna* was the creation of Mūlasarvāstivādin monastics who needed dharma tales to tell, particularly on those occasions when they were invited to someone's house for a meal, but this possibility is given significant support.

This hypothesis would also explain the strong genealogical connection between the avadānas in the *Divyāvadāna* and their counterparts in the *Mūlasarvāstivāda-vinaya,* as well as the erasure and marginalization of some of the legal content in the *Divyāvadāna* versions of these stories. For example, while the Meṇḍhaka story in the *Mūlasarvāstivāda-vinaya* contains a technical discussion regarding the propriety and mechanics of accepting certain kinds of offerings (see appendix 1), this section is elided completely in the *Divyāvadāna.* A similar elision also occurs in the *Svāgata-avadāna.* As Satoshi Hiraoka (1998: 423–24) observes,

> It seems virtually certain that...the compiler of the Divy. skillfully omitted the sections of the establishment of the Vinaya rule and the commentary on it, directly connecting the part quoted above with the story of Svāgata's past. Thus he produced a story that looks natural and preserves the typical style of an avadāna.

Taking all of this information into account, perhaps the development of these avadānas can be explained as follows: With the routinization and increase in lay-monastic interactions, or at least with the desire for such ends, there came the need for good, easily accessible stories to be told on those numerous occasions when monks were enjoined to discourse on the dharma.[81] Since these monks were familiar with the stories found in their vinaya, they reworked these very narratives—transforming them from accounts of the origins of monastic rules to accounts of the workings of karma—to meet the didactic needs of preaching to novice monks and lay disciples. One can speculate that since these stories were not easily accessible for monks to learn and consult because of the tremendous size as well as lack of systemization and revision of the *Mūlasarvāstivāda-vinaya* (Schopen 1994b: 69), they were eventually anthologized into more accessible volumes.[82] It is also possible that these stories were frequently recited, and as the need to recount them grew, they were codified into their own collections to canonize those stories that were considered appropriate or efficacious to tell.[83] These stories became known as avadānas and, judging by the name of the present collection, the *Divyāvadāna*—"Divine Stories"—this collection was one of great importance, or at least had pretensions to be so. Regardless of whether this text was really important, or merely self-important, it offers the reader an excellent and entertaining way of engaging with early Buddhist moral thought.

A Summary of the Stories

1. The Story of Koṭikarṇa
Koṭikarṇa-avadāna
The caravan leader Śroṇa Koṭikarṇa encounters people from his hometown who have been reborn as hungry ghosts and sees them experiencing the results of their karma. Asked to intercede on behalf of their family members who aren't following the true dharma, Śroṇa Koṭikarṇa returns home, does as he has been instructed, and eventually becomes a monk. Śroṇa Koṭikarṇa later meets the Buddha and, following the directions of his instructor, the venerable Mahākātyāyana, asks him questions about monastic regulations.

2. The Story of Pūrṇa
Pūrṇa-avadāna
A wealthy merchant with three sons suffers a serious illness before being cured by a slave girl. As per her request, she bears him a child, who is named Pūrṇa. This son of a slave girl is mistreated by some of his half-brothers, and the household soon splits apart. Though Pūrṇa is now destitute, he is diligent and clever, and in time becomes a wealthy merchant and friend to the king. Pūrṇa eventually becomes a monk, receives teachings from the Buddha, and travels to Śroṇāparāntaka. The rest of the monastic community later meets him in Sūrpāraka, where they have been invited for a meal.

3. The Story of Maitreya
Maitreya-avadāna
The Buddha has the sacrificial post of King Mahāpraṇāda unearthed so that it can be glimpsed by the monastic community, but the monk Bhaddālin barely notices it. In response to questions about Bhaddālin's behavior, the Buddha tells the story of how and why in the past King Mahāpraṇāda disposed of the sacrificial post. The Buddha then tells a story about the future concerning the Buddha Maitreya and the disappearance of the post, and then another story about previous events that will culminate in Maitreya becoming a buddha.

4. The Story of a Brahman's Daughter
Brāhmaṇadārikā-avadāna
A brahman's daughter sees the Buddha and, filled with faith, offers him some barley meal as alms. The Buddha then explains that as a result of her offering she will eventually become a solitary buddha. The woman's husband hears of this prediction and approaches the Buddha in angry disbelief. The Buddha, however, proves to him the truth of his words, and the brahman becomes a stream-enterer.

5. The Story of a Brahman's Panegyric
Stutibrāhmaṇa-avadāna
A brahman sees the Buddha and, filled with faith, praises him with a verse. The Buddha then explains that as a result of his offering he will eventually become a solitary buddha. In response to questions about this course of events, the Buddha tells the story of how this brahman in a previous life had likewise offered a verse of praise.

6. The Story of a Brahman Named Indra
Indrabrāhmaṇa-avadāna
A brahman named Indra is told by the Buddha where he can find a post of sandalwood the height of the Buddha. The brahman retrieves it and, with the permission of the Buddha, uses it to celebrate a festival that comes

to be known as the Indramaha. In what follows, the Buddha travels to Toyikā and there sits down upon the spot where the Buddha Kāśyapa lies buried, hence creating a site that is doubly venerable. Pilgrims come to venerate the shrine, and the Buddha explains the value of their offerings. A festival is established there that comes to be known as the Toyikāmaha.

7. The Story of a Woman Dependent on a City for Alms
Nagarāvalambikā-avadāna
The venerable Mahākāśyapa accepts the offering of a leprous beggar woman, allowing her to earn great merit. Śakra tries to do likewise, but is thwarted by Mahākāśyapa. Hearing of the results of the leprous beggar's actions, King Prasenajit tries to replicate her success, but is thwarted by a bowl-carrying beggar, leading to a peculiar assignation of merit by the Buddha. The Buddha then tells of King Prasenajit's deeds in a past life that resulted in his becoming king.

8. The Story of Supriya
Supriya-avadāna
After paying off a thousand robbers who repeatedly rob the monastic community, the Buddha converts those robbers, and they become monks. The Buddha then tells the story of when he trained those robbers once before in a previous life. He was the great caravan leader Supriya, and after being robbed by those same one thousand robbers, he undertook the arduous journey to find riches that could satisfy everyone's needs.

9. The Chapter on the Great Fortune of the Householder Meṇḍhaka
Meṇḍhakagṛhapativibhūti-pariccheda
The householder Meṇḍhaka and his family possess great merit, and so the Buddha sets off to their home in the city of Bhadraṅkara to teach them the dharma. Hearing of this, some heretics enact a plan to ruin Bhadraṅkara and make sure that no one meets the Buddha when he arrives there. Nevertheless, the Buddha circumvents their plans and offers teachings to the community that has amassed there.

10. The Story of Meṇḍhaka
Meṇḍhaka-avadāna
The Buddha explains the deeds performed by Meṇḍhaka and his family in a past life that led them to their present condition. The Buddha tells of a famine in the past when Meṇḍhaka and his family offered the little food they had to a solitary buddha and, as a result, came to possess magical powers.

11. The Story of Aśokavarṇa
Aśokavarṇa-avadāna
A bull about be butchered breaks free and comes to the Buddha for protection, and the Buddha purchases his freedom. The Buddha explains that since the bull cultivated faith in him, he will eventually become a solitary buddha. The Buddha then tells of deeds done by the bull in his previous life as a robber that led him to be reborn as an animal.

12. The Miracle Sūtra
Prātihārya-sūtra
Prompted by the evil Māra, six heretics challenge the Buddha to a competition of miracles in the city of Śrāvastī. The Buddha accepts the challenge and agrees to meet after seven days. Meanwhile, King Prasenajit's brother Kāla is falsely accused of consorting with one of the king's wives, and his hands and feet are cut off. Ānanda restores them by the power of his words. On the seventh day, the Buddha displays a miracle at Śrāvastī that defeats the heretics. After the heretics flee, the Buddha offers teachings to those who have assembled before him.

13. The Story of Svāgata
Svāgata-avadāna
In the city of Śuśumāragiri, the householder Bodha has a son named Svāgata who turns out to be ill fated, causing death and destruction for his family. Svāgata goes to Śrāvastī and is forced to join the ranks of beggars, suffering greatly because of his bad karma. Svāgata meets the

Buddha, who arranges for him to overcome some of his bad karma and become a monk. The Buddha, Svāgata, and the monastic community then travel to Śuśumāragiri, where Svāgata defeats an evil nāga and then returns back to Śrāvastī, where he unknowingly consumes liquor and gets drunk. The Buddha observes this and explains to the other monks what Svāgata did in a past life that has resulted in the difficulties he has faced in this lifetime.

14. The Story of a Wretched Pig
Sūkarika-avadāna
A divine being about to fall from heaven and be reborn as a pig laments his fate, and Śakra, out of compassion, convinces him to take refuge in the Buddha. As a result of his taking refuge, the divine being is reborn among the gods of Tuṣita heaven, a realm even higher than the one Śakra inhabits.

15. The Story of One Foretold to Be a Wheel-Turning King
Cakravartivyākṛta-avadāna
The Buddha observes a monk performing rituals at a stūpa and explains to the other monks that, as a result of this deed, this monk will become a wheel-turning king in a future life. The other monks, not wanting such a fate, refrain from such practices, and then the Buddha offers them instructions.

16. The Story of Two Parrot Chicks
Śukapotaka-avadāna
Two parrot chicks who frequently receive Buddhist teachings are killed by a cat, but not before taking refuge in the Buddha, the dharma, and the community. In response to a question about their fate, the Buddha explains that they have been reborn among the gods and will one day be reborn as solitary buddhas.

17. The Story of Māndhātā
Māndhātā-avadāna
After making the decision to enter final nirvāṇa, the Buddha tells the story of King Māndhātā. The king, full of hubris, conquered the earth and then the heavens, but then his magical powers were destroyed. The Buddha goes on to explain some of the deeds that Māndhātā did in past lives that resulted in his successes in this one.

The Divyāvadāna

(STORIES 1–17)

दिव्यावदान

Om! Praise to all the glorious buddhas and bodhisattvas!

1. The Story of Koṭikarṇa

KOṬIKARṆA-AVADĀNA[84]

Śroṇa Koṭikarṇa's Birth

THE LORD BUDDHA was staying in the city of Śrāvastī at the Jeta Grove in the park of a man named Anāthapiṇḍada (Almsgiver to the Poor). Meanwhile in Aśmāparāntaka,[85] in the village of Vāsava, there lived a householder named Balasena (Having a Powerful Army). He was rich, wealthy, and prosperous, with vast and extensive holdings. Truly, he rivaled the god Vaiśravaṇa in wealth.

The householder Balasena brought home a girl from an appropriate family as his wife, and with her he fooled around, enjoyed himself, and made love. Having no son but eager for one, he prayed to the likes of Śiva, Varuṇa, Kubera, Śakra, and Brahmā, as well as a park deity, a forest deity, a crossroads deity, and a deity who received oblations. He also prayed to his hereditary deity, who shared the same nature as him and who constantly followed behind him.

There is a popular saying that as a result of such prayers, sons are born and daughters as well. But this isn't the case. If this were the case, then every man would have a thousand sons, just like a wheel-turning king. Instead, it's because of the presence of three conditions that sons are born and daughters as well. Which three? The mother and father must come together in love; the mother must be healthy and fertile; and a being seeking rebirth must be standing by.[86] It's because of the presence of these three conditions that sons are born and daughters as well. Nevertheless, the householder Balasena remained devoted to such prayers.

Meanwhile, there was a being about to enter his last existence who was benevolent, who had grasped the path of liberation, who had turned toward nirvāṇa and away from saṃsāra,[87] [2] who wasn't desirous of worldly things, who had turned his back on all states and realms of existence as well as rebirth,[88] and who would be possessing his last body. He died and fell from a community of the gods[89] and entered the womb of the householder Balasena's wife.

Now an intelligent woman tends to possess five special characteristics. Which five?

She knows when a man is in love,
  and she knows when he is indifferent;
she knows when the time is right,
  and she knows when she is fertile;
she knows when life has entered her womb;[90]
she knows from whom life has entered her womb;
and she knows if it's a boy, and she knows if it's a girl.

If it's a boy, it settles on the right side of the womb. If it's a girl, it settles on the left side of the womb.

In high spirits, the householder Balasena's wife informed her husband: "Congratulations, dear husband! I'm pregnant! And since it has settled on the right side of my womb, it will definitely be a boy."

Likewise in high spirits, he uttered this inspired utterance:

So it is that I may finally get to see my son's face,
  a sight I've long desired to see!
May my son not be ignoble.
May he perform those duties I expect of him.
May he, having been supported by me, support me in return.
May he be the one to claim my inheritance.
May my family lineage be long lasting.

> And may he, when we are dead and gone, make offerings, either few or many, as well as perform meritorious deeds, and then direct the reward [in our names][91] with these words—"This [merit][92] shall follow these two wherever they are born and wherever they go."[93]

Knowing that his wife was pregnant, the householder Balasena kept her in the upper story of their palatial home, free from any restraints, with all the necessities for the cold in the cold season and all the necessities for the heat in the hot season. She was given the foods that doctors prescribed, those not too bitter, not too sour, not too salty, not too sweet, not too pungent, and not too astringent, and those foods free from bitterness, sourness, saltiness, sweetness, pungency, and astringency. Her body was adorned with strings and necklaces of pearls, and like a nymph wandering in the divine Nandana Grove, she moved from bed to bed and from seat to seat, never descending to the ground below.[94] And she heard no unkind words until the fetus matured.

After eight or nine months, she gave birth. A boy was born who was beautiful, good-looking, and attractive, radiant with a golden complexion, who had a parasol-shaped head, lengthy arms, a large and broad forehead, joined eyebrows, a prominent nose, and who was adorned on one ear with a jewel-studded earring.

The householder Balasena [3] sent for some jewel experts and told them, "Gentlemen, determine the value of this jewel."[95]

"The value of this jewel[96] can't be determined," they said.

As a rule, if the value of a jewel can't be determined, it's valued at ten million. So they said, "Householder, this jewel[97] is worth ten million."

Then his relatives came together and assembled. For three weeks, that is twenty-one days, they celebrated the occasion of the boy's birth in full and then they selected a name for him.

"What should this boy's name be?"

"The boy was born wearing a jewel stud worth ten million and under the stars of the constellation of Śravaṇa (Hearing).[98] Therefore, the boy's name should be Śroṇa Koṭikarṇa (Born under Śravaṇa with an Ear Worth Ten Million)."

On the very day that Śroṇa Koṭikarṇa was born, two sons were also born to servants of the householder Balasena. He named one of them Dāsaka (Servant) and the other Pālaka (Protector).

Śroṇa Koṭikarṇa was given over to eight nurses—two shoulder nurses, two playtime nurses, two nursemaids, and two wet nurses. Raised by these eight nurses, who nourished him with milk, yogurt, fresh butter, clarified butter, butter scum, and other special provisions that were very pure, he grew quickly like a lotus in a lake.

When he grew up, he was entrusted to teachers to learn writing and then arithmetic, accounting, matters relating to trademarks,[99] and to debts, deposits, and trusts. [He was also educated][100] in the science of building-sites and the science of jewels. In each of the eight sciences, he became learned and well versed, capable of explaining and expounding upon them.

Śroṇa Koṭikarṇa the Caravan Leader

Meanwhile, on Śroṇa Koṭikarṇa's behalf, his father had three residences built—one for the cold season, one for the hot season, and one for the rainy season; he had three parks built—one for the cold season, one for the hot season, and one for the rainy season; and he had three harems established—senior, intermediate, and junior.[101]

Śroṇa Koṭikarṇa would stay on the upper story of his palatial home, and there he would fool around, enjoy himself, and make love, accompanied by music played only by women. The householder Balasena, on the other hand, was always engaged in the business of farming. Koṭikarṇa saw that his father was always engaged in the business of farming and said, "Dad, why are you always engaged in the business of farming?"

"Son," he said, "you stay on the upper story of our palatial home, [4] and you fool around, enjoy yourself, and make love, accompanied by music played only by women. If I, likewise, were to fool around, enjoy myself, and make love, it wouldn't take long for our wealth to diminish, give out, and finally be exhausted."

Śroṇa Koṭikarṇa reflected, "He's criticizing me for my own good."[102] So he said, "Dad, if that's the case, I'll leave. I'll set sail in the great ocean."

"Son," his father said, "I have so many jewels that even if you make use of them as you would sesames, rice, jujube berries, and *kulattha* beans, they still won't be exhausted."

"Dad," he said, "give me permission to take some goods and set sail in the great ocean."

Realizing that he was absolutely determined, Balasena gave his permission. Then the householder Balasena had bells rung in the village of Vāsava for the following proclamation: "Whoever among you is eager to set sail in the great ocean with Śroṇa Koṭikarṇa as your caravan leader, all the while exempt from customs and freight fees, gather up goods for export across the great ocean." Five hundred merchants then gathered up goods for export across the great ocean.

The householder Balasena reflected, "By which vehicle should Śroṇa Koṭikarṇa travel?" He reflected further, "What about elephants? Elephants are nice to sit on, but they're difficult to maintain. Horses are also nice to sit on, but they're also difficult to maintain. Donkeys, though, have good memories and are also nice to sit on. He should travel by donkey."[103]

His father sent for him and said, "Son, you shouldn't travel at the front of the caravan nor at the rear. If a robber is strong, he'll attack the front of the caravan. If he's weak, he'll attack the rear. You should go in the middle of the caravan. For if the caravan leader dies, how can you still call it a caravan?"[104] He also spoke with Dāsaka and Pālaka. "Sons," he said, "don't leave Śroṇa Koṭikarṇa behind under any circumstances!"

Some time later, Śroṇa Koṭikarṇa, after performing auspicious rituals and benedictions for a safe journey, approached his mother, fell prostrate at her feet, and said, "Mother, I'm going. Farewell! I'm setting sail in the great ocean."

She began to cry.

"Mother," he said, "why are you crying?"

His mother, her face rainy with tears, said, "Son, will I ever see my dear son alive again?"

Śroṇa Koṭikarṇa reflected, "I set off auspiciously, [5] but now she speaks such inauspicious words!" Then, in anger, he said, "Mother, I performed auspicious rituals and benedictions before setting off for the great ocean. And you do such inauspicious things! Don't you see what terrible realms of existence there are?"

"Son," she said, "you have committed an act of harsh speech. Confess your sin as sin. Maybe then this bad karma will diminish, give out, and finally be exhausted."

He confessed his sin as sin, and she forgave him.

Then Śroṇa Koṭikarṇa, having once again performed auspicious rituals and benedictions, loaded many goods for export across the ocean in carts, carriers, containers, and baskets, and on camels, bulls, and donkeys, and then set out for the great ocean. He passed through marketplaces, hamlets, villages, towns, and trading centers, one after another, until he arrived at the banks of the great ocean. Then he carefully outfitted an ocean-going ship and set sail in the great ocean to find his fortune.[105]

With the help of a favorable wind, he arrived at Ratnadvīpa (Jewel Island). There he closely examined each jewel and then filled his boat with them as though they were sesames, rice, jujube berries, and *kulattha* beans. Then, with the help of a favorable wind, he arrived back in Jambudvīpa (Black Plum Island) successfully completing his voyage.[106]

Right there, on the shore of the ocean, the caravan set up camp. The caravan leader Śroṇa Koṭikarṇa took Dāsaka and Pālaka off to one side, away from the middle of the caravan, and there they began to tally their income and expenditures.

After some time, Śroṇa Koṭikarṇa said to Dāsaka, "Dāsaka, see what the caravan is doing." He went there, and seeing that the caravan was asleep, he went to sleep there as well.

"Dāsaka is taking a long time," Śroṇa Koṭikarṇa thought. So he said to Pālaka, "Pālaka, see what the caravan is doing."

He went there as well,[107] and seeing that the members of the caravan were unloading cargo, he also began to unload cargo. Dāsaka reflected, "Pālaka will send for the caravan leader." Pālaka, in turn, reflected, "Dāsaka will send for the caravan leader." That very night the caravan finished unloading the cargo and set off. As for the caravan leader, he became very tired, lay down, and fell asleep.

Meanwhile, the caravan traveled on until daybreak.

"Gentlemen, where is the caravan leader?" they asked each other.

"He travels up front."

So they went up front and asked, "Where is the caravan leader?"

"He brings up the rear."

Then they went to the rear and asked, [6] "Where is the caravan leader?"

"He travels in the middle."

So they went to the middle of the caravan and asked once again, but he wasn't there either.

"I thought that Pālaka would send for the caravan leader," Dāsaka said.

"Well," Pālaka said, "I thought that Dāsaka would send for the caravan leader."

"Friends, we haven't done well to leave the caravan leader behind. Come! Let's go back."

"Friends, if we go back," they said, "every single one of us will straightaway meet some disaster.[108] Come! Let's agree that no one will inform Śroṇa Koṭikarṇa's parents until all the merchandise is stored away." They agreed and then continued on their way.

Now Śroṇa Koṭikarṇa's parents heard that Śroṇa Koṭikarṇa had returned, so they went out to meet him.

"Where is the caravan leader?" they asked.

"He travels in the middle."

So they went to the middle of the caravan and asked, "Where is the caravan leader?"

"He brings up the rear," they said.

Then they went to the rear of the caravan and asked, "Where is the caravan leader?"

"He travels up front."

And so the merchants kept them confused until all the merchandise was stored away. Then they said, "Mother,[109] we forgot the caravan leader behind."

Then one person came to Śroṇa Koṭikarṇa's parents and said, "Śroṇa Koṭikarṇa has returned!" They gave him a reward and then went out to meet their son, but they didn't see him. Then another person came to them and said, "Mother![110] Congratulations! Śroṇa Koṭikarṇa has returned!" They gave him a reward as well and then went out to meet their son, but they didn't see him. And so they began never to believe anyone again.

In parks, and in their community halls and temples, Śroṇa Koṭikarṇa's parents presented and established umbrellas, fans, water pots, and shoes that were inscribed with these letters: "If Śroṇa Koṭikarṇa is still alive, this is for his speedy return, for his quick return. Otherwise, if he has died and passed away, this is so that the life that he has been born into shall be followed by another, even better existence." Crying from grief, Śroṇa Koṭikarṇa's parents went blind.

Meanwhile the caravan leader Śroṇa Koṭikarṇa, touched and warmed by the sun's rays, woke up and saw nothing of the caravan, except for his donkey cart.[111] So he got on the donkey cart and set off. Then at night, a dusty wind blew [7] that covered up and concealed the path. The donkeys had good memories though. Repeatedly sniffing at the path,[112] they plodded along slowly.

The caravan leader reflected, "Why are they plodding along so slowly?" With this in mind, he began to beat them with his goad. The donkeys became agitated and confused and were no longer mindful. They set off on the wrong path and continued until they reached a forest of *śāla* trees.[113] Suffering from thirst, with pained looks on their faces and their tongues hanging out, they continued on. Seeing them, Śroṇa Koṭikarṇa felt compassion. He reflected, "If I don't set them free, I'll straightaway meet some disaster. Who has such a cruel heart and so little concern for the next world that he'd whip the bodies of these donkeys with a goad?"

He set them free.

"From now on," he said, "may you eat grass whose fresh upper part hasn't already been eaten and that hasn't already been trampled! May you may drink water that isn't dirty! And may cool winds blow on you from all four directions!" After setting them free, Śroṇa Koṭikarṇa set out by foot.

Śroṇa Koṭikarṇa in the Realm of Hungry Ghosts

After a while Śroṇa Koṭikarṇa saw a tall and lofty iron city. There at the gate to the city stood a man who was black, cruel, and fierce, with red eyes and a massive body,[114] brandishing an iron staff in his hands. Śroṇa Koṭikarṇa approached the man and, having approached, asked him, "Friend, is there any water here?"

The man remained silent.

Again he asked, "Is there any water here in this city?"

Once again the man remained silent.

The caravan leader entered the city and called out the words, "Water! Water!"[115] Soon five thousand hungry ghosts who looked like scorched wooden pillars, raised-up skeletons covered with hair from head to toe, with stomachs like mountains[116] and mouths like pinholes, surrounded Śroṇa Koṭikarṇa.

"Caravan leader," they said, "you're compassionate. We're suffering from thirst. Give us water!"

"Friends," he said. "I'm looking for water as well. Where is there water that I can give you?"

"Caravan leader, this is a city of hungry ghosts," they said. "How could there be water here? In the last twelve years, it's only now, from you, that we even hear the words 'Water! Water!'"

"Friends, who are you?" he asked. "What deed led you to be reborn here?"

"Śroṇa, the people of Jambudvīpa are difficult to convince. You won't believe us." [8]

"Friends, I can see what's before my eyes. Why wouldn't I believe you?"

Then they uttered this verse:

> We were abusive and scornful,
> we were greedy and stingy.
> We didn't make even the smallest offerings.
> That's why we've come to the ancestral realm.[117]

"Go, Śroṇa! You're very powerful because of your merit. Have you ever seen anyone who entered a city of hungry ghosts leaving it safe and sound?"

He set out and continued on his way until he saw that man again at the gate to the city. "Friend," he said to him, "it would have been good [if][118] you'd have informed me that this is a city of hungry ghosts. Then I wouldn't have entered it."

"Go, Śroṇa!" he said to him. "You're very powerful because of your merit. That's how you entered a city of hungry ghosts and left it safe and sound."

Śroṇa Koṭikarṇa set out and continued on his way until he saw another tall and lofty iron city. There too, at the gate to the city, stood a man who was black and fierce, with red eyes and a massive body,[119] brandishing an iron staff in his hands. Śroṇa Koṭikarṇa approached him and, having approached, said, "Friend, is there any water here in this city?"

The man remained silent.

Again he asked, "Is there any water here in this city?"

The man remained silent.

The caravan leader entered the city and again said the words, "Water! Water!" Soon many thousands of hungry ghosts who looked like scorched wooden pillars, raised-up skeletons covered with hair from head to toe, with stomachs like mountains[120] and mouths like pinholes, surrounded Śroṇa Koṭikarṇa.

"Śroṇa, you're compassionate. We're suffering from thirst. Give us water!"

"Friends," he said. "I'm looking for water as well. Where is there water that I can give you?"

"Śroṇa, this is a city of hungry ghosts," they said. "How could there be water here? In the last twelve years, it's only now, from you, that we even hear the words 'Water! Water!'"

"Friends, who are you?" he asked. "What deed led you to be reborn here?"

"Śroṇa," they said, "the people of Jambudvīpa are difficult to convince. You won't believe us."

"Friends," he said, "I can see what's before my eyes. [9] Why wouldn't I believe you?"

Then they uttered this verse:

> We were intoxicated with the pride of good health,
> intoxicated with the pride of wealth and indulgence.[121]
> We didn't make even the smallest offerings.
> That's why we've come to the ancestral realm.[122]

"Go, Śroṇa! You have meritorious karma.[123] Have you ever seen or heard of anyone who entered a city of hungry ghosts leaving it alive, safe and sound?"

He set out and continued on his way until he saw that man at the gate to the city again. "Friend," he said to him, "it would have been good if you'd have informed me that this is a city of hungry ghosts. Then I wouldn't have entered it."

"Go, Śroṇa!" he said. "You're very powerful because of your merit. Have you ever seen or heard of anyone who entered a city of hungry ghosts leaving it alive, safe and sound?"

Śroṇa Koṭikarṇa set out and continued on his way until sunset, when he saw a flying mansion. [On it][124] were four nymphs, all beautiful, good-looking, and attractive. And there was a single man who was beautiful, good-looking, and attractive, wearing armlets, earrings, colorful garlands, ornaments, and scented creams, who was fooling around, enjoying himself, and making love with them. They saw Śroṇa Koṭikarṇa from a distance and began to call out to him: "Welcome, Śroṇa! Aren't you thirsty or hungry?"

He reflected, "This must be a god or a nāga or a yakṣa!" Then he said, "Noble one, I am thirsty. I am hungry."

So they gave him plenty of water and fed him.[125] He stayed on the flying mansion until sunrise. Then the man said to him,[126] "Śroṇa, get down now. It's going to get dangerous here."

Śroṇa got down and stood off to one side. Then, when the sun arose, the flying mansion disappeared. The nymphs disappeared as well. Then four black-spotted dogs appeared. They threw the man face down on the ground and began ripping the bones out of his back[127] and eating them. They continued doing this until sunset. Then, once again, the flying mansion appeared and the nymphs appeared as well. And once again the man fooled around, enjoyed himself, and made love with them.

Śroṇa approached them and asked, "Who are you? What deed led you to be reborn here?"

"Śroṇa," they said, "the people of Jambudvīpa are difficult to convince. You won't believe us." [10]

"I can see what's before my eyes," he said. "Why wouldn't I believe you?"

"Śroṇa, I was a shepherd in the village of Vāsava. I used to slaughter sheep and sell their meat. That's how I made my living. The noble Mahākātyāyana, out of compassion for me, came and said, 'Friend, the consequence of this deed will be most undesirable. Stop this evil practice that goes against the true dharma!' But I didn't heed his words and stop. Again and again he tried to dissuade me. 'Friend,' he said, 'the consequence of this deed will be most undesirable. Stop this evil practice that goes against the true dharma!' Even then I didn't abstain. 'Friend,' he asked me, 'do you slaughter these sheep during the day or at night?' 'Noble one,' I said, 'I slaughter them during the day.' And he said, 'Friend, at night why don't you observe the moral code?' So I accepted the moral code from him and observed it at night. Since at night I observed the moral code, as a result of that action, at night I experience divine pleasure, just as you've seen. Since during the day I slaughtered sheep, as a result of that action, during the day I experience suffering, just as you've also seen."

Then he uttered this verse:

> By day I crushed the lives of others,
> at night I adhered to the virtues of morality.
> The result of that action is that now
> I experience good and evil.

"Śroṇa, will you go to the village of Vāsava?"

"Yes, I'll go."

"My son lives there. He slaughters sheep for a living. Tell him, 'I have seen your father. He says that the consequence of this deed will be most undesirable. Stop this evil practice that goes against the true dharma!'"

"Friend, as you said before, 'The people of Jambudvīpa are difficult to convince.' He won't believe me."

"Śroṇa, if he doesn't believe you, tell him, 'Your father says that underneath the slaughtering pen a pot full of gold is buried.[128] Retrieve it and use it to enjoy yourself fully. And from time to time offer alms to the noble Mahākātyāyana and then direct the reward in our names. Maybe then this bad karma will diminish, give out, and finally be exhausted.'"

Śroṇa Koṭikarṇa set out and continued on his way until sunrise, when he saw another flying mansion. On it was a single nymph [11] who was beautiful, good-looking, and attractive. And there was a single man who was beautiful, good-looking, and attractive, wearing armlets, earrings, colorful garlands, ornaments, and scented creams, who was fooling around, enjoying himself, and making love with her. The man saw Śroṇa Koṭikarṇa from a distance and began to call out to him: "Welcome, Śroṇa! Aren't you thirsty? Aren't you hungry?"

He reflected, "This must be a god or a nāga or a yakṣa." Then he said, "I am thirsty and hungry."

So the man gave him plenty of water and fed him.[129] He stayed on the flying mansion until sunset. Then the man said to him: "Get down now. It's going to get dangerous here."

Śroṇa Koṭikarṇa had already seen enough danger, so he got down and stood off to one side. Then, when the sun set, the flying mansion disappeared. The nymph disappeared as well. Then a giant centipede appeared. It wrapped its body around the man's body seven times and began eating from the top of his head.[130] It stayed like that until sunrise. Then, once again, the flying mansion appeared and the nymph appeared as well. And once again the man, who was beautiful, good-looking, and attractive, fooled around, enjoyed himself, and made love with her.

Śroṇa Koṭikarṇa approached the man and asked, "Who are you? What deed led you to be reborn here?"

"Śroṇa," he said, "the people of Jambudvīpa are difficult to convince. You won't believe me."

"I can see what's before my eyes," he said. "Why wouldn't I believe you?"

"If that's the case,"[131] the man said, "[then listen to this]. I was a brahman in the village of Vāsava. And I was an adulterer. The noble Mahākātyāyana, out of compassion for me, came and said, 'Friend, the consequence of this deed will be most undesirable. Stop this evil practice that goes against the true dharma!' But I didn't take his advice and stop. Again and again he tried to dissuade me. But just as before, I didn't abstain from that evil practice that goes against the true dharma. 'Friend,' he asked me, 'do you commit adultery during the day or at night?' 'Noble one,' I said to him, 'only at night.' And he said, 'Friend, during the day why don't you observe the moral code?' So I accepted the moral code from him and observed it during the day. Since I accepted the moral code from the noble Kātyāyana and observed it during the day, as a result of that action, during the day I experience divine pleasure, just as you've seen. [12] Since at night I committed adultery, as a result of that action, at night I experience suffering, just as you've also seen."

Then he uttered this verse:

> At night I was entranced by others' wives,
> by day I adhered to the virtues of morality.
> The result of that action is that now
> I experience good and evil.

"Śroṇa, will you go to the village of Vāsava?[132] There my son is a brahman adulterer. Tell him, 'I have seen your father. He says that the consequence of this deed will be most undesirable. Stop this evil practice that goes against the true dharma!'"

"Friend, as you yourself said before, 'The people of Jambudvīpa are difficult to convince.' Who will believe what I say?"

"Śroṇa, if he doesn't believe you,[133] tell him, 'Your father says that underneath the fire altar for the *agniṣṭoma* sacrifice, a pot full of gold is buried.[134] Retrieve it and use it to enjoy yourself fully. And from time to time offer alms to the noble Mahākātyāyana and then direct the reward in our names. Maybe then this bad karma will diminish, give out, and finally be exhausted.'"

Śroṇa Koṭikarṇa set out and continued on his way until he saw yet another flying mansion. On it was a single woman who was beautiful, good-looking, and attractive, wearing armlets, earrings, colorful garlands, ornaments, and scented creams. Four hungry ghosts were bound to the four corner-posts of her bed. She saw Śroṇa Koṭikarṇa from a distance and began to call out to him: "Welcome, Śroṇa! Aren't you thirsty? Aren't you hungry?"

He reflected, "This must be a deity or a female nāga or yakṣa." Then he said, "Noble woman, I am thirsty. I am hungry."

She massaged him, then gave him plenty of water and food as well. Then she said, "Śroṇa, if these hungry ghosts ask you for anything,[135] don't give it to them!" With that said, she entered the flying mansion, wanting to let him see with his own eyes what the respective karmas of those beings would produce.[136]

Meanwhile, those hungry ghosts began to plea, "Śroṇa, you're compassionate. We're hungry. Give us some food."

Śroṇa tossed some food to one of them, and it turned into dung beetles.[137] He tossed some to another, and when that hungry ghost began to eat it, it turned into balls of iron.[138] He tossed some to another, and when that hungry ghost began to eat it, it turned into the hungry ghost's own flesh. Then he tossed some to yet another, and it turned into pus and blood.

The woman emerged because of the putrid smell.[139] "Śroṇa," she said, "you were forbidden by me! Why did you give them food? [13] What can I say of my compassion? Your compassion is greater."[140]

"Sister," he said, "who are these people to you?"

"This is my husband, this is my son, this is my daughter-in-law, and this is my maidservant," she said.

"Who are you?" he asked. "What deed led to be reborn here?"

"Śroṇa," she said, "it is said that the people of Jambudvīpa are difficult to convince. You won't believe me."

"I can see what's before my eyes. Why wouldn't I believe you?"

"I was a brahman woman in the village of Vāsava," she said. "At night, when the moon appeared in a particular constellation,[141] I prepared some fine foods. The noble Mahākātyāyana, out of compassion for me, entered the village of Vāsava for alms. I saw him. He instilled faith through his body and through his mind. At the sight of him, my mind was filled with faith,[142] and being filled with faith, I offered him alms. Then this thought occurred to me: 'I'll share my joy with my husband. He'll be happy.' Later my husband bathed and came in. 'Dear husband,' I said, 'rejoice! I gave alms to the noble Mahākātyāyana.' He was furious. 'We still haven't given alms to any brahmans, nor have we honored our relatives with the appropriate offerings, yet you give the first and finest share of alms to that lousy, shaven-headed ascetic?' He became indignant and said, 'Why doesn't that lousy, shaven-headed ascetic eat dung beetles instead?' As a result of that action, whatever food he eats turns into dung beetles.

"Then this thought occurred to me: 'I'll share my joy with my son as well. He'll be happy.' 'Son,' I said to him, 'rejoice! I gave alms to the noble Mahākātyāyana.' He too was furious. 'We still haven't given alms to any brahmans, nor have we honored our relatives with the appropriate offerings, yet you give away the first and finest share of alms to that lousy, shaven-headed ascetic?' He also became indignant, and he said, 'Why doesn't that lousy, shaven-headed ascetic eat balls of iron instead?' As a result of that action, whatever food he eats turns into balls of iron.

"At night, when the moon appeared in a particular constellation, my relatives sent me some food as a gift, which I entrusted to my daughter-in-law. She ate the best of the food that had been offered and then presented me with the crumbs. I sent a message to those relatives: 'Why do you send me crumbs as a gift as though there were a famine going on?' Then they sent a message to me: [14] 'We didn't send you crumbs. We sent you only fine foods as a gift.' So I said to my daughter-in-law, 'Young woman, isn't it true that you ate the best of the food that we received as a gift and then presented me with the crumbs?' She said, 'Wouldn't eating the food that was sent to you as a gift be like eating my own flesh?'[143] As a result of that action, whatever food she eats turns into her own flesh.

"At night, when the moon appeared in a particular constellation, I handed over some fine foods [to the young woman][144] [who was our maidservant] to deliver to my relatives as a gift. Along the way, the young woman ate the best of the food that was intended as a gift and then presented them with the crumbs. They sent a message to me: 'Why do you send us crumbs as a gift as though there were a famine going on?' Then I sent a message to them: 'I didn't send you crumbs. I sent you only fine foods.' So I said to the young woman: 'Young woman, isn't it true that you ate the best of the food that was intended as a gift for my relatives and then gave them the crumbs?' She said, 'Wouldn't eating the food that you sent as a gift be like eating pus and blood?' As a result of that action, whatever food she eats turns into pus and blood.

"Then this thought came to me, 'I should take rebirth where I can see [my husband, my son, my daughter-in-law, and my maidservant] all experiencing the results of their respective karma.' Since I gave alms to the noble Mahākātyāyana, I should have been reborn in the excellent company of the gods of Trāyastriṃśa (Thirty-Three). Instead, because of the power of this improper fervent aspiration, I became a hungry ghost, though of great power.

"Śroṇa, will you go to the village of Vāsava? There my daughter makes her living as a prostitute. Tell her, 'I have seen your father, mother, brother, sister-in-law, and maidservant. They say that the consequence of this deed will be most undesirable. Stop this practice that goes against the true dharma!'"

"Sister, as you yourself said, 'The people of Jambudvīpa are difficult to convince.' She won't believe me."[145]

"Śroṇa, if she doesn't believe you, tell her, 'In the old house where your father used to live, there are four iron jars filled with gold, and in the middle of them is a golden water-pitcher. They say that you should retrieve them and use them to enjoy yourself fully. And from time to time offer alms to the noble Mahākātyāyana and then direct the reward in our names. Maybe then this bad karma [15] will diminish, give out, and finally be exhausted.'"

Śroṇa Koṭikarṇa promised her.

Wandering about in this way, twelve years had already passed.

"Śroṇa," she said to him, "will you go to the village of Vāsava?"

"Yes, sister. I'll go." Meanwhile, he passed his time right there on the flying mansion.[146]

She then ordered those same hungry ghosts [who had previously been her husband, son, daughter-in-law, and maidservant]. "All of you," she said, "while Śroṇa Koṭikarṇa is asleep, go and place him in his father's park in the village of Vāsava. Then come back."

So they placed him in his father's park in the village of Vāsava.

Śroṇa Koṭikarṇa Returns to the Village of Vāsava

When Śroṇa Koṭikarṇa woke up, he saw bells, umbrellas, and fans inscribed with these letters: "If Śroṇa Koṭikarṇa is still alive, this is for his speedy return, for his quick return. If he has died and passed away, this is so that the life that he has been born into shall be followed by another, even better existence."

He reflected, "If my parents have accepted that I'm dead, why should I go home again? Instead, I'll go away. I'll go forth as a monk under the noble Mahākātyāyana." Then Śroṇa Koṭikarṇa approached the venerable Mahākātyāyana.

The venerable Mahākātyāyana saw Śroṇa Koṭikarṇa from a distance, and at the sight of him, he said this to Śroṇa Koṭikarṇa: "Come, Śroṇa! Welcome! Śroṇa, have you seen this world and the next world as well?"

"Bhadanta Mahākātyāyana, I have seen them," he said. "Bhadanta Mahākātyāyana, may I renounce, take ordination, and become a monk according to the dharma and monastic discipline that have been so well expressed. May I follow the religious life in your presence."[147]

"Śroṇa," the noble one said, "first fulfill those promises that you made previously.[148] Deliver those messages as you received them."

He approached the shepherd. "Friend," he said, "I have seen your father. He says that the consequence of this deed will be most undesirable. Stop this practice that goes against the true dharma!"

"Sir, it's now been twelve years since my father died. Has anyone ever been seen coming back from the next world?"

"Friend, I am such a person. I have come back."

He didn't believe him.

"Friend, if you don't believe me, this is what your father said: 'Underneath the slaughtering pen is a pot filled with gold. Retrieve it and use it to enjoy yourself fully. And from time to time offer alms to the noble Mahākātyāyana [16] and then direct the reward in our names. Maybe then this bad karma will diminish, give out, and finally be exhausted.'"

"I've never heard such a thing before," he reflected. "I'll go and see. If it's there, all this must be true." He went and dug it up. He found that everything was just as Śroṇa Koṭikarṇa had said.[149] And then he believed.

After that Śroṇa Koṭikarṇa approached the adulterer. Having approached, he said, "Friend, I have seen your father. He says that the consequence of this deed will be most undesirable. Stop this evil practice that goes against the true dharma!"

"Sir, it's now been twelve years since my father died. Have you ever seen anyone who has gone to the next world and then come back?"

"Friend, I am such a person. I have come back."

He didn't believe him.

So he said, "Friend, if you don't believe me, your father buried a pot filled with gold underneath the fire altar for the *agniṣṭoma* sacrifice. He says that you should retrieve it and use it to enjoy yourself fully. And from time to time offer alms to the noble Mahākātyāyana and then direct the reward in our names. Maybe then this bad karma will diminish, give out, and finally be exhausted."

"I've never heard about this before," he reflected. "I'll go and see. If it's there, all this must be true." He went and dug it up. He found that everything was just as Śroṇa Koṭikarṇa had said. And then he believed.

Then Śroṇa Koṭikarṇa approached the prostitute. Having approached, he said: "Sister, I have seen your mother, father, brother, sister-in-law, and maidservant. They say that the consequence of this deed will be most undesirable. Stop this evil practice that goes against the true dharma!"

"Sir," she said, "it's been twelve years since my parents died. Have you ever seen anyone who has gone to the next world and then come back?"

"I am such a person," he said. "I have come back."

She didn't believe him.

"Sister," he said, "if you don't believe me,[150] in the old house where your father used to live are four iron jars filled with gold, and in the middle of them is a golden water-pitcher. They say that you should retrieve them and use them to enjoy yourself fully. And from time to time offer alms to the noble Mahākātyāyana and then direct the reward in our names. Maybe then this bad karma will diminish, [17] give out, and finally be exhausted."

"I've never heard about this before," she reflected. "I'll go and see. If it's there, all this must be true." She went and dug it up. She found that everything was just as Śroṇa Koṭikarṇa had said. And then she believed.

Śroṇa Koṭikarṇa reflected, "The whole world believes in gold, but no one believes in me." Then he smiled.[151]

In his childhood, Śroṇa Koṭikarṇa's teeth had been fixed with gold, so the prostitute recognized him. "This must be the noble Śroṇa Koṭikarṇa. This is how your sisters know you to be."[152] She went and informed his parents, "Mother! Father! Koṭikarṇa has returned!" But many had informed them likewise, and they no longer believed in anyone. "Young woman," they said, "you mock us as well."[153]

Then Śroṇa Koṭikarṇa himself went to his parents. Standing in the gateway to their house, he cleared his throat.[154] That great being had a golden voice, and that sound of his filled the entire house. They recognized him by his voice. Then his parents[155] hugged him and began to cry.[156] The film over their eyes was suffused with tears.[157] Once again, they began to see.

"Mother, Father," he said, "permit me. Because of my right belief, I want to go forth as a monk from home to homelessness."

"Son," they said, "crying with grief over you, we became blind. Now, thanks to you, our sight has been restored. As long as we live, you are not to go forth as a monk. After we die, then you may go."

Hearing the dharma from the venerable Mahākātyāyana, Śroṇa Koṭikarṇa directly experienced the reward of the stream-enterer. His parents were established in the taking of the refuges as well as in the precepts. Thereafter Śroṇa Koṭikarṇa studied [the four fundamental collections of the Buddha's discourses known as] the Āgamas and directly experienced the reward of the once-returner. His mother and father were established in the [four noble] truths.[158]

Śroṇa Koṭikarṇa Becomes a Monk

After some time, Śroṇa Koṭikarṇa's parents died. He then gave his wealth to the destitute, to orphans, and to the pitiable, making the poor rich, and then he approached the venerable Mahākātyāyana. [18] Having approached, he venerated with his head the feet of the venerable Mahākātyāyana and then stood at a respectful distance. Standing at a respectful distance, Śroṇa Koṭikarṇa said this to the venerable Mahākātyāyana: "Noble Mahākātyāyana, may I now renounce[159] according to the dharma and monastic discipline that have been so well expressed. May I follow the religious life in the presence of the Blessed One." And so he was initiated by the venerable Mahākātyāyana. After he was initiated, he studied the *mātṛkā*s and directly experienced the reward of the nonreturner.

In the region of Aśmāparāntaka,[160] there were very few monks. A quorum of ten monks could only be filled with difficulty. Therefore, Śroṇa Koṭikarṇa was kept as a novice monk for three months.

As a rule,[161] the disciples of lord buddhas have two assemblies each year—one at the time of the full moon in the month of Āṣāḍha [in late June, early July], when the rainy season begins, and the other at the time of the full moon in the month of Kārtika [in late October, early November]. Those who assemble in the month of Āṣāḍha, when the rainy season begins, learn and master certain teachings, as well as yoga and meditation. They then pass the rainy season in various villages, hamlets, towns, districts, and capitals. Those who assemble at the time of the full moon in the month of Kārtika report what they have learned and, moreover, ask questions about topics in the sūtras, monastic discipline, and *mātṛkās*.[162] The senior disciples do likewise.

Those monks who were the students and pupils of the venerable Mahākātyāyana learned and mastered certain teachings, as well as particular kinds of yoga and meditation. They then passed the rainy season in various villages, hamlets, towns, districts, and capitals. After the three months of the rainy season, with their robes fixed and readied, they took their bowls and robes and approached the venerable Mahākātyāyana. Having approached, they venerated with their heads the feet of the venerable Mahākātyāyana and then sat down at a respectful distance. Sitting down at a respectful distance, they reported what they had learned and, afterward, asked questions. The quorum of ten monks was filled. It then ordained Śroṇa Koṭikarṇa, after which he learned [the threefold collection of scripture known as] the Tripiṭaka. Then, by ridding himself of all defilements, he directly experienced arhatship. Becoming an arhat,[163]

he was free from attachment in the three realms
  [of desire, form, and formlessness];
[he regarded clods of earth and gold as equal in value;
he possessed equanimity toward the sky
  and the palm of his hand;
he didn't distinguish between being cut by a blade
  and being anointed with sandalwood paste;
the eggshell of his ignorance was broken by knowledge;
he obtained the special knowledges, superhuman faculties,
  and analytic insights;
and he was averse to worldly attainments, temptations,
  and honors.
He became worthy of respect, honor,] and obeisance
  [from the gods, including Indra and Upendra].[164]

Meanwhile the students and pupils of the venerable Mahākātyāyana [19] paid their respects to the venerable Mahākātyāyana and then said this to him: "We have seen you and paid our respects to you, our instructor. Now we'll go and pay our respects to the Blessed One."

"Do so, my children," he said. "For perfectly awakened tathāgata arhats are certainly to be seen and certainly to be offered respect."

Śroṇa Koṭikarṇa Visits the Buddha

At that time Śroṇa Koṭikarṇa was seated in the venerable Mahākātyāyana's assembly. As one of those assembled,[165] the venerable Śroṇa Koṭikarṇa got up from his seat, properly arranged his robe on one shoulder, kneeled with his right knee on the ground, bowed toward the venerable Mahākātyāyana with his hands respectfully folded, and said this to the venerable Mahākātyāyana: "Thanks to you, my instructor,[166] I have seen the Blessed One through his dharmic form but not through his physical form. I too am going, my instructor. I shall see the Blessed One through his physical form as well."

"You may do so, my child," he said. "For it is as difficult to get a glimpse of perfectly awakened tathāgata arhats, my child, as it is of a flower from an *udumbara* tree. On my behalf, venerate with your head the feet of the Blessed One, and ask him whether he is healthy and so on, and whether he is comfortable and at ease.[167] Then ask him these five questions:

[1] In the region of Aśmāparāntaka, Bhadanta,[168] there are very few monks. A quorum of ten monks can only be filled with difficulty. Considering this, how should we proceed [with the ordination process]?

[2] The ground is rough with the prickly grains of the cattle-thorn bush.[169]

[3] In the region of Aśmāparāntaka,[170] such things are used for mats and rugs as sheepskin, cowhide, deerskin, and goatskin. In other regions, such things are used for mats and rugs as *eraka* grass,

tree bark, silk, and cotton.[171] In the very same way, [as it has already been said], in the region of Aśmāparāntaka,[172] such things are used for mats and rugs as sheepskin and so on.

[4] People there are truly devoted to water[173] and are preoccupied with bathing.[174]

[5] If a monk sends another monk robes, once they've been sent off from here and if they are not delivered to their intended recipient [in the requisite time], for whom do these robes cause a serious misdeed involving forfeiture?[175]

With his silence, the venerable Śroṇa Koṭikarṇa agreed to the venerable Mahākātyāyana's request. [20]

Now in the morning, after that night had passed, the venerable Śroṇa Koṭikarṇa got dressed, took his bowl and robe, and entered the village of Vāsava for alms. Eventually, by and by, he reached Śrāvastī. Then the venerable Śroṇa Koṭikarṇa put away his bowl and robe, washed his feet, and approached the Blessed One. Having approached, he sat down at a respectful distance. Then the Blessed One addressed the venerable Ānanda: "Ānanda, go and prepare seats for the Tathāgata and Śroṇa Koṭikarṇa in one of the buildings in the monastery."

"Yes, Bhadanta," he said. The venerable Ānanda then made the arrangements as such for the Tathāgata and Śroṇa Koṭikarṇa and then approached the Blessed One. Having approached, he said this to the Blessed One: "Bhadanta, I have prepared seats for the Tathāgata and Śroṇa Koṭikarṇa in the same building. Now the Blessed One may do as the time permits."

Then the Blessed One approached the building in which Śroṇa Koṭikarṇa would be staying,[176] entered that building, and sat down. There he made his mindfulness fully present and looked into it.[177]

Meanwhile, the venerable Śroṇa Koṭikarṇa was washing his feet outside of the building. He then entered the building, sat down, crossed his legs, and likewise made his mindfulness fully present. The Blessed

One and the venerable Śroṇa Koṭikarṇa passed that night together in noble silence.[178] Then, when that night turned into dawn, the Blessed One addressed the venerable Śroṇa Koṭikarṇa: "Śroṇa, may the dharma that I myself have fully known, understood, and expressed inspire you to recite."

Given the opportunity by the Blessed One, the venerable Śroṇa, following the Aśmāparāntaka intonation,[179] recited passages at length and out loud[180] from *The Inspired Utterances (Udāna), The Farther Shore (Pārāyaṇa),* and *Discerning the Truth (Satyadṛś),* as well as *The Verses of Śaila (Śailagāthā), The Sage's Verses (Munigāthā),* and *Discourses Concerning the Goal (Arthavargīya Sūtras).*[181]

When the Blessed One was sure that Śroṇa Koṭikarṇa had finished his recitation, he said this to the venerable Śroṇa Koṭikarṇa: "Excellent! Excellent, Śroṇa! Sweet is the dharma that you have spoken and presented! It is that which I myself have fully known, understood, and expressed."

Then it occurred to the venerable Śroṇa Koṭikarṇa, "This is the appropriate time to address the Blessed One with the words of my instructor."[182] [21] With this in mind, he got up from his seat, [properly arranged his robe on one shoulder, kneeled with his right knee on the ground,] bowed [toward the Blessed One with his hands respectfully folded,] and said to the Blessed One:[183] "In the region of Aśmāparāntaka,[184] in the village of Vāsava, there lives the venerable Mahākātyāyana, who is my instructor. He venerates with his head the feet of the Blessed One and asks whether you are healthy and so on and whether you are comfortable. He also asks five questions:

{[1] In the region of Aśmāparāntaka, Bhadanta, there are very few monks. A quorum of ten monks can only be filled with difficulty. Considering this, how should we proceed with the ordination process?

[2] The ground is rough with the prickly grains of the cattle-thorn bush.

[3] In the region of Aśmāparāntaka, such things are used for mats and rugs as sheepskin, cowhide, deerskin, and goatskin. In other regions, such things are used for mats and rugs as *eraka* grass, tree bark, silk, and cotton. In the very same way, as it has already been said, in the region of Aśmāparāntaka, such things are used for mats and rugs as sheepskin and so on.

[4] People there are truly devoted to water and are preoccupied with bathing.

[5] If a monk sends another monk robes, once they've been sent off from here and if they are not delivered to their intended recipient in the requisite time, for whom do these robes cause a serious misdeed involving forfeiture?}[185]

Then the Blessed One said this to Śroṇa Koṭikarṇa, "Śroṇa, this is not the appropriate time for answering your questions. There will be an assembly of the community.[186] That will be the appropriate time for answering questions."

The Blessed One got up early the next morning and then sat down in front of the community of monks in the seat specially prepared for him. The venerable Śroṇa Koṭikarṇa approached the Blessed One, venerated with his head the feet of the Blessed One, and then stood at a respectful distance. Standing at a respectful distance, he said this to the Blessed One: "In the region of Aśmāparāntaka,[187] in the village of Vāsava, there lives the venerable Mahākātyāyana, who is my instructor. He venerates with his head the feet of the Blessed One and asks whether you are healthy and so on and whether you are comfortable. He also asks five questions:

{[1] In the region of Aśmāparāntaka, Bhadanta, there are very few monks. A quorum of ten monks can only be filled with difficulty. Considering this, how should we proceed with the ordination process?

[2] The ground is rough with the prickly grains of the cattle-thorn bush.

[3] In the region of Aśmāparāntaka, such things are used for mats and rugs as sheepskin, cowhide, deerskin, and goatskin. In other regions, such things are used for mats and rugs as *eraka* grass, tree bark, silk, and cotton. In the very same way, as it has already been said, in the region of Aśmāparāntaka, such things are used for mats and rugs as sheepskin and so on.

[4] People there are truly devoted to water and are preoccupied with bathing.

[5] If a monk sends another monk robes, once they've been sent off from here and if they are not delivered to their intended recipient in the requisite time, for whom do these robes cause a serious misdeed involving forfeiture?}[188]

"I give my permission as follows," the Blessed One said.[189]

[1] In the lands beyond the border, ordinations may be performed by five monks, if at least one of them is a master of the monastic discipline.

[2] Sandals are to be worn that are lined with just a single *palāśa* leaf, not with two or three. If it gets worn out, it should be disposed of and a new one should be procured.

[3] [Skins may be used.][190]

[4] One may bathe frequently.

[5] If a monk sends another monk robes, once they've been sent off from here and if they are not delivered to their intended recipient [in the requisite time], no one has committed a serious misdeed involving forfeiture.[191]

Then the venerable Upāli asked the Lord Buddha: "Bhadanta, the Blessed One has said that in the lands beyond the border, ordinations may be performed by five monks if at least one of them is a master of the monastic discipline. Regarding this rule, where is the border? Where is beyond the border?"

"To the east, Upāli, there is a city called Puṇḍavardhana.[192] East of that is a mountain[193] called Puṇḍakakṣa. Past that is beyond the border. To the south, there is a city called Sarāvatī (Full of Reeds). Past that is a river called Sarāvatī.[194] That is the border. Past that is beyond the border. [22] To the west, there are two brahman villages called Sthūṇa (Pillar) and Upasthūṇaka (Lesser Pillar).[195] That is the border. Past that is beyond the border. To the north is the mountain called Uśīragiri (Mountain Covered with Uśīra Grass).[196] That is the border. Past that is beyond the border."

Śroṇa Koṭikarṇa's Past Life

[Those monks in doubt asked the Lord Buddha, the remover all doubts,] "Bhadanta, what deed did the venerable Śroṇa Koṭikarṇa do [that resulted in his being born in a family that was rich, wealthy, and prosperous, with a jewel-studded earring fastened to him, and in his going forth as a monk in the Blessed One's order where, by getting rid of all his defilements, he directly realized arhatship?]"[197]

And the Blessed One spoke.

Long ago, [monks, in the city of Vārāṇasī],[198] there arose in the world the perfectly awakened tathāgata arhat named Kāśyapa, who was a blessed one and a teacher. At that time in Vārāṇasī there was a husband and wife. In the presence of the perfectly awakened Kāśyapa, they accepted the taking of the refuges as well as the precepts.

When the perfectly awakened Kāśyapa had completed all the duties of a buddha and passed into the realm of remainderless nirvāṇa, King Kṛkin[199] had a shrine built for him of four kinds of jewels that was a league in height on all sides.[200] For repairing breaks and fissures there, the king had those taxes and tributes collected at the eastern gate of the city given directly to the stūpa. When King Kṛkin died, his son named Sujāta (Well Born) was installed as king. The ministers presented him with only meager taxes and tributes. So he addressed his ministers.

"What is the reason that you've presented me with such meager taxes and tributes? Aren't taxes and tributes collected in our realm?"

"My lord," they said, "from where can taxes and tributes be collected? My lord, the old king arranged for the taxes and tributes collected at the eastern gate to be used for repairing breaks and fissures in the stūpa. If my lord permits, we will discontinue these taxes and tributes."

"Gentlemen," the king replied, "what was done by my father was done by a lord. It wasn't done by Brahmā."[201]

They reflected, "If my lord permits, we'll make it so that automatically no taxes and tributes are ever collected there." Then they permanently closed the eastern gate. No longer were taxes and tributes collected there. Soon cracks began to appear in the stūpa.

Meanwhile, that husband and wife became old, but still they remained there taking care of the stūpa.

At that time, a caravan leader from the North Country took up his goods and came to Vārāṇasī. He saw the stūpa. Cracks and fissures had appeared in it. At the sight of it, he asked, "Mother, Father, whose stūpa is this?"

"The perfectly awakened Kāśyapa's," they said.

"Who had it built?" [23]

"King Kṛkin."

"Didn't the king make any arrangements for repairing the breaks and fissures in this stūpa?"

"Yes, he made arrangements," they said. "Those taxes and tributes collected at the eastern gate of the city used to be given for repairing the breaks and fissures in the stūpa. Then King Kṛkin died, and his son Sujāta was installed as king. He discontinued those taxes and tributes. That's why cracks and fissures have appeared in the stūpa."

The caravan leader had a jeweled earring in one ear. He took off the jeweled earring and gave it to them. "Mother, Father," he said, "with this earring, repair the breaks and fissures in the stūpa. After I've disposed of my goods, I'll come back. Then I'll give you even more."

The old couple sold the earring and with the money repaired the breaks and fissures in the stūpa.[202] What was left over was set aside.

Then, one day, after the caravan leader had disposed of his goods, he returned. He saw that the stūpa had become a sight one never tires of seeing. And at the sight of it, his faith became even greater. Filled with faith, he asked, "Mother, Father, did you incur any debt?"

"No, my son," they said, "we didn't incur any debt. In fact, what was left over remains set aside."[203] Filled with faith, he gave the wealth that remained from the sale of his earring and a little more to the stūpa. Then he performed a great ceremony and made this fervent aspiration: "By this root of virtue may I be born in a family that is rich, wealthy, and prosperous; and may I obtain such virtues so that I may please and not displease just such a teacher as this one!"

Coda

"What do you think, monks? That caravan leader was none other than Śroṇa Koṭikarṇa. Since he made offerings to the stūpa of the perfectly awakened Kāśyapa and then made a fervent aspiration, as a result of that action, he was born in a family that was rich, wealthy, and prosperous, and he went forth as a monk in my order, where, by ridding himself of all defilements, he directly experienced arhatship. And as a teacher—who is equal in speed and equal in strength with the perfectly awakened Kāśyapa, and who is equally dedicated to religious duties and who has attained an equal universality—I am pleased and not displeased by Śroṇa Koṭikarṇa.

"And so, monks, the result of absolutely evil actions is absolutely evil, the result of absolutely pure actions is absolutely pure, and the result of mixed actions is mixed. Therefore, monks, because of this, you should reject absolutely evil actions and mixed ones as well, and strive to perform only absolutely pure actions. [24] It is this, monks, that you should learn to do."

"Bhadanta," the monks asked, "what deed did the venerable Śroṇa Koṭikarṇa do that resulted in his witnessing terrible realms of existence in this lifetime?"

"He committed the act of harsh speech in the presence of his mother," the Blessed One said. "As a result of that action, he witnessed terrible realms of existence in this lifetime."

This was said by the Blessed One. With their minds uplifted, the monks welcomed the words of the Blessed One.

So ends the *Koṭikarṇa-avadāna,* the first chapter in the glorious *Divyāvadāna.*

2. *The Story of Pūrṇa*

PŪRṆA-AVADĀNA

Bhava and His Sons

THE LORD BUDDHA was staying in the city of Śrāvastī at the Jeta Grove in the park of a man named Anāthapiṇḍada (Almsgiver to the Poor). Meanwhile, in the city of Sūrpāraka, there lived a householder named Bhava (Affluence). He was rich, wealthy, and prosperous, with vast and extensive holdings, and had amassed a wealth like the god Vaiśravaṇa. Truly, he rivaled Vaiśravaṇa in wealth.

The householder Bhava brought home a girl[204] from an appropriate family as his wife, and with her he fooled around, enjoyed himself, and made love. After some time, from his fooling around, enjoying himself, and making love, his wife became pregnant. Eight or nine months later she gave birth. A boy was born. For three weeks, that is twenty-one days, they celebrated the occasion of his birth in full and then they selected a name for him.

"What should the boy's name be?"

"This boy is the son of the householder Bhava," his relatives said. "Therefore he should be given the name Bhavila (Little Bhava)."

Once again from his fooling around, enjoying himself, and making love, a son was born. He was given the name Bhavatrāta (Bhava's Protector). Then another son was born to him. He was given the name Bhavanandin (Bhava's Joy). [25]

After some time, the householder Bhava became sick. He spoke with very harsh words, and so he was shunned by his wife and even his sons. But he had a servant girl, and she reflected, "In many hundreds of different ways,[205] my master has accumulated pleasurable things. Now he has become sick, and he is shunned by his wife and even his sons.[206] It wouldn't be right for me to neglect my master as well."

So she went to a doctor and said, "Sir, do you know the householder Bhava?"

"Yes, I know him. What of him?"

"He has developed some kind of sickness, and he is shunned by his wife and even his sons. Please prescribe some medicine for him."

"My daughter," he said, "you said that he is shunned by his wife and even his sons. Then who attends to him?"

"I attend to him," she said. "Now please prescribe some inexpensive medicines."[207]

So he offered a prescription: "This is the medicine for him."

Thereafter she took a little from her share from the house, and she attended to him.[208]

He became healthy, and he reflected, "I was neglected by my wife and sons. That I am alive is due to this young woman. I should repay her kindness."

"Young woman," he said to her, "I was shunned by my wife and even my sons. That I managed to live is entirely due to you. Let me offer you a reward."[209]

"Master," she said, "if you are pleased with me, then let me have sex with you."

"What's the point of your having sex with me?" he said. "I can offer you five hundred *kārṣapaṇa* coins and send you off as a free woman."

"Noble one,"[210] she said, "even if I go far away or to the next world,[211] I'll still be a slave. But if I have sex with the son of a noble man, then I will be a free woman."

Realizing that she was absolutely determined, he said, "When you're in a fertile period, let me know."

The next time she was in good health and in a fertile period, she let him know. The householder Bhava made love with her, and she became pregnant. From the very day that she became pregnant, all the aspirations and all the endeavors of the householder Bhava were fulfilled. [26]

After eight or nine months, she gave birth. A boy was born who was beautiful, good-looking, and attractive, radiant with a golden complexion, who had a parasol-shaped head,[212] lengthy arms, a broad forehead, joined eyebrows, and a prominent nose. On the very day that the boy was born, all the aspirations and all endeavors of the householder Bhava became fulfilled to an even greater degree.

Then his relatives came together and assembled. For three weeks, that is twenty-one days, they celebrated the occasion of his birth in full [and then they selected a name for him.

"What should this boy's name be?"

"From the very day that his mother became pregnant with him," his relatives said, "all the aspirations and all the endeavors of the householder Bhava became fulfilled. And on the very day that he was born, all the aspirations and all the endeavors of the householder Bhava became fulfilled to an even greater degree. Therefore he should be given the name Pūrṇa (Fulfilled)."][213] And so he was given the name Pūrṇa.

The boy Pūrṇa was given over to eight nurses—two shoulder nurses, [two playtime nurses, two nursemaids, and two wet nurses. Raised by these eight nurses, who nourished him with milk, yogurt, fresh butter, clarified butter, butter scum, and other special provisions that were very pure,][214] he grew quickly like a lotus in a lake.

When he grew up, he was entrusted to teachers to learn writing and then arithmetic, accounting, matters relating to trademarks, and to debts, deposits, and trusts. [He was also educated][215] in the science of building-sites, the science of jewels,[216] the science of elephants, the science of horses, the science of young boys, and the science of young girls. In each of the eight sciences, he became learned and well versed, capable of explaining and expounding upon them.[217]

Then the householder Bhava married off his other sons in the appropriate order, beginning with Bhavila. They became excessively attached to their wives, they stopped working, and they were obsessed with fashion.[218] As a result, the householder Bhava sat lost in thought, with his cheek in his hand.[219]

His sons saw him and asked, "Father, why do you sit there lost in thought, with your cheek in your hand?"

"Sons," he said, "I didn't get married and settle down until I had accumulated a hundred thousand gold coins. Yet you disregard your work, you're excessively attached to your wives, and you're obsessed with fashion. After I die, this house will be a place of misery. Why shouldn't I be lost in thought?"

Bhavila was wearing a jeweled earring. He took it off, put on a wooden earring instead, and made this promise: "I won't put on a jeweled earring again until I've earned a hundred thousand gold coins."

Another did the same with a lac earring. Another with a tin earring. And so, in time, the names by which they were known—Bhavila, Bhavatrāta, and Bhavanandin—disappeared. In their place appeared Dārukarṇin (Wood Earring), Stavakarṇin (Lac Earring), and Trapukarṇin (Tin Earring). Then the brothers took some goods for trade [27] and set off for the great ocean.

"Father," Pūrṇa said, "I'm going off to the great ocean as well."

"Son," he said, "you're still a child. Stay right here. Do business in a shop."

So he stayed right there. As for his brothers, they successfully completed their voyages and then returned. When they had recovered from the toil of their travels, they said, "Father, calculate the worth of our goods."

He made the calculations—each one of them had come to have one hundred thousand gold coins.

As for Pūrṇa, he had conducted his business affairs there in Sūrpāraka honestly and according to dharma,[220] and he had accumulated a hundred thousand gold coins and even more. Pūrṇa fell prostrate at the feet of his father and said, "Dad, calculate the worth of the merchandise that's found in my shop."

"Son," he said, "you've stayed right here. What of yours is there to calculate?"

"Father," he said, "just make the calculations. Only then will the truth be known."[221]

He made the calculations, and leaving aside the gold that had served as the capital for his business[222]—which he had earned honestly—there was a hundred thousand [gold coins][223] and even more. The householder Bhava was full of joy and pleasure, and he reflected, "This being is very powerful because of his merit. That's how he could stay right here and earn this much gold."

After some time, the householder Bhava became sick. "After my death," he reflected, "these sons of mine will split apart. A plan needs to be devised."

"My sons," he said to them, "gather some pieces of wood."

So they gathered some pieces of wood.

"Now light a fire with them," he said.

So they lit a fire with them.

Then the householder Bhava said, "One by one, remove those flaming pieces of wood." So they removed them, and the fire was extinguished.

"My sons," he said, "did you see that?

"Yes, father, we saw it."

Then he uttered this verse:

> Embers together burn bright.
> Brothers together do the same.
> Separated they die down—
> as with embers, so with men.

My sons, after my death, you shouldn't listen to women:

A household is split apart by women.
Cowards[224] are split apart by threatening words.
A prayer is split apart when wrongly used.
And joy is split apart by greed.[225]

The others departed,[226] but Bhavila stayed right there.

"Son," he said to him, "you should never leave Pūrṇa. That being is very powerful because of his merit." And with the words

All that is accumulated is lost in the end,
what goes up comes down in the end,
what comes together comes apart in the end,
and what lives must die in the end [28]

...he died. They adorned his funeral bier with pieces of blue, yellow, red, and white cloth, and in accordance with many rites,[227] brought him to the cremation ground and committed him to flames. Then, casting off their grief, they said, "When our father was alive, our lives were dependent on him. If we continue to disregard our work, the house will sink in ruin. That wouldn't be right.[228] We really should take our goods and go abroad."

"If that's so," Pūrṇa said, "I'll go as well."

"You stay right here and do business in a shop," they said. "We'll be the ones to go." So they took their goods and went abroad.

Entrusted with all the responsibilities, Pūrṇa stayed right there in Sūrpāraka.

The Household Splits Apart

Now it is customary that in the houses of rich lords, an allowance for expenses is distributed daily. So the brothers' wives would send off their servant girls to get the allowance. But Pūrṇa would be surrounded by the well-to-do, guildmasters, caravan leaders, and others from such professions. So the servant girls wouldn't get a chance. Only after they had attended upon him[229] and departed would Pūrṇa give the servant girls their daily allowance for expenses. The servant girls would take a long time to return and as such were scolded. So they explained the situation in detail.

"This is what happens to those in whose families the sons of slave girls control the wealth as if they were lords!" they said.

"You should go when you know the time is right," Bhavila's wife said to her servant girl.

When she knew that the time was right, she went and quickly got the daily allowance. But the other girls[230] still took a long time. They questioned her, and she gave them a full account.[231] Then they began to go with her, and they too received the daily allowance quickly.

"How is it that you now return so quickly?" the women of the house said to them. "May our older brother's wife enjoy good health![232] When her servant girl goes to Pūrṇa, she gets the daily allowance right away. So we go with her."

Unable to bear it, they said, "This is what happens to those in whose families the sons of slave girls control the wealth as if they were lords!"

After some time, Bhavila, Bhavatrāta, and Bhavanandin successfully completed their voyage and returned from the great ocean together, united and complimenting each other.

"My dear," Bhavila asked his wife, "did Pūrṇa take good care of you?" [29]

"Like a brother or a son," she said.

As for the other two, when asked by their husbands, they said, "This is what happens to those in whose families the sons of slave girls control the wealth as if they were lords!"

The brothers reflected, "Women split apart friends."

At one time, Pūrṇa opened up a shop selling cloth from Vārāṇasī.[233] Shortly thereafter Bhavila's son went there, and Pūrṇa clothed him in twin pieces of Banarsi cloth. Seeing this, the wives of the other two brothers sent off their sons, but in the meanwhile Pūrṇa closed the shop selling cloth from Vārāṇasī and opened up a shop selling secondhand cloth.[234] As fate would have it, they arrived and Pūrṇa clothed them with secondhand cloth.

Seeing this, the two women said to their husbands, "Did you see that! Vārāṇasī cloth is given to some and secondhand cloth to others."

The two men gave the following explanation: "What is all this? It must be that Pūrṇa closed down the shop selling Banarsi cloth and opened up a shop selling secondhand clothes."

After some time, Pūrṇa opened up a shop selling sugar. Bhavila's son went there, and he got a piece of sugar.[235] Seeing this, the wives of the other two brothers sent off their sons. As fate would have it, they went into the shop selling molasses that Pūrṇa had opened, and they got some molasses. The two women saw this, and they caused such a rift between their husbands that they eventually began to divide up the household.[236] The two brothers conferred with each other.

"We're completely at a loss. Let's divide the household."

"Let's inform our older brother," one of them said.

"First we should consider how we'll divide things up," the other said.

Both of them thought this over in their minds—"One of us gets the house and the fields. One gets the shop and the foreign holdings.[237] And one gets little Pūrṇa. If our older brother takes the house and fields, we can provide for ourselves with the shop and the foreign holdings. If he takes the shop and the foreign holdings, then we can provide for ourselves with the house and the fields and keep Pūrṇa completely under our control."[238]

After the two of them had conversed as such, they went to Bhavila.

"Brother, we're completely at a loss. Let's divide up the household."

"You should examine this situation carefully," he said. [30] "Women split apart households."

"We've already examined it,"[239] the two of them said. "Let's divide it up."

"If that's the case," he said, "call together members of the family [to mediate]."[240]

"We've already divided up everything," the two of them said. "One of us gets the house and the fields. One gets the shop and the foreign holdings. And one gets little Pūrṇa."

"You won't offer a share to Pūrṇa?" Bhavila said.

"He's the son of a slave girl," the other two said. "Who would give him a share? He's one of the things we divided up. If it's agreeable to you, then take him."

Bhavila reflected, "My father said to me, 'Even if you have to sacrifice all of your possessions, you should hold on to Pūrṇa.' So I'll take Pūrṇa." With this in mind, he said, "Very well then. I'll have little Pūrṇa."[241]

Then the brother who got the house and the fields, making haste, went to the house and said, "Older brother's wife,[242] get out!" She went out.

"Don't ever enter the house again."

"Why?"

"We've divided up the household. [The house is mine now]."

The brother who got the shop and the foreign holdings, likewise making haste, went to the shop and said, "Hey little Pūrṇa, step down!" Pūrṇa stepped down.

"Don't ever climb up here again."

"What's the reason?"

"We've divided up [the household].[243] [The shop is mine now]."

And so Bhavila's wife, along with Pūrṇa, set off for the home of some relatives. The children were hungry and began to cry.

"Pūrṇa," she said, "give the children some breakfast."

"Give me a *kārṣāpaṇa* coin," he said.

"You did business with so many hundreds of thousands of gold coins," she said. "Isn't there enough for the children's breakfast?"

"How was I to know that there'd be a situation like this in your house?"[244] Pūrṇa said. "If I'd have known, I would have collected many hundreds of thousands of gold coins."

The Value of Gośīrṣa Sandalwood

Now it is customary that women tie brass *kārṣāpaṇa* coins[245] in the hem of their clothes. So she gave him a small measure of brass coins and said, "Bring back some breakfast." He took it and set off for the marketplace.

Meanwhile a man carrying a load of wood that the tides had jettisoned onto the seashore approached him, overrun with cold and shaking.

Pūrṇa saw him and asked, "Friend, why are you shaking like that?"

"I don't know," he said. "I picked up this load, and since then my condition has been like this." [31]

Now Pūrṇa was an expert in the science of wood. He began to examine that load of wood, and he saw that there was some *gośīrṣa* sandalwood in it.

"Friend," he said to him, "what price will you sell this for?"

"Five hundred *kārṣāpaṇa* coins."

Pūrṇa bought the load of wood,[246] removed the *gośīrṣa* sandalwood, and went to the marketplace. With a saw, he cut off four pieces. These he sold, to be made into powder, for one thousand *kārṣāpaṇa* coins. Then he gave the man his five hundred *kārṣāpaṇa* coins and said, "Bhavila's wife lives in such-and-such house. Bring the load of wood there and say that Pūrṇa sent it."[247]

The man brought the load of wood there and explained to Bhavila's wife what had transpired. She beat her chest and said, "Just because he has lost his wealth, has he also lost his senses? 'Bring some cooked food,' I say, and he sends wood for cooking. But there's nothing at all to be cooked!"

With some of the *kārṣāpaṇa* coins that remained, Pūrṇa acquired such necessities of life as a manservant, a maidservant, cows, water buffalo, clothes, and also some cooked food. These he brought and presented to Bhavila and his wife. He made the household quite content.

Meanwhile the King of Sūrpāraka became sick with a high fever. His doctors prescribed *gośīrṣa* sandalwood, so his ministers began to search for it. In the marketplace, they listened to one person after another.

Then they went to Pūrṇa and said, "Do you have any *gośīrṣa* sandalwood?"

"Yes," he said.

"What price will you sell it for?" they said.

"One thousand *kārṣāpaṇa* coins," he said.

They bought it for one thousand *kārṣāpaṇa* coins, applied a paste made from it upon the king, and the king regained his health.

The king reflected, "What sort of king is he who doesn't have any *gośīrṣa* sandalwood in his home?"[248] Then the king asked, "Where is this from?"

"My lord, it's from Pūrṇa."

"Send for little Pūrṇa."

So a messenger went to him and said, "Pūrṇa, my lord summons you."

He began to think: "Why does the king summon me?" Then he reflected, "It's because of the *gośīrṣa* sandalwood that the king became healthy. That's why he summons me. By all means I should go and take some *gośīrṣa* sandalwood with me."

Having hidden three pieces of *gośīrṣa* sandalwood under his clothes and grasping one piece in his hand, he went to the king.

"Pūrṇa," the king asked, "is there any more *gośīrṣa* sandalwood?

"My lord," he said, "there is this piece."

"What is the price of it?" [32]

"My lord, a hundred thousand gold coins."

"Is there more?"

"There is, my lord." Then he showed him those three other pieces.

The king ordered his ministers: "Give Pūrṇa four hundred thousand gold coins."

"My lord," Pūrṇa said, "just give three. One piece is a gift to my lord."

And so he gave him three.

"Pūrṇa," the king said, "I am quite satisfied. Tell me, what reward may I offer you?"[249]

"If my lord is satisfied with me," Pūrṇa said, "may I live in my lord's kingdom undisturbed."

The king ordered his ministers: "Gentlemen, from now on, orders may be given even to princes, but not as such to Pūrṇa."

Pūrṇa and the Merchant Guild

Meanwhile five hundred merchants, having successfully completed their voyage, left the great ocean and arrived in the city of Sūrpāraka. The merchant guild in the city made an agreement: "None of us who are here together should go and approach the merchants independently. Only the group as a collective shall buy their wares."[250]

"Let's inform Pūrṇa as well," others said.

"What does that wretch have that he should be informed?"[251]

Now at that time Pūrṇa had gone outside of the city, and he heard that five hundred merchants, having successfully completed their voyage, had left the great ocean and arrived in the city of Sūrpāraka. Without even entering the city, he approached them.

"Gentlemen," he asked, "what merchandise is this?"

"This and that," they said.

"What's the price?"

"Caravan leader," they said, "you've traveled far and wide.[252] It's you who should be asked that question."

"Even if that is the case, you should still name a price."

They indicated a price of one million eight hundred thousand gold coins.

"Gentlemen," he said, "take three hundred thousand as a deposit. This is my price. I'll give you the remainder later."

"Very well then."

He had three hundred thousand brought and gave it to them. He then affixed his seal to the merchandise and departed.

Meanwhile the merchant guild sent some men as their agents: "See what merchandise there is." They went and asked, "What merchandise is there?"

"This and that."

"Well, our storerooms and warehouses are full."[253]

"Whether they be full or not, this merchandise has already been sold."

"To whom?"

"To Pūrṇa."

"Will you get much profit selling it all to Pūrṇa?"[254] [33]

"What he gave as a deposit," they said, "you wouldn't even give as the full price."

"What did he give as a deposit?"

"Three hundred thousand gold coins."

"He has really cheated his brothers!" The agents returned and informed the merchant guild.

"The goods have been sold."

"To whom?"

"To Pūrṇa."

"Will they get much profit selling it all to Pūrṇa?"

"What he gave as a deposit you wouldn't even give as the full price."

"What did he give as a deposit?"

"Three hundred thousand gold coins."

"He has really cheated his brothers!"

The merchant guild sent for him and said, "Pūrṇa, the merchant guild made an agreement that no one should buy from the merchants independently. Only the merchant guild should do the buying. So why did you buy from them?"

"Gentlemen," he said, "when you made the agreement, why wasn't I or my brother informed?[255] You alone made the agreement. You alone can abide by it."

The merchant guild became furious and restrained him in the heat of the sun so that he would pay the fine of sixty *kārṣāpaṇa* coins.[256] The king's men saw him standing in the sun and they informed the king.

"Gentlemen," the king said, "summon those men of the merchant guild."

So they summoned them.

"Gentlemen," the king said, "why did you restrain Pūrṇa in the heat of the sun?"

"My lord," they said, "the merchant guild made an agreement that no one would buy goods independently. Yet he bought them independently."

"My lord," Pūrṇa said, "question them as to whether, when they made the agreement, either I or my brother was informed."

"No, my lord," they said. ["We did not inform them."]

"Gentlemen," the king said, "Pūrṇa speaks rightly."

The merchant guild was put to shame and released Pūrṇa.

Pūrṇa and the Buddha

After some time, a need arose on behalf of the king for some of that merchandise. He summoned the merchant guild and said, "Gentlemen, I need such and such an item of merchandise. Give it to me."

"My lord," they said, "it belongs to Pūrṇa."

"Gentlemen," the king said, "I do not give orders to him. You yourselves should buy it from him and then give it to me."

They sent a messenger to Pūrṇa: "The merchant guild summons you."

"I'm not coming," he said.

Then the entire merchant guild as a collective went to his house and stood at his door. Again they sent a messenger—"Pūrṇa, come out. [34] The merchant guild is standing at your door."

Full of pride and without giving in, he went out.[257]

"Caravan leader," the merchant guild said, "give us some of the goods you have for the same price you paid."

"A fine merchant I'd be," he said, "were I to give you goods at the same price I paid for them!"[258]

"Caravan leader," they said,[259] "give it to us then for twice the price. The merchant guild is honorable."

"The merchant guild is to be honored," he reflected. "I'll give it to them." So he gave it to them at twice the price.

Pūrṇa then gave those foreign merchants[260] one million five hundred thousand gold coins.[261] The rest he sent off to his home.

He reflected, "Can I fill a water pot with a dewdrop? I'll set sail in the great ocean."

He had bells rung in the city of Sūrpāraka for the following proclamation: "Friends, merchants of Sūrpāraka, listen here! The caravan leader Pūrṇa is setting sail in the great ocean. Whoever among you is eager to set sail in the great ocean with Pūrṇa as your caravan leader, while being exempt from customs, transit, and freight fees,[262] gather up goods for export across the great ocean." Five hundred merchants then gathered up goods for export across the great ocean.

Then the caravan leader Pūrṇa, after performing auspicious rituals and benedictions for a safe journey, set sail in the great ocean surrounded by five hundred merchants.

Once he had successfully completed his voyage, he returned. And it went on like this six times. Word then spread all around that six times Pūrṇa set sail in the great ocean, successfully completed his voyage, and returned.

Meanwhile some merchants from Śrāvastī took their goods and went to the city of Sūrpāraka. Having recovered from the toil of their travels, they approached the caravan leader Pūrṇa. Having approached, they said, "Caravan leader, let us set sail together in the great ocean."

"Gentlemen," he said, "have you seen or heard of anyone who has successfully completed a voyage and returned from the great ocean six times and then set sail a seventh time?"

"Pūrṇa," they said, "we have come from far away on your account. But if you won't set sail—well, you're the authority."

He reflected, "Though I'm not in need of wealth, I'll set sail for their benefit." So with them he set off into the great ocean.

When that night turned into dawn, they recited passages at length and out loud from *The Inspired Utterances (Udāna)*, *The Farther Shore (Pārāyaṇa)*, and *Discerning the Truth (Satyadṛś)*,[263] [35] as well as *The Verses of the Elder Monks (Sthaviragāthā)*, *The Verses of Śaila*

(Śailagāthā), The Sage's Verses (Munigāthā), and *Discourses Concerning the Goal (Arthavargīya Sūtras).*[264] He heard them and said, "Gentlemen, you sing beautiful songs."

"Caravan leader," they said, "these aren't songs! This is the word of the Buddha."[265]

Hearing the word "Buddha," which he had never heard before, goosebumps arose over his entire body. Full of respect, he asked, "Gentlemen, who is this one called Buddha?"

They said, "There is an ascetic named Gautama, a son of the Śākyas from the Śākya clan, who shaved off his hair and beard, put on red clothes, and with right belief, went forth from home to homelessness. He has fully awakened to unsurpassed perfect awakening. It is he, caravan leader, who is called Buddha."

"Gentlemen, where is this Blessed One staying now?"

"Caravan leader, in the city of Śrāvastī at the Jeta Grove in the park of a man named Anāthapiṇḍada.

Pūrṇa put him in his heart, and with those men, set sail in the great ocean. After successfully completing another voyage, he returned.

Meanwhile his brother Bhavila reflected, "Pūrṇa must be exhausted from traveling the great ocean. His marriage should be arranged."

"Tell me, brother," he said to him. "The daughter of which rich man or caravan leader shall I ask in marriage on your behalf?"

"I'm not looking for sensual pleasures. If you permit me, I'll go forth as a monk."

"When there was nothing to live on in our house,[266] you didn't go forth as a monk. Why do you want to go forth as a monk now?"[267]

"Brother," Pūrṇa said, "back then it didn't suit me. But now it's the right thing to do."

Realizing that he was absolutely determined, Bhavila gave his permission.

"Brother," Pūrṇa said, "the great ocean has many dangers and few pleasures. Many set sail; few return. You shouldn't set sail in the great ocean under any circumstances. You have great wealth that you have earned honestly, while that of your brothers has been earned dishonestly. Even if they say, 'Let's live together!' you shouldn't live with them." With that said, he took his attendant and set off for Śrāvastī. In due course, he arrived there.

Once he was settled in a park in Śrāvastī, he sent a messenger to the householder Anāthapiṇḍada. He went and informed the householder Anāthapiṇḍada: "Householder, the caravan leader Pūrṇa is staying in a park, and he wants to see the householder."

The householder Anāthapiṇḍada [36] reflected, "He must have become weary of ships so now he travels overland." Then he asked, "Friend, how large an amount of goods has he brought?"

"How could he have any goods? Only a single servant accompanies him. There is just he and I."

Anāthapiṇḍada reflected, "It wouldn't right for me to usher in such an important person without the appropriate honors." So, with great honor, he ushered him in, then had him massaged, bathed, and fed.

As the two of them sat there talking freely, Anāthapiṇḍada asked, "Caravan leader, what's your purpose in coming here?"

"For the first time,[268] householder, I want to renounce, take ordination, and become a monk according to the dharma and monastic discipline that have been so well expressed."

Then the householder Anāthapiṇḍada puffed up his chest, extended his right arm, and uttered this inspired utterance:

Oh Buddha!
Oh dharma!
Oh community!
Oh the clearly expressed dharma![269]

"Even today there are important men like you who abandon large followings of family and relatives, vast treasuries and granaries, and want to renounce, take ordination, and become monks according to the dharma and monastic discipline that have been so well expressed."

At that time the Blessed One was seated in front of an assembly of many hundreds of monks, and he was teaching the dharma. The Blessed One saw the householder Anāthapiṇḍada coming with a gift, and at the sight of this, he addressed the monks: "That, monks, is the householder Anāthapiṇḍada, and he is coming with a gift. For a tathāgata, there is no gift that compares with the gift of new disciples."

The householder Anāthapiṇḍada then venerated the feet of the Blessed One, and with the caravan leader Pūrṇa, sat down at a respectful distance. Sitting down at a respectful distance, the householder Anāthapiṇḍada said this to the Blessed One: "Bhadanta, this is the caravan leader Pūrṇa. He wants to renounce, take ordination, and become a monk according to the dharma and monastic discipline that have been so well expressed. May the Blessed One, out of compassion for him, initiate and ordain him."

With his silence the Blessed One agreed to the householder Anāthapiṇḍada's request. Then the Blessed One addressed the caravan leader Pūrṇa: "Come, O monk! Follow the religious life!" [37] As soon as the Blessed One finished speaking, there he stood—head shaved, garbed in monastic robes, bowl and water pot in hand, with a week's growth of hair and beard, and with the disciplined deportment of a monk who had been ordained for one hundred years.[270]

> "Come," the Tathāgata said to him.
> With head shaved and body wrapped in robes,
> he instantly attained tranquility of the senses,
> and so he remained by the will of the Buddha.[271]

Brief Instructions in the Dharma

Now, after some time, the venerable Pūrṇa approached the Blessed One.[272] Having approached, he venerated with his head the feet of the Blessed One and then stood at a respectful distance. Standing at a respectful distance, the venerable Pūrṇa said this to the Blessed One:

"It would be good for me if the Blessed One would teach the dharma in brief. That way, having listened to the dharma in brief from the Blessed One, I may live alone, secluded, attentive, ardent, and resolute. For the very reason that the nobly born shave off hair and beard, put on red clothes, and with right belief, go forth from home to homelessness, may I too renounce and go forth as a monk so that in this lifetime I myself can also understand and directly experience the culmination of the unsurpassed religious life. [May I one day say,] 'Birth is exhausted for me, the religious life has been lived, what was to be done has been done. I will know no other existence beyond this one.'"

Thus addressed, the Blessed One said this to the venerable Pūrṇa: "Excellent, Pūrṇa! It is excellent indeed, Pūrṇa, that you speak as such:

> It would be good for me if the Blessed One would teach the dharma in brief. [That way, having listened to the dharma in brief from the Blessed One, I may live alone, secluded, attentive, ardent, and resolute. For the very reason that the nobly born shave off hair and beard, put on red clothes, and with right belief, go forth from home to homelessness, may I too renounce and go forth as a monk so that in this lifetime I myself can also understand and directly experience the culmination of the unsurpassed religious life. May I one day say, 'Birth is exhausted for me, the religious life has been lived, what was to be done has been done.][273] I will know no other existence beyond this one.'

"Therefore, Pūrṇa, listen to this. Concentrate well and closely. I will speak—

"There are, Pūrṇa, forms perceptible to the eye that are desirable, agreeable, pleasing, charming, connected with sense pleasures, and alluring. And if a monk, after seeing them, rejoices in them, welcomes them, clings to them, and remains clinging to them—then, from rejoicing in them, welcoming them, clinging to them, and remaining clinging to them, enjoyment arises. With enjoyment there arises the satisfaction of enjoyment. When there is the satisfaction of enjoyment, passion arises.[274] When there is passion for enjoyment, bondage to passion for enjoyment arises. A monk who is in bondage to passion for enjoyment, Pūrṇa, is said to be far from nirvāṇa.

"There are, Pūrṇa, sounds perceptible to the ear, smells perceptible to the nose, tastes perceptible to the tongue, objects of touch perceptible to the body, and mental objects perceptible to the mind, all of which are desirable, agreeable, pleasing, [38] charming, connected with sense pleasures, and alluring. And if a monk, after seeing them,[275] [rejoices in them, welcomes them, clings to them, and remains clinging to them—then, from rejoicing in them, welcoming them, clinging to them, and remaining clinging to them, enjoyment arises. With enjoyment there arises the satisfaction of enjoyment. When there is the satisfaction of enjoyment, passion arises. When there is passion for enjoyment, bondage to passion for enjoyment arises. A monk who is in bondage to passion for enjoyment, Pūrṇa,][276] is said to be far from nirvāṇa.

"There are, Pūrṇa, forms perceptible to the eye that are desirable, agreeable, pleasing, charming, [connected with sensual pleasure, and alluring. But if a monk, after seeing them, does not rejoice in them, does not welcome them, and does not cling to them—then, from not rejoicing in them, not welcoming them, and not clinging to them, enjoyment does not arise. When there is no enjoyment, the satisfaction of enjoyment does not arise. When there is no satisfaction of enjoyment, passion does not arise. Where there is no passion for enjoyment, bondage to passion for enjoyment does not arise. A monk who is not in bondage to passion for enjoyment, Pūrṇa, is said by the virtous to be near to nirvāṇa.

"There are, Pūrṇa, sounds perceptible to the ear, smells perceptible to the nose, tastes perceptible to the tongue, objects of touch perceptible to the body, and mental objects perceptible to the mind, all of which are desirable, agreeable, pleasing, charming, connected with sense pleasures, and alluring. But if a monk, after seeing them, does not rejoice in them, does not welcome them, and does not cling to them—then, from not rejoicing in them, not welcoming them, and not clinging to them, enjoyment does not arise. When there is no enjoyment, the satisfaction of enjoyment does not arise. When there is no satisfaction of enjoyment, passion does not arise. When there is no passion for enjoyment, bondage to passion for enjoyment does not arise. A monk who is not in bondage to passion for enjoyment, Pūrṇa,][277] is said by the virtuous[278] to be near to nirvāṇa.

"Pūrṇa, with these brief instructions, I urge you on. Where do you want to live? Where do you want to make a home?"

"Bhadanta, now that the Blessed One has urged me on with these brief instructions, I want to live in the region of Śroṇāparāntaka, to make a home in the region of Śroṇāparāntaka."

"Pūrṇa, the people of Śroṇāparāntaka are fierce, violent, cruel, abusive, scornful, and insulting. Pūrṇa, if the people of Śroṇāparāntaka abuse, scorn, and insult you face to face with harsh and wicked lies,[279] what would you think of that?"[280]

"Bhadanta, if the people of Śroṇāparāntaka abuse, scorn, and insult me face to face with harsh and wicked lies, this is what I will think: 'The people of Śroṇāparāntaka are virtuous! The people of Śroṇāparāntaka are loving! They may abuse, scorn, and insult me face to face with harsh and wicked lies, but at least they don't attack me with their hands or clumps of dirt.'"

"Pūrṇa, the people of Śroṇāparāntaka are fierce, [violent, cruel, abusive, scornful,][281] and insulting. Pūrṇa, if the people of Śroṇāparāntaka attack you with their hands or with clumps of dirt, what would you think of that?"

"Bhadanta, if the people of Śroṇāparāntaka attack me with their hands or with clumps of dirt, this is what I will think: 'The people of Śroṇāparāntaka are virtuous! The people of Śroṇāparāntaka are loving! They may attack me with their hands or with clumps of dirt, but at least they don't attack me with clubs or swords.'"

"Pūrṇa, the people of Śroṇāparāntaka are fierce, [violent, cruel, abusive, scornful,][282] and insulting. Pūrṇa, if the people of Śroṇāparāntaka attack you with clubs or swords, what would you think of that?"

"Bhadanta, if the people of Śroṇāparāntaka attack me with clubs or swords, this is what I will think: 'The people of Śroṇāparāntaka are virtuous! The people of Śroṇāparāntaka are loving! They may attack me with clubs or swords, [39] but at least they don't completely deprive me of my life!'"

"Pūrṇa, the people of Śroṇāparāntaka are fierce, [violent, cruel, abusive, scornful,][283] and insulting. Pūrṇa, if the people of Śroṇāparāntaka completely deprive you of life, what would you think of that?"

"Bhadanta, if the people of Śroṇāparāntaka completely deprive me of my life, this is what I will think: 'There are disciples of the Buddha who are so tormented, ashamed,[284] and disgusted by this stinking body that they will even wield a knife against themselves, consume poison, hang themselves to death, or fling themselves off a cliff. The people of Śroṇāparāntaka are virtuous! The people of Śroṇāparāntaka are loving! With little pain, they will liberate me from this stinking body!'"

"Excellent! Excellent, Pūrṇa! Possessed of such patience and gentleness,[285] Pūrṇa, you are able to live in the region of Śroṇāparāntaka, make a home in Śroṇāparāntaka. Go Pūrṇa. Become liberated and then liberate others! Cross over and then help others cross over![286] Breathe easy and help others breathe easy![287] Attain final nirvāṇa and then help others attain final nirvāṇa!"

The venerable Pūrṇa rejoiced and delighted in the words of the Blessed One, venerated with his head the feet of the Blessed One, and then left the Blessed One's presence.

Pūrṇa in Śroṇāparāntaka

Now in the morning, after that night had passed, the venerable Pūrṇa got dressed, took his bowl and robe, and entered Śrāvastī for alms. After wandering through Śrāvastī for alms, he finished his meal, and in the afternoon returned from his almsround. He then put away the bedding and seat that he had used, collected his bowl and robe, and wandering toward the region of Śroṇāparāntaka, eventually arrived there.

In the morning, the venerable Pūrṇa got dressed, took his bowl and robe, and entered Śroṇāparāntaka for alms. Just then a certain hunter on the hunt emerged with bow in hand. The hunter saw him and reflected, "This is inauspicious. I see a shaven-headed ascetic." With this in mind, he drew his bowstring to his ear and charged the venerable Pūrṇa. The venerable Pūrṇa saw him, and at the sight of him, he opened up his robe and [gesturing toward his stomach] said, "Friend, [40] I have entered here for the sake of *this* which is hard to fill.[288] Attack me here!"[289] Then he uttered this verse:

> For the sake of which
> birds wander in a thicket,
> wild animals move toward a trap,
> men bearing arrows, spears, and lances
> forever perish in battle,
> and poor pitiful fish, fallen on dark days,
> swallow the hook...
> It is for the sake of that—the stomach—
> that I have come here from far away
> into this cesspool of wickedness.

The hunter reflected, "This renunciant possesses such patience and gentleness. Why should I attack him?" With this thought in mind, he became full of faith. Then the venerable Pūrṇa taught him the dharma and established him in the taking of the refuges as well as in the precepts.[290] Pūrṇa also led five hundred others to become lay male disciples and five hundred to become lay female disciples. In addition, he had five hundred monasteries built, and he inspired donations of[291] many hundreds of chairs, seats, cushions, woolen blankets,[292] pillows, and shawls.

After three months, he directly experienced the three special knowledges with his body.[293] Becoming an arhat,

he was free from attachment in the three realms
  [of desire, form, and formlessness];
[he regarded clods of earth and gold as equal in value;
he possessed equanimity toward the sky
  and the palm of his hand;
he didn't distinguish between being cut by a blade
  and being anointed with sandalwood paste;
the eggshell of his ignorance was broken by knowledge;
he obtained the special knowledges, superhuman faculties,
  and analytic insights;
and he was averse to worldly attainments, temptations,
  and honors.][294]
He became worthy of respect, honor, and obeisance
  from the gods, including Indra and Upendra.

The Gośīrṣa Sandalwood Forest

After some time, the wealth of Dārukarṇin's [né Bhavila's] brothers diminished, gave out, and finally became exhausted.

Those two [went to their older brother and] said, "He's gone from our house, appearing like he did as an omen of bad luck.[295] Come now. Let's live together."

"Who is it that appeared as an omen of bad luck?" he said.

"Little Pūrṇa,"[296] the two brothers said.

"Prosperity indeed has left my house![297] Pūrṇa didn't appear as any omen of bad luck."

"Whether he be prosperity itself or bad luck—come now, let's live together."

"The two of you earned your wealth dishonestly," he said. "Mine was earned honestly. I won't make a home together with the two of you."

"That son of a slave girl has set sail again and again in the great ocean and accumulated wealth that you boast of enjoying. But how capable are you of setting sail in the great ocean?"

The two of them made him cling to his pride.

He reflected, "I'll set sail in the great ocean as well."

Then, [acting as a caravan leader, he performed auspicious rituals and benedictions for a safe journey] and set sail in the great ocean [surrounded by five hundred merchants].[298] In time the winds propelled the boat to a *gośīrṣa* sandalwood forest.

"Gentlemen," the captain said, "the *gośīrṣa* sandalwood forest that one hears of—this is it. [41] Take the best of what's here."

At that time the *gośīrṣa* sandalwood forest was under the protection of the yakṣa Maheśvara, but he had gone to an assembly for yakṣas. Meanwhile five hundred axes began felling trees in the *gośīrṣa* sandalwood forest.[299] A yakṣa called Apriya (Unkind) saw these five hundred axes felling trees in the *gośīrṣa* sandalwood forest, and at the sight of this, he approached the yakṣa Maheśvara. Having approached, he said this to the yakṣa Maheśvara: "As the officer in charge, you should know that five hundred axes are felling trees in the *gośīrṣa* sandalwood forest. Do what you need to do. Do what must be done."

The yakṣa Maheśvara became furious, adjourned the assembly of yakṣas, produced a huge hurricane with all its dangers,[300] and then set out for the *gośīrṣa* sandalwood forest.

"Listen up, merchants of Jambudvīpa (Black Plum Island)!" the captain announced. "The danger of a huge hurricane that you hear of—this is it! What do you think?"

The merchants were frightened, scared, and agitated, and with gooseflesh bristling, they began to pray to the gods:

> Śiva, Varuṇa, Kubera, Vāsava, and others![301]
> Antigods, mortals, serpents, yakṣas, and demon lords!
> We have met with a great danger that is catastrophic.
> May those without fear now be our protectors!

Some men praised Śacī's husband,
others Brahmā, Hari, or Śaṅkara,[302]
gods of the ground, the trees, or forests.
Assailed by the wind and *piśācas*,[303]
they begged for protection.

Yet Dārukarṇin remained unconcerned.

"Caravan leader," the merchants said, "we're in trouble, difficulty, and danger. How is it that you remain unconcerned?"

"Gentlemen," he said, "my brother told me this: 'The great ocean has few delights and many dangers. Blind with desire, many set sail; few return. You shouldn't set sail in the great ocean for any reason.' But I disregarded his words and set sail in the great ocean. What can I do now?"

"Who is your brother?" [42]

"Pūrṇa."

"Gentlemen," the merchants said, "the noble Pūrṇa is very powerful because of his merit. Let's take refuge in him alone!"

In one voice all of them released the cry, "Praise to the noble Pūrṇa! Praise! Praise to the noble Pūrṇa!"

Now there was a venerable deity who was full of faith in the noble Pūrṇa, and she approached the noble Pūrṇa. Having approached, she said this to him: "Noble one, your brother is in trouble, difficulty, and danger. Focus your attention." So he focused his attention.[304]

Then the venerable Pūrṇa entered a state of meditative concentration such that when his mind was concentrated, he disappeared from Śroṇāparāntaka and reappeared upon the great ocean, sitting with his legs crossed in meditation on the edge of his brother's boat. Then the hurricane receded as though it had bounced off Mount Sumeru.

The yakṣa Maheśvara reflected, "In the past, any boat touched by that hurricane was tossed and split apart as though it were made of *tūla* cotton. What is this yoga by which the hurricane has now receded as though it had bounced off Mount Sumeru?" He began to look here and there until he saw the venerable Pūrṇa sitting with his legs crossed on the edge of the boat. At the sight of him, he said, "Noble Pūrṇa, why are you harassing me?"

"I am subject to old age [and death] as well,"[305] the venerable Pūrṇa said. "Why do you torment me like this? If I hadn't amassed so many virtues, you would have reduced my brother to nothing more than a name."

"Noble one," the yakṣa Maheśvara said, "this *gośīrṣa* sandalwood forest is preserved for the use of a wheel-turning king."

"What do you think, officer? Is a wheel-turning king somehow better than a perfectly awakened tathāgata arhat?"

"Noble one, has a blessed one arisen in the world?"

"Yes, one has arisen."

"If so, then may that which has not been fulfilled be fulfilled."

Then those merchants, whose lives had gone and come back again, cultivated faith in the venerable Pūrṇa, filled their boat with *gośīrṣa* sandalwood, and set off. In due course, they arrived at the city of Sūrpāraka.

Then the venerable Pūrṇa said to his brother, "If a ship successfully completes its voyage because of the power of someone's name, the ship should go to him. Divide the jewels among the merchants.[306] I'll take the *gośīrṣa* sandalwood [43] and use it to have a palace built for the Blessed One with upper stories made of sandalwood."[307]

And so Bhavila divided the jewels among the merchants. Then the venerable Pūrṇa began to construct a palace with upper stories of *gośīrṣa* sandalwood. He summoned craftsmen and said, "Gentlemen, for your daily wage would you rather accept five hundred *kārṣāpaṇa* coins or a measure of *gośīrṣa* sandalwood powder the size of a cat's paw?"

"Noble one," they said, "a measure of *gośīrṣa* sandalwood the size of a cat's paw."

And so in a short time a palace with sandalwood upper stories was built.

A Meal in Sūrpāraka

"Gentlemen," the king said, "the palace is beautiful! Everything to be done has been done."

The shavings and powder that were left over were then ground up and presented there at the palace to be used as a salve. Pūrṇa then made all the brothers forgive each other and said to them, "Invite the community of monks led by the Buddha and feed them."

"Noble one, where is the Blessed One?"

"In Śrāvastī."

"How far is Śrāvastī from here?"

"More than a hundred leagues."

"Let's first ask the king's permission."

"Yes, you should do that."

So they approached the king and, having approached, bowed their heads respectfully and said, "My lord, we want to invite the community of monks led by Buddha and feed them. May my lord make arrangements to assist us."

"That would be excellent," the king said. "And so it shall be. I will make the arrangements."

Then the venerable Pūrṇa climbed onto the roof of that place of refuge, stood facing the Jeta Grove, kneeled with both knees on the ground, strew flowers, and waved incense. Then a park attendant[308] gave him a golden pitcher, and he began to offer worship.

> O you of pure virtue,[309] whose intellect is so very pure,
> who always sees the intentions in an offering of food!
> Look upon those who have no protector, virtuous one!
> Have pity and come here!

Then, by the Buddha's innate power and the divine power of deities, those flowers formed an overhead flower-canopy and traveled off to the Jeta Grove. There they stopped in the area of the elders, while the incense appeared like the peak of a cloud and the water from the pitcher like a stick made of beryl.[310]

Now the venerable Ānanda was skilled in reading signs, so he respectfully cupped his hands together and asked the Blessed One: "Blessed One, where has this invitation come from?" [44]

"From the city of Sūrpāraka, Ānanda."

"Bhadanta, how far away is the city of Sūrpāraka?"

"More than a hundred leagues, Ānanda."

"Shall we go?"

"Ānanda, inform the monks that whoever is eager to go to the city of Sūrpāraka tomorrow to eat should take a tally stick."

"Yes, Bhadanta," the venerable Ānanda replied, consenting to the Blessed One's request. Then he took a tally stick and stood in front of the Blessed One. The Blessed One also took a tally stick along, as did the most senior monks.

At that time another venerable Pūrṇa, the elder Kuṇḍopadhānīyaka (One Who Uses a Water Pot as a Pillow),[311] who had been liberated by wisdom,[312] was seated in that very assembly. As one of those assembled, he also began to take a tally stick. The venerable Ānanda responded to him with these verses:

> Venerable one, this is not a meal
> in the house of the King of Kośala
> or in the home of Sudatta
> or in the residence of Mṛgāra.[313]
>
> The city of Sūrpāraka is
> more than one hundred leagues from here.
> One should use magical powers to go there.
> So be silent, little Pūrṇa.

Since little Pūrṇa was only liberated by wisdom, he had not generated magical powers. It occurred to him, "Though I have spewed up, spit out, abandoned, and driven away the whole mass of defilements, I am still dejected, for I still don't possess the magical powers common even to heretics." Just then he built up his strength and generated magical powers, and before the venerable Ānanda could give a tally stick to the third elder, he stretched out his arm, which was like the trunk of an elephant, and took a tally stick for himself. Then he uttered these verses:

> Not through physical stature or learning
> nor by virtue of brute force, O Gautama,
> not even through powerful words or wishes does one attain
> in this world possession of the six superhuman faculties.
>
> It is through the various powers of tranquility,
> virtue, insight, and the powers of meditation that
> the six superhuman faculties are examined by those like me,
> whose youth has been crushed by old age.[314]

Then the Blessed One addressed the venerable Ānanda: "Monks, this monk is foremost among those monks that are my disciples in coming forward and taking tally sticks.[315] [45] Of those who take tally sticks, Pūrṇa—the elder Kuṇḍopadhānīyaka—is first of all."

The Blessed One then addressed the venerable Ānanda: "Ānanda, go and inform the monks as follows—'Though I have said, monks, that you should live with your virtues concealed and your sins exposed, that city of Sūpāraka is propped up by heretics. Whoever of you has obtained magical powers should make use of them to go to the city of Sūrpāraka to eat a meal.'"

"Yes, Bhadanta," the venerable Ānanda replied, consenting to the Blessed One's request. Then he informed the monks: "Venerable ones, the Blessed One has said the following—'Though I have said, monks, that you should live with your virtues concealed and your sins exposed, [that city of Sūrpāraka is propped up by heretics. Whoever of you has obtained magical powers should make use of them to go to the city of Sūrpāraka] to eat a meal.'"[316]

Meanwhile the king of Sūrpāraka had the city of Sūrpāraka cleared of stones, pebbles, and gravel; sprinkled with sandalwood-scented water; adorned with small pots filled with various kinds of fragrant incense; festooned with rows of silk banners; and strewn with a variety of flowers. It was beautiful.

Now the city of Sūrpāraka had eighteen gates, and the king had seventeen sons. The princes, in the height of splendor, were stationed one to a gate. And at the main gate, with great royal pomp, was stationed the king, sovereign of Sūrpāraka, along with the venerable Pūrṇa, Dārukarṇin, Stavakarṇin, and Trapukarṇin.

Just then, making use of their magical powers, some monks arrived, some bearing leaf plates, some bearing leaf trays, and some bearing bowls.[317]

Seeing them, the king said, "Bhadanta Pūrṇa, has the Blessed One arrived?"

"Your majesty," the venerable Pūrṇa said, "these are monks bearing leaf plates, bearing leaf trays, and bearing bowls. The Blessed One is not here yet."

Then, making use of many varieties of meditation and meditative absorption, the most senior monks arrived.

"Bhadanta Pūrṇa," he asked again, "has the Blessed One arrived?"

"Your majesty," the venerable Pūrṇa said, "the Blessed One is not here. Those monks are his most senior disciples."

Then, at that time, one of the lay devotees uttered this verse:

Some ride beautiful lions or tigers,
elephants, horses, nāgas, or bulls;
some jeweled flying mansions or mountains,
trees or sparkling chariots of many colors.

Others, like rain clouds in the sky
adorned with tendrils of lightning,
rise up through their magical powers,
as if pleased to be going to the city of the gods. [46]

Some rise up, breaking through the earth,
others descend from the surface of the sky,
and some magically appear in their seats.
Look at the power of those who possess magical powers!

The Buddha's Journey to Sūrpāraka

Meanwhile the Blessed One, [still in the city of Śrāvastī at the Jeta Grove,] washed his feet outside of the monastery, entered the monastery, and sat down in the seat specially prepared for him, holding his body upright and making his mindfulness fully present. Then the Blessed One, with his mind resolute, put his foot down in his perfumed chamber, and the earth moved in six different ways: it quivered, quavered, and quaked; it shifted, shuddered, and shook.

The east rose up and the west sank down.
The west rose up and the east sank down.
The south rose up and the north sank down.
The north rose up and the south sank down.
The ends rose up and the middle sank down.
The middle rose up and the ends sank down.

"Noble Pūrṇa," the king asked the venerable Pūrṇa, "what is this?"

"Your majesty," he said, "the Blessed One, with his mind resolute, has put down his foot in his perfumed chamber. This is why the earth has moved in six different ways."

Then the Blessed One sent forth brilliant rays of light the color of gold such that Jambudvīpa became suffused in golden light.

With his eyes wide open with wonder, the king once again asked, "Noble Pūrṇa, what is this?"

"Your majesty," he said, "the Blessed One has sent forth brilliant rays of light the color of gold."

Now the Blessed One was self-controlled and his followers were self-controlled, he was calm and his followers were calm.[318] Along with five hundred arhats,[319] he set out toward Sūrpāraka.

At that time a deity who lived in the Jeta Grove grabbed a branch of a *bakula* tree and stood behind the Blessed One shading him.

Then the Blessed One, knowing her inclinations, propensities, makeup, and nature, gave her a discourse on the dharma that penetrated the four noble truths. When that deity heard this, with her thunderbolt of knowledge she broke through that mountain which is the false view of individuality that arises with its twenty peaks of incorrect views, and directly experienced the reward of the stream-enterer.

Meanwhile in a certain place there lived five hundred housewives. They saw the Lord Buddha,

who was adorned with the thirty-two marks of a great man,
whose body was radiant with the eighty minor marks,
who was adorned with a halo extending an arm's length, [47]
whose brilliance was greater than a thousand suns,
and who, like a mountain of jewels that moved,
    was beautiful from every side.

At the sight of him, great faith arose in them for the Buddha. Now it is law of nature that

twelve years' practice of quiescence meditation
does not produce such peace of mind—
nor does the birth of a son for one who has no son,
the sight of a treasure trove for one who is destitute,
or a royal coronation for one who desires kingship.

None of these produce such well-being
as when a being who has accumulated roots of virtue
sees a buddha for the first time.

The Blessed One, perceiving that it was time to train these housewives, sat down in front of the community of monks in the seat specially prepared for him.

As for those women, they venerated with their heads the feet of the Blessed One and then sat down at a respectful distance. Then the Blessed One, knowing their inclinations, propensities, makeup, and nature, [gave them a discourse on the dharma that penetrated the four noble truths. When they heard this, with their thunderbolts of knowledge they broke though that mountain which is the false view of individuality that arises with its twenty peaks of incorrect views,][320] and directly experienced the reward of the stream-enterer.

Having seen the truth, three times they uttered this inspired utterance:

What the Blessed One has done for us, Bhadanta,
  neither our mothers nor our fathers have done,
  nor any king,
  nor any dear ones, kinsmen, or relatives,
  nor any deities or deceased ancestors,
  nor ascetics or brahmans.
Oceans of blood and tears have dried up!
Mountains of bones have been scaled!
The doors to the lower realms of existence have been closed!
We have been established among gods and mortals!
We have surpassed those who have crossed over![321]
And so, we take refuge in the Lord Buddha, in the dharma,
  and in the community of monks.
May the Blessed One consider us as disciples.

Then, getting up from their seats, they bowed toward the Blessed One with their hands respectfully folded and said this to the Blessed One: "What a good thing it would be if the Blessed One would give us something here that we could serve."

Then the Blessed One made use of his magical powers and presented them with some of his hair and nails. They, in turn, established a stūpa for the Blessed One's hair and nails.

The deity who lived in the Jeta Grove then established that *bakula* branch in the terrace around that stūpa[322] and said to the Blessed One, "Blessed One, I will stay here and serve the stūpa." And she stayed right there.

Some know that place as the "Housewife's Stūpa," others as the "Bakula Terrace." Even today monks who venerate shrines venerate it.

Then the Blessed One departed.

Meanwhile, in a certain hermitage, there lived five hundred seers. Their hermitage was well provided with flowers, fruit, and water. They were intoxicated with pride and didn't respect anyone. [48] Then the Blessed One, perceiving that it was time to train these seers, approached that hermitage. Having approached, he made use of his magical powers and destroyed the flowers and fruits from the hermitage, dried up the water, ploughed under the verdant meadows,[323] and broke down the altars.

Those seers, with cheek in hand, sat there lost in thought.

"Great seers," the Blessed One said, "why do you sit there lost in thought?"

"Blessed One," they said, "you are a field of merit on two feet. You entered this place, and such is our condition."

"What?" the Blessed One said.

"Blessed One," they said, "our hermitage, which was well provided with flowers, fruit, and water, has been destroyed. Please restore it to how it was before."

"Very well then," the Blessed One said.[324]

Then the Blessed One withdrew his magical powers, and all was restored to how it was before.

The seers were filled with awe and cultivated faith in their hearts for the Blessed One.

Then the Blessed One, knowing their inclinations, propensities, makeup, and nature, gave them a discourse on the dharma that penetrated the four noble truths. When they heard this, the five hundred seers directly experienced the reward of the nonreturner and gained magical powers.

Then, bowing toward the Blessed One with their hands respectfully folded, they said this to the Blessed One: "Bhadanta, may we renounce, take ordination, and become monks according to the dharma and monastic discipline that have been so well expressed. May we follow the religious life in the presence of the Blessed One."

Then the Blessed One addressed them uttering the "Come, O monk" formula for ordination: "Come, O monks! Follow the religious life!" As soon as the Blessed One finished speaking, there they stood—head shaved, garbed in monastic robes, bowl and water pot in hand, with a week's growth of hair and beard, and the disciplined deportment of a monk who had been ordained for one hundred years.

> "Come," the Tathāgata said to them.
> With heads shaved and bodies wrapped in robes,
> they instantly attained tranquility of the senses,
> and so they remained by the will of the Buddha.[325]

After striving, struggling, and straining, they came to understand that ever-turning five-spoked wheel [of saṃsāra; they dealt a final blow to rebirth in all realms of saṃsāra because these were subject to decay and decline, scattering and destruction; and by ridding themselves of all defilements, they directly experienced arhatship. Becoming arhats,

> they were free from attachment in the three realms
>   of desire, form, and formlessness;

they regarded clods of earth and gold as equal in value;
they possessed equanimity toward the sky
and the palm of their hands;
they didn't distinguish between being cut by a blade
and being anointed with sandalwood paste;
the eggshell of their ignorance was broken by knowledge;
they obtained the special knowledges, superhuman faculties,
and analytic insights;
and they were averse to worldly attainments, temptations,
and honors.]
They became worthy of respect, [honor, and obeisance
from the gods, including Indra and Upendra.][326]

Then that seer who had been their instructor said, "Blessed One, I have deceived a great many people with this costume of a seer. Now I will lead them to have faith in the Blessed One, and then I will go forth as a monk."

Then those five hundred seers and the five hundred monks from before encircled the Blessed One, forming the shape of a crescent moon. [49] He then made use of his magical powers and set off high into the sky. In due course, he arrived at Mount Musalaka.

At that time on Mount Musalaka there lived a seer named Vakkalin (Bark-Wearer). From a distance, that seer saw the Blessed One,

who was adorned with the thirty-two marks of a great man,
[whose body was radiant with the eighty minor marks,
who was adorned with a halo extending an arm's length,
whose brilliance was greater than a thousand suns,
and who, like a mountain of jewels that moved,][327]
was beautiful from every side.

As soon as he saw him, his mind became filled with faith in the presence of the Blessed One. Full of faith, he thought, "I really should descend from the mountain so that I can approach the Blessed One to see him. But then the Blessed One will pass right by me in his search for new disciples. Suppose I throw myself from the mountain." So he threw himself from the mountain.

Now lord buddhas are always alert. And so, the Blessed One made use of his magical powers and received him. Then the Blessed One, knowing his inclinations, propensities, makeup, and nature, gave him a discourse on the dharma such that when he heard it, Vakkalin directly experienced the reward of the nonreturner and gained magical powers.

Then he said this to the Blessed One: "Bhadanta, may I renounce, take ordination, and become a monk according to the dharma and monastic discipline that have been so well expressed. [May I follow the religious life in the presence of the Blessed One."

Then the Blessed One addressed him uttering the "Come, O monk" formula for ordination: "Come, O monk! Follow the religious life!" As soon as the Blessed One finished speaking, there he stood—head shaved, garbed in monastic robes, bowl and water pot in hand, with a week's growth of hair and beard, and the disciplined deportment of a monk who had been ordained for one hundred years.

> "Come," the Tathāgata said to him.
> With head shaved and body wrapped in robes,
> he instantly attained tranquility of the senses,
> and so he remained by the will of the Buddha.][328]

Then the Blessed One addressed the monks: "O monks, this monk Vakkalin is foremost among my monks who are zealously devoted in their belief in me."

Then the Blessed One, surrounded by those one thousand monks and performing various miraculous deeds as he went, arrived in the city of Sūrpāraka. The Blessed One reflected, "If I enter the city through one gate, those at the other gates will be distressed. I really should make use of my magical powers to enter the city." And so, making use of his magical powers, he rose up high into the sky and then descended into the middle of the city of Sūrpāraka.

Then the king, who was the sovereign of Sūrpāraka, the venerable Pūrṇa, Dārukarṇin, Stavakarṇin, Trapukarṇin, and those seventeen sons[329] with their respective retinues approached the Blessed One, as did many hundreds and thousands of beings. The Blessed One, followed by those many hundred and thousands of beings, then approached the palace with its upper stories of sandalwood. Having approached, he sat down in front of the community of monks in the seat specially prepared for him. Not seeing the Blessed One,[330] [50] the people began to break down the palace and its upper stories of sandalwood.

The Blessed One reflected, "If the palace with its upper stories of sandalwood is broken, donors will have their merit impeded. Suppose I magically transform it into a palace made of crystal." So the Blessed One magically transformed it into a palace made of crystal.

Then the Blessed One, knowing the assembly's inclinations, propensities, makeup, and nature, gave them a discourse on the dharma such that when they heard it, many hundreds and thousands of beings attained great distinction. Some produced roots of virtue conducive to liberation; some roots of virtue conducive to attaining the four stages of penetrating insight; some directly experienced the reward of the stream-enterer; some the reward of the once-returner; some the reward of the nonreturner; and some rid themselves of all defilements and thereby directly experienced arhatship. Some set their minds on attaining awakening as a disciple, some awakening as a solitary buddha, and some unsurpassed perfect awakening. Almost the entire assembly was affected and became favorably inclined toward the Buddha, intent on the dharma, and well disposed toward the community.

Then Dārukarṇin, Stavakarṇin, and Trapukarṇin[331] prepared fine foods, both hard and soft, prepared the seats, and had a messenger inform the Blessed One that it was now the appropriate time: "It is time, Bhadanta. The food is ready. Now the Blessed One may do as the time permits."

The Buddha and the Nāga Kings

At that time, there lived in the great ocean two nāga kings, Kṛṣṇa and Gautama. They reflected, "The Blessed One teaches the dharma in the city of Sūrpāraka. Let's go and listen to the dharma." Then those two, with a retinue of five hundred nāgas, produced five hundred rivers and set out for the city of Sūrpāraka.

Now lord buddhas are always alert. So the Blessed One reflected, "If those two nāga kings, Kṛṣṇa and Gautama, come to the city of Sūrpāraka, they will defile it."[332] And so, the Blessed One addressed the venerable Mahāmaudgalyāyana: "Mahāmaudgalyāyana, on behalf of the Tathāgata, go and accept [from Pūrṇa's brothers] some 'irregular' almsfood.[333] Why is that? For me, Maudgalyāyana, there are five types of irregular alms. What are these five? The almsfood of a monk who is a visitor at a monastery, of one setting out on a trip, of one who is sick, of an attendant to the sick, and of the acting caretaker of a monastery." In this instance, the Blessed One himself was taking care of the monastery.[334]

Then the Blessed One, accompanied by Maudgalyāyana approached the two nāga kings, Kṛṣṇa and Gautama. [51] Having approached, he said, "Nāga lords, pay attention. Spare the city of Sūrpāraka from defilement."[335]

"Bhadanta," they said, "we come with such faith that we could never harm any living being, even a tiny biting ant, let alone the crowds of people who live in the city of Sūrpāraka."

Then the Blessed One gave the two nāga kings, Kṛṣṇa and Gautama, a discourse on the dharma such that when they heard it, they took refuge in the Buddha, they took refuge in the dharma and in the community, and they accepted the precepts.

Then the Blessed One began to take his meal.

Every one of the nāgas reflected, "What a good thing it would be if the Blessed One would drink water from my river!"

The Blessed One reflected, "If I drink water from just one of them, the rest of them would think otherwise [and turn away from the dharma].[336] A plan needs to be devised."

And so, the Blessed One addressed the venerable Mahāmaudgalyāyana: "Maudgalyāyana, go to the confluence of those five hundred rivers and bring back from there a bowlful of water."

"Yes, Bhadanta," the venerable Maudgalyāyana replied, consenting to the Blessed One's request. So at the confluence of those five hundred rivers, he took a bowlful of water and then approached the Blessed One. Having approached, he presented him the bowlful of water. The Blessed One accepted it and partook of it.

Maudgalyāyana's Mother

Then the venerable Maudgalyāyana reflected, "Previously the Blessed One said,

> Monks, a mother and father undertake such hardships for the sake of a son. They nurture, nourish, and foster him, they give him mother's milk, and they show him the wondrous Jambudvīpa. Were a son to care for[337] his mother with half his energy and father with the other half for a full one hundred years; or to give his mother and father all the gems, pearls, beryl, conch, quartz,[338] coral, silver, gold, emeralds, sapphires,[339] red pearls,[340] and right-spiraling conch shells found on this great earth; or to establish them in various forms of lordship and dominion—with this, that son would still not have sufficiently served or obliged his mother and father. But a son who inspires, trains, introduces, and establishes his mother and father who are without faith into the riches of

> faith; who inspires, trains, introduces, and establishes his mother and father who are unvirtuous into the riches of virtue, [52] who are greedy into the riches of sacrifice, who are unwise into the riches of wisdom—with this, that son would have served and obliged his mother and father sufficiently.

"And yet I never performed such a good deed for my mother. I should focus my attention on where my mother has been reborn."[341] He began to focus his attention, and then he saw that she had been reborn in the world system of Marīcika (Mirage).

"Who will train her?" he reflected. He saw that it would be the Blessed One. Then it occurred to him, "We have come here from far away [after many births].[342] I really should inform the Blessed One of this matter." So he said this to the Blessed One: "Bhadanta, previously the Blessed One said, 'Monks, a mother and father undertake such hardships for the sake of a son.' Well, my mother has been reborn in the world system of Marīcika, and she is to be trained by the Blessed One. Therefore, out of compassion, may the Blessed One train her."

"Maudgalyāyana," the Blessed One said, "let's go, but making use of whose magical powers?"

"By making use of mine, Blessed One."

Then the Blessed One and the venerable Mahāmaudgalyāyana set their feet on the peak of Mount Sumeru and set off. In seven days they arrived at the Marīcika world system. That noble daughter[343] saw the venerable Mahāmaudgalyāyana from a distance, and at the sight of him, she anxiously approached him and said, "Ah, after a long time I see my dear son again!"

"Bhadanta,"[344] the people said, "this renunciant is an old man, and this is a young woman. How can she be his mother?"

"Gentlemen," the venerable Maudgalyāyana said, "these elements of mine [that make me who I am] were fostered by her.[345] Therefore this young woman is my mother."

Then the Blessed One, knowing that virtuous daughter's inclinations, propensities, makeup, and nature, gave her a discourse on the dharma that penetrated the four noble truths. When that virtuous daughter heard this, with her thunderbolt of knowledge she broke through that mountain which is the false view of individuality that arises with its twenty peaks of incorrect views, and directly experienced the reward of the stream-enterer. Having seen the truth, three times she uttered this inspired utterance:

> [What the Blessed One has done for the likes of us, Bhadanta,
> neither our mothers nor our fathers have done,
> nor any king,
> nor any dear ones, kinsmen, or relatives,
> nor any deities or deceased ancestors,
> nor ascetics or brahmans.
> Oceans of blood and tears have dried up!
> Mountains of bones have been scaled!
> The doors to the lower realms of existence have been closed!
> We have been established] among gods and mortals![346]

And then she said,

> Because of your power,[347]
> closed is the truly terrifying path
> to the lower realms of existence,
> defiled as it is by many sins.
> Open is the realm of heaven,
> which is filled with merit.
> I have found the path to nirvāṇa!
>
> From taking refuge in you,
> today I have obtained
> freedom from sin and[348]

a pure and fully purified vision. [53]
I have attained that beloved state,
so beloved to the noble ones,
and crossed to the far shore
of the sea of suffering.

O you who are honored in this world
by demons, mortals, and gods,
and freed from birth,
old age, sickness, and death,
even in a thousand lives
seeing you is extremely rare.
O Sage, seeing you today
brings great results!

"I have crossed over, Bhadanta! I have crossed over. And so, I take refuge in the Blessed One, in the dharma, and in the community of monks. Hereafter and for as long as I live and breathe, consider me a faithful disciple who has taken the refuges. May the Blessed One, along with the noble Mahāmaudgalyāyana, now accept alms from me."

The Blessed One accepted that noble daughter's invitation with his silence.

Now when the noble daughter was sure that the Blessed One and the venerable Mahāmaudgalyāyana were comfortably seated, she served and indulged them, with her own hands, with hard and soft foods, both fresh and fine. [When she had served and indulged them, with her own hands, with many courses of hard and soft foods, both fresh and fine,][349] and was sure that the Blessed One had finished eating, washed his hands, and set aside his bowl, she sat down in front of the Buddha, taking a lower seat, to listen to the dharma.

Then the Blessed One gave her a discourse on the dharma. The venerable Mahāmaudgalyāyana collected the Blessed One's bowl and washed it for him.[350]

"Mahāmaudgalyāyana," the Blessed One said, "let's go."

"Yes, Blessed One. Let's go."

"By means of whose magical powers?"

"Those of the Blessed One, the Tathāgata."

"If that is so, then focus your attention on the Jeta Grove."

"We have already arrived, Blessed One! We have arrived!"

"Yes, we have arrived, Maudgalyāyana."[351]

Then, his intellect overcome with wonder, he said, "Blessed One, what is the name of this magical power?"

"*Mind-speed,*[352] Maudgalyāyana."

"Bhadanta, I didn't know that the dharmas of the Buddha were so profound.[353] Had it been known to me, my mind would not have turned away from unsurpassed perfect awakening,[354] even if my body were ground into bits the size of sesame seeds.[355] What can I do now? I am like kindling that has already burned up."

Those monks in doubt asked the Lord Buddha, the remover of all doubts, "Bhadanta, what deed did the venerable Pūrṇa do so that he was born in a family that was rich, wealthy, and prosperous? What deed did he do so that he was born in the womb of a slave girl, then went forth as a monk, and by ridding himself of all defilements [54] directly experienced arhatship?"

"Monks," the Blessed One said, "the deeds that the monk Pūrṇa has performed and accumulated have now come together, and their conditions have matured.[356] They remain before him like an oncoming flood and will certainly come to pass. Those deeds were performed and accumulated by Pūrṇa. Who else will experience their results? For those deeds, monks, that are performed and accumulated, monks, do not mature outside of oneself, neither in the element of earth nor in the element of water, in the element of fire or in the element of wind. Instead, those deeds that are done, both good and bad, mature in the aggregates, the elements, and the sense bases that are appropriated when one is reborn.[357]

Actions never come to naught,
even after hundreds of millions of years.[358]
When the right conditions gather and the time is right,
then they will have their effect on embodied beings."

Pūrṇa Speaks Harshly

Long ago, monks, in this present auspicious age, when people lived for twenty thousand years, there arose in the world a perfectly awakened buddha named Kāśyapa,

who was perfect in knowledge and conduct,
a sugata,
a knower of the world,
an unsurpassed guide for those in need of training,
a teacher of gods and mortals,
a buddha,
and a blessed one.

That lord buddha stayed near the city of Vārāṇasī. Pūrṇa went forth as a monk into his order. He became a master of [the threefold collection of scripture known as] the Tripiṭaka, and he engaged himself in the duties of the community in accordance with the dharma.[359]

Once one of the arhats was appointed as the acting caretaker of the monastery. He began sweeping the monastery, but the sweepings were scattered here and there by the wind. He reflected, "Let the work wait until the wind calms down."

Now Pūrṇa, while engaged in community duties, saw that the monastery had not been swept. In a fit of rage, he committed an act of harsh speech: "Who is the son of a slave girl whose turn it is to be caretaker of the monastery?" The arhat heard this and reflected, "He's having a fit. Let it be for a while. I'll inform him later."

When Pūrṇa's fit had passed, he approached Pūrṇa and said, "Do you know who I am?"

"I know," he said, "that you have gone forth as a monk in the order of the perfectly awakened Kāśyapa, and so have I."

"That very well may be so," he said, "but since going forth as a monk, I have done what should be done and become released from all bonds to existence.[360] But you have committed an act of harsh speech. [55] Confess your sin as sin. Maybe then this bad karma will diminish, give out, and finally be exhausted."

Pūrṇa then confessed his sin as sin.

Now Pūrṇa would have been reborn in hell and then as a slave girl's son, but [because he confessed his sin as sin] he was not reborn in hell. Instead, for five hundred births he was reborn in the womb of a slave girl. Even now, in his last birth, he was again reborn in the womb of a slave girl. But since he attended to the community, he was born in a family that was rich, wealthy, and prosperous. And since he read and studied and worked for the welfare of many,[361] he went forth as a monk in my order and, by ridding himself of all defilements, directly experienced arhatship.

"And so, monks, the result of absolutely evil actions is absolutely evil, the result of absolutely pure actions is absolutely pure, and the result of mixed actions is mixed. Therefore, monks, because of this, you should reject absolutely evil actions and mixed ones as well, and strive to perform only absolutely pure actions. It is this, monks, that you should learn to do."

This was said by the Blessed One. With their minds uplifted, the monks welcomed the words of the Blessed One.

So ends the *Pūrṇa-avadāna,* the second chapter in the glorious *Divyāvadāna.*

3. *The Story of Maitreya*

MAITREYA-AVADĀNA

When the Magadhan king Ajātaśatru (Having No Enemies), the son of Queen Videhī, had a bridge of boats[362] constructed for his mother and father, then the Licchavis of Vaiśālī had a bridge of boats constructed for the sake of the Blessed One.

The nāgas reflected, "We really should lay our bodies down and have the Blessed One cross the Gaṅgā River over a bridge made of our serpent hoods."[363] They then constructed a bridge of their serpent hoods.

Regarding this, the Blessed One addressed the monks: "Whoever among you, monks, is eager to go from Rājagṛha to Śrāvastī, crossing the Gaṅgā River by the bridge of boats of the Magadhan king Ajātaśatru, the son of Queen Videhī, cross that way. And whoever, [56] monks, wishes to cross by the bridge of boats of the Licchavis of Vaiśālī, cross that way. As for me, I will cross the Gaṅgā River, together with the venerable monk Ānanda, by the bridge made of nāgas' serpent hoods."

And so, some crossed over the bridge of boats of the Magadhan king Ajātaśatru, the son of Queen Videhī, and others over the bridge of boats of the Licchavis of Vaiśālī. As for the Blessed One, he crossed, together with the venerable Ānanda, over the bridge made of nāgas' serpent hoods.

Now at that time one of the Buddha's lay disciples uttered these verses:

Those who build a bridge,
leaving behind the shallows,
cross oceans and rivers.
The people bound a raft;
the wise simply crossed.[364]

The Lord Buddha has crossed,
the brahman remains on shore.
Here the monks swim across,
the disciples bind a raft.

What is the use of a well
if water is all around?
If the root of thirst is cut,
what can one go and search for?

In a certain place, the Blessed One saw an elevated tract of land.[365] At the sight of it, he addressed the venerable [Ānanda]:[366] "Ānanda, do you want to see a sacrificial post that is one thousand arm-lengths high, sixteen bow-shots across,[367] variegated with many jewels, divine, and made entirely of gold? It is the one that King Mahāpraṇāda (Great Cry), after making offerings and performing meritorious deeds, immersed in the Gaṅgā River."

"Yes, Blessed One. For this it is the right time. Sugata, for this it is the right occasion. The Blessed One should raise the sacrificial post so that the monks may see it."

Then the Blessed One with his hand—which had the emblems of the wheel, the svastika, and the *nandyāvarta;* which had webbed fingers; which had come into being by performing many hundreds of meritorious deeds; and which brought comfort to the fearful[368]—touched the earth.

The nāgas reflected, "Why did the Blessed One touch the earth? Ah—so that those who want to see the sacrificial post can see it."

Then the nāgas raised the sacrificial post, and the monks began to look at it. But the venerable Bhaddālin, unconcerned, just sewed his robe.

Then the Blessed One addressed the monks: [57] "Monks, contemplate the appearance of this sacrificial post, its height and width, for it will disappear." And then it disappeared.[369]

The monks asked the Lord Buddha, "Look, Bhadanta. The monks looked at the sacrificial post, but the venerable Bhaddālin, unconcerned, just sewed his robe. Is this because he's free from desire or because he paid respect to it previously? If it's because he's free from desire—well, there are others here who are also free from desire. If it's because he paid respect to it previously—how did he pay respect to it?"[370]

"Monks," the Blessed One said, "it is because he is free from desire and because he paid respect to it previously."

"How did he pay respect to it?"

Mahāpraṇāda and the Sacrificial Post

Long ago, monks, there was a king named Praṇāda (Cry) who was a close friend of Śakra, lord of the gods. Without a son and yet desiring one, he sat lost in thought, his cheek in his hand. "I have great riches, but I have no son," he thought. "After my death, the royal lineage will be broken."

Śakra saw him and asked, "Friend, why do you sit there lost in thought, your cheek in your hand?"

"Kauśika," he said, "I have great riches, but I have no son. After my death, the royal lineage will be broken."

"Friend, don't worry," Śakra said. "If there's a divine being[371] destined to fall from divine existence, I'll urge him to become your son."[372]

It is a law of nature that when a divine being is destined to fall from divine existence, five omens appear—his unsoiled clothes get soiled, his fresh garlands wither, a bad smell emerges from his mouth,[373] sweat oozes from both of his armpits, and he takes no comfort[374] in his throne. Meanwhile, these five omens appeared for one of the divine beings.

"Friend," Śakra, lord of the gods, said to him, "take rebirth in the womb of King Praṇāda's principal queen."

"Kauśika, that's madness!" he said. "Kings commit many offenses. Don't let me end up in hell having ruled a kingdom unjustly."

"Friend, I'll remind you," Śakra said.

"Kauśika, lords are careless and indulge in many pleasures."

"This is true, my friend. Nevertheless, I'll remind you."

That divine being then took rebirth in the womb of King Praṇāda's principal queen. On the very day that he took rebirth, [58] a large crowd of people released a cry. After eight or nine months, she gave birth. A boy was born who was beautiful, good-looking, and attractive, radiant with a golden complexion, who had a parasol-shaped head, lengthy arms, a broad forehead, joined eyebrows, and a prominent nose.

His relatives came together and assembled to select a name for him. "What should this boy's name be?"

"On the very day that this boy descended into his mother's womb," the relatives said, "a large crowd of people released a cry. And on the very day that he was born, a large crowd of people also released a cry. So let the boy's name be Mahāpraṇāda (Great Cry)." And so he was given the name Mahāpraṇāda.

The boy Mahāpraṇāda was given over to eight nurses—two shoulder nurses, two nursemaids, two wet nurses, and two playtime nurses. Raised by these eight nurses, who nourished him with milk, yogurt, fresh butter, clarified butter, butter scum, and other special provisions that were very pure, he grew quickly like a lotus in a lake.

When he grew up, he was entrusted to teachers to learn writing and then arithmetic, accounting, matters relating to trademarks, and to debts, deposits, and trusts, the science of building-sites,[375] the science of wood, the science of jewels, the science of elephants, the science of horses, the science of young men, and the science of young women. In each of the eight sciences, he became learned and well versed, capable of explaining and expounding upon them. He also became skilled in those topics regarding arts and administration that are applicable to those kṣatriya kings who have been duly consecrated[376] and who have obtained lordship, might, and power in their respective regions. This enables them to conquer and rule the great sphere of the earth. That is to say, he became skilled in the art of training elephants, riding horseback, driving chariots, using a bow and arrow, marching, decamping, handling an elephant, tossing a lasso, throwing a lance, wielding a club, punching, head-butting, and kicking,[377] striking from a distance, striking vital points, piercing a target, delivering vigorous blows, and the five subjects of knowledge.[378]

Now it is a truism that a son doesn't make a name for himself [59] as long as his father is still alive. After some time, King Praṇāda died and Mahāpraṇāda was established as king. He ruled justly for a short while but then began to rule unjustly.

Then Śakra, lord of the gods, said, "Friend, I urged you to become the son of King Praṇāda. Don't rule unjustly lest you end up in hell."

After ruling justly for a short while, once again he began to rule unjustly.

A second time as well Śakra said, "Friend, I urged you to become the son of King Praṇāda. Don't rule unjustly lest you end up in hell."

"Kauśika," he said, "we kings are known to be careless. We indulge in many pleasures and are quick to forget. Establish some mark for us, so that when we see it, we'll make offerings and perform meritorious deeds. We aren't able to perform meritorious deeds without some reminder."

Then Śakra, lord of the gods, gave an order to the divinely born Viśvakarman: "Go, Viśvakarman, to the palace of King Mahāpraṇāda. Create a divine circular garden with your magic, and erect there a sacrificial post that is one thousand arm-lengths high, sixteen bow-shots across, variegated with many jewels, and made entirely of gold."

Then the divinely born Viśvakarman magically created a divine circular garden and there erected a sacrificial post that was one thousand arm-lengths high, variegated with many jewels, divine, and made entirely of gold.

King Mahāpraṇāda then had a hall for almsgiving[379] built and appointed his maternal uncle Aśoka as the sacrificial post's attendant. All of the people living in Jambudvīpa (Black Plum Island) without exception were eager to see the sacrificial post, so they would come, eat, and look at the sacrificial post. And they wouldn't do their respective jobs. The crops went completely to ruin. No royal taxes or tributes could be raised, and so the ministers could only bring in meager taxes and tributes.

"Gentlemen," King Mahāpraṇāda asked, "why have you brought in such meager taxes and tributes?"

"My lord, the people living in Jambudvīpa come, eat, and look at the sacrificial post. And they don't do their respective jobs. The crops have gone completely to ruin, so no royal taxes and tributes have been raised."

"Then the hall for almsgiving shall be brought completely to ruin as well!" the king said.

So the ministers destroyed it. [60] But still the people would come, eat the food that they brought,[380] and remain gazing at the sacrificial post. And they wouldn't do their respective jobs. Again the crops went completely to ruin, and still no taxes or tributes were raised.

"Gentlemen," the king asked, "how is it that the halls for almsgiving have been brought completely to ruin and still no taxes and tributes are raised?"

"My lord," the ministers said, "the people [come,] eat the food they bring, and remain gazing at the sacrificial post. And they don't do their respective jobs. The crops have gone completely to ruin, so no taxes and tributes have been raised."

Then King Mahāpraṇāda, after making offerings and performing meritorious deeds, immersed the sacrificial post in the Gaṅgā River.

"What do you think, monks? Aśoka, King Mahāpraṇāda's maternal uncle, was none other than the monk Bhaddālin. This is how he paid respect to the sacrificial post."

"And how, Bhadanta, will that sacrificial post disappear?"

The Story of Maitreya

Monks, in a future time, men will live for eighty thousand years. Those men who live for eighty thousand years will have a king named Śaṅkha (Conch) who is self-controlled, a wheel-turning king,[381] a conqueror of the four corners of the earth, a just and virtuous ruler, and a possessor of the seven treasures. These seven treasures of his will have the form of the most-treasured wheel, the most-treasured elephant, the most-treasured horse, the most-treasured jewel, the most-treasured woman, the most-treasured householder, and the most-treasured counselor. And he will have a full one thousand sons who are brave, heroic, in excellent physical condition, and who can crush enemy armies. He will conquer the sea-bound earth without violence and without weapons, and then rule there justly and evenhandedly so that it will be entirely fertile, without enemies, and without oppression.[382]

There will be a brahman priest of King Śaṅkha named Brahmāyus (Age of Brahmā). He will have a wife named Brahmavatī (Possessing Brahmā). Suffusing the world with loving kindness,[383] she will give birth to a son named Maitreya (Loving Kindness).

The young brahman Brahmāyus will instruct eight thousand brahman youths in the recitation of brahmanical mantras. He will then pass these brahman youths on to Maitreya. The young brahman Maitreya will also instruct these eighty thousand brahman youths [61] in the recitation of brahmanical mantras.

At that time, there will be four great kings who possess four great treasures:

Piṅgala among the Kaliṅgas,
Pāṇḍuka in Mithilā,
Elāpatra in Gandhāra
And Śaṅkha in the city of Vārāṇasī.[384]

They will take that sacrificial post and present it to King Śaṅkha. King Śaṅkha will then pass it on to the brahman Brahmāyus, the brahman Brahmāyus will then pass it on to the young brahman Maitreya, and the young brahman Maitreya will then pass it on to those brahman youths. Those brahman youths will then break the sacrificial post into many pieces and divide them up.

Then the brahman Maitreya will see the impermanence of that sacrificial post, and deeply moved he will take refuge in the forest. On the very day that he'll take refuge in the forest, he will suffuse the world with loving kindness and attain supreme knowledge. He will be known as the perfectly awakened Maitreya. On the very day that the perfectly awakened Maitreya will attain supreme knowledge, King Śaṅkha's seven treasures will disappear.

Thereafter, King Śaṅkha, with a retinue of eighty thousand vassal kings, will renounce, following the perfectly awakened renunciant Maitreya. The most-treasured woman, named Viśākhā (Branchless), with a retinue of eighty thousand women, will also renounce, following the perfectly awakened renunciant Maitreya.

Then the perfectly awakened Maitreya, with a following of 800 million monks,[385] will approach Mount Gurupādaka (Teacher's Feet), where the skeleton of the monk Kāśyapa remains undisturbed. Mount Gurupādaka will then open itself up for the perfectly awakened Maitreya, whereupon the perfectly awakened Maitreya will take the undisturbed skeleton of the monk Kāśyapa with his right hand, put it into his left hand, and thus teach the dharma to the disciples of the Buddha: "Monks," he will say, "when people lived for one hundred years, there arose in the world a teacher named Śākyamuni, who declared the disciple named Kāśyapa to be the best of those who have few desires, the best of those who are satisfied, and the best of those who preach [the ascetic code known as] the virtues of the purified. When Śākyamuni passed into final nirvāṇa, the disciple Kāśyapa organized a communal recitation of his teachings."

The monks there will see this and be deeply moved. [62] They will think, "Now how can a person with a body so small amass such virtues?"[386]

Because of this deeply moving experience, they will directly experience arhatship. There will be 960 million arhats who will have directly experienced the virtues of the purified. And when they have that deeply moving experience, the sacrificial post will disappear.[387]

King Vāsava, King Dhanasammata, and the Buddha Ratnaśikhin

"What, Bhadanta, is the cause and condition for the simultaneous[388] appearance in the world of the two jewels?"

"It is because of the power of a fervent aspiration," the Blessed One said.

"Blessed One, how was that fervent aspiration made?"

Long ago, monks, in a time gone by,[389] a king named Vāsava (Born of Wealth) ruled a kingdom in the Middle Country that was thriving, prosperous, and safe, with plenty of food and crowds of people, and where the trees always had flowers and fruit. There the [rain] god would offer showers of rain in just the right amount at the appropriate times, and there was an exceedingly rich harvest.

In the North Country a king named Dhanasammata (Considerable Wealth) also ruled a kingdom that was thriving, prosperous, and safe, with plenty of food and crowds of people, and where the trees always had flowers and fruit. There too the [rain] god would offer showers of rain in just the right amount at the appropriate times, and there was an exceedingly rich harvest.

Then one day a son was born to King Vāsava[390] with a jewel-studded topknot. After celebrating his birthday in full, they gave him the name Ratnaśikhin (Jeweled Topknot). One day, upon seeing an old man, a sick man, and a dead man, he was shaken and took refuge in the forest. On the very day that he took refuge in the forest, he attained supreme knowledge. He came to be known as the perfectly awakened Ratnaśikhin.

Now one day King Dhanasammata went out on the roof of his palace and stood there surrounded by his cabinet of ministers. "Gentlemen," he addressed his ministers, "is there any other king who has a kingdom just as we have—one that is thriving, prosperous, and safe, with plenty of food and crowds of people, where the trees always have flowers and fruit, where the [rain] god offers showers of rain in just the right amount at the appropriate times, and where there is an exceedingly rich harvest?"

There were some traders from the Middle Country who had taken their goods and come to the North Country. They said, "There is, my lord—a king named Vāsava in the Middle Country."

As soon as he heard this, King Dhanasammata became furious with jealousy, and furious as he was with jealousy, he addressed his ministers: "Gentlemen, [63] prepare the four branches of the military for battle! I will crush his kingdom."

After King Dhanasammata had the four branches of his military readied for battle—the elephant corps, the cavalry, the chariot corps, and the infantry—he came to the Middle Country and stood in wait on the southern bank of the Gaṅgā.

King Vāsava heard that King Dhanasammata had readied the four branches of his military for battle—the elephant corps, the cavalry, the chariot corps, and the infantry—and that he had come to the Middle Country and now stood in wait on the southern bank of the Gaṅgā. And having heard this, he readied the four branches of his own military for battle—the elephant corps, the cavalry, the chariot corps, and the infantry—and stood in wait on the northern bank of the Gaṅgā.

Now the perfectly awakened Ratnaśikhin, knowing that it was time to train these two kings, went to dwell for a night on the banks of the Gaṅgā River. Then the perfectly awakened Ratnaśikhin had a worldly thought.

It is a law of nature that when a lord buddha has a worldly thought, Śakra, Brahmā, and the other gods know the blessed one's thought with their minds.

Śakra, Brahmā, and the other gods then approached the perfectly awakened Ratnaśikhin. Having approached, they venerated with their heads the feet of the perfectly awakened Ratnaśikhin and then sat down at a respectful distance.

A tremendous light arose from the power of their appearance. King Dhanasammata saw this, and at the sight of it, asked his ministers, "Gentlemen, what is that tremendous light in King Vāsava's realm?"

"My lord," they said, "a perfectly awakened buddha named Ratnaśikhin has arisen in King Vāsava's realm. Śakra, Brahmā, and the other gods have gone to see him. It is because of this that a great light has arisen. He possesses great magic and great power. This is his power."

"Gentlemen," King Dhanasammata said, "what sort of misfortune can I inflict upon someone in whose realm has arisen such a field of merit on two feet that even Śakra, Brahmā, and the other gods go to see him?"

So he sent a messenger to King Vāsava with this message: "Friend, please come. I won't do anything to you. You are very powerful because of your merit. In your realm is that field of merit on two feet, the perfectly awakened Ratnaśikhin, whom even Śakra, Brahmā, and the other gods go to see. Instead, I will come, embrace you, and then go. This way there will be mutual goodwill between us."

Now King Vāsava didn't trust King Dhanasammata. [64] He approached the perfectly awakened Ratnaśikhin and, having approached, venerated with his head the feet of the perfectly awakened Ratnaśikhin and then sat down at a respectful distance. Sitting down at a respectful distance, King Vāsava then said this to the perfectly awakened Ratnaśikhin: "Bhadanta, this message was sent to me by King Dhanasammata—'Dear friend, please come. I won't do anything to you. I will come, embrace you, and then go. This way there will be mutual goodwill between us.' How should I respond to this?"

"Go, your majesty," the perfectly awakened Ratnaśikhin said. "It will be fine."

"Lord, should I fall prostrate at his feet?"

"Your majesty, kings are great because of their power. They should be bowed down to."[391]

King Vāsava then venerated with his head the feet of the perfectly awakened Ratnaśikhin, got up from his seat, and departed. He approached King Dhanasammata and, having approached, fell prostrate at the feet of King Dhanasammata. King Dhanasammata then embraced him, inspired trust in him, and sent him away.

King Vāsava then approached the perfectly awakened Ratnaśikhin. Having approached, he venerated with his head the feet of the perfectly awakened Ratnaśikhin and then sat down at a respectful distance. Sitting down at a respectful distance, King Vāsava then said this to the perfectly awakened Ratnaśikhin: "Bhadanta, at whose feet do all kings fall prostrate?"

"At those of a wheel-turning king, your majesty."

King Vāsava then got up from his seat, properly arranged his robe on one shoulder, bowed toward the perfectly awakened tathāgata Ratnaśikhin with his hands respectfully folded, and said this to him: "May the Blessed One, along with the community of monks, accept this invitation to eat at my home tomorrow."

[The perfectly awakened Ratnaśikhin accepted King Vāsava's invitation with his silence. Then King Vāsava, realizing that by his silence the perfectly awakened Ratnaśikhin had accepted his invitation, venerated with his head the feet of the perfectly awakened Ratnaśikhin, got up from his seat, and left the perfectly awakened Ratnaśikhin's presence.][392]

That very night King Vāsava prepared hard and soft foods, both fresh and fine, and then at daybreak he got up, prepared the seats, and distributed pitchers of water. Then he had a messenger inform the perfectly awakened Ratnaśikhin that it was now the appropriate time: "It is time, Bhadanta. The food is ready. Now the Blessed One may do as the time permits."

Later in the morning the perfectly awakened Ratnaśikhin got dressed, [65] took his bowl and robe, and leading the community of monks that surrounded him, approached the place where King Vāsava was offering food. Having approached, he sat down in front of the community of monks in the seat specially prepared for him.

Now when King Vāsava was sure that the perfectly awakened Ratnaśikhin was comfortably seated, he served and indulged him, with his own hands, with hard and soft foods, both fresh and fine. When he had served and indulged him, with his own hands, with many courses of hard and soft foods, both fresh and fine, and was sure that the Blessed One, the perfectly awakened Ratnaśikhin, had finished eating, washed his hands, and set aside his bowl, he fell prostrate at his feet, and began to make a fervent aspiration: "Bhadanta, by this root of virtue may I be a wheel-turning king." Immediately a conch sounded.

The perfectly awakened Ratnaśikhin then said this to King Vāsava: "Your majesty, when people live for eighty thousand years, you will be a wheel-turning king named Śaṅkha (Conch)." Then there arose a great shout and uproar.

When King Dhanasammata heard the commotion, he asked his ministers, "Gentlemen, what's this commotion heard in King Vāsava's realm?"

They came to him and explained: "My lord, the people are pleased, satisfied, and delighted because the perfectly awakened Ratnaśikhin has predicted that Vāsava will be a king in a wheel-turner's kingdom. That's why there is such a commotion."

Now King Dhanasammata approached the perfectly awakened Ratnaśikhin. Having approached, he venerated with his head the feet of the perfectly awakened Ratnaśikhin and then sat down at a respectful distance. Sitting down at a respectful distance, King Dhanasammata then said this to the perfectly awakened Ratnaśikhin: "Bhadanta, at whose feet do all wheel-turning kings fall prostrate?"

"At those of a perfectly awakened tathāgata arhat, your majesty."

King Dhanasammata then got up from his seat, properly arranged his robe on one shoulder, bowed toward the perfectly awakened tathāgata Ratnaśikhin with his hands respectfully folded, and said this him: "May the Blessed One, along with the community of monks, accept this invitation to eat at my home tomorrow."

The perfectly awakened Ratnaśikhin accepted King Dhanasammata's invitation with his silence. Then King Dhanasammata, realizing that by his silence the perfectly awakened Ratnaśikhin had accepted his invitation, [66] venerated with his head the feet of the perfectly awakened Ratnaśikhin, [got up from his seat,][393] and left the perfectly awakened Ratnaśikhin's presence.

That very night King Dhanasammata prepared hard and soft foods, both fresh and fine, and then at daybreak he got up, prepared the seats, and distributed pitchers of water. Then he had a messenger inform the perfectly awakened Ratnaśikhin that it was now the appropriate time: "It is time, Bhadanta. The food is ready. Now the Blessed One may do as the time permits."

Later in the morning the perfectly awakened Ratnaśikhin got dressed, took his bowl and robe, and leading the community of monks that surrounded him, approached the place where King Dhanasammata was offering food. Having approached, he sat down in front of the community of monks in the seat specially prepared for him.

Now when King Dhanasammata was sure that the perfectly awakened Ratnaśikhin was comfortably seated at the head of the community of monks, he served and indulged them, with his own hands, with hard and soft foods, both fresh and fine. When he had served and indulged them, with his own hands, with many courses of hard and soft foods, both fresh and fine, and was sure that the perfectly awakened Ratnaśikhin had finished eating, washed his hands, and set aside his bowl, he fell prostrate at his feet, suffused this whole world with loving kindness, and began to make a fervent aspiration: "By this root of virtue may I be a teacher in the world, a perfectly awakened tathāgata arhat."

"Your majesty," the perfectly awakened Ratnaśikhin said, "when people live for eighty thousand years, you will be a perfectly awakened tathāgata arhat named Maitreya."

Because of the power of these fervent aspirations, two jewels will appear in the world.[394]

This was said by the Blessed One. With their minds uplifted, those monks welcomed the words of the Blessed One.

So ends the *Maitreya-avadāna,* the third chapter in the glorious *Divyāvadāna.* [67]

4. *The Story of a Brahman's Daughter*

BRĀHMAṆADĀRIKĀ-AVADĀNA

THE BLESSED ONE arrived in Nyagrodhikā (Home of a Banyan Tree). Then in the morning the Blessed One got dressed, took his bowl and robe, and entered Nyagrodhikā for alms.

Meanwhile a brahman's daughter from Kapilavastu had come to stay in Nyagrodhikā. That brahman's daughter saw the Blessed One,

who was adorned with the thirty-two marks of a great man,
whose brilliance was greater than a thousand suns,
and who, like a mountain of jewels that moved,
was beautiful from every side.

As soon as she saw him, it occurred to her, "This is the Blessed One, the delight of the Śākya clan, who abandoned his kingdom, his vast harem, his vast treasuries and granaries. Leaving behind a lineage of wheel-turning kings,[395] he went forth as a renunciant, and now he wanders for alms. If he'll accept barley meal as alms from me, then I'll give it to him."

Then the Blessed One, understanding her thoughts with his mind, held out his bowl to her. "If you have anything to spare, my sister, please fill my bowl." Then even greater faith arose in her. Realizing that the Blessed One knew her thoughts with his mind, with intense faith she offered the Blessed One some alms of barley meal.

Then the Blessed One displayed his smile.

The Buddha's Smile

Now it is a law of nature that whenever lord buddhas manifest their smiles, rays of blue, yellow, red, and white light, and those the color of topaz, rubies, diamonds, beryl, sapphires, crystals, red pearls, right-spiraling conch shells, quartz, coral, gold, and silver emerge from their mouths, some going downward and some going upward. Those that go downward enter the various hells down to the Avīci (Ceaseless Torture)—the Sañjīva (Reviving), the Kālasūtra (Black Thread), the Saṅghāta (Crushing), the Raurava (Shrieking), the Mahāraurava (Loud Shrieking), the Tapana (Heat), the Pratāpana (Extreme Heat), the Avīci (Ceaseless Torture), the Arbuda (Blistering), the Nirarbuda (Blisters Bursting), the Aṭaṭa (Chattering Teeth), the Hahava (Ugh!), the Huhuva (Brrr!), the Utpala (Blue Lotus), the Padma (Lotus), and the Mahāpadma (Great Lotus). [68] Becoming cold, they fall in the hot hells, and becoming hot, they fall in the cold hells. In this way, at that moment, those rays of light alleviate the particular torments of those beings who dwell in these various hells. And so they think, "Friends, have we died and passed away from this place? Have we been reborn somewhere else?"

Then, in order to engender their faith, the Blessed One manifests a magical image of himself for them to see. Seeing this magical image, they think, "Friends, we haven't died and passed away from this place, nor have we been born someplace else. Instead, it's this person who we've never seen before; it's by his power that our particular torments are alleviated." Cultivating faith in their minds toward this magical image, they then cast off that karma still to be suffered in these hells and take rebirth among gods and mortals, where they become vessels for the [four noble] truths.

Those rays of light that go upward, enter the various divine realms[396]—Cāturmahārājika (Four Groups of the Great Kings), Trāyastriṃśa (Thirty-Three), Yāma (Free from Conflict), Tuṣita (Content), Nirmāṇarati (Delighting in Creation), Paranirmitavaśavartin (Masters of Others' Creations), Brahmakāyika (Brahmā's Assembly), Brahmapurohita (Brahmā's Priests), Mahābrahmaṇa (Great Brahmā), Parīttābha (Limited Splendor), Apramāṇābha (Immeasurable Splendor), Ābhāsvara (Radiant), Parīttaśubha (Limited Beauty), Apramāṇaśubha (Immeasurable Beauty), Śubhakṛtsna (Complete Beauty), Anabhraka (Unclouded), Puṇyaprasava (Merit Born), Bṛhatphala (Great Result), Abṛha (Not Great), Atapa (Serene), Sudṛśa (Good-Looking), Sudarśa (Clear Sighted), and finally Akaniṣṭha (Supreme). There they proclaim [the truth of] impermanence, suffering, emptiness, and no-self. And they utter these two verses:

> Strive! Go forth!
> Apply yourselves to the teachings of the Buddha!
> Destroy the army of death
> as an elephant would a house of reeds.
>
> Whoever diligently follows
> this dharma and monastic discipline
> will abandon the endless cycle of rebirth
> and put an end to suffering.

Then those rays of light, having roamed through the great thousand third-order thousand world-system, come together directly behind the Blessed One.

> If the Blessed One wants to reveal the past,
> they vanish into him from behind.
> If he wants to predict the future,
> they vanish into him from the front.
> If he wants to predict a rebirth in hell,
> they vanish into the sole of a foot.
> If he wants to predict a rebirth as an animal,
> they vanish into a heel.

If he wants to predict a rebirth as a hungry ghost,
  they vanish into a big toe.
If he wants to predict a rebirth as a mortal, [69]
  they vanish into his knees.
If he wants to predict a reign of an armed wheel-turning king,
  they vanish into his left palm.
If he wants to predict a reign of a wheel-turning king,
  they vanish into his right palm.[397]
If he wants to predict an awakening as a disciple,
  they vanish into his mouth.
If he wants to predict an awakening as a solitary buddha,
  they vanish into the circle of hair between his eyebrows.
If he wants to predict unsurpassed perfect awakening,
  they vanish into his *uṣṇīṣa*.

In this case, those rays of light circumambulated the Blessed One three times and then vanished into the circle of hair between his eyebrows.

The venerable Ānanda then respectfully cupped his hands together and addressed the Blessed One:

A bundle of diverse light rays,
variegated with a thousand colors,
comes forth from your mouth.
They illuminate every direction,
as though the sun were rising.

And then he uttered these verses:

Without pride, free from grief and passion,
buddhas are the cause of greatness in the world.[398]
Not without reason do victors, defeaters of the enemy,
display a smile, white like the conch or lotus root.

O you who are resolute, an ascetic, the best of victors,[399]
you know at once with your mind the desires of your listeners.
Destroy their doubts that have arisen, O best of sages,
with words excellent, enduring, and virtuous.

Masters, awakened ones,
those with the patience of an ocean or great mountain
do not display a smile without reason.
Masses of people yearn to hear why it is
that resolute ones display a smile.

"It is like this, Ānanda," the Blessed One said. "It is like this. Perfectly awakened tathāgata arhats do not manifest a smile, Ānanda, without proper cause and reason. Ānanda, did you see that brahman's daughter in whom faith had arisen who gave me some barley meal as alms?"

"Yes, Bhadanta, I saw her."

"That brahman's daughter, Ānanda, by this root of virtue will not suffer a karmic downfall for thirteen eons. [70] Then what? After cycling through saṃsāra, being reborn again and again among gods and mortals, in her last life, her last existence, her last body, her last incarnation, she will become a solitary buddha named Supraṇihita (Resolute)."

The Buddha and the Brahman Girl's Husband

Word then spread all around that a certain brahman's daughter in whom faith had arisen had offered some barley meal as alms to the Blessed One, and that the Blessed One had predicted that she would attain awakening as a solitary buddha.

Now during this time her husband had gone into the forest to gather flowers and firewood. He heard that his wife had offered some barley meal as alms to the ascetic Gautama, and that this ascetic Gautama had predicted that she would attain awakening as a solitary buddha. Hearing this, he was infuriated and approached the Blessed One. Face to face with the Blessed One, he exchanged the customary greetings and pleasantries, and then said to the Blessed One, "Honorable Gautama, have you been to my house?"

"Yes, brahman, I have been there."

"Is it true that my wife offered you barley meal as alms and that you predicted that she would attain awakening as a solitary buddha?"

"That is true, brahman."

"Gautama, you abandoned a wheel-turner's kingdom and went forth as a renunciant. How is it that now you knowingly tell lies for the sake of some alms of barley meal? Who will believe you that this is the fruit of such a small seed?"

"In that case, brahman, I will ask you a question, and you should answer it as best you can.[400] What do you think, brahman, have you ever seen something that was truly amazing?"

"Set aside for now, Gautama, any other truly amazing things. Listen for a moment to this truly amazing thing that I saw right here in Nyagrodhikā. In the eastern part of Nyagrodhikā, Gautama, there is a banyan *(nyagrodha)* tree for which the city of Nyagrodhikā is named. Underneath it, five hundred carts can fit without touching or pushing up against each other."

"What is the size of the seed[401] of that banyan tree?" asked the Blessed One. "How big is it? Is it the size of a marsh?"

"No,[402] Gautama."

"Is it the size of a grass mat? An oil-pressing wheel? A wagon wheel? Or a cow basket? A *bilva* fruit? Or even a wood apple?" [71]

"No,[403] Gautama, it's just a quarter of the size of a mustard seed."

"Who will believe you that from a seed this size arises such a big tree?"

"Whether honorable Gautama believes me or not, it was there before my eyes.[404] There was a field in a place,[405] Gautama, that was soft, with soil rich and fertile. And there was a fresh, vigorous, and undamaged seed that was easily sown.[406] From time to time the [rain] god produced rain, and so this great banyan tree came into being.

Then, at that moment,[407] the Blessed One uttered these verses:

Just as a field and seed[408] were there before your eyes, brahman,
karma and its results are right before the eyes of tathāgatas.
Just as you see, brahman, that a seed is small but a tree is very large,
I too see, brahman, that a seed is small but the results are great.

The Blessed One then stuck out his tongue from his mouth so that it covered the entire sphere of his face up to his hairline. Then he said to the brahman, "What do you think, brahman, would a person who can stick out his tongue from his mouth and cover the entire sphere of his face[409] knowingly tell lies, even for the sake of hundreds of thousands of wheel-turner's kingdoms?"

"No, Gautama."

Then [the Blessed One][410] uttered this verse:

How could this tongue of mine tells lies;
it speaks with honesty and truth.
Things are as I say, brahman.[411]
Know that I am the Tathāgata.

The brahman became filled with faith. Then the Blessed One, knowing his inclinations, propensities, makeup, and nature, gave him a discourse on the dharma that penetrated the four noble truths. When the brahman heard this, with his thunderbolt of knowledge he broke through that mountain which is the false view of individuality that arises with its twenty peaks of incorrect views, and directly experienced the reward of the stream-enterer. "I have crossed over, Bhadanta! I have crossed over! [72] And so, I take refuge in the Blessed One, in the dharma, and in the community of monks. Hereafter, and for as long as I live and breathe, consider me a faithful disciple who has taken the refuges." And then the brahman, having rejoiced and delighted in the words of the Blessed One, venerated with his head the feet of the Blessed One, got up from his seat, and went out.

This was said by the Blessed One.

So ends the *Brāhmaṇadārikā-avadāna,* the fourth chapter in the glorious *Divyāvadāna.*

5. *The Story of a Brahman's Panegyric*

STUTIBRĀHMAṆA-AVADĀNA

THE BLESSED ONE arrived in Hastināpura. There, from a distance, a certain brahman [saw][412] the Blessed One, who was adorned with the thirty-two marks of a great man,

whose body was radiant with the eighty minor marks,
who was adorned with a halo extending an arm's length,
whose brilliance was greater than a thousand suns,
and who, like a mountain of jewels that moved,
was beautiful from every side.

At the sight of the Blessed One, he approached and began to praise him in verse:

A golden complexion, a pleasure to the eyes,
a source of joy, endowed with all virtues,
a god superior to the gods,
a guide for those people who need training—
you have crossed to the far shore of the ocean of existence!

Then the Blessed One displayed his smile.

The Buddha's Smile

Now it is a law of nature that whenever lord buddhas manifest their smiles, [rays of blue, yellow, red, and white light, and those the color of topaz, rubies, diamonds, beryl, sapphires, crystals, red pearls, right-spiraling conch shells, quartz, coral, gold, and silver emerge from their mouths, some going downward and some going upward. Those that go downward enter the various hells down to Avīci (Ceaseless Torture)—Sañjīva (Reviving), Kālasūtra (Black Thread), Saṅghāta (Crushing), Raurava (Shrieking), Mahāraurava (Loud Shrieking), Tapana (Heat), Pratāpana (Extreme Heat), Avīci, Arbuda (Blistering), Nirarbuda (Blisters Bursting), Aṭaṭa (Chattering Teeth), Hahava (Ugh!), Huhuva (Brrr!), Utpala (Blue Lotus), Padma (Lotus), and Mahāpadma (Great Lotus). Becoming cold, they fall in the hot hells, and becoming hot, they fall in the cold hells. In this way, at that moment, those rays of light alleviate the particular torments of those beings who dwell in these various hells. And so they think, "Friends, have we died and passed away from this place? Have we been reborn somewhere else?"

Then, in order to engender their faith, the Blessed One manifests a magical image of himself. Seeing this magical image, they think, "Friends, we haven't died and passed away from this place, nor have we been born someplace else. Instead, it's this person whom we've never seen before; it's by his power that our particular torments are alleviated." Cultivating faith in their minds toward this magical image, they then cast off that karma still to be suffered in these hells and take rebirth among gods and mortals, where they become vessels for the four noble truths.

Those rays of light that go upward enter the various divine realms—Cāturmahārājika (Four Groups of the Great Kings), Trāyastriṃśa (Thirty-Three), Yāma (Free from Conflict), Tuṣita (Content), Nirmāṇarati (Delighting in Creation), Paranirmitavaśavartin (Masters of Others' Creations), Brahmakāyika (Brahmā's Assembly), Brahmapurohita (Brahmā's Priests), Mahābrahmaṇa (Great Brahmā), Parīttābha (Limited Splendor), Apramāṇābha (Immeasurable Splendor), Ābhāsvara (Radiant), Parīttaśubha (Limited Beauty), Apramāṇaśubha (Immeasurable Beauty), Śubhakṛtsna (Complete Beauty), Anabhraka (Unclouded), Puṇyaprasava (Merit Born), Bṛhatphala (Great Result), Abṛha (Not Great), Atapa (Serene), Sudṛśa (Good-Looking), Sudarśa (Clear Sighted), and finally Akaniṣṭha (Supreme). There they proclaim the truth of impermanence, suffering, emptiness, and no-self. And they utter these two verses:

> Strive! Go forth!
> Apply yourselves to the teachings of the Buddha!
> Destroy the army of death
> as an elephant would a house of reeds.
>
> Whoever diligently follows
> this dharma and monastic discipline
> will abandon the endless cycle of rebirth
> and put an end to suffering.

Then those rays of light, having roamed through the great thousand third-order thousand world-system, come together directly behind the Blessed One.

> If the Blessed One wants to reveal the past,
> they vanish into him from behind.
> If he wants to predict the future,
> they vanish into him from the front.
> If he wants to predict a rebirth in hell,
> they vanish into the sole of a foot.
> If he wants to predict a rebirth as an animal,
> they vanish into a heel.

If he wants to predict a rebirth as a hungry ghost,
they vanish into a big toe.
If he wants to predict a rebirth as a mortal,
they vanish into his knees.
If he wants to predict a reign of an armed wheel-turning king,
they vanish into his left palm.
If he wants to predict a reign of a wheel-turning king,
they vanish into his right palm.
If he wants to predict an awakening as a disciple,
they vanish into his mouth.
If he wants to predict an awakening as a solitary buddha,
they vanish into the circle of hair between his eyebrows.
If he wants to predict unsurpassed perfect awakening,
they vanish into his *uṣṇīṣa*.

In this case, those rays of light circumambulated the Blessed One three times][413] and then vanished into the circle of hair between the Blessed One's eyebrows.

The venerable Ānanda then respectfully cupped his hands together and addressed the Blessed One:

A bundle of diverse light rays,
variegated with a thousand colors,
comes forth from your mouth.
They illuminate every direction,
as though the sun were rising.

And then he uttered these verses:

Without pride, free from grief and passion,
buddhas are the cause of greatness in the world. [73]
Not without reason do victors, defeaters of the enemy,
display a smile, white like the conch or lotus root.

O you who are resolute, an ascetic, and an excellent victor,[414]
you know at once with your mind the desires of your listeners.
Destroy their doubts that have arisen, O best of sages,
with words excellent, enduring, and virtuous.

Masters, awakened ones,
those with the patience of an ocean or great mountain
do not display a smile without reason.
Masses of people yearn to hear why it is
that resolute ones display a smile.

"It is like this, Ānanda," the Blessed One said. "It is like this. Perfectly awakened tathāgata arhats do not manifest a smile, Ānanda, without proper cause and reason. Ānanda, did you see that brahman who praised the Tathāgata with a verse?"

"Yes, Bhadanta, I saw him."

"By this root of virtue he will not suffer a karmic downfall for twenty eons. Instead,[415] being reborn again and again[416] among gods and mortals, in his last existence, his last body, his last incarnation, he will become a solitary buddha named Stavārho (Worthy of Eulogy).

Those monks in doubt asked the Lord Buddha, the remover of all doubts, "Look, Bhadanta. This brahman praised the Blessed One with a single verse, and the Blessed One predicted that he would attain awakening as a solitary buddha."

"Monks," the Blessed One said, "not only now, but in the past [as well],[417] he praised me with a single verse. At that time I established him in charge of five excellent villages. Listen to this. Concentrate well and closely. I will speak."

Brahmadatta and the Poet

Long ago, monks, in a time gone by, a king named Brahmadatta ruled in the city of Vārāṇasī. It was thriving and prosperous, with plenty of food and crowds of people. This king was also very fond of poets.

Now in Vārāṇasī there was a certain brahman poet. His wife said to him, "Husband, it's the cold season. Go and say some favorable words[418] to the king. Maybe then he'll offer us some shelter from the cold." So he departed. [74]

Meanwhile the king had mounted the back of his elephant and set out.

The brahman reflected, "Should I praise the king or his noble elephant?" It occurred to him, "This noble elephant is dear and beloved to the whole world. Setting aside the king for now, I'll praise his noble elephant." He then uttered this verse:

A body equal in form to Indra's elephant,
handsome and with excellent features—
you are honored with royal splendor,[419]
O great and mighty elephant,
your appearance is magnificent by any standard of beauty.[420]

Then the king, filled with pleasure,[421] uttered this verse:

My mighty elephant is dear and beloved,
instilling joy and stealing the sight of men.
You speak words in his praise,
and so I grant you five excellent villages.

"What do you think, monks? That noble elephant was none other than me at that time and at that juncture. [That brahman poet was none other than this brahman poet at that time and at that juncture].[422] Back then he praised me with a single verse, and I caused him to be put in charge of five excellent villages. Now he praises me with a single verse, and I foretell his future awakening as a solitary buddha."

This was said by the Blessed One. With their minds uplifted, the monks welcomed the words of the Blessed One.

So ends the *Stutibrāhmaṇa-avadāna,* the fifth chapter in the glorious *Divyāvadāna.*

6. *The Story of a Brahman Named Indra*

INDRABRĀHMAṆA-AVADĀNA

THE BLESSED ONE arrived in Śrughnā. Now in Śrughnā there lived a brahman named Indra, and being proud that he was handsome, youthful, and learned,[423] he boasted that no one was his equal.

Meanwhile in a certain place in Śrughnā, the Blessed One sat down in front of the community of monks in the seat specially prepared for him and taught the dharma. The brahman named Indra heard that the ascetic Gautama had arrived in Śrughnā, and it occurred to him, "It is heard that the ascetic Gautama is handsome, good-looking, and attractive. [75] I'll go and see whether or not he is more handsome than me." He went off, and then he saw the Blessed One,

> who was adorned with the thirty-two marks of a great man,
> whose body was radiant with the eighty minor marks,
> who was adorned with a halo extending an arm's length,
> whose brilliance was greater than a thousand suns,
> and who, like a mountain of jewels that moved,
> was beautiful from every side.

At the sight of him, it occurred to him, "The ascetic Gautama may be more beautiful than me, but he isn't taller." Then he tried to behold the Blessed One's head, but he couldn't grasp its full extent. So he climbed up to a higher place.

Then the Blessed One addressed the brahman Indra: "Enough of this, brahman! You'll just exhaust yourself. Even if you climb to the summit of Mount Sumeru, you can't look down upon the Tathāgata's head.[424] You'll just exhaust yourself even more, and you still won't see it. Besides, haven't you heard that in this world, which is filled with gods and antigods, the heads of lord buddhas can't be looked down upon? But still, if you desire to see the extent of the Tathāgata's body, [then listen to this.]

"Underneath the fire pit in your home where the *agnihotra* offering is made, there lies a post made of *gośīrṣa* sandalwood. Retrieve it and then measure it. That is the measure of the body received from the mother and father of the Tathāgata."

The brahman Indra reflected, "I've never heard something so outrageous before![425] I'll go and see." He went there right away and began to dig underneath the fire pit for the *agnihotra*. Everything was just as the Buddha had said. He was filled with faith. "Certainly the ascetic Gautama is omniscient," he reflected. "I'll go and pay my respects to him." Possessed of faith as he now was, he approached the Blessed One. Having approached the Blessed One and, face to face, exchanged the customary greetings and pleasantries, he then sat down at a respectful distance. Then the Blessed One, knowing his inclinations, propensities, makeup, and nature, gave him a discourse on the dharma that penetrated the four noble truths. [When the brahman Indra heard this,][426] with his thunderbolt of knowledge he broke through that mountain which is the false view of individuality that arises with its twenty peaks of incorrect views, and directly experienced the reward of the stream-enterer. Having seen the truth, he said, "I have crossed over, Bhadanta! I have crossed over! And so, I take refuge in the Blessed One, in the dharma, and in the community of monks. Hereafter and for as long as I live and breathe, [76] consider me a faithful disciple who has taken the refuges."[427]

Then the brahman Indra got up from his seat, properly arranged his robe on one shoulder, bowed toward the Blessed One with his hands respectfully folded, and said this to the Blessed One: "If the Blessed One permits, I shall celebrate a festival with this post made of *gośīrṣa* sandalwood."

"Go, brahman," the Blessed One replied. "You have my permission. Celebrate the festival."[428]

Then in a remote place, with great respect, he raised that post and a festival was celebrated. Realizing that this festival would promote virtue, brahmans and householders bound *kuśa* grass[429] for offerings.[430] Since this festival with a post was celebrated by the brahman Indra, it came to be known as the Indramaha—the Indramaha (Indra Festival).[431]

The Incident at Toyikā[432]

The Blessed One then addressed the venerable Ānanda: "Come, Ānanda, let us go to Toyikā (Watering Hole)."

"Yes, Bhadanta," the venerable Ānanda replied, consenting to the Blessed One's request.

Then the Blessed One arrived in Toyikā. There in that place a brahman was ploughing his fields. The brahman saw the Lord Buddha,

> who was adorned with the thirty-two marks of a great man,
> whose body was radiant with the eighty minor marks,
> who was adorned with a halo extending an arm's length,
> whose brilliance was greater than a thousand suns,
> and who, like a mountain of jewels that moved,
> was beautiful from every side.

At the sight of him, he reflected, "If I go to Lord Gautama and pay my respects, my work will suffer. If I don't go to him and pay my respects, my merit will suffer. Isn't there any skillful way wherein neither my work nor my merit will suffer?" Then this thought occurred to him: "I will pay my respects standing right here. This way neither my work nor my merit will suffer." Standing right there and still holding his goad-post,[433] he paid his respects: "I pay my respects to Lord Buddha!"

The Blessed One then addressed the venerable Ānanda: "Ānanda, this brahman has a great opportunity to put an end to worldly existence.[434] If he only had the proper experience, knowledge, and insight,[435] it would have occurred to him that in this place lies the undisturbed skeleton of the perfectly awakened Kāśyapa. Hence, he could have venerated me and, in this way, have venerated two perfectly awakened buddhas. [77] How is that? In this place, Ānanda, lies the undisturbed skeleton of the perfectly awakened Kāśyapa.

Then the venerable Ānanda very quickly folded his upper garment into four as a seat and then said this to the Blessed One: "May the Blessed One please sit down on this seat that I have specially prepared. In this way this piece of earth will be made use of by two perfectly awakened buddhas—previously by the perfectly awakened Kāśyapa and at present by the Blessed One."

The Blessed One sat down in that seat specially prepared for him, and having sat down, he addressed the monks: "Monks, do you want to see the undisturbed body of the perfectly awakened Kāśyapa?"

"Yes, Blessed One. For this it is the right time. Sugata, for this it is the right occasion. May the Blessed One display the undisturbed body of the perfectly awakened Kāśyapa to the monks. At the sight of it, the monks can cultivate faith in their minds."

Then the Blessed One had a worldly thought.

Now it is a law of nature that any time a lord buddha has a worldly thought, all creatures, even tiny biting ants, know the blessed one's thought with their minds.

The nāgas reflected, "What is the reason that the Blessed One has had a worldly thought? So that those who want to see the undisturbed body of the perfectly awakened Kāśyapa can see it."[436] Then they raised the undisturbed body of the perfectly awakened Kāśyapa.

The Blessed One then addressed the monks: "Contemplate its appearance, monks, for it will disappear." And then it disappeared.

Practices of Faith at Toyikā[437]

King Prasenajit heard that the Blessed One had raised the undisturbed body of the perfectly awakened Kāśyapa for the disciples to see. And having heard this, he became curious. So, with the women of his harem as well as with princes, ministers, military commanders, townspeople, and villagers, he set out to see it. Likewise, Virūḍhaka, the householder Anāthapiṇḍada, the head officials Ṛṣidatta and Purāṇa, Viśākha Mṛgāramātā, and many hundreds of thousands of other people set out to see it, some out of curiosity, others impelled by former roots of virtue. [78] But in the meantime, it had disappeared. They heard that the undisturbed bodily remains of the perfectly awakened lord Kāśyapa had disappeared. And having heard this, they felt miserable and were dejected. "Our coming here has been in vain," they thought.

One of the lay disciples then began to circumambulate that place. And with his mind, he formed this thought: "How much merit will I get from respectfully walking around this place?"[438]

Then the Blessed One, knowing with his mind the thoughts of that lay disciple and that large crowd of people, uttered this verse so that they wouldn't have any regrets:

> Hundreds of thousands of gold coins or nuggets
> are not equal to the wise man, faithful in mind,
> who walks around shrines of a buddha.

One of the lay disciples then offered a lump of clay at this place and thus formed this thought: "Elsewhere[439] the Blessed One has explained how much merit is earned from respectfully walking around a shrine of a buddha. But how much merit will there be from offering a lump of clay?"

Then the Blessed One, knowing with his mind his thoughts as well, uttered this verse:

> Hundreds of thousands of gold coins or nuggets
> are not equal to one, faithful in mind,
> who places a single lump of clay
> at a shrine of a buddha.

After hearing this, many hundreds of thousands of beings placed lumps of clay there as offerings. Others put pearls and flowers there, and thus formed this thought: "The Blessed One has said how much merit is earned from respectfully walking around a shrine of a buddha and from offering a lump of clay. But how much merit will we get from offering pearls and flowers?"

Then the Blessed One, knowing with his mind their thoughts as well, uttered this verse:

> Hundreds of thousands of gold coins or nuggets
> are not equal to one, faithful in mind,
> who places heaps of pearls and lovely flowers
> at shrines of a buddha.

Others festooned the area there with garlands and formed this thought, "The Blessed One has said how much merit is earned from offering pearls and flowers. But how much merit will we get from festooning the area with garlands?"

Then the Blessed One, knowing with his mind their thoughts as well, uttered this verse: [79]

> Hundreds of thousands of gold vehicles or nuggets
> are not equal to the wise man, faithful in mind,
> who festoons with garlands
> shrines of a buddha.

Others gave oil-lamp trees[440] there and formed this thought, "The Blessed One has said how much merit is earned from festooning this area with garlands. But how much merit will we get from giving oil lamps?"

Then the Blessed One, knowing with his mind their thoughts as well, uttered this verse:

> Hundreds of thousands of millions of gold pieces or nuggets
> are not equal to the wise man, faithful in mind,
> who makes a gift of oil lamps
> at shrines of a buddha.

Others sprinkled perfume and thus with their minds formed this thought: "The Blessed One has said how much merit is earned from offering oil lamps. But how much merit will we get from sprinkling perfume?"

Then the Blessed One, knowing with his mind their thoughts as well, uttered this verse:

> Hundreds of thousands of piles of gold or gold nuggets
> are not equal to the wise man, faithful in mind,
> who sprinkles perfume
> at shrines of a buddha.

Others raised up umbrellas, flags, and banners there [and formed this thought, "The Blessed One has said how much merit is earned from respectfully walking around a shrine of a buddha, from offering a lump of clay, from placing pearls and flowers, from festooning this area with garlands, from offering oil lamps, and from sprinkling the area with perfume. But how much merit will we get from raising up umbrellas, flags, and banners?"

Then the Blessed One, knowing with his mind their thoughts as well, uttered these verses:

Hundreds of thousands of gold mountains
equal to Mount Meru
are not equal to one, faithful in mind,
who raises umbrellas, flags, and banners
at shrines of a buddha.

This is the tribute declared
on behalf of the immeasurable Tathāgata,
ocean-like in perfect awakening,
the unsurpassed caravan leader.

It occurred to them, "This is the amount of merit that the Blessed One has said will be earned from acts performed on behalf of a blessed one who has passed into final nirvāṇa. But how much merit will be earned in the case of one still living?"

Then the Blessed One,][441] knowing with his mind their thoughts as well, uttered these verses:

One may honor a buddha still living
as well as one passed into final nirvāṇa.
Making one's mind equally faithful,
here there is no difference in merit.

In this way buddhas are inconceivable,
and the dharma of buddhas inconceivable as well.
For those faithful in the inconceivable,
the result is likewise inconceivable.

It is not possible to understand the extent
of the virtues of those who are inconceivable,
of those who turn the unobstructed wheel of dharma[442]
of perfectly awakened buddhas.

Then the Blessed One gave a discourse on the dharma to that great crowd of people such that when they heard it many hundreds of thousands of beings attained great distinction. Some set their minds on attaining awakening as a disciple, some on awakening as a solitary buddha, and some on unsurpassed perfect awakening; some reached the summit and attained the summit stages,[443] [80] some attained the heat stages, and some the tolerance stages in accord with truth;[444] some directly experienced the reward of the stream-enterer, some the reward of the once-returner, and some rid themselves of all defilements and thereby directly experienced arhatship. Almost everyone was affected and became favorably inclined toward the Buddha, intent on the dharma, and well disposed toward the community.

Then the householder Anāthapiṇḍada said this to the Blessed One: "If the Blessed One permits, I will arrange a festival here."

"Householder, I give my permission. Make the arrangements."

Then the householder Anāthapiṇḍada arranged a festival. In time it came to be known as the Toyikāmaha (Toyikā Festival).

This was said by the Blessed One. With their minds uplifted, the monks welcomed the words of the Blessed One.

So ends the *Indrabrāhmaṇa-avadāna,* the sixth chapter in the glorious *Divyāvadāna.*

7. *The Story of a Woman Dependent on a City for Alms*

NAGARĀVALAMBIKĀ-AVADĀNA

After wandering through the Kośala countryside, the Blessed One arrived in Śrāvastī. Once in Śrāvastī, he stayed in the Jeta Grove in the park of a man named Anāthapiṇḍada (Almsgiver to the Poor).

Now the householder Anāthapiṇḍada heard that the Blessed One, after wandering through the Kośala countryside, had arrived in Śrāvastī, and that in Śrāvastī he stayed in the Jeta Grove in Anāthapiṇḍada's park. When he heard this, he approached the Blessed One and, having approached, venerated with his head the feet of the Blessed One and then sat down at a respectful distance. With a discourse on the dharma, the Blessed One instructed, incited, inspired, and delighted the householder Anāthapiṇḍada, who was seated at a respectful distance. After he instructed, incited, inspired, and delighted him in many ways with this discourse on the dharma, he became silent.

The householder Anāthapiṇḍada then got up from his seat, properly arranged his robe on one shoulder, bowed toward the Buddha with his hands respectfully folded, and said this to the Blessed One: [81] "May the Blessed One, along with the community of monks, accept this invitation to eat at my home tomorrow." With his silence, the Blessed One accepted the householder Anāthapiṇḍada's invitation. Then the householder Anāthapiṇḍada, realizing that by his silence the Blessed

One had accepted his invitation, rejoiced and delighted in the words of the Blessed One, venerated with his head the feet of the Blessed One, left the Blessed One's presence, and approached his home. Having approached, he addressed his gatekeeper: "Listen here! Don't let any non-Buddhist renunciants enter until the community of monks led by the Buddha has finished eating. After that, I'll allow the non-Buddhist renunciants to enter."

"Yes sir," the gatekeeper replied, consenting to the householder Anāthapiṇḍada's request.

That very night the householder Anāthapiṇḍada prepared hard and soft foods, both fresh and fine, and then at daybreak he got up, prepared the seats, and distributed pitchers of water. Then he had a messenger inform the Blessed One that it was now the appropriate time: "It is time, Bhadanta. The food is ready. Now the Blessed One may do as the time permits."

Later in the morning the Blessed One got dressed, took his bowl and robe, and leading the community of monks that surrounded him, approached the place where the householder Anāthapiṇḍada was offering food. Having approached, he sat down in front of the community of monks in the seat specially prepared for him.

Now when the householder Anāthapiṇḍada was sure that the community of monks led by the Buddha was comfortably seated, he served and indulged them, with his own hands, with hard and soft foods, both fresh and fine. When he had served and indulged them, with his own hands, with many courses of hard and soft foods, both fresh and fine, and was sure that the Blessed One had finished eating, washed his hands, and set aside his bowl, he sat down in front of the Buddha, taking a lower seat, to listen to the dharma.

The Venerable Mahākāśyapa and a Leprous Beggar Woman

Meanwhile the venerable Mahākāśyapa left behind his forest shelter and with his long hair and beard and his coarse robe went to the Jeta

Grove.[445] Seeing that the Jeta Grove was empty, he asked the acting caretaker of the monastery, "Where is the community of monks led by the Buddha?"

"The householder Anāthapiṇḍada has invited them for a meal," he explained.

"I'll go there then," the venerable Mahākāśyapa reflected. [82] "There I can partake of almsfood and pay my respects to the community of monks led by the Buddha." He then went to the householder Anāthapiṇḍada's home.

"Sir, stay where you are!" the gatekeeper said. "You are not to enter."

"Why is that?"

"The householder Anāthapiṇḍada has ordered me not to allow any non-Buddhist renunciants to enter until the community of monks led by the Buddha has finished eating. After that, he'll allow the non-Buddhist renunciants to enter."

"This is a great opportunity for someone like me," the venerable Mahākāśyapa reflected. "Here the brahmans and householders are believers, and they don't know me as an ascetic of the Śākya clan. I'll go then and do good deeds for the poor." With this in mind, he went to the park. Then he reflected, "Now whom should I do a good deed for today?"

Meanwhile a certain woman dependent on the city for alms,[446] who was afflicted with leprosy and was pained and diseased with rotten limbs, was wandering for alms. The venerable Mahākāśyapa approached her, though she had only the foamy water from boiled rice[447] that she herself had received as alms. Then she saw the venerable Mahākāśyapa, who instilled faith through his body and through his mind and was calm in his actions.

"Surely I've never served one so worthy of an offering before," she reflected. "And so my condition is as it is. If the noble Mahākāśyapa will take pity on me and accept this rice water of mine, then I should give it to him."

Then the venerable Mahākāśyapa, understanding her thoughts with his mind, held out his begging bowl. "If you have anything to spare, my sister, please put it in my bowl."

Cultivating faith in her mind, she poured some rice water into his bowl. Then a fly fell in. She began to take it out when one of her fingers fell off into the rice water. She reflected, "Although the noble one, out of respect for my feelings, hasn't thrown this rice water away, he won't partake of it."

Then the venerable Mahākāśyapa, understanding her thoughts with his mind, sat down against the base of a wall and, right before her eyes, began to eat.

She reflected, "Although the noble one, out of respect for my feelings, has partaken of this, he won't think of this food as a proper meal."

Then the venerable Mahākāśyapa, understanding her thoughts, said this to that woman who was dependent on the city for alms: "Sister, I am happy![448] I can pass the whole day and night on the food that you have given me."[449]

She became very excited. "The noble Mahākāśyapa [83] has accepted alms from me!" Then, while cultivating faith in her mind for the venerable Mahākāśyapa, she died and was reborn among the gods of Tuṣita (Content).

Śakra's Attempted Offering

Though Śakra, lord of the gods, saw the woman offering rice water, cultivating faith in her mind, and then dying, he didn't see where she was reborn. He began to look through the various hells, but he didn't see her. Then he looked through the realms of animals, hungry ghosts, and mortals, and among the gods of Cāturmahārājika (Four Groups of the Great Kings) and Trāyastriṃśa (Thirty-Three), but still he didn't see her. This is the case because gods can look and come to know[450] what is below them but not what is above them. So Śakra, lord of the gods, approached the Blessed One and, having approached, asked a question in verse:

Where is that woman who rejoiced,
giving rice water to Kāśyapa,
while the great being Kāśyapa
was wandering about for alms?

The Blessed One replied:

There[451] among those gods named Tuṣita,
who have success in all they desire,
is that woman who rejoiced,
giving rice water to Kāśyapa.

Then it occurred to Śakra, lord of the gods, "These mortals can't see the results of merit and demerit[452] before their eyes, and yet they make offerings and perform meritorious deeds. I can see[453] the results of merit right before my eyes, since I am appointed in the results of my own merit. So why shouldn't I make offerings and perform meritorious deeds? This noble Mahākāśyapa has pity for the poor, for orphans, for the destitute, and for beggars. I really should offer him alms."

With this in mind, Śakra magically created a dilapidated, broken-down house in which crows lurked, on a road where poor people lived. Then he magically transformed himself into a weaver dressed in hempen rags and wearing a rumpled turban. With cracked hands and feet, he began to weave. The divine maiden Śacī, bearing the disguise of a weaver's wife, also began to weave on a loom. Near her, divine ambrosia stood ready.

Now the venerable Mahākāśyapa, having pity for the destitute, for orphans, and for beggars, went to their homes one after another. [84] "This is so sad," he thought as he stood at their doorways holding out his bowl. Then Śakra, lord of the gods, filled his bowl with divine ambrosia.

Then it occurred to the venerable Mahākāśyapa,

Divine ambrosia is his food,
and yet this is the extent of his home.
Considering this sharp contrast,
my heart is filled with doubt.

It is in fact a law of nature that the knowledge and insight of arhats does not operate unless they focus their attention.[454] Mahākāśyapa began to focus his attention, and then he saw that it was Śakra, lord of the gods.

"Kauśika," he said, "why do you create obstacles for those beings who suffer, especially when the Blessed One himself, a perfectly awakened tathāgata arhat, has completely uprooted[455] that arrow of doubt and uncertainty that you have cultivated for so long?"

"Noble Mahākāśyapa, you ask why I create obstacles for those beings who suffer. Well, these mortals can't see the results of merit before their eyes, and yet they make offerings and perform meritorious deeds. I can see the results of merit right before my eyes. So why shouldn't I make offerings?[456] Indeed the Blessed One has said,

Meritorious deeds are to be performed.
Not performing meritorious deeds brings suffering.[457]
Those who perform meritorious deeds[458]
can rejoice in this world and in the next.

From then on the venerable Mahākāśyapa began to enter households for alms only after focusing his attention. Meanwhile Śakra, lord of the gods, would float in the air, and as the venerable Mahākāśyapa would wander for alms, he would fill his begging bowl with divine ambrosia. The venerable Mahākāśyapa, in turn, would flip his bowl over and the food would spill out.

The monks explained this situation to the Blessed One.

The Blessed One said, "Therefore, I permit a begging-bowl cover to be used."

King Prasenajit of Kośala's Offerings

Word spread all around that a certain woman who was dependent on the city for alms had offered rice water to the noble Mahākāśyapa and that she had been reborn among the Tuṣita gods. Then King Prasenajit of Kośala heard that a certain woman who was dependent on the city for alms had offered rice water to the noble Mahākāśyapa and that she had been reborn among the Tuṣita gods.[459] When he heard this, he approached the Blessed One. Having approached, he venerated with his head the feet of the Blessed One and then sat down at a respectful distance. The Blessed One instructed, incited, inspired, and delighted King Prasenajit of Kośala, [85] who was seated at a respectful distance, with a discourse on the dharma. After he instructed, incited, inspired, and delighted him in many ways with this discourse on the dharma, he became silent. King Prasenajit of Kośala then got up from his seat, properly arranged his robe on one shoulder, bowed toward the Blessed One with his hands respectfully folded, and said this to the Blessed One: "May the Blessed One, on behalf of the noble Mahākāśyapa, accept food from me for seven days." With his silence, the Blessed One accepted King Prasenajit of Kośala's invitation. Then King Prasenajit of Kośala, realizing that by his silence the Blessed One had accepted his invitation, left the Blessed One's presence.

That very night King Prasenajit of Kośala prepared hard and soft foods, both fresh and fine, and then at daybreak he got up, prepared the seats, and distributed pitchers of water. Then he had a messenger inform the Blessed One that it was now the appropriate time: "It is time, Bhadanta. The food is ready. Now the Blessed One may do as the time permits."

Later in the morning the Blessed One got dressed, took his bowl and robe, and leading the community of monks that surrounded him, approached the place where King Prasenajit of Kośala was offering food. Having approached, he sat down in front of the community of monks in the seat specially prepared for him.

Now when King Prasenajit of Kośala was sure that the community of monks led by the Buddha was comfortably seated, he served and indulged them, with his own hands, with hard and soft foods, both fresh and fine.

Meanwhile a bowl-carrying beggar stood in the area of the elders cultivating faith in his mind. "This king," he thought, "can see the results of merit right before his eyes since he is appointed in the results of his own merit. Yet he is still unsatisfied with this merit, so he makes more offerings and performs more meritorious deeds."

Now when King Prasenajit of Kośala had served and indulged the community of monks led by the Buddha, with his own hands, with many courses of hard and soft foods, both fresh and fine, and was sure that the Blessed One had finished eating, washed his hands, and set aside his bowl, he then sat down in front of the Buddha, taking a lower seat, to listen to the dharma.

Then the Blessed One said, "Your majesty, in whose name shall I assign the reward from the offering—in your name or in the name of that person who has earned more merit than you?"

"The Blessed One has eaten the food that I've offered as alms," the King reflected. [86] "Who else could have earned more merit than me?" With this in mind, he said, "Blessed One, may the Blessed One assign the reward from the offering in the name of that person who has earned more merit than me."

The Blessed One then assigned the reward in the name of that bowl-carrying beggar. And it went on like this for six days.

Then on the sixth day[460] the king sat lost in thought, with his cheek in his hand. "The Blessed One eats the food that I offer as alms," he thought, "and then assigns the reward in the name of a bowl-carrying beggar."

His ministers saw him and asked, "Why do you sit there lost in thought, with your cheek in your hand?"

"Gentlemen," the king said, "why shouldn't I be lost in thought? The Blessed One eats the food that I offer as alms and then assigns the reward in the name of a bowl-carrying beggar!"

Then one old minister said, "Don't worry. We'll take care of things so that tomorrow the Blessed One will assign the reward only in the name of my lord."

The ministers then ordered the workers as follows: "Tomorrow you are to prepare and keep ready an abundance of fine food so that half may fall in the monks' bowls and half on the ground."[461]

On the next day, the ministers kept ready an abundance of fine food. Then when the community of monks led by the Buddha was comfortably seated, they began to serve them. Half of the food fell in the monks' bowls, and half on the ground. Those bowl-carrying beggars ran forward, thinking, "We'll take what's fallen on the ground!" But the people who were serving food didn't let them.

Then that one bowl-carrying beggar said, "Though the king has an abundance of food and wealth, there are others like us who are suffering and longing for it. Why then isn't it being given away? What's the use of throwing it away without making use of it?"

That bowl-carrying beggar's mind became distracted. It wasn't possible for him to cultivate faith in his mind as he did before.

Meanwhile the king fed the community of monks led by the Buddha, and thinking that the Blessed One wouldn't assign the reward from the offering in his name, he departed without even waiting to hear the reward assigned.

Then the Blessed One assigned the reward from the offering in the name of King Prasenajit of Kośala:

> In the case of a king with an army of
> elephants, horses, chariots, and foot soldiers
> who protects a city and its people— [87]
> now you see the power of offering even
> dry and bland rice gruel as alms.

Then the venerable Ānanda said this to the Blessed One: "Many, many times, Bhadanta, the Blessed One has eaten at the home of King

Prasenajit of Kośala and assigned the reward from an offering in someone's name. But I don't remember a reward ever being assigned like this before."

"Ānanda," the Blessed One asked, "do you want to hear about the karmic bonds of King Prasenajit of Kośala, beginning with his offering of some bland rice gruel?"

"Yes, Blessed One. For this it is the right time. Sugata, for this it is the right occasion. May the Blessed One describe the karmic bonds of King Prasenajit of Kośala, beginning with his offering of some bland rice gruel. Hearing the words of the Blessed One, the monks will keep them in mind."

Then the Blessed One addressed the monks:

Long ago, monks, in a certain market town,[462] there lived a householder. He brought home a girl from an appropriate family as his wife, and with her he fooled around, enjoyed himself, and made love. From his fooling around, enjoying himself, and making love, a son was born. The boy was raised and nourished and eventually became quite clever.

One day that householder said to his wife, "My dear, this son of ours will bring us debt and take away our wealth.[463] I'll take some goods for trade and go abroad."

"Yes, dear husband," she said. "You should do that."

So the householder took some goods and went abroad, and right there met with an untimely death. The householder had few possessions; the householder's wealth was completely lost. His son became miserable.

Now the householder had a friend, and this friend spoke to the boy's mother: "Let this son of yours protect my field. I can provide him with food without any difficulty."[464]

"Yes, that would be good."

The boy began to protect the man's field. And the man, with no difficulties, began to provide him with food.[465] Then one day it was a lunar holiday.

The boy's mother reflected, [88] "Today the householder's wife will be busy feeding friends, relations, and relatives as well as ascetics and brahmans. I'll go during the peak hours[466] and bring food to my boy." Then, during the peak hours, she went and informed the householder's wife of the matter.

"I don't give anything to ascetics, brahmans, or even to my relatives," she said angrily. "Do you think I'm going to give anything to a servant? Leave things as they are for now. Tomorrow I'll give him twice as much."[467]

"I won't let my son go hungry," the boy's mother reflected. Since she had prepared some bland rice gruel for herself,[468] she took it and went to the field.[469] Her son saw her from far away.

"Mom," he said, "do have anything tasty to eat?"

"Son," she said, "I don't even have the usual, everyday food with me today. I prepared some bland rice gruel for myself, brought it, and came here. You should eat it."

"Put it down and go," he said. So she put it down and went away.

When no buddhas are born, solitary buddhas can arise in the world. They have pity for the poor and neglected, they live in remote areas, and they alone are worthy of people's offerings.

Meanwhile a solitary buddha arrived in that country. The householder's son saw this solitary buddha, who instilled faith through his body and through his mind and was calm in his actions.

"Surely I've never served such a righteous being so worthy of offerings before," he reflected. "And so my condition is as it is. If he will accept some bland rice gruel from me, then I should give it to him."

Then that solitary buddha, understanding with his mind the thoughts of the householder's son, held out his begging bowl. "Friend, if you have anything to spare, please put it in my bowl."

With great faith he offered that bland rice gruel to the solitary buddha.

"What do you think, monks? That poor man was none other than King Prasenajit of Kośala at that time and at that juncture. Since he offered some bland rice gruel to that solitary buddha as alms, because of that action, six times he will have kingship, lordship, and dominion among the Trāyastriṃśa gods, and six times, right here in Śrāvastī, he will be a kṣatriya king who has been duly consecrated. And because of the karma that remains, he has now become a kṣatriya king who has been duly consecrated. [89] His offering of alms has come to fruition.

It is with reference to this that I say:

> In the case of a king with an army of
> elephants, horses, chariots, and foot soldiers
> who protects a city and its people—
> now you see the power of offering even
> dry and bland rice gruel as alms."

Word spread all around that the Blessed One had revealed the karmic bonds of King Prasenajit, beginning with his offering of some bland rice gruel. King Prasenajit heard this, so he approached the Blessed One. Having approached, he venerated with his head the feet of the Blessed One and then sat down at a respectful distance. The Blessed One instructed, incited, inspired, and delighted King Prasenajit of Kośala, who was seated at a respectful distance, with a discourse on the dharma. After he instructed, incited, inspired, and delighted him in many ways with this discourse on the dharma, he became silent.

King Prasenajit of Kośala then got up from his seat, properly arranged his robe on one shoulder, bowed toward the Buddha with his hands respectfully folded, and said this to the Blessed One: "May the Blessed One, along with the community of monks, accept my offering of enough provisions of robes, begging bowls, bedding and seats, and medicines to cure the sick to last the three months of the rainy season."

With his silence the Blessed One accepted King Prasenajit of Kośala's invitation.

For those three months, King Prasenajit of Kośala offered delicious food to the community of monks led by the Buddha and provided each and every monk with hundreds and thousands of garments. He also collected millions of jars of oil and was all set to give out oil-lamp trees. Then, at the time of distributing these things and performing a ceremony, there was a great commotion.

A Suffering Beggar Woman's Offering

A certain woman who was dependent on the city for alms was suffering greatly. While wandering for alms with an empty bowl, she heard a great uproar. And when she heard it, she asked, "Gentlemen, what is this great commotion and uproar?"

"For three months King Prasenajit of Kośala has given food to the community of monks led by the Buddha," others reported. "He has also provided each and every monk with hundreds and thousands of garments. Now he has collected millions of jars of oil and is all set to give out oil-lamp trees."

Then it occurred to that woman who was dependent on the city for alms, "This King Prasenajit of Kośala isn't satisfied with his merit, so he still makes offerings and performs meritorious deeds. [90] I really should collect oil from someplace so that I can offer a lamp to the Blessed One as well." Then she begged a little bit of oil in a broken bowl, lit a lamp, and placed it where the Buddha would do his walking meditation. Falling prostrate at his feet, she made this fervent aspiration:

> By this root of virtue, just as this lord Śākyamuni arose in the world when people lived for one hundred years as a teacher named Śākyamuni, likewise, may I, too, when people live for one hundred years, be a teacher, that very Śākyamuni. As that excellent pair, Śāriputra and Maudgalyāyana, were his first pair of disciples, the monk Ānanda his personal attendant, Śuddhodana his father, Mahāmāyā his mother, [Kapilavastu his city],[470] and Prince Rāhulabhadra his son, [likewise, may the excellent pair Śāriputra and Maudgalyāyana also be my

> first pair of disciples, the monk Ānanda my personal attendant, Śuddhodana my father, Mahāmāyā my mother, Kapilavastu my city, and Prince Rāhulabhadra my son.][471] And as this Blessed One will pass into final nirvāṇa and his relics be distributed, likewise, may I, too, pass into final nirvāṇa and may my relics be distributed.

Then all the lamps went out save the lamp that she had lit, which continued to shine.

It is a rule that the personal attendants of lord buddhas do not go to bed until lord buddhas go to bed. The venerable Ānanda reflected, "It is impossible and inconceivable that lord buddhas would go to sleep in the light. I really should put out that lamp." He began to put it out with his hand, but he wasn't able to. Then he tried with the edge of his robe, then with a fan, but he still wasn't able to put it out.

Then the Blessed One addressed the venerable Ānanda: "What are you trying to do, Ānanda?"

"Blessed One," he said, "the thought occurred to me that it is impossible and inconceivable that lord buddhas would go to sleep in the light, and that I should put out that lamp. So I began to put it out with my hand, but I wasn't able to. Then I tried with the edge of my robe, then with a fan, but I still wasn't able to."

"Ānanda," the Blessed One said, "you'll just exhaust yourself. Even if gale-force Vairambhaka winds[472] were to blow, they wouldn't be able to put it out, much less the movement of a hand, the edge of a robe, or a fan. This is so precisely because this lamp was lit by that woman with a great resolution of mind. Moreover, Ānanda, when people live for one hundred years, that woman will be a perfectly awakened tathāgata arhat named Śākyamuni. The excellent pair, Śāriputra and Maudgalyāyana, will be her first pair of disciples, the monk Ānanda her personal attendant,[473] Śuddhodana her father, Mahāmāyā her mother, Kapilavastu her city, and Prince Rāhulabhadra her son. [91] She will pass into final nirvāṇa and her relics will be distributed."

This was said by the Blessed One. With their minds uplifted, the monks welcomed the words of the Blessed One.

So ends the *Nagarāvalambikā-avadāna,* the seventh chapter in the glorious *Divyāvadāna.*

8. The Story of Supriya

SUPRIYA-AVADĀNA

THE LORD BUDDHA was staying in Śrāvastī at the Jeta Grove in the park of a man named Anāthapiṇḍada (Almsgiver to the Poor). There he was respected, honored, revered, and venerated by kings, royal ministers, the well-to-do, townspeople, brahmans, householders, guildmasters, caravan leaders, gods, nāgas, yakṣas, antigods, heavenly birds, kinnaras, and great snakes. Thus praised by gods, nāgas, yakṣas, antigods, heavenly birds, kinnaras, and great snakes, the Lord Buddha, along with the community made up of his disciples, received provisions of robes, begging bowls, bedding and seats, and medicines to cure the sick.

There in the Jeta Grove in the park of Anāthapiṇḍada, the Blessed One had come to pass the rainy-season retreat. When the day of the ceremony to mark the end of the rainy season finally arrived, many of the merchants living in Śrāvastī approached the Blessed One. Having approached, they venerated with their heads the feet of the Blessed One and then sat down at a respectful distance. The Blessed One instructed, incited, inspired, and delighted those many merchants living in Śrāvastī, seated as they were at a respectful distance, with a discourse on the dharma. After he instructed, incited, inspired, and delighted them in many ways with this discourse on the dharma, he became silent. Then those many merchants from Śrāvastī rejoiced and delighted in the words of the Blessed One, venerated with their heads the feet of the Blessed One, and left the Blessed One's presence.

Next they approached the venerable Ānanda. Having approached, [92] they venerated with their heads the feet of the venerable Ānanda and then sat down at a respectful distance. The venerable Ānanda instructed, incited, inspired, and delighted those many merchants living in Śrāvastī with a discourse on the dharma. After he instructed, incited, inspired, and delighted them in many ways with this discourse on the dharma, he became silent.

Then those merchants got up from their seats, properly arranged their robes on one shoulder, bowed toward the venerable Ānanda with their hands respectfully folded, and said this to the venerable Ānanda: "Noble Ānanda, now that the Blessed One has finished the rainy-season retreat, have you heard which region he'll travel through? That way we can prepare the necessary goods for his journey."

As a rule, merchants living in the six major cities[474] prepare goods for the travels of lord buddhas in whichever direction they desire to go.

"Why don't you ask the Lord Buddha?" the venerable Ānanda asked.

"Lord buddhas are very difficult to approach, and their presence is difficult to bear. We can't ask the Blessed One."

"Friends, I also find lord buddhas very difficult to approach and their presence difficult to bear. I can't ask the Blessed One either."

"If lord buddhas are difficult to approach and their presence is difficult to bear for Bhadanta Ānanda as well, how does Bhadanta Ānanda know that the Blessed One will go in one direction or another?"

"Gentlemen, either by a sign or by some indirect reference."

"How about if it's by a sign?"

"The Blessed One will sit facing in the direction that he wants to go. That's how it is with a sign."

"How about if it's by an indirect reference?"

"He will praise some particular region. That's how it is with an indirect reference."

"These days which direction, Bhadanta Ānanda, does the Blessed One sit facing? And which region does the Blessed One praise?"

"Friends, these days the Blessed One sits facing Magadha, and he praises the region of Magadha. Now friends, there are eighteen benefits to traveling with a buddha. Which eighteen? There is no fear of fire; no fear of water; no fear of lions; no fear of tigers; no fear of leopards, hyenas, or enemy armies; no fear of thieves; no fear of transit, freight, or passage fees; and no fear of humans or nonhumans. And from time to time, one sees divine forms, hears divine sounds, perceives great flashes of light, [93] and hears predictions about oneself. There are dharmic pleasures and material pleasures as well. Truly, journeying with a buddha leads to good health."[475]

Those many merchants living in Śrāvastī rejoiced and delighted in the words of the venerable Ānanda, venerated with their heads the feet of the venerable Ānanda, then got up from their seats and departed.

One Thousand Robbers in a Forest

As a rule, as long as lord buddhas are living, surviving, and passing time, they are intent on helping others and impelled by their great compassion. From time to time they travel through forests, rivers, mountains, cremation grounds, and the countryside. In this instance, the Lord Buddha wanted to travel through the Magadha countryside.

After the ceremony marking the end of the rainy-season retreat had been performed, the Blessed One addressed the venerable Ānanda: "Ānanda, go and inform the monks as follows—'Seven days from now the Tathāgata will travel through the Magadha countryside. Whoever among you is eager to travel through the Magadha countryside with the Tathāgata should ready his robes.'"

"Yes, Bhadanta," the venerable Ānanda replied, consenting to the Blessed One's request. Then he informed the monks: "Venerable ones, seven days from now the Blessed One will travel through the Magadha countryside. Whoever among you is eager to travel through the Magadha countryside with the Blessed One should ready his robes."

Then the Blessed One, leading the community of monks that surrounded him, together with many merchants, brahmans, and householders from Śrāvastī, set off on a journey through the Magadha countryside.

Now those many merchants from Śrāvastī approached the Blessed One. Having approached, they venerated with their heads the feet of the Blessed One and then said this to him: "While we're on the way between Śrāvastī and Rājagṛha, may the Blessed One, along with the community of monks, please accept provisions from us of robes, begging bowls, bedding and seats, and medicines to cure the sick."

The Blessed One accepted this invitation from those many merchants from Śrāvastī with his silence. Then those many merchants from Śrāvastī, knowing by the Blessed One's silence that he had accepted their invitation, left the Blessed One's presence. [94]

So the Blessed One set out. Meanwhile, on the way between Śrāvastī and Rājagṛha, a thousand robbers were staying in a large forest. Those thousand robbers saw the Blessed One surrounded by the members of the caravan and leading the community of monks. At the sight of this, they spoke among themselves: "The Blessed One and the community made up of his disciples can go. We'll rob the rest of the caravan." After giving this some thought, they all quickly charged toward the caravan.

"Gentlemen," the Blessed One said to them, "what are you planning to do?"

"Bhadanta, we're robbers who live in the forest. We don't have farms, businesses, or cows to look after. This is the way that we make a living. Now the Blessed One and the community made up of his disciples can go. We'll rob the rest of the caravan."

The Blessed One said, "This caravan depends on me. Instead of robbing it, figure out how much the caravan is worth as a whole and then take the equivalent in gold."[476]

"Okay," the thousand robbers agreed. "Let it be as you say."

Those merchants in the caravan who were lay disciples of the Buddha figured out how much the whole caravan was worth and informed the robbers: "It comes to this many hundreds and thousands."

Then, in order to pay those thousand robbers the ransom for the caravan, the Blessed One showed them where there was treasure buried underground. The thousand robbers took as much gold as the caravan was worth. The rest vanished on the spot. In this way the Blessed One saved the caravan from the thousand robbers.

Eventually the Blessed One arrived in Rājagṛha. After some time, the Blessed One, once again surrounded by the members of the caravan and leading the community of monks, left Rājagṛha and set out for Śrāvastī. Just as before, a ransom was paid to those thousand robbers for the caravan. And it went on like this a second, third, fourth, fifth, and sixth time as well. As the Blessed One came and went, he protected the caravan from those thousand robbers and paid them off. But on the seventh time, the Blessed One left Śrāvastī and set out for Rājagṛha leading the community of monks, yet without the caravan. Those thousand robbers saw that the Lord Buddha was leading the community of monks without the caravan. At the sight of this, they conversed among themselves.

"The Blessed One can go. We'll rob the community of monks."

"Why's that?"

"It's only the Blessed One that gives us gold."

With that said, they charged as fast as they could and began to rob the monks. [95]

"My children," the Blessed One said, "these are my disciples."

"As the Blessed One very well knows," the robbers said, "we're robbers who live in the forest. We don't have farms, businesses, or cows to look after. This is the way that we make a living."

Then the Blessed One showed the robbers where there was a huge treasure trove buried underground. "My children," he said, "take as much wealth as you can."

Those thousand robbers took as much gold for themselves as they could from that huge treasure trove. The rest vanished on the spot.

Now after the Blessed One had satisfied those thousand robbers with as much wealth as they could take, he continued on and eventually arrived in Rājagṛha.

Then this thought occurred to those robbers: "All the prosperity and good fortune that we have is due to the Lord Buddha. We really should feed the Blessed One along with the community made up of his disciples right here in this place."

Meanwhile there is nothing that lord buddhas [do not know, see, realize, and understand. It is a law of nature that lord buddhas have][477] great compassion,

they have a single guardian [which is mindfulness],
they are the singularly heroic,
they preach nondualism,
they abide in the meditative states of tranquility and insight,
they are expert in the three kinds of objects for self-control,
they have planted the soles of their feet well
  on the four bases of success,
they have crossed the four floods [of corruptions],
they have long since developed an expertise in the four means
  of attracting beings to the religious life,
they are powerful with the ten powers,
they are confident with the four confidences,
they roar the lion-like roar that is far-reaching, majestic,
  and perfect,
they have destroyed the five [bad] qualities,
they help others obtain release from the five aggregates
  [which are the basis of clinging to existence],
they have crossed over the five realms of existence,
they have shattered the six sense objects,[478]
they reside alone,[479]
they are famous for their fulfillment
  of the six perfections,

they are replete with the flowers of the seven factors
of awakening,
they grant the requisites for the seven meditative concentrations,
they are teachers of the noble eightfold path,
they lead individuals on the noble path,
they are expert in attaining the nine successive states
of quiescence meditation,
they help others unbind the nine bonds to existence,
they have fame that fills up the ten directions,
and they are superior to the thousand gods who have control
over others.[480]

Three times in the night and three times in the day—all together six times in the night and day—lord buddhas observe the world with their buddha vision and think:

For whom with roots of virtue unplanted shall I plant them?
For whom with roots of virtue already planted
shall I cause them to develop?
Who will encounter trouble?
Who will encounter difficulty?
Who will encounter danger?
Who will encounter trouble, difficulty, and danger?
Who shall I release from trouble, difficulty, and danger?
Who is inclined toward a terrible realm of existence?
Who is prone toward a terrible realm of existence?
Who is disposed toward a terrible realm of existence?
Who shall I lift up from a terrible realm of existence
and establish in heaven and liberation? [96]
To whom, mired in the mud of sense pleasures,
shall I offer a helping hand?
For whom shall I make the world, which is already adorned
with the rising of a Buddha, fruitful?

Who, without noble wealth, shall I establish in the lordship
and dominion of noble wealth?
Who will get worse?
Who will get better?

Although the sea, home to monsters,
may allow the time of the tides to pass,
the Buddha never allows the time to pass
for training his beloved children.[481]

Just as a mother looks after an only child,
whom she loves dearly, and protects his life,
the Tathāgata looks after those to be trained,
his future disciples, and protects their minds.

Abiding in the mind of the Omniscient One,
like the loving cow searching for her missing calves,
the cow of compassion never tires of searching
for her tender calves in need of training,
lost as they are in the suffering of existence.

Now the Blessed One was self-controlled
and his followers were self-controlled,
he was calm and his followers were calm,
he was excellent and his followers were excellent,
he was liberated and his followers were liberated,
he was confident and his followers were confident
[he was disciplined and his followers were disciplined,
he was an arhat and his followers were arhats,
he was without attachment
and his followers were without attachment,
and he instilled faith and his followers instilled faith.

He was like a bull surrounded by a herd of cows,
like a royal elephant surrounded by a herd of elephant cubs,
like a lion surrounded by a carnivorous pack,
like a royal goose surrounded by a gaggle of geese,
like an eagle surrounded by a flock of birds,
like a learned brahman surrounded by an assembly of students,
like an eminent doctor surrounded by a group of patients,
like a warrior surrounded by a troop of soldiers,
like a guide surrounded by a group of travelers,
like a caravan leader surrounded by a company of merchants,
like a guildmaster surrounded by townspeople,
like a vassal king surrounded by a cabinet of ministers,
like a wheel-turning king surrounded by a thousand sons,
like the moon surrounded by a constellation of stars,
like the sun surrounded by a thousand rays of light,
like the great king Dhṛtarāṣṭra surrounded by a group
of celestial musicians,
like the great king Virūḍhaka surrounded by a group
of *kumbhāṇḍa*s,
like the great king Virūpākṣa surrounded by a group of nāgas,
like the great king Dhanada surrounded by a group of yakṣas,
like Vemacitrin surrounded by a group of antigods,
like Śakra surrounded by a group of gods,
and like Brahmā surrounded by the gods of Brahmakāyika
(Brahmā's Assembly).

He was like an ocean but calm,
like a cloud but full of water,
and like a mighty elephant but without pride or passion.
His senses were well restrained,
his deportment and demeanor were unflappable,
he was adorned with the thirty-two marks of a great man,
and his body was radiant with the eighty minor marks.

His form was adorned with a halo extending an arm's length,
his brilliance was greater than a thousand suns,
and like a mountain of jewels that moved,
he was beautiful from every side.

He was endowed with the ten powers,
the four confidences,
the three special applications of mindfulness,
and great compassion.][482]

Then the Blessed One, considering that it was the proper time to train those robbers, left Rājagṛha, and leading the community of monks that surrounded him, in due course arrived at that forest of *śāla* trees. Those thousand robbers saw the Lord Buddha, together with the community made up of his disciples, coming from a distance. At the sight of them, they cultivated faith in their minds and approached the Blessed One. Having approached, they fell prostrate at the feet of the Blessed One and said this to him: "May the Blessed One, along with the community of monks, accept this invitation to eat in our homes tomorrow."

With his silence, the Blessed One accepted the invitation of those thousand robbers. Then those thousand robbers, knowing by the Blessed One's silence that he had accepted their invitation, left the Blessed One's presence.

That very night those thousand robbers prepared hard and soft foods, both fresh and fine, and then at daybreak they got up, prepared the seats, and distributed pitchers of water. Then they had a messenger inform the Blessed One that it was now the appropriate time: "It is time, Bhadanta. The food is ready. Now the Blessed One may do as the time permits." [97]

Later in the morning the Blessed One got dressed, took his bowl and robe, and leading the community of monks that surrounded him, approached the place where those thousand robbers were offering food. Those thousand robbers then washed the feet of the community of monks led by the Buddha with sandalwood-scented water. With his hands and feet washed, the Blessed One sat down in front of the community of monks in the seat specially prepared for him.

Now when those thousand robbers were sure that the community of monks led by the Buddha was [comfortably][483] seated, they served and indulged them with their own hands, with hard and soft foods, both fresh and fine. And when they were sure[484] that the Blessed One had finished eating, washed his hands, and set aside his bowl, they then sat down in front of the Blessed One, taking lower seats, to listen to the dharma.

Then the Blessed One, realizing their inclinations and propensities, and knowing their makeup and nature, gave them a discourse on the dharma such that when they heard it, those thousand robbers, seated right there in their seats, with the thunderbolt of knowledge, broke through that mountain which is the false view of individuality that arises with its twenty peaks of incorrect views, and directly experienced the reward of the stream-enterer. Having seen the truth, they said,

What has been done for us, Bhadanta,
neither our mothers nor our fathers have done,
nor any king,
nor any deities, or deceased ancestors,
nor any ascetics or brahmans,
nor any kinsmen or relatives.
It is all due to the Blessed One, our virtuous friend.
Our feet, which were sinking in the realms of hell, the animal realm, and the realm of hungry ghosts, have been lifted up!
We've been established among gods and humans!
Saṃsāra has come to end!
Oceans of blood and tears have dried up!
Mountains of bones have been scaled!
Bhadanta, may we renounce, take ordination, and become monks according to the dharma and monastic discipline that have been so well expressed.
May we follow the religious life in the presence of the Blessed One.

Then the Blessed One said in his Brahmā-like voice, "Come, my children, follow the religious life." As soon as the Blessed One finished speaking, their heads were suddenly shaven.[485] [Becoming arhats,]

> they were free from attachment in the three realms
> [of desire, form, and formlessness];
> they regarded clods of earth and gold as equal in value;
> they possessed equanimity toward the sky
> and the palms of their hands;
> they didn't distinguish between being cut by a blade
> and being anointed with sandalwood paste;
> the eggshell [of their ignorance] was broken by knowledge;
> they obtained the special knowledges, superhuman faculties,
> and analytic insights;
> and they were averse to worldly attainments, temptations,
> and honors.
> They became worthy of respect, honor, and obeisance
> from the gods, including Indra and Upendra.

Those monks in doubt asked the Lord Buddha, the remover of all doubts, [98] "Look, Bhadanta. Is it true that the Blessed One satisfied those thousand robbers with wealth seven times and then established them in the unsurpassed supreme security that is nirvāṇa?"

"Yes, monks," the Blessed One said, "not only now, but in the past as well, I paid those same thousand robbers a ransom for a caravan and its many thousands of goods—but I wasn't able to fully satisfy them. Then, after performing many hundreds and thousands of difficult deeds, after one hundred years, I completed the journey to Badaradvīpa. It is a difficult journey to make for gods and humans; it is even difficult to accomplish for Śakra, Brahmā, and the other gods. Then I satisfied those same thousand robbers with gold, silver, beryl, crystal, and the like, with special jewels, and with those special things that were the objects of their desire. Afterward, I established all the inhabitants of Jambudvīpa (Black Plum Island) on the tenfold path of virtuous actions. Listen to this."

The Beloved Supriya

Long ago, monks, in a time gone by, right here in Jambudvīpa, in the city of Vārāṇasī, a king named Brahmadatta ruled a kingdom that was thriving and safe, with plenty of food and crowds of people, that was free from quarrel and strife, with no hustle and bustle, thieves, famine, or diseases. He watched over the kingdom as if it were an only child whom he loved dearly.

Now at that time in Vārāṇasī there lived a caravan leader named Priyasena (Beloved Commander), who was rich, wealthy, and prosperous. Truly, he rivaled the god Vaiśravaṇa in wealth. He brought home a girl from an appropriate family as his wife, and with her he fooled around, enjoyed himself, and made love.

Meanwhile a certain being who was very powerful because of his vast merit[486] died and passed away from an excellent community of the gods. He entered the womb of the caravan leader Priyasena's wife.

Now an intelligent woman here in this world tends to possess five special characteristics. Which five?

> She knows when a man is in love;
> she knows when the time is right,
>   and she knows when she is fertile;
> she knows when life has entered her womb;
> she knows from whom life has entered her womb;[487]
> and she knows if it's a boy, and she knows if it's a girl.

If it's a boy, the fetus settles on the right side of the womb. If it's a girl, it settles on the left side of the womb.

In high spirits, the caravan leader Priyasena's wife informed her husband: [99] "Congratulations, dear husband! I'm pregnant! And since the fetus has settled on the right side of my womb, it will definitely be a boy."

Likewise in very high spirits, he uttered this inspired utterance:

> So it is that I may finally get to see my son's face,
> a sight I've long desired to see!
> May my son not be ignoble.
> May he perform those duties I expect of him.
> May he, having been supported by me, support me in return.
> May he be the one to claim my inheritance.
> May my family lineage be long lasting.
>
> And may he, when we are dead and gone, make offerings and perform meritorious deeds on our behalf, and then direct the reward in our names with these words—"This merit shall follow these two wherever they are born and wherever they go."

Knowing that she was pregnant, the caravan leader Priyasena kept his wife in the upper story of their palatial home, free from any restraints, with all the necessities for the heat in the hot season and all the necessities for the cold in the cold season. She was given the foods that doctors prescribed, those not too cold, not too hot, not too bitter, not too sour, not too salty, not too sweet, not too pungent, and not too astringent, and those foods free from bitterness, sourness, saltiness, sweetness, pungency, and astringency. Her body was adorned with strings and necklaces of pearls, and like a nymph wandering in the divine Nandana Grove, she moved from bed to bed and from seat to seat, never descending to the ground below.[488] And she heard no unkind words until the fetus matured.

After eight or nine months, she gave birth. A boy was born who was beautiful, good-looking, and attractive, radiant with a golden complexion, who had a parasol-shaped head, lengthy arms, a broad forehead, joined eyebrows, a prominent nose, and a firm and toned body as strong as an athlete's.

Then his relatives came together and assembled. For three weeks, that is twenty-one days and nights, they celebrated the occasion of his birth and then they selected a name for him.

"What should this boy's name be?"

"The boy is the son of the caravan leader Priyasena. Therefore the boy's name should be Supriya (Greatly Beloved)."

The boy Supriya was entrusted to eight nurses—two wet nurses, two shoulder nurses, two nursemaids, and two playtime nurses. Raised by these eight nurses, who nourished him with milk, yogurt, fresh butter, clarified butter, butter scum, and other special provisions that were very pure, he grew quickly like a lotus in a lake.

When he grew up, [100] he was entrusted to teachers to learn writing and then arithmetic, accounting, matters relating to trademarks, and to debts, deposits, and trusts. He was educated in the science of elephants, the science of horses, the science of jewels, the science of wood, the science of cloth,[489] the science of men, the science of women, and the sciences of various commodities. He knew all the scriptures, he was skilled in all the arts and proficient in all crafts, he knew the languages of all creatures, and he knew the fates of those in all realms of existence.[490] [And in each of the eight sciences][491] he was learned and well versed, capable of explaining and expounding upon them. His intellect was singularly sharp and acute, and with his knowledge, he was like fire ablaze.

He also became skilled in those topics regarding arts and administration that are applicable to those kṣatriya kings who have been duly consecrated and who have obtained lordship, might, and power in their respective regions. This enables them to conquer and rule the great sphere of the earth. That is to say, he became skilled in riding on an elephant's neck, riding horseback, driving chariots, handling weapons and a bow, attacking, decamping, handling an elephant, throwing a lance, knowing what is to be cut, knowing what is to be broken, punching, head-butting, shooting by sound, piercing a target, striking vital points, delivering vigorous blows, and the five subjects of knowledge.

Now it is a truism that a son doesn't make a name for himself as long as his father is still alive. Well, one day the caravan leader Priyasena fell sick. Though treated with medicines made from roots, stalks, leaves, flowers, and fruits, he continued to get worse.

> All that is accumulated is lost in the end,
> what goes up comes down in the end,
> what comes together comes apart in the end,
> and what lives must die in the end.

And so, he died. After the caravan leader Priyasena had died, Brahmadatta, the king of Kāśi, anointed Supriya as the chief caravan leader.

Supriya the Caravan Leader and One Thousand Robbers

In his capacity as a caravan leader, Supriya made this great promise: "All beings I will satisfy with wealth." But there wasn't much to give and there were many supplicants. After a few days, his wealth gave out and was finally exhausted.

Now as chief caravan leader, Supriya reflected, "There isn't much to give and there are many supplicants. After a few days, my wealth will give out and finally be exhausted. I really should get an ocean-going ship ready and then set sail in the great ocean to find more wealth." [101]

Then the chief caravan leader Supriya got an ocean-going ship ready, and together with five hundred merchants, set sail in the great ocean. Eventually, they reached Ratnadvīpa (Jewel Island), collected jewels, and at last they emerged from the great ocean, safe and sound. They then loaded their goods onto vehicles on land and set off toward Vārāṇasī. When they were in the middle of the wilds of the forest, they met up with a thousand robbers.

Eager to rob them, those robbers charged as fast as they could.

The caravan leader Supriya looked at them and said, "Gentlemen, what are you planning to do?"

"Caravan leader," they said, "you alone may go. You'll be safe and sound. We'll rob the rest of the caravan."

"Gentlemen," the caravan leader said, "this caravan depends on me. You shouldn't rob it."

Thus addressed, the robbers said, "We're robbers who live in the forest. We don't have farms, businesses, or cattle to look after. This is the way that we make a living."

"Gentlemen, figure out how much the caravan is worth," the caravan leader Supriya said to them, "and I'll pay you that much on its behalf."

Then the merchants, after consulting with each other, figured out how much wealth they had among them and informed the robbers: "It comes to this many hundreds and thousands."

Then the caravan leader Supriya offered his own things to buy back the caravan's goods, and thus he saved the caravan from the robbers. And it went on like this a second, third, fourth, fifth, and a sixth time as well. Each time the caravan leader Supriya protected the caravan from those same thousand robbers and paid them off. Then on the seventh time, the caravan leader Supriya set sail once again in the great ocean. After successfully completing his voyage, while he was on his way back, in the middle of the wilds of the forest, he was again overtaken by those same thousand robbers. Eager to rob him, the robbers charged him as fast as they could. Then the caravan leader Supriya looked at them and said, "Gentlemen, I am Supriya the caravan leader."

"Great caravan leader," the robbers said, "you know very well that we're robbers that live in the forest. We don't have farms, businesses, or cows to look after. This is the way that we make a living."

Then the caravan leader Supriya remembered his promise from before, and with a firm commitment to that promise, offered his goods to those thousand robbers. The great caravan leader Supriya reflected, [102] "These robbers hoard whatever wealth they can get. Though I made a great promise that I would satisfy all beings with wealth, under these circumstances I can't even satisfy these thousand robbers with wealth. How can I possibly satisfy all beings with wealth?" Lost in this thought, he drifted into sleep.

Supriya Receives Instructions

Meanwhile the great being Supriya, who was very powerful because of his vast merit, who was magnanimous, trying to fulfill the desires of all beings, and who had set out for the benefit of the world, was approached by a very powerful deity. She consoled him: "Caravan leader, don't be sad. This fervent aspiration of yours will be successful. Great caravan leader, right here in Jambudvīpa there is a great trading center called Badaradvīpa (Jujube Island), which is inhabited by nonhumans and presided over by very powerful people. And in Badaradvīpa are the very best jewels, which can fulfill the various desires of all beings. Only if the great caravan leader can complete the journey to Badaradvīpa can he fulfill this great promise. Still, this great promise would be difficult to fulfill even for Śakra, Brahmā, and the rest of the gods, let alone for a human being." With these words, the deity vanished on the spot.

Now the great caravan leader wasn't able to ask that deity which direction Badaradvīpa was in or how one got there. So when the caravan leader Supriya had awakened from his sleep, it occurred to him, "How good it would be if that deity would show herself again! She has to point out the direction and the way to go to the great trading center Badaradvīpa!" Lost in this thought, he drifted into sleep once again.

Now that deity knew that Supriya was a great being who was very powerful because of his vast merit, that he was firmly committed to his generous promise, that he had great courage and heroism, and that he never gave up.[492] So she approached him and said, "Caravan leader, don't be sad. In the west, great caravan leader, after steering clear of five hundred small islands, one comes upon seven great mountains, which are tall and lofty, and seven great rivers. After one traverses these, making use of one's physical strength, this is who and what one encounters—

- [a mountain and an ocean called] Anulomapratiloma (Going This Way and That)
- [a mountain and an ocean called] Āvarta (Whirlpool)
- [the demon] Śaṅkhanābha (Conch-Like Navel) and Śaṅkhanābhī [the magical herb that he controls]
- a mountain [and an ocean called] Nīloda (Blue Water)
- Mount Tārakākṣa (Starry-Eyed)
- [the demon] Nīlagrīva (Blue Neck)
- [an ocean called] Vairambha (Gale)
- the Tāmra Forest (Forest of Copper Tāmra Trees) [103]
- a bamboo thicket
- seven thorny mountains
- a river of acid
- Mount Triśaṅku (Triple-Pointed Peak)
- Mount Ayaskīla (Iron Nail)
- the river Aṣṭādaśavakra (Eighteen Bends)
- [a mountain and a] river called Ślakṣṇa (Smooth)
- Mount[493] Dhūmanetra (Smokey-Eyed)
- Mount Saptāśīviṣa (Seven Venomous Snakes)
- and lastly, a river with the same name

"There is a great ocean called Anulomapratiloma, and in the great Anulomapratiloma Ocean, where no humans can live, Anulomapratiloma winds blow this way and that. A person who is very powerful and is protected by a deity who is very powerful can make use of his great powers of merit, strength, and mind, take a great raft, and set sail in the great Anulomapratiloma Ocean. He can travel forward for a month, but for the next full day he'll be brought back by opposing winds. It will happen like this a second and a third time as well. While being taken along and brought back, if he meets up with a central current of water—since he is protected by the power of loving kindness and since he has set out for the benefit of the world—he'll thus emerge from the ocean, pass out of danger, and free himself.

"After successfully crossing the great Anulomapratiloma Ocean, he'll come upon a mountain also called Anulomapratiloma. On the great Mount Anulomapratiloma, which is inhabited by nonhumans, winds called Anulomapratiloma blow this way and that, blinding a person and making him lose consciousness. Whoever maintains himself with his strength should search for the herb called Amoghā on that great mountain, then take it and apply it to his eyes and smear it on his head.[494] Then he should leave the great mountain called Anulomapratiloma. If he follows this procedure, he won't lose his senses, and he'll pass over the great Mount Anulomapratiloma and be safe and sound. If he doesn't follow this procedure or if he doesn't find the herb or if he finds it but doesn't take it, he'll lose his senses for six months and he'll be crazy as well. Or else he'll fall from on high and die.

"After successfully crossing the great Mount Anulomapratiloma, he'll come upon a great ocean called Āvarta. There blow violent winds that stir up the water. A person who is very powerful as a result of his vast merit and who is protected by a deity can make use of his great powers of merit, strength, mind, and body, take a great raft, [104] and set sail in the great Āvarta Ocean. The ocean will spin him around seven times in a whirlpool and then come to a pause. Having traveled a league in distance, he'll emerge in a second whirlpool. The ocean will then spin him around seven times in that whirlpool and again come to pause. Likewise, in a third,[495] fourth, fifth, and sixth whirlpool, the ocean will spin him around seven times and then come to a pause, and he'll travel a league before he emerges. Since he is protected by the power of loving kindness, and since he has set out for the benefit of the world, he'll thus emerge from the ocean, pass out of danger, and free himself.

"After successfully navigating the great Āvarta Ocean, he'll come upon a mountain called Āvarta that is inhabited by nonhumans. A demon named Śaṅkha (Conch)[496] lives there. He is fierce, he is a killer, and he's big and strong. A league above him is the herb called Śaṅkhanābhī. It emits smoke during the day and fire at night, and it is protected by a nāga. That nāga sleeps during the day and wanders about at night. Protecting himself and without physically disturbing the nāga, that person should make use of the power of the herb, the power of mantras, and the power of his merit, and take the nāga's Śaṅkhanābhī herb during the day while he's sleeping peacefully. Having taken it, he should apply it to his eyes and smear it on his head. He should then climb up Mount Āvarta. If he follows this procedure, he'll cross Mount Āvarta without being harassed by the demon Śaṅkhanābha, and he'll be safe and sound. If he doesn't follow this procedure, if he doesn't take the herb, or if he finds it but doesn't take it, the demon will kill him.

"After crossing Mount Āvarta, he'll come upon the great ocean called Nīloda—it is deep and it appears deep.[497] In the great Nīloda Ocean there lives a demon named Tārākṣa. He has red eyes and flaming hair, his feet, teeth, and eyes are deformed, and his stomach protrudes like a mountain. If he's asleep, then his eyes are open and they look like newly risen suns. His in-breaths and out-breaths are huge, making the noise *guru-guru,*[498] like the growl of thunder in the clouds or when lightning flashes. If he's awake, then his eyes are shut. At that time, there on that shore of the great Nīloda Ocean, that person should search for the herb called Mahāmakarī (Great Crocodile),[499] [105] take it, apply it to his eyes, and smear it on his head. He should then take a great raft, and when he knows that the water demon Tārākṣa is asleep, uttering the words of the mantras that make up the great spell known as Eraṇḍa, which was uttered by buddhas in the past, he should approach the water demon. If he doesn't follow this procedure, if he doesn't take the herb, or if he finds it but doesn't take it, then the water demon Tārākṣa will first weaken him, then disturb his mind, and in the end completely and utterly destroy him.

"After successfully crossing the great Nīloda Ocean, he'll come upon a great mountain also called Nīloda. A demon named Nīlagrīva lives there. He has five hundred followers, he is terribly strong and fierce, and he is a killer. The great Mount Nīloda is completely dark, with no chasms, openings, or fissures. It's all closed up.[500] It's one solid mass. Now at that time if that person stares at it without blinking, it will ruin his eyes and render him unconscious. A league above him there is a strange-looking herb called Amoghā (Never Failing). It's in the possession of a nāga. That nāga's sight is poisonous, as is his breath, and his touch and bite are poisonous as well.[501] When he sleeps, he emits smoke. Any animal or bird that this smoke happens to touch will die. Considering this, that man should wash himself fully and refrain from eating. Then, while protecting himself with thoughts filled with loving kindness and compassion, thoughts free from malice, and without disturbing the nāga's body, he should take the herb. Having taken it, he should apply it to his eyes and smear it on his head. Following this procedure, with full awareness, he should climb Mount Nīloda. This way he won't go blind and he won't lose consciousness. And the *guhyaka* demigods won't attack his body. If he doesn't follow this procedure, if he doesn't take the herb, or if he finds it but doesn't take it, then the demon Nīlagrīva will kill him.

"After successfully crossing Mount Nīloda, he'll come upon the great ocean called Vairambha. In the great Vairambha Ocean blow gale-force winds called Vairambha that stir up the water. Even the likes of crocodiles, tortoises, *vallaka* monsters, and porpoises, as well as hungry ghosts, *piśāca*s, and *kumbhāṇḍa* and *kaṭapūtana* spirits don't dare go there, to say nothing of human beings. Having left behind the great Vairambha Ocean, to the north, he'll come upon the great Tāmra Forest, which is many leagues in length and width. In the middle of the Tāmra Forest is a large grove of *śāla* trees [106] and a large well. A huge serpent named Tāmrākṣa (Copper Eyed) lives there. He is fierce, he is a killer, he smells terrible, and he is five leagues long. He sleeps for six months at a stretch. When he sleeps he sprays spittle for a league around him. When he's awake though, there's less spittle.

Above him is a great bamboo thicket. In the bamboo thicket is a great stone slab. Making use of his strength and digging it up, that man will come upon a cave. In the cave is an herb called Sammohinī (Making One Senseless). It is ablaze both day and night. He should take it, apply it to his eyes, and smear it on his head. Then, when he knows that the serpent Tāmrākṣa is asleep, he should make use of the power of the herb or the power of mantras and approach the serpent's home. If he follows this procedure, he'll pass through and be safe and sound, undisturbed by the serpent Tāmrākṣa. Afterward, eating roots and fruit, he can proceed.

"After crossing the great Tāmra Forest, he'll come upon seven mountains covered in thorny bamboo. He should bind his feet with copper strips,[502] and making use of his strength, traverse those mountains. Then he'll come upon seven acid rivers. On their banks is a great forest of silk-cotton trees. He should bind together planks of silk-cotton wood to make a raft, then board it and cross the rivers without touching the water. If he touches the water, the limb that touched it will rot and fall off.

"After successfully crossing the seven acid rivers, he'll come upon a mountain called Triśaṅku. On Mount Triśaṅku, there are triple-pointed thorns called Triśaṅkava, which are sharp—very sharp. With this in mind, that person should bind his feet with copper strips, tie them on with rattan straps, and then cross over the mountain.

"After crossing Mount Triśaṅku, he'll come upon a river also called Triśaṅku. There, too, in the water are thorns called Triśaṅkava, which are sharp and eighteen fingers long. That person should bind planks of silk-cotton wood together to make a raft, and without touching the water, he should cross the river there. If he falls in, right there, he'll straightaway meet his death. As there is a Mount Triśaṅku, there is likewise a river called Triśaṅkukā. And as there is a Mount Ayaskīla, so too is there a river called Ayaskīlā.

"After crossing the Ayaskīlā River, he'll come upon a mountain called Aṣṭādaśavakra. It's tall, it's covered on all sides, and it has no passageways. There is no way to cross it unless one climbs a tree and travels along the treetops.

"After crossing Mount Aṣṭādaśavakra, he'll come upon a river with eighteen bends called Aṣṭādaśavakrikā, which is filled with different kinds of crocodiles. It's almost round in shape. At that time, he should tie up a rattan cord and then use it to cross.[503] If he falls in, he'll straightaway meet his death. [107]

"After crossing the Aṣṭādaśavakrikā River, he'll come upon a mountain called Ślakṣṇa. Mount Ślakṣṇa has soft slopes, is tall, and has no passageways. There is no way to get around it. Considering this, he should make a stairway of iron nails and use it to cross over.[504]

"After crossing Mount Ślakṣṇa, he'll come upon a river also called Ślakṣṇā, which is filled with different kinds of crocodiles. That river is covered up. At that time, he should tie up rattan cords and use them to cross. If he falls, he'll straightaway meet his death.

"After crossing the Ślakṣṇā River, he'll come upon a mountain called Dhūmanetra that emits smoke. It churns out smoke. Any animals or birds that happen to touch this smoke die. Mount Dhūmanetra is tall with great pitfalls and no passageways. That person should search around there for a cave. After finding that cave, he should make use of the power of the herb and the power of mantras to open the door to the cave. That cave is completely filled with snakes, and the sight of those snakes is poisonous as is their touch. Now above Mount Dhūmanetra is a large pool of water. In that pool of water is a great stone slab. Making use of his strength, he should lift it up, and he'll come upon another cave. In that cave is an herb called Sañjīvanī (Life Giving) and a gem, Jyotīrasa (Exuding Light), that shines like a lamp. He should take that herb and smear himself with it from head to foot. Then he should take that herb and enter the previous cave. Making use of the power of the herb and the power of mantras, and because of the effect of the herb, [he can proceed, and] the snakes won't climb up on his body. In this way it's possible to cross the mountain.

"After crossing Mount Dhūmanetra, he'll come upon the Saptāśīviṣa

Mountains. Making use of the power of the herb and the power of mantras, he should cross the Saptāśīviṣa Mountains.

"After crossing the Saptāśīviṣa Mountains, he'll come upon the Saptāśīviṣa Rivers. There is a snake there named Tīkṣṇagandha (Sharp Smelling). In those rivers that person should look for a piece of flesh. Now on the banks of those snake-filled rivers is a forest of silk-cotton trees. He should therefore bind planks of silk-cotton wood together to make a raft, cover himself with a piece of flesh, and board the raft. Then, because of the smell of meat, the snakes will stay on the opposite shore.

"After crossing the Saptāśīviṣa,[505] he'll come upon a large mountain called Sudhāvadāta (White as Lime),[506] which is tall and lofty. He should climb it.

"There you'll see a large patch of ground whose surface is golden in color, which is adorned with flowers, fruit, and shade trees. And you'll see the countryside of Rohitaka (Red), which is thriving and safe, with plenty of food and crowds of people. [108] And you'll also see the great city of Rohitaka. It is twelve leagues long and seven leagues wide; it is surrounded by seven ramparts and adorned with sixty-two gates; it is resplendent with hundreds and thousands of homes, and its streets, roads, squares, crossroads, and marketplaces are all well laid out. And in Rohitaka there are lutes such as the *vīṇā, vallikī,* and *mahatī,* and there is always the sound of melodious singing that is pleasant to the ears. It is prosperous with many kinds of goods; it is crowded with people who are always happy; it has a park, an assembly hall, and a lotus pool, like those of Indra and Upendra; it has a pond made even more beautiful by geese, swans, ducks, and *cakravāka* birds; it is inhabited by a great king; and it is served by merchants who are great men.

"A caravan leader named Magha (Generous) lives there who is beautiful, good-looking, and attractive as well as learned, wise, and intelligent. He is also rich, wealthy, and prosperous, with vast and extensive holdings, and has amassed a wealth like the god Vaiśravaṇa. Truly, he rivals Vaiśravaṇa in wealth. He knows how to go from island to island, traveling by ship in the great ocean. He'll tell you about the great trading center called Badaradvīpa, and he'll point out the signs that tell of what is to come. If you follow this procedure that I've explained, you won't come to grief. In this way, great caravan leader, performer of the most difficult of deeds, you can fulfill this promise of yours and make good on your commitment that is as firm as Mount Sumeru, Mount Malaya, and Mount Mandara. This great promise would be difficult to fulfill even for Śakra, Brahmā, and the rest of the gods, let alone for human beings."

With these words, the deity vanished on the spot.

Supriya's Journey

Now after the caravan leader Supriya heard what the deity had to say, he woke up from his sleep and was filled with great wonder. He thought, "This deity must have performed many hundreds and thousands of the most difficult kinds of deeds and in the past completed the journey to Badaradvīpa. If this deity completed the journey, then she must be able to perform difficult deeds. If she is in the process of completing the journey, however, then she must have come across people who can perform the most difficult deeds and who have, by performing many hundreds and thousands of such difficult deeds, completed the journey to Badaradvīpa. I must perform this very difficult deed, though even just by setting out for the benefit of the world, my efforts will have good results. If I perform many hundreds and thousands of difficult deeds and complete this journey to the great trading center Badaradvīpa, I will do a great service to the world. [109] There have been people who performed many hundreds and thousands of difficult deeds and in the past completed this journey to Badaradvīpa. I'm human just as they were. They completed it, so why can't I?"

Upon reflection, the great caravan leader Supriya—who was firmly committed to his promise, whose courage and heroism never tired, who never gave up, who was very powerful as a result of his vast merit, and who had set out for the benefit of the world—remembered the instructions as they had been pointed out to him. Then, preserving in his mind the firm commitment to his promise, with great strength, all alone, and without anyone's help, he successfully crossed the five hundred small islands as he was instructed. Likewise, he successfully crossed all those dangerous places that had been listed in detail, such as the seven great mountains and the seven great rivers. Following the procedure that had been explained, he survived on roots, bulbs, and fruit, tied two planks together to form a raft,[507] and after twelve full years arrived in the great city of Rohitaka. Standing in a park, he addressed one of the men there: "Friend, is there a caravan leader named Magha living here in this great city of Rohitaka?"

"There is, my friend," he said. "But he's afflicted with a terrible illness. It's quite likely that this sickness will kill him."

Then the great caravan leader Supriya thought, "Oh no! I hope the great caravan leader Magha doesn't die before I get to see him! Who else will tell me how to go to the great trading center Badaradvīpa!" With this in mind, he quickly went to the caravan leader Magha's house, but there he was stopped at the door. He couldn't get in to see the great caravan leader. Now it's a law of nature that bodhisattvas are experts in arts and administration. So, claiming that he was a doctor, he was allowed to enter.

Since the great caravan leader Supriya knew the accounts in the chapters of the Ayurveda regarding those with terminal illnesses,[508] he saw that the caravan leader Magha would die after six months. Realizing this, the great caravan leader Supriya studied medical treatises, and on his own prescribed efficacious medical treatments of roots, stalks, leaves, flowers, and fruits to alleviate his illness. He also made him very happy by speaking precisely and eloquently, and by telling tales from the scriptures. In addition, he entertained him with various stories that were pleasing to hear.[509] With dexterity, humility, cleverness, and sweetness, Supriya attended to Magha, with devotion and respect, like a good son would his father.[510] [110] Soon things became more tolerable and comfortable for the caravan leader Magha, and he regained his senses.

After the great caravan leader Magha regained his senses, he said this to the great caravan leader Supriya: "Where are you from? Clearly you are smart in practice and theory; handsome, good-looking, and attractive; as well as learned, wise, and intelligent. You're also a good speaker; knowledgeable and well versed in all the scriptures; skilled in all the arts, and knowing the languages of all creatures as well their body language. What are you by birth? What is your ancestry? Why have you come to this country inhabited by nonhumans?"

Spoken to in this way, the caravan leader Supriya said, "Excellent! Excellent, great caravan leader! The time has finally come for the great caravan leader to ask me about my hereditary status, my family, my ancestry, and the reason that I've come here." Then the great caravan leader Supriya gave the caravan leader Magha a detailed account of his hereditary status, his family, his ancestry, and the reason that he had come there. Afterward, he made this request: "May the caravan leader help me to see the great trading center Badaradvīpa. This way I may fulfill my desires, make good on the promise to which I'm firmly committed, and fulfill the desires of all beings."

After the great caravan leader Magha heard that the great caravan leader Supriya had set out for the benefit of others and was firmly committed to his promise, such things as he'd never heard before, he stared at him for a long time, unblinkingly and with great astonishment, and then said this to him: "You're young and yet your passion is the dharma. I can see that your heroism is extraordinary, not of the kind found in mortals. You've left Jambudvīpa and crossed mountains, oceans, and rivers, places where no humans live, to arrive here. And this is a place where nonhumans meet their end, to say nothing of human beings. You look to me to be a god or one of the gods disguised as a man. Now there is nothing difficult left for you to do, nothing you won't be able to accomplish. I'm afflicted with a terrible illness, however, and I'm about to die. And yet you've come. But still, considering that you've set out for the benefit of others, who wouldn't sacrifice himself for you? And so, my son, quickly get an excellent ship and make sure everything is in order so that we'll have a proper vehicle for our journey."[511]

"Okay, caravan leader," the great caravan leader Supriya replied, consenting to the great caravan leader Magha's request. [111] Then he got an excellent ship and made sure everything was in order. Once again he approached the great caravan leader Magha and, having approached, said this to him: "My lord, I've got us an excellent ship and made sure everything is in order. Now the great caravan leader may do as the time permits."

Well, the great caravan leader Magha was determined to go to the great trading center Badaradvīpa, even though his family, relations, children, and wife, friends, confidants, kinsmen, and relatives, as well as the king of Rohitaka and his workers tried to prevent him from going. He tied two planks together to form a raft and, accompanied by the caravan leader Supriya, quickly boarded the excellent ship and set sail in the great ocean.

Then the great caravan leader Magha addressed the great caravan leader Supriya: "I'm very sick. I can't travel standing up. You should make a bed for me so that I can travel lying down. Moreover, in this great ocean there are signs of various kinds that foretell of what is to come, so you should keep me informed of the color and condition of the water."

After traveling many hundreds of leagues, the great caravan leader Supriya saw water that was completely white. At the sight of this, he informed the caravan leader Magha: "Great caravan leader, there is something you should know. I see water that is pure white."

Thus addressed, the caravan leader Magha said, "Great caravan leader, the water isn't really pure white. Instead, if you look to your right, you can see a great mountain made of lime. It's because of this that the water is colored. And there are mines there that contain twenty-one minerals. Heat up some of this water[512] and you'll get gold, silver, and beryl. Some people even come here from Jambudvīpa, take some jewels, and return. This is the first sign that foretells of the great trading center Badaradvīpa."

Continuing on, the great caravan leader Supriya saw water that was the color of weapons' metal.[513] At the sight of this, he informed the caravan leader Magha: "Great caravan leader, there is something you should know. I see water the color of weapons' metal."

"The water isn't really the color of weapons' metal," the caravan leader Magha said. "If you look to your right, you can see a great mountain made of weapons' metal. It's because of this that the water is colored. Here as well there are many mines containing minerals. Heat up some of this water and you'll get gold, silver, beryl, and crystal. [112] Some people even come here from Jambudvīpa, take some jewels, and return. This is the second sign that foretells of the great trading center Badaradvīpa."

Likewise, they came across an iron mountain, a copper mountain, a silver mountain, a gold mountain, a crystal mountain, and a mountain made of beryl.

Then the great caravan leader Supriya saw water that was blue, yellow, red, and white, and he saw the lamp flames blazing in the water. At the sight of this, he informed the caravan leader Magha: "Great caravan leader, there is something you should know. I see water that is blue, yellow, red, and white, and in the water are lamps with flames ablaze."

Thus addressed, the great caravan leader Magha said, "Great caravan leader, the water isn't blue, yellow, red, and white, nor is there anything like lamps ablaze. If you look to your right, you can see a mountain made of four kinds of jewels. It's because of this that the water is colored. As for those things blazing like lamps, they are actually herbs ablaze underwater. Here too there are many mines containing minerals. Heat up some of this water and you'll get gold, silver, beryl, and crystal. Some people even come here from Jambudvīpa, take some jewels, and return. This is the tenth sign that foretells of the great trading center Badaradvīpa. However, great caravan leader, I know only these ten signs on the way going to the great trading center Badaradvīpa. After this, I don't know any more."

Thus addressed, the great caravan leader Supriya said, "When will we finally arrive at the great trading center Badaradvīpa?"

"Supriya," the caravan leader Magha said, "I've never seen the whole of the great trading center Badaradvīpa. But I've heard from great caravan leaders of the past who were worn out, advanced in years, and past their prime that after this, one should leave the water and go west, traveling on land."

As he spoke he felt the presence of death, so he said to the great caravan leader Supriya, "I feel the presence of death. You should therefore bring this excellent ship near the shore, lower the anchor,[514] and then perform a funeral ceremony for my body."[515]

Then the great caravan leader Supriya brought the excellent ship near the shore and lowered the anchor. Meanwhile, the great caravan leader Magha died.

When the great caravan leader Supriya realized that the caravan leader Magha had died, he brought him ashore and performed a funeral ceremony for his body. [113] "Now I'll board my excellent ship and go," he thought. But then the wind broke the ship's anchor, and the ship was carried away. So instead, the great caravan leader Supriya set out on land, through a forest to the right of that mountain made of four kinds of jewels. There he survived on roots and fruit. After traveling many leagues, he saw a smooth mountain whose slopes were tapered, gradually getting steeper as they rose. It was unclimbable. Nevertheless, the great caravan leader Supriya smeared his feet with honey and climbed up and over it. Then he continued on for many more leagues, with roots and fruit as his only food, until he saw a great mountain, tall and lofty. He looked for a way through but he didn't find one, and there was no one to tell him how to find a way through. Then, lost in his thoughts, he was overcome by sleep.

Supriya Receives Additional Instructions, and His Journey Continues

Now on that mountain lived a yakṣa named Nīlāda (Dark Blue Devourer). He reflected, "This bodhisattva has set out for the benefit of the world, but now he suffers. I really should offer him my help." Considering this, he said this to the great caravan leader Supriya: "Great caravan leader, from here go one league to the east, and you'll see three mountain summits whose slopes are tapered, gradually getting steeper and narrower as they rise. There you should make a bamboo ladder[516] and cross over them."

Now when the great caravan leader Supriya woke up from his sleep, he made a bamboo ladder and crossed over those three peaks. Setting out once again, the great caravan leader Supriya saw a crystal mountain that was smooth, without anything to hold on to, and impassable for any human being. He didn't see any way to climb it. With this in mind, he sat there for a day and a night, lost in thought.

On that mountain lived a yakṣa named Candraprabha (Moonlight). Realizing that the caravan leader, who had set out for the benefit of the world, who followed [the great vehicle known as] the Mahāyāna, and whose mind was full of faith, was lost in thought, he approached and consoled him: "The great caravan leader shouldn't be sad. Go a quarter of a league to the east and you'll find a great sandalwood forest. In that sandalwood forest is a great stone slab. Use your strength to dig it up, and you'll see a cave. In that cave is an herb called Prabhāsvarā (Luminous) that has five special qualities. No blade can penetrate the body of a person who possesses this herb, nor can any nonhuman enter his body and possess him. The herb produces strength and power, and it supplies light. [114] With this light, you'll see stairs made of four kinds of jewels. Use these stairs to cross over the crystal mountain. After you've crossed over the crystal mountain, that Prabhāsvarā herb will disappear. Don't grieve, cry, or lament about this." When the yakṣa Candraprabha had finished giving these instructions to the great caravan leader Supriya, he vanished on the spot.

After the great yakṣa Candraprabha had consoled him and directed him on the right path, the great caravan leader Supriya followed the procedure that had been explained and crossed the crystal mountain. After he crossed, the Prabhāsvarā herb disappeared. Setting out again, the great caravan leader Supriya saw a great golden city that had a park and a lotus pool. Then the great caravan leader Supriya went to the gate of the city, but he saw that the city was all closed up. At the sight of this, he went to the park and thought, "Though I've seen the city, it's as though it's empty." Wondering when it would it be time to go to the great trading center Badaradvīpa, he was overcome by sleep.

Now the deity who had previously approached the great caravan leader Supriya realized that he was depressed, so at the time when night turns to dawn, she approached him once again. She consoled him and praised him: "Excellent! Excellent, great caravan leader! You have crossed great oceans, mountains, rivers, and forests that are impassable for humans and nonhumans alike! You have now arrived at the great trading center Badaradvīpa, which neither humans nor nonhumans frequent. It is inhabited by very powerful men. Still, don't be careless. Guard your senses, your eyes and so on, and cultivate mindfulness of the body. When tomorrow comes, knock three times at the gate to the city. Out will come four kinnara girls who are beautiful, good-looking, and attractive; clever and sweet; sound in all parts of their bodies; distinguished with their stunning beauty; adorned with all kinds of ornaments; skilled in joking, playing, lovemaking, dancing, singing, and making music; and skilled in the arts as well. They'll flatter you very much, and this is what they'll tell you:

> Come to us, great caravan leader! Welcome, great caravan leader! Be our lord for we have no lord, be our master for we have no master, be our haven for we have no haven, be our

> shelter for we have no shelter, be our protector for we have no protector, be our refuge for we have no refuge, be our last resort for we have no last resort. And all these are yours—these banquet halls, [115] wine cellars, wardrobes full of garments, bedchambers, and beautiful parks. And these many jewels from Jambudvīpa are yours as well—gems, pearls, beryl, conch, quartz, and coral, silver and gold, emeralds, sapphires, red pearls, and right-spiraling conch shells. These jewels are for you. And now you should fool around, enjoy yourself, and make love to us.

"Nevertheless, you should consider them as mothers, or you should consider them as sisters or daughters. You should condemn the tenfold path of evil actions and praise the tenfold path of virtuous actions. Even being greatly tempted by them, you shouldn't have any thoughts of desire. If you have such thoughts, you'll straightaway meet your death. If your mindfulness is firmly in place, your efforts will be successful. Then, if they offer you a precious gem as a reward for your noble words, make sure that you ask them this: 'Sisters, what is the power of this jewel?' Likewise, you will arrive at a second kinnara city, and out will come eight kinnara girls even more beautiful than the ones before. There, too, follow the procedure that I just explained. Eventually you will arrive at a fourth kinnara city, and out will come thirty-two kinnara girls even more beautiful, good-looking, and attractive than the ones before. They will rival divine nymphs in beauty. In their loveliness, each will be one in a million. There, too, follow the procedure that I just explained."

With that said, that deity vanished on the spot.

Supriya and the Kinnaras

Now the great caravan leader Supriya woke up from his sleep feeling excellent and glad at heart. After getting up early in the morning, he arrived at the golden city of the kinnaras. He approached the threshold of the gate and knocked three times. When the great caravan leader had knocked at the gate three times, out came four kinnara girls who were beautiful, good-looking, and attractive; clever and sweet; sound in all parts of their bodies; distinguished with their stunning beauty; [116] skilled in joking, playing, lovemaking, dancing, singing, and making music; and skilled in the arts as well.

> "Come to us, great caravan leader!" they said. "Welcome, great caravan leader! Be our lord for we have no lord, be our master for we have no master, be our haven for we have no haven, be our shelter for we have no shelter, be our refuge for we have no refuge, be our protector for we have no protector, be our last resort for we have no last resort. And all these are yours—these banquet halls, wine cellars, wardrobes full of garments, bedchambers, beautiful parks, beautiful groves, and beautiful lotus pools. And these jewels from Jambudvīpa are yours as well—gems, pearls, beryl, conch, quartz, and coral, silver and gold, emeralds, sapphires, red pearls, and right-spiraling conch shells. These jewels are for you. And now you should fool around, enjoy yourself, and make love to us."

Even as all those kinnara girls closely embraced the great caravan leader Supriya, his mindfulness remained firmly in place. Then they led him into the golden city, brought him up to the palace, and sat him down in a seat that had been prepared. After sitting down, the great caravan leader Supriya condemned the tenfold path of evil actions and praised the tenfold path of virtuous actions. Even though they tempted him greatly, the great caravan leader couldn't be made to stumble.

The kinnara girls were pleased and said, "It's amazing! You're so young and yet your passion is the dharma! You aren't attached or bound up with desires!" Then they presented him with many jewels.

Drawn in, as they were, by his discourse on the dharma,[517] they gave him a very special jewel as a reward for his noble words.

Then the great caravan leader Supriya inquired into the power of that jewel: "Sisters, what is the power of this jewel?"

"Caravan leader," they said, "there is something you should know. On the *upoṣadha* day that comes on the full moon, you should fully bathe and observe the *upoṣadha* vows and then mount this most-treasured jewel atop a flagpole. For a thousand leagues all around, anyone who desires something—whether gold or golden things, food, clothing, drink, particular ornaments, people or animals, vehicles or conveyances, wealth or grain—should think of that thing and then give voice to his desire. As soon as he thinks of something and then gives voice to it, whatever thing he wants will come down from the sky. That is the power of this jewel."

Then the great caravan leader Supriya instructed, incited, inspired, and delighted the kinnara girls with a discourse on the dharma; [117] addressed them as though they were his mother, sisters, or daughters; and then left that golden kinnara city.

Next the great caravan leader Supriya saw a silver kinnara city that had a park, a forest, and a lotus pool. There too the caravan leader Supriya knocked three times at the gate, and eight kinnara girls came out.

> "Come to us, great caravan leader!" they said as well. "Welcome, great caravan leader! Be our lord for we have no lord, [be our master for we have no master, be our haven for we have no haven, be our shelter for we have no shelter, be our refuge for we have no refuge, be our protector for we have no protector, be our last resort for we have no last resort. And all these are yours—these banquet halls, wine cellars, wardrobes full of garments, bedchambers, beautiful parks, beautiful groves, and beautiful lotus pools. And these jewels from Jambudvīpa are yours as well—gems, pearls, beryl, conch, quartz, and coral, silver and gold, emeralds, sapphires,

> red pearls, and right-spiraling conch shells. These jewels are for you. And now you should fool around, enjoy yourself, and make love to us."

Even as all those kinnara girls closely embraced the great caravan leader Supriya, his mindfulness remained firmly in place. Then they led him into the golden city, brought him up to the palace, and sat him down in a seat that had been prepared. After sitting down, the great caravan leader Supriya condemned the tenfold path of evil actions and praised the tenfold path of virtuous actions. Even though they tempted him greatly, the great caravan leader couldn't be made to stumble.

The kinnara girls were pleased and said, "It's amazing! You're so young and yet your passion is the dharma! You aren't attached or bound up with desires!" Then they presented him with many jewels].[518] Drawn in, as they were, by his discourse on the dharma, they also offered him a most-treasured jewel, this one even more special than the one before. Its power rained down for two thousand leagues.

Then the great caravan leader Supriya instructed, incited, inspired, and delighted the kinnara girls with a discourse on the dharma; addressed them as though they were his mother, sisters, or daughters; and then left that silver kinnara city.

Eventually the great caravan leader Supriya arrived at a third kinnara city, this one made of beryl. There too he knocked at the gate three times, and sixteen kinnara girls came out. They were even more beautiful and attractive than the ones he'd seen before. Drawn in, as they were, by his discourse on the dharma, they also gave him a jewel as a reward for his noble words, this one even more special than the one that preceded it. Its power extended for three thousand leagues. Then the great caravan leader Supriya inquired into the power of that jewel: "Sisters, what is the power of this jewel?"

["Caravan leader,"] the kinnara girls said, ["there is something you should know. On the *upoṣadha* day that comes on the full moon, you should fully bathe and observe the *upoṣadha* vows and then mount this most-treasured jewel atop a flagpole. For three thousand leagues all around, anyone who desires something—whether gold or golden things, food, clothing, drink, particular ornaments, humans or animals, vehicles or conveyances, wealth or grain—should think of that thing and then give voice to his desire. As soon as he thinks of something and then gives voice to it, whatever thing he wants will come down from the sky. That is the power of this jewel."][519]

Then the great caravan leader Supriya instructed, incited, inspired, and delighted the kinnara girls with a discourse on the dharma; addressed them as though they were his mother, sisters, or daughters; and then left that third kinnara city.

The great caravan leader Supriya then saw a fourth kinnara city, this one made of four kinds of jewels. It was laid out well with parks, gardens, palatial buildings, temples, lotus pools, and tanks, and it was well planned with streets, roads, squares, crossroads, and marketplaces. It was fragrant with burning incense, and it was made beautiful by singing, instrumental music, and the sweet voices of young girls. It was also made beautiful by a rampart and arched gates that were studded with diamonds, beryl, and gold. The great caravan leader Supriya knocked at the gate three times, and when he had knocked at the gate three times, thirty-two kinnara girls came out. They were even more beautiful and good-looking than the ones he'd seen before. They rivaled divine nymphs in beauty. In their loveliness, each was one in a million.

> "Come to us, great caravan leader!" they said as well. [118] "Welcome, great caravan leader! Be our lord for we have no lord, be our master for we have no master, be our haven for we have no haven, be our shelter for we have no shelter, be our refuge for we have no refuge, be our protector for we have no protector, be our last resort for we have no last resort. And all these are yours—these banquet halls, wine cellars, wardrobes full of garments, bedchambers, beautiful parks,

beautiful groves, and beautiful lotus pools. And all these many jewels from Jambudvīpa are yours as well—gems, pearls, beryl, conch, quartz, and coral, silver and gold, emeralds, sapphires, red pearls, and right-spiraling conch shells. These jewels are for you, and so are we. And now you should fool around, enjoy yourself, and make love to us."

There too the great caravan leader Supriya, with his mindfulness firmly in place, fully satisfied those kinnara girls with the dharma in its precise wording.[520] Once all the kinnara girls were satisfied, they closely embraced the great caravan leader Supriya. Then they led him into the kinnara city made of four kinds of jewels, brought him up to the palace, and sat him down in a seat specially prepared. After sitting down, the great caravan leader Supriya condemned the tenfold path of evil actions and praised the tenfold path of virtuous actions. Even though they tempted him greatly, the great caravan leader couldn't be made to stumble.

The kinnara girls were pleased and said, "It's amazing! You're so young and yet your passion is the dharma! You aren't attached or bound up with desires!" Then they presented him with many jewels. Drawn in, as they were, by his discourse on the dharma, they also offered him a jewel as a reward for his noble words. It was the most excellent in Jambudvīpa, it was priceless, with endless virtues and powers, and it was the best of what there was in the great trading center Badaradvīpa.[521]

"Great caravan leader," they said, "our brother Badara, king of the kinnaras, gave this most-treasured jewel to us. In this great trading center of Badaradvīpa, it exists as a sign, an emblem, and ornament."

Then the great caravan leader Supriya said, "What is the power of this jewel?"

"Caravan leader," they said, "there is something you should know. You should observe the *upoṣadha* vows, securely mount this most-treasured jewel atop a flagpole, raise it up, and ring the bells in all of Jambudvīpa for the following proclamation—'Friends, men and women who live in Jambudvīpa, listen here! Whoever among you desires anything in particular [119]—whether gold or golden things, jewels, food or drink, clothing, foodstuffs, particular ornaments, humans or animals, conveyances or vehicles, wealth or grain—think of that thing and then give voice to your desire. Because of the power of that jewel, as soon as you think of something and then give voice to it, whatever thing you want will come down from the sky.'

"But there's more. In this world there are great dangers such as these—the danger of kings and robbers, fire and water, humans and nonhumans, lions, tigers, leopards,[522] and hyenas, yakṣas, demons, hungry ghosts, and *piśācas*, *kumbhāṇḍa*, *pūtana*, and *kaṭapūtana* spirits, calamities and plagues, droughts and famines. Yet when this special jewel is raised, these catastrophes won't occur."

After they finished speaking, the kinnara girls congratulated the great caravan leader Supriya: "Excellent! Excellent, great caravan leader! You have crossed great oceans, mountains, rivers, and forests! You have fulfilled your great promise to which you have been so firmly committed! Your belief has brought rewards! You've kept your senses guarded and completed the journey to the great trading center Badaradvīpa! Now you've obtained this special jewel, the best in Jambudvīpa, which can fulfill the desires of all people. Yet the way that you've come could lead even nonhumans to their end, let alone mere mortals. We'll show you a better way that will allow you to return to Vārāṇasī quickly. Listen to this and concentrate. We'll explain it to you.

"To the west of here, after crossing seven mountains, you'll come upon a large, tall mountain. On that mountain lives a demon named Lohitākṣa (Red Eyes). He is fierce and he is a killer. And that mountain, which is inhabited by nonhumans, lets loose a dark, black wind that sparks with fire. There you should mount this jewel atop a flagpole and continue on your way. The power of the jewel will free you from any calamities in the making.

"After crossing that great mountain, you'll come upon another mountain. On that mountain lives a nāga named Agnimukha (Fire Mouth). Once he smells you, he'll hurl flaming bolts of lightning for seven days and nights. On that mountain seek out a jewel cave and enter it. After seven nights, the evil nāga will sleep. While the evil nāga is sleeping, ascend the mountain. [120] There you will see a plateau that is neither tilled nor sown and yet produces rice with perfect grains and no husk or husk powder and that is clean and fragrant and four fingers wide when bunched together.

"Now on either the eighth or fifteenth day of the lunar month, the royal horse Bālāha (Cloud)[523] partakes of that rice, and then feeling comfortable, healthy, and strong, with all his senses satisfied, puffs up his chest and utters this inspired utterance: 'Who is going to the other side? Who is going to the other side? Whom shall I lead to the other side? Whom can I deliver to Jambudvīpa safe and sound?' You should approach him and say this: 'I am going to the other side. Lead me to the other side! Deliver me to Vārāṇasī safe and sound.'"

Supriya's Journey Home

The great caravan leader Supriya then instructed, incited, inspired, and delighted the kinnara girls with a discourse on the dharma, greeted them as though they were his mother or daughters, and then following the way that had been pointed out and the procedure that had been explained, eventually arrived at the plateau. There the royal horse Bālāha was grazing, and while doing so he asked, "Who is going to the other side? Who is going to the other side? Whom shall I lead to the other side? Whom can I deliver to Jambudvīpa safe and sound?"

Then the great caravan leader Supriya approached the royal horse Bālāha. Having approached, he properly arranged his robe on one shoulder, kneeled with his right knee on the ground, bowed toward the royal horse Bālāha with his hands respectfully folded, and said this to him: "I am going to the other side. I am going to the other side. Lead me! Deliver me to Vārāṇasī safe and sound."

Thus addressed, the royal horse Bālāha said this to the great caravan leader Supriya: "Great caravan leader, once you've climbed on my back do not look around. You must keep your eyes shut." With that said, the royal horse Bālāha lowered his back. Then the great caravan leader Supriya mounted the royal horse Bālāha, did as he was instructed, and in just a few seconds, a few instants, a few moments, arrived back in Vārāṇasī. He got down in his very own park. Having gotten down from the royal horse Bālāha, the great caravan leader Supriya circumambulated him three times and then venerated his hooves. The royal horse Bālāha then congratulated the great caravan leader Supriya: "Excellent! Excellent, great caravan leader! You have crossed great oceans, mountains, rivers, and forests! You have fulfilled your great promise to which you have been so firmly committed! [121] Your travels have been successful! You've kept your senses guarded and completed the journey to the great trading center Badaradvīpa! Now you've obtained this special jewel, the best in Jambudvīpa, which can fulfill the desires of all people. Special beings who have set out for the benefit of others do just the same." With that said, the royal horse Bālāha departed.

Supriya Fulfills His Promise

Just after the royal horse Bālāha departed, the great caravan leader Supriya went and entered his home. The citizens of Vārāṇasī as well as Brahmadatta, the king of Kāśi, heard that after a full one hundred years the great caravan leader Supriya had completed his journey, fulfilled his wish, and arrived back home. And having heard this, Brahmadatta, the king of Kāśi, was pleased. The townspeople, in turn, praised the great caravan leader Supriya.

Those thousand robbers from before, and other people as well who desired wealth, also heard that the great caravan leader Supriya had completed his journey, fulfilled his wish, and now returned. Having heard this, they approached the great caravan leader Supriya and said this to him: "Our wealth is all gone."

Thus addressed, the great caravan leader looked around, his eyes filled with loving kindness, and informed all of them as follows: "My friends, go back to your respective kingdoms. You who desire anything in particular should focus your mind on it and then give voice to your desire." Having heard this, they departed.

Now on the *upoṣadha* day that comes on the full moon, the great caravan leader Supriya fully bathed and observed the *upoṣadha* vows. Then he mounted the first most-treasured jewel that he obtained atop a flagpole and gave voice to his desire. For a thousand leagues all around, whatever beings wanted was produced. As soon as someone would speak, whatever that person desired would rain down upon him. Those beings had all their desires fulfilled. Then the great caravan leader Supriya established those thousand robbers on the tenfold path of virtuous actions.

Meanwhile Brahmadatta, the king of Kāśi, died. The townspeople and ministers consecrated the great caravan leader Supriya as king. At the time that he was consecrated, the great king Supriya mounted the second most-treasured jewel atop a flagpole. In the same way as before, but now for two thousand leagues all around, whatever beings wanted was produced. As soon as someone would speak, whatever that person desired would rain down upon him. [122] As for the third most-treasured jewel, it was also hoisted atop a flagpole following the procedure that had been explained. As a result, those particular things that beings wanted came raining down. In this way, for three thousand leagues all around, women and men were fully satisfied with the things they had desired.

After some time, on one of the *upoṣadha* days that comes on the full moon, the great king Supriya, who was the lordship incarnate of Jambudvīpa, fully bathed and observed the *upoṣadha* vows. Then he had bells rung in all of Jambudvīpa for the following proclamation—"For the benefit of the women and men who live in Jambudvīpa and desire particular things, King Supriya has had the most-treasured jewel mounted atop a flagpole. It is the best of what there is in the great trading center Badaradvīpa, and it will make all those things one wants rain down."

Later, when the best of the most-treasured jewels in Jambudvīpa had been mounted atop a flagpole, the entire multitude of people living in Jambudvīpa were fully satisfied with the special things that they desired. When the people living in Jambudvīpa were fully satisfied with these things, King Supriya established them on the tenfold path of virtuous actions. Then he established his eldest son as a royal authority, lord, and sovereign, and as a royal sage he followed the religious life, cultivated the four Brahmā states, and destroyed sensual desire for objects of desire. Abiding for the most part in this state, he was reborn an inhabitant of the Brahmā World and became the great Brahmā himself.

Coda

"What do you think, monks?" the Blessed One said.

That great caravan leader named Supriya was none other than
me, following the path of the bodhisattva at that time and
at that juncture.
Those thousand robbers were these very thousand monks.
That first deity was the perfectly awakened Kāśyapa,
who was a bodhisattva at that time and at that juncture.
That great caravan leader Magha was none other than
the monk Śāriputra at that time and at that juncture.
That great yakṣa named Nīloda was none other than
the monk Ānanda at that time and at that juncture.
The yakṣa Candraprabha was none other than
the monk Aniruddha at that time and at that juncture.
The great yakṣa named Lohitākṣa was none other than
Devadatta at that time and at that juncture.
The nāga named Agnimukha was none other than
the wicked Māra at that time and at that juncture.
And the royal horse Bālāha was the bodhisattva Maitreya
at that time and at that juncture.

"Back then, monks, firmly committed to my promise as I was, [123] I protected the caravan seven times from those thousand robbers in order to fulfill my promise. Realizing that the robbers weren't completely satisfied, I made good on that promise to which I was firmly committed. Having performed many hundreds and thousands of difficult deeds, I completed my journey to the great trading center Badaradvīpa; I satisfied with wealth all of Jambudvīpa, beginning with those thousand robbers; and then I established those robbers on the tenfold path of virtuous actions. Now too, performing many hundreds and thousands of difficult deeds, I acquired supreme knowledge, and while performing acts of loving kindness and compassion, protected this caravan seven times from those thousand robbers. Realizing that these thousand robbers weren't completely satisfied, I satisfied them with whatever wealth I could find and established them in the unsurpassed supreme security that is nirvāṇa. I established many hundreds and thousands of gods and humans as well as hundreds and thousands and millions of yakṣas, demons, hungry ghosts, *piśāca*s, *kumbhāṇḍa, pūtana,* and *kaṭapūtana* spirits in the taking of the refuges as well as in the precepts."

This was said by the Blessed One. With their minds uplifted, the monks welcomed the words of the Blessed One.

So ends the *Supriya-avadāna*, the eighth chapter in the glorious *Divyāvadāna*.

9. *The Chapter on the Great Fortune of the Householder Meṇḍhaka*

MEṆḌHAKAGṚHAPATIVIBHŪTI-PARICCHEDA

THIS INCIDENT occurred in Śrāvastī. At one time in the city of Bhadraṅkara (Conferring Prosperity) there lived six people who possessed great merit: the householder Meṇḍhaka (Ram), Meṇḍhaka's wife, Meṇḍhaka's son, Meṇḍhaka's daughter-in-law, Meṇḍhaka's servant, and Meṇḍhaka's maid.[524]

How was it known that the householder Meṇḍhaka possessed great merit? If he looked at an empty treasury or granary, as soon as he looked it would become full. Thus it was known that the householder Meṇḍhaka possessed great merit.

And how about Meṇḍhaka's wife? She would prepare a small dish for one person, [124] and it could feed hundreds and thousands of people. Thus it was known about Meṇḍhaka's wife.

And how about Meṇḍhaka's son? He had a purse tied to his hips that contained five hundred coins. Whether he gave away a hundred or a thousand coins, it would remain completely full. It wouldn't diminish. Thus it was known about Meṇḍhaka's son.

And how about Meṇḍhaka's daughter-in-law? She would prepare a fragrance for one person, and it would suffice for hundreds and thousands of people. Thus it was known about Meṇḍhaka's daughter-in-law.

And how about Meṇḍhaka's servant? When he ploughed a single furrow, seven furrows would be ploughed. Thus it was known about Meṇḍhaka's servant.

And how was it known that Meṇḍhaka's maid possessed great merit? When she took care of[525] a single object, it would become sevenfold—when she looked after one of anything, it would become seven. Thus it was known that Meṇḍhaka's maid possessed great merit.

The Buddha Sets Out to Instruct Meṇḍhaka

It is a law of nature that lord buddhas have great compassion,
they are intent on doing good deeds for mankind,
they have a single guardian [which is mindfulness],
they abide in the meditative states of tranquility and insight,
they are expert in the three objects for self-control,
they have crossed the four floods [of corruptions],
they have planted the soles of their feet well
  on the four bases of success,
they have long since developed an expertise in the four means
  of attracting beings to the religious life,
they have destroyed the five [bad] qualities,
they have crossed over the five realms of existence,
they have acquired the six [good] qualities,
have fulfilled the six perfections,
they are replete with the flowers of the seven factors
  of awakening,
they are teachers of the eightfold path,
they are expert in attaining the nine successive states
  of quiescence meditation,
they are powerful with the ten powers,
they have fame that fills up the ten directions,
and they are superior to the thousand gods who have control
  over others.

As lord buddhas observe the world with their buddha vision, three times in the night and three times in the day—six times in the night and day all together—knowledge and insight arise as to the following:

Who will get worse?
Who will get better?
Who will encounter trouble?
Who will encounter difficulty?
Who will encounter danger?
Who will encounter trouble, difficulty, and danger?
Who is inclined toward a terrible realm of existence?
Who is prone toward a terrible realm of existence?
Who is disposed toward a terrible realm of existence?
Who shall I lift up from the path leading to a terrible realm
of existence and establish in the fruits of heaven and
in liberation?
To whom, mired in the mud of sense pleasures,
shall I offer a helping hand?
Who, without noble wealth, shall I establish in the lordship
and dominion of noble wealth?
For whom with roots of virtue unplanted shall I plant them? [125]
For whom with roots of virtue already planted
shall I cause them to mature?
For whom with roots of virtue already matured
shall I cause them to be released?
And for whom, with sight fully obscured by the dark film
of ignorance, shall I purify the eyes with the collyrium stick
of knowledge?

Although the sea, home to monsters,
may allow the time of the tides to pass,
the Buddha never allows the time to pass
for training his beloved children.

Abiding in the mind of the Omniscient One,
like the loving cow searching for her missing calves,
the cow of compassion never tires of searching
for her tender calves in need of training,
lost as they are in the impasse of existence.

The Blessed One reflected, "The householder Meṇḍhaka together with his family lives in the city of Bhadraṅkara. The time for his training awaits like a ripe boil for the fall of the knife. I really should travel through the Bhadraṅkara countryside."

And so the Blessed One addressed the venerable Ānanda: "Ānanda, go and inform the monks as follows—'The Tathāgata, monks, will travel through the Bhadraṅkara countryside. Whoever among you is eager to travel through the Bhadraṅkara countryside with the Tathāgata should take up his robes.'"

"Yes, Bhadanta," the venerable Ānanda replied, consenting to the Blessed One's request. Then he informed the monks: "Venerable ones, the Tathāgata will travel through the Bhadraṅkara countryside. Whoever among you is eager to travel through the Bhadraṅkara countryside with the Tathāgata should take his up robes."

"Yes, venerable one," those monks replied to the venerable Ānanda's request, and then, following close behind him, departed.

Now the Blessed One was self-controlled
  and his followers were self-controlled,
he was calm and his followers were calm,
he was liberated and his followers were liberated,
he was confident and his followers were confident,
he was disciplined and his followers were disciplined,
he was an arhat and his followers were arhats,
he was without attachment
  and his followers were without attachment,
and he instilled faith and his followers instilled faith.

He was like a bull surrounded by a herd of cows,
like a lion surrounded by a carnivorous pack,[526]
like a royal goose surrounded by a gaggle of geese,
like an eagle surrounded by a flock of birds, [126]
like a learned brahman surrounded by an assembly of students,
like an eminent doctor surrounded by a group of patients,
like a warrior surrounded by a troop of soldiers,
like a guide surrounded by a group of travelers,[527]
like a caravan leader surrounded by a group of merchants,
like a guildmaster surrounded by townspeople,
like a vassal king surrounded by a cabinet of ministers,
like a wheel-turning king surrounded by a thousand sons,
like the moon surrounded by a constellation of stars,
like the sun surrounded by a thousand rays of light,
like the great king Dhṛtarāṣṭra surrounded by a group
of celestial musicians,
like the great king Virūḍhaka surrounded by a group
of *kumbhāṇḍa*s,
like the great king Virūpākṣa surrounded by a group of nāgas,
like the great king Dhanada surrounded by a group of yakṣas,
like Vemacitrin surrounded by a group of antigods,
like Śakra surrounded by a group of gods,
and like Brahmā surrounded by the gods of Brahmakāyika
(Brahmā's Assembly).

He was like an ocean but calm,
like a cloud but full of water,[528]
and like a mighty elephant but without pride or passion.
His senses were well restrained,
his deportment and demeanor were unflappable,
[he was adorned][529] with the thirty-two marks of a great man,
and his body was radiant with the eighty minor marks.

[He was endowed][530] with the ten powers,
the four confidences,
the three special applications of mindfulness,
and with great compassion.

Thus endowed with a mass of virtues, the Lord Buddha set out traveling through the countryside on his way to the city of Bhadraṅkara.

Some Heretics Devise a Plan

In the past the Blessed One had performed a great miracle in Śrāvastī, put a group of heretics to shame, made both gods and mortals happy, and satisfied the hearts of good people. Those heretics, having lost their influence, then took refuge in neighboring lands. Some of those heretics went and settled in the city of Bhadraṅkara.

Now those heretics heard that the ascetic Gautama was coming, and having heard this, they were troubled. They spoke among themselves: "In the past the ascetic Gautama drove us out of the Middle Country. If he comes here, he'll surely drive us away from this place as well. We need to devise a plan."

They approached a house that usually provided them with food and said, "Pious Gain! Pious Gain!"[531]

"What's this?" they asked.

"Farewell. We're going."

"Why?"

"We've seen your good fortune. We don't want to see your misfortune."

"Noble ones, will misfortune befall us?"

"Friends, the ascetic Gautama is coming, hurling his razor-like thunderbolt, making many women childless widows."[532]

"Noble ones, if this is so, then at the very time when you should stay, [127] you're abandoning us. Please stay! Don't go."

"Why should we stay?"[533] they asked. "You won't listen to us."

"Noble ones, speak and we'll listen."

"Drive all the people away from the areas around Bhadraṅkara," they said, "and force them to live in the city of Bhadraṅkara. Plough under the grassy meadows, break down the altars, cut down any trees with fruits or flowers, and pollute the water sources with poison."

"Noble ones, please stay. We'll do everything you ask."

So they stayed.

Those others then drove all the people away from the areas around Bhadraṅkara and forced them to live in the city of Bhadraṅkara. They ploughed under the grassy meadows, broke down the altars, cut down any trees with fruit or flowers, and polluted the water sources with poison.

Then Śakra, lord of the gods, reflected, "It isn't right for me to ignore this inhospitable treatment of the Blessed One. Indeed, over the course of three incalculable ages, after fulfilling the six perfections by performing many hundreds and thousands of difficult deeds, he has attained supreme knowledge. And now the Blessed One, the most distinguished person in the world and the winner of all debates, will travel through a deserted countryside! I really should strive to make things agreeable for the Blessed One and the community made up of his disciples." So he ordered the divine beings of the storm clouds: "Go to the areas around Bhadraṅkara and dry up the poisonous water sources!" Then he ordered the divine beings of the rain clouds: "Refill the water sources with water possessing the eight good qualities!" And then he said to the gods of Cāturmahārājika (Four Groups of the Great Kings): "Settle the Bhadraṅkara countryside!"

The divine beings of the storm clouds then dried up the poisonous water. Those of the rain clouds filled up these wells, ponds, reservoirs, pools, and tanks with water possessing the eight good qualities. And the Cāturmahārājika gods settled all the areas around the city of Bhadraṅkara. The countryside became thriving and prosperous.

Meanwhile the heretics, meeting up with some people from the city, sent them off as spies: "Go and see what sort of condition the countryside is in."

These spies went and saw that the countryside was greatly thriving and prosperous. Upon their return, they said, "Gentlemen, we've never seen the countryside so thriving and prosperous before!"

"So you have seen this for yourselves, my friends,"[534] the heretics said. [128] "Well, whoever can convert nonsentient beings, can't he convert you as well?"[535]

"What are you saying?"[536]

"Gentlemen, a final farewell! This is the last you'll see of us. We're going."[537]

"Noble ones," they said, "please stay! What can the ascetic Gautama do to you? He is a renunciant and you are renunciants as well, and both of you survive on alms. Do you think he'll eat those alms meant for you?"[538]

"We'll stay on the condition that you agree that no one will go to see the ascetic Gautama," the heretics said. "Whoever approaches him will be fined sixty *kārṣāpaṇa* coins."

The people consented, and the agreement was accepted.

The Buddha Instructs the Residents of Bhadraṅkara

Then [the Blessed One,][539] after wandering through the countryside, arrived in the city of Bhadraṅkara. In the city of Bhadraṅkara, he stayed in a resting house in the south.

At that time, there was a brahman girl from Kapilavastu who'd gotten married and come to the city of Bhadraṅkara. While on top of a retaining wall, she saw the Blessed One [standing][540] in the darkness.

"This is the Blessed One," she reflected, "the delight of the Śākya clan, who abandoned the kingdom of the Śākya clan and went forth as a renunciant. Now he stands in the darkness.[541] If there were a ladder here, I'd take a lamp and climb down to him."

Then the Blessed One, understanding her thoughts with his mind, magically created a ladder. Pleased, satisfied, and delighted, she took a lamp, climbed down that ladder, and approached the Blessed One.

Having approached, she placed the lamp in front of the Blessed One, venerated with her head the feet of the Blessed One, and then sat down to listen to the dharma. Then the Blessed One, knowing her inclinations, propensities, makeup, and nature, [gave her a discourse on the dharma] that penetrated the four noble truths. [When the brahman girl heard this, with her thunderbolt of knowledge she broke through that mountain which is the false view of individuality that arises with its twenty peaks of incorrect views, and directly experienced the reward of the stream-enterer. "I have crossed over, Bhadanta! I have crossed over! And so, I take refuge in the Blessed One, in the dharma, and in the community of monks. Hereafter and for as long as I live and breathe,][542] consider me a faithful disciple who has taken the refuges."

Then the Blessed One said this to the girl: "Come, young girl. Go to the householder Meṇḍhaka, and having gone to him, offer my greetings. Then say, 'Householder, I have come here on your account and yet you keep your door closed. Is it proper to treat a guest as you have?' If he says, 'The community has made an agreement,' then say, 'Your son has a purse tied to his hips that contains five hundred coins. Whether he spends a hundred or a thousand, [129] it remains completely full. It doesn't diminish. Aren't you able to pay sixty *kārṣāpaṇa* coins to come out?'"

"Very well, Bhadanta," the girl replied, consenting to the Blessed One's request, and then she set out. [Then the Blessed One exercised his power] so that no one at all noticed the girl as she went to the householder Meṇḍhaka.[543] Arriving there, she said, "Householder, the Blessed One offers you his greetings."

"I pay homage to the Lord Buddha," he said.

"Householder, the Blessed One has said that I should say: 'Householder, I have come here on your account and yet you keep your door closed. Is it proper to treat a guest as you have?'"

"Young girl," he said, "the community has agreed that no one will go to see the ascetic Gautama, and that whoever does will be fined sixty *kārṣāpaṇa* coins."

"Householder, the Blessed One says that your son has a purse tied to his hips that contains five hundred coins. Whether he spends a hundred or a thousand, it remains completely full. It doesn't diminish. Aren't you able to pay sixty *kārṣāpaṇa* coins to come out?"

"Nobody knows this," he reflected. "The Blessed One must be omniscient. I'll go." He placed sixty *kārṣāpaṇa* coins at the door, climbed down the ladder that the brahman girl had pointed out, and approached the Blessed One. Having approached, he venerated with his head the feet of the Blessed One and then sat down in front of the Blessed One to listen to the dharma. Then the Blessed One, knowing the householder Meṇḍhaka's inclinations, propensities, makeup, and nature, gave him a discourse on the dharma that penetrated the four noble truths. When he heard this, the householder Meṇḍhaka [broke through that mountain which is the false view of individuality that arises with its twenty peaks of incorrect views],[544] and directly experienced the reward of the stream-enterer. Having seen the truth, he asked, "Blessed One, will all the people living in the city of Bhadraṅkara attain such virtues as well?"

"Householder," the Blessed One said, "thanks to you practically everyone will attain them."

Then the householder Meṇḍhaka venerated with his head the feet of the Blessed One and left the Blessed One's presence. After going home, he made a pile of *kārṣāpaṇa* coins in the middle of the city, and then uttered the following verse:

Whoever wants to see the Victor,
who has conquered desire and hatred,
who is free from all bonds,
incomparable, compassionate, and pure,[545] [130]
may he go quickly, with a steadfast and resolute heart.
I will give him the money that he needs.

"Householder," the people said, "is seeing the ascetic Gautama very beneficial?"

"Yes, it's very beneficial," he said.

"If that's the case," they said, "just as the community made this agreement, the community itself can rescind it. Is there any opposition here?"

They then rescinded the agreement and began to leave. But as they were jostled up against one another, they couldn't leave. So the yakṣa Vajrapāṇi (Thunderbolt in Hand), out of compassion for those beings to be trained, threw his thunderbolt. A part of the retaining wall collapsed. Many hundreds of thousands of beings departed, some out of curiosity, others impelled by former roots of virtue. They went out, and having venerated the feet of the Blessed One, sat down in front of him. Then the assembly gathered all around the Blessed One.[546] Then the Blessed One made his way through the assembly,[547] sat down in front of the community of monks in the seat specially prepared for him, and gave a discourse on the dharma that caused roots of virtue to be planted in the minds of many beings. Hearing this, some beings directly experienced the reward of the stream-enterer[548] and some accepted the taking of the refuges as well as the precepts.

Rules for Eating at Improper Times

Since the Blessed One discoursed on the dharma for a long time, the proper time for eating passed.

"Blessed One," the householder Meṇḍhaka said, "please take your meal."

"Householder," the Blessed One said, "the proper time for eating has passed."

"Blessed One," he said, "when it isn't the proper time for eating, what is permissible to eat?"

"Clarified butter, molasses, sugar, and beverages," the Blessed One said.

Then the householder Meṇḍhaka sent for cooks and said, "Quickly, prepare for the Blessed One those foods that can be eaten when the proper time for eating has passed." So they prepared foods that could be eaten when the proper time for eating had passed. Then the householder Meṇḍhaka satisfied the community of monks led by the Buddha with food and drink that could be consumed at an improper time for eating.

The Blessed One then established the householder Meṇḍhaka and his followers in the [four noble] truths, instructed the residents of that market town according to their capabilities, and departed.[549]

This was said by the Blessed One. With their minds uplifted, the monks welcomed the words of the Blessed One.

So ends the *Meṇḍhakagṛhapativibhūti-pariccheda*, the ninth chapter in the glorious *Divyāvadāna*. [131]

10. The Story of Meṇḍhaka

MEṆḌHAKA-AVADĀNA

THOSE MONKS in doubt asked the Lord Buddha, the remover of all doubts, "Bhadanta, what deeds did Meṇḍhaka (Ram), Meṇḍhaka's wife, Meṇḍhaka's son, Meṇḍhaka's daughter-in-law, Meṇḍhaka's servant, and Meṇḍhaka's maid do so that the six of them became well known and possessed of great merit, so that they saw the [four noble] truths in the presence of the Blessed One, and so that the Blessed One was pleased and not displeased with them?"

"Monks," the Blessed One said, "the deeds that they themselves have performed and accumulated have now come together, and their conditions have matured. They remain before them like an oncoming flood and will certainly come to pass. Those deeds were performed and accumulated by them. Who else will experience their results? For those deeds that are performed and accumulated, monks, do not mature outside of oneself—neither in the element of earth nor in the element of water, in the element of fire or in the element of wind. Instead, those deeds that are done, both good and bad, mature in the aggregates, the elements, and the sense bases that are appropriated when one is reborn.

Actions never come to naught,
even after hundreds of millions of years.
When the right conditions gather and the time is right,
then they will have their effect on embodied beings."

A Famine in Vārāṇasī

Long ago, monks, in a time gone by, in the city of Vārāṇasī, a king named Brahmadatta ruled a kingdom that was thriving, prosperous, and safe, with plenty of food and crowds of people, that was free from quarrel and strife, with no hustle and bustle, thieves or diseases, that was rich in rice and sugarcane, cows and buffalo, and was entirely without enemies. He watched over the kingdom as if it were his only son.

One time the soothsayers in Vārāṇasī predicted that there would be a drought for twelve years[550] and that there would be three kinds of famine: Box, White Bone, and Living-by-the-Stick.

It is called Box because at that [time][551] people place seeds in a casket, storing them for the sake of future generations. "After we have died," they think, "future generations will make a collection of seeds with this."[552] Since it involves a casket, it is called Box. [132]

The second famine is called White Bone because at that time people gather together bones and boil them until those bones become white. Then they drink that decoction. Hence it is called the White Bone famine.[553]

Then there is the famine called Living-by-the-Stick. At that time, people use sticks to drag corn and hardened molasses out of holes.[554] Then they boil them in a large pot of water and drink them. Since it involves a stick, it is called Living-by-the-Stick.

At that time, King Brahmadatta had bells rung in Vārāṇasī for the following proclamation: "Friends, citizens of Vārāṇasī, listen here! Soothsayers predict a twelve-year drought. There will be Living-by-the-Stick, Box, and White Bone famines. Those of you who have enough food for twelve years should stay. Those who don't should go where they please. When the danger of famine is over and once again there is plenty of food, then you should return."[555]

At that time in Vārāṇasī there was a certain householder who was rich, wealthy, and prosperous, with an extended family. He summoned the officer in charge of his granaries and said, "Friend, will there be enough food for me and my family[556] for twelve years?"

"Yes sir, there will be," he said.

So he remained right where he was, and in a short while the famine followed. His granaries[557] were exhausted, and all his attendants passed away. He survived with five others. Then the householder cleaned out his granaries and managed to gather one measure of grain. His wife put that grain in a pot and cooked it.

When no buddhas are born, solitary buddhas can arise in the world. They have pity for the poor and neglected, they live in remote areas, and they alone are worthy of people's offerings.

Meanwhile a certain solitary buddha, after wandering throughout the countryside, arrived in Vārāṇasī. In the morning he got dressed, took his bowl and robe, and entered Vārāṇasī for alms. As for the householder, he sat to take his meal with the five others.[558]

Now the solitary buddha, after wandering for alms in due course, arrived at that householder's home. The householder saw the solitary buddha, who instilled faith through his body and through his mind, and at the sight of him, he reflected, "Even if I eat[559] this food, I will surely die. I really should give my share to this renunciant." [133] So he said to his wife, "Dear wife, I will offer my share to this renunciant."

She reflected, "If my husband doesn't eat, how can I eat?" So she said, "Dear husband, I will offer him my share as well." Thinking such thoughts, the householder's son, daughter-in-law, servant, and maid each gave up their respective shares. Then all of them together presented the solitary buddha with alms.

Those great beings teach the dharma through deeds not words. So like a royal goose with outstretched wings, he flew up high into the sky and began to perform the miraculous deeds of causing fire and heat, making rain and lightning.

Magic quickly wins over the ordinary person. Like trees cut down at the roots, they fell prostrate at his feet and began to make fervent aspirations.[560]

The householder began to make a fervent aspiration: "Since I have served someone so worthy of offerings from good people,[561] by this root of virtue, if [I look at][562] empty granaries may they become full as soon as I see them. And may I obtain such virtues so that I may please and not displease a teacher even more distinguished than this one!"

Then his wife began to make a fervent aspiration: "Since I have served this person who is so worthy of offerings from good people, by this root of virtue, if I prepare a dish for one person, even if a hundred partake of it, or even a thousand, may it not be exhausted until I've finished making use of it.[563] And may I obtain such virtues so that I may please and not displease a teacher even more distinguished than this one!"

Then his son began to make a fervent aspiration: "Since I have served this person who is so worthy of offerings from good people, by this root of virtue may the purse tied around my hips that contains five hundred [coins],[564] whether I give away a hundred or a thousand, not suffer a loss. May it remain completely full and not diminish. And may I obtain such virtues so that I may please and not displease a teacher even more distinguished than this one!"

Then his daughter-in-law began to make a fervent aspiration: "Since I have served this person who is so worthy of offerings from good people, [134] by this root of virtue, even if I prepare a scent for one, a hundred or a thousand will be able to smell it.[565] And may it not diminish until I'm finished making use of it. And may I obtain such virtues so that I may please and not displease a teacher even more distinguished than this one!"

Then his servant began to make a fervent aspiration: "Since I have served this person who is so worthy of offerings from good people, by this root of virtue, even if I plough a single furrow, may seven furrows be plowed. And may I obtain such virtues so that I may please and not displease a teacher even more distinguished than this one!"

Then his maid began to make a fervent aspiration: "Since I have served this person who is so worthy of offerings from good people, by this root of virtue, if I take hold of one of anything,[566] may seven be produced. And may I obtain such virtues so that I may please and not displease a teacher even more distinguished than this one!"

And so in this way they made their fervent aspirations. And that great being, the solitary buddha, having had compassion for them,[567] then made use of his magical powers, rose up high into the sky, and set out over the palace.

Now at that time, King Brahmadatta was standing on the roof of his palace. As the solitary buddha was moving along, making use of his magical powers, his shadow fell on King Brahmadatta. The king raised his head up and began to look about. He saw that solitary buddha, and it occurred to him, "Surely this great being has dug up the roots of poverty for someone with the great ploughshare of his magical powers. I have great hope."[568]

Then that householder began looking at his granaries until he saw that they were full. He addressed his wife: "My fervent aspiration has now been fulfilled! Now let's see about yours."

Then the maid began to prepare a single measure of grain, and it turned into seven measures. His wife then prepared a dish for one person, and though all of them partook of it,[569] it remained just as it was. Neighbors and many hundreds and thousands of other beings then partook of it as well,[570] and it still remained just as it was. In just the same way the fervent aspirations of the householder's son, daughter-in-law, and servant were also accomplished.

Then the householder had bells rung in Vārāṇasī for the following proclamation: [135] "Friends, please come if you need food!"

A great shout and uproar arose in Vārāṇasī. The king heard it and said, "Gentlemen, what's this great shout and uproar?"

"My lord," the ministers explained, "such-and-such a householder has opened up his granaries."

The king summoned him and said,[571] "When the whole world has died then you open up your granaries?"

"My lord, whose granaries have been opened? It's just that on this very day I have sown a seed and on this very day it has born fruit."[572]

"How is that?" the king asked.

The householder then explained to him in detail what had happened.

"Householder," the king asked, "did you present that great being with alms?"

"Yes, my lord. I presented them myself."

Filled with faith,[573] the king uttered this verse:

> Oh! This field is so fertile and faultless!
> A seed sown today bears fruit today as well!

Coda

"What do you think, monks? The householder, the householder's wife, the householder's son, the householder's daughter-in-law, the householder's servant, and the householder's maid were none other than the householder Meṇḍhaka, Meṇḍhaka's wife, Meṇḍhaka's son, Meṇḍhaka's daughter-in-law, Meṇḍhaka's servant, and Meṇḍhaka's maid. Since each of them served the solitary buddha and made a fervent aspiration, as a result of that action, the six of them have come to possess great merit and in my presence have seen the [four noble] truths. And I have been their teacher, more distinguished than hundreds and thousands and millions of solitary buddhas, and I have been pleased and not displeased by them.

"And so, monks, the result of absolutely evil actions is absolutely evil, the result of absolutely pure actions is absolutely pure, and the result of mixed actions is mixed. So then, this is to be learned: 'You should reject absolutely evil actions and mixed ones as well, and strive to perform only absolutely pure actions.' It is this, monks, that you should learn to do."

This was said by the Blessed One. With their minds uplifted, the monks welcomed the words of the Blessed One.

So ends the *Meṇḍhaka-avadāna,* the tenth chapter in the glorious *Divyāvadāna.* [136]

11. The Story of Aśokavarṇa

AŚOKAVARṆA-AVADĀNA

THUS I HAVE HEARD. At one time the Blessed One was respected, honored, revered, and venerated by kings, ministers, the well-to-do, townspeople, guildmasters, caravan leaders, gods, nāgas, yakṣas, antigods, heavenly birds, kinnaras, and great snakes. Thus praised by gods, nāgas, yakṣas, antigods, heavenly birds, kinnaras, and great snakes, the Lord Buddha—who was renowned and possessed great merit—received provisions of robes, begging bowls, bedding and seats, and medicines to cure the sick. He stayed in Vaiśālī with the community made up of his disciples in the Kūṭāgāra hall on the banks of the Markaṭahrada (Monkey Pool).

At one time the Licchavis of Vaiśālī made the following agreement: "Gentlemen, on the fifteenth, eighth, and fourteenth days of each fortnight, animals are to be slaughtered, since on those days men come looking for meat."

On one of those days a certain butcher took a large bull outside of the city for slaughter. A large crowd of people wanting meat followed close behind him saying, "Kill the bull quickly! We want meat!"

"I'm going to," the butcher replied. "Just give me a minute."

When the bull heard such cruelly uttered ignoble words, he was frightened, terrified, agitated, and his hair stood on end. Pacing back and forth, he looked about and thought, "I'm in trouble, difficulty, and danger. I have no protection and no refuge. Who can give me the precious gift of life?" And so in this way, looking distressed, he stood there, in search of protection.

In the morning the Blessed One got dressed, took his bowl and robe, and leading the community of monks that surrounded him, entered Vaiśālī for alms. The bull saw the Lord Buddha,

who was adorned with the thirty-two marks of a great man,
whose body was radiant with the eighty minor marks,
who was adorned with a halo extending an arm's length,
whose brilliance was greater than a thousand suns,
and who, like a mountain of jewels that moved,
was beautiful from every side. [137]

As soon as he saw him, being in the presence of the Blessed One, his mind was filled with faith. Then, with his mind filled with faith, he reflected, "This special being instills faith! He will be able to save my life. I really should approach him."

Looking at the Blessed One, the bull fixed his mind on the thought, "This is my refuge!" At that very moment, he ran forward, breaking through the sturdy straps that restrained him, and approached the Blessed One. Having approached, he fell to his knees at the feet of the Blessed One and with his tongue began to lick his feet. The butcher, a man of cruel deeds, followed close behind brandishing a sword.

The Blessed One said this to the ruthless butcher: "Friend, identify with this bull. Give him the gift of life."

"Bhadanta," he said, "I can't give him the gift of life. Why's that? I paid a lot of money for him, and I have a big family to support."

"If you are reimbursed," the Blessed One said, "will you set him free?"

"Yes, Blessed One," he said. "I'll set him free."

Then the Blessed One had this worldly thought: "How good it would be if Śakra, lord of the gods, would come and bring three thousand *kārṣāpaṇa* coins!" As soon as the Blessed One had this thought,

Śakra, lord of the gods, stood before the Blessed One having brought three thousand *kārṣāpaṇa* coins.

Then the Blessed One said this to Śakra, lord of the gods: "Kauśika, offer these *kārṣāpaṇa* coins, three times the bull's value, to this butcher." Then Śakra, lord of the gods, gave those three thousand *kārṣāpaṇa* coins to the butcher as the price of the bull. The butcher accepted those three thousand *kārṣāpaṇa* coins as the price of the bull, and being pleased, satisfied, and delighted, venerated with his head the feet of the Blessed One, released the bull from his restraints, and then departed. Śakra, lord of the gods, venerated with his head the feet of the Blessed One and vanished on the spot.

The bull, whose life had gone and come back again, was filled with even more faith in the Blessed One. He circumambulated the Blessed One three times and then remained close to the Blessed One staring intently at his face. Then the Blessed One smiled. [138]

The Buddha's Smile

Now it is a law of nature that whenever lord buddhas manifest their smiles, rays of blue, yellow, red, and white light, and those the color of topaz, rubies, diamonds, beryl, sapphires, crystals, red pearls, right-spiraling conch shells, quartz, coral, gold, and silver emerge from their mouths, some going downward and some going upward. Those that go downward enter the various hells—Sañjīva (Reviving), Kālasūtra (Black Thread), Raurava (Shrieking), Mahāraurava (Loud Shrieking), Tapana (Heat), Pratāpana (Extreme Heat), Avīci (Ceaseless Torture), Arbuda (Blistering), Nirarbuda (Blisters Bursting), Aṭaṭa (Chattering Teeth), Hahava (Ugh!), Huhuva (Brrr!), Utpala (Blue Lotus), Padma (Lotus), down to Mahāpadma (Great Lotus). Becoming cold, they fall in the hot hells, and becoming hot, they fall in the cold hells. In this way, those rays of light alleviate the particular torments of those beings who dwell in these various hells. And so they think, "Friends, have we died and passed away from this place? Have we been reborn somewhere else?"

Then, in order to engender their faith, the Blessed One manifests a magical image of himself. Seeing this magical image, they think, "Friends, we haven't died and passed away from this place nor have we been born someplace else. Instead, it's this person whom we've never seen before; it's by his power that our particular torments are alleviated." Cultivating faith in their minds toward this magical image, they then cast off that karma still to be suffered in these hells and take rebirth among gods and mortals, where they become vessels for the [four noble] truths.

Those rays of light that go upward enter the various divine realms[574] —Cāturmahārājika (Four Groups of the Great Kings), Trāyastriṃśa (Thirty-Three), Yāma (Free from Conflict), Tuṣita (Content), Nirmāṇarati (Delighting in Creation), Paranirmitavaśavartin (Masters of Others' Creations), Brahmakāyika (Brahmā's Assembly), Brahmapurohita (Brahmā's Priests), Mahābrahmaṇa (Great Brahmā), Parīttābha (Limited Splendor), Apramāṇābha (Immeasurable Splendor), Ābhāsvara (Radiant), Parīttaśubha (Limited Beauty), Apramāṇaśubha (Immeasurable Beauty), Śubhakṛtsna (Complete Beauty), Anabhraka (Unclouded), Puṇyaprasava (Merit Born), Bṛhatphala (Great Result), Abṛha (Not Great), Atapa (Serene), Sudṛśa (Good-Looking), Sudarśa (Clear Sighted), and finally Akaniṣṭha (Supreme). There they proclaim the truth of impermanence, suffering, emptiness, and no-self. And they utter these two verses:

Strive! Go forth!
Apply yourselves to the teachings of the Buddha!
Destroy the army of death
as an elephant would a house of reeds. [139]

Whoever diligently follows
this dharma and monastic discipline
will abandon the endless cycle of rebirth
and put an end to suffering.

Then those rays of light, having roamed through the billion world-systems, come together directly behind the Blessed One.

If the Blessed One wants to reveal the past,
they vanish into the Blessed One from behind.
If he wants to predict the future,
they vanish into him from the front.
If he wants to predict a rebirth in hell,
they vanish into the sole of a foot.
If he wants to predict a rebirth as an animal,
they vanish into a heel.
If he wants to predict a rebirth as a hungry ghost,
they vanish into a big toe.
If he wants to predict a rebirth as a mortal,
they vanish into his knees.
If he wants to predict a reign of an armed wheel-turning king,
they vanish into his left palm.
If he wants to predict a reign of a wheel-turning king,
they vanish into his right palm.
If he wants to predict a rebirth as a god,
they enter his navel.
If he wants to predict an awakening as a disciple,
they vanish into his mouth.
If he wants to predict an awakening as a solitary buddha,
they vanish into the circle of hair between his eyebrows.
If he wants to predict unsurpassed perfect awakening,
they vanish into his *uṣṇīṣa*.

In this case, those rays of light circumambulated the Blessed One three times and then vanished into the circle of hair between the Blessed One's eyebrows.

The venerable Ānanda then respectfully cupped his hands together and addressed the Blessed One:

A bundle of diverse light rays,
variegated with a thousand colors,
comes forth from your mouth.
They illuminate every direction,
as though the sun were rising.

And then he uttered these verses:

Without pride, free from grief and passion,
buddhas are the cause of greatness in the world.
Not without reason do victors, defeaters of the enemy,
display a smile, white like the conch or lotus root.

O you who are resolute, an ascetic, and an excellent victor,[575]
you know at once with your mind the desires of your listeners.
Destroy their doubts that have arisen, O best of sages,
with words excellent, enduring, and virtuous. [140]

Masters, awakened ones,
those with the patience of an ocean or great mountain
do not display a smile without reason.
Masses of people yearn to hear why it is
that resolute ones display a smile.

"It is like this, Ānanda," the Blessed One said. "It is like this. Perfectly awakened tathāgata arhats do not manifest a smile, Ānanda, without proper cause and reason. Ānanda, did you see that bull?"

"Yes, Bhadanta, I saw him."

"That bull, Ānanda, his mind filled with faith in the presence of the Tathāgata, will die after seven days and be reborn among the Cāturmahārājika gods, where he will be the son of the great king named Vaiśravaṇa. Then, having passed away from there, he will be reborn among the Trāyastriṃśa gods as the son of Śakra, lord of the gods. Having passed away from there, he will be reborn among the Yāma gods as the son of Lord Yāma. Having passed away from there, he will be reborn among the Tuṣita gods as the son of Lord Tuṣita. Having passed away from there, he will be reborn among the Nirmāṇarati gods as the son of the divinely born Sunirmāṇarati (Greatly Delighting in Creation). Having passed away from there, he will be reborn among the Paranirmitavaśavartin gods as the son of the divinely born Vaśavartin (Master). Continuing in this way, he will not suffer a karmic downfall for ninety-nine thousand eons. Then, having experienced divine pleasure among the gods in the sphere of desire, in his last life, his last existence, his last body, his last incarnation, he will take on human form. He will be the king named Aśokavarṇa (Praised as Griefless), a wheel-turning king, a conqueror of the four corners of the earth, a just and virtuous ruler possessing the seven treasures. These seven treasures of his will have the form of the most-treasured wheel, the most-treasured elephant, the most-treasured horse, the most-treasured jewel, the most-treasured woman, the most-treasured householder, and the most-treasured counselor. And he will have a full one thousand sons who are brave, heroic, in excellent physical condition, and who can crush enemy armies. He will conquer the vast sea-bound earth without violence and without weapons, and then rule there justly and evenhandedly so that it will be entirely fertile, without enemies, and without oppression. At that time he will make offerings, renounce his wheel-turner's kingdom, shave off his hair and beard, [put on][576] red clothes, and with just the right belief, [141] go forth from home to homelessness. Then he will directly experience awakening as a solitary buddha and become the solitary buddha named Aśokavarṇa."

The venerable Ānanda then respectfully cupped his hands together and asked the Blessed One: "Bhadanta, what deed did this bull do that resulted in his being reborn as an animal? And what deed did he do that will result in his experiencing divine-like[577] pleasure and in his attainment of awakening as a solitary buddha?"

"Ānanda," the Blessed One said, "the deeds that this very bull has performed and accumulated have now come together, and their conditions have matured. They remain before them like an oncoming flood and will certainly come to pass. Those deeds were performed and accumulated by the bull. Who else will experience their results? For those deeds that are performed and accumulated, Ānanda, do not mature outside of oneself—neither in the element of earth nor in the element of water, in the element of fire or in the element of wind. Instead, those deeds that are done, both good and bad, mature in the aggregates, the elements, and the sense bases that are appropriated when one is reborn.

> Actions never come to naught,
> even after hundreds of millions of years.
> When the right conditions gather and the time is right,
> then they will have their effect on embodied beings."

The Perfectly Awakened Vipaśyin and the Five Hundred Rogues

Long ago, Ānanda, in a time gone by, in the ninety-first age, there arose in the world a perfectly awakened buddha named Vipaśyin (Visionary),

> who was perfect in knowledge and conduct,
> a sugata,
> a knower of the world,
> an unsurpassed guide for those in need of training,
> a teacher of gods and mortals,
> a buddha,
> and a blessed one.

He stayed near the capital Bandhumatī (Abode of Relatives) in a wooded area. Not far from him, there lived sixty forest monks who survived on almsfood. All of them were free from attachment, free from hate, and free from delusion.

Meanwhile five hundred rogues, wandering here and there, arrived at this place, and it occurred to them, "These great beings who have gone forth as monks enjoy themselves in places like this. If we don't kill them, we'll never be able to live comfortably in this region. Not that these great beings will inform anyone else; they're busy improving the welfare of all beings. But important people do approach them. They'll have us handed over to the king, and then we'll be imprisoned and die. So how should we proceed?"

One of the rogues was cruel at heart and had abandoned any concern for the next world. [142] He said, "Without killing them how can we be safe?" And so the rogues killed those monks.

Coda

"Having done this wicked and evil deed, those rogues were reborn in the lower realms of existence for ninety-one eons. Practically all were reborn in the realms of hell or animals, each time being killed by a sword. The robber who at that time incited the others was none other than the bull. As a result of that action, during all that time he was never reborn in a favorable realm of existence. But now since his mind is filled with faith in my presence, as a result of that action, he will experience divine-like pleasure and attain awakening as a solitary buddha. And so it is, Ānanda, that having faith in mind toward tathāgatas produces results that can't even be imagined. What to say of making a fervent aspiration? So then, Ānanda, this is to be learned: 'Bit by bit, moment by moment, even for just a snap of the fingers, we should bring to mind the attributes of the Tathāgata.' It is this, Ānanda, that you should learn to do."

Then the venerable Ānanda rejoiced and delighted in the words of the Blessed One and then uttered these verses before the monks:

How great is the compassion of the lord!
He is omniscient and benevolent,
his affection such a great wonder!
It is indeed our good fortune.

He set free that bull,
trapped in great danger,
and predicted for him a divine existence
and a future as a solitary victor.[578]

This was said by the Blessed One. With their minds uplifted, the monks welcomed the words of the Blessed One.

So ends the *Aśokavarṇa-avadāna,* the eleventh chapter in the glorious *Divyāvadāna.* [143]

12. The Miracle Sūtra

PRĀTIHĀRYA-SŪTRA

The Blessed One was staying in the city of Rājagṛha at the bamboo grove in Kalandakanivāpa.[579] There he was respected, honored, revered, and venerated by kings, royal ministers, the well-to-do, townspeople, guildmasters, caravan leaders, gods, nāgas, yakṣas, antigods, heavenly birds, kinnaras, and great snakes. He was also praised by gods, nāgas, yakṣas, antigods, heavenly birds, kinnaras, and great snakes. Renowned and possessing great merit, the Lord Buddha, along with the community made up of his disciples, received provisions, both divine and human, of robes, begging bowls, bedding and seats, and medicines to cure the sick. And the Blessed One remained detached from these, like a lotus leaf from water.

The Six Heretics Plan a Miracle Competition with the Buddha

At that time in the city of Rājagṛha there lived six teachers—including Pūraṇa—who didn't know everything but claimed they did. They were Pūraṇa Kāśyapa; Maskarin, the son of Gośālī; Sañjayin, the son of Vairaṭṭī; Ajita Keśakambala; Kakuda Kātyāyana; and Nirgrantha, the son of Jñāti. One day those six heretics, including Pūraṇa, assembled and sat down in a discussion hall, and this is the conversation that ensued:

"Friends, as you know, before the ascetic Gautama arose in the world, we were respected, honored, revered, and venerated by kings, royal ministers, brahmans, householders, townspeople, villagers, guildmasters, and caravan leaders. We also received provisions of robes, begging bowls, bedding and seats, and medicines to cure the sick. But since the ascetic Gautama has arisen in the world, it's the ascetic Gautama who is respected, honored, revered, and venerated by kings, royal ministers, brahmans, householders, villagers, the well-to-do, guildmasters, and caravan leaders. And it's the ascetic Gautama, along with the community made up of his disciples, who receives provisions of robes, begging bowls, bedding and seats, and medicines to cure the sick. [144] Whatever benefits and respect we had have been completely and utterly destroyed.

"We have magical powers[580] and can speak knowledgeably.[581] The ascetic Gautama, on the other hand, only alleges that he has magical powers and can speak knowledgeably. One who speaks knowledgeably should [compete] with another who speaks knowledgeably in making use of magical powers and displaying miracles that are beyond the capability of ordinary mortals.[582] If the ascetic Gautama makes use of his magical powers and displays a single miracle that is beyond the capability of ordinary mortals, we'll display two. If the ascetic Gautama displays two, we'll display four. If the ascetic Gautama displays four, we'll display eight. If the ascetic Gautama displays eight, we'll display sixteen. If the ascetic Gautama displays sixteen, we'll display thirty-two. As many miracles as the ascetic Gautama displays, through his magical powers, that are beyond the capability of ordinary mortals, we'll continue to display two or three times that many. The ascetic Gautama should come halfway here, and we'll go halfway there. And in that place, let us [compete] with the ascetic Gautama in making use of magical powers and displaying miracles that are beyond the capability of ordinary mortals."[583]

Meanwhile it occurred to the evil Māra, "I have attacked the ascetic Gautama many times, but I've never found a weak spot. I really should attack these heretics instead." With this in mind, he magically took on the appearance of Pūraṇa. He then rose up high into the sky and performed the miraculous deeds of causing fire and heat, making rain and lightning. Then he addressed Maskarin, the son of Gośālī:

> Maskarin, as you know, I possess magical powers and I can speak knowledgeably. The ascetic Gautama, on the other hand, only alleges that he has magical powers and can speak knowledgeably. One who speaks knowledgeably should compete with another who speaks knowledgeably in making use of magical powers and displaying miracles that are beyond the capability of ordinary mortals. If the ascetic Gautama makes use of his magical powers and displays a single miracle that is beyond the capability of ordinary mortals, I'll display two. If the ascetic Gautama displays two, I'll display four. If the ascetic Gautama displays four, I'll display eight. If the ascetic Gautama displays eight, I'll display sixteen. If the ascetic Gautama displays sixteen, I'll display thirty-two. As many miracles as the ascetic Gautama displays, through his magical powers, that are beyond the capability of ordinary mortals, let us continue to display twice that many. [145] The ascetic Gautama should come halfway here, and I'll go halfway there. And in that place, let us compete with the ascetic Gautama in making use of magical powers and displaying miracles that are beyond the capability of ordinary mortals.

Then it occurred to the evil Māra: "I have attacked the ascetic Gautama many times, but I've never found a weak spot. I really should attack these heretics instead." With this in mind, he magically took on the appearance of Maskarin. He then rose up high into the sky and performed the miraculous deeds of causing fire and heat, making rain and lightning. Then he addressed Sañjayin, the son Vairaṭṭī:

> Sañjayin, as you know, I possess magical powers and I can speak knowledgeably. The ascetic Gautama, on the other hand, only alleges that he has magical powers and can speak knowledgeably. One who speaks knowledgeably should compete with another who speaks knowledgeably in making use of magical powers and displaying miracles that are beyond the capability of ordinary mortals. If the ascetic Gautama makes use of his magical powers and displays a single miracle that is beyond the capability of ordinary mortals, I'll display two. If the ascetic Gautama displays two, I'll display four. If the ascetic Gautama displays four, I'll display eight. If the ascetic Gautama displays eight, I'll display sixteen. If the ascetic Gautama displays sixteen, I'll display thirty-two. As many miracles as the ascetic Gautama displays, through his magical powers, that are beyond the capability of ordinary mortals, I'll continue to display twice that many. The ascetic Gautama should come halfway here, and I'll go halfway there. And in that place, I shall compete with the ascetic Gautama in making use of magical powers and displaying miracles that are beyond the capability of ordinary mortals.

In this way, the heretics were all troubled by one another. Each one of them said to himself, "But I haven't obtained magical powers."

Then Pūraṇa and those five other teachers, who were sure that they knew everything, approached the king of Magadha, Śreṇya Bimbisāra. Having approached, they said this to him:

> Please be informed, my lord, that we have magical powers and can speak knowledgeably. The ascetic Gautama, on the other hand, only alleges that he has magical powers and can speak knowledgeably. One who speaks knowledgeably should compete with another who speaks knowledgeably in making use of magical powers and displaying miracles that

are beyond the capability of ordinary mortals. If the ascetic Gautama makes use of his magical powers and displays a single miracle that is beyond the capability of ordinary mortals, [146] we'll display two. If the ascetic Gautama displays two, we'll display four. If the ascetic Gautama displays four, we'll display eight. If the ascetic Gautama displays eight, we'll display sixteen. If the ascetic Gautama displays sixteen, we'll display thirty-two. As many miracles as the ascetic Gautama displays, through his magical powers, that are beyond the capability of ordinary mortals, we'll continue to display two or three times that many. The ascetic Gautama should come halfway here, and we'll go halfway there. And in that place, allow us to compete with the ascetic Gautama in making use of magical powers and displaying miracles that are beyond the capability of ordinary mortals.

Thus addressed, the Magadhan king, Śreṇya Bimbisāra, said this to those heretics: "You'll be corpses before your magic works on the Blessed One!"[584]

Later on, Pūraṇa and those five other teachers, who didn't know everything but were sure they did, beseeched the Magadhan king, Śreṇya Bimbisāra, once again—this time while he was on the road.

My lord, we have magical powers and can speak knowledgeably. The ascetic Gautama, on the other hand, only alleges that he has magical powers and can speak knowledgeably. One who speaks knowledgeably should compete with another who speaks knowledgeably in making use of magical powers and displaying miracles that are beyond the capability of ordinary mortals. [If the ascetic Gautama makes use of his magical powers and displays a single miracle that is beyond the capability of ordinary mortals, we'll display two. If the ascetic Gautama displays two, we'll display four. If the

> ascetic Gautama displays four, we'll display eight. If the ascetic Gautama displays eight, we'll display sixteen. If the ascetic Gautama displays sixteen, we'll display thirty-two. As many miracles as the ascetic Gautama displays, through his magical powers, that are beyond the capability of ordinary mortals, we'll continue to display two or three times that many. The ascetic Gautama should come halfway here, and we'll go halfway there].[585] And in that place, let us compete with the ascetic Gautama in making use of magical powers and displaying miracles that are beyond the capability of ordinary mortals.

Thus addressed, the Magadhan king, Śreṇya Bimbisāra, said this to those mendicant heretics: "If you request this of me a third time, I'll banish you from the kingdom!"

Then it occurred to those heretics, "This Magadhan king, Śreṇya Bimbisāra, is a disciple of the ascetic Gautama. Forget about Bimbisāra. King Prasenajit of Kośala is impartial. When the ascetic Gautama goes to Śrāvastī, we'll go there and challenge[586] him to make use of his magical powers and display miracles that are beyond the capability of ordinary mortals." With these words, they departed.

Then the Magadhan king, Śreṇya Bimbisāra, addressed one of his men: "Go quickly, my man! Get an excellent carriage ready! I'll board and go to see the Blessed One and pay my respects." [147]

"Very well, my lord," the man replied, consenting to the Magadhan king Śreṇya Bimbisāra's request. Then he quickly readied an excellent carriage and approached the Magadhan king, Śreṇya Bimbisāra. Having approached, he said this to him: "An excellent carriage has been readied for my lord. Now my lord may do as the time permits."

Then the Magadhan king, Śreṇya Bimbisāra, boarded the excellent carriage and left Rājagṛha to go to see the Blessed One and pay his respects in the Blessed One's presence. After covering as much ground as he could by carriage, he got down from the carriage and entered the grove on foot. When the Magadhan king, Śreṇya Bimbisāra, saw the Blessed One, he immediately removed his five royal insignia—that is to say, his turban, his umbrella, his precious sword, his yak-tail fan, and his colorful sandals. Having removed those five royal insignia, he approached the Blessed One. Having approached, he venerated with his head the feet of the Blessed One and then sat down at a respectful distance. When the Blessed One was sure that he was seated at a respectful distance, he instructed, incited, inspired, and delighted the Magadhan king, Śreṇya Bimbisāra, with a discourse on the dharma. After he instructed, incited, inspired, and delighted him in many ways with this discourse on the dharma, he became silent. Then the Magadhan king, Śreṇya Bimbisāra, rejoiced and delighted in the words of the Blessed One, venerated with his head the feet of the Blessed One, and then left the Blessed One's presence.

The Buddha Sets Out for Śrāvastī

Then it occurred to the Blessed One, "Where did each perfectly awakened buddha in the past display a great miracle for the benefit of sentient beings?"

Some deities informed the Blessed One: "Bhadanta, we've heard as well that in the past each perfectly awakened buddha displayed a great miracle for the benefit of sentient beings."

The Blessed One then looked and came to know that in the past each perfectly awakened buddha displayed a great miracle for the benefit of sentient beings in Śrāvastī. And so the Blessed One addressed the venerable Ānanda: "Ānanda, go and inform the monks as follows—'The Tathāgata will travel through the Kośala countryside. Whoever among you is eager to travel through the Kośala countryside with the Tathāgata [148] should wash, stitch, and dye his robes.'"

"Yes, Bhadanta," the venerable Ānanda replied, consenting to the Blessed One's request. Then he informed the monks: "Venerable ones, the Blessed One will travel through the Kośala countryside. Whoever among you is eager to travel through the Kośala countryside with the Tathāgata should wash, stitch, and dye his robes."

Now the Blessed One was self-controlled
  and his followers were self-controlled,
he was calm and his followers were calm,
he was liberated and his followers were liberated,
he was confident and his followers were confident,
he was disciplined and his followers were disciplined,
he was an arhat and his followers were arhats,
he was without attachment
  and his followers were without attachment,
and he instilled faith and his followers instilled faith.

He was like a bull surrounded by a herd of cows,
like a royal elephant surrounded by a herd of elephant cubs,
like a lion surrounded by a carnivorous pack,
like a royal goose surrounded by a gaggle of geese,
like an eagle surrounded by a flock of birds,
like a learned brahman surrounded by an assembly of students,
like an eminent doctor surrounded by a group of patients,
like a warrior surrounded by a troop of soldiers,
like a guide surrounded by a group of travelers,[587]
like a caravan leader surrounded by a company of merchants,
like a guildmaster surrounded by townspeople,
like a vassal king surrounded by a cabinet of ministers,
like a wheel-turning king surrounded by a thousand sons,
like the moon surrounded by a constellation of stars,
like the sun surrounded by a thousand rays of light,
like the great king Virūḍhaka surrounded by a group
  of *kumbhāṇḍa*s,
like the great king Virūpākṣa surrounded by a group of nāgas,
like the great king Dhanada surrounded by a group of yakṣas,

like the great king Dhṛtarāṣṭra surrounded by a group
of celestial musicians,
like Vemacitrin surrounded by a group of antigods,
like Śakra surrounded by a group of gods,
and like Brahmā surrounded by the gods of Brahmakāyika
(Brahmā's Assembly).

He was like an ocean but calm,
like a cloud but full of water,
and like a mighty elephant but without pride or passion.
His senses were well restrained,
his deportment and demeanor were unflappable,
and he possessed the many special qualities of a buddha.

And so the Blessed One, leading a large community of monks, set off on a journey to Śrāvastī. Traveling along, with many hundreds and thousands of deities following behind him, he eventually arrived in Śrāvastī. Once in Śrāvastī, he stayed at the Jeta Grove in the park of a man named Anāthapiṇḍada (Almsgiver to the Poor).

The Buddha and the Heretics Prepare to Meet

The heretics heard that the ascetic Gautama had gone to Śrāvastī, and having heard this, they set out for Śrāvastī as well. When they arrived in Śrāvastī, they said this to King Prasenajit of Kośala: [149]

Please be informed, my lord, that we have magical powers and can speak knowledgeably. The ascetic Gautama, on the other hand, only alleges that he has magical powers and can speak knowledgeably. One who speaks knowledgeably should compete with another who speaks knowledgeably in making use of magical powers and displaying miracles that are beyond the capability of ordinary mortals. If the ascetic

> Gautama makes use of his magical powers and displays a single miracle that is beyond the capability of ordinary mortals, we'll display two. If the ascetic Gautama displays two, we'll display four. If the ascetic Gautama displays four, we'll display eight. If the ascetic Gautama displays eight, we'll display sixteen. If the ascetic Gautama displays sixteen, we'll display thirty-two. As many miracles as the ascetic Gautama displays, through his magical powers, that are beyond the capability of ordinary mortals, we'll continue to display two or three times that many that are beyond the capability of ordinary mortals. The ascetic Gautama should come halfway here, and we'll go halfway there. And in that place, let us compete with the ascetic Gautama in making use of magical powers and displaying miracles that are beyond the capability of ordinary mortals.

Thus addressed, King Prasenajit of Kośala said this to those heretics: "Bear with me, gentlemen, while I go to see the Blessed One." Then King Prasenajit of Kośala addressed one of his men: "Go quickly, my man! Get an excellent carriage ready! I'll board immediately and go to see the Blessed One and pay my respects."

"Very well, my lord," that man replied, consenting to King Prasenajit of Kośala's request. Then he quickly readied an excellent carriage and approached King Prasenajit of Kośala. Having approached, he said this to him: "An excellent carriage has been readied for my lord. Now my lord may do as the time permits."

Then King Prasenajit of Kośala boarded the excellent carriage and left Śrāvastī to go to see the Blessed One and pay his respects in the Blessed One's presence. After covering as much ground as he could on his carriage, he got down from the carriage and entered the grove on foot. He approached the Blessed One and, having approached, venerated with his head the feet of the Blessed One [150] and then sat down at a respectful distance. After sitting down at a respectful distance,

King Prasenajit of Kośala said this to the Blessed One: "Bhadanta, some heretics are challenging the Blessed One to make use of his magical powers and display miracles that are beyond the capability of ordinary mortals. For the benefit of sentient beings, the Blessed One should make use of his magical powers and display a miracle that is beyond the capability of ordinary mortals. The Blessed One should put these heretics to shame! He should make gods and mortals happy! And he should satisfy the hearts and minds of good people!"

Thus addressed, the Blessed One said this to King Prasenajit of Kośala: "Your majesty, I don't teach the dharma to my disciples by saying, 'Monks, for the benefit of those brahmans and householders who come to you, make use of your magical powers and display a miracle that is beyond the capability of ordinary mortals.' Instead, I teach the dharma to my disciples in this way—'Monks, you should live with your virtues concealed and your sins exposed.'"

A second time and a third as well, King Prasenajit of Kośala said this to the Blessed One: "For the benefit of sentient beings, the Blessed One should make use of his powers and display a miracle that is beyond the capability of ordinary mortals. He should put these heretics to shame! The Blessed One should make gods and mortals happy! And he should satisfy the hearts and minds of good people!"

It is a law of nature that while lord buddhas live, exist, remain alive, and pass time, they must perform these ten indispensable deeds. Each respective lord buddha will not pass into final nirvāṇa

> until he foretells of a future Buddha,
> until another being makes a resolution, never to be betrayed,
> to attain unsurpassed perfect awakening,
> until he has instructed all those whom he was destined
> to instruct,
> until he has passed three quarters of his existence,
> until he has drawn a strict line [between good and evil],[588]
> until he has designated a pair as his principal disciples,

until he has displayed his descent, accomplanied by deities,
into the city of Sāṅkāśya,[589]
until he has, in the company of his disciples, explained former
karmic bonds at the great Lake Anavatapta,
until he has established his mother and father
in the [four noble] truths,
and until he has displayed a great miracle at Śrāvastī.

Then it occurred to the Blessed One, "It is this last indispensable deed that the Tathāgata must perform." With this in mind, he addressed King Prasenajit of Kośala: "Go, your majesty. Seven days from now, before the eyes of a large crowd of people, the Tathāgata will make use of his magical powers and display, for the benefit of sentient beings, a miracle that is beyond the capability of ordinary mortals."

Then King Prasenajit of Kośala said this to the Blessed One: [151] "If the Blessed One permits, I will have a miracle pavilion built for the Blessed One."

Then it occurred to the Blessed One, "In what place did each perfectly awakened buddha in the past display a great miracle for the benefit of sentient beings?"

Some deities informed the Blessed One: "Between Śrāvastī and the Jeta Grove, Bhadanta. That's where, in the past, each perfectly awakened buddha displayed a great miracle for the benefit of sentient beings."

Then the Blessed One himself looked and came to know that it was, in fact, between Śrāvastī and the Jeta Grove that in the past each perfectly awakened buddha displayed a great miracle for the benefit of sentient beings. And so the Blessed One agreed to King Prasenajit of Kośala's request with his silence. Then, knowing by the Blessed One's silence that he had agreed to his request, King Prasenajit of Kośala said this to the Blessed One: "In which place, Bhadanta, should I have a miracle pavilion built?"

"Between Śrāvastī and the Jeta Grove, your majesty."

Then King Prasenajit of Kośala rejoiced and delighted in the words of the Blessed One, venerated with his head the feet of the Blessed One, and left the Blessed One's presence.

Afterward King Prasenajit of Kośala said this to the heretics: "Gentlemen, please be informed that seven days from now the Blessed One will make use of his magical powers and display a miracle that is beyond the capability of ordinary mortals."

Then it occurred to those heretics, "During these seven days will the ascetic Gautama attain some faculty that he hasn't yet attained? Or will he run away? Or will he try to find more supporters?"[590] It occurred to them, "There's no way that the ascetic Gautama will run away, nor is there any way that he'll attain some special faculty that he hasn't yet attained. No doubt the ascetic Gautama will try to find more supporters. In the meantime, we'll find more supporters for ourselves."

With this in mind, they called on the mendicant named Raktākṣa (Red Eyes) who was very skilled in the art of magic. They explained the matter to the mendicant Raktākṣa in detail. Then they said,

> Raktākṣa, there is something you should know. We have called on the ascetic Gautama to make use of his magical powers. He has said that [152] seven days from now he will make use of his magical powers and display a miracle that is beyond the capability of ordinary mortals. No doubt the ascetic Gautama will try to find more supporters. In the meantime, you should find supporters for us among those who follow the religious life with you.[591]

The mendicant Raktākṣa agreed to do so. Then he approached various heretics, ascetics, brahmans, wanderers, and mendicants. Having approached, he explained the matter to those various heretics, ascetics, brahmans, wanderers, and mendicants in detail. Then he said,

> Friends, there is something you should know. We have called on the ascetic Gautama to make use of his magical powers.

> He has said that seven days from now he will make use of his magical powers and display a miracle that is beyond the capability of ordinary mortals. No doubt the ascetic Gautama will try to find more supporters. In the meantime, you should form an alliance with those who follow the religious life.[592] Then, seven days from now, you should go to a place outside of Śrāvastī.

They also agreed to do so.

Now on a certain mountain there lived five hundred seers. The mendicant Raktākṣa approached those sages and, having approached, explained the matter to them in detail. Then he said,

> Friends, there is something you should know. The ascetic Gautama has been called on to make use of his magical powers. He has said that seven days from now he will make use of his magical powers and display a miracle that is beyond the capability of ordinary mortals. No doubt the ascetic Gautama will try to find more supporters. In the meantime, you should form an alliance with those who follow the religious life with you. Then, seven days from now, you should come to Śrāvastī.

They agreed to do so as well.

There was, at that time, a mendicant named Subhadra (Lucky) who possessed the five superhuman faculties. His home was in Kuśinagarī, but he would pass his days at the great Lake Anavatapta. Now the mendicant Raktākṣa approached the mendicant Subhadra and, having approached, explained the matter to him in detail. Then he said,

> Subhadra, there is something you should know. We have called on the ascetic Gautama to make use of his magical powers. He has said that seven days from now he will make

> use of his magical powers and display a miracle that is beyond the capability of ordinary mortals. No doubt the ascetic Gautama will try to find more supporters. You should form an alliance with others who follow the religious life with you. [153] Then, seven days from now, you should come to Śrāvastī.

"You were mistaken to challenge the ascetic Gautama to make use of his magical powers," Subhadra said. "Why is that? These days my home is in Kuśinagarī, but I pass my days at the great Lake Anavatapta. The ascetic Gautama has a student named Śāriputra, and he has a novice named Cunda. Cunda also passes his days there at the great Lake Anavatapta. The deities that live at Anavatapta don't consider any duties as important as their duties toward him. Here is one example. On one occasion, after wandering here in Kuśinagarī for alms, I took my bowl of almsfood and went to the great Lake Anavatapta. The deity residing there at Anavatapta drew water from the great Lake Anavatapta, but she didn't offer any to me, even though I was [sitting][593] at a respectful distance. Meanwhile Cunda, who was still just a senior monk's subordinate, had taken the rags that he used to cover himself and had also gone to the great Lake Anavatapta. The deity residing there at Anavatapta washed his ragged clothes and then anointed herself with the water that she wrung out. Now, we aren't even equal to a disciple of a disciple of the ascetic Gautama, yet you've challenged him to make use of his magical powers and display a miracle that is beyond the capability of ordinary mortals. You haven't done well to challenge the ascetic Gautama to make use of his magical powers and display a miracle. Considering what I've seen, I'm sure that the ascetic Gautama possesses great magic and great power."

"Well, since you're siding with the ascetic Gautama," Raktākṣa said, "there's no need for you to go."

"No," Subhadra said. "I definitely won't be going."

The Story of Prince Kāla

Now King Prasenajit of Kośala had a brother named Kāla (Dark One), who was handsome, good-looking, and attractive, trustworthy and virtuous at heart. One day Kāla walked out of the main gate of King Prasenajit of Kośala's palace as one of the women confined to the king's harem was standing on one of the terraces of the palace. When she saw the prince, she threw a wreath of flowers, which landed upon him.

Now the world is made up of friends, enemies, and those who are indifferent. Consequently, some people went and informed the king: "There is something you should know, my lord. Kāla has solicited a woman in my lord's harem."

King Prasenajit of Kośala was violent, impetuous, and merciless. Without further examination, he gave his men the following order: "Go quickly, gentlemen! Cut off Kāla's hands and feet."

"Very well, my lord," the men replied, consenting to King Prasenajit of Kośala's request. [154] Then, in the middle of the marketplace, they cut off Kāla's hands and feet. He cried in pain. The suffering he experienced was sharp, intense, excruciating, and heart-rending.

Seeing Prince Kāla like this, a large crowd of people began to wail.

Meanwhile Pūraṇa and the other Nirgranthas arrived there.

"Noble ones," Kāla's relatives said to them, "appeal to the truth so that you can restore Prince Kāla to the way he was before!"

"He is a disciple of the ascetic Gautama," Pūraṇa said. "Gautama will restore him to the way he was before by virtue of the dharma of the ascetics.

Then it occurred to Prince Kāla, "I'm in trouble, difficulty, and danger, yet the Blessed One doesn't pay attention to me." With this in mind, he uttered this verse:

> How is it that the lord of the world
> doesn't know the danger I'm in?

Praise to him who is free from passion,
who has compassion for all beings!

Now lord buddhas are always alert. And so, the Blessed One addressed the venerable Ānanda: "Go, Ānanda! Take your outer robe, and with an attending monk following behind you, approach[594] Kāla, the king's brother. Having approached, put Prince Kāla's hands and feet back in their proper place. Then say,

Among those beings who have no feet, two feet, or many feet, and among those who have form or have no form, and among those who are conscious, are without consciousness, or are neither-conscious-nor-without-consciousness, a perfectly awakened tathāgata arhat is said to be the best.

Among those dharmas that are conditioned or are unconditioned, detachment is said to be the best.

Among communities, groups, gatherings, or assemblies, a community made up of a tathāgata's disciples is said to be the best.[595]

By this truth, by this declaration of truth, may your body be restored to the way it was before!"

"Yes, Bhadanta," the venerable Ānanda replied, consenting to the Blessed One's request. Then he took his outer robe and, with an attending monk following behind him, approached Kāla, the king's brother. Having approached, he restored Prince Kāla's hands and feet to their proper place. [155] Then he said,

Among those beings who have no feet, two feet, four feet, or many feet, [and among those who have form or have no form, and among those who are conscious, are without consciousness,][596] or are neither-conscious-nor-without-consciousness, a perfectly awakened tathāgata arhat is said to be the best.

Among those dharmas that are conditioned or are unconditioned, detachment is said to be the best.

Among communities, groups, gatherings, or assemblies, the community made up of a tathāgata's disciples is said to be the best.

By this truth, by this declaration of truth, may your body be restored to the way it was before!

As soon as he spoke these words, Prince Kāla's body was restored to the way it was before. Such is the Buddha's innate power and the divine power of deities. Deeply moved, Prince Kāla directly experienced the reward of the nonreturner and acquired[597] magical powers. In return, he presented a park to the Blessed One and began to serve him. Since his body had been cut into pieces, he came to be known as the gardener Gaṇḍaka (Pieces).

King Prasenajit of Kośala presented him with all kind of offerings, but Kāla told him, "I want nothing to do with you. I only serve the Blessed One."

The Miracle at Śrāvastī

Meanwhile, between Śrāvastī and the Jeta Grove, King Prasenajit of Kośala had a miracle pavilion built for the Blessed One. It extended hundreds and thousands of hands in length so that it could accommodate the four [assemblies].[598] A lion throne was specially prepared for the Blessed One. The other disciples, those of the heretics, had separate pavilions built for Pūraṇa and the other Nirgranthas.

When the seventh day came, King Prasenajit of Kośala had all the land between the Jeta Grove and the Blessed One's miracle pavilion cleared of stones, pebbles, and gravel. The air was darkened by the smoke of incense powder;[599] umbrellas, flags, and banners were raised; and the ground was sprinkled with fragrant waters and strewn with a variety of flowers. It was beautiful. Here and there flower pavilions were also readied.

On the morning of the seventh day, the Blessed One got dressed, took his bowl and robe, and entered Śrāvastī for alms. After wandering through Śrāvastī for alms, he finished his meal and in the afternoon returned from his almsround. Then he put away his bowl and robe, [156] washed his feet outside the monastery, and entered the monastery to retreat into meditation.

Then King Prasenajit of Kośala, along with many hundreds of followers, many thousands of followers, many hundreds and thousands of followers, approached the Blessed One's miracle pavilion. Having approached, he sat down in the seat specially prepared for him. The heretics, also surrounded by a large crowd of people, approached their pavilions as well. Having approached, they each sat down in their respective seats. After sitting down, they said this to King Prasenajit of Kośala: "As you can see,[600] my lord, we're the ones who have arrived. Where is the ascetic Gautama now?"

"Gentlemen, just be patient for a moment. The Blessed One will be arriving shortly." Then King Prasenajit of Kośala addressed a young brahman named Uttara (Higher): "Uttara, go and approach the Blessed One. After approaching, on my behalf, venerate with your head the feet of the Blessed One and ask him whether he is healthy, at ease, and light on his feet, whether he has had a pleasant journey and whether he is feeling strong and comfortable, and whether there is anything to find fault with and whether he is feeling relaxed. Then say, 'Bhadanta, King Prasenajit of Kośala said this as well: "Bhadanta, the heretics have arrived. Now the Blessed One may do as the time permits."'"

"Very well, my lord," the young brahman Uttara replied, consenting to King Prasenajit of Kośala's request. Then he approached the Blessed One. Having approached the Blessed One and, face to face, exchanged the customary greetings and pleasantries, he then sat down at a respectful distance. After sitting down at a respectful distance, the young brahman Uttara said this to the Blessed One: "Bhadanta, King Prasenajit of Kośala venerates with his head the feet of the Blessed One and asks whether you are healthy, at ease and light on your feet, whether you have had a pleasant journey and whether you are feeling strong and comfortable, and whether there is anything to find fault with and whether you are feeling relaxed."

"May King Prasenajit of Kośala be happy, young brahman, and you as well."

"Bhadanta, King Prasenajit of Kośala said this as well: 'Bhadanta, the heretics have arrived. Now the Blessed One may do as the time permits.'"

Thus addressed, the Blessed One said this to the young brahman: "Young brahman, I'll be arriving there today." Then the Blessed One exercised his power so that the young brahman Uttara [rose up] from where he was and set off high into the sky toward King Prasenajit of Kośala.

King Prasenajit of Kośala saw the young brahman Uttara high in the sky, coming toward him. [157] At the sight of him, he said this to the heretics: "The Blessed One has made use of his magical powers and displayed a miracle that is beyond the capability of ordinary mortals! You should display one as well."

"A large crowd of people has assembled here, your majesty," the heretics said. "How do you know for sure who displayed this miracle, us or the ascetic Gautama?"

Then the Blessed One entered a state of meditative concentration such that when his mind was concentrated, a flame issued through the hole on the bolt to his door. This, in turn, fell upon the Blessed One's miracle pavilion, and the whole miracle pavilion caught on fire. The heretics saw that the Blessed One's miracle pavilion had caught on fire, and at the sight of this, said this to Prasenajit of Kośala: "Your majesty, the ascetic Gautama's miracle pavilion has just caught on fire! Go and have it put out right away." But the fire, before it was even touched by water, extinguished itself before the entire miracle pavilion was burned down. Such is the Buddha's innate power and the divine power of deities.

Then King Prasenajit of Kośala said this to the heretics: "The Blessed One has made use of his magical powers and displayed a miracle that is beyond the capability of ordinary mortals! You should display one as well."

"A large crowd of people has assembled here, your majesty," the heretics said. "How do you know for sure who displayed this miracle, us or the ascetic Gautama?"

Then the Blessed One sent forth a brilliant golden light that suffused the entire world in a majestic splendor. King Prasenajit of Kośala saw that the entire world was suffused with a majestic splendor, and at the sight of this, addressed the heretics: "The Blessed One has made use of his magical powers and displayed a miracle that is beyond the capability of ordinary mortals! You should display one as well."

"A large crowd of people has assembled here, your majesty," the heretics said. "How do you know for sure who displayed this miracle, us or the ascetic Gautama?"

The gardener Gaṇḍaka, who had taken a *karṇikāra* tree from the island of Uttarakuru (Northern Kuru), now placed it in front of the Blessed One's miracle pavilion. Likewise, the park attendant Ratnaka, who had brought an *aśoka* tree from Gandhamādana (Intoxicating Fragrance),[601] placed that tree behind the Blessed One's miracle pavilion. [158]

Then King Prasenajit said this to the heretics: "The Blessed One has made use of his magical powers and displayed a miracle that is beyond the capability of ordinary mortals! You should display one as well."

"A large crowd of people has assembled here, your majesty," the heretics said. "How do you know for sure who displayed this miracle, us or the ascetic Gautama?"

Then the Blessed One focused his mind in such a way that when he put his foot down on the ground, the great earth began to move. The great thousand third-order thousand world-system, and so this great earth teetered, tottered, and tremored in six different ways: it quivered, quavered, and quaked; it shifted, shuddered, and shook.

> The west rose up and the east sank down.
> [The east rose up and the west sank down.][602]
> The south rose up and the north sank down.
> The north rose up and the south sank down.
> The middle rose up and the ends sank down.
> The ends rose up and the middle sank down.

And the sun and the moon were shining, blazing, and radiant. Various wonderful and fantastic things also appeared. Deities in the sky threw divine lotuses down on the Blessed One—red, blue, and white ones—and they threw *agaru,* sandalwood, and *tagara* that had been pounded into powders, as well as *tamāla* leaves and flowers from the divine coral tree. They also made their divine instruments resound and threw cloth streamers.[603]

Then it occurred to those seers, "Why has the great earth begun to move?" And then it occurred to them, "No doubt those who follow the religious life with us have called on the ascetic Gautama to make use of his magical powers." With this in mind, those five hundred seers set out for Śrāvastī. As they were approaching, the Blessed One exercised his power so that there was only a single path on which they could travel.[604] From a distance, those seers saw the Blessed One adorned with the thirty-two marks of a great man.

> He was like the dharma embodied,
> like a sacrificial fire that had been fed with oblations,
> like a lamp placed in a golden vessel,
> like a mountain of gold that moved,
> and like a golden object variegated with many jewels.

That is to say, they saw the Lord Buddha,
whose great intellect is expansive and quick,
spotless and stainless.

Twelve years' practice of quiescence meditation
does not produce such peace of mind in the yoga practitioner—
nor does the birth of a son for one who has no son,
the sight of a treasure trove for one who is destitute,
or a royal coronation for one who desires kingship. [159]
None of these produce such well-being
as when those whose roots of virtue were planted
  by a previous buddha
see a buddha in their present life for the first time.

Then those sages approached the Blessed One. Having approached, they venerated with their heads the feet of the Blessed One and then stood at a respectful distance. Standing at a respectful distance, those sages said this to the Blessed One: "Bhadanta, may we renounce, take ordination, and become monks according to the dharma and monastic discipline that have been so well expressed. After we renounce, may we follow the religious life in the presence of the Blessed One."

Then the Blessed One called on them with his Brahmā-like voice: "Come, O monks! Follow the religious life!" As soon as the Blessed One spoke, there they stood—heads shaved, garbed in monastic robes, bowls and water pots in their hands, with a week's growth of hair and beard, and the disciplined deportment of monks who had been ordained for one hundred years.

"Come," the Tathāgata said to them.
With heads shaved and bodies wrapped in robes,
they instantly attained tranquility of the senses,[605]
and so they remained by the will of the Buddha.[606]

Meanwhile the Blessed One, who was respected, honored, revered, and venerated with the offerings and honors accorded to gods and mortals, who was surrounded by arhats, and who was attended by seven groups [of gods][607] and a large crowd of people, approached the miracle pavilion. Having approached, he sat down in front of the community of monks in the seat specially prepared for him. Then, from the Blessed One's body emerged rays of light that illuminated the entire miracle pavilion in a light the color of gold. The householder Lūhasudatta (Stingy Benefactor) then got up from his seat, properly arranged his robe on one shoulder, kneeled with his right knee on the ground, bowed toward the Blessed One with his hands respectfully folded, and said this to the Blessed One: "The Blessed One needn't concern himself. I will make use of my magical powers and display, in the presence of these heretics, a miracle that is beyond the capability of ordinary mortals.[608] I will put these heretics to shame! I will make gods and mortals happy with the dharma! And I will satisfy the hearts and minds of good people!"

"Householder, these heretics didn't challenge you to make use of your magical powers. They challenged me. I will make use of my magical powers and display a miracle that is beyond the capability of ordinary mortals. Otherwise, given the situation, [160] the heretics will say that the ascetic Gautama has no magical powers and can't display a miracle that is beyond the capability of ordinary mortals. They will say that it is one of his disciples, a householder, one who wears the white clothes of a layperson, who possesses magical power. Sit back down in your seat, householder."

The householder Lūhasudatta sat back down in his seat. Then others followed the householder Lūhasudatta's example—Kāla, the brother of the king; the park attendant Rambhaka; Ṛddhila's mother, the lay devotee, who was still a senior monk's subordinate; Cunda, who was also still a senior monk's subordinate; and the nun Utpalavarṇā (Lotus Complexion). Then the venerable Mahāmaudgalyāyana got up from his seat, properly arranged his robe on one shoulder, bowed toward the Blessed One with his hands respectfully folded, and said this to the Blessed One: "The Blessed One needn't concern himself. I will make use of my magical powers and display, in the presence of these heretics, a miracle that is beyond the capability of ordinary mortals. I will subdue these heretics! I will make gods and mortals happy with the dharma! And I will satisfy the hearts and minds of good people!"

"You are fully capable, Maudgalyāyana, of subduing these heretics with the dharma. But these heretics haven't challenged you to make use of your magical powers. I will make use of my magical powers and display, for the benefit of sentient beings, a miracle that is beyond the capability of ordinary mortals. I will put these heretics to shame! I will make gods and mortals happy! And I will satisfy the hearts and minds of good people! Sit back down in your seat, Maudgalyāyana."

The venerable Maudgalyāyana sat back down in his seat. Then the Blessed One addressed King Prasenajit of Kośala: "Your majesty: who wants[609] the Tathāgata to make use of his magical powers and display, for the benefit of sentient beings, a miracle that is beyond the capability of ordinary mortals?"

Then King Prasenajit of Kośala got up from his seat, properly arranged his robe on one shoulder, kneeled with his right knee on the ground, bowed toward the Blessed One with his hands respectfully folded, and said this to the Blessed One: "It is I, Bhadanta, who wants the Blessed One to make use of his magical powers and display a miracle that is beyond the capability of ordinary mortals. The Blessed One should make use of his magical powers and [display],[610] for the benefit of sentient beings, a miracle that is beyond the capability of ordinary mortals! He should put these heretics to shame! He should make gods and mortals happy! And he should satisfy the hearts and minds of good people!" [161]

Then the Blessed One entered a state of meditative concentration such that when his mind was concentrated, he disappeared from his seat, rose up high in the sky in the eastern direction, and appeared in the four bodily postures—that is to say, walking, standing, sitting, and lying down. Then he entered into the state of mastery over the element of fire.[611] When the Lord Buddha had entered into the state of mastery over the element of fire, different kinds of light emerged from his body—they were blue, yellow, red, white, crimson, and the color of crystal. He displayed many other miracles as well. He made his lower body blaze in flames, and then a shower of cold water rained down from his upper body. What he displayed in the east, he then displayed in the south, and likewise in all four directions. After making use of his magical powers and displaying these four miracles in the four directions, he withdrew those magical powers that he had activated and sat down in the seat that had been specially prepared for him. After sitting down, the Blessed One said this to King Prasenajit of Kośala: "This magical power, your majesty, is common to all the disciples of the Tathāgata." Then the Blessed One addressed King Prasenajit of Kośala a second time: "Your majesty, who is it who wants the Tathāgata to make use of his magical powers and display, for the benefit of sentient being, an extraordinary miracle that is beyond the capability of ordinary mortals?"

Then King Prasenajit of Kośala got up from his seat, properly arranged his robe on one shoulder, kneeled with his right knee on the ground, bowed toward the Blessed One with his hands respectfully folded, and said this to the Blessed One: "It is I, Bhadanta, who wants the Blessed One to make use of his magical powers and display, for the benefit of sentient beings, an extraordinary miracle that is beyond the capability of ordinary mortals. The Blessed One should put these heretics to shame! He should make both gods and mortals happy! And he should satisfy the hearts and minds of good people!"

Then the Blessed One had a worldly thought. Now it is a law of nature that if a lord buddha has a worldly thought, all creatures, even tiny biting ants, know the blessed one's thought with their minds. But when they have an otherworldly thought, it is inaccessible even to solitary buddhas, to say nothing of a buddha's disciples.

Then it occurred to Śakra, Brahmā, and the other gods, "Why has the Blessed One had a worldly thought?" And it occurred to them, "He wants to display a great miracle at Śrāvastī for the benefit of sentient beings." [162] Then Śakra, Brahmā, and the other gods, along with many hundreds and thousands of deities, knowing with their minds this thought of the Blessed One, with the same ease that a strong man can flex and unflex his arm, disappeared from the world of gods and reappeared standing in front of the Blessed One. Some of the gods, led by Brahmā, then circumambulated the Blessed One three times, venerated with their heads the feet of the Blessed One, and sat down to his right. Other gods, led by Śakra, circumambulated the Blessed One three times, venerated with their heads the feet of the Blessed One, and sat down to his left. The two nāga kings, Nanda and Upananda,[612] magically created a lotus that had a thousand leaves and was the size of a wagon wheel, made entirely of gold and with a stalk of diamonds, and presented it to the Blessed One. The Blessed One sat down on the pericarp of that lotus. Then, crossing his legs and holding his body upright, he made his mindfulness fully present and magically created above that lotus another lotus on which the Blessed One also sat with his legs crossed. And he did the same in front of that lotus, behind it, and to the side of it. In this way the Blessed One created an array of buddhas rising up to the abode of the gods of Akaniṣṭha (Supreme) such that there was an entire assembly of lord buddhas.[613] Some of these magically created buddhas were walking, some were standing, some were sitting, and some were lying down. Some, as well, entered into the state of mastery over the element of fire and were performing the miraculous deeds of causing fire and heat, making rain and lightning. Others were asking questions, and others were answering them. They uttered[614] these two verses:

> Strive! Go forth!
> Apply yourselves to the teachings of the Buddha!
> Destroy the army of death
> as an elephant would a house of reeds.

Whoever diligently follows
this dharma and monastic discipline
will abandon the endless cycle of rebirth
and put an end to suffering.

Then the Blessed One exercised his power so that the entire world, even young children, could see the multitude of buddhas, without any obstructions, all the way up to the abode of the Akaniṣṭha gods. Such is the Buddha's innate power and the divine power of deities.

At that moment the Blessed One addressed the monks: [163] "Monks, contemplate the appearance of this array of buddhas, standing in order, one on top of another,[615] for in an instant it will disappear." And then, in an instant, it disappeared. The Blessed One then withdrew those magical powers that he had activated and sat down in the seat that had been specially prepared for him. At that time, after sitting down, the Blessed One uttered these verses:

The glowworm shines
as long as the sun doesn't rise,
but as soon as the sun comes up,
he is distressed by the sun's prowess[616]
and won't shine on his own.

Likewise the sophists shined
as long as the Tathāgata didn't arise,
but when the Perfectly Awakened One shined in the world,
the sophists no longer shined,
nor did their disciples.

Then King Prasenajit of Kośala said this to the heretics: "The Blessed One has made use of his magical powers and displayed a miracle that is beyond the capability of ordinary mortals! You should display one as well."

Thus addressed, the heretics fell silent and stood there, with thoughts only of fleeing.

Once again King Prasenajit of Kośala said this to the heretics: "The Blessed One has made use of his magical powers and displayed a miracle that is beyond the capability of ordinary mortals! You should display one as well."

Thus addressed, the heretics started elbowing each other and saying, "Stand up! Stand up!" But no one stood up.

The Heretics Flee

Now at that time the great general Pāñcika was seated in that assembly. As one of those assembled, it occurred to Pāñcika, the leader of the yakṣa army, "These deluded fools are going to harass the Blessed One and the community of monks for a long time." With this in mind, he created and unleashed a great tempest of wind and rain. That tempest of wind and rain hurled the heretics' pavilions out of sight. Tormented by the lightning and the rain, the heretics fled in all directions. Many hundreds and thousands of other beings, also tormented by the violent rain, approached the Blessed One. Having approached, they venerated with their heads the feet of the Blessed One and then sat down at a respectful distance. The Blessed One then exercised his power so that not even a single drop of water fell on the assembly. Those hundreds of thousands of beings, sitting at a respectful distance, then uttered this inspired utterance:

> Oh Buddha!
> Oh dharma!
> Oh community!
> Oh the clearly expressed dharma! [164]

Then Pāñcika, the leader of the yakṣa army, told the heretics, "Hey, you deluded fools! Take refuge in the Blessed One, in the dharma, and in the community of monks!" But as they were fleeing they said, "Hah! We're taking refuge in the mountains! We're taking refuge among the trees, behind walls, and in parks!"

Then, at that time, the Blessed One uttered these verses:

> Many people, frightened with fear,
> take refuge in the mountains,
> or in forests, or in parks,
> or in the shrines of sacred trees.
>
> But this isn't the best refuge;
> it isn't the most excellent one.
> Recourse to this refuge doesn't
> release one from all suffering.
>
> Whoever takes refuge in the Buddha,
> in the dharma, and in the community,
> sees, with his wisdom,
> the four noble truths—
>
> suffering, the arising of suffering,
> its destruction, and how to get beyond it—
> and he sees the noble eightfold path,
> bestowing safety and leading to nirvāṇa.
>
> This is the best refuge,
> this is the most excellent one.
> Recourse to this refuge
> releases one from all suffering.

Then it occurred to Pūraṇa, "The ascetic Gautama will convert my disciples." With this in mind, while he was running away, he said, "I will explain to you the essence of the teachings!" And while on the run, he tried to convince them of heretical views, such as that the world is finite, it's infinite, it's both finite and infinite, and it's neither finite nor infinite; and that the soul is the body, the soul is something else, and the body is something else.[617]

Elaborating on these heretical views, he began to convince them. One of the people there said, "The world is transient."

"It's eternal," said another.

"It's transient and eternal."

"The soul is the body."

"The soul is something else."

"The body is something else."

Like this, they fought and quarreled, disagreed and argued. Pūraṇa, however, was terrified and began to run away. As he was running away, a eunuch saw him approaching on the path.[618] When the eunuch saw him, he uttered this verse: [165]

> Where are you coming from empty-handed,
> like a carriage builder's ram with his horns cut off?[619]
> Having known that very dharma taught by the Victor,
> you still wander about like a weaver's donkey.[620]

Then Pūraṇa said,

> The time has come for me to go,
> but my body has little strength.
> I've had feelings,
> leading to happiness and suffering—
> the arhats' knowledge of this world
> is unimpeded.[621]
>
> I have come a long way.
> I've come out of intense darkness,
> and now thirst befalls me.[622]

Tell me this, eunuch,
where is a pool with cold water?

And the eunuch replied,

There is a cold pool right here,
dazzling with lotuses and filled with water.
Vile ascetic, debased and wicked man,
don't you see this lotus pool before you?

And Pūraṇa said,

You are neither a man nor a woman.
You have neither a beard nor breasts.
Your voice is broken, but you're not a *cakravāka* bird.
That's why it's said that you're mentally disturbed.

Then the Nirgrantha Pūraṇa tied a pot of sand around his neck and threw himself into the cold pool. Right there he met his death.

Meanwhile, as the other Nirgranthas were searching for Pūraṇa, they saw a courtesan coming toward them on the road and asked her, "Miss, did you see someone coming this way, one named Pūraṇa? He wears only the clothes of the dharma[623] and eats just a few spoonfuls of food as per his vow."

The courtesan said,

Doomed to a bad rebirth, destined for hell,
he slinked about empty-handed.
Pūraṇa lies here decomposing,
with his hands and feet turning white.

And they said,

Miss, don't speak like that.
You haven't spoken well.
Clad only in the clothes of the dharma,
that sage follows the dharma in full.[624]

The courtesan said,

How wise could he be?
This man, with his genitals intact,
wandered naked in the village
before the eyes of the people.

Whoever follows a dharma like this,
with his condition dangling in front of him,
should have both his ears cut off
with a sharp knife by the king.

Then the Nirgranthas approached the lotus pool filled with cold water. Those Nirgranthas saw Pūraṇa Kāśyapa, in the pool, dead. And seeing that his time had come, [166] they lifted him out of the pool, laid him down at a respectful distance, and departed.

The Buddha Instructs the Assembly

Meanwhile, the Blessed One magically created an image of the Buddha, endowed with the thirty-two marks of a great man, with a shaven head and clad in monastic robes. It is a law of nature that lord buddhas make decisions in conversation with magical images that they have created. If a disciple creates a magical image, however, when the disciple speaks, the magical image only repeats what he says.[625] When the disciple is silent, the magical image is also silent.

When a disciple is speaking,
all magical images of his creation
repeat what he says.
When he is silent, all are silent.

If the Blessed One questions a magical image that he has created, the Blessed One['s magical image] gives the answer.[626] This is a natural law for perfectly awakened tathāgata arhats.

Then the Blessed One, knowing the inclinations, propensities, makeup, and nature of that large crowd of people in whom faith had arisen, gave them a discourse on the dharma that penetrated the four noble truths such that many hundreds and thousands of beings [accepted][627] the taking of the refuges as well as the precepts. Some attained the heat stages, some the summit stages, some the tolerance stages, and some the highest worldly dharma stages. Some directly experienced the reward of the stream-enterer; some the reward of the once-returner; some the reward of the nonreturner; and some went forth as monks and, by ridding themselves of all defilements, directly experienced arhatship. Some planted the seeds for the great awakening of a disciple, and others planted the seeds for the awakening as a solitary buddha. Almost the entire assembly became favorably inclined toward the Buddha, intent on the dharma, and well disposed toward the community. Then, after the Blessed One had transformed the assembly so that it was favorably inclined toward the Buddha, intent on the dharma, and well disposed toward the community, he got up from his seat and departed.

Fortunate are those people in the world
who have taken refuge in the Buddha.
Those people who have served the Buddha[628]
will one day attain nirvāṇa.

Those who offer even a few services
to the Victor, to the Guide,

will come to a wonderful heaven.
They will find the eternal abode.

This was said by the Blessed One. With their minds uplifted, the monks welcomed the words of the Blessed One.

So ends the *Prātihārya-sūtra,* the twelfth chapter in the glorious *Divyāvadāna.* [167]

13. The Story of Svāgata

SVĀGATA-AVADĀNA

At one time the Lord Buddha was staying in the city of Śrāvastī at the Jeta Grove in the park of a man named Anāthapiṇḍada (Almsgiver to the Poor). At that same time, in the city of Śiśumāragiri,[629] there lived a householder named Bodha (Knowledge), who was rich, wealthy, and prosperous, with vast and extensive holdings, and had amassed a wealth like the god Vaiśravaṇa. Truly, he rivaled Vaiśravaṇa in wealth.

The Householder Bodha Has a Daughter

The householder Bodha brought home a girl from an appropriate family as his wife, and with her he fooled around, enjoyed himself, and made love. After some time, from his fooling around, enjoying himself, and making love, his wife became pregnant. She was kept in the upper story of their palatial home, free from any restraints, and she was provided with the necessities appropriate to the seasons. She was given the foods that doctors prescribed, those not too bitter, not too sour, not too salty, not too sweet, not too pungent, and not too astringent, and those foods free from bitterness, sourness, saltiness, sweetness, pungency, and astringency. Her body was adorned with strings and necklaces of pearls, and like a nymph wandering in the divine Nandana Grove, she moved from bed to bed and from seat to seat, never descending to the ground below.[630] And she heard no unkind words until the fetus matured.

After eight or nine months, she gave birth. A girl was born who was beautiful, good-looking, and attractive, and sound in all parts of her body. For three weeks, that is twenty-one days, they celebrated the occasion of her birth in full and then they selected a name for her that was appropriate to her particular complexion and constitution. Raised on the laps of nurses, who nourished her with milk, yogurt, fresh butter, clarified butter, butter scum, and other special provisions that were very pure, she grew quickly like a lotus in a lake.

When she grew up, she became a beautiful girl whose conduct, behavior, and demeanor befitted her youth. She brightened her home like a goddess and filled her friends, acquaintances, and relatives as well as her immediate family with joy. Hearing such accounts of her splendor, princes living in various foreign countries, sons of ministers, sons of householders, rich men, sons of guildmasters, and sons of caravan leaders [168] sent messengers to ask for her hand in marriage. The more requests that were made, the more pleased the householder Bodha became. He reflected, "I won't give her to any suitor because of his good looks, nor because of his skill in the arts or because of his sovereign power. Instead, I'll give her to whoever has as virtuous a family and as much wealth as I have." This is the way he thought.

The householder Anāthapiṇḍada heard that in Śiśumāragiri there was a householder named Bodha, that his daughter was beautiful and young, and that she had been asked to marry the sons of foreigners, kings, ministers, householders, and rich men as well as the sons of guildmasters and caravan leaders. Having heard this, it occurred to him, "I'll ask her to marry my son as well. Some day the householder Bodha will give her away in marriage." With this in mind, he sent messengers to her. The householder Bodha thought about the householder Anāthapiṇḍada's good conduct and wealth and gave her to him for marriage. The householder Anāthapiṇḍada married off his son with great pomp.

The Householder Bodha Has a Son

Now, once again, as the householder Bodha fooled around, enjoyed himself, and made love with his wife, his wife became pregnant. On the very day that she became pregnant, there arose for the householder Bodha many hundreds of misfortunes. He summoned soothsayers and said, "Gentlemen, look and see whose fault it is that these hundreds of misfortunes have arisen for me."

The soothsayers considered the situation and said unanimously, "Householder, it's the fault of whoever has entered your wife's womb. You should get rid of him."

Hearing this, the householder Bodha became greatly distressed. "Gentlemen," he said, "I won't get rid of what is welcome."

The soothsayers said farewell and departed.

Now the householder Bodha, though tormented by the thought of abandoning his child,[631] put up with the situation because he was afraid of being denounced publicly. The more the fetus grew, the more hundreds of misfortunes arose for the householder Bodha. He reflected, "Who wants to listen to such things?" And he thought, "I'll go and stay in the garden." Then he said to his servants, "If some really big disaster comes up, let me know. Otherwise, don't bother." With that said, he went to the garden and stayed there until his wife gave birth. [169] A son was born. One of the men went off in a hurry to the householder Bodha. The householder Bodha saw him coming from a distance and reflected, "Since he's coming in a hurry there must have been some disaster." With this in mind, he asked anxiously, "Friend, why do you come in such a hurry?"

"Householder, congratulations! You're now father to a son!"

"Friend," he said, "even though this son of mine has given rise to hundreds of misfortunes, still he is welcome."

Immediately a second man, likewise in a great hurry, with his eyes filled with tears, approached the householder Bodha. Filled with anxiety at the thought of more misfortunes, he asked him as well, "Friend, why do you come in such a hurry?"

The man, choked with tears, his voice stuck in his throat, spoke with drawn out words full of pity and distress. "Householder, there's been a fire in your house. All your possessions have been burned up."

With a mind state hardened from hearing of misfortunes over and over again, he said, "Friend, this was destined to happen. Don't despair. Be silent."

Now his relatives, following popular custom, began to deliberate on a name—but with contempt.

"What should this boy's name be?"

"Give him one that is suitable to his family," some of them said.

Others said, "Considering that just as he entered the womb he brought destruction upon the householder Bodha's home and its many riches, what kind of name can he be given that would be suitable to his family? Well, since his father greeted him with the word "welcome" *(svāgata)* as soon as he was born, let the boy's name be Svāgata (Welcome)." And so he was given the name Svāgata.

The Ill-Fated Svāgata

The more that Svāgata grew, the more the householder Bodha's wealth, supply of grain, gold and golden things, maids, servants, workers, and laborers diminished, gave out, and finally became exhausted. Then one day the householder Bodha died. His wife died as well. Their house, which had been repaired, again burned in a fire. Whatever wealth they had of grain and so on that was in the marketplace and in the fields was also destroyed by fire. As for his workers who had taken goods and gone abroad, while they crossed the great ocean some of them were shipwrecked, [170] some had their goods become unsaleable, and some straightaway met their deaths. Some had their things stolen by robbers while they were deep in the wilderness, some had their valuables taken away by calculating customs officers as they arrived at the outskirts of cities, and some, as they arrived in trading centers, had all their goods taken away by the king's appointees on trumped-up charges. Some also stayed right where they were on hearing of the householder Bodha's death. As for his relatives, some died, some ran away, and some stayed right where they were but wouldn't even talk to Svāgata. As for his maids, servants, workers, and laborers, some died, some ran away, and some stayed right where they were and became dependent on others for work. They wouldn't even acknowledge Svāgata's name.

An old maid who had been with the family a long time, however, out of gratitude continued to serve Svāgata. She entrusted him to a writing teacher to learn the letters. She reflected, "The householder Bodha's home and its many riches, its large following of family and relatives, and its many maids, servants, workers, and laborers have given out and finally become exhausted. Only Svāgata and I remain. What I'd like to know is whose evil deeds have brought on this misery, Svāgata's or mine?"

In Svāgata's name, she put some rice in a pot and prepared a meal. It went bad. Then she prepared some more in the same way in her own name, and it turned out just fine. "He's the ill-fated one," she reflected. "It's his fault that the householder Bodha's home and its many riches, its large following of family and relatives, its many maids, servants, workers, and laborers have given out and finally become exhausted. I'm not going back. But where will I stay? If I don't run away now, though, I'm completely done for." With this in mind, she took whatever valuables were there and fled.

Dogs entered the empty house and began to fight. Then a vagrant passed by the place. He heard the dogs fighting and reflected, "There are dogs fighting in the householder Bodha's home. Maybe it's empty.[632] I'll have a look." He went in and saw that it was empty. [171] He took whatever was left from there and then departed.

Now when Svāgata realized that it was his mealtime, he left the writing school and came home to eat. He saw that his house was empty. Since his thoughts were overcome with a desire to eat and since he was tormented with hunger, he began to call out, "Mom! Mom!" No one replied. He looked here and there, all around the house, then lost hope and left.

Not far from his house was another house where Svāgata's relatives stayed. He went there [surreptitiously] and soon a quarrel broke out among them. After they finished quarreling, they calmed down and spoke among themselves: "Friends, it used to be that when we saw each other, we felt love. Now there's hatred. Let's see if anyone has come." They began to search the house. Eventually they found Svāgata.

"Friends," some of them said, "Svāgata has come here."

"He isn't Svāgata," the others said. "He's Durāgata (Unwelcome). It's his fault that we started quarreling."

They then took him by the neck and threw him out. He went somewhere else and soon was thrown out from there as well. Eventually, he joined some beggars. Wherever they went[633] for alms, they were abused and thrown out. Disappointed, with empty hands and empty bowls, they came and sat in empty temples and pavilions and at the roots of trees.

"Friends," they asked each other, "in the past wherever we'd go we'd always come back with our hands full and our bowls full. Now what's happened? Why do we come back disappointed, with empty hands and empty bowls?"

"Some ill-fated person must have joined us," some of them said. "That's why we come back here with empty hands and empty bowls."

"That's right," the others said. "Let's divide into two groups and then enter [the city for alms]."

On the following day, they divided into two groups and entered [the city for alms]. Those whom Svāgata was among were abused and thrown out just as before. Disappointed, with empty hands and empty bowls, they returned to their homes. But the others came back with their hands full and bowls full. Those who came back with empty hands and empty bowls once again divided into two groups and entered [the city for alms]. Those whom Svāgata was among [172] came back with empty hands and empty bowls just as before. In this way, they divided into two groups, again and again, until eventually Svāgata and another beggar entered [the city for alms] and came back with empty hands and empty bowls, while the others came back with their hands full and bowls full. Then all the beggars began to converse among themselves.

"Friends, this ill-fated person has joined us! That's why we come back with empty hands and bowls empty. Let's throw him out!" So they beat him soundly, broke a begging bowl over his head, and then threw him out.

Svāgata Goes to Śrāvastī

Meanwhile a merchant from Śrāvastī, a friend of the householder Bodha, took his goods and came to Śiśumāragiri. He went to the marketplace, [saw] Svāgata with a begging bowl in his hands, recognized his face, and said, "Son, are you the son of the householder Bodha?"

"Yes, uncle," he said. "I am his unwelcome son."

The merchant stood silently for a moment. Then, with his eyes filled with tears, he said, "Son, have your parents died? And your relatives?"

"As for my relatives," he said, "some of them died, and some still live right here but won't even talk to me."

"And your maids, servants, workers, and laborers?"

"Some of them died, some ran off, and some have stayed here and became dependent on others for work. But they won't even talk to me. Most of the wealth that was left was burned in a fire. Merchants and workers took some [goods],[634] though, and crossed the great ocean in search of wealth abroad. There some had their goods become unsaleable, and some straightaway met their deaths. Some had their things stolen by robbers while they were deep in the wilderness, some had their valuables taken away by calculating customs officers as they arrived at the outskirts of cities, and some, as they arrived in trading centers, had all their goods taken away by the king's appointees on trumped-up charges. Some also stayed right where they were when they heard of the householder Bodha's death."

The merchant let out a long and deep sigh. Then he said, "Son, why don't you go to Śrāvastī?"

"Uncle, what's the use of going there?"

"Son, the householder Anāthapiṇḍada is there. His son married your sister. She'll support you."

"Uncle," he said, "if that's the case, I'll go."

The merchant gave him two *kārṣāpaṇa* coins and said, [173] "Son, take care of yourself with these while I dispose of my goods. Then we'll go together."

Svāgata tied those two *kārṣāpaṇa* coins securely in the hem of his worn-out clothes, but as a result of his [bad] karma, he forgot about them. Just as before, from some places he got food and from other places he got nothing. He was constantly tormented with hunger.

Meanwhile that merchant disposed of his goods, received other goods in exchange, and set off, forgetting about Svāgata.[635] Svāgata, nevertheless, set off along with him. Soon the members of the caravan began to quarrel and the bulls began to fight. "Friends," the members of the caravan said, "check the caravan! That Durāgata better not have come here!" While they were checking the caravan, they found him. They punched him, slapped him, and so on, grabbed him by the neck and began to throw him out.[636] While he was being thrown out, he began to wail. The caravan leader heard the commotion and began to look about. He saw that Svāgata was being thrown out.

"Friends," he said, "don't throw him out. He's the son of a friend of mine."

"Caravan leader," they said, "it's his fault that the householder Bodha's home and its many riches, with its friends, acquaintances, and relatives were all destroyed. How can we go along with him? In every respect you're the leader of this caravan, but if he goes, we're not going."

"Son, there's a large group of people here against you," the caravan leader said to him. "The members of the caravan are agitated. Follow one stage behind us. I'll put out food for you."

Svāgata stood silently [in acquiescence], his throat choked with tears.[637] And his mind, under the influence of his previous misdeeds,[638] was tormented with a grief and suffering that rivaled what he felt at the loss of his parents.

The caravan set off, and Svāgata began to follow one stage behind them. The caravan leader would tie up food for him in leaf plates and then bury some of it in the ground and hide some of it among the branches and leaves of trees. But whatever food he'd put in the ground would be eaten by jackals [and][639] other animals, and whatever food he'd put on the branches of trees would be eaten by birds and monkeys. As before, sometimes Svāgata got food and sometimes he got nothing. [174]

Now it is impossible and inconceivable that a being in his last existence should die without attaining special faculties.[640] Anyway, it was with difficulty Svāgata reached Śrāvastī. And once outside of Śrāvastī, he rested near a well.

Meanwhile a servant girl who lived near Svāgata's sister was in need of water, so she took a pot and went to that same well. She recognized Svāgata by his face. Then she stared at him for a long time and, with a face full of sadness and pity, said, "Boy, are you the son of the householder Bodha of Śuśumāragiri?"

"Sister, know that I am,"[641] he said.

With tears filling her eyes and choking her throat, she beat her chest. Then, with drawn-out words full of compassion and pity, she began to ask, "Are your parents dead?"

"Yes, they're dead."

"Your relatives?"

"Some of them died, some ran away, and some still live right where they were before but won't even talk to me."

"And your maids, servants, workers, and laborers?"

"Some of them died, some ran off, and some stayed right where they were and became dependent on others for work. But they won't even talk to me. Most of the wealth was burned in a fire. Some of it, though, was taken by other workers who crossed the great ocean in search of wealth abroad. There too, some of them were shipwrecked, some had their goods become unsaleable, and some straightaway met their deaths. Some had their things stolen by robbers while they were deep in the wilderness, some had their valuables taken away by calculating customs officers as they arrived at the outskirts of cities, and some, as they arrived in trading centers, had all their goods taken away by the king's appointees on trumped-up charges. Some also stayed right where they were when they heard of the householder Bodha's death."

She let out a long and deep sigh. Then she said, "Stay right here while I tell your sister." She then went and told her in secret.

"What kind of goods does he have?" Svāgata's sister asked. "Where are his goods from?"

"He has a stick in his hand and a begging bowl."

Svāgata's sister gave her some expensive clothes for him. Then she gave her some *kārṣāpaṇa* coins as well and said, "He should be told that if he meets up with one of his nephews or nieces he should give them these *kārṣāpaṇa* coins. That way the relatives won't get suspicious."

The servant girl took the clothes and *kārṣāpaṇa* coins, went to him, and said, [175] "These clothes and *kārṣāpaṇa* coins were sent by your sister, and she said that if you meet with one of your nephews or nieces you should give them these *kārṣāpaṇa* coins. That way the relatives won't get suspicious."

"This is excellent," he said. And with that said, he remained silent. The girl left. Then he reflected, "The householder Anāthapiṇḍada has a large immediate family. My father also has a large family." Then he thought about having to talk with each of them one by one.[642] "My sister will talk for a long time," he reflected. Pained with hunger, and tired and exhausted from the road, he just couldn't do it. "I'll get something to eat first. When I'm satisfied, I'll be able to speak more easily." Then he went to a liquor store, and there he drank some alcohol that gets one very drunk. Once he was drunk, he went to a park and fell asleep.

It's quite common in Śrāvastī for thieves to go roaming through the parks every day. If they see a man sleeping, they kick him. If he wakes up, they tell him, "Hey you, haven't you heard that in Śrāvastī thieves go roaming through the parks every day?" If they see a man sleeping, they tell him to get up and go. If he doesn't wake up, they rob him and take off.

So the thieves kicked Svāgata, but he didn't wake up. Then they robbed him and left. When the intoxication wore off and he woke up, he saw that he was covered with the same worn-out clothes.

Meanwhile his sister reflected, "He's really late. There must be a reason for it." She sent the girl off again. "Girl, go," she said. "He's late. See why he hasn't come." She went and saw that he'd been robbed and was still in the same old clothes. She hurried back and told her, "Miss, he's been robbed and he's still in the same old clothes."

She reflected, "It's his fault that the householder Bodha's home and its many riches, with its friends, acquaintances, and relatives, were all destroyed. If I allow him to enter here, given the situation, my[643] father-in-law's house will straightaway meet disaster. He can't be allowed to enter." With this in mind, she also scorned him.

Svāgata Joins the Beggars

As for Svāgata, because of his previous misdeeds he forgot [about his sister]. Instead, he joined some other beggars. [176] Wherever they entered for alms, they were abused and thrown out. Disappointed, with empty hands and empty bowls, they came and sat in empty temples and pavilions and at the roots of trees.

"Friends," they asked each other, "in the past wherever we'd go we'd always come back with our hands full and our bowls full. Now what's happened? Why do we come back disappointed, with empty hands and empty bowls?"

"Some ill-fated person must have joined us," some of them said. "That's why we come back here with empty hands and empty bowls."

"That's right," the others said. "Let's divide into two and then enter [the city for alms]."

On the following day, they divided into two groups and entered [the city for alms]. Those whom Svāgata was among were abused and thrown out just as before. Disappointed, they returned with empty hands and empty bowls. But the others came back with their hands full and bowls full. Those who came back with empty hands and empty bowls once again divided into two groups and entered [the city for alms]. Those whom Svāgata was among came back with empty hands and bowls empty just as before. In this way, they divided into two groups again and again until eventually Svāgata and another beggar entered [the city for alms] and came back with empty hands and empty bowls, while the others came back with their hands full and bowls full. Then all the beggars began to converse among themselves.

"Friends, this ill-fated person has joined us! That's why we come back with empty hands and empty bowls. Let's throw him out!" So they beat him soundly, broke a begging bowl over his head, and then threw him out.

Meanwhile the householder Anāthapiṇḍada invited the community of monks led by the Buddha into his home for a meal. He ordered the doorkeeper, "Don't let any beggars enter until the community of monks led by the Buddha has finished eating. I'll feed them afterward." All those beggars who relied on his house [for food] gathered together and began to enter. The doorkeeper stopped them.

"Friend," they said, "it's because of us that this householder is well known as the householder Anāthapiṇḍada (Almsgiver to the Poor). What is this? Why are you stopping us from entering?" [177]

"The householder has given an order," he said, "that no beggars are to be allowed to enter until the community of monks led by the Buddha has finished eating. He'll feed you afterward."

"Friends," they said, "we've never been stopped here before. Have a look for him! That unwelcome one better not have come here!"[644] And so they began to search. Eventually they found him hiding. Then they began to shout, "Friends, the unwelcome one is hiding here!" They beat him soundly, threw him out, and in a fit of rage whacked him on the head with a begging bowl, breaking his skull. He backed off and began to cry.[645] Then they grabbed him by his hands and feet and threw him on a pile of garbage. "Durāgata, stay here!" they said. With his blood streaming out, he stayed right there on that pile of garbage.

Svāgata Meets the Buddha

Now in the morning the Blessed One got dressed, took his bowl and robe, and leading the community of monks that surrounded him, approached the householder Anāthapiṇḍada's home. The Blessed One saw Svāgata lying on that pile of garbage. His fingers were rough and dirty, his hair was long, and his body was smeared with dirt; he was skinny, with hardly any strength, and he was wearing dirty, tattered clothes. Blood was streaming from his broken head, as flies attacked the wounds all over his body. At the sight of him, the Blessed One addressed the monks: "Rejoice, monks, in rebirths in all realms of existence! Rejoice in the means for rebirth in all realms of existence! For this is the condition of a being in his last existence."[646]

Then the Blessed One addressed Svāgata: "My son, would you like the leftover food from an almsbowl?"

"Yes, Blessed One. I'd like it."

Then the Blessed One addressed the venerable Ānanda: "Ānanda, set aside some of the food in your bowl for Svāgata."

"Yes, Bhadanta," the venerable Ānanda replied, consenting to the Blessed One's request.

The Blessed One then approached the place where the householder Anāthapiṇḍada was offering food. Having approached, he sat down in front of the community of monks in the seat specially prepared for him. When the householder Anāthapiṇḍada was sure that the community of monks led by the Buddha was comfortably seated, he served and indulged them, [178] with his own hands, with hard and soft foods, both fresh and fine.[647] When he had served and indulged them, with his own hands, with many courses of hard and soft foods, both fresh and fine, and was sure that the Blessed One had finished eating, washed his hands, and set aside his bowl, he then sat down in front of the Blessed One, taking a lower seat, to listen to the dharma. The venerable Ānanda, however, forgot to set aside some of the food in his bowl for Svāgata.[648]

It is the nature of lord buddhas that they are always alert. Then the Blessed One stood up. As the venerable Ānanda began to take the Blessed One's bowl, he saw that in the bowl some food had been carefully set aside.[649] At the sight of this, his memory came back to him. Since he possessed the essence of dharma through the words [of the Blessed One], he began to cry.[650]

"Ānanda, why are you crying?" the Blessed One asked.

"Bhadanta," he said, "I've never violated an order of the Blessed One before."

"What did you do?"

"I didn't set aside any food in my bowl for Svāgata."

"Ānanda," the Blessed One said, "it's not that you weren't mindful of my order. The deeds that Svāgata himself [has performed and accumulated][651] have now come together, and their conditions have matured. They remain before him like an oncoming flood and will certainly come to pass. That's why you forgot. Don't be sad anymore. Go, call for him to come here."

The venerable Ānanda went and began to call for him. Many people responded. Svāgata had also forgotten that the Blessed One had promised to have some almsfood set aside for him. He reflected, "Who is this person of meritorious karma that the Blessed One, the teacher of the three worlds, pays attention to and calls for?"

Then the venerable Ānanda went and informed the Blessed One. "Blessed One, when I said Svāgata (Welcome) many people responded. I don't know whom to call for."

"Go, Ānanda," the Blessed One said. "Go and say that Svāgata, the son of the householder Bodha of Śuśumāragiri, should come forward."

The venerable Ānanda went there and said in a loud voice, "Svāgata, the son of the householder Bodha of Śuśumāragiri, should come forward."

When Svāgata heard his father's name, he remembered his own name. After getting up slowly, with the help of a walking stick, he uttered these verses:

> The name "Svāgata" is long gone.
> How could it have followed me here? [179]
> My misfortune must be finished.
> Good fortune must be on the way.
>
> You are all-knowing, the master
> of those who take refuge in you.
> Welcome are those noble ones
> who delight in your teachings.
>
> But I have no luck.
> I'm shunned by all my relatives.
> I am wretched and pitiable,
> struck as I am by the arrow of grief.

The venerable Ānanda then took Svāgata and approached the Blessed One. Having approached, he said this to the Blessed One: "This, Bhadanta, is Svāgata." Then the Blessed One consoled Svāgata, who was tormented with hunger, and said, "Son, eat the food that is left in this bowl."

When Svāgata saw it, he reflected, "It's fortunate that the Blessed One, the teacher of the three worlds, has turned his attention to me. But only a little bit of food has been set aside in his bowl. What will I eat?"

The Blessed One, knowing Svāgata's thoughts with his mind, said, "My child, even if your stomach were as vast as the ocean and you ate handfuls of food the size of Mount Sumeru, this food in my bowl would never diminish, it would never be exhausted. So eat as you like until you're satisfied."

Svāgata ate until he was satisfied. When he was brought back to his senses, he began to stare intently at the Blessed One's face.

The Blessed One said, "Svāgata, my child, are you satisfied?"

"I'm satisfied, Blessed One."

"If that is so, my child, then take this last mouthful of food and my bowl will disappear."

When Svāgata took that last mouthful of food, the bowl disappeared. The Blessed One then assigned the reward from the offering and departed.[652]

That being who was in his last existence followed close behind the Blessed One until the Blessed One entered the monastery and sat down in front of the community of monks in the seat specially prepared for him. Svāgata, in turn, venerated with his head the feet of the Blessed One and then sat down at a respectful distance.

The Blessed One reflected, "I will send him for flowers. His [bad] karma must be destroyed."

With this in mind, he addressed Svāgata: "Svāgata, my child, do you have any *kārṣāpaṇa* coins?"

"No, I don't, Blessed One."

"Svāgata, my child, look in the hem of your clothes."

He began to search in the hem of his clothes, and he found two *kārṣāpaṇa* coins. "Blessed One," he said, "I have two *kārṣāpaṇa* coins."

"My child, go and get some blue lotuses from the gardener Gaṇḍaka and then come back."[653]

Svāgata then approached the gardener Gaṇḍaka. [180] Seeing him coming from a distance, he was exasperated. "That unwelcome Durāgata has come!" he reflected. "Surely this means misfortune for me." With this in mind, he shouted, "Hey Durāgata! Why are you coming here?"

Then Svāgata uttered this verse:

> I need blue lotuses,
> not any other kind of lotus.

For I have been sent by the best of sages,
who is renowned and all-knowing.

After saying these words, he turned around and began to leave. Then the gardener Gaṇḍaka uttered this verse:

Come! Please come if you're a messenger
of that sage who is tranquil at heart!
He is worthy of the honor of gods and mortals,
and worthy of the honor of the most honorable as well.

Following these words, he said, "Are you a messenger of the Buddha?"

"Yes, I'm a messenger of the Buddha."

"Why have you come?"

"For flowers."

"If you're a messenger of the Buddha, take whatever you like."

So Svāgata collected a bundle of blue lotuses and then approached the Blessed One.

"My child," the Blessed One said, "distribute them to the monks."

He began to distribute them to the monks, but the monks wouldn't accept them.

"Monks," the Blessed One said, "accept this most fragrant of things. His [bad] karma must be destroyed by what he sees."[654]

So the monks accepted them, and when they accepted them, they bloomed.

In the past Svāgata had practiced the extraordinary type of meditation known as blue *kṛtsna*.[655] And now as he stood in the area of the elders and saw those flowers and began to consider them closely, that blue *kṛtsna* appeared to him again.

Then the Blessed One said to him, "My child, won't you go forth as a monk?"

"Yes, Blessed One," he said. "I'll go forth as a monk."

The Blessed One initiated and ordained him and gave him a subject for contemplation. After striving, struggling, and straining, he came to understand that ever-turning five-spoked wheel of saṃsāra; he dealt a final blow to rebirth in all realms of saṃsāra, since they are subject to decay and decline, scattering and destruction; and by ridding himself of all defilements, he directly experienced arhatship. Becoming an arhat,

he was free from attachment in the three realms
  [of desire, form, and formlessness];
he regarded clods of earth and gold as equal in value;
he possessed equanimity toward the sky
  and the palm of his hand;
he didn't distinguish between being cut by a blade
  and being anointed with sandalwood paste;
the eggshell of his ignorance was broken by knowledge;
he obtained the special knowledges, superhuman faculties,
  and analytic insights;
and he was averse to worldly attainments, temptations,
  and honors.
He became worthy of respect, honor, and obeisance
  from the gods, including Indra and Upendra. [181]

Having attained arhatship, he experienced the pleasure of liberation, and at that time, he uttered these verses:

Out of compassion, the hero,
the seer of what is real,
bound me in the snares of his skillful means
and lifted me from suffering,
like an old elephant from the mud.

I was Svāgata (Welcome),
then later Durāgata (Unwelcome).

I came at first, Master,
when I heard your great teachings.[656]

I am now Svāgata (Welcome), evidently,
no longer Durāgata (Unwelcome).
I will now maintain this body,
which is golden and free from corruptions.[657]

I have obtained the [three] jewels![658]
For those who desire heaven and liberation,
it is always best to associate with virtuous friends,
since they wish to benefit others.

The Buddha Goes to Śuśumāragiri

When the venerable Svāgata had gone forth as a monk according to the dharma and monastic discipline that have been so well expressed, word spread all around that the ascetic Gautama had initiated the unwelcome beggar Durāgata as a monk. Heretics heard this, and they were rude, abusive, and disrespectful. "The ascetic Gautama has said that his order instills faith all around. But how is this supposed to instill faith all around? Now beggars, even ones like Durāgata, go forth as monks in it!"

Meanwhile there is nothing that lord buddhas do not know, see, realize, and understand. So the Blessed One reflected, "When there is a senior disciple who is great like Mount Sumeru, many people experience faith. Hence Svāgata's virtues should be manifested.[659] But where should it be done? In that very place where he fell [from welcome]." With this in mind, he addressed Ānanda: "Ānanda, go and inform the monks as follows—'The Tathāgata, monks, will travel through the Bharga countryside. Whoever among you is eager to travel through the Bharga countryside with the Tathāgata should take up his robes.'"

"Yes, Bhadanta," the venerable Ānanda replied, consenting to the

Blessed One's request. Then he announced to the monks, "Venerable Ones, the Blessed One will travel through the Bharga countryside. Whoever among you is eager to travel through the Bharga countryside with the Blessed One should take up his robes." [182]

Now the Blessed One was self-controlled
and his followers were self-controlled,
he was calm and his followers were calm,
he was liberated and his followers were liberated,
he was confident and his followers were confident,
he was disciplined and his followers were disciplined,
he was an arhat and his followers were arhats,
he was without attachment
and his followers were without attachment,
and he instilled faith and his followers instilled faith.

He was like a bull surrounded by a herd of cows,
like a royal elephant surrounded by a herd of elephant cubs,
like a lion surrounded by a carnivorous pack,
like a royal goose surrounded by a gaggle of geese,
like an eagle surrounded by a flock of birds,
like a learned brahman surrounded by an assembly of students,
like an eminent doctor surrounded by a group of patients,
like a warrior surrounded by a troop of soldiers,
like a guide surrounded by a group of travelers,[660]
like a caravan leader surrounded by a company of merchants,
like a guildmaster surrounded by townspeople,
like a vassal king surrounded by a cabinet of ministers,
like a wheel-turning king surrounded by a thousand sons,
like the moon surrounded by a constellation of stars,
like the sun surrounded by a thousand rays of light,
like the great king Dhṛtarāṣṭra surrounded by a group
of celestial musicians,

like the great king Virūḍhaka surrounded by a group
of *kumbhāṇḍa*s,
like the great king Virūpākṣa surrounded by a group of nāgas,
like the great king Dhanada surrounded by a group of yakṣas,
like Vemacitrin surrounded by a group of antigods,
like Śakra surrounded by a group of gods,
and like Brahmā surrounded by the gods of Brahmakāyika
(Brahmā's Assembly).

He was like an ocean but calm,
like a cloud but full of water,
and like a mighty elephant but without pride or passion.
His senses were well restrained,
his deportment and demeanor were unflappable,
he was adorned with the thirty-two marks of a great man,
and his body was radiant with the eighty minor marks.
His form was adorned with a halo extending an arm's length,
his brilliance was greater than a thousand suns,
and like a mountain of jewels that moved,
he was beautiful from every side.

He was endowed with the ten powers,
the four confidences,
the three special applications of mindfulness,
and great compassion.

Surrounded by great disciples such as Ājñāta Kauṇḍinya, Bāṣpa, Mahānāma, Aniruddha, Śāriputra, Maudgalyāyana, Kāśyapa, Ānanda, and Raivata, the Blessed One, together with a large community of monks, approached Śuśumāragiri. He then continued traveling until he eventually arrived in Śuśumāragiri. Once in Śuśumāragiri, he settled down at the deer park in the Bhīṣaṇikā (Frightening) Grove.

The brahmans and householders of Śuśumāragiri heard that the

Blessed One, after traveling through the Bharga countryside, had now arrived in Śuśumāragiri, and that now in Śuśumāragiri, he was staying in the deer park at the Bhīṣaṇikā Grove. Having heard this, they gathered and assembled—community joining community, group joining group—left Śuśumāragiri, and approached the Blessed One. [183] Having approached, they venerated with their heads the feet of the Blessed One and then sat down at a respectful distance. The Blessed One instructed, incited, inspired, and delighted the brahmans and householders of Śuśumāragiri with a discourse on the dharma. After he instructed, incited, inspired, and delighted them in many ways with this discourse on the dharma, he became silent. The brahmans and householders of Śuśumāragiri then got up from their seats, properly arranged their robes on one shoulder, bowed toward the Blessed One with their hands respectfully folded, and said this to the Blessed One: "May the Blessed One, along with the community of monks, accept this invitation to eat in our homes tomorrow."

The Blessed One accepted the invitation of the brahmans and householders of Śuśumāragiri with his silence. Then the brahmans and householders of Śuśumāragiri, realizing that by his silence the Blessed One had accepted their invitation, rejoiced and delighted in the words of the Blessed One, venerated with their heads the feet of the Blessed One, and then left the Blessed One's presence.

That very night the brahmans and householders of Śuśumāragiri prepared hard and soft foods, both fresh and fine, and then at daybreak they got up, prepared the seats, and distributed pitchers of water. Then they had a messenger inform the Blessed One that it was now the appropriate time: "It is time, Bhadanta. The food is ready. Now the Blessed One may do as the time permits."

Later in the morning the Blessed One got dressed, took his bowl and robe, and leading the community of monks that surrounded him, approached the place where the brahmans and householders of Śuśumāragiri were offering food. Having approached, he sat down in the seat specially prepared for him.

Now when the brahmans and householders of Śuśumāragiri were sure that the community of monks led by the Buddha was comfortably seated, they served and indulged them, with their own hands, with hard and soft foods, both fresh and fine. When they had served and indulged them, with their own hands, with many courses of hard and soft foods, both fresh and fine, and were sure that the Blessed One had finished eating, washed his hands, and set aside his bowl, they then sat down in front of the Blessed One, taking lower seats, to listen to the dharma.

Then the Blessed One instructed, incited, inspired, and delighted the brahmans and householders of Śuśumāragiri with a discourse on the dharma. [184] After he instructed, incited, inspired, and delighted them in many ways with this discourse on the dharma, he became silent.

Svāgata and the Nāga Aśvatīrthika

Now the brahmans and householders of Śuśumāragiri said this to the Blessed One: "Bhadanta, the Blessed One has subdued evil nāgas and evil yakṣas in many towns and in many countries. The nāga Aśvatīrthika (Guardian where Horses Ford)[661] is hateful though we're not hateful, hostile though we're not hostile, and malicious though we're not malicious. He always destroys our crops as soon as they arise, and he does the same to our women and men, boys and girls, cows and buffaloes, goats and rams. How good it would be if the Blessed One, out of compassion for us, would subdue him!"

The Blessed One agreed to the request of the brahmans and householders of Śuśumāragiri; he agreed to their request with his silence. Now after the Blessed One had agreed to the request of the brahmans and householders of Śuśumāragiri, he got up from his seat and departed. Then the Blessed One went to the monastery and sat down in front of the community of monks in the seat specially prepared for him. After sitting down, the Blessed One addressed the venerable

Ānanda: "Ānanda, go and inform the monks as follows—'Whoever among you is eager to subdue the nāga Aśvatīrthika should take a tally stick.' Then distribute the tally sticks."

"Yes, Bhadanta," the venerable Ānanda replied, consenting to the Blessed One's request. Then he made the announcement to the community of monks and began to distribute the tally sticks among the community of monks led by the Buddha. The Blessed One, however, didn't take a tally stick. Then the senior monks began to focus their attention on why the Blessed One hadn't taken a tally stick. They saw that he wanted the venerable Svāgata's virtues to be manifested, so they didn't take any either.

Then the venerable Svāgata began to focus his attention on why the Blessed One didn't take a tally stick nor did any of the most senior monks. He saw that the Blessed One wanted his virtues to be manifested. "I shall fulfill the wish of the teacher," he thought. "I shall take a tally stick." Then he got up halfway out of his seat, stretched out his arm, which was like the trunk of an elephant, and took a tally stick.

Now lord buddhas will ask questions even though they know the answers. So the Lord Buddha asked the venerable Ānanda, [185] "Ānanda, which monk took a tally stick?"

"Svāgata did, Bhadanta," he said.

"Ānanda," the Blessed One said, "go and tell the monk Svāgata that this nāga is evil and that he should protect himself from physical harm."

"Yes, Bhadanta," the venerable Ānanda replied, consenting to the Blessed One's request. Then he approached the venerable Svāgata and, having approached, said this: "Venerable Svāgata, the Blessed One has said that this nāga is evil and that you should protect yourself from physical harm."

"Venerable Ānanda," he said, "the teacher's order is not to be violated. Even if Jambudvīpa (Black Plum Island) were filled with nāgas like Aśvatīrthika, crowded together like sugarcane, bamboo, and reeds, they still wouldn't be able to move even a single hair on my body. So how will the nāga Aśvatīrthika cause me physical harm?"

The venerable Ānanda wished him good health and departed.

Now in the morning, after that night had passed, the venerable Svāgata got dressed, took his bowl and robe, and entered Śuśumāragiri for alms. After wandering through Śuśumāragiri for alms, he approached the home of the nāga Aśvatīrthika. The nāga Aśvatīrthika saw the venerable Svāgata from a distance, and at the sight of him, he reflected, "Has this foolish ascetic heard news that I'm dead? Is that why he comes to my home?" Then again he reflected, "He is a visitor. Let him come and stay for a while."

The venerable Svāgata then went to the nāga Aśvatīrthika's pond, set down his bowl and robe off to one side, washed his feet, cleaned his hands, strained some water, collected some dried out leaves, sat down, and then began to eat his food. The nāga Aśvatīrthika ignored him, however, since he considered him a guest. The venerable Svāgata reflected, "Evil nāgas that aren't irritated cannot be tamed. Therefore, I'll irritate him." He then washed his bowl and threw the dishwater into the pond.

The nāga Aśvatīrthika got irritated. "I ignored this ascetic when he arrived," he reflected. "I even ignored him while he was eating. But now he's thrown filthy dishwater into my home!" Seething with anger, he thought, "Only his name will be left after I get through with him!" He then rose up high into the sky [186] and began to hurl weapons such as the discus, spear, battle ax, and javelin upon the venerable Svāgata.

But the venerable Svāgata had entered into a state of loving kindness. As a result, those weapons turned into divine blue, red, and white lotuses, lilies, and coral-tree flowers, and fell [harmlessly, as offerings,] on his body.[662] The nāga Aśvatīrthika then began to let loose a rain of hot coal. This turned into flowers from the divine coral tree, and they too began to fall [harmlessly, as offerings,] on the venerable Svāgata's body. Then the nāga Aśvatīrthika began to send forth a rain of dust. It turned into divine *agaru* powder, sandalwood powder, and *tamāla*-leaf powder, and began to fall [just as the others did]. Then the nāga Aśvatīrthika, as a result of his overwhelming anger, began to emit smoke. The venerable Svāgata, as a result of his magical powers, also began to emit smoke. Then the nāga Aśvatīrthika, as a result of his overwhelming anger, began to emit fire. The venerable Svāgata then entered into the state of mastery over the element of fire. Once this happened, as a result of the nāga Aśvatīrthika's anger and the venerable Svāgata's magical powers, a tremendous flash of light appeared.

When the brahmans and householders of Śuśumāragiri saw this, they got excited and began to look here and there. "Friends," they said, "the Blessed One is subduing the nāga Aśvatīrthika! Come on, let's have a look!"

Many hundreds and thousands of beings went out to look. Monks were standing right there as well, and they also began to look at that great light. Then the Blessed One addressed the monks: "Monks, this monk Svāgata is foremost among those monks that are my disciples who repeatedly attain mastery over the element of fire."

When the nāga Aśvatīrthika's pride and arrogance had disappeared and his arsenal of weapons was exhausted, he began to flee. The venerable Svāgata then magically created fire all around him. In whichever direction the nāga Aśvatīrthika turned, he saw that it was on fire and ablaze, that it flared into a single fiery mass. Frightened by this magically created fire in front of him and behind him, he saw that he had no protection and was unsafe everywhere—except for the area around the venerable Svāgata. There it was safe and cool. So he approached the venerable Svāgata [187] and, having approached, said this to him: "Enough, Bhadanta Svāgata! Why do you torment me?"

"Subject to old age as I am,"[663] he said, "I wouldn't torment you. Yet you torment me. If I hadn't amassed so many virtues, you would have reduced me today to nothing more than a name."

"Bhadanta Svāgata," he said, "command me. What should I do?"

"Friend, go to the Blessed One and accept from him the taking of the refuges as well as the precepts."

"Very well, Bhadanta Svāgata," he said. "I'll do so."

Then the venerable Svāgata took the nāga Aśvatīrthika and

approached the Blessed One. Having approached, he venerated with his head the feet of the Blessed One and then sat down at a respectful distance. Sitting down at a respectful distance, the venerable Svāgata said this to the Blessed One: "This is the nāga Aśvatīrthika."

Then the Blessed One addressed the nāga Aśvatīrthika: "Friend, because of your depravity in the past you were reborn in this lower, animal realm. So now you're intent on death and destruction. You take the lives of others. You live by endangering the lives of others. After you die and fall from this existence, what will be your destiny? What kind of rebirth will you have? What will be your future?"

"Blessed One," he said, "command me. What should I do?"

"Accept from me the taking of the refuges as well as the precepts," the Blessed One said. "And offer safety to the brahmans and householders of Śuśumāragiri."

"I take refuge in the Blessed One and I accept the precepts," he said. "And from this day onward, I offer safety to the brahmans and householders of Śuśumāragiri."

Then the brahmans and householders of Śuśumāragiri took a large offering and approached the Blessed One. Having approached, they venerated with their heads the feet of the Blessed One and then sat down at a respectful distance. Sitting down at a respectful distance, the brahmans and householders of Śuśumāragiri said this to the Blessed One: "Bhadanta, has the Blessed One subdued the nāga Aśvatīrthika?"

"Brahmans and householders," the Blessed One said, "I haven't subdued the nāga Aśvatīrthika. The monk Svāgata has."

"Which monk, Bhadanta?"

"One who is a resident of this very place—the son of the householder Bodha."

Now people in the world desire success and spurn misfortune.

"He's my brother's son," some of them said. [188]

"He's my sister's son," others said.

"He's my friend's son," still others said.

Then the brahmans and householders of Śuśumāragiri got up from their seats, properly arranged their robes on one shoulder, bowed toward the Blessed One with their hands respectfully folded, and said this to the Blessed One: "On behalf of Bhadanta Svāgata, may the Blessed One, along with the community of monks, accept food from us for seven days."

The Blessed One accepted the invitation of the brahmans and householders of Śuśumāragiri with his silence. Then the brahmans and householders of Śuśumāragiri, realizing that by his silence the Blessed One had accepted their invitation, venerated with their heads the feet of the Blessed One, and left the Blessed One's presence.

Svāgata and the Elephant's Liquor

Now in Śuśumāragiri there had been a brahman named Ahituṇḍika (Snake Charmer) who was a friend of the householder Bodha, but he'd fled out of fear of the nāga Aśvatīrthika and gone to Śrāvastī. There King Prasenajit of Kośala placed him in charge of liquor for the elephants.[664] One day he came to Śuśumāragiri on some business and heard that the monk Svāgata, the son of the householder Bodha, had subdued the nāga Aśvatīrthika. After hearing this, he approached the venerable Svāgata. Having approached, he venerated with his head the feet of the venerable Svāgata and then sat down at a respectful distance. The brahman then said this to the venerable Svāgata: "May the noble Svāgata accept this invitation to eat at my home tomorrow."

"Brahman," the venerable Svāgata said, "it's on my account that the brahmans and householders of Śuśumāragiri have invited the community of monks led by the Buddha to eat with them for seven days. Therefore I can't accept your invitation."

"Noble one, if you can't accept my invitation now," the brahman said, "then at least when you're in Śrāvastī partake of alms from my home before any other."

"And so it shall be," he said.

Then the brahman venerated his feet and departed.

Now after the Blessed One had stayed in Śuśumāragiri as long as he pleased, he set off traveling toward Śrāvastī. Traveling along, he eventually arrived in Śrāvastī. Once in Śrāvastī, he settled down in the Jeta Grove in the park of Anāthapiṇḍada. The householder Anāthapiṇḍada heard that the Blessed One, [189] after traveling through the Bharga countryside, had now arrived in Śrāvastī and was staying right there in his very own park. Having heard this, he left Śrāvastī and approached the Blessed One. Having approached, he venerated with his head the feet of the Blessed One and then sat down at a respectful distance. The Blessed One instructed, incited, inspired, and delighted the householder Anāthapiṇḍada who was seated at a respectful distance with a discourse on the dharma. After he instructed, incited, inspired, and delighted him in many ways with this discourse on the dharma, he became silent. The householder Anāthapiṇḍada then got up from his seat, properly arranged his robe on one shoulder, bowed toward the Blessed One with his hands respectfully folded, and said this to the Blessed One: "May the Blessed One, along with the community of monks, accept this invitation to eat at my home tomorrow."

With his silence, the Blessed One accepted the householder Anāthapiṇḍada's invitation. Then the householder Anāthapiṇḍada, realizing that by his silence the Blessed One had accepted his invitation, rejoiced and delighted in the words of the Blessed One, venerated with his head the feet of the Blessed One, and left the Blessed One's presence.

The brahman Ahituṇḍika also heard that the Blessed One, after traveling through the Bharga countryside, had now arrived in Śrāvastī and was staying right there in the Jeta Grove in the park of Anāthapiṇḍada. Having heard this, he approached the venerable Svāgata and, having approached, said this to him: "May the noble one accept this invitation to eat at my home tomorrow."

With his silence, the venerable Svāgata accepted that brahman's invitation. Then that brahman, realizing that by his silence the venerable Svāgata had accepted his invitation, got up from his seat and departed.

That very night the householder Anāthapiṇḍada prepared hard and soft foods, both fresh and fine, and then at daybreak he got up, prepared the seats, and distributed pitchers of water. Then he had a messenger inform the Blessed One that it was now the appropriate time: "It is time, Bhadanta. The food is ready. Now the Blessed One may do as the time permits."

Later in the morning the Blessed One got dressed, took his bowl and robe, and leading the community of monks that surrounded him, approached the householder Anāthapiṇḍada's home.

As for that brahman, he had prepared rich foods for the venerable Svāgata. In the morning the venerable Svāgata got dressed, took his bowl and robe, and approached that brahman's home. [190] Having approached, he sat down in the seat specially prepared for him. When the venerable Svāgata was sitting at a respectful distance,[665] the brahman served him rich foods. Then the brahman reflected, "The noble Svāgata has eaten rich foods that he won't be able to digest. I'll offer him a drink [to help with his digestion]." With this in mind, he said this to the venerable Svāgata: "Noble one, the food you have eaten is rich. Have something to drink. A drink will help your digestion."

"Very well," he said. "I'll do so."

The brahman Ahituṇḍika prepared a drink for the venerable Svāgata and then placed a finger of elephant's liquor in it.[666]

Now the knowledge and insight of arhats does not operate unless they focus their attention. And so the venerable Svāgata drank that drink. Then he assigned the reward from the offering and left for the marketplace in Śrāvastī, which was covered with grass mats. After he passed the marketplace, he was overcome[667] by the sun's heat and shaken by the alcohol. He collapsed on the ground.

Now lord buddhas are always alert. So the Blessed One magically created a leaf hut [over the venerable Svāgata] so that no one would see him and refute their faith in the teachings.

When Anāthapiṇḍada was sure that the community of monks led by the Buddha was comfortably seated, he served and indulged them, with his own hands, with hard and soft foods, both fresh and fine. When he had served and indulged them, with his own hands, with many courses of food, and was sure that the Blessed One had finished eating, washed his hands, and set aside his bowl, he then sat down in front of the Blessed One, taking a lower seat, to listen to the dharma. The Blessed One instructed, incited, inspired, and delighted the householder Anāthapiṇḍada with a discourse on the dharma, then got up from his seat and departed. Eventually he arrived at that place [where the monk Svāgata was]. Then the Blessed One withdrew those magical powers that he had activated and addressed the monks: "Monks, this is the monk Svāgata who subdued the fierce nāga Aśvatīrthika. Now could he even take the poison out of food that has gone bad?"[668]

"No, Bhadanta."

"Monks, there are these and other transgressions involved in drinking alcohol. That is why monks should not drink or distribute alcohol."

Then the Blessed One woke up the venerable Svāgata, who was sleeping off the alcohol's effects, and said this: "Svāgata, what is this?"

"Lack of attention, Blessed One. Lack of attention, Sugata."

Then the Blessed One took the venerable Svāgata, [191] went to the monastery, and sat down in front of the community of monks in the seat specially prepared for him.[669] After he sat down, he addressed the monks: "Monks, those who regard me as an authority[670] shouldn't drink or distribute alcohol, even the tiny amount on the tip of a blade of *kuśa* grass."

Those monks in doubt asked the Lord Buddha, the remover of all doubts, "Bhadanta, what deed did the venerable Svāgata do so that he was born in a family that was rich, wealthy, and prosperous? What deed did he do so that he became a beggar and came to be known as the unwelcome Durāgata? What deed did he do so that he went forth as a monk in the Blessed One's order, rid himself of all defilements, and thereby directly experienced arhatship, and then was recognized as being foremost of those who repeatedly attain mastery over the element of fire?"

"Monks," the Blessed One said, "the deeds that the monk Svāgata himself has performed and accumulated have now come together, and their conditions have matured. They remain before him like an oncoming flood and will certainly come to pass. Those deeds were performed and accumulated by Svāgata. Who else will experience their results? For those deeds that are performed and accumulated, monks, do not mature outside of oneself, neither in the element of earth nor in the element of water, in the element of fire or in the element of wind. Instead, those deeds that are done, both good and bad, mature in the aggregates, elements, and sense bases that are appropriated when one is reborn.

Actions never come to naught,
even after hundreds of millions of years.
When the right conditions gather and the time is right,
then they will have their effect on embodied beings."

The Householder and the Solitary Buddha

Long ago, monks, in a certain market town, there lived a householder who was rich, wealthy, and prosperous, with vast and extensive holdings. Truly, he rivaled the god Vaiśravaṇa in wealth. One day, surrounded by his friends, acquaintances, and relatives as well as his immediate family, he went out to a park.

When no buddhas are born, solitary buddhas can arise in the world. They have pity for the poor and neglected, they live in remote areas, and they alone are worthy of people's offerings.

Meanwhile a certain solitary buddha, after traveling through the countryside, arrived in that market town. Sick from the exhaustion of traveling and from an imbalance of his bodily humors, he entered the park in search of alms. The householder was exasperated when he saw him. [192]

"Gentlemen!" he ordered his men. "Throw out this renunciant!"

None of them dared to throw him out.

The householder was furious. So with his own hands, he grabbed that great being by the neck and threw him out. "Go live among the beggars!" he said to him.

The solitary buddha was very weak and fell to the ground. He reflected, "This poor householder is [spiritually] beaten and battered. He should be rescued." With this in mind, he rose up high into the sky and began to perform the miraculous deeds of causing fire and heat, making rain and lightning.

Magic quickly wins over the ordinary person. Like a tree cut down at the roots, the householder fell prostrate at his feet[671] and said, "Come down! Come down, O you who are worthy of great offerings! Offer me a helping hand, for I am mired in the mud of depravity!"

Out of kindness for the householder, the solitary buddha came down. Then the householder honored him with offerings and made this fervent aspiration: "Although I have committed an offense against someone so worthy of offerings from good people, may I not suffer from this deed. But since I have also performed a good deed, by this root of virtue may I be reborn in a family that is rich, wealthy, and prosperous; and may I obtain such virtues so that I may please and not displease a teacher even more distinguished than this one!"

Coda

"What do you think, monks?" the Blessed One said. "That householder was none other than the monk Svāgata at that time and at that juncture. Since he served a solitary buddha, he was reborn in a family that was rich, wealthy, and prosperous. Since he committed an offense against him, he became a beggar for five hundred births. Even now, even in his last existence, he became a beggar once again. Since he made a fervent aspiration, he went forth as a monk in my order, rid himself of all defilements, and thereby directly experienced arhatship. And as his teacher, one who is more distinguished than hundreds and thousands and millions of solitary buddhas, I have been pleased and not displeased by him. In the past he had gone forth as a monk under the perfectly awakened lord Kāśyapa, renouncing in the presence of that monk whom the perfectly awakened lord Kāśyapa recognized as being foremost of those who repeatedly attain mastery over the element of fire. At that time he practiced the religious life for as long as he lived but never amassed many virtues. At the time of his death, he made a fervent aspiration: [193]

> Since I have followed the religious life for as long as I've lived under the unsurpassed perfectly awakened lord Kāśyapa, who is worthy of great offerings, by this root of virtue may the perfectly awakened lord Kāśyapa make the following prediction about the brahman Uttara (Higher): "When people live for one hundred years, brahman, you will be a perfectly awakened tathāgata arhat named Śākyamuni." And may I go forth as a monk in his order and, by ridding myself of all defilements, directly experience arhatship. In the same way that the perfectly awakened lord Kāśyapa recognized my teacher as being foremost of those who repeatedly attain mastery over the element of fire, may the lord Śākyamuni, the sovereign of the Śākyas, recognize me as being foremost of those who repeatedly attain mastery over the element of fire.

"Now, by the power of this fervent aspiration, the Tathāgata has recognized him as being foremost of those who repeatedly attain mastery over the element of fire.

"And so, monks, the result of absolutely evil actions is absolutely evil, the result of absolutely pure actions is absolutely pure, and the result of mixed actions is mixed. Therefore, monks, because of this, you should reject absolutely evil actions and mixed ones as well, and strive to perform only absolutely pure actions. It is this, monks, that you should learn to do."

This was said by the Blessed One. With their minds uplifted, the monks welcomed the words of the Blessed One.

So ends the *Svāgata-avadāna,* the thirteenth chapter in the glorious *Divyāvadāna.*

14. The Story of a Wretched Pig

SŪKARIKA-AVADĀNA

It is a law of nature that when a divine being is destined to fall from divine existence, five omens appear—his unsoiled clothes get soiled; his unwithered garlands wither; a bad smell emerges from his body; sweat appears in both of his armpits; and, lastly, a divine being destined to fall takes no comfort in his throne.[672]

Now there was a divine being destined to fall [194] who was rolling about on the ground. As he rolled around and about, he lamented mournfully, "Ah Mandākinī River! Ah lotus pond! Ah water tank! Ah Caitraratha Grove! Ah Pāruṣyaka Grove! Ah Nandana Grove! Ah Miśrakā Grove! Ah Pāriyātraka Grove! Ah Pāṇḍukambala Rock! Ah divine assembly hall! Ah Sudarśana!"[673]

Śakra, lord of the gods, saw that divine being rolling around and about all over the ground, and at the sight of that divine being, he approached him. Having approached, he said this to him: "My friend, why do you roll around and about all over the ground, lamenting mournfully, 'Ah Mandākinī River! Ah lotus pond! Ah water tank! Ah Caitraratha Grove! Ah Pāruṣyaka Grove! Ah Nandana Grove! Ah Miśrakā Grove! Ah Pāriyātraka Grove! Ah Pāṇḍukambala Rock! Ah divine assembly hall! Ah Sudarśana!'?"

Thus addressed, the divine being said this to Śakra, lord of the gods: "Kauśika, though I have been experiencing divine pleasure, seven days from now I will be reborn in a pig's womb in the city of Rājagṛha! For many years there I will have to feed on shit and piss."

Then Śakra, lord of the gods, out of compassion, said this to that divine being: "Come, my friend. Take refuge in the Buddha, the best of men. Take refuge in the dharma, the best of those things free from attachment. And take refuge in the community, the best of assemblies."

That divine being, terrified of being reborn as an animal and terrified of death, said this to Śakra, lord of the gods: "Kauśika, I take refuge in the Buddha, the best of men. I take refuge in the dharma, the best of those things free from attachment. And I take refuge in the community, the best of assemblies." Then that divine being, having embraced the three refuges, died and passed away and was reborn among the gods of Tuṣita (Content).[674]

It is a law of nature that gods can look and come to know what is below them but not what is above them. Śakra, lord of the gods, then began looking for that divine being. "Has that divine being been reborn in a wretched pig's womb or not?" he thought. Then he looked and saw that he hadn't been reborn among animals or hungry ghosts. So he looked to see if he had been reborn among the realms of hell, but he hadn't been reborn there either. He then looked to see if he had been reborn in the company of mortals. [195] He also hadn't been reborn there. He then began to look among the gods of Cāturmahārājika (Four Groups of the Great Kings) and Trāyastriṃśa (Thirty-Three). He didn't see him there either.

Then Śakra, lord of the gods, with his curiosity aroused, approached the Blessed One. Having approached, he venerated with his head the feet of the Blessed One and then sat down at a respectful distance. Sitting down at a respectful distance, Śakra, lord of the gods, said this to the Blessed One:

> Bhadanta, I saw a divine being here who was destined to fall from divine existence rolling about on the ground and lamenting mournfully, "Ah Mandākinī River! Ah lotus pond!

Ah water tank! Ah Caitraratha Grove! Ah Pāruṣyaka Grove! Ah Nandana Grove! Ah Miśrakā Grove! Ah Pāriyātraka Grove! Ah Pāṇḍukambala Rock! Ah divine assembly hall! Ah Sudarśana!" I said to him, "My friend, why do you grieve, lament, cry, and beat your chest so much? Why are you in such a daze?" He said, "Kauśika, seven days from now I will abandon divine pleasure and be reborn in a wretched pig's womb in the city of Rājagṛha. For many years there I will have to feed on shit and piss." Then I said this to him, "Go, my friend. Take refuge in the Buddha, the best of men. Take refuge in the dharma, the best of those things free from attachment. And take refuge in the community, the best of assemblies." He said, "Kauśika, I take refuge in the Buddha, the best of men. I take refuge in the dharma, the best of those things free from attachment. And I take refuge in the community, the best of assemblies." With that said, that divine being died. Where, Bhadanta, was that divine being reborn?

"Kauśika," the Blessed One said, "the gods called Tuṣita have success in all they desire. He is enjoying himself as a god there, having taken the three refuges here."[675]

At that time Śakra, lord of the gods, with his mind uplifted, uttered these verses:

Those who take refuge in the Buddha
do not have a bad rebirth.
Abandoning human bodies,
they take up divine bodies.

Those who take refuge in the dharma
do not have a bad rebirth.
Abandoning human bodies,
they take up divine bodies. [196]

Those who take refuge in the community
do not have a bad rebirth.
Abandoning human bodies,
they take up divine bodies.[676]

Then the Blessed One, approving of these words of Śakra, lord of the gods, said, "Quite so, Kauśika. Quite so—

Those who take refuge in the Buddha
do not have a bad rebirth.
Abandoning human bodies,
they take up divine bodies.

Those who take refuge in the dharma
do not have a bad rebirth.
Abandoning human bodies,
they take up divine bodies.

Those who take refuge in the community
do not have a bad rebirth.
Abandoning human bodies,
they take up divine bodies."

Śakra, lord of the gods, rejoiced and delighted in the words of the Blessed One. Then he venerated with his head the feet of the Blessed One, circumambulated the Blessed One three times, and bowing to the Blessed One with hands respectfully folded and cupped, vanished on the spot.[677]

So ends the *Sūkarika-avadāna,* the fourteenth chapter in the glorious *Divyāvadāna.*

15. The Story of One Foretold to Be a Wheel-Turning King

CAKRAVARTIVYĀKṚTA-AVADĀNA

THE LORD BUDDHA was staying in the city of Śrāvastī at the Jeta Grove in the park of a man named Anāthapiṇḍada (Almsgiver to the Poor). As a rule, while lord buddhas are living, existing, and passing time, there are stūpas for their hair and nails. When lord buddhas are withdrawn for meditation, monks perform ceremonies at these stūpas for hair and nails. Then some monks enter [towns] for alms, and some experience the pleasures of meditation, liberation, and meditative concentration and absorption.

One time the Lord Buddha was withdrawn for meditation. In the evening time, a certain monk prostrated himself with all his limbs at a stūpa for the Buddha's hair and nails. Then, bringing to mind the Tathāgata with his attributes, he cultivated faith in his mind as he thought,

The Blessed One is just like this—
a tathāgata,
an arhat,
a perfectly awakened being,
perfect in knowledge and conduct,
a sugata,
a knower of the world,
an unsurpassed guide for those in need of training,

a teacher of gods and mortals,
a buddha,
and a blessed one.[678] [197]

In the evening, the Blessed One came out of meditative seclusion and sat down in front of the community of monks in the seat specially prepared for him. The Blessed One saw that monk prostrating himself with his entire body at that stūpa for hair and nails and cultivating a faithful mind. At the sight of him, he addressed the monks:[679] "Monks, look at this monk who prostrates himself with his entire body at this stūpa for hair and nails and cultivates a faithful mind."[680]

"Yes, Bhadanta."

"As many grains of sand as there are in that space between the land that this monk has tread upon and the stratum of the golden wheel, which is eighty thousand leagues down below, this monk will enjoy that many thousands of reigns as a wheel-turning king."

Then it occurred to those monks, "One cannot count the grains of sand in a pit that is a man's height in depth; what then of those in the eighty thousand leagues leading down to the stratum of the golden wheel? Who can pass such a long time stuck in saṃsāra?" So from then on those monks never again made offerings to a stūpa for hair and nails.

Then the Blessed One, knowing with his mind the thoughts of those monks, addressed the monks: "Saṃsāra, monks, is without beginning or end for those beings hindered by ignorance, fettered by desire, and bound by the chains of desire—they are reborn over and over again for a very long time. The very beginning of suffering is not known."

The venerable Upāli then asked the Lord Buddha, "As the Blessed One has said, 'This monk has such a mass of merit.' In what way, Bhadanta, will such a mass of merit[681] diminish, give out, and finally be exhausted?"

"Upāli, I see no injury and harm more terrible than when one follower of the religious life entertains bad thoughts toward another follower of the religious life.[682] In this way, Upāli, these great roots of virtue will diminish, give out, and finally be exhausted. So then, Upāli, you should put this into practice: 'We won't even have bad thoughts toward a burnt stump,[683] let alone a body with sensory consiousness.'"

This was said by the Blessed One. With their minds uplifted, the monks rejoiced.

So ends the fifteenth chapter in the glorious *Divyāvadāna,* in which it is foretold that a certain monk will be a wheel-turning king. [198]

16. *The Story of Two Parrot Chicks*

ŚUKAPOTAKA-AVADĀNA

THIS INCIDENT occurred in Śrāvastī. One day the householder Anāthapiṇḍada (Almsgiver to the Poor) acquired two parrot chicks. He brought them home, then taught them to speak, reared and nourished them, and instructed them in the language of humans. The venerable Ānanda frequently visited these two parrot chicks and gave them a discourse on the dharma that penetrated the four noble truths—namely, this is suffering, this is the origin of suffering, this is the cessation of suffering, and this is the path that leads to the cessation of suffering. The most senior monks would also approach the householder Anāthapiṇḍada's home, such as Śāriputra, Maudgalyāyana, Kāśyapa, Ānanda, and Raivata. As those senior monks approached time and again, those parrot chicks learned their names.

One time the venerable Śāriputra arrived at the householder Anāthapiṇḍada's home. The two parrot chicks saw the venerable Śāriputra, and at the sight of him, they addressed the members of the household: "Friends,[684] the elder Śāriputra is coming! Prepare a seat for him." They also did the same when they saw the venerable Mahāmaudgalyāyana, Kāśyapa, and Raivata. And when they saw the venerable Ānanda, they said, "Our teacher Ānanda is coming! Prepare a seat for him."

One time the Blessed One arrived at the householder Anāthapiṇḍada's home. The two parrot chicks saw the Blessed One coming from a distance. He instilled faith and was worthy of faith, he was restrained at heart and in his senses, his mind was possessed of extreme tranquility, and he blazed with splendor like a golden pillar. At the sight of him, they quickly addressed the members of the household. "Friends,"[685] they cooed in a sweet and pleasing voice, "the Blessed One is coming! Prepare a seat for him."

Then, to do a good deed for the two parrot chicks, the Blessed One entered that house and sat down in the seat specially prepared for him. [199] After sitting down, the Blessed One gave a discourse on the Dharma that penetrated the four noble truths and established those two parrot chicks in the taking of the refuges as well as in the precepts. Then the Blessed One, having instructed, incited, inspired, and delighted the two parrot chicks and the members of the household with this discourse on the Dharma, got up from his seat and went out.

Afterward, as the members of the household were wandering about, the two parrot chicks were acting carelessly and were seized by a cat. With looks of pain on their faces as their vital points were pierced and their joints were broken, they said, "Praise to the Buddha! Praise to the dharma! Praise to the community!" And with that said, they died and were reborn among the gods of Cāturmahārājika (Four Groups of the Great Kings).

Meanwhile, in a certain place, the Blessed One smiled. The venerable Ānanda saw the Blessed One manifesting his smile, and at the sight of the Blessed One, he said this to him: "Perfectly awakened tathāgata arhats do not manifest a smile, Bhadanta, without proper cause and reason. Bhadanta, what is the proper cause and reason for your manifesting a smile?"

"It is like this, Ānanda. It is like this. Perfectly awakened tathāgata arhats do not manifest a smile without proper cause and reason. Ānanda, did you see those two parrot chicks?"

"Yes, Bhadanta. I saw them."

"As soon as I left, Ānanda, those two parrot chicks were killed by a cat. With their awareness focused on the Buddha, the dharma, and the community, they died and were reborn among the Cāturmahārājika gods."

That same morning many monks got dressed, took their bowls and robes, and entered Śrāvastī for alms. As those many monks were wandering in Śrāvastī for alms, they heard those two parrot chicks in the householder Anāthapiṇḍada's home saying "Praise to the Buddha! Praise to the dharma! Praise to the community!" as they were killed by a cat. Having heard this, after wandering in Śrāvastī for alms and after finishing their meals and returning from their almsrounds, they put away their bowls and robes, washed their feet, and then approached the Blessed One. Having approached, they venerated with their heads the feet of the Blessed One and then sat down at a respectful distance. Sitting down at a respectful distance, those many monks [200] said this to the Blessed One: "Bhadanta, all of us here [were wandering in Śrāvastī for alms, when we heard][686] those two parrot chicks in the householder Anāthapiṇḍada's home saying 'Praise to the Buddha! Praise to the dharma! Praise to the community!' as they were killed by a cat. Bhadanta, what is their destiny? What kind of rebirth will they have? What will be their future?"

"Monks," the Blessed One said, "those two parrots, as a result of taking refuge, will be reborn thirty-six times among the Cāturmahārājika gods, and they will be reborn thirty-six times among the gods of Trāyastriṃśa (Thirty-Three), Yāma (Free from Conflict), Tuṣita (Content), Nirmāṇarati (Delighting in Creation), and Paranirmitavaśavartin (Masters of Others' Creations). After being reborn again and again as beings among the gods in the six spheres of desire,[687] in their last life, their last existence, their last incarnation, they will take human form. Then they will attain awakening as solitary buddhas and become the solitary buddhas Dharma and Sudharma (Good Dharma). In just this way, monks, listening to the dharma has great results and great benefits, what to say of discoursing on the dharma or clearly understanding the dharma? So then, monks, this is to be learned: 'We shall be devoted to listening to the dharma.'[688] It is this, monks, that you should learn to do."

This was said by the Blessed One. With their minds uplifted, the monks welcomed the words of the Blessed One.

So ends the *Śukapotaka-avadāna,* the sixteenth chapter in the glorious *Divyāvadāna.*

17. The Story of Māndhātā

MĀNDHĀTĀ-AVADĀNA

The Buddha Decides to Pass into Final Nirvāṇa[689]

THUS I HAVE HEARD. At one time the Blessed One was staying in the city of Vaiśālī at the Kūṭāgāra Hall on the banks of the Markaṭahrada (Monkey Pool). One morning the Blessed One got dressed, took his bowl and robe, and entered Vaiśālī for alms. After wandering through Vaiśālī for alms, he finished his meal and in the afternoon returned from his almsround. [201] Then he put away his bowl and robe, and approached the Cāpāla Shrine. Having approached, he sat down at the base of a tree for a daytime rest. Then the Blessed One addressed the venerable Ānanda.

"Ānanda, beautiful is Vaiśālī, as is the land of Vṛji, the Cāpāla Shrine, the Seven Mangoes Shrine, the Many Children Shrine,[690] the Gautama Banyan Tree Shrine, the *śāla* forest, the Putting Aside Burdens Shrine, and the Tying a Crest Shrine of the Mallas! Jambudvīpa (Black Plum Island) is wonderful, and sweet is the life of humans!

"Ānanda, whoever has practiced, developed, and cultivated the four bases of success may, if he so desires, live for a full eon or what remains of an eon.[691] The Tathāgata, Ānanda, has practiced, developed, and cultivated the four bases of success.[692] If he desires, the Tathāgata may live for a full eon or what remains of an eon."

Thus addressed, the venerable Ānanda remained silent. A second time and a third as well, the Blessed One addressed the venerable

Ānanda: "Ānanda, beautiful is Vaiśālī, as is the land of Vṛji, the Cāpāla Shrine, the Seven Mangoes Shrine, the Many Children Shrine,[693] the Gautama Banyan Tree Shrine, the *śāla* forest, the Putting Aside Burdens Shrine, and the Tying a Crest Shrine of the Mallas! Jambudvīpa is wonderful, and sweet is the life of humans!

"Ānanda, whoever has practiced, developed, and cultivated the four bases of success may, if he so desires, live for a full eon or what remains of an eon. The Tathāgata, Ānanda, has practiced, developed, and cultivated the four bases of success. If he desires, the Tathāgata may live a full eon or what remains of an eon."

And for a second time and a third as well, the venerable Ānanda remained silent. Then it occurred to the Blessed One, "The monk Ānanda is possessed by the evil Māra. Three times a clear and obvious suggestion was made apparent, but he still wasn't able to understand that suggestion. This is because he is possessed by the evil Māra."

Then the Blessed One addressed the venerable Ānanda: "Ānanda, go and rest at the base of some other tree. Let's not crowd together here while we're resting." [202]

"Yes, Bhadanta," the venerable Ānanda replied, consenting to the Blessed One's request. Then he sat down at the base of another tree for a daytime rest.

Meanwhile, the evil Māra approached the Blessed One and, having approached, said this to the Blessed One: "The Blessed One should pass into final nirvāṇa. The time has come for the final nirvāṇa of the Sugata."

"Evil one, why do you speak like this—'The Blessed One should pass into final nirvāṇa. The time has come for the final nirvāṇa of the Sugata'?"

"There was one time, Bhadanta,[694] when the Blessed One was staying in the village of Uruvilvā on the banks of the Nairañjanā River, at the base of a bodhi tree, just after becoming perfectly awakened. At that time I approached the Blessed One and, having approached, said to the Blessed One, 'Blessed One, you should pass into final nirvāṇa.

The time has come for the final nirvāṇa of the Sugata.' And the Blessed One said,

> Evil one, I shall not pass into final nirvāṇa until my disciples are learned, wise, disciplined, and confident, able to refute with the dharma those who come to expound false doctrines, and able—as monks, nuns, male and female lay devotees—to completely purify their own views. And, furthermore, they shall follow the religious life so that it will be widespread, popular, and pervasive,[695] and so that it will be made perfectly clear to gods and mortals.

"Now, Bhadanta, the Blessed One's disciples are learned, wise, disciplined, and confident, able to refute with the dharma those who have come to expound false doctrines, and able—as monks, nuns, male and female lay devotees—to completely purify their own views. And, furthermore, the religious life is now widespread, popular, and pervasive, and it has been made perfectly clear to gods and mortals. Therefore, I say this—'The Blessed One should pass into final nirvāṇa. The time has come for the final nirvāṇa of the Sugata.'"

"You needn't worry, evil one. It isn't long now. After the three months of the rainy season, the Tathāgata will pass into the realm of remainderless nirvāṇa."

Then it occurred to the evil Māra, "Aha! The ascetic Gautama will finally pass into final nirvāṇa." With this in mind, he was pleased, satisfied, delighted, excited, and full of joy and pleasure. Then he vanished on the spot.

Then it occurred to the Blessed One, "Who is to be trained face to face with the Tathāgata? Supriya, king of celestial musicians, and the mendicant Subhadra. [203] After the three months of the rainy season their various faculties will reach maturity and they will live in comfort. One who is to be trained by a disciple can be trained by a tathāgata, but one who is to be trained by a tathāgata cannot be trained by a disciple."

Then it occurred to the Blessed One, "Suppose I enter a state of meditative concentration such that when my mind is concentrated, in full control of the conditions for life, I relinquish the conditions for an unabridged life."

Then the Blessed One entered a state of meditative concentration, and when his mind was concentrated and he was in full control of the conditions for life, he began to relinquish the conditions for an unabridged life. As soon as the conditions for an unabridged life had been relinquished,[696] there was a great earthquake. Meteors fell, the sky looked like it was on fire, and the drums of the gods thundered in the air. As soon as the conditions for an unabridged life had been relinquished, six signs appeared among the gods belonging to the sphere of desire. Flowering trees withered, jeweled trees withered, trees bearing ornaments withered. Thousands of homes shook, the peaks of Mount Sumeru crumbled, and divine musical instruments[697] were dealt a blow.

Then the Blessed One emerged from that state of meditative concentration, and at that time uttered the following verse:

> Abandoning the condition for existence,
> and with it both higher and lower rebirths,[698]
> the Sage, with inward joy
> and absorbed in meditative concentration,
> broke through becoming
> as a chick does its shell.[699]

As soon as the Blessed One had relinquished the conditions for an unabridged life, the gods belonging to the six spheres of desire made an agreement and then set off into the Blessed One's presence, to see him and to venerate him. The Blessed One gave a discourse on the dharma such that many hundreds and thousands of deities saw the [four noble] truths, and having seen the truth, they returned to their homes.

As soon as the Blessed One had relinquished the conditions for an unabridged life, many hundreds and thousands of seers arrived from mountains, valleys, hills, and caves. The Blessed One initiated them, saying, "Come, O monks! Follow the religious life!" After striving and struggling, they rid themselves of all defilements and thereby directly experienced arhatship.

As soon as the Blessed One had relinquished the conditions for an unabridged life, many nāgas, yakṣas, celestial musicians, kinnaras, and great snakes approached the Blessed One's presence to see the Blessed One. [204] The Blessed One then gave a discourse on the dharma such that many nāgas, yakṣas, celestial musicians, kinnaras, and great snakes accepted the taking of the refuges as well as the precepts. Thereafter they returned to their homes.

In the evening, the venerable Ānanda came out of meditative seclusion[700] and approached the Blessed One. Having approached, he venerated with his head the feet of the Blessed One and then stood at a respectful distance. Standing at a respectful distance, the venerable Ānanda said this to the Blessed One: "Bhadanta, what is the cause, what is the reason for a great earthquake?"

"There are eight, Ānanda. There are eight reasons for a great earthquake. Which eight? Ānanda, this great earth is established on water, water is established on wind, and wind is established on sky. Ānanda, at that time when violent winds blow in the sky, they stir up the water, and the stirred-up water shakes the earth. This, Ānanda, is the primary cause, the primary reason for a great earthquake.

"Now the next case, Ānanda: A monk who possesses great magic and great power and who takes a small portion of earth as a basis for meditative consciousness and does the same for the immeasurable ocean can, if he desires, cause the earth to shake. Likewise, a deity who possesses great magic and great power and who takes a small portion of earth as a basis for meditative consciousness and does the same for the immeasurable ocean can, if she desires, cause the earth to shake. This is the second cause, the second reason for a great earthquake.

"Now the next case, Ānanda: At that time when a bodhisattva falls from among the gods of Tuṣita (Content) and descends into his mother's womb, there is an earthquake, and all the world is ablaze with a great flash of light. Even those in-between places in the world that are blindingly dark glooms of darkness, where the sun and moon, so magical and so powerful, can't see their own light,[701] even they at that time are ablaze with a great flash of light. Then, in this light, those beings who have been reborn there see one another and come to this understanding—'Friends, other beings have been reborn here as well! Friends, other beings have been reborn here as well!' This, Ānanda, is the third cause, [205] the third reason for a great earthquake.

"Now the next case, Ānanda: At that time when a bodhisattva emerges from his mother's womb, there is a great earthquake, and all the world is ablaze with a great flash of light. Once again, even those in-between places in the world that are blindingly dark glooms of darkness, where the sun and moon, so magical and so powerful, can't see their own light, even they at that time are ablaze with a great flash of light. Then, in this light, those beings who have been reborn there see one another and come to this understanding—'Friends, other beings have been reborn here as well! Friends, other beings have been reborn here as well!' This, Ānanda, is the fourth cause, the fourth reason for a great earthquake.

"Now the next case, Ānanda: At that time when a bodhisattva attains supreme knowledge, there is a great earthquake, and all the world is ablaze with a great flash of light. Once again, even those in-between places in the world that are blindingly dark glooms of darkness, where the sun and moon, so magical and so powerful, can't see their own light, even they at that time are ablaze with a great flash of light. Then, in this light, those beings who have been reborn there see one another and come to this understanding—'Friends, other beings have been reborn here as well! Friends, other beings have been reborn here as well!' This, Ānanda, is the fifth cause, the fifth reason for a great earthquake.

"Now the next case, Ānanda: At that time when a tathāgata turns the wheel of dharma, with its twelve links, three times,[702] there is a very great earthquake, and all the world is ablaze with a great flash of light. Once again, even those in-between places in the world that are blindingly dark glooms of darkness, where the sun and moon, so magical and so powerful, can't see their own light, even they at that time are ablaze with a great flash of light. Then, in this light, those beings who have been reborn there see one another and come to this understanding—'Friends, other beings have been reborn here as well! Friends, other beings have been reborn here as well!' This, Ānanda, is the sixth cause, [206] the sixth reason for a great earthquake.

"Now the next case, Ānanda: At that time when a tathāgata, in full control of the conditions for life, relinquishes the conditions for an unabridged life, there is a great earthquake. Meteors fall, the sky looks like it is on fire, the drums of the gods thunder in the air, and this whole world is ablaze with a great flash of light. Once again, even those in-between places in the world that are blindingly dark glooms of darkness, where the sun and moon, so magical and so powerful, can't see their own light, even they at that time are ablaze with a great flash of light. Then, in this light, those beings who have been reborn there see one another and come to this understanding—'Friends, other beings have been reborn here as well! Friends, other beings have been reborn here as well!' This, Ānanda, is the seventh cause, the seventh reason for a great earthquake.

"Now the next case, Ānanda: Not long from now, the Tathāgata will pass into the realm of remainderless nirvāṇa. At that time, there will be a great earthquake. Meteors will fall, the sky will look like it is on fire, the drums of the gods will thunder in the air, and this whole world will be ablaze with a great flash of light. Once again, even those in-between places in the world that are blindingly dark glooms of darkness, where the sun and moon, so magical and so powerful, can't see their own light, even they at that time will be ablaze with a great flash of light. Then, in this light, those beings who have been reborn there will see one another and come to this understanding—'Friends, other beings have been reborn here as well! Friends, other beings have been reborn here as well!' This, Ānanda, is the eighth cause, the eighth reason for a great earthquake."

Then the venerable Ānanda said this to the Blessed One: "Bhadanta, as I understand the meaning of what the Blessed One has said, right here the Blessed One, who is in full control of the conditions for life, must have relinquished the conditions for an unabridged life."

"It is like this, Ānanda," the Blessed One said. "It is like this. At this moment, Ānanda, the Tathāgata, who is in full control of the conditions for life, has relinquished the conditions for an unabridged life."

"Bhadanta, face to face and in person I have listened to the Blessed One, and face to face with him, I have understood this: 'Whoever has practiced, developed, and cultivated the four bases of success may, if he[703] so desires, [207] live for a full eon or what remains of an eon.' Bhadanta, the Blessed One has practiced, developed, and cultivated the four bases of success. If he desires, the Tathāgata may live for a full eon or what remains of an eon. The Blessed One should stay for a full eon. Otherwise the Sugata should stay for the remainder of an eon."

"Ānanda, the fault is yours. The misdeed is yours. Even when the Tathāgata made apparent a clear and obvious suggestion not less than three times, it was you who wasn't able to respond[704] to this suggestion. This is because you are possessed by the evil Māra. What do you think, Ānanda? Would the Tathāgata speak words that are ambiguous?"

"No, Bhadanta."

"That's right, Ānanda. That's right. It is impossible and inconceivable, Ānanda, that the Tathāgata would speak words that are ambiguous. Ānanda, go to the monks staying near the Cāpāla Shrine and gather them all together in the assembly hall."

"Yes, Bhadanta," the venerable Ānanda replied, consenting to the Blessed One's request. Ānanda then went to the monks staying near the Cāpāla Shrine, gathered them all together in the assembly hall, and then approached the Blessed One. Having approached, he venerated with his head the feet of the Blessed One and stood at a respectful distance. Standing at a respectful distance, the venerable Ānanda said this to the Blessed One: "Bhadanta, those monks staying near the Cāpāla Shrine have all gathered together and are seated in the assembly hall. Now the Blessed One may do as the time permits."

Then the Blessed One approached the assembly hall and, having approached, sat down in front of the community of monks in the seat specially prepared for him. Once seated, the Blessed One addressed the monks: "Monks, impermanent are all conditioned things. They are unstable, unreliable, and subject to change. And this, monks, is sufficient to condition all conditioned things. Abstain from them![705] Now then, monks, after my passing, those dharmas that offer benefit in the here and now, pleasure in the here and now, benefit in the life to come, and pleasure in the life to come, should be understood and mastered by the monks so that they can be preserved, preached, and promulgated. In this way the religious life may be long-standing, [208] popular, and pervasive, and as such made perfectly clear to gods and mortals.

"Now, monks,[706] there are dharmas that offer benefit in the here and now, pleasure in the here and now, benefit in the life to come, and pleasure in the life to come. They should be understood and mastered by the monks so that they can be preserved, preached, and promulgated. In this way, the religious life may be long-standing, popular, and pervasive, and as such made perfectly clear to gods and mortals. These are the four applications of mindfulness, the four proper efforts, the four bases of success, the five spiritual faculties, the corresponding five powers, the seven factors of awakening,[707] and the eightfold noble path. It is these dharmas, monks, that offer benefit in the here and now, pleasure in the here and now, benefit in the life to come, and pleasure in the life to come, which should be understood and mastered by the monks so that they can be preserved, promulgated, and preached. In this way, the religious life may be long-standing, popular, and pervasive, and as such made perfectly clear to gods and mortals. Ānanda, go to Kuśigrāmaka!"

"Yes, Bhadanta," the venerable Ānanda replied, consenting to the Blessed One's request.

As the Blessed One approached the forest at Vaiṣālī, he looked about intently, as an elephant would look, turning his whole body to the right.

Then the venerable Ānanda said this the Blessed One: "It is not without cause and reason, Bhadanta, that perfectly awakened tathāgata arhats look about intently, as elephants would look, turning their whole bodies to the right. What is the cause, Bhadanta, what is the reason for looking about as would an elephant?"

"It is like this, Ānanda. It is like this. It is not without proper cause and reason that perfectly awakened tathāgata arhats look about intently, as elephants would look, turning their whole bodies to the right. Ānanda, this is the Tathāgata's last sight of Vaiśālī. Never again, Ānanda, will the Tathāgata come to Vaiśālī. Instead, he will go to the Yamakaśāla (Twin Śāla Trees) Grove in the land[708] of the Mallas to pass into final nirvāṇa."

At that time, one of the monks uttered this verse: [209]

Lord, this is your last sight of Vaiśālī.
The Sugata, the Buddha, will not come to Vaiśālī again.

He will go to the Yamakaśāla Grove
in the land of the Mallas for final nirvāṇa.[709]

When the Blessed One spoke these words—"This is the Tathāgata's last sight of Vaiśālī"—the many deities living in the forest at Vaiśālī began to shed tears.

"Blessed One," the elder Ānanda said, "how can the rainy season have started without a single cloud?"

"Since the deities living in the forest at Vaiśālī will be separated from me," the Blessed One said, "they have begun to cry."

Those deities in Vaiśālī then uttered these words:[710] "The Blessed One will pass into final nirvāṇa! Never again will he come to Vaiśālī!"

Hearing the words of those deities, many hundreds and thousands of beings from Vaiśālī approached the Blessed One's presence. Then the Blessed One, knowing their inclinations, propensities, makeup, and nature, gave them a discourse on the dharma such that many hundreds and thousands of beings accepted the refuges as well as the precepts. Some obtained the reward of the stream-enterer; some the reward of the once-returner; and some the reward of the nonreturner. Some went forth as monks and obtained arhatship. Some set their minds on attaining awakening as a disciple. Some set their minds on attaining awakening as a solitary buddha. Some set their minds on attaining unsurpassed perfect awakening. And some accepted the refuges as well as the precepts. Almost the entire assembly became favorably inclined toward the Buddha, intent on the dharma, and well disposed toward the community.

The elder Ānanda then respectfully folded and cupped his hands together and said this to the Blessed One: "Look, Bhadanta. Since the Blessed One has set out for final nirvāṇa, he has established many hundreds and thousands of deities in the [four noble] truths. Many hundreds and thousands of seers from many mountains, valleys, hills, and caves have arrived here, and the Blessed One has initiated them as monks. After striving, struggling, and straining, they have rid themselves of all defilements and thereby directly experienced arhatship. Many gods, nāgas, yakṣas, celestial musicians, kinnaras, and great snakes have accepted the taking of the refuges as well as the precepts. Many hundreds of thousands of beings from Vaiśālī have been established in the reward of the stream-enterer, some in the reward of the once-returner, [210] and some in the reward of the nonreturner. Some have gone forth as monks, and having gone forth, obtained arhatship. And some have been established in the taking of the refuges as well as in the precepts."

"What a wonder it is, Ānanda, that today, right here, I have offered such training to disciples—for I am omniscient, with knowledge of all forms, mastery over supreme knowledge and the objects of knowledge, without craving or clinging to existence, and permanently rid of all evil propensities and the false beliefs of 'me,' 'mine,' 'I am.' In a previous time, Ānanda, I was filled with attachment, with hate, and with delusion, and I wasn't liberated from birth, old age, sickness, death, sorrow, lamentation, suffering, grief, or despair. However, experiencing the presence of death, I delivered a sermon on karma such that many hundreds of thousands of beings left behind the household life and went forth as seers would do.[711] Cultivating the four Brahmā states and abandoning their mass of aspirations,[712] and for the most part abiding in this state, they were reborn as inhabitants of the Brahmā World.[713] Listen to this."

The Ascendancy of King Māndhātā

Long ago, Ānanda, there was a king named Upoṣadha.[714] On King Upoṣadha's head there was a swelling that was soft, very soft, like *tūla* or *karpāsa* cotton.[715] But it didn't cause any trouble. When it became ripe, it burst and a young man was born who was beautiful, good-looking, and attractive, endowed with the thirty-two marks of a great man.

Now King Upoṣadha had sixty thousand wives, and all of their breasts began to flow with milk. "Suckle from me! Suckle from me!" each of them said. Since he was born from a head *(mūrdhataḥ)* he came to be known as Mūrdhātā (Born from a Head). And since "Suckle me *(māṃ dhaya)*! Suckle me *(māṃ dhaya)*!" was said, he also came to be known as Māndhātā (Suckle Me). Others say, though, that some know him as Mādhātā.

While Prince Māndhātā was playing the games of youth, six Śakras died and passed away.[716] After he was appointed crown prince, six more Śakras died and passed away.

Once Māndhātā went off to the countryside, and while he was there in the countryside his father became sick. Though treated with medicines made from roots, leaves, stalks, and flowers, his father continued to get worse. Then his ministers dispatched this message—"Your father is sick. Come and accept royal power from our lord."[717] But before he could come, his father died. His ministers then dispatched another message—"Your father has met his death. Come and accept royal power from our lord." [211]

"If my father has died," he reflected, "what's the use of my returning?"

Then another message arrived—"Come and accept royal power from our lord."

"If it is in accordance with dharma that I acquire royal power," he said, "then may the royal coronation come here!"

"My lord," the ministers said, "a jeweled mosaic[718] is needed [for a royal coronation]."

Now Māndhātā had an attendant, a yakṣa named Divaukasa (Sky Dweller). He brought a jeweled mosaic, and when he had brought that jeweled mosaic, the ministers then said, "My lord, a royal palanquin is also needed." So Divaukasa brought a royal palanquin. Then the ministers said, "A coronation must be performed in a king's palace."

"If it is in accordance with dharma that I acquire royal power," he said, "then may the palace come here!"

And so, on its own, the palace came to that place. Since it arrived on its own—arrived on its own *(svayam āgataṃ)*—that place came to be known as Sāketa—Sāketa (Self-Arrived).[719] Thereafter, the ministers as well as the military commanders, townspeople, and villagers arrived, bringing with them the coronation water.

"My lord," they said, "accept this coronation water."

"Mortals shall affix my royal insignia?" he said. "If it is in accordance with dharma that I acquire royal power, may immortals affix my royal insignia!" So immortals affixed his royal insignia. Then the seven treasures appeared before him—the most-treasured wheel, the most-treasured elephant, the most-treasured horse, the most-treasured jewel, the most-treasured counselor, the most-treasured woman, and, as the seventh, the most-treasured householder. He also had a full one thousand sons who were brave, heroic, in excellent physical condition, and who could crush enemy armies.

Near Vaiśālī was a beautiful forest where five hundred seers, each possessing the five superhuman faculties, would meditate. And there in that forest lived many birds and animals. Now, meditative practices are hindered by noise. And as those birds were constantly alighting, they made a lot of noise.

In that forest there was also a seer named Durmukha (Foul Mouthed). He became angry and he said, "May the wings of these cranes wither away!" As a result of that seer's anger, the wings of those birds withered away, and they then began to walk about on foot.

Meanwhile the king, who was touring the countryside, saw those birds moving about on foot. So he asked his ministers, "Why do they move about on foot?"

"My lord," the ministers said, "meditative practices are hindered by noise. [212] As a result of a seer's anger, the wings of these birds have withered away."

"Are there really seers such as this," the king said, "with no compassion for living beings?" Then the king ordered his ministers, "Go, gentlemen! Tell those seers to leave my realm."

So the ministers said to the seers: "These are the king's orders—'You are not to live in my kingdom. Gentlemen, you must leave my realm.'"

"He is lord of the four islands," they reflected. "Let's go to the slopes of Mount Sumeru." So they went and settled there.

Now, King Mūrdhātā's ministers were thinkers, evaluators, and examiners. And having thought, evaluated, and examined, each of them was said to cultivate various arts and administrative works. And so those thinkers, evaluators, and examiners came to be known as wise counselors—wise counselors.[720] They also began to work the fields.

While touring the countryside, the king saw them working the fields. "What are these people doing?" the king asked.

"My lord," the ministers said to the king, "these people cultivate grain and so on. That way there will be plants."

"People cultivate crops in my kingdom?" the king said. And so he said, "Let there be a rain of twenty-seven kinds of seeds!"

As soon as King Mūrdhātā had this thought, a rain of twenty-seven kinds of seeds fell.

King Mūrdhātā then asked the people in the countryside, "This is a result of whose meritorious deeds?"[721]

"My lord's and our own," they said.

Then the people began to cultivate fields of *karpāsa* cotton, and again while touring the countryside, King Mūrdhātā asked a question. "What are these people doing?" the king said.

"My lord," the ministers said, "these people are cultivating fields of *karpāsa* cotton."

"Why?" the king said.

"For cloth, my lord," the ministers said.

Then the king said, "People cultivate fields of *karpāsa* cotton in my kingdom? If that is so, let there be a rain of *karpāsa* cotton!"

As soon as King Mūrdhātā had this thought, a rain of *karpāsa* cotton fell.

Again the king asked the people in the countryside, [213] "This is a result of whose meritorious deeds?"

"My lord's and our own," they said.

Thereafter, those people began to spin that *karpāsa* cotton.

"What are these people doing?" the king said.

"My lord," the ministers said, "they need thread."

Then the king said, "People spin thread in my kingdom? Let there be a rain of thread!"

As soon as King Mūrdhātā had this thought, a rain of thread fell.

Again the king said, "This is a result of whose meritorious deeds?"

"My lord's and our own," they said.

Then, by and by, they began to weave cloth.

"What are these people doing?" the king said.

"My lord," the ministers said, "they are weaving cloth. They need cloth."

Then the king reflected, "People weave cloth in my kingdom? Let there be a rain of cloth!"

As soon as King Mūrdhātā had this thought, there was a rain of cloth.

Again the king said, "This is a result of whose meritorious deeds?"

"My lord's and our own," the people in the countryside said.

Then the king reflected, "The people do not know the power of my meritorious deeds." And it occurred to King Māndhātā, "I possess Jambudvīpa, which is thriving, prosperous, and safe, with plenty of food and crowds of people. I possess the seven treasures—the most-treasured wheel, the most-treasured elephant, the most-treasured horse, the most-treasured jewel, the most-treasured householder, the most-treasured woman, and, as the seventh, the most-treasured counselor. I have a full one thousand sons who are brave, heroic, in excellent physical condition, and who can crush enemy armies. How good it would be if for a week a rain of gold would fall inside my harem without even a single *kārṣāpaṇa* coin falling outside of it!"

As soon as King Mūrdhātā had this thought, a rain of gold fell for a week inside his harem. Not even a single *kārṣāpaṇa* coin fell outside of it. As in the case of a being possessed of great magic and great power who has performed meritorious and virtuous deeds, he now experienced the result of his own merit.

Again the king said, "This is a result of whose meritorious deeds?"

"My lord's and our own," they said.

Then King Mūrdhātā said, "Gentlemen, you are mistaken. [214] If you would have said previously, 'This is a result of my lord's meritorious deeds!' I would have caused a rain of jewels to fall over the whole of Jambudvīpa. Each of you would have been able to take as many jewels as you desired."

During that time while King Mūrdhātā ruled his great kingdom, six Śakras died and passed away.

Now King Mūrdhātā had an attendant, the yakṣa Divaukasa, and King Mūrdhātā said to him, "Is there any place on any other island that is not under my command that I should command?"

"My lord," Divaukasa said, "there is an island named Pūrvavideha (Eastern Videha). It is thriving, prosperous, and safe, with plenty of food and crowds of people. My lord himself should go there and command that place as well."

Then it occurred to King Mūrdhātā, "I possess Jambudvīpa, which is thriving, prosperous, and safe, with plenty of food and crowds of people. I possess the seven treasures—the most-treasured wheel, the most-treasured elephant, the most-treasured horse, the most-treasured jewel, the most-treasured woman, the most-treasured householder, and, as the seventh, the most-treasured counselor. I have a full one thousand sons who are brave, heroic, and in excellent physical condition, and who can crush enemy armies. A rain of gold fell for a week inside my harem. Now one hears that there is an island named Pūrvavideha. I really should go there as well and govern."

As soon as he had that thought, King Māndhātā, surrounded by his one thousand sons and accompanied by his seven treasures, his attendant, and an army of 180 million soldiers, rose up high in the sky. Then King Māndhātā went to the island of Pūrvavideha, and there on the island of Pūrvavideha, King Māndhātā alighted. In short order, King Mūrdhātā controlled[722] the island of Pūrvavideha. While he was in control there, six Śakras died and passed away. Again the king addressed the yakṣa Divaukasa.

"Divaukasa, is there any place on any other island that I don't command?"

"My lord," Divaukasa said, "there is an island named Aparagodānīya (Western Pasturage). It is thriving, prosperous, and safe, with plenty of food and crowds of people. My lord should go there as well and govern."

Then it occurred to King Mūrdhātā, "I possess Jambudvīpa, which is thriving, prosperous, and safe, with plenty of food and crowds of people. I possess the seven treasures. I have a full one thousand sons [215] who are brave, heroic, in excellent physical condition, and who can crush enemy armies. A rain of gold fell for a week inside my harem. As in the case of a being possessed of great magic and great power who has performed meritorious and virtuous deeds, I now experience the result of my own merit. Now one hears that there is an island named Aparagodānīya that is thriving, prosperous, and safe, with plenty of food and crowds of people. I really should go there as well and govern."

As soon as he had that thought, King Māndhātā, surrounded by one thousand sons and accompanied by his seven treasures, his attendant, and an army of 180 million soldiers, rose up high in the sky. Then King Māndhātā went to the island of Aparagodānīya, and in short order, King Māndhātā governed Aparagodānīya. While he was governing there, six Śakras died and passed away.

Then King Māndhātā asked the yakṣa Divaukasa, "Is there any other island, Divaukasa, that is not under my command?"[723]

"My lord, there is an island named Uttarakuru (Northern Kuru), and there the people have no sense of ownership and no belongings. My lord should go there as well and govern with his army."[724]

Then it occurred to King Māndhātā, "I possess Jambudvīpa, which is thriving, prosperous, and safe, with plenty of food and crowds of people. I possess the seven treasures. I have a full one thousand sons who are brave, heroic, in excellent physical condition, and who can crush enemy armies. A rain of gold fell for a week inside my harem. And now it is heard that there is an island named Uttarakuru, and that the people there have no sense of possession and no belongings. I really should go there as well and govern with the help of my army."

As soon as he had that thought, King Māndhātā, surrounded by one thousand sons and accompanied by his seven treasures, his attendant, and an army of 180 million soldiers, rose up high in the sky. As King Māndhātā was going along the slopes of Mount Sumeru, he saw trees of various colors hung with wreaths. At the sight of this, he addressed the yakṣa Divaukasa: "Divaukasa, what are those trees of various colors hung with wreaths?"

"My lord, those are wish-fulfilling trees that bear cloth for the people of Uttarakuru. And so the people of Uttarakuru wear clothes made from those trees. My lord should go there and dress himself with clothes made from those wish-fulfilling trees."

Hearing this, King Māndhātā addressed his ministers: [216] "Officers, do you see those trees of various colors that are hung with wreaths?"

"Yes, my lord."

"Officers, those are wish-fulfilling trees that bear cloth for the people of Uttarakuru. And so the people of Uttarakuru wear clothes made from those trees. You should go there and dress yourselves with sets of clothes from those wish-fulfilling trees."

As King Māndhātā was going along the slopes of Mount Sumeru, he saw a patch of ground that was bright white. At the sight of this, he addressed the yakṣa Divaukasa: "Divaukasa, what is that bright white patch of ground?"

"My lord, it is a paddy that was neither sown nor cultivated and yet produces full grains of rice for the people of Uttarakuru.[725] And so the people of Uttarakuru eat those full grains of rice that were neither sown nor cultivated. My lord should go there and partake of those full grains of rice that were neither sown nor cultivated."

Then King Māndhātā went to the island of Uttarakuru, and there on the island of Uttarakuru, King Māndhātā alighted. And there on the island of Uttarakuru, King Māndhātā governed with the help of his army.

While he was governing there, with the help of his army, six Śakras died and passed away. Then King Māndhātā addressed the yakṣa Divaukasa: "Is there any other island that is not under my command?"

"No there isn't, my lord. But there are, it is heard, the gods of Trāyastriṃśa (Thirty-Three). They live long, they're beautiful, they abound in bliss, and since long ago they've lived in lofty flying mansions. My lord should approach those Trāyastriṃśa gods to see them."

Then it occurred to King Māndhātā, "I possess Jambudvīpa, which is thriving, prosperous, and safe, with plenty of food and crowds of people. I possess the seven treasures. I have a full one thousand sons who are brave, heroic, and in excellent physical condition, and who can crush enemy armies. A rain of gold fell for a week inside my harem. I governed the island of Pūrvavideha. I governed the island of Aparagodānīya. On the island of Uttarakuru, I governed with the help of my army. And now, it is heard, there are the Trāyastriṃśa gods. They live long, they're beautiful, they abound in bliss, and since long ago they've lived in lofty flying mansions. I really should approach those Trāyastriṃśa gods to see them."

As soon as he had that thought, King Māndhātā, surrounded by one thousand sons and accompanied by his seven treasures, his attendant, and an army of 180 million soldiers, rose up high in the sky. [217]

Now Sumeru, the king of mountains, is surrounded by seven golden mountains. On Mount Nimindhara, one of those golden mountains, the king alighted. While he governed there with the help of his army, six Śakras died and passed away.

After Mount Nimindhara, he alighted on the golden Mount Vinataka (Causing One to Bend). While he governed there with the help of his army, six Śakras died and passed away.

After Mount Vinataka, he alighted on the golden Mount Aśvakarṇagiri (Peaks Like Horse's Ears). While he governed there with the help of his army, six Śakras died and passed away.

After Mount Aśvakarṇagiri, he alighted on the golden Mount Sudarśana (Good-Looking). While he governed there with the help of his army, six Śakras died and passed away.

After Mount Sudarśana, he alighted on the golden Mount Khadiraka (Home to Khadira Trees). While he governed there with the help of his army, six Śakras died and passed away.

After Mount Khadiraka, he alighted on the golden Mount Īṣādhāra (Plow Holder). While he governed there with the help of his army, six Śakras died and passed away.

After Mount Īṣādhāra, he alighted on the golden Mount Yugandhara (Yoke Holder). While he governed there with the help of his army, six Śakras died and passed away.

After Mount Yugandhara, he flew up high in the sky.

Now there on the slopes of Mount Sumeru, five hundred seers were meditating. When they saw the king coming, they said, "Friends, here he comes, that evil king!"

The seer named Durmukha was there, and he took water in his

cupped hands and flung it. This stopped the army. Leading the army was the most-treasured counselor, and he said to the seers,

> Go away![726] This brahman is wretched!
> This won't work everywhere.
> This is King Mūrdhātā himself.
> These aren't just cranes from Vaiśālī.

Now when the king arrived in that district, he said, "Who stopped the army?"

"My lord," the most-treasured counselor said, "a seer stopped the army."

Then the king said, "What is most loved by these seers?"

"Seers most love their matted hair," the most-treasured counselor said.

"Then may the matted hair of seers wither away!" said the king. "And may my army fly through the sky."

And so the matted hair of those seers withered away, and King Mūrdhātā's army set off through the sky.[727] [218]

Now Sumeru, the king of mountains, descended down 80,000 leagues into the golden earth and rose up 80,000 leagues from the water, so that in total its height was 160,000 leagues.[728] Each of its sides measured 80,000 leagues so that its total circumference was 320,000 leagues. It was beautiful, good-looking, and attractive, and it was made of four kinds of jewels. On its summit was the city of the Trāyastriṃśa gods called Sudarśana (Good-Looking). Five defenses had been established for the Trāyastriṃśa gods:

> Water-inhabiting nāgas,
> Karoṭapāṇi (Bowl-in-Hand) gods,
> Mālādhāra (Bearing Garlands) gods,
> Sadāmatta (Ever-Intoxicated) gods,
> and the four great kings.[729]

First the water-inhabiting nāgas blocked King Mūrdhātā's troops. So King Mūrdhātā came to that place and said, "Who blocked my army?"

"My lord," they said, "it's the water-inhabiting nāgas."

"Animals wage war with me?" the king said. "For this, the water-inhabiting nāgas shall become my attendants!" Then those nāgas became King Mūrdhātā's followers, marching in front of him.

As the nāgas proceeded, the Karoṭapāṇi gods arrived. The Karoṭapāṇi gods united with the nāgas, and again the army was stopped.

"Who stopped the army?" King Mūrdhātā said.

"My lord," they said, "it's the Karoṭapāṇi gods. They stopped the army."

"Then the Karoṭapāṇi gods shall become my attendants as well!" King Mūrdhātā said. And so they marched in front of him. As they were marching along with the nāgas, the Mālādhāra gods arrived.

"Gentlemen," the Mālādhāra gods asked, "why are you marching?"

"The king of mortals is coming," they said.

So the Mālādhāra gods joined forces with the nāgas and the other gods, and again the army was stopped.

Then King Māndhātā arrived at that place and said, "Gentlemen, what is this?"

"My lord," they said, "it's the doing of the Mālādhāra gods."

"Then the Mālādhāra gods shall become my attendants as well!" the king said. And so the Mālādhāra gods along with the nāgas and the other gods began to march in front of Mūrdhātā. As they were marching, the Sadāmatta gods arrived.

"Gentlemen," the Sadāmatta gods asked, "why are you marching?" [219]

The nāgas, the Karoṭapāṇi gods, and the other gods said, "The king of mortals is coming."

So the Sadāmatta gods united with the Karoṭapāṇi gods and with the other gods and nāgas, and once again the army was stopped.

Then King Māndhātā arrived at that place and said, "Who blocked the army?"

"My lord," they said, "it's the Sadāmatta gods."

"Then the Sadāmatta gods shall become my attendants as well!" the king said. And so the Sadāmatta gods along with the other gods and nāgas began to march in front of him.

As they were marching, the gods known as four great kings arrived and said, "Gentlemen, why are you marching?"

The various nāgas and gods who had become followers, marching in front of the king, said, "The king of mortals is coming."

The four great kings reflected, "This being is very powerful because of his merit. It isn't possible to oppose him." Then the four great kings informed the Trāyastriṃśa gods: "Gentlemen, Mūrdhātā, the king of mortals, is coming."

Then the Trāyastriṃśa gods reflected, "This being is very powerful as a result of merit. It isn't possible to oppose him. Let us go and receive him respectfully." Then the Trāyastriṃśa gods went and received him respectfully.

While ascending the summit of Mount Sumeru, King Mūrdhātā saw a stretch of dark blue forest aloft like a streak of clouds. At the sight of this, he addressed the yakṣa Divaukasa: "Divaukasa, what is that stretch of dark blue forest aloft like a streak of clouds?"

"My lord, that is the *kovidāra* grove of the gods known as Pāriyātraka. This is where the Trāyastriṃśa gods, moved and captivated by the five divine sense pleasures, fool around, enjoy themselves, and make love for the four months of the rainy season.[730] My lord should go there, and being moved and captivated by the five divine sense pleasures, fool around, enjoy himself, and make love."

Having heard this, King Mūrdhātā addressed his ministers: "Officers, do you see that stretch of dark blue forest aloft like a streak of clouds?"

"Yes, my lord."

"That is the *kovidāra* grove of Trāyastriṃśa gods known as Pāriyātraka. There the Trāyastriṃśa gods, moved and captivated by the five divine sense pleasures, fool around, enjoy themselves, and make love for the four months of the rainy season. [220] Officers, you should go there, and being moved and captivated by the five divine sense pleasures, fool around, enjoy yourselves, and make love."

While ascending the summit of Mount Sumeru, King Mūrdhātā saw something bright white aloft like a mass of clouds. At the sight of this, he addressed the yakṣa Divaukasa: "Divaukasa, what is this bright white thing aloft like a mass of clouds?"

"My lord, that is the divine assembly of the Trāyastriṃśa gods known as Sudharmā (Good Dharma). There the Trāyastriṃśa gods and the four great kings come together and assemble to consider, evaluate, and examine what is beneficial and what is just for gods and mortals. My lord should go there."

Having heard this, King Mūrdhātā addressed his ministers: "Officers, do you see that bright white thing aloft like a mass of clouds?"

"Yes, my lord."

"That is the divine assembly of the Trāyastriṃśa gods known as Sudharmā. There the Trāyastriṃśa gods and the four great kings come together and assemble to consider, evaluate, and examine what is beneficial and what is just for gods and mortals. Officers, you should go there."

Sudarśana: The City of the Trāyastriṃśa Gods

The city of the Trāyastriṃśa gods known as Sudarśana is 2,500 leagues in length, 2,500 leagues in width, 10,000 leagues in circumference, and surrounded on all sides by seven gold ramparts. These ramparts are two and a half leagues in height, and they are fitted with four kinds of coping:[731] gold, silver, beryl, and crystal. On top is a single watchtower.[732]

The portion of land inside the city of Sudarśana is beautiful, good-looking, and attractive, and it is colorful and variegated with many hundreds of colors. The land is soft, very soft, like *tūla* or *karpāsa* cotton, yielding with each footstep, rising again when the foot is lifted. And it is strewn knee-deep with a pile of flowers from the divine coral tree. As the wind arises, old flowers are swept away and new ones are spread out.

The city of Sudarśana has 999 gates. [221] Stationed at each gate are five hundred yakṣas wearing dark clothes and clad in ornamented armor. They protect the Trāyastriṃśa gods and add great beauty.

The roads in the city of Sudarśana are 2,500 leagues long and twelve leagues wide. They are beautiful, good-looking, and attractive, strewn with golden sand, sprinkled with sandalwood-scented water, and affixed with nets of gold.[733]

All around various lotus pools have been built. These lotus pools are formed from four kinds of bricks: those of gold, silver, crystal, and beryl. The railings that surround these lotus pools have transverse bars, crossbars, and bases made of crystal. Those railings made of crystal have transverse bars, crossbars, and bases made of beryl.[734]

These lotus pools are filled with cold water that is like honey; they are covered with blue, red, and white lotuses, and as well as white lilies; and they resound with the sweet and agreeable sounds of shape-shifting shore birds. All around these lotus pools are various flowering and fruit-bearing trees that are well formed, well arranged, and covered with wreaths, as though a skilled garland-maker or a garland-maker's student had placed garlands on top of them or carefully arranged them with flowers as ornaments. They resound with the sweet and agreeable sounds of shape-shifting land-born birds.

In the city of Sudarśana there are four kinds of wish-fulfilling trees that produce cloth: blue, yellow, red, and white ones. These wish-fulfilling trees produce four kinds of fine material, and these fine materials yield four kinds of clothes:[735] blue, yellow, red, and white ones. Whenever a god or a daughter of the gods desires them, as soon as that thought comes to mind, they appear in hand.

There are also four kinds of ornament trees: those that produce ornaments for hands and for feet, and those that produce ones to be concealed and to be exposed. Whenever a god or a daughter of the gods desires [them], as soon as that thought comes to mind, they appear in hand.

There are also four kinds of trees that produce musical instruments: those that produce bamboo flutes, three-stringed lutes, and *sughoṣakas*.[736]

Whenever a god or a daughter of the gods desires them, as soon as that thought comes to mind, they appear in hand.

There are also four kinds of divine nectar: blue, yellow, red, and white. Whenever a god or a daughter of the gods desires them, as soon as that thought comes to mind, they appear in hand.

There is honey, honey wine, liquor from *kadamba* blossoms, and other beverages.[737] There are homes, penthouse apartments, summer chambers, palatial open-air platforms,[738] observation points, and galleries. [222] There is also a dining room[739] that is made radiant by groups of women, served by communities of nymphs numbering in the thousands, and filled with the sounds of music. It is there that the Trāyastriṃśa gods fool around, enjoy themselves, and make love, experiencing the results of their merit.

The divine assembly hall of the Trāyastriṃśa gods is known as Sudharmā. It is three hundred leagues in length, three hundred leagues in width, and hence nine hundred leagues all around. It is beautiful, good-looking, and attractive, made of crystal, and it rises above the city four and a half leagues. Inside are seats that have been specially prepared for the Trāyastriṃśa gods. There are seats for each of the thirty-two underlords, and a thirty-third for Śakra, lord of the gods.

At the very end of all these gods, a seat had been specially prepared for King Mūrdhātā.

King Māndhātā among the Gods

The Trāyastriṃśa gods went out to receive King Mūrdhātā respectfully with an offering. Those beings, who were very powerful because of their merit, entered according to rank; the others remained outside.

King Mūrdhātā reflected, "Of all those seats that have been specially prepared, that final seat must be mine." Then it occurred to King Mūrdhātā, "How good it would be if Śakra, lord of the gods, offered me half of his seat!"

As soon as King Māndhātā had that thought, Śakra, lord of the gods, gave half of his seat to King Māndhātā. King Mūrdhātā then took up half of the seat of Śakra, lord of the gods.[740] When King Mūrdhātā and Śakra, lord of the gods, were both sitting on the same seat, there wasn't any distinction, difference, or disparity between them, not in height, breadth, loveliness of complexion, or timber and quality of voice. The only difference was that Śakra, lord of the gods, never blinked.

While King Mūrdhātā stayed among the Trāyastriṃśa gods, thirty-six Śakras died and passed away. Then a war broke out between the gods and antigods.[741] First the antigods were defeated, so they closed the gates to the city of the antigods. Then the five defenses of the gods were defeated, so the gods closed the gates to their city as well. At this point, the gods and the antigods both became confused.

"What is this, gentlemen?" King Mūrdhātā said to the Trāyastriṃśa gods. "The gods seem extremely confused."

"The antigods have broken through our five defenses," [223] the Trāyastriṃśa gods said, "so we've closed our gates."

"Men," King Mūrdhātā said, "bring me my bow." And so his bow was brought to him.

Taking up his bow, he sounded his bowstring. The antigods heard the sound of his bowstring, and having heard this, the antigods said, "Whose bowstring has sounded?"

"The bowstring of King Mūrdhātā has sounded," they heard it said.

When they heard this, they were in awe.

Then King Mūrdhātā departed from that divine city. As the gods were being routed by the antigods, he readied himself for battle.

As a rule, when the gods and antigods do battle, their chariots are aloft in the sky, and neither of them has any advantage or disadvantage.

Then King Mūrdhātā rose up into the sky and stood above all of the antigods.

"Who's that who has risen up into the sky above us?" the antigods said.

"That's the king of mortals," they heard it said. "His name is Mūrdhātā."

And then they reflected, "This being is very powerful as a result of his merit. It's his chariot that moves in the sky above us."

Defeated, subdued, and vanquished, the antigods were forced to flee, and they entered the antigod city.

"Who won?" King Mūrdhātā said.

"My lord has won," his ministers said.

And then the king reflected, "I am greater than the Trāyastriṃśa gods." Then it occurred to King Mūrdhātā,

> I possess Jambudvīpa.
> I possess the seven treasures.
> I have a full one thousand sons.
> A rain of gold fell for a week inside my harem.
> I governed the island of Pūrvavideha.
> I governed the island of Aparagodānīya.
> With the help of my army, I governed among the people
> of Uttarakuru.
> I mastered the Trāyastriṃśa gods.
> I entered Sudharmā, the divine assembly.
> And Śakra, lord of the gods, gave me half of his seat.

"How good it would be if I could oust Śakra, lord of the gods, causing him to fall from his position, so that I myself could establish kingship, lordship, and dominion over gods and mortals!"

As soon as King Mūrdhātā had this thought, his magical powers were destroyed and he alighted on Jambudvīpa. There he suffered from a severe affliction, experiencing the painful sensation of the presence of death. [224]

Then King Mūrdhātā's cabinet of ministers and chief ministers, royal officials, and comrades in counsel approached King Mūrdhātā. Having approached, they said this to King Mūrdhātā: "After my lord passes away, there may be future inhabitants[742] who ask, "What did King Mūrdhātā pronounce at the time of his death?"

"Officers, after I pass away, if someone approaches you and asks, 'Gentlemen, what did King Mūrdhātā pronounce at the time of his death?' tell them this: 'Gentlemen, King Mūrdhātā possessed the seven treasures, and making use of the four magical powers that humans can attain,[743] he established kingship, lordship, and dominion over the four islands and then surmounted the Trāyastriṃśa gods. Nevertheless, he met his death still unsatisfied with the objects of the five senses.

Even with a rain of *kārṣāpaṇa* coins,
satisfaction isn't found among sense pleasures.
The wise man knows that sense pleasures
yield little enjoyment and cause great suffering.

Even among divine sense pleasures,
he finds no pleasure at all.
The disciple of a perfectly awakened buddha
is pleased at the demise of craving.

Even a mountain of gold
equal to the Himālayas
is not enough wealth for a single person.
Knowing this, a wise man should act accordingly.

How can one who beholds the suffering
that is caused by sense pleasures
ever take delight in sense pleasures?[744]
Understanding attachment, the thorn in this world,
one who is steadfast should learn to remove it.'"[745]

When the people heard that King Mūrdhātā was sick and set to die, ministers and villagers as well as many hundreds and thousands of beings approached King Mūrdhātā to see him. The king offered various discourses on the dharma to those people. He told a tale of the dangers of sense pleasures and he told of the dangers of household life. Sense pleasure thus became so detested that many hundreds and thousands of beings went forth in the presence of seers, abandoning the household life, and took refuge in the forest. Having gone forth in the manner of seers, they cultivated the four Brahmā states and destroyed sensual desire for objects of desire. Abiding for the most part in this state, they were reborn as inhabitants of the Brahmā World. [225]

The Buddha Gives a Timetable

"Ānanda, from the time that Mūrdhātā played the games of youth through his time as crown prince and then sovereign, while he lived in Jambudvīpa, on the island of Pūrvavideha, on the island of Aparagodānīya, among the Uttarakurus, and upon the seven golden mountains, up until he surmounted the Trāyastriṃśa gods, 1,400 Śakras died and passed away.

"Monks, the lifespan of Śakra, lord of the gods, is like this: One year for mortals equals one day and night for the Trāyastriṃśa gods. Now a month has thirty such days and nights, a year has twelve months, and the lifespan of the Trāyastriṃśa gods is one thousand divine years. Hence, according to human calculation, Śakra's lifespan is 360,000 years."[746]

Identifications

"At that time and at that juncture, Ānanda, when King Mūrdhātā surmounted the Trāyastriṃśa gods and thought, 'How good it would be if Śakra, lord of the gods, would invite me to occupy half of his seat,' the monk Kāśyapa was Śakra, lord of the gods.

"At that time and at that juncture, Ānanda, when this thought occurred to King Mūrdhātā, 'I really should oust Śakra, lord of the gods, causing him to fall from his position so that I myself may have kingship, lordship, and dominion over gods and mortals,' the perfectly awakened Kāśyapa was Śakra, lord of the gods. This malicious thought occurred in that very powerful being, and as a result, his magical powers were destroyed and he alighted on Jambudvīpa. There he suffered from a severe affliction, experiencing the painful sensation of the presence of death.

"At that time and at that juncture, Ānanda, I myself was King Mūrdhātā. Ānanda, I was filled with attachment, with hate, and with delusion, and I wasn't liberated from birth, old age, sickness, death, sorrow, lamentation, suffering, grief, or despair. At the time of my death, however, I delivered a sermon such that many hundreds of thousands of beings left behind the household life and went forth as monks under the guidance of seers. Abandoning sensual desire for objects of desire, and abiding for the most part in this state, they were thus reborn in the Brahmā World.

"Now—as one who is omniscient, with mastery over supreme knowledge and the objects of knowledge, and who had set out to attain nirvāṇa [226]—I delivered a discourse on the dharma such that many hundreds and thousands of deities were established in the [four noble] truths. Many hundreds and thousands of seers were initiated with the "Come, O monk" formula for ordination. After striving, struggling, and straining, they rid themselves of all defilements and thereby obtained arhatship. Many gods, nāgas, yakṣas, celestial musicians, antigods, heavenly birds, kinnaras, and great snakes were established in the taking of the refuges as well as in the precepts. Some of those many hundreds of thousands of beings from Vaiśālī were established in the reward of the stream-enterer, some in the reward of the once-returner, and some in the reward of the nonreturner. Some went forth as monks and obtained arhatship. Some set their minds on attaining awakening as a disciple, some on awakening as a solitary buddha, and some on unsurpassed perfect awakening. And some accepted the refuges as well as the precepts."

Those monks in doubt asked the Lord Buddha, the remover of all doubts, "Bhadanta, what deeds did King Mūrdhātā do so that as a result of those deeds as soon as he had a thought, there was a shower of gold in his harem for seven days?"

And the Blessed One spoke.

A Guildmaster's Son Meets Lord Sarvābhibhū

Long ago, monks, in a time gone by, there arose in the world a tathāgata arhat named Sarvābhibhū (Overpowering All),

who was perfect in knowledge and conduct,
a sugata,
a knower of the world,
an unsurpassed guide for those in need of training,
a teacher of gods and mortals,
a buddha,
and a blessed one.

At that time a certain guildmaster's son had just settled down. In that region, it was a custom that a newly married girl was presented to the bridegroom in a carriage. Strewn with flower [ornaments] made of four kinds of jewels, and then laden as such, she would be given to her husband.[747] She would then take her husband and go to her home. And so, the guildmaster's son accepted those flowers made of four kinds of jewels, got into that vehicle, and set out for the home of his father-in-law. While he was on his way, he came face to face with the perfectly awakened Sarvābhibhū, who was traveling along through the countryside. At the sight of the perfectly awakened Sarvābhibhū, who was adorned with the thirty-two marks of a great man and who was a sight one never tires of seeing, great faith arose in him. Since his mind had been made faithful, he got down from his vehicle and bedecked the Blessed One with those flowers made of four kinds of jewels. [227] When those flowers were in the perfectly awakened Sarvābhibhū's possession, they were magically transformed into the shape of a wagon wheel.[748] They formed a covering that went wherever he went and stopped wherever he stopped.

Filled with faith, the guildmaster's son uttered these verses:

By virtue of this gift to a great one,
may I be a buddha, a sugata, a self-made man.
Having crossed, may I help great masses of people to cross,
those unable to cross under previous great victors.

I have bedecked the great sage
Lord Sarvābhibhū with very lovely flowers,
and I have made this lofty fervent aspiration,
longing for this highest awakening.[749]

[Then the Buddha said to the monks,]

As a result of that act of mine,
I have obtained awakening,
auspicious and supreme.
And for the mighty King Mūrdhātā,
a shower of gold fell for a week.

"As a result of that very act, my city became lovely and golden. It became the beautiful capital of [King] Mahāsudarśana (Very Handsome) known as Kuśāvatī."

Those monks in doubt asked the Lord Buddha, the remover of all doubts, "Bhadanta, what sort of deed did King Mūrdhātā do so that as a result of that deed he established kingship, lordship, and dominion over the four islands and surmounted the Trāyastriṃśa gods?"

And the Blessed One spoke.

The Merchant Otkarika Meets Lord Vipaśyin

Long ago, monks, in a time gone by, there arose in the world a perfectly awakened tathāgata arhat named Vipaśyin (Visionary). Now the perfectly awakened Vipaśyin, after traveling through the countryside, eventually arrived at the capital Bandhumatī (Abode of Relatives). In the morning the perfectly awakened Vipaśyin got dressed, took his bowl and robe, and entered Bandhumatī for alms.

In Bandhumatī there was a certain merchant named Otkarika (Affluent).[750] At the sight of Lord Vipaśyin, whose form was a sight one never tired of seeing, great faith arose in him. Possessed of faith, he took a handful of mung beans and tossed them in Lord Vipaśyin's bowl. Four mung beans fell into his bowl, while one hit the rim[751] and fell on the ground. What was left didn't reach the bowl at all. Not reaching it, they fell on the ground. Then the merchant, possessed of faith, made a fervent aspiration: [228]

By virtue of this gift to a great one,
may I be a buddha, a sugata, a self-made man.
Having crossed, may I help great masses of people to cross,
those who couldn't cross under previous great victors.

The Blessed One said, "The merchant Otkarika was none other than me at that time and at that juncture. Possessed of faith, I threw a handful of mung beans into the perfectly awakened Vipaśyin's bowl, and of that handful, four mung beans fell into his bowl and the rest fell on the ground. As a result of that action, I established kingship, lordship, and dominion over the four islands. As for that mung bean that hit the rim of his bowl and fell on the ground—as a result of that action, I surmounted the Trāyastriṃśa gods. Monks, if that mung bean had fallen in his bowl, given the situation, I would have established kingship, lordship, and dominion over gods and mortals alike.

"The merchant Otkarika, at that time and at that juncture, was none other than King Mūrdhātā. And King Mūrdhātā was none other than me at that time and at that juncture. Since offerings made to a greatly compassionate lord buddha are very well rewarded, very beneficial, very glorious, and very extensive, awakening can occur in this existence. So what should be done? Offering should be made to the Buddha, dharma, and community, and proper fervent aspirations should be made as well."

This was said by the Blessed One. With their minds uplifted, the monks welcomed the words of the Blessed One.

So ends the *Māndhātā-avadāna,* the seventeenth chapter in the glorious *Divyāvadāna.*

Appendix 1

Addendum to *Meṇḍhakagṛhapativibhūti-pariccheda*

In the *Mūlasarvāstivāda-vinaya*, "The Chapter on the Great Fortune of the Householder Meṇḍhaka" and "The Story of Meṇḍhaka"—chapters 9 and 10 of the *Divyāvadāna*—are linked together by the following passage, which is filled with monastic technical terms. I base my translation on the Sanskrit text found in the *Gilgit Manuscripts* (iii 1, 248.7–249.17).[752]

"Blessed One," the householder Meṇḍhaka said, "please allow *kārṣā-paṇa* coins to be accepted for medicinal provisions and so on."[753]

"Yes," the Blessed One said, "they should be accepted."

Though the Blessed One said that the *kārṣāpaṇa* coins should be accepted, the monks didn't know by whom or how they should be accepted.

"Let it be done by the monk who officiates over offerings,"[754] the Blessed One said. But a monk who officiated over offerings was not present. So the Blessed One said, "Let it be done by a novice."

Then the venerable Udāli[755] asked the Lord Buddha, "Bhadanta, the Blessed One has said that a novice is not to receive a gift of gold or silver.[756] This is the tenth precept. Yet now the Blessed One has said that a novice may accept them. How can this be?"

"Udāli," the Blessed One said, "it is with reference to a gift that I said it is not to be accepted. Therefore, a novice may accept it, but not if he will take the gift for himself."

Then the householder Meṇḍhaka said, "Blessed One, please accept this boiled rice mixed with hardened molasses."

"It should be accepted," the Blessed One said. But the monks didn't know by whom or how it should be accepted. So the Blessed One said, "If there is no householder[757] present, either a novice or a monk should watch over it for seven days[758] and then carry it with him." But the monks did not know how it should be watched over. [249]

So the Blessed One said, "Wash your hands, and then have them offer the gift. Place it in your left hand and cover it with your right hand. Then stand in front of a monk and say: 'Venerable ones, pay attention.[759] I, named so-and-so, will watch over this medicine for seven days for the sake of myself and those who follow the religious life with me.' Do this a second and a third time as well."

Then the venerable Udāli asked the Lord Buddha, "Bhadanta, the Blessed One said that the hardened molasses should be looked after for seven days. Who should partake of it?"

"Five kinds of people, Udāli. One who is traveling, one who is fasting, one who is sick, the supervisor of a monastery, and the junior monk who does menial work."[760]

Now some monks set out on a journey through the countryside. They mixed hardened molasses together with some rice and also with some barley meal, and as they were traveling they wanted to eat it. With hesitation, they did eat it. Monks then informed the Blessed One of this matter.

"Monks," the Blessed One said, "it is not permissible to take this sweet worldly pleasure and make a meal of it.[761] Whatever has been mixed with rice should be separated out and then eaten. That which has been mixed with barley meal should be made into a liquid, by adding water, and then eaten." But even when water was added, the latter could not be separated. So the Blessed One said, "It should be scraped with a bamboo reed and then washed in water."

Even doing that, however, he was unable to make it free from its sweet taste.

The Blessed One said, "It should be well purified, mixed with water, and then drunk."

Appendix 2

The Cosmos According to the *Divyāvadāna*

Buddhist cosmology normally divides life within saṃsāra into three realms—the desire realm, the form realm, and the formless realm. The *Divyāvadāna* mentions the various existences and heavens in the desire realm as well as the seventeen heavens in the form realm, but it doesn't mention the four spheres in the formless realm, which are populated by a class of gods with minds but no physical bodies.

These three realms are inhabited by five types of beings: gods, humans, hungry ghosts, animals, and hell beings. Other Buddhist cosmologies include a realm of antigods (*asuras*) between those of humans and hungry ghosts. The *Divyāvadāna* mentions the antigods and Vemacitrin, one of their chiefs, but they do not seem to inhabit their own level of existence.

Other materials also describe a correspondence between psychology and cosmology, such that one's state of mind corresponds to one's level of existence. For example, beings in the desire realm *(kāmadhātu)* tend to have thoughts within the sphere of desire *(kāmāvacara)*, and beings that attain high levels of meditative awareness psychically visit, as it were, the levels of existence of higher classes of beings. The *Divyāvadāna*, however, does not discuss this connection.

The chart that follows presents the various types of beings, the realms and levels of existence that they inhabit, and their average lifespans.[762] Please read it as two long columns.

TYPE OF BEING	LIFESPAN	REALM
Gods *(deva)*		FORMLESS REALM *arūpadhātu*
Naivasañjñānāsañjñāyatana (Sphere of Neither Consciousness nor Unconsciousness)	84,000 eons	
Ākiñcanyāyatana (Sphere of Nothingness)	60,000 eons	
Vijñānānantyāyatana (Sphere of Infinite Consciousness)	40,000 eons	
Ākāśānantyāyatana (Sphere of Infinite Space)	20,000 eons	
Gods *(deva)*		FORM REALM *rūpadhātu*
Akaniṣṭha (Supreme)[763]	16,000 eons	
Sudarśa (Clear Sighted)	8,000 eons	
Sudṛśa (Good-Looking)	4,000 eons	
Atapa (Serene)	2,000 eons	
Abṛha (Not Great)	1,000 eons	
Bṛhatphala (Great Result)	500 eons	
Puṇyaprasava (Merit Born)	250 eons	
Anabhraka (Unclouded)	125 eons	
Śubhakṛtsna (Complete Beauty)	64 eons	
Apramāṇaśubha (Immeasurable Beauty)	32 eons	
Parīttaśubha (Limited Beauty)	16 eons	
Ābhāsvara (Radiant)	8 eons	
Apramāṇābha (Immeasurable Splendor)	4 eons	
Parīttābha (Limited Splendor)	2 eons	
Mahābrahmaṇa (Great Brahmā)	1 eon	
Brahmapurohita (Brahmā's Priests)	1/2 eon	
Brahmakāyika (Brahmā's Assembly)	1/3 eon	
Human Beings *(manuṣya)*	variable	DESIRE REALM *kāmadhātu*
FOUR ISLANDS *(caturdvīpa)*		
Jambudvīpa (Black Plum Island) in the south		
Pūrvavideha (Eastern Videha) in the east		
Aparagodānīya (Western Godānīya) in the west		
Uttarakuru (Northern Kuru) in the north		
Hungry Ghosts *(preta)*	unspecified	
Animals *(tiryagyoni)*	unspecified	
Hell Beings *(naraka)*	unspecified	
COLD HELLS		
Arbuda (Blistering)[765]		
Nirarbuda (Blisters Bursting)		
Aṭaṭa (Chattering Teeth)		
Hahava (Ugh!)		
Huhuva (Brrr!)		
Utpala (Blue Lotus)[766]		
Padma (Lotus)		
Mahāpadma (Great Lotus)		
HOT HELLS		
Sañjīva (Reviving)		
Kālasūtra (Black Thread)		
Saṅghāta (Crushing)		
Raurava (Shrieking)		
Mahāraurava (Loud Shrieking)		
Tapana (Heat)		
Pratāpana (Extreme Heat)		
Avīci (Ceaseless Torture)		

DESIRE REALM
kāmadhātu

Gods *(deva)*

SIX HEAVENS

Paranirmitavaśavartin (Masters of Others' Creations)	9,219,000,000 years
Nirmāṇarati (Delighting in Creation)	2,304,000,000 years
Tuṣita (Content)	576,000,000 years
Yāma (Free from Conflict)	144,000,000 years
Trāyastriṃśa (Thirty-Three) home to Śakra, lord of the gods	36,000,000 years[764]
Cāturmahārājika (Four Groups of the Great Kings)	9,000 years

Four Great Kings

Kubera = Vaiśravaṇa = Dhanada (Bestower of Wealth)
guardian of the north and lord of the yakṣas

Dhṛtarāṣṭra (One Whose Kingdom Is Secure)
guardian of the east and lord of celestial musicians

Virūḍhaka (Sprouted)
guardian of the south and lord of the *kumbhāṇḍa*s

Virūpākṣa (Ugly Eyes)
guardian of the west and lord of the nāgas

Sadāmatta Gods (Ever-Intoxicated)

Mālādhāra (Bearing Garlands)

Karoṭapāṇi (Bowl-in-Hand)

Appendix 3

Divyāvadāna and *Mūlasarvāstivāda-vinaya* Concordance

Twenty-one of the thirty-eight stories in the *Divyāvadāna* are preserved within the Tibetan canon. The appendix shows their location.

P Peking edition of the Tibetan Tripiṭaka
D Derge edition of the Tibetan Tripiṭaka
GM *Gilgit Manuscripts*. See Dutt 1984.

1. *Koṭikarṇa-avadāna*
   P: Carmavastu 41/97, 1, 3; khe 237a3 ff.
   D: ka 251b3 ff.
   GM: iii 4, 159.4–193.20

2. *Pūrṇa-avadāna*
   P: Bhaiṣajyavastu 41/112, 4, 8; khe 276a8 ff.
   D: ka 295b4 ff.
   GM: —

3. *Maitreya-avadāna*
   P: Bhaiṣajyavastu 41/130, 5, 2; ge 26b2 ff.
   D: kha 28b4 ff.
   GM: —

4. *Brāhmaṇadārikā-avadāna*
   P: Bhaiṣajyavastu 41/155, 3, 5; ge 88a5 ff.
   D: kha 95a7 ff.
   GM: —

5. *Stutibrāhmaṇa-avadāna*
P: Bhaiṣajyavastu 41/161, 3, 7; ge 103a7 ff.
D: kha 112a5 ff.
GM: —

6. *Indrabrāhmaṇa-avadāna*
P: Bhaiṣajyavastu 41/161, 5, 7; ge 104a7 ff.
D: kha 113a6 ff.
GM: iii 1, 73.16–76.2 (= Divy 76.10–80.9)

7. *Nagarāvalambikā-avadāna*
P: Bhaiṣajyavastu 41/180, 4, 2; ge 151a2
D: kha 162b5 ff.
GM: iii 1, 79.3–91.6

8. *Supriya-avadāna*
P: —
D: —
GM: —

9. *Meṇḍhakagṛhapativibhūti-pariccheda*
P: Bhaiṣajyavastu 41/250, 4, 3; nge 26a3 ff.
D: ga 28a5 ff.
GM: iii 1, 241.1–248.6

10. *Meṇḍhaka-avadāna*
P: Bhaiṣajyavastu 41/252, 2, 8; nge 30a5 ff.
D: ga 32b2 ff.
GM: iii 1, 249.18–255.10

11. *Aśokavarṇa-avadāna*
P: —
D: —
GM: —

12. *Prātihārya-sūtra*
P: —
D: —
GM: —

13. *Svāgata-avadāna*
P: Vinayavibhaṅga 43/149, 1, 8; te 17a8 ff.
D: nya 19a1 ff.
GM: iii 4, 159.3–193.20

14. *Sūkarika-avadāna*
P: —
D: —
GM: —

15. *Cakravartivyākṛta-avadāna*
P: —
D: —
GM: —

16. *Śukapotaka-avadāna*
P: —
D: —
GM: —

17. *Māndhātā-avadāna* (Divy 200.20–210.13)
P: Vinayakṣudraka 44/216, 4, 7; ne 236a7 ff.
D: da 247b4 ff.
GM: —

Māndhātā-avadāna (Divy 210.13–225.10)
P: Bhaiṣajyavastu 41/183, 3, 6; ge 158a6 ff.
D: kha 169b6 ff.
GM: —

Notes

1 Tatelman (2000: 1) equates it with Aparānta, explaining that it "corresponds to much of the present Indian state of Gujarat."

2 B. C. Law (1976: 264–65) notes that it may be identified with the village of Urel near modern-day Bodh Gaya.

3 Mosley 1998: 26.

4 One frequently represented practice involves seeing objects that are "agents of faith" *(prāsādika),* such as buddhas, images of buddhas, arhats, and stūpas, and making offerings to them. See Rotman 2003b.

5 For more on the specific nature and definition of avadānas, see Speyer 1992: ii, i–cx; Winternitz 1993: 266–67; Weeraratne 1966; Prakash 1970: 3–5; Sarkar 1981: 45–52 and 1990: xxiv–xxvii; Sharma 1985: 3–7 and 1992: 6–8; Ohnuma 1997: 20–25; Hiraoka 1998: 433n21; and, most notably, Tatelman 2000: 4–10.

6 For example, as Joel Tatelman (2000: 7) explains, "for the 'story of the past' some avadānas substitute a 'prediction' *(vyākaraṇa):* typically, at the conclusion of the story, when the protagonist vows to become a buddha or *pratyekabuddha* ['solitary buddha'] or arhat, the Buddha confirms the accuracy of the vow and reveals the name by which that individual will be known."

7 Divy 23.27–24.1, 55.9–13, 135.21–25, 193.12–16, 289.20–24, 314.4–8, 348.3, 465.7–9, etc., *bhikṣava ekāntakṛṣṇānām ekāntakṛṣṇo vipākaḥ ekāntaśuklānāṃ dharmāṇām ekāntaśuklo vipākaḥ vyatimiśrāṇāṃ vyatimiśraḥ | tasmāt tarhi bhikṣava ekāntakṛṣṇāni karmāṇy apāsya vyatimiśrāṇi caikāntaśukleṣv eva karmasv ābhogaḥ karaṇīyaḥ | ity evaṃ vo bhikṣavaḥ śikṣitavyam.*

8 For more on the literary history of stories about Pūrṇa, see Tatelman 2000: 12–27. For more on the story in art, see Schlingloff 1989 and 1991.

9 See Ellis 1966: 8, 385–886; Welbon 1968: 178; and Osthoff 1996.

10 For a translation of the play, see Sykes 1950: 151–76.

11 Divy 82.13–14, *kāyaprāsādikaś cittaprāsādikaḥ.*

12 Divy 432.9–10, *svaiḥ karmabhir vañcitaḥ.*

13 See, for example, Sharma 1985: 20; Cunningham 1879: plates XXVII-12, XXXIV-2; Vogel 1910: 47ff.; Rhi 1991; and Borromeo 1992.

14 With regard to the date of the *Divyāvadāna,* scholars frequently cite Moriz Winternitz's (1993: 274) claim that the *Divyāvadāna* "as a whole, could not have come into existence earlier than the 4th century A.D." or P. L. Vaidya's (1959a: xi) claim that it is

"sage to hold that the *Divyāvadāna,* in its present form, came into existence between 200 and 350 A.D." With regard to the text's sectarian affiliation, A. C. Banerjee (1979: 19) claims that it "is a work of the Mūlasarvāstivāda school." Vaidya (1959a: x), citing Banerjee, nevertheless explains that "it is now proved beyond doubt that the *Divyāvadāna* is a work belonging to the Sarvāstivāda School." I will explain more about the relationship between the Sarvāstivādins and the Mūlasarvāstivādins (and the confusion that ensues) in what follows.

15 Winternitz 1993: 277.

16 Divy 1.4–5; cf. 24.11–12, 167.3–4, 262.8–9, etc., *āḍhyo mahādhano mahābhogo vistīrṇaviśālaparigrahaḥ.* All of these references occur on the first page of an avadāna.

17 Divy 62.8–9, 62.12–13, 131.16–17, 435.6–7, etc., *ṛddhaṃ ca sphītaṃ ca kṣemaṃ ca subhikṣaṃ cākīrṇabahujanamanuṣyaṃ ca.*

18 Divy 3.12–16, 99.24–28, 441.21–25, etc., *aṣṭābhir dhātrībhir unnīyate vardhyate kṣīreṇa dadhnā navanītena sarpiṣā sarpimaṇḍenānyaiś cottaptottaptair upakaraṇaviśeṣaiḥ.*

19 For more on this dehistoricizing strategy, see Pollock 1985. Cf. Speyer 1992: i, xvi–xvii.

20 See, for example, Sastri 1945; Prakash 1970; and Sharma 1985. Bongard-Levin 1971 and Upreti 1995 are more successful.

21 For a useful comparison, see Steven Collins's discussion of "the Pali imaginaire" and why he treats it "as a stable and cohesive ideology throughout the traditional period, in relationship to historical change in South Asia" (1998: 72–73; cf. 72–89).

22 Ginzburg 1980: 24.

23 This manuscript is unlabeled by Cowell and Neil.

24 This is the manuscript that Eugène Burnouf utilized in his *Introduction a l'histoire du buddhisme indien* (1844).

25 To borrow David Hult's (1991: 116–17) terminology, Cowell and Neil followed the Bédierian mode of text editing (i.e., "the detection of the single 'best' manuscript") and not the Lachmannian one (i.e., "the reconstruction of an author's original text").

26 For more on these avadānamālās and later avadāna compositions, see Speyer 1992: ii, xii–xiv, xxi–c; Winternitz 1993: 280; Bongard-Levin and Volkova 1965: 7; Tatelman 2000: 10; and Lewis 2000.

27 Divy 664, *iti śrīdivyāvadāne aśokāvadānamālāyāṃ ṣaṣṭho 'dhyāyaḥ.* As a point of comparison, the following story (Divy 664) concludes with "So ends the *Maṇicūḍaavadāna* ('The Story of Maṇicūḍa'), the seventh chapter in the glorious *Divyāvadānamālā*" *(iti śrīdivyāvadānamālāyāṃ maṇicūḍāvadānaṃ saptamo 'dhyāyaḥ).*

28 Divy viii, *iti śrīdivyāvadānoddhṛta<m> aṣṭamīvratamāhātmyakuśāvadānaṃ samāptam.* Mitra (1981: 274–75) also notes another manuscript that "contains two works, both in the Newari language, one a translation of the story of Kuśa of the *Vīrakuśa Avadāna* and the other the *Aṣṭamīvrata-kathā,* or story in praise of the Aṣṭamī fast. Both are said to be extracts from the *Divya Avadāna* translated into the Nepalese language by Amṛtānanda." For more on the *Aṣṭamīvratakathā,* see Mitra 1981: 266.

29 Hans Jorgensen edited and translated this text in 1931 and titled it the *Vicitrakarṇikāvadānoddhṛta* ("Selected from the *Vicitrakarṇikāvadāna*"), a name reminiscent of the title *Śrīdivyāvadānoddhṛta* ("Selected from the Glorious *Divyāvadāna*") found in the *Vīrakuśāvadāna* colophon. Cf. Lienhard 1963.

30 At the end of the *Koṭikarṇa-avadāna* ("The Story of Koṭikarṇa"), Cowell and Neil (Divy 24n1) explain that "the words *iti śrīdivyāvadāne* ['in the glorious *Divyāvadāna*'] are always omitted in ABC. We give them from DE." Likewise, manuscripts A, B, and C end with the words "So ends the *Maitrakanyaka-avadāna*" *(maitrakanyakāvadānaṃ samāptam),* signifying the end of the last story, but not the end of the work itself.

31 Cf. Weeraratne 1966: 649; Sharma 1975: 31–32, 1985: 56–57; and Sarkar 1990: xxviii.

32 Hahn's hypothesis that Gopadatta, the author of the *Saptakumārikāvadāna* ("The Story of the Seven Maidens"), is also the author of this work is convincing, though yet to be verified (Klaus 1983: 5–22).

33 In this regard, some scholars have argued that the compiler of the *Divyāvadāna* made use of Kumāralāta's *Kalpanāmaṇḍitikā* (Winternitz 1993: 277 and Vaidya 1959a: xi), but the reverse is also possible. Cf. Huber 1904: 709–26; Lévi 1907: 106; and Lüders 1926: 71–132.

34 Nevertheless, it does seem that copyists or later editors incorporated some verses from Kṣemendra's *Avadānakalpalatā,* which was composed in the eleventh century, into the *Kunāla-avadāna* (Bongard-Levin and Volkova 1965: 5), the *Sudhanakumāra-avadana* (Jaini 1989: 325), and the *Rūpāvatī-avadāna* (Dimitrov 2007: 7–15).

35 This needn't be an insurmountable problem for the historian. As Joel Rosenberg (1975; cited in Alter 1981: 19–20) remarks regarding the construction of the Torah, "It may actually improve our understanding of the Torah to remember that it is quoting documents, that there is, in other words, a purposeful documentary montage that must be perceived as a unity, regardless of the number and types of smaller units that form the building blocks of its composition. Here, the final weight of literary interest falls upon the activity of the final redactor, whose artistry requires far more careful attention than has hitherto been accorded."

36 Fourteen of these stories occur in the *Vinayavastu,* while seven have parallels in the *Vinayavibhaṅga* and *Vinayakṣudraka*. For a list and their locations, see appendix 3. Cf. Panglung 1981: xv–xvi.

37 Ms. H 303b10, *iti divyāvadānamālāyāṃ sumāgadhānām avadānaṃ trayacatvāriṃsaḥ samāptaḥ*. For more on the *Sumāgadhāvadāna*, see Iwamoto 1968.

38 This manuscript of the *Divyāvadānamālā* begins with the same first seven stories as the *Divyāvadāna* and then proceeds with *Maitrakanyaka-avadāna* (H 33a3–37a2), which is the thirty-eighth story in the *Divyāvadāna*, though the version here is completely different. Story 9 is the *Śaśaka-avadāna* ("The Story of the Rabbit") (H 37a2–39a10; cf. *Avadānaśataka*, no. 37 and *Jātaka*, no. 316), which is also not included in the *Divyāvadāna*. What follows is mixture of stories from the *Divyāvadāna*—e.g., no. 10, *Meṇḍhaka-avadāna;* no. 11, *Aśokavarṇa-avadāna* ("The Story of Aśokavarṇa"); no. 12, *Prātihārya-sūtra*—and stories from other sources—e.g., no. 31, *Maṇicūḍa-avadāna* (Handurukande 1967); no. 33, *Chinnabhaktabrāhmaṇa-avadāna* ("The Story of the Fasting Brahman") (Mitra 1981: 314–15); no. 42, *Suvarṇavarṇa-avadāna* ("The Story of Suvarṇavarṇa") (cf. Roy 1971).

39 For example, at the end of the *Pūrṇa-avadāna,* manuscripts A, B, and C (Divy 55n2) read *iti pūrṇāvadānaṃ dvitīyam,* while manuscript H 20b3 reads *iti pūrṇāvadānaṃ dvitīyaḥ*. Likewise at the end of the *Koṭikarṇa-avadāna,* manuscripts A, B, and C (Divy 24n1) read *iti koṭīkarṇāvadānaṃ prathamaḥ,* while manuscript H 9a6 reads *iti śroṇakoṭī,* and then the rest is blotted out quite thoroughly.

40 Ms. H 74a4 reads *vaihāyasena tiṣṭhanti - - - nya na kasyacit,* with three distinctive dashes, while Divy 223.10 contains the more complete reading of *vaihāyasena tiṣṭhanti teṣām anyonyaṃ na kasyacit.* Since ms. A reads *kaścasyacid* and mss. BC read *kaścisya cid* (Divy 223n3), ms. H appears to be from a different text lineage. Cowell and Neil's reading is likely from ms. D, which ms. H often seems to follow.

41 See, for example, Divy 1.18 and 51.10–11 in the accompanying translation.

42 In the middle of the *Pāṃśupradāna-avadāna,* ms. H 129a7–8 preserves || *iti upaguptāvadānaṃ ṣaḍviṃśatiṃ*||, though it is crossed out, while Divy 364.16, after *kāryānurodhāt,* preserves only a "||." Cf. Aśokāv 28.19; trans. in Strong 1989: 198. Cowell and Neil (Divy 364n5) observe that the manuscripts of the text that they use "put || after *kāryānurodhāt* and connect it with the preceding sentence." My guess is that the "||" that remains in the *Divyāvadāna* is likely a holdover from a reading much like the one preserved in ms. H.

43 Ali 1997: 27.

44 As Baums (2002: 291) notes, however, "It seems safe to say that our manuscript did not contain the *Divyāvadāna* in the form we know it...it is most likely that the *Jyotiṣkāvadāna* fragments are from an avadāna collection not identical to the *Divyāvadāna.*" My thanks to Jens-Uwe Hartmann for information about avadānas in the Schøyen Collection.

45 See, for example, Gnoli 1977–78: ii, xvii–xxi and Schopen 1997: 212, 235–36 and 1995: 122.

46 Giuseppe Tucci (1971) provides an extended account of the textual parallels and possible precursors for the avadānas in the *Divyāvadāna.* Also helpful in this regard is Leslie Grey's *A Concordance of Buddhist Birth Stories.*

47 See Divy 20.23–24 and 34.29–35.1.

48 See Dutt 1930: 15; Mukhopadhyaya 1963: lx–lxi; and Strong 1989: 36–37.

49 See Dutt 1987: 241, 252 and 1930: 25; and Strong 1989: 31.

50 *Śikṣāsamuccaya* 148.13–149.4, *āryasarvāstivādānāṃ ca paṭhayate.* For a complete translation of this passage, see Śāntideva 1971: 147–48.

51 See, for example, Przyluski 1923: 8–9; Ch'en 1945–47: 221; Frauwallner 1956: 24–42; Lamotte 1988: 168–79; Mukherjee 1984; and Hirakawa 1990: 122–23.

52 The compelling question for historians, however, might not be who came first, the Sarvāstivādins or the Mūlasarvāstivādins, but what was at stake in being considered the *authentic* Sarvāstivādins. An instructive parallel is the ongoing debate in New York City about which Ray's Pizza is the original Ray's Pizza, what such a distinction means, and why so many pizza parlors in the city make use of the name. As John Tierney (1991) explains, "The results of a *New York Times* investigation in 1987 were summed up most poignantly by an employee at one Ray's pizzeria who, after saying that Ray couldn't come to the phone, finally broke down and confessed, 'There is no Ray, really.' The situation was existentially disquieting, but also liberating. It meant that Ray's pizzerias could be opened by people of all nations and first names. The only real obstacle was finding a block that didn't already have a Famous Ray's, World Famous Ray's, Original Ray's, Famous Original Ray's, Ray Bari's, Real Ray's or One and Only Famous Ray's." Regardless of its origin and pedigree, Ray's Pizza has become emblematic of New York City. In the proposed East Village retail complex in Las Vegas it is given pride of place, and in the television show *Futurama,* New York City one thousand years in the future is home to the Famous Original Ray's Supreme Court. As one con-

cerned Ray's proprietor observed, "The frightening thing is that someday all pizza will be Ray's pizza. Think about it" (Giest 1987). In the early centuries of the Common Era, "the Sarvāstivāda school was the most widely extended group of schools in India" (Banerjee 1994: 5), it enjoyed the many benefits of royal patronage, and it produced an enormous body of literature (Banerjee 1979). Perhaps Sarvāstivādin hegemony in North India, regardless of who were the *first* Sarvāstivādins, led to an internal struggle between Sarvāstivādin subsects to differentiate themselves within a world in which it might appear that one day *all* Buddhists will be Sarvāstivādin.

53 While the differences between the stories in the *Divyāvadāna* and their counterparts in the *Mūlasarvāstivāda-vinaya* are not major, they may be significant—for example, why does the story of Aśoka in the *Mūlasarvāstivāda-vinaya* emphasize Kashmir and the version in the *Divyāvadāna* emphasize Mathura (Przyluski 1914: 495–522)? Cf. Strong 1985: 878–79.

54 Various representations of stories from the *Divyāvadāna*, however, do suggest some contours to this cultural construct. For example, there may have been a connection between the Mūlasarvāstivādins and the Bhadāyanīya (or Bhadāvanīya) branch of Sarvāstivādins who were prominent at Pauni in the western Deccan (Mirashi 1981: 144). This could explain the large carved panels at Bhājā, between Mumbai and Pune, that seem to represent the *Māndhātā-avadāna* (Gyani 1951; Agrawala 1965; cf. Dehejia 1972: 115–16). Considering that the caves at Bhājā date to the first or second centuries B.C.E.—before the period tentatively ascribed for the production of the *Divyāvadāna*—the identification of these panels, if true, signifies an earlier circulation for this story and perhaps for the other narratives of the *Divyāvadāna* as well. Since Buddhist narratives were rarely represented in sculpture in the western Deccan (Ray 1986: 189), these panels may also testify to the wide-ranging importance of this story. Representations of the narrative, for example, also occur on the railings around a stūpa at Amarāvatī circa 150 C.E. (Sivaramamurti 1942: 293). These panels at Bhājā may also signify an old connection between Buddhism in the northern plains and in the western Deccan. Representations of Dipaṅkara in the two places also suggest this possibility (Vasant 1991). Nevertheless, certain passages in the *Divyāvadāna* indicate a northern bias against the western Deccan, perhaps attesting to a friction between Buddhists in these two places. While the western Deccan is generally described as a place connected with trade and wealth (Divy 576.20–25 and Upreti 1995: 26, 54), Aparānta, a Sātavāhana stronghold from the time of Ptolemy (Ray 1986: 55), receives a scathing critique. In the *Pūrṇa-avadāna,* the Buddha warns "the people of Śroṇāparāntaka are fierce, violent, cruel, abusive, scornful, and insulting" (Divy 38.8–10).

55 Rushdie 1990: 17.

56 For an instructive parallel example, see Ronald Davidson's (1990: 303–5) account of how Sarvāstivādin abhidharma texts came to be elevated to canonical status.

57 See, respectively, Hofinger 1982 and Hartmann 1985.

58 Salomon (1999: 36; cf. 1999: 147n17) explains that "in many cases, the individual recitations end with an abbreviation formula such as *vistare sarva karya*, 'The whole [story] is to be done [i.e., recited] in full (e.g., frag. 25, r, line 26); *vistare janidave siyadi*, '[The story] should be known [i.e., recalled] in full' (frag. 4, part 7, v, line 4); or the frequent but enigmatic *sarva vistare yaśayupamano siyadi* (frag. 1, part 2, v, line 74) or *vistare jaṇidave yaśayupamano siyadi* (frag. 4, part 6, v, line 30), whose interpretation remains to be fully clarified."

As Timothy Lenz (personal communication) explains, the frequent but enigmatic expression *vistare* [|] *yaṣayupamano siyadi,* equivalent to *yathopamāno syāt* in Classical Sanskrit, is open to a number of interpretations, including, "And so on. It should be done according to the appropriate model"; "It should be extended according to the appropriate model"; "And so on. There should be an appropriate analogy"; or "It should be extended according to an appropriate analogy." In an avadāna fragment that corresponds to the *Vessantara-jātaka*, a similar expression—*yaṣayupamano sarvo*—occurs, which Salomon (1999: 38–39) translates as "the whole [introductory portion is to be recited] according to the usual pattern." In the same fragment the more conventional expression meaning "the verse is to be recited in full"—*gatha vi(stare*)*—also occurs. And so, there is no shortage of instructions to the reciter.

59 See Speyer 1992: ii, xvi–xviii. Furthermore, as Salomon (1999: 140n29) notes, "this Gāndhārī avadāna style has much in common with the simpler narrative style of the Sanskrit prose avadānas, as seen, for example, in some sections of the *Divyāvadāna*."

60 This conjecture is further supported by notations on the manuscripts that seem to indicate that these avadānas were copied en masse (Salomon 1999: 71–76). For example, "*sarva ime avada*[*na*] [*aca*] *(likhidaga*),* 'all these avadānas have been written'" (1999: 74). "According to this theory," Salomon (1999: 74) hypothesizes, "the scribe who had been assigned to make new copies of the texts contained in our scrolls would have marked them, after he had finished recopying them, as 'written' *(likhidaga),* that is, 'copied,' to indicate that they could be discarded."

61 Schopen (1994a: 552–53) suggests that during this period the vinaya had not yet been composed or was in the process of being composed, but also possible is that vinaya masters preserved the vinaya without recourse to writing, while avadānists, who were engaged in the novel practice of creating stories, relied on the new medium of writing to preserve their new genre of composition.

62 More recently Salomon (2006: 370) has claimed that "early Buddhist manuscript traditions may have been ritual and symbolic as well as—perhaps even rather than—practical." Early avadāna texts are so brief and schematic (e.g., Vorobyova-Desyatovskaya 2000) that it is hard to know how they were used or what purpose they served. They very well could have been exercises or tests for an avadānist in training (Lenz 2003: 110). Regardless of the purpose in writing them down, however, the stories they referenced were very likely meant to be recited.

63 For more on how avadānas may have been used in practice, see Tatelman 2000: 11–12.

64 Moore 1998: 260.

65 Divy 71.25, 75.24–25, 79.25, etc., *dharmadeśanā.*

66 Divy 97.12, 310.27, 462.11, etc., *dharmadeśanā.* Such discourses on the Dharma, however, are not restricted to mealtime. The Buddha also offers these teachings to those who approach him on other occasions (Divy 71.25, 75.24–25, 79.25, etc.).

67 Divy 183.29, 190.20, 285.11, 542.27, etc., *dharmyayā kathayā.*

68 Divy 338.19, *bahubollakāḥ.*

69 Cf. Dutt 1940: 173 and Law 1925: 104–5.

70 Divy 312.15–16, *ārya kiṃ nivartayase tvaṃ piṇḍakenārthī aham api puṇyenāsminn evodyāne vihara piṇḍakenāvighātaṃ karomīti.* Vaidya (Divy-V 193.8) emends to *nivartase.* Cf. Speyer 1902: 130 and Divy 238.29–239.4.

71 Divy 183.29–30, 285.1011, 542.27–28, *saṃdarśayati samādāpayati samuttejayati saṃpraharṣayati.*

72 Divy 235.24–236.1, *tatra gṛhe kālena kālaṃ bhikṣavo bhikṣuṇyaś ca piṇḍapātaṃ praviśya parikathāṃ kurvanti | sa dārakas tāṃ parikathāṃ śrutvā tasyāṃ velāyāṃ na rodity avahitaśrotras tūṣṇībhūtvā tāṃ dharmaśravaṇakathāṃ śṛṇoti | pratyavasṛteṣu bhikṣubhikṣuṇīṣu ca punaḥ pipāsāduḥkhaṃ pratisaṃvedayamāno rodituṃ pravṛttaḥ.*

73 Edgerton (BHSD), citing this passage, suggests "religious talk," "sermon," or "dialogue." Rhys Davids and Stede (PTSD) offer "'round-about tale,' exposition, story, esp. religious tale." Cf. Divy 92.18 where *parikathā* seems to mean "indirect reference."

74 Divy 241.25–26, *icchatha bhikṣavo 'sya dharmaruceḥ pūrvikāṃ karmaplotim ārabhya dharmīkathāṃ śrotum.*

75 Divy 97.29–98.1, 131.1–2. 191.6–7, etc., *bhikṣavaḥ saṃśayajātāḥ sarvasaṃśayacchettāraṃ buddhaṃ bhagavantaṃ papracchuḥ.*

76 Divy 69.17–20, 73.3–6, 139.27–30, etc.,

> *tat kālaṃ svayam adhigamya dhīra buddhyā*[a] |
> *śrotṝṇāṃ śramaṇa jinendra*[b] *kāṅkṣitānām* |
> *dhīrābhir munivṛṣa vāgbhir uttamābhiḥ* |
> *utpannaṃ vyapanaya saṃśayaṃ śubhābhiḥ* ||

[a]Following Divy-V 42.21, etc., and Aśokāv 33.21. Divy 69.17, etc., *dhīrabuddhyā.*
[b]Following Divy-V 42.22, etc., and Aśokāv 33.21. Divy 69.17–18, etc., *śramaṇajinendra.*

77 See, for example, Divy 237.17–19 and 303.12–303.27.

78 Wendy Doniger (1998: 84–88) likewise describes the "multivocality" of myths, which allows them to contain a variety of perspectives regarding the events that they depict.

79 Divy 241.28–30, *bhagavān dharmarucim ārabhya bhikṣūṇāṃ dharmīkathāṃ kuryāt | bhagavataḥ śrutvā bhikṣavo dhārayiṣyati.*

80 Georges Dreyfus (2003: 114–15) notes, however, that among contemporary Tibetan monastics the study of vinaya is often deferred, sometimes indefinitely. As he explains, "When monks begin their careers, they are enthusiastic and pure, but do not know the monastic discipline. Instead of studying it immediately, they wait for ten or fifteen years. When they finally turn to Vinaya, they understand what they should have done—but it is too late. By then they have become blasé and have lost their enthusiasm for monastic life."

81 See, for example, Schopen 1997: 75.

82 The mahāsūtras may well have shared a similar history. Like the avadānas in the *Divyāvadāna,* these mahāsūtras were circulating separately in the canon and were then culled and codified as a particular class of document, though not as a particular genre. The reason for this codification appears to be connected with the use of these documents as protection texts, for they apparently had powerful apotropaic effects. Perhaps they were compiled for the use of "protectionists," akin to avadānists, who would use these stories in some rites or rituals. Also noteworthy is that some of these mahāsūtras appear to be uniquely Mūlasarvāstivādin (Skilling 1994: 92–95), and many involve merchants. For more on these mahāsūtras, see Peter Skilling's (1994: 1–220) very thorough introduction to his mahāsūtra edition. For descriptions of other summaries or compendiums of the *Mūlasarvāstivāda-vinaya* (e.g., Guṇaprabha's *Vinayasūtra,* Nāgārjuna's *Āryamūlasarvāstivādiśrāmaṇerakārikā*), see Schopen 1994b: 33. Cf. Salomon 2006: 368.

83 This proposed genealogy, that recitations of stories from the vinaya gave rise to the multi-leveled accounts known as avadānas, exemplifies Todorov's (1990: 13–26) theory that speech acts give rise to literary genres, and new literary genres are merely transformations of old literary genres.

84 For a translation of a Chinese version of this story, see Chavannes 1910–34: ii, 237–66 and iv, 172–74.

85 Following GM iii 4, 184.6, 186.5, 186.7, 186.11, 188.16–17, 189.9–10. Divy 1.3, *'smāt parāntake* (mss., *'pasmārāntake*). There is great variation in the form that this term takes in this story (e.g., *apasmārāntaka, asyāparāntaka, asmāparāntaka, parāntaka*). Cowell and Neil emend each variant to *asmāt parantaka* (e.g., Divy 18.6, 19.16–17, 19.19), while the version of the story in the *Gilgit Manuscripts* preserves *aśmāparāntaka*. The Tibetan version of the story concurs with the latter (cf. Shackleton Bailey 1950–51: 172 and Divy 703). It (N 264b2; cited in GM iii 4, 186n3) reads *rdo can zhes bgyi b'i yul gye mtha' na*. Aśmāparāntaka appears to be a conjunct of two place names—Aśma (as in Pāli, Assaka; Skt., Aśmaka or Aśvaka) and Aparānta. These two areas are in proximity to each other in what is now Maharashtra. Judging by the variation of its form in the *Divyāvadāna,* this designation may not have been well known by the text's scribes.

86 For more on these three conditions, see *Milindapañha* 123–30 (trans. in Horner 1969: 172–82) and Collins 1982: 210–13.

87 Following GM iii 4, 160. 1–2, read *gṛhītamokṣamārgo 'ntarmukho nirvāṇe*. Divy 1.18, *gṛhītamokṣamārgāntoṇmukho na nirvāṇe*. Ms. A reads *-mārgānte sukhaḥ*. Ms. D reads *-margānte mukhaḥ*. Ms. H 1a8 reads *-mārgān mukhe nirvāṇe*.

88 Divy 2.1, *anarthikaḥ sarvabhavagativyupapattiparāṅmukhaḥ*. GM iii 4, 160.2–3, "he had no desire for any state or realm of existence nor death or rebirth" *(anarthikaḥ sarvabhavagaticyutyupapattiṣu).* The Tibetan (Shackleton Bailey 1950: 167–68) concurs.

89 Following GM iii 4, 160.3, read *devanikāyāt*. Cf. Divy 98.21. The Tibetan (Shackleton Bailey 1950: 168) concurs. Divy 2.2, "from one of the communities of beings" *(anyatamasmāt sattvanikāyat).*

90 Divy 2.6, *yasya sakāśād garbham avakrāmati*. Likewise GM iii 4, 160.7. Nevertheless, Divy 98.24 reads *yasyāḥ sakāśād garbho 'vakrāmati*. This is probably a better reading, though *yasyāḥ* should be emended to *yasya*.

91 Following GM iii 4, 161.1, add *asmākaṃ nāmnā*. Divy 2.16 (omitted).

92 Although the referent for the neuter indexical "this" *(idam)* isn't supplied, the implied subject seems to be "merit." Cf. GM iii 1, 220.20–221.1, "Then the Blessed One, with a voice having five qualities, commenced to assign the reward in the name of those hungry ghosts: 'May that merit from this gift go to the hungry ghosts'" *(tato bhagavān pañcāṅgena svareṇa teṣāṃ nāmnā dakṣiṇām ādeṣṭuṃ pravṛttaḥ | ito dānād dhi yat puṇyaṃ tat pretān upagacchatu)*. See also *Saṅghabhedavastu* i, 199.25. For more on these passages, see Schopen 1994a: 545.

93 Cp. Vogel and Wille's translation of a parallel passage from the Tibetan version of the *Pravrajyāvastu* (1984: 15): "Having made us (funeral) presents—whether they are few or many—after we shall have died and met our death, (and thus) having done good works, may he allocate the (profit of his every) gift in (our) name, (saying): 'This shall follow the two (parents) to where they go after rebirth.'"

94 Following GM iii 4, 161.7–8, read *anavatarantīm adharimāṃ bhūmim*. One could also take this to mean "never descending to the ground floor," since it's clear that the woman's husband keeps her upstairs. I suspect the implication here is that the woman

enjoys a divine existence, for her feet never touch the ground, one of the attributes of divinity. Divy 2.23, "treading only on the upper grounds" *(avataratīm uparimāṃ bhūmim)*. The corresponding Tibetan (D ka 252b7) reads *khri nas khri dang khri'u nas khri'ur rgyu zhing shod kyis gzhir mi 'bab ste* —> Skt., <*piṭhāt piṭhaṃ carantīṃ nāvatarantīm adharimāṃ bhūmim*>. Cf. *Avadānaśataka* i, 15.5–6, 197.7–8, 277.6–7, etc., *mañcān mañcaṃ pīṭhāt pīṭham anavatarantīm adharimāṃ bhūmim*. See also Ch'en 1945–47: 248–49n7.

95 Following the Tibetan (Shackleton Bailey 1950: 168), read *rin po che rin thang chod cig* —> Skt., <*ratnasya*>. Divy 3.1, "of these jewels" *(ratnānām)*. Likewise GM iii 4, 161.14.

96 Following the Tibetan (Shackleton Bailey 1950: 168), read *rin po che rin thang chod cig* —> Skt., <*ratnasya*>. Divy 3.2, "of these jewels" *(ratnānām)*. Likewise GM iii 4, 161.14.

97 Divy 3.4, *ratnasya*. Cp. GM iii 4, 161.17, "these jewels" *(ratnānām)*.

98 For more on the constellation of Śravaṇa, see Divy-V 351, vv. 198–201.

99 Divy 3.18, *mudrā*. Perhaps this refers to the knowledge of different trademarks impressed on seals and sealings (Roy 1971: 153). Cf. Divy 32.24, "he affixed his trademark [to the merchandise]" *(svamudrālakṣitaṃ ca kṛtvā)* and Divy 279.13, "he dropped his seal ring" *(tenāṅgulimudrā kṣiptā)*. Edgerton (BHSD) as well as Rhys Davids and Stede (PTSD, s.v. *muddā*), however, suggest that it means "hand calculation," which would coincide well with the previous two skills. For more on this list of subjects, see Roy 1971: 152–58 and Sastri 1945: 9–10.

100 Following Divy 100.4, add *paryavadātaḥ*. Divy 3.19 (omitted).

101 Divy 3.23–24, *jyeṣṭhakaṃ madhyamaṃ kan[ī]yasam*. This might also be translated as "one quite big, one of moderate size, and one rather small." Cf. Divy 442.10 and 523.38, *jyeṣṭhaṃ madhyaṃ kanīyasam*.

102 Divy 4.4, *mamaivārthaṃ codanā kriyate*. Likewise GM iii 4, 163.6. Speyer (1902: 106) suggests *mamaiveyaṃ codanā kriyate*.

103 Likewise GM iii 4, 164.1–3. The Tibetan (Shackleton Bailey 1950: 168–69), however, reads "If you travel by elephant, elephants are difficult to care for and difficult to maintain. Horses as well are difficult to care for and difficult to maintain. But donkeys are easy to nourish and they have good memories" *(gal te glang po che'i bzhon pas 'gro na ni de shin tu bskyang dka' zhing dgang dka'o | rta yang shin tu...dka'o | bong bu gso sla zhing dran pa dang ldan pas...* —> Skt., <*saced dhastibhir hastinaḥ sudūrakṣyā durbharāś ca aśvā api sudūrakṣyā durbharāś ca gardabhāḥ supoṣāḥ smṛtimantaś ca*>*)*.

104 Divy 4.22, *na ca te sārthavāhe hate sārtho vaktavyaḥ*. GM iii 4, 164.7, *na cet hate sārthavāhe hataḥ sārtho bhavet* (ms., *na madhye | madhye sārthasya vastavyaṃ hate sārthavāhe*). The Tibetan (Shackleton Bailey 1950: 169) reads *ded dpon bcom pa'i tshe tshong pa rnams bcom zhes bya'o* —> Skt., <*hate sārthavāhe sārtha iti vaktavyam*>. Speyer (1902: 107) suggests *na ca te sārthikebhyaḥ so 'rtho vaktavyaḥ*. That is, "but don't tell the merchants about it." Bloomfield (1920: 347) suggests *na ca te sārthe hataḥ sāthavāho vaktavyaḥ*, which he loosely translates as, "It shall not happen that you, the leader of the caravan, shall come to grief."

105 Divy 5.11–12, *nipuṇataḥ sāmudraṃ yānapātraṃ pratipādya*. Cf. 100.27–28, *yan nv ahaṃ samudraṃ yānapātraṃ samudānīya*.

106 Divy 5.15, *saṃsiddhayānapātraḥ*. Tatelman (2000: 57) translates this trope as "his ship safe and sound." While *yānapātra* can refer to "ship" (cf. Divy 5.12), my sense is that

this trope means that he returned with "his ship intact" and "his voyage successful." Considering how often in the *Divyāvadāna* someone bemoans the dangers of the ocean (e.g., Divy 35.21, 41.26, 103.35) or dies in a shipwreck (Divy 169.30–170.2, 172.18–20, 174.15–18), this is no mean feat.

107 Vaidya (Divy-V 3.23) omits Divy 5.20–22.

108 Divy 6.7, *sarva evānayena vyasanam āpatsyāmaḥ*. In Pāli, the equivalent expression occurs in compound, *anayavyasana,* and this is how it is referred to by Edgerton (BHSD). He translates it as "misfortune and disaster." In the *Divyāvadāna,* however, the compound is broken, *anayena vyasanam,* rendering this translation possible but not probable. The Tibetan, with its word-for-word translation, offers little additional insight (e.g., D 75b6, *de nyid du tshul ma yin pas sdug bsngal bar gyur to* —> Skt., *tatraiva anayena vyasanam āpannaḥ* | Divy 87.20). Though I generally translate *anayena* in this trope as "straightaway," the term is particularly difficult to translate consistently. Consider these three cases: (1) When Śroṇa Koṭikarṇa reflects on the consequences of beating his donkeys (Divy 7.7–8), *anayena* might be rendered "because of bad judgment." (2) Yet, when a large group of pigs meet with "misfortune" *(vyasanam),* there is no indication that this occurred because of their bad judgment (Divy 505.10–11). Here *anayena* seems to mean "untimely" or "unfortunate." (3) When directions are given to the caravan leader Supriya, he is repeatedly advised to be careful when crossing dangerous places, lest he fall in and die (e.g., Divy 106.23–24, 106.30–107.1, 107.5–6). Here the emphasis seems to be that this misfortune will occur "straightaway." Charles Malamoud's observations about the term *vyasana*—the other key term in this trope—might help explain the first two senses of *anayena*. In the *Arthaśāstra,* he explains, "calamities *[vyasana]* are of two kinds: those that arise from *daiva,* from the will or pleasure of the gods, and those which are human in their essence. The former are the handiwork of misfortune *(an-aya)*. In the latter case, however, it is the king's bad policies *(a-naya)* that would be incriminating." Cf. *Arthaśāstra* 8.1.1–4, 6.2.6–12; trans. in Kangle 1972: 385, 317. Considering how difficult it often is to determine whether fate or karma is responsible for an event, I generally prefer translating *anayena* in this trope as "straightaway."

109 Likewise GM iii 4, 166.20. The Tibetan (Shackleton Bailey 1950: 169), however, reads "mother and father" *(yab yum* —> Skt., *<amba tāta>)*.

110 GM iii 4, 167.3 doesn't include this sentence. The Tibetan (Shackleton Bailey 1950: 169) reads "mother and father" *(yab yum* —> Skt., *<amba tāta>)*.

111 GM iii 4, 167.11–12, "...except for his two donkeys standing there. He harnessed them and set off" *(nānyatra tāveva gardabhāvavatiṣṭhataḥ | sa tau yojayitvā samprasthitaḥ)*.

112 Following the Tibetan (Shackleton Bailey 1950: 169), read *lam* —> Skt., *<mārgam>*. Divy 7.2, "smell" *(gandham)*. GM iii 4, 167.13 (omitted).

113 Following GM iii 4, 167.14, read *anyatamā śālāṭavīm*. The Tibetan (Shackleton Bailey 1950: 169) concurs. Divy 7.5–6, *anyatamāśāṭavī*.

114 Following GM iii 4, 168.6, read *udbaddhapiṇḍaḥ* (ms., *udbandhapiṇḍakāyaṣṭhi*). Divy 7.14, "a body full of holes" *(udviddhapiṇḍaḥ)*.

115 Divy 7.19, *iti śabdo niścāritaḥ*. In the *Divyāvadāna,* words that are "called out" *(niścārita)* are often regretted. Forms of this verb are quite common when "harsh" *(khara)* words are uttered (e.g. Divy 5.5–6, 24.4–5, 54.20–21), and it also occurs when words are spoken with anger (Divy 253.15). For a counter example, see Divy 281.4.

116 Following GM iii 4, 168.11, read *parvatasaṃnibhodaraiḥ*. Divy 7.21, *parvatodarasaṃnibhaiḥ*.

117 Divy 8.4, *pitṛlokam*. GM iii 4, 169.7, "realm of hungry ghosts" *(pretalokam)*.

118 Following Divy 9.8, add *yadi*. Divy 8.8 (omitted). Likewise GM iii 4, 169.11.

119 Following GM iii 4, 169.16, read *udbaddhapiṇḍaḥ*. Divy 8.13, "a body full of holes" *(udviddhapiṇḍaḥ)*.

120 Following GM iii 4, 170.1, read *parvatasaṃnibhodaraiḥ*. Divy 8.20, *parvatodarasaṃnibhaiḥ*.

121 Divy 9.3, *ye dhanabhogamadena*. GM iii 4, 170.11, "youth and indulgence" *(yauvanabhogena)*. The Tibetan (Shackleton Bailey 1950: 169) reads "youth and wealth" *(lang tsho longs spyod —>* Skt., *<yauvanadhana>)*, though *longs spyod* could also refer to *bhoga*.

122 Divy 9.4, *pitṛlokam*. GM iii 4, 170.12, "realm of hungry ghosts" *(pretalokam)*.

123 Divy 9.5, *puṇyakarmā*. Likewise GM iii 4, 170.13. The Tibetan (Shackleton Bailey 1950: 169, however, reads "you have the power of merit" *(bsod nams kyi mtho chen po dang ldan pas —>* Skt., *<puṇyamaheśākhyas tvam>)*.

124 Following Divy 10.30, add *tatra*. The Tibetan (Shackleton Bailey 1950: 169–70) concurs. Divy 9.23 (omitted).

125 Divy 9.19, *sa taiḥ snāpito bhojitaḥ*. The term *snāpita* generally means "bathed," but I think the sense here is that he was given copious amounts of water—enough, perhaps, to immerse himself.

126 GM iii 4, 171.10, "They said to him" *(sa tair uktaḥ)*.

127 Divy 9.25, *pṛṣṭhavaṃśān utpāṭyotpāṭya bhakṣitaḥ*. GM iii 4, 171.14, *pṛṣṭhavaṃśāny utpāṭyotpāṭya bhakṣitāni*. The Tibetan (Shackleton Bailey 1950: 170) reads *rgyab kyi sha lpags —>* Skt., *<pṛṣṭhatvaṅ māṃsān>*.

128 Divy 10.25, *asisūnādhastāt*. GM iii 4,173.3, *asisthānādhastāt* (ms., *pitrosya sūnāyām adhastāt*). The Tibetan (N 258b3; cited in GM iii 4, 173n1) reads *ral gris bsad pa'i sa'i 'og na —>* Skt., *<asivadhyasthānādhastāt>*. Vaidya (Divy-V 6.27) emends to *asti sūnādhastāt*.

129 Divy 11.7, *tena*. GM iii 4, 173. 15, "those two" *(tābhyām)*.

130 Divy 11.13, *uparimastikaṃ bhakṣayantī sthitā yāvat*. GM iii 4, 174. 2, *uparimastakaṃ bhakṣitaṃ yāvat*. To be grammatically correct, one should read either *sā* for *tayā* or *bhakṣitam* for *bhakṣayantī*. The Tibetan (Shackleton Bailey 1950: 170) reads *steng du dbyung ste | des...klad rgyas za bar byed do —>* Skt., *<upariṣṭhān mastakam>*. However, Lokesh Chandra (2001) and J. S. Negi (1993–) translate *klad gyas* with *mastakaluṅga*, a Sanskrit term referring to the membranes around the brain. Perhaps the giant centipede is eating through the man's meninges.

131 Divy 11.20, *yadi evam*. GM iii 4, 174.10 (omitted).

132 Following Divy 10.19 and 15.3, one would expect the response, "Yes, I'll go" *(gamiṣyāmi)*.

133 Following GM iii 4, 175.12, read *yadi na*. Divy 12.9, *yan na*.

134 Following Divy 10.25, read *tava pitā kathayati*. The Tibetan (Shackleton Bailey 1950: 170) concurs. Though Cowell and Neil (Divy 12.10) emend the *Divyāvadāna* to read *tava pitrā*, mss. ABCD (Divy 12n2) and ms. H 4b12 read *pitā*, suggesting that *kathayati* may have been mistakenly dropped. GM iii 4, 175.13, however, reads *tava pitrā*.

135 Divy 12.22, *yadi ete kiṃcin mṛgayanti*. Though I generally translate √*mṛg* as "to look for," such as when Śroṇa explains to the hungry ghosts who surround him that he too

is looking for water (Divy 7.25), here and in what follows (Divy 12.24) I take the verb to mean "to ask for" or "to plead." This reading seems more likely, considering that the four hungry ghosts are bound to bedposts and probably unable to wander far.

136 Divy 12.22–23, *teṣāṃ sattvānāṃ karmasvakatām*. GM iii 4, 176.4–5, *teṣāṃ sattvānāṃ karma svakṛtam* (ms., *karmaścakatām*).

137 Divy 12.25–26, *busaplāvī*. The Tibetan (N 259b5; cited in GM iii 4, 176n5) reads "chaff" *(phub ma),* but my sense is that it is something that "jumps" or "swims" *(plāvī)* in "chaff" or "dry cow-dung" *(busa)*. Cf. BHSD.

138 Divy 12.26–27, *aparasya kṣiptam ayoguḍaṃ* [mss. *-guḍāṃ*] *bhakṣayitum ārabdhaḥ*. While this might be translated more literally as "he tossed some to another, and he began to eat balls of iron," my sense is that the food given to these hungry ghosts transforms according to their particular karma, and it is this transformed food that they eat. Cf. Divy 12.27, 13.17–18, 13.24–25, 14.5–6, 14.14–15.

139 Divy 12.28–29, *sā visragandhena nirgatā*. GM iii 4, 176.9–10, "She saw Śroṇa leaving because of the putrid smell" (*sā paśyati visragandhena nirgatam* [ms., *sā paśyati gandhena nirgataḥ*]).

140 Divy 12.29–13.1, *kiṃ mama kāruṇikayā tvam eva kāruṇikataraḥ*. GM iii 4, 176.11, *kiṃ mama karuṇayā tvam eva kāruṇikataraḥ*. The Tibetan (Shackleton Bailey 1950: 170) reads *ci kho mo'i snying rje las khyod kyi snying rje lhag gam* —> Skt., <*kiṃ me kāruṇikayā* (?)> or perhaps <*mama kāruṇikāyāḥ*>. Shackleton Bailey suggests "Is your pity greater than my pity?"

141 Divy 13.7, *nakṣatrarātryāṃ pratyupasthitāyām*. As Sharmistha Sharma (1992:12) observes in her book on the *Śārdūlakarṇa-āvadāna,* it was believed that "definite food is favourable as an offering and perhaps also for consumption during the period when [the] moon dwells upon a particular constellation."

142 Divy 13.9–10, *cittam abhiprasannaṃ dṛṣṭvā*. Grammatically awkward.

143 Divy 14.4–5, *kiṃ svamāṃsaṃ na bhakṣayati yā tvadīyāni praheṇakāni bhakṣayati*. GM iii 4, 178.8–9, *kiṃ na svamāṃsāni bhakṣayati yāhaṃ tvadīyāni praheṇakāni bhakṣayāmi*.

144 Following GM iii 4, 178.11, read *dārikāyā haste*. Divy 14.6 (omitted).

145 Following Divy 10.24, read *nābhiśraddadhāsyati*. Divy 14.24, "they won't believe me" *(nābhiśraddadhāsyanti)*.

146 Divy 15.4, *uṣitaḥ*. GM iii 4, 179.19, "boarded" *(adhirūḍhaḥ)*.

147 Divy 15.19–20, *bhavato 'ntike*. GM iii 4, 180.15, "in the presence of the Blessed One" *(bhagavato 'ntike)*. The Tibetan (Shackleton Bailey 1950: 170) concurs. Though *antike* literally means "in the presence of" (as in Skt. *samīpe*), it sometimes functions more loosely as "under," "in," or "in reference to" (cf. BHSD, s.v. *antike*). Perhaps in this trope, "under your supervision" or "under your guidance" would be appropriate. In the Upaniṣads, for example, we find parallel expressions such as *brahmacaryaṃ bhagavati vatsyāmi* (*Chāndogya Upaniṣad* iv.4.3). Nevertheless, I generally translate *antike* literally, perhaps to a fault. While a literal reading of the term would clearly be a mistake in some instances (e.g., Divy 534.9–11), I'm not so sure in other instances (e.g., Divy 10.11–12, 11.28). The text places a premium on being in the presence of beings such as buddhas and arhats. See, for example, "The Incident at Toyikā" (Divy 76.10ff.).

148 Divy 15.20, *taṃ tāvat pūrvikāṃ pratijñāṃ paripūraya*. GM iii 4 180.16, *taṃ tāvat pūrvikāṃ pratijñāṃ paripūraya* (ms., *tat tāvat pūrikāṃ pratijñāṃ smara pūraya*). The

Tibetan (Shackleton Bailey 1950: 170–71) reads *dran par byos la snga na ji skad spring zhing bzung ba* —> Skt., <*śroṇa smaryatāṃ tāvat pūrvikāṃ pratijñāṃ paripūraya*>.

149 Divy 16.4–5, *yāvat tat sarvaṃ tat tathaiva*. Likewise GM iii 4, 181.8. The Tibetan (Shackleton Bailey 1950: 171) reads "he saw that everything was just as Śroṇa Koṭikarṇa had said" *(brkos nas ji tsam na mthong ba dang thams cad de kho na bzhin du gyur te* —> Skt., <*yāvat paśyati sarvaṃ tat tathaiva*>*)*. Cf. Divy 16.18–19, 17.3.

150 The Tibetan (Shackleton Bailey 1950: 171) reads "they said" here (Divy 16.26) and not in the next sentence (Divy 16.28) as it appears in the Sanskrit.

151 Divy 17.6, *tena vaipuṣpitam*. GM iii 4, 182, *[vaipu]ṣpitam*. The Tibetan (N 262b7; cited in GM iii 4, 182n2) reads *'dzum phyung ba* —> Skt., <*smitam*>.

152 Read *syād āryaḥ śroṇaḥ koṭikarṇa evaṃ te bhaginījanaḥ saṃjānate*. Divy 17.7–8, *syād āryaḥ śroṇaḥ koṭikarṇa eva te bhaginījanaḥ saṃjānate* (mss. AC, *śroṇaḥ koṭikarṇaḥ sa janaḥ saṃjānate*). GM iii 4, 182.20–183.1, *syād āryaḥ śroṇa koṭikarṇaḥ eva me [bhagini] saṃjānīte*. The Tibetan (Shackleton Bailey 1950: 171) reads "'This must be the noble Śroṇa Koṭikarṇa.' Thus those young women recognized him" *(des ngo shes par gyur nas dpon po [']gro bzhin skyes rna ba bye ba ri yin nam | sring mo bdag ni skye bo dag gis de ltar shes so* —> Skt., <*syād āryaḥ śroṇa koṭikarṇaḥ | evaṃ māṃ bhaginī janaḥ saṃjānate*>*)*. Cf. Divy 174.7–8, *evaṃ mā[ṃ] bhāginījana saṃjānīta iti*.

153 Divy 17.11, *utprāsayasi*. Likewise GM iii 4, 183.4. The Tibetan (N 263a1; cited in GM iii 4, 183n2) reads "announce" *(sbron pa)*. Shackleton Bailey (1950: 171) says that this line is missing in the Tibetan.

154 Divy 17.12, *utkāśanaśabdaḥ kṛtaḥ*. According to Edgerton (BHSD), who follows the Tibetan from *Mahāvyutpatti* §2799, *utkāśanaśabda* means "conspicuous, vigorous pronouncement." The standard meaning for the term, however, seems to apply here and at Divy 517.26, 517.27. Perhaps it should be read as *utkāsaśabda*, which Edgerton (BHSD, s.v. *utkāsa*) remarks might have the same sense as *utkāsana* ("clearing the throat").

155 Read *tau*. Divy 17.14, *te*. GM iii 4, 183.6 reads likewise, though the manuscripts (GM iii 4, 183n4) read *te*.

156 The Tibetan (Shackleton Bailey 1950: 171–72) reads "Then he himself went [to his parents], and said, 'Mother, Father, I pay my respects!' Śroṇa Koṭikarṇa had a lovely voice, so they recognized him by his voice. They hugged him and began to cry" *(ji tsam na de rang nyid 'ongs te yab yum phyag 'tshal lo zhes smras pa dang | de dbyig gi nga ro can zhig pas de gnyis kyis skad las ngo shes nas de'i mgul nas 'jus te ngu bar brtams pa dang*— > Skt., <*yāvad asau svayam eva gatvā kathayati | amba tāta vande iti | hiraṇyasvaro 'sau tābhyāṃ svareṇa pratyabhijñātaḥ | tau tasya kaṇṭhe ruditum ārabdhau*>*)*.

157 Read *tayor*. Divy 17.14, *teṣām*. GM iii 4, 183.7 reads likewise.

158 Here the *Gilgit Manuscripts* (iii 4, 183n5) add *abhidharmamadhotam | anāgāmiphalaṃ sākṣātkṛtam | tasya kālāntareṇa mātāpitarau kālagatau | sa tam...* Dutt, however, does not include this in his edition of the text.

159 Divy 18.4, *pravrajyām* (mss., *pravrajya*). GM iii 4, 184.2, "renounce, take ordination, and become a monk" *(pravrajyām upasampadaṃ bhikṣubhāvam)*. Cf. Divy 15.19.

160 Following GM iii 4, 184.6, read *aśmāparāntakeṣu janapadeṣu*. Divy 18. 6–7, *asmāt parāntakeṣu janapadeṣu*.

161 Cf. Divy 489.8–10.

162 GM iii 4, 184.14 omits *sutrasya vinayasya mātṛkāyāḥ*.

163 The following descriptions of an arhat are discussed in Bloomfield 1920: 339–42. For an account of their Tibetan translations, see Ch'en 1945–47: 264n86.

164 Following GM iii 4, 185.4–7 (cf. Divy 97.25–28,180.25–28, 240.23–27, 282.1–5). Divy 18.26, "and so on" *(yāvat)*. Upendra is a name for Viṣnu or Kṛṣṇa. He is Indra's younger brother, and hence, as his name indicates, has the position of vice Indra *(upa + indra)*.

165 Divy 19.6–7, *tasyām eva parṣadi saṃniṣaṇṇo 'bhūt saṃnipatitaḥ*. Likewise GM iii 4, 185.13–14 and Divy 44.9–10. Cf. Divy 163.18–19, *tasyām eva parṣadi saṃnipatito 'bhūt saṃnipatitaḥ*.

166 Divy 19.10–11, *dṛṣṭo mayopādhyāyānubhāvena*. GM iii 4, 185.17 reads likewise, though the manuscripts (GM iii 4, 185n5) omit *anubhāvena*. The Tibetan (Shackleton Bailey 1950: 172) concurs.

167 For the fuller version of these pleasantries, see Divy 156.12–15.

168 Following GM iii 4, 186.5, read *aśmāparāntakeṣu bhadanta janapadeṣu*. Divy 19.16–17, *asmāt parāntakeṣu bhadanta janapadeṣu*.

169 Divy 19.19, *kharā bhūmī gokaṇṭakā dhānāḥ*. GM iii 4, 186.7, *kharā bhūmigokaṇṭakādhānā* (ms., *kharā bhadanta bhūmi kaṇṭakādhānāḥ*). Cowell and Neil (Divy 704) offer this translation: "[the ground is rough] and thorns the only corn." However, in the corresponding passage in the Pāli *Vinaya* (i, 195), we find "the top layer of soil has been trampled by the hooves of cattle" *(kaṇhuttarā bhūmi kharā gokaṇṭakahatā)*. For more on this, see the commentary to the *Aṅguttara-nikāya* (*Manorathapūraṇī* ii, 225.11–15). My sense is that in this passage in the *Divyāvadāna*, *gokaṇṭaka* (like the attested *gokaṇta*) refers to the cattle-thorn bush *(Asteracantha lonigolia)*. Monier-Williams (SED) also cites *gokṣura, gokṣuraka,* and *gokharu* ("like a razor to cows") as having the same meaning. Likewise in Hindi, there is *gokharu* ("cruel to the cow"), which is said to refer to the plant *Ruellia longifolie* and its fruit as well as to the plant *Tribulus lanuginosus* and its thorny seed. Still another way to understand this expression is that the fruit of this *gokaṇṭaka* bush was actually desirable to cows, for it is an attested kind of synonym *(adhivacana)* in Pāli that "thorns" can be understood as "pleasures." For example, the *Saṃyutta-nikāya* (iii, 169) preserves, "That which is pleasant and agreeable is said, in the monastic discipline of the noble ones, to be a thorn" *(yaṃ piyarūpaṃ sātarūpam ayaṃ vuccati ariyassa vinaye kaṇṭako)*. For more on this, see Dhadphale 1980: 174–77.

170 Following GM iii 4, 186.7, read *aśmāparantakeṣu janapadeṣu*. Divy 19.19–20, *asmākam aparāntakeṣu janapadeṣu*.

171 Divy 19.22–23, *erako merako jandurako mandurakaḥ*. The Tibetan (N 264b4–5; cited in GM iii 4, 186n7) reads *bal stan dang shing shun gyi stan dang sren [srin?] bal gyi stan dang ras bal gyi [stan?] dag mchis pa* —> Skt., <*kocavavalkalakacakārpāsika* (?)>. Agrawala (1966: 68) suggests that they are made from eraka grass, wool, the coarse hair of animals, and woolen materials used for covering horses. The corresponding passage in the Pāli *Vinaya* (i, 196.6) reads *sethyathāpi bhante majjhimeṣu janapadeṣu eragu moragu majjhāru jantu*. According to Divy 704, the Pāli commentary explains these as "grass creepers" *(tiṇajātiyo)*. Cf. Edgerton (BHSD, s.v. *eraka*) and the *Mahāvyutpatti* (§9180–83).

172 Following GM iii 4, 186.7, read *aśmāparantakeṣu janapadeṣu*. Divy 19.19–20, *asmākam aparāntakeṣu janapadeṣu*.

173 Divy 19.25, *udakastabdhikāḥ*. GM iii 4, 187.1, "people there think that water purifies them" *(udakaśuddhikāḥ)*.

174 Divy 19.25, *snātopavicāraḥ*. GM iii 4, 187.1–2, *snānasamudācārāḥ*.

175 Divy 19.25–27, *bhikṣur bhikṣoś cīvarakāni preṣayati itaś cyutāni tatrāsamprāptāni kasyaitāni naiḥsargikāni.* The Pāli *Vinaya* (i, 196) reads "At present, Bhante, people offer robes to monks who are outside the boundary, with the message that this robe should be given to such-and-such monk. After going there, they announce as follows: 'Venerable ones, such-and-such people have given this robe to you.' They're hesitant and don't accept it, thinking, 'Don't let it happen that we'll commit a *nissaggiya* offense'" *(etarahi bhante manussā nissīmagatānaṃ bhikkhūnaṃ cīvaraṃ denti imaṃ cīvaram itthannāmassa demā ti | te āgantvā ārocenti itthannāmehi te āvuso manussehi cīvaraṃ dinnaṃ ti | te kukkuccāyantā na sādiyanti mā no nissaggiyam ahosīti).* For other translations of this passage, see Rhys Davids and Oldenberg 1987: ii, 34 and Horner 1938–66: iv, 263. In the *Prātimokṣa-sūtra* of the Mūlasarvāstivāda, thirty such *niḥsargika-pāyantika* offenses are listed (Prebish 1975: 65–75).

176 Divy 20.13–14, *yena śroṇasya koṭikarṇasya vihāras tenopasaṃkrāntaḥ.* Likewise GM iii 4, 187.15–16. The Tibetan (Shackleton Bailey 1950: 172–73), however, reads "Then the Blessed One and Śroṇa Koṭikarṇa approached the building" *(de nas bcom ldan 'das dang gro bzhin skyes rna ba bye ba ri gtsug lag khang gang na ba der gshegs te* —> Skt., *<atha bhagavāñ chroṇaś ca koṭikarṇo yena vihāras tenopasaṃkrāntau>).*

177 GM iii 4, 187.16 omits *paśyati.*

178 Following GM iii 4, 188.4–5, read *āryasya tūṣṇībhāvenātināmitavān.* Divy 20.19, "They accepted [each other] in noble silence" *(āryeṇa tūṣṇībhavenādhivāsitavān).* The Tibetan (N 265a7; cited in GM iii 4, 188n2) reads *'phags pa'i mi smra bas de'i mtshan mo 'das par mdzad do.*

179 Following GM iii 4, 188.8–9, read *aśmāparāntikayāsvaraguptikayā.* Divy 20.22–23, *asmāt parāntikayā guptikayā.*

180 Divy 20.24, *vistareṇa svareṇa.* This could also mean "in full and with correct intonation" or "in a loud voice."

181 GM iii 4, 188.9–10, "as well as *The Verses of Śaila, The Sage's Verses, The Elder Monk's Verses, The Elder Nun's Verses,* and *Discourses Concerning the Goal*" *(śailagāthāmunigāthāsthaviragāthāsthavirīgāthārthavargīyāṇi ca sutrāṇi).*

182 Divy 20.29–21.1, *upādhyāyasya vacasārocayitum.* GM iii 4, 188.15, *upādhyāyasya vacasārādhayitum.*

183 Following Divy 19.8–9. Divy 21.1, "and so on" *(yāvat).*

184 Following GM iii 4, 188.16–17, read *aśmāparāntakeśu janapadeṣu.* Divy 21.2, *asmāt parantakeṣu janapadeṣu.*

185 Following Divy 19.16–27. Divy 21.5, "These are to be recited in detail" *(vistareṇoccārayitavyāni).*

186 GM iii 4, 189.5, "a question should be asked amid the community" *(saṃghamadhye praśnaḥ pṛcchyet).*

187 Following GM iii 4, 189.9–10, read *aśmāparāntakeṣu janapadeṣu.* Divy 21.12, *asmāt parantakeṣu janapadeṣū.*

188 Following Divy 19.16–27. Divy 21.15–16, "These are now to be recited in detail as they were stated before up to 'for whom do [these robes] cause serious misdeeds involving forfeiture'" *(vistareṇoccārayitavyāni yathā pūrvam uktāni yāvat kasya naiḥsargikāni).*

189 I have changed the order of the Buddha's five injunctions so that they match the venerable Mahākātyāyana's questions. The Buddha responds, following my numbering: 1, 4, 2, 3, 5.

190 Following GM iii 4, 189n4, add *carmā dhārayitavyām*. The Tibetan (Shackleton Bailey 1950: 173; D ka 266a6) concurs. Divy 21.20 (omitted). Dutt emends the *Gilgit Manuscripts* to read as one answer. GM iii 4, 189.16–17, "If one gets worn out, it should be patched and then both of them may be worn" *(sā cet kṣayadharmiṇī bhavati argalakaṃ dattvā dhārayitavye)*. The manuscript reading, however, seems to indicate two answers. GM iii 4, 189n4, *sacet kṣiyadharmiṇyau bhavataḥ arghaṭakam vārayitavye carmā dhārayitavyām*. The Tibetan (N 266a5; cited in GM iii 4, 189n4) reads *lhan pas btab ste bcang bar bya 'o*.

191 Hiraoka (1998: 3) offers this translation: "When a monk hands over his garment to another monk, if the garment does not reach [the latter monk] even though it already leaves [the former], there is no violation of forfeiture for anyone."

192 GM iii 4, 190.3, *puṇḍravardhana*. Puṇḍavardhana is presumably a variant for Puṇḍravardhana, the capital of the Puṇḍra homeland, which roughly corresponds with modern-day north Bengal. Puṇḍravardhana seems to correspond with the ruins of Mahāsthān (or Mahāsthāngarh), which lies seven miles north of the town of Bogra (Law 1976: 246–48). Monier-Williams (SED, s.v. *puṇḍravardhanam*) equates it with modern Bengal and Bihar. For more on these boundaries of the Middle Country, see Law 1976: 12–13 and Dutt 1987: 231–32.

193 GM iii 4, 190.4, "forest" *(dāva)*.

194 GM iii 4, 190.5, *śarāvatī*. The precise locations of the city and river by this name are still unknown.

195 B. C. Law (1976: 129, s.v. *sthāneśvara*), following S. N. Majumdar, suggests that Sthūṇa may be identified with Sthāneśvara (Sthāniśvara).

196 According to Law (1976: 132, s.v. *uśīradhvaja*), "Usīnārā mentioned in Pāli Literature and Uśīnaragiri mentioned in the *Kathāsaritsāgara* are doubtless identical with the Uśīragiri of the *Divyāvadāna* and Uśīradhvaja of the *Vinaya Texts*." Law identifies it with the Siwalik range.

197 Following GM iii 4, 190.9–13, read *bhikṣavaḥ saṃśayajātāḥ sarvasaṃśayacchettāraṃ buddhaṃ bhagavantaṃ pṛcchanti | kiṃ bhadantāyuṣmatā śroṇena koṭikarṇena karma kṛtaṃ yasya karmaṇo vipākenāḍhye mahādhane mahābhoge kule jāto ratnapratyupatikayā karṇe āmuktikayā bhavataḥ śāsane pravrajya sarvakleśaprahāṇād arhattvaṃ sākṣātkṛtam*. Divy 22.3–4, *iti vistaraḥ*.

198 Following GM iii 4, 190.14, read *bhūtapūrvaṃ bhikṣavo vārāṇasyāṃ nagaryām*. Divy 22.4, "Long ago, and so on" *(bhūtapūrvaṃ yāvat)*.

199 For additional stories about King Kṛkin and Kāśyapa in Sanskrit sources (cited in Schopen 1997: 47n31), see GM iii 1, 191, 195, 200; iii 2, 77–78; iii 4, 190–93; *Avadānakalpalatā* i, 95, vv. 147–48; i, 145, vv. 132–33; i, 279, vv. 16–17; *Avadānaśataka* ii, 76, 124–25 (trans. in Feer 1891: 316, 359); and *Ratnamālāvadāna* 132. See also *Dhammapada-aṭṭhakathā* iii, 29–31 (trans. in Burlingame 1921: ii, 280–81) and the vinayas of the Mahāsāṅghikas, Mahīśāsakas, and Dharmaguptakas (trans. from the Chinese in Bareau 1962: 257–67). For scholarly accounts, see Handurukande 1970 and 1976; Hofinger 1982: 225n1; Schopen 1997: 28–29, 131–32; and Strong 1999.

200 GM iii 4, 191.4–5, "a league in circumference and half a league in height" *(samantād yojanam ardhayojanam ardhayojanam uccatvena)*.

201 Divy 22.20–21, *yan mama pitrā kṛtaṃ devakṛtaṃ na tu brahmakṛtaṃ tat*. I take this to mean that an edict of a king, unlike one by Brahmā, is not permanently binding. However, GM iii 4 191.14–15, "that which was done by my father should be taken as done by Brahmā himself" (*yan mama pitrā kṛtaṃ tad eva brahmakṛtam* [ms. *tad eva*

kṛtaṃ brahmakṛtam]). The Tibetan (Shackleton Bailey 1950: 173) reads *yab kyis gang mdzad pa de ni tshangs pas byas pa'o | de ni brgya byin gyis byas pa'o* —> Skt., <*yan mama pitrā kṛtaṃ brahmakṛtaṃ tat śakrakṛtaṃ tat*>.

202 Read *tābhyām*. Divy 23.10, *taiḥ*.

203 Divy 23.16, *kiṃ tu aparam utsarpitaṃ tiṣṭhati*. Cowell and Neil (Divy 705) offer this translation: "No debt has been incurred by us, but something has been saved." Edgerton (BHSD, s.v. *utsarpita*) translates this as "We have not incurred any debt, but the rest remains put aside as left over."

204 Divy 24.13, *kalatram*. Vaidya (Divy-V 15.3) emends to *kulatram*. Perhaps he preferred the latter's more obvious etymology (i.e., "one who guards the family.").

205 Divy 25.4, *upāyaśataiḥ*. The Tibetan (Shackleton Bailey 1950: 174) reads "in many hundreds and thousands of ways" *(thabs brgya stong du mas* —> Skt., <*upāyaśatasahasraiḥ*>*)*.

206 Divy 25.4, *sa idānīm*. Vaidya (Divy-V 15.13) emends to *sedānīm*, a mistaken double sandhi.

207 Divy 25.12, *alpamūlyāni*. This conjecture by Cowell and Neil (25n3) follows the emendation of Burnouf (1844: 236n1). Burnouf bases his emendation on the Tibetan (Shackleton Bailey 1950: 174), which reads *ci nas sman rin chung ba zhig ston cig*. Mss. ABCD read *asya mūlyāni*.

208 Divy 25.14, *tatas tayā kiṃcit svabhaktāt tasmād eva gṛhād apahṛtyopasthānaṃ kṛtam*. Mss. ABC and ms. H 9b2, however, omit *svabhaktāt*—hence, "Then she took a little from that very home and began treatment." The Tibetan (Shackleton Bailey 1950: 174) reads *de nas des bdag rang gi rgyags las kyang cung zad sbyar khyim de nyid nas kyang cung zad brkus nas* —> Skt., <*kiṃcit svabhaktāt samudānīya kiṃcit tasmād*>. My sense is that she took a little from her "share" *(bhakta)*, and this may be understood as either "wages" or "food." If it is the former, perhaps she used that money to purchase the inexpensive medicines about which she had inquired. If it is the latter, perhaps she made use of her allotment of food or provisions to provide for Bhava. It is also possible that the food she served him was itself the medicine that had been prescribed. Burnouf (1844: 236) translates this as "La jeune fille prenant quelque chose sure ses provisions personnelles et faisant quelques larcins à la maison de son maître, se mit à le soigner." Tatelman (2000: 47) translates it as "She collected some [appropriate herbs] from her own supplies, took others from the household supplies and began treatment."

209 Divy 25.19–20, *ahaṃ te varam anuprayacchāmīti*. The Tibetan (Shackleton Bailey 1950: 174), however, reads *khyod mchog ci 'dod pa sbyin gyis smros shig*, which probably indicates the same Sanskrit reading that occurs on Divy 32.5: "Tell me, what may I offer you as a reward?" *(ahaṃ vada kiṃ te varam anuprayacchāmīti)*.

210 Divy 25.23, *āryaputra*. The Tibetan (Shackleton Bailey 1950: 174) reads "master" *(jo bo* —> Skt., <*svāmin*>*)*. Generally the term *āryaputra* is used as a vocative in the *Divyāvadāna* by wives who are addressing their husbands. In what follows, I translate the term quite literally as "the son of a noble man." Tatelman (2000: 47) translates it as "a man of the upper classes."

211 Divy 25.23, *dūram api param api gatvā*. Ms. B (Divy 25n5) omits *param api*. The Tibetan (Shackleton Bailey 1950: 174) reads *bdag rgyangs bkum par mchis kyang*, which Shackleton Bailey tentatively translates as "though I go far away (or) die."

212 Divy 26.3, *chattrākāraśīrṣaḥ*. Peter Khoroche (1989: 261) explains that "the comparison of the head with a parasol is to emphasize its perfect roundness at birth." Ananda

Coomaraswamy (1995: 42), citing the *Divyāvadāna,* explains that "the expression 'with a head, or rather, cranium *like* an umbrella' has a definite meaning: it is an assimilation of the top of the head to the Sky or Roof of the Universe, 'with its rays'...represented by the 'ribs' of the umbrella, of which the stick is the spine of the Universal Man and the Axis of the Universe."

213 Following Divy 24.17–19 and 58.5–10 (modified accordingly). Divy 26.8, "and so on as before" *(pūrvavat yāvat).*

214 Following Divy 3.13–16. Divy 26.10, "and so on in full" *(vistareṇa yāvat).*

215 Following Divy 100.4, add *paryavadātaḥ*. Divy 26.14 (omitted).

216 Divy 26.12–13, *vastuparīkṣāyāṃ ratnaparīkṣāyām.* The Tibetan (Shackleton Bailey 1950: 174) reads "the science of building-sites, the science of cloth, the science of jewels, the science of wood" *(gzhi brtag pa dang | ras brtag pa dang | rin po che brtag pa dang | shing rtag pa dang* —> Skt., <*vastuparīkṣāyāṃ vastraparīkṣāyāṃ ratnaparīkṣāyāṃ dāruparīkṣāyām*>*).* Cp. Divy 58.18–21, 100.1–3, 441.28–442.1. Though "the science of wood" is not listed here in the *Divyāvadāna,* it is mentioned later in the story as one of Pūrṇa's areas of expertise (Divy 31.1).

217 Divy 26.14, *udghaṭakaḥ*. Vaidya (Divy-V 16.7) emends to *uddhaṭakaḥ,* probably in the sense of "expert in quoting."

218 Divy 26.17, *maṇḍanaparamā vyavashitāḥ.* To use an antiquated term, they were "dandies"—what one might today refer to as "fashionistas."

219 Divy 26.18, *kare kapolaṃ dattvā cintāparo vyavasthitaḥ*. This trope, writes Schopen (2000: 158nV.4), is "of very common occurrence of considerable importance for 'reading' Buddhist art... In the texts the posture is invariably associated with dejection, disconsolation, despair, anxiety, grief and depression. When the contexts are clear the same holds for the art."

220 Following the Tibetan (Shackleton Bailey 1950: 174–75), read *chos dang mthun pas bsgyur bas* —> Skt., <*vyavahāratā*>. The Tibetan, however, leaves out the term *nyāyena*. Divy 27.6–7, *purṇenāpi tatraiva dharmeṇa nyāyena vyavahāritā sātirekā suvarṇalakṣā samudānītā*. Vaidya (Divy-V 16.20) emends to *vyavaharitāḥ sātirekāḥ suvarṇalakṣāḥ samudānītāḥ*.

221 Read *tathā hi*. Divy 27.10, *tathāpi*.

222 Divy 27.11, *nyāyopārjitasya suvarṇasya mūlyaṃ varjitasya*. Though *mūla* occurs in the *Divyāvadana* meaning "capital" (e.g., Divy 504.2), the term *mūlya* generally means "value" or "price." Here, however, it seems to mean "capital" or "production cost." It is, more literally, the "root money"—what is commonly referred to as "seed money."

223 Following the Tibetan (Shackleton Bailey 1950: 175), add *gser 'bum* —> Skt., <*suvarṇa*>. Divy 27.12 (omitted).

224 Divy 27.25, *kātarāḥ*. The Tibetan (Shackleton Bailey 1950: 175) reads *sngar ma rnams* —> Skt., <*cāturāḥ*(?)>. Tatelman (2000: 49) translates this as "clever men."

225 Since the householder Bhava realized that after his death his sons would "split apart" (*bhedaṃ gamiṣyanti* | Divy 27.15–16), he now recites this verse (repeatedly using a form of the verb √*bhid*) to demonstrate the dangers that such a coming apart would yield.

226 Following the Tibetan (Shackleton Bailey 1950: 175), read *de dag gzhan ni dong ngo* —> Skt., <*te 'nyā niṣkrāntā*>. Divy 27.26, *te niṣkrāntāḥ*. As Tatelman (2000: 83n23) observes, "According to the fifth century painting of this scene found at Kizil in Central Asia (Schlingloff 1991: fig. 3), these 'others' include Pūrṇa and the two other brothers as well as Bhava's wife and Pūrṇa's own mother (the slave-girl)."

227 Divy 28.2, *mahatā saṃskāreṇa.* The same trope on Divy 486.23 reads *mahatā satkāreṇa.*

228 Divy 28.5, *na śobhanaṃ bhaviṣyati.* The Tibetan (Shackleton Bailey 1950: 175) reads *nye du rnams kyis kyang dbyas (dpyas?) par 'gyur gyis,* which Shackleton Bailey translates as "We shall be blamed [insulted?] by our kinsmen."

229 Divy 28.13, *upasthāya.* The Tibetan (Shackleton Bailey 1950: 175) reads "they got up" *(langs te dong bar gyur pa —> Skt., <utthāya>).*

230 Divy 28.19, "girls" *(kanyāḥ).* The Tibetan (Shackleton Bailey 1950: 175) reads "others" *(gzhan dag ni —> Skt., <anyāḥ>).* Vaidya (Divy-V 17.19) likewise emends to *anyāḥ.*

231 Divy 28.19–20, *tayā samākhyātam.* Shackleton Bailey (1950: 175) suggests emending the Sanskrit to read "'How is it that you get [the daily allowance] so quickly?' She gave them a complete account" *(tvaṃ kathaṃ śīghraṃ labhase | tayā sarvaṃ samākhyātam).* He does remark, however, that in the Tibetan "the whole passage is considerably expanded."

232 Following the Tibetan (Shackleton Bailey 1950: 175), read *jo mo thu mo snyun[g] mi mnga' bar gyur cig* —> Skt., <*jyeṣṭhabhartṛkāyā*>. Divy 28.22, *jyeṣṭhabhavikāyā.* Ms. A reads *jyeṣṭhaparicaryāyā.* Ms. D and H 10b10 read *jyeṣṭhabharikāyā.* Ms. C reads *jyeṣṭhaparicaryābharikāyā.* As Cowell and Neil (Divy 28n3) observe, "paricaryā seems a gloss." Cf. Divy 30.11–12.

233 Divy 29.4–5, *kāśikavastrāvārī udghāṭitā.* Though this might be taken more literally as "a shop [selling] cloth from Vārāṇasī opened up," my sense is that it refers to Pūrṇa's shop, which would transform according to its merchandise. It would "open up" *(udghāṭita)* as a shop selling cloth from Vārāṇasī until that consignment ran out. It would then "close" *(ghaṭṭita)* and another "shop" *(āvārī)* would open in its place. The shop, in short, was named after the merchandise it contained. Tatelman (2000: 51) and Burnouf (1844: 241) translate these terms similarly.

234 Divy 29.7, *phuṭṭakavastra.* The precise meaning of *phuṭṭaka* is unclear (cf. BHSD), though presumably it refers to a kind of cloth that is less valued than the cloth produced in Vārāṇasī. Vārāṇasī was (and still is) famous for its silk (cf. Divy 316.27). Perhaps *phuṭṭaka* should be understood as *spṛṣṭaka* or *sphuṭaka*—clothing that is "used" and "worn" or "split apart" and "worn out."

235 Divy 29.14, *śarkarākhodakaḥ.* Cowell and Neil (Divy 679) translate *khodaka* as "pot," though Edgerton suggests that the term "could be related to Amg. khoda (in khododage), khoya, sugar-cane; or even to Skt. kṣoda, piece...any of these mgs. would make possible sense. Uncertain." Vaidya (Divy-V 18.3) suggests emending to *modaka,* a sweet made of sugar, flour, and spices. Since *śarkarā* originally referred to a "small stone" or "pebble," perhaps this should be translated as a "rock of sugar," as in present-day rock candy. Cf. Divy 297.13–14, which reads "candied sugar" *(khaṇḍaśarkarā).*

236 Here and in what follows (Divy 29.17, 29.18, 29.28, 30.1, 30.13) *gṛha* refers to the family and its holdings (i.e., its estate). This is differentiated from *gṛhagata,* as I describe in what follows.

237 Divy 29.21–22, *ekasya gṛhagataṃ kṣetragatam ca | ekasyāvārigatena deśāntaragataṃ ca.* Following Edgerton (BHSD, s.v. *gata*), one might translate this either as "the house(s) and the field(s)" and so on, or "what's in the house(s) and in the field(s)" and so on. The sense here of *gata* seems to be "X and what it contains."

238 Neither of the two younger brothers even consider the possibility that their eldest

brother Bhavila will choose option 3—that is, Pūrṇa. They imagine that he'll either take option 1 (i.e., the house and the fields) or option 2 (i.e., the shop and the foreign holdings), and that they'll get the other and, as a consolation prize, Pūrṇa.

239 Following the Tibetan (Shackleton Bailey 1950: 175), read *bdag cag gis brtags zin gyis* —> Skt., <*parīkṣitam asmābhiḥ*>. Divy 30.1–2, *pratyakṣīkṛtam.*

240 Divy 30.3–4, *āhūyantāṃ kulāni.* The Tibetan (Shackleton Bailey 1950: 175) reads *gzu bo mi lnga zhig bos shig,* which Shackleton Bailey translates as "Call five arbiters." Burnouf (1844: 242n2) and Tatelman (84n37) are both unclear as to the meaning here. Tatelman remarks that "given the importance of the merchant's guild later in the story, one might even infer 'members of the guild.'"

241 Divy 30.10, *evaṃ bhavatu mama pūrṇaka iti.* The Tibetan (Shackleton Bailey 1950: 175) reads "If that is so, then I'll have little Pūrṇa" *(gal te de lta[r?] na gang po ni kho bos bkur ro* —> Skt., <*yady evaṃ bhavatu mama pūrṇaka iti*>*).*

242 Following the Tibetan (Shackleton Bailey 1950: 176), read *mna' ma thu mo phyung shig* —> Skt., <*jyeṣṭhabhātṛke*>. Divy 30.11, *jyeṣṭhabhavike.* Mss. CD read *jyeṣṭhabharike.*

243 Following Divy 30.13, add *gṛham.* The Tibetan (Shackleton Bailey 1950: 176) concurs. Divy 30.15–16, *asmābhir bhājitam.*

244 Pūrṇa seems to be apportioning blame to Bhavila's wife, for he says "in your house" *(yuṣmākaṃ gṛhe)* not "in our house." Though Pūrṇa has been ousted from his home and his shop by his brothers, perhaps he is like his brother Bhavila in assuming that women are the cause of household dissent.

245 Divy 30.23, *ārakūṭākārṣāpaṇān.* Here the Tibetan (Shackleton Bailey 1950: 176) reads "a small measure of brass coins" *(ma sha ka sgyu ma can dag* —> Skt., <*ārakūṭamāṣakān*>*),* as it does in the sentence that follows (Divy 30.24).

246 Although Pūrṇa has "bought" *(gṛhītvā)* the load of wood, he apparently did so on credit, for he doesn't pay the man until later. Cf. Divy 31.20. Tatelman (2000: 53) translates this as "Pūrṇa [accepted this price], took the load of yellow sandalwood and carried it off."

247 Read *preṣitam iti.* Divy 31.8, *preṣita iti.*

248 Divy 31.21–22, *kīdṛso 'sau rājā yasya gṛhe gośīrṣacandanaṃ nāsti.* The Tibetan (Shackleton Bailey 1950: 176) reads *gang gi khyim na tsan dan sa mchog yod pa'i khyim de ci 'dra ba zhig yin,* which Shackleton Bailey translates as "What sort of house is it in which there is *gośīrṣa* sandal?" Though Shackleton Bailey tends to prefer those readings found in the Tibetan, he does note that in this case "the Sanskrit may well be right." I agree. Vaidya (Divy-V 19.13) omits the term *rājā.*

249 In much the same way that Pūrṇa "satisfied" *(saṃtoṣita)* his family with food and the basic necessities, he led the king to "become satisfied" *(parituṣṭa)* with his gift of a piece of sandalwood. Likewise, just as Bhava—Pūrṇa's father—offered his servant girl a reward for providing him with the medicine that saved his life, the king of Sūrpāraka offered Pūrṇa a reward for the same reason.

250 Here the Tibetan (Shackleton Bailey 1950: 176) adds *gal te song na de la kār ṣā pa ṇa drug bcu dbab bo,* which Shackleton Bailey translates as "If he does so he shall be fined sixty *kārṣāpaṇas.*" Burnouf (1844: 245) and Tatelman (2000: 54) both add this sentence in their translations.

251 Divy 32.14, *śabdyata iti.* Vaidya (Divy-V 19.18) emends to *śabdāyata iti.*

252 Divy 32.19, *dūram api param api gatvā.* This idiom also occurred previously in this story (Divy 25.23), and there I translated it as "even if I go far away or to the next

world..." The Tibetan (cf. Shackleton Bailey 1950: 174) likewise offers different translations in both cases.

253 The Tibetan (Shackleton Bailey 1950: 176) reads "with such [merchandise]" *(bdag cag la 'di 'dra bas ni —>* Skt., *<asmākam īdṛśena [dravyeṇa]>).* Divy 32.26, *asmākam api.*

254 Following the Tibetan (Shackleton Bailey 1950: 176), read *gang po la btsongs na —>* Skt., *<purṇasyāntike>.* Divy 33.1, *purṇasyāntikād.*

255 The Tibetan (Shackleton Bailey 1950: 176) omits the negative.

256 Divy 33.12–14, *tato baṇiggrāmeṇa saṃjātāmarseṇa ṣaṣṭeḥ kārṣāpaṇāṇām arthāyātape dhāritaḥ.* Though Edgerton tentatively translates *ātape dhāritaḥ* as "he was assessed a fine," here I follow Tatelman (2000: 85), who in turn follows Burnouf (1844: 246) and the Chinese translation (T 1448: vol. XXIV, p. 10c20–22).

257 Divy 34.1–2, *sa sāhaṃkāraḥ kāmakāram adattvā nirgataḥ.* Cowell and Neil (Divy 34n1) suggest *kāmakāramadatvān.* The Tibetan (Shackleton Bailey 1950: 177) reads *de nga rgyal dang nyam[s?] du shed dang bcas pa'i dregs pas byung ba dang* —> Skt, *<sa sāhaṃkārakāmakāramadatvān* (?)>.

258 Divy 34.3–4, *yathākrītam.* Vaidya (Divy-V 20.26) emends to *yathākṛtam.*

259 Vaidya (Divy-V 20.27) omits Divy 34.4–6.

260 Divy 34.7, *teṣāṃ baṇijām.* Vaidya (Divy-V 20.27) emends to *teṣāṃ vaṇijyam.*

261 This is how much he owed the merchants after giving them 300,000 gold coins as a deposit. Now he has paid up in full.

262 For more on these kinds of fees, see Agrawala 1966: 71.

263 Divy 34.29, *udānāt pārāyaṇāt satyadṛśaḥ.* Tatelman (2000: 85n57) emends to *udānaṃ pārāyaṇam satyadṛṣṭim.* Cf. Lévi 1915: 417–18.

264 Lamotte (1988: 162) explains that "all these works have their correspondents in the Pāli *Khuddaka*. The *Dharmapadagāthā* or *Udāna[varga]* correspond to the *Dhammapada*. The *Munigāthā* are probably the *Munigāthā* of the Aśokan edict at Bhābra... and the *Munisutta* of the *Suttanipāta* (i, 12). The *Satyadṛta* (variant: *Satyadṛśa*), although not yet identified, possibly refers to the eulogy of the 'Truth, voice of the Immortal,' which is the subject of the *Subhāsitasutta* of the *Suttanipāta* (iii, 3). The *Śailagāthā* are the equivalent of the *Selasutta* of the *Suttanipāta* (iii, 7). The *Arthavargīyāṇisūtrāṇi* are the sixteen *sutta* of the *Aṭṭ[ha]kavagga* of the *Suttanipāta* (iv). The *Pārāyaṇa* is chapter V of the *Suttanipāta*. Finally, the *Sthaviragāthā* and *Sthavirī-* correspond respectively to the *Thera-* and *Therīgāthā* of the Pāli collection" (slightly modified). For more on these texts and their extant counterparts, see Lévi 1915.

265 Divy 35.4, *naitāni gītāni kiṃtu khalv etad buddhavacanam.* Vaidya (Divy-V 21.11) omits *gītāni.* The Tibetan (Shackleton Bailey 1950: 177) reads *lags so | 'on ci | de ni sangs rgyas kyi*[*s*] *bka'o,* for which Shackleton Bailey suggests *naitāni gītāni | kiṃ nu khalv etad | buddhavacanam* (?). Following the Tibetan, Tatelman (2000: 58) translates this as "Caravan-leader, these are not [mere] songs! How could you possibly think that? These are the words of the Awakened One, the Buddha!"

266 Divy 35.18, *värttā.* Vaidya (Divy-V 21.20) emends to *vārtā.*

267 Divy 35.19, *kimartham.* Vaidya (Divy-V 21.21) emends to *kāmārtham.*

268 Divy 36.8, *apūrveṇa.* Edgerton (BHSD) suggests "extraordinarily," "in a high degree," but this is the only passage cited. Cowell and Neil (Divy 673) suggest "suddenly." The term is omitted in the Tibetan (Shackleton Bailey 1950: 177).

269 Following Divy 163.29–164 and Divy 558.2–3, read *aho saṃghaḥ aho dharmasya*

svākhyātatā. The Tibetan (Shackleton Bailey 1950: 177) concurs. Divy 36.11–12, *aho saṃghasya svākhyātatā.*

270 The implication is that these new initiates don't look like rank novices, whose heads would be freshly shaven, and they don't act like them either.

271 Following Vaidya's emendation (Divy-V 22.20), read *evaṃ sthitaḥ*. Divy 37.5, *naiva sthitaḥ*. Cp. Divy 48.24 and 159.12, *naiva sthitā*, which Vaidya (Divy-V 29.32 and 98.22) emends to *evaṃ sthitā*, and Divy 342.2, *nopasthitā,* which Vaidya (Divy-V 211.23) also emends to *evaṃ sthitā.*

272 For another translation of the following section (Divy 37.5–40.14), see E. J. Thomas 1950: 40–43. In addition, writes Tatelman (2000: 86n65), "The Mūlasarvāstivādin version (Schmithausen 1987: 311–13) is preserved in the Chinese *Saṃyuktāgama* (T 99, chüan 13: vol. II, pt. 2, p. 89b1–c23); the very similar Theravādin *sutta* is found at *Majjhima-nikāya* iii, 267–70... and at *Saṃyukta-nikāya* iv, 60–63" (slightly modified).

273 Following Divy 37.9–15. Divy 37.19, "and so on as before" *(pūrvavat yāvat).*

274 Read *saṃrāga* for each of the following repetitions of *sarāga,* though the differences between the two terms are minimal. Divy 37.25–27, *nandīsaumanasye sati sarāgo bhavati | nandīsarāge sati nandīsarāgasaṃyojanaṃ bhavati | nandīsarāgasaṃyojanasaṃyuktaḥ pūrṇa bhikṣuḥ.* The Tibetan (Shackleton Bailey 1950: 177) reads *kun du chags par 'gyur ro | kun du chags pa yod na kun du sbyor bar 'gyur te | dga' ba dang | kun du chags pa dang | kun du sbyor ba dang ldan par gyur pa'i dge slong ni...* —> Skt. <*nandīsaumanasye sati saṃrāgo bhavati | saṃrāge sati saṃyojanaṃ bhavati | nandīsaṃrāgasaṃyojanasaṃyukto bhikṣuḥ...*>.

275 Divy 38.1–2, *tāṃś ca bhikṣur dṛṣṭvā*. Perhaps "after seeing them" should be deleted or revised to "after hearing them, smelling them, etc." Tatelman (2000: 61) translates this as "becoming aware of these."

276 Following Divy 37.22–27. Divy 38.2, "and so on as before" *(pūrvavat yāvat).*

277 The text is abbreviated here (Divy 38.3–4) with the expression "and so on as before" *(pūrvavat yāvat),* but it isn't clear what precisely has been abbreviated. I adapt the previous passage in accordance with the Tibetan, following both Burnouf (1844: 252) and Tatelman (2000: 61–62).

278 Divy 38.4, *śuklapakṣenāntike nirvāṇasyety ucyate*. For more on the term *śuklapakṣa* in this passage and the troubles it seems to have given Burnouf (1844: 225n1), Thomas (1950: 41), and Edgerton (BHSD), see Tatelman 2000: 86n69.

279 Divy 38.11, *asatyayā*. The Tibetan (Shackleton Bailey 1950: 177) reads "indecent" *(tshogs par me dbyung ba'i —> <asabhyayā>).* Likewise at Divy 38.14 and 38.17.

280 Divy 38.12, *tasya*. The Tibetan (Shackleton Bailey 1950: 177) reads *de la* —> Skt. <*tatra*>. The Tibetan, likewise, reads *tatra* for *tasya* on Divy 38.12, 38.15, 38.21, 38.23, 38.30, and 39.4.

281 Following Divy 38.9–10. Divy 38.19, "and so on as before" *(pūrvavat yāvat).*

282 Following Divy 38.9–10. Divy 38.26, "and so on as before" *(pūrvavat yāvat).*

283 Following Divy 38.9–10. Divy 39.2, "and so on" *(yāvat).*

284 Read *jehrīyamāṇā*. Divy 39.7, *jehriyante*. The Tibetan (Shackleton 1950: 178) reads *lus rnag can 'dis | skyo ba dang | ngo tsha ba | dang rnam par smod pa gang dag.*

285 Following Edgerton (BHSD, s.v. *saurabhya*), read *sauratyena*. Divy 39.12, *saurabhyena.*

286 Divy 39.14, *tīrṇas tāraya*. I translate this expression literally, thought Tatelman (2000: 87n77) is right that the idea here is to "cross over the ocean of birth-and-death *(saṃsāra, bhava).*"

287 Divy 39.14–15, *āśvasta āśvāsaya.* The idea here is that one should recover from a breathlessness, a kind of suffocation or claustrophobia, caused by the stresses of living in this world. In the *Pabbajā-sutta* in the *Suttanipāta,* for example, a young man decides to leave the confined life of a householder for the less confined life of a wandering Buddhist renunciant. As the text explains (*Suttanipāta* 72, v. 406), "'Cramped is this household life. Passion is everywhere like dust,' he thought. 'But for the renunciant, living in the open air, the sky is the limit.' Seeing this was so, he went forth as a monk" *(sambādho 'yaṃ gharāvāso rajassāyatanaṃ iti abbhokāso va pabbajjā iti disvāna pabbaji).* In this case, however, inhalation also entails inspiration, as in the archaic sense of the latter term. Elsewhere I translate variants of this term with forms of "to console."

288 Divy 39.29–40.1, *asya duṣpūrasyārthe praviśāmi.* Though the object that is "hard to fill" *(duṣpūrasyārthe)* is not directly mentioned, the referent is no doubt the stomach. Bhartṛhari (cf. PSED, s.v. *piṭharī*) also makes the same allusion in his epigrams—*jaṭharapiṭharī duṣpūreyaṃ karoti viḍambanām.*

289 In the previous section, Pūrṇa expressed his willingness to succumb to a variety of attacks, such as those by club or by sword, even if they resulted in his death. Here Pūrṇa once again expresses that same willingness, even pushing away his robe so that he would be even more vulnerable to the hunter's already drawn arrow.

290 Divy 40.8, *śikṣāpadeṣu.* Vaidya (Divy-V 24.20) emends to *śikṣāpadeśeṣu.*

291 Divy 40.11, *anupradāpitāni.* Cowell and Neil (Divy 40n3) query *anupradatāni.* Ms. A reads *anupradatāni* (?). Ms. D reads *anupradātāni.* Mss. BC reads *anupradāmitāni.* Divy 550.23 has *dāpitāni* in a parallel passage.

292 Following Edgerton (BHSD, s.vv. *uccaka, kocava*), read *vṛṣikocava* or *vṛṣikākocava.* Divy 40.10–11, *vṛṣikoccaka.*

293 It is unclear here (Divy 40.11–12) whether it is Pūrṇa or the hunter who attains arhatship. Burnouf (1844: 255) understands the hunter to be the subject of the sentence, while Thomas (1950: 43), the Theravādin versions of the story, and the Chinese recension understand it to be Pūrṇa. For details, see Tatelman 2000: 87–88n85.

294 Following Divy 282.1–4. Divy 40.13, "and so on" *(yāvat).*

295 Divy 40.16, *kālakarṇin.* More literally this expression means "black-eared," though it is an attested idiom for an evil omen. Tatelman's (2000: 88n91) remarks here are instructive: "Since *kāla* also means 'death,' one could also translate *kālakarṇin* as 'he who wears death in his ear'. In this passage, the brothers and Bhavila are talking at cross purposes: the former regard Pūrṇa's departure as the end of their 'bad luck,' while Bhavila feels Pūrṇa's absence as the departure of good fortune. Recall also that the three brothers have long been named for the types of earrings they wear [Divy 26.24–29]. Thus the pair here express their animosity toward Pūrṇa by means of an ironic symmetry with their own nicknames." For more on this term, see Agrawala 1966: 69–70. See also DPPN, s.v. *kālakaṇṇī.*

296 Divy 40.18, *pūrṇakaḥ | śrīr sā...* Vaidya (Divy-V 24.27) emends to *pūrṇakaśrīḥ.*

297 What he means here is that he is no longer blessed with the good fortune that is *śrī,* not that he has lost all of his money. He refers to Pūrṇa as though he were "prosperity" *(śrī)* incarnate, like Śrī the goddess of wealth, otherwise known as Lakṣmī.

298 Following Divy 34.15–17 (modified accordingly). Divy 40.26, *pūrvavat yāvat.*

299 Divy 41.4., *voḍhum ārabdhāni.* The Tibetan (Shackleton Bailey 1950: 178) reads *de nas sa mchog gi tshal sta re lnga [b]rgya tsam gyis bcod par brtsams so,* which Shackleton

Bailey translates as "Then they began to cut the sandal forest with five hundred axes." Likewise, in what follows, he notes, "in [Divy 41].6 *vahato dṛṣṭvā* becomes *gcod par mthong ngo* and *vahanti* in [Divy 41.]9, *'gums na* ('respectful' equivalent of *gcod na*)." M. G. Dhadphale (personal correspondence) has suggested to me that these instances of √*vah* might signify √*vaḍḍh*, since in some Prakrits, when there is a conjunct of a consonant and its aspirate (e.g., *da* + *dha*), the consonants drop out and just the aspirate remains (e.g., *da* + *dha* = *ha*). Even an aspirate consonant can reduce to just its aspiration, as in the case of the Prakrit epic, the *Gauḍavaho* (i.e., *Gauḍavadho* —> *Gauḍavaho*). Hence, *voḍhum* might signify *voḍḍhum*, *vahanti* would be *vaḍḍhanti* (cf. PTSD, s.v. *vaddheti*), and *vahataḥ* would be *vaḍḍhataḥ*.

300 Following Divy 41.13–14, read *mahākālikāvātabhayam*. Divy 41.11, *mahāntaṃ kālikāvātabhayam*.

301 Following the Tibetan (Shackleton Bailey 1950: 179), read *zhi ba dang* [*ni*] *chu lha lus ngan nor lha sogs* —> Skt., <*śivavaruṇakuveravāsavādyā-*>. This corrects the verse to the *puṣpitāgrā* metre. Divy 41.16, *śivavaruṇakuveraśakrabrahmādyā-*.

302 Śacī's husband is Indra; Hari is another name for Viṣṇu; and Śaṅkara refers to Śiva.

303 Divy 41.21–22, *vātapiśācadaṣṭhāḥ*. Vaidya (Divy-V 25.19) emends to *vātapiśācadasthāḥ* and in brackets suggests *yakṣāḥ*.

304 As we read elsewhere in the *Divyāvadāna* (e.g., Divy 84.6–7, 190.8, 492.9–10), "the knowledge and insight of arhats does not operate unless they focus their attention." In other words, Pūrṇa must focus his attention in order to see his brother's situation. Though the specific act of what I translate as "focusing the attention" *(samanvāhara)* is unclear, it seems to involve collecting *(āhara)* oneself, and then gathering *(sam)* and directing *(anu)* one's attention. For more on this term, see Edgerton (BHSD, s.v. *samanvāharati*). For more on this trope, see my footnotes to Divy 83.7 and Divy 84.6–7.

305 Divy 42.17, *jarādharmāham*. Cf. Divy 187.2.

306 This passage seems to have been abbreviated. Cf. Divy 232.25–233.16.

307 Divy 43.1, *candanamālaṃ prāsādam*. Quite likely the bases of such "palaces" *(prāsāda)* were made of stone and the upper stories were built of wood. For more on the architecture of these buildings, see Coomaraswamy 1928: 268–69 and Meister 1988–89.

308 Divy 43.20, *ārāmikena*. The Tibetan (Shackleton Bailey 1950: 180) reads *khyim pa zhig*, for which Shackleton Bailey suggests Skt., *āgārika*. Tatelman (2000: 68) follows the Tibetan and translates the term as "lay-disciple."

309 Read *viśuddhaśīlin* to restore to *upajāti* meter. Divy 43.22, *viśuddhaśīla*.

310 Divy 43.27, *vaidūryaśalākāvat*. Considering that Ānanda reads this apparition as a de facto invitation to a meal and then distributes *śalākās*—in this case meaning "tally sticks"—there does seem to be some homology between the *śalākā* that magically appears before the monks and those that the monks take to indicate their willingness to go to the city of Sūrpāraka for a meal. Edgerton (BHSD, s.v. *śalākā*) suggests "like a sliver of *vaiḍūrya* (in color)." Burnouf (1844: 259) translates it as "aiguilles de lapis-lazuli" and Tatelman (2000: 68) as "a staff of lapis lazuli."

Though *vaiḍūrya* is often translated as "lapis lazuli" or "cat's eye," the term and its equivalents are used in Sanskrit, Prakrit, and Tibetan literature to refer to objects that are the color of water (as above), as well as blue, green, and yellow. Unlike lapis lazuli or cat's eye, beryl can range in color from pale green to light blue (e.g., aquamarine), or from yellow to white (e.g., chrysoberyl). For an excellent discussion of the term, see Winder 1987.

311 "This Pūrṇa," writes Tatelman (2000: 89n109), "is given the same epithet in the *Sumāgadhāvadāna* (Iwamoto 1978: 68). The term may be meant to suggest strict adherence to an ascetical life-style." For various parallels in the Pāli materials, see DPPN, s.v. Kuṇḍadhāna Thera.

312 Divy 44.9, *prajñāvimuktaḥ*. This term, following Tatelman (2000: 89–90n110), "refers to one who has attained arhatship through intellectual analysis or intuition without attaining the higher yogic 'absorptions' *(samāpatti),* which alone confer such powers as flight, clairvoyance, etc. The 'insight-liberated' individual is one of seven types of practitioners classified according to temperament (*Majjhima-nikāya* i, 477–80) and, according to *Saṃyutta-nikāya* i, 191, by far the most common. On the seven types, see Saṅgharakshita 1967: 154–58 and Gombrich 1996: 96–134" (slightly modified).

313 Following the Tibetan (Shackleton Bailey 1950: 180), read *rab sbyin* —> Skt., <*sudatta*>. Divy 44.13, *sujātasya*. Sudatta is Anāthapiṇḍada's given name. Cf. Edgerton (BHSD, s.v. *sujāta*). The King of Kośala in this instance is King Prasenajit, and Mṛgāra is his chief minister.

314 Divy 44.25, *jarayā hi*. The Tibetan (Shackleton Bailey 1950: 180) reads *rga bas dar yal gyur kyang* —> Skt., <*jarayāpi*>.

315 Divy 44.28, *caitya śalākāgrahaṇe*. Tatelman (2000: 69), following Burnouf (1844: 261), reads *caitya* in the sense of an object of veneration and translates this expression as "in the matter of taking ecclesiastical food-tickets." Yet the term *caitya* in this context is odd—to quote Tatelman (2000: 90n117), "its precise function here is unclear." I read *caitya* instead as *ca etya*, a conjunction and a gerund, rather than a noun.

316 Following Divy 45.4–6. Divy 45.9, "and so on as before" *(pūrvavat yāvat).*

317 Divy 45.17–18, *yāvat patracārikā ṛddhyā haritacārikā bhājanacārikāś cāgatāḥ*. Agrawala (1966: 71–72) discusses this passage in great depth, and explains that "the real meaning is that *cārika* denoted persons who formed part of a procession holding various auspicious objects in their hands or who moved on the back of auspicial animals or in chariots or appeared seated in *vimānas* ['flying mansions'], all of them moving at the head of the procession in an order." An earlier version of this account had appeared as an article, and in it Agrawala (1964) quotes Edgerton's full entry from the BHSD (s.v. *cārika*) before refuting it. Tatelman (2000: 70) translates this as "Just then, monks, seated in [vehicles fashioned from] leaves, from tree-branches and from water-pots began to arrive, flying in by means of their psychic powers." Yutaka Iwamoto (1968: 84–85) likewise translates a similar passage in the *Sumāgadhāvadāna*. Yet in the verse that follows (Divy 45.27–28), monks are said to have recourse to a variety of vehicles, though *patra, harita,* and *bhājana* are not among them. More likely is that the monks arrive with various implements to accept the meal that they came to Sūrpāraka to receive. This may be why *patracārikā, haritacārikā,* and *bhājanacārikā* occur in this passage with the variants *patravārikā, haritavārikā,* and *bhājanavārikā* (Divy 45n2). The last of these terms, *bhājanavārika*—"the monastery official in charge of bowls"—is cited in the *Mahāvyutpatti* (§9069). The Tibetan (Burnouf 1844: 261n2) translates these terms as *lo ma 'dri ma, shing tshe 'dri ma,* and *sngang spyad 'dri ma*. The term *patra* here is probably similar to the Hindi *patrāvali*—a plate made with stitched-together

leaves. The term *harita,* though unattested in this context, may refer to some kind of leafy branch like a banana leaf.

318 This is the typical beginning of a long stock passage that describes the Buddha and the monks in his entourage (e.g., Divy 125.25–126.14, 148.8–148.24, 182.1–182.21). I do not include it in my translation, however, since there is no indication here that the remainder of the passage is to be supplied.

319 Divy 46.20, *arhacchataiḥ*. Vaidya (Divy-V 28.21) emends to *arhacchāntaiḥ*.

320 Following Divy 46.23–26 (slightly modified). Divy 47.10, "and so on" *(yāvat).*

321 Divy 47.16, *atikrāntātikrāntāḥ*. But the manuscripts (Divy 47n4) read *atikrāntābhikrāntaḥ*. The Tibetan (Shackleton Bailey 1950: 180) reads *'phags so | mngon par 'phags so*, for which Shackleton Bailey suggests Skt., *atikrāntābhikrāntāḥ*. In the same trope elsewhere (Divy 311.5–6), we find *abhikrānto 'haṃ bhadantābhikrāntaḥ*.

322 Following the Tibetan (Shackleton Bailey 1950: 180), read *'khor sar* —> Skt., <*medhyāṃ*>. This is confirmed by Bendall (Divy 660) in his description of fragments from the *Divyāvadāna*. Divy 47.23, *yaṣṭyām*. Tatelman (2000: 72) follows the Tibetan reading, and the Tibetan sense of the term (cf. Burnouf 1844: 265n2), and translates this as "...planted that *bakula* branch in the path around that *stūpa*." For more on the placement of a "terrace" *(medhi)* and "post" *(yaṣṭi)* in the architecture of a stūpa, see Divy 244.9–12.

323 Following the Tibetan (Shackleton Bailey 1950: 180–81), read *ne'u gsing rnams ni glogs* —> Skt., <*kṛṣṭam*>. Divy 48.3, *kṛṣṇam*. Cf. Divy 127.5, where within the same trope occurs *śādvalāni kṛṣata*.

324 The Tibetan (Shackleton Bailey 1950: 181) reads "The Blessed One said, 'Seers, has your hermitage, which was well provided with flowers, fruit, and water, been destroyed? Shall it be restored to how it was before?' 'Let it be so, Blessed One'" *(bcom ldan 'das kyis bka' stsal pa | drang srong dag bsti gnas me tog dang 'bras bu dang chu phun sum tshogs pa ci ste ma rung | ji sngon gyi ji lta ba de bzhin du bya 'am | bcom ldan 'das mdzad du gsol* —> Skt., <*bhagavān āha | ṛṣayaḥ kiṃ puṣpaphalasalilasaṃpannam āśramapadaṃ vinaṣṭam | kiṃ yathāpaurāṇaṃ bhavatu | bhavatu bhagavan*>*).* Divy 48.7–10, *bhagavān āha kiṃ*[a] *| te kathayanti | bhagavan puṣpaphalasalilasaṃpannam āśramapadaṃ vinaṣṭaṃ yathāpaurāṇaṃ bhavatu | bhavatu ity āha bhagavān.*[b]

[a] In his description of fragments from the *Divyāvadāna*, Bendall (Divy 661) reads *āha maharṣayaḥ kim*.

[b] Though the manuscripts (Divy 48n2) read *bhavatu bhagavān*, Cowell and Neil have added *ity āha*. Bendall (Divy 661) likewise reads *bhavatu bhagavān,* which lends additional support to the Tibetan reading of this passage.

325 Following Vaidya's emendation (Divy-V 29.32), read *evaṃ sthitā*. Divy 48.24, *naiva sthitā*.

326 Following Divy 180.22–28 (modified accordingly). Divy 48.25, "and so on as before" *(pūrvavat yāvat).*

327 Following Divy 67.5–7. Divy 49.5, "and so on as before" *(pūrvavat yāvat).*

328 Following Divy 48.17–24 (modified accordingly). Divy 49.15–17, *pūrvavat yāvad bhagavatā ehibhikṣukayā pravrājito yāvan naiva sthito buddhamanorathena*. Though one would expect *ābhāṣitaḥ* for *pravrājitaḥ* (cf. Divy 48.19, 281.23, 341.27, 558.12), one does find *ehibhikṣukayā pravrājitāḥ pūrvavat yāvat* at Divy 463.25–26.

329 The Tibetan (Shackleton Bailey 1950: 181) reads "princes" *(rgyal po'i sras* —> Skt., *rājapūtrāḥ).*

330 Divy 50.1, *apaśyan*. The manuscript fragments examined by Bendall (Divy 661) read "saw" *(apaśyat),* and the Tibetan (Shackleton Bailey 1950: 181) concurs, but this is a much less desirable reading. It is crucial here that the people *can't* see the Buddha. Tatelman (2000: 76; 92n148) concurs and likewise translates the text as is.

331 Divy 50.14, *trapukarṇī ca praṇītam*. However, the manuscript fragments examined by Bendall (Divy 661) read *trapukarṇī suci praṇītam*, substituting "excellent" *(suci)* for "and" *(ca),* and the Tibetan (Shackleton Bailey 1950: 181) concurs.

332 Divy 50.23, *agocarīkariṣyataḥ*. Although the CPD cites *agocara* as meaning both "improper pasture" and "behavior not to be indulged in," Edgerton (BHSD, s.v. *agocara*) cites only the latter of the two meanings. While the former meaning can be explained by breaking up the term as "not" *(a)* "a pastureland" *(gocara)*—in short, undesirable if not uninhabitable—the latter meaning is less apparent. M. G. Dhadphale (personal communication) suggests that *agocara* in this latter sense may represent a mis-Sanskritization of Pāli *āgucārin*, a "wrong" *(āgu)* "doer" *(cārin)*—what should have been Skt. *āgaścārin*. This seems all the more likely in this passage, which provides the two references given by Edgerton, because what is being discussed is nāgas. As the CPD notes, *āgu* is "mostly used in etym[ological] expl[anations] of nāga." For example, as we read in *Sutta Nipāta* (SN 88, v. 522), a nāga is one who "does no wrong in the world" *(āguṃ na karoti kiñci loke)*. But in this context, nāga is an epithet of a buddha or an arhat, not a serpent who lives in the ocean. Perhaps what we have in the *Divyāvadāna* is an explanation that while real *nāgās*, such as buddhas and arhats, "do no wrong," *wrong* is precisely what those other nāgas do. With the term *agocarīkariṣyataḥ,* both meanings may have been at play, though Edgerton is right to stress the latter. Edgerton (BHSD, s.v. *agocarī-karoti*) translates this passage as "take heed for the city of S[ūrpāraka] that no wrong behavior (i.e. injury to the inhabitants, [Divy] 51.3–5) takes place." Tatelman (2000: 76) captures this ambivalence well with his translation: "they will wreak havoc." The Buddha may have been concerned that the nāgas would misbehave and that they would ruin Sūrpāraka.

333 Divy 50.25, *ātyayikapiṇḍapātam*. Following Edgerton (BHSD, s.v. *ātyayika*) and Burnouf (1844: 628), Tatelman (2000: 93n158) explains that "the term 'irregular' (or 'special' or 'transgressive' or 'untimely') almsfood *(ātyayikapiṇḍapāta)* refers to a meal taken in a manner or at a time—for example, after noon, when monks are not supposed to take solids—which violates strict Vinaya regulations, but which irregularity is justified by circumstances." Tatelman then goes on to posit a sequence of events that might explain the Buddha's rather cryptic remark: "if he is to intercept the nāgas, the Buddha cannot take the time to have lunch at the home of Pūrṇa's brothers. Instead, he has Maudgalyāyana fetch his meal. When Maudgalyāyana returns with the food, the Buddha takes it with him, meets up with the nāgas, admonishes and instructs them, and only then eats. Finally, he accepts a beverage—the part of the meal he did not bring with him—from his new lay-disciples."

334 Divy 50.28, *upadhau*. Vaidya (Divy-V 31.8) emends to *upādhau*. Edgerton (BHSD, s.v. *upadhi*) translates this as "the Lord was acting in regard to material things (of the assembly of monks), in the function of an *upadhi-vārika*"—that is, "an acting caretaker of a monastery." It was, in other words, his turn to be property master, the one responsible for managing and protecting the offerings given to the community. The Tibetan reads *upadhivāraka* as *dge skos* (*Mahāvyutpatti* §9067)—one monitoring "virtue" *(dge ba)*—or a close variant such as *dge bskos,* which Jäschke (1987) explains as "censor, and

at the same time provost and beadle in a monastery, who has to watch over strict order, and to punish transgressors." Cf. Schopen 1996: 97n35. M. G. Dhadphale (personal communication) suggests that *upadhi* may be connected to *upādāna,* in the sense of "receiving" or "acquiring," just as *praṇidhi* is connected to *praṇidhāna,* though one would still have to explain the added aspiration (i.e., *d* to *dh*). Edgerton notes that *vārika* occurs in the names of various monastic officials (e.g., *bhājanavārika, pānīyavārika, śayanāsanavārika*) in the sense of "charged with," "superintendent of," and "one who watches over." But *vārika* can also mean "turn." Hence, these monastic titles may refer to someone whose turn it was to be in charge of something, whether "bowls" *(bhājana)* or "bedding and seats" *(śayanāsana).*

335 Divy 51.2, *nagaraṃ mā 'gocarībhaviṣyati.* Vaidya (Divy-V 31.9–10) emends to *nagaram agocarībhaviṣyati.*

336 Divy 51.10–11, *yady ekasyaiva pānīyaṃ pāsyāmi.* This is a conjecture. Ms. A reads *yady eva bhagavānīyam.* Ms. C reads *yady eta bhavānīyam.* Ms. D reads *yad deśayeyaṃ pānīyam.* Ms. B is corrupt. Ms. H 1921 reads *yady ekasya pānīya pāsyāmi.* Bendall's manuscript (661), *yadi ekasya pānīyam.* The Tibetan (Shackleton Bailey 1950: 182) reads *gal te gcig gi chu gsol na ni des na gzhan dag gzhan du sems par 'gyur bas* —> Skt., <*yady ekasya pānīyaṃ pāsyāmy apareṣām*>.

337 Divy 51.23, *parikaret.* Vaidya (Divy-V 31.23) emends to *paricaret.* The Tibetan (Shackleton Bailey 1950: 182) reads *khur du thogs sam,* for which Shackleton Bailey suggests Skt., *pariharet.* This would work quite well if on Divy 51.22 we emended *ekenāṃśena* to *ekenāṃsena.* This could be taken as "Were a son to carry his father on one shoulder and his mother on the other shoulder for a full one hundred years."

338 Divy 51.24, *śilā.* Edgerton (BHSD) explains that it probably means "crystal." The *Mahāvyutpatti* (§5955) equates it with the Tibetan *man shel.*

339 Divy 51.25, *musāragalva* (mss. BCD, *susāragalva*). This term no doubt refers to a kind of precious stone, but it is unclear which one—perhaps coral, emerald, or cat's eye. Edgerton (BHSD) notes that "in recent years most interpreters of Buddhist Hybrid Sanskrit have left the exact meaning undetermined." The *Mahāvyutpatti* (§5956) offers *spug* as the Tibetan equivalent. Lokesh Chandra (2001) translates *spug* with *karketana,* a Sanskrit term for a precious though indistinct gemstone, offering little additional insight.

340 Divy 51.25, *lohitakā.* Apparently the same as *lohitamuktā,* which the *Mahāvyutpatti* (§5953) translates with the Tibetan *mu tig dmar po.*

341 Divy 52.4, *yad aham.* The Tibetan (Shackleton Bailey 1950: 182) suggests Skt., *yan nv aham.*

342 Divy 52.7, *dūraṃ vayam ihāgatāḥ.* Though the literal meaning of the Sanskrit here is clear, its figurative meaning is not. Burnouf (1844: 271) translates this as "Nous sommes ici bien loin de cet univers." Tatelman (2000: 78) translates it as "We in this world are far away from there."

343 Edgerton (BHSD) and Tatelman (2000: 78) take *bhadrakanyā* as a proper name.

344 Divy 52.19, *bhadantaḥ.* The Tibetan (Shackleton Bailey 1950: 182) reads "gentlemen" *(shes ldan dag* —> Skt., <*bhavantaḥ*>*).*

345 Divy 52.21, *anayā.* Vaidya (Divy-V 32.7) emends to *anyāḥ.*

346 Following Divy 47.11–16. Divy 52.27, "and so on as before" *(pūrvavat yāvat).*

347 Divy 52.28, *tavānubhāvāt.* The term *anubhāva,* Schopen (2000: 147nII.18) writes, "is frequently found in association with the Buddha himself in the form of *buddhānu-*

bhāvena, and has crucial bearing on how this figure was understood... At a minimum, the term seems to refer to the power, force, or ability to effect and affect things which are external to oneself—people, events, etc. It appears to be as much magical as moral, and in fact overlaps and is sometimes paired with *ṛddhi.*" With that said, it may be more appropriate to translate *anubhāva* as "the effects of power" or "innate power," though I generally translate it as simply "power."

348 Following Vaidya's emendation (Divy-V 32.14) as well as Shackleton Bailey's suggestion (1950: 182), read *apetadoṣam.* Likewise Divy 555.3. Divy 52.30, *apetadoṣā.*

349 Following Divy 65.6–7. Divy 53.13 (omitted).

350 Divy 53.18, *nirmādayati.* Vaidya (Divy-V) 32.25 emends to *niryātayati.* Cf. Edgerton (BHSD, s.v. *nirmādayati*). Perhaps *nirmādayati* is connected with *nirmardayati* or *nirmālayati.* Cf. Divy 345.28–346.1.

351 Read *āgatāḥ smo bhagavan | āgatā maudgalyāyana | tataḥ.* Divy 53.20–21, *āgatāḥ smo bhagavan | āgatā | maudgalyāyanas tataḥ.*

352 Divy 53.22, *manojavā.* This term also appears later in the text (Divy 636.27) in a list of various kinds of magic, but it is not defined. Edgerton (BSHD) observes only that it is a "name of a kind of magic."

353 Divy 53.22–23, *na mayā bhadanta vijñātam evaṃ gambhīram evaṃ gambhīrā buddhadharmāḥ.* The Tibetan (Shackleton Bailey 1950: 182–83) suggests Skt., <*na mayā bhadanta vijñātam evaṃ gambhīrā buddhadharmā*>.

354 Following the Tibetan (Shackleton Bailey 1950: 182–83), read Skt., <*nābhaviṣyat*>. Divy 53.25, *abhaviṣyat.*

355 As Shackleton Bailey (1950: 183) observes, "Maudgalyāyana means that had he realized the grandeur of the Buddha's *dharmas* he would have striven for Buddhahood *(samyaksaṃbodhi)* instead of stopping short at the attainment of Arhatship." Cowell and Neil (Divy 705) offer a translation of this passage that Shackleton Bailey is right to describe as "altogether astray."

356 Divy 54.2–3, *labdhasaṃbhārāṇi pariṇatapratyayāni.* Though *saṃbhāra* can have the technical meaning of "equipment" or "prerequisite" for awakening, I follow the Tibetan (cf. D nya 34b4) and translate the term here in its nontechnical sense. Tatelman (2000: 80) offers this translation of the passage (Divy 54.1–3): "Monks, the monk Pūrṇa performed and accumulated many deeds, the bases of which are about to ripen, which exist in a multitude and the effects of which are inevitable." In a similar instance, Ch'en (1945–47: 297n226) offers this translation: "O monks, acts were performed by Svāgata which accumulated and reached their fullness, whose causes have matured, which approached him like a flood, and which were inevitable in their results."

357 Divy 54.6, *api tūpātteṣv eva.* As Cowell and Neil (Divy 54n1) observe, "The MSS. read here and elsewhere *bhūpānteṣv eva* or perhaps *bhūyānteṣv eva*" (e.g., Divy 131.11, 141.11, 191.16, 282.15). Their conjecture "is based on the fact that *tū* and *tt* are sometimes written in the MSS. like *bhū* and *nt.*" Edgerton (BHSD, s.v. *dhātu*) notes that this emendation is "probable." Burnouf (1844: 35n1) suggests emending to *api bhūtāntṣv eva.* If we follow Cowell and Neil's emendation, *upātta* might be explained as the past passive participle of *upa* + *ā* + √*dā.* This would have the sense of "collected" or "brought forward," likely related to the technical notion of *upādāna* as it figures in interdependent arising (cf. BHSD, s.v. *upādāna*). Tatelman (2000: 80–81) offers a somewhat free translation of this trope (Divy 54.6–8): "Rather deeds that are performed and accumulated manifest their effects in the [five] constituents of the per-

sonality, in states of mind, in the whole complex of embodied experience, where they were performed, and these results may be wholesome or unwholesome."

358 Following Divy 131.13, 191.19, 282.17, read *kalpakoṭiśatair api*. Divy 54.9, *api kalpaśatair api*.

359 Following the Tibetan (Shackleton Bailey 1950: 183), read *sde snod gsum par gyur te | chos bzhin gyis dge 'dun gyi zhal ta ba byed do* —> Skt., <*tripiṭakaḥ saṃvṛttaḥ saṃghasya ca*>. Divy 54.15–16, *tripiṭakasaṃghasya ca dharmavaiyāvṛtyaṃ karoti*.

360 Divy 54.26, *yan mayā caraṇīyaṃ tat kṛtam ahaṃ sakalabandhanābaddhaḥ*. The Tibetan (Shackleton Bailey 1950: 183–84) reads "Since going forth as a monk, I have done what should be done and become released from all bonds [to existence]. But you are still bound by all these bonds" *(kho bos ni rab tu byung ba'i bya ba byas te | 'ching ba mtha' dag las grol ba yin la | khyod ni 'ching ba mtha' dag gis bcings pa yin pas* —> Skt., <*pravrajya karaṇīyaṃ tat kṛtam ahaṃ sakalabandhanābaddhas tvaṃ sakalabandhanabaddhaḥ*>*)*.

361 Divy 55.7–8, *skandhakauśalaṃ ca kṛtam*. The Tibetan (D ka 63b2) reads *phung po la mkhas pa dang | khams la mkhas pa dang | skye mched la mkhas pa dang | rten cing 'brel par 'byung ba la mkhas pa dang | gnas dang gnas ma yin pa la mkhas par bya'o* —> Skt., <*skandhakauśalaṃ dhātukauśalam āyatanakauśalaṃ pratītyasamutpādakauśalaṃ bhavābhavakauśalam* (?)>.

362 Divy 55.17, *naukramaḥ*. This peculiar term seems to refer to a collection of boats strung together, though Edgerton (BHSD) posits that it may refer to a navigatable passageway for ships. Elsewhere it seems to refer to a particular kind of raft (Strong 1992: 324n29).

363 Divy 55.19, *vinipatitaśarīrāḥ*. This expression also suggests that nāgas have "bodies" *(śarīra)* that have "fallen" *(vinipatita)* in the hierarchy of saṃsāra. As embodied beings, they inhabit a lower karmic realm than gods and mortals. Cf. Divy 333.8.

364 Divy 56.8,

> *ye taranty arṇavaṃ saraḥ setuṃ kṛtvā visṛjya palvalāni |*
> *kolaṃ hi janāḥ prabandhitā uttīrṇā medhāvino janāḥ ||*

As Shackleton Bailey (1951: 82) notes, "The obscurity of the couplet remains in the Tibetan version which, however, suggests *ke cit (kha cig)* was read for *ye* and *janaḥ prabandhati (skye bo rnams ni gzings 'cha')* for *janāḥ prabandhitā*." For instances of this verse in Pāli, see the *Udāna* (90/§8.6.16; trans. in Masefield 1994: 178) and its commentary (*Paramatthadīpanī* i, 424) and the *Mahāparinibbāna-sutta* in the *Dīgha-nikāya* (ii, 89/§16.1.34; trans. in Walshe 1987: 239) and its commentary (*Sumaṅgalavilāsinī* 543). In the latter, Buddhaghosa interprets *saram* as "craving" *(taṇhā)* and *setu* as "the noble path" *(ariyamaggo)*. These Pāli versions also preserve a variation in tense in the second couplet: "People bind a raft, the wise have crossed already" *(kullaṃ hi jano pabandhati tiṇṇā medhāvino janā)*. For more on this verse, see Dhadphale 1980: 181–82.

365 Following Cowell and Neil's conjecture (Divy 56n3), read *unnatonnatam*. The Tibetan (Shackleton Bailey 1951: 82) concurs. Divy 56.14, *uttatonnatam*.

366 Following the Tibetan (Shackleton Bailey 1951: 82), add *tshe dang ldan pa kun dga' bo la* —> Skt., <*ānandam*>. Divy 56.15 (omitted).

367 Cowell and Neil (Divy 56) follow ms. B, *tiryak ṣoḍaśapravedhaḥ*. Likewise ms. H 20b11. Ms. A reads *tiryakvyāmaveṣṭanena*. Ms. D reads *sahasraṃ tiryak vyāmaveṣṭa-*

nena. Ms. C. reads *vyāmasahasraṃ tiryak* ṣoḍaśa *vyāmaveṣṭanena* pravedhaḥ. These unitalicized words are, as Cowell and Neil (Divy 56n5) observe, "dotted as if superfluous" in the manuscript. The Tibetan (Shackleton Bailey 1951: 82) reads *sboms su 'dom drug cu yod pa* —> Skt., <*tiryak ṣaṣṭivyāmaḥ*>. Cp. Divy 59.16, *vyāmasahasraṃ tiryakṣoḍaśapravedham.*

368 Following the Tibetan (Shackleton Bailey 1951: 82), read *dbugs 'byin par mdzad pa phyag gis* —> Skt., <*āśvāsanakareṇa kareṇa*>. Divy 56.22, *bhītānām āśvāsanakareṇa.*

369 The Tibetan (Shackleton Bailey 1951: 82) omits this sentence and the one before it.

370 Following Divy 57.8, read *kutra anena paryupāsitam.* The Tibetan (Shackleton Bailey 1951: 82) concurs. Divy 57.6, "How was this respect paid and by whom?" *(kutra kena paryupāsitam iti).*

371 Divy 57.17, *devaputraḥ.* In certain cases, *putra* means "a real one" or "the quintessential," as in the Hindi, *ullū ka paṭṭha*—"a real owl." Here, however, the opposite seems to be the case. A *devaputra* seems to be a god of lesser standing than a *deva.* A more literal translation would be "son of god," but this rendering is unduly loaded with Christian connotations. I translate it either as "divine being" or "divinely born."

372 Divy 57.17–18, *tat te putratve samādāpayiṣyāmi.* The Tibetan (Shackleton Bailey 1951: 83) reads *de khyod kyi bu bskor bar bya'o* —> Skt., <*taṃ te*>.

373 The Tibetan (Shackleton Bailey 1951: 83) reads "body" *(lus las* —> Skt., <*kāyāt*>*).* Cf. Divy 193.21, "a bad smell emerges from his body" *(daurgandhaṃ kāyena niṣkrāmati).*

374 Divy 57.21, *dhṛtim.* The Tibetan (Shackleton Bailey 1951: 83) reads "joy" *(dga'* —> Skt., <*prītim*>*).*

375 Divy 58.17, *vastuparīkṣāyām.* Ms. D, however, reads "knowledge of cloth" *(vastraparīkṣā).* Nilakantha Sastri (1945: 10) prefers this latter reading, while Sitaram Roy (1971: 154) prefers the former.

376 Divy 58.21, *mūrdhnabhiśiktānām.* While this term could be translated more literally as "anointed on the head," the *Divyāvadāna* (Divy 544.2–6) makes it clear this refers to a royal coronation ceremony.

377 Divy 58.26, *muṣṭibandhe padabandhe śikhābandhe.* Edgerton (BHSD) takes these expressions to refer to methods of holding a bow. The *Mahāvyutpatti* (§4978, §4980) explains *muṣṭibandha* as a "grasping posture" *('dzin stangs),* and it explains *pādabandha (=padabandha)* as a "step-posture" *(gom stangs)* or "step-manner" *(gob stabs).* Likewise, the *Mahāvastu* (ii.82.17; trans. in Jones 1976: ii, 79) uses *muṣṭisaṃbandha* in a similar sense, though Jones translates the term as "the range of his fist."

378 Following the *Mahāvyutpatti* (§4996) and Edgerton (BHSD, s.v. *sthāna*), understand as *vidyāsthāna.* Divy 58.27, *sthāna.* Cf. Divy 100.2 ff. 442.5 ff. For another translation of this passage, see Schiefner 1988: 52–53.

379 The "hall for almsgiving" *(dānaśālā)* was, presumably, where the king would make offerings to his subjects. Judging from this story, it may have functioned something like a soup kitchen.

380 Divy 60.1, *svapathy adanam ādāya bhuktvā.* Perhaps emend to *svapathyādanam.* The Tibetan (Shackleton Bailey 1951: 83) reads "they brought their own food" *(rang rang gi rgyags blangs nas* —> Skt., <*svaṃ svaṃ adanam ādāya*>*).*

381 Divy 60.15 (= ms. B), *saṃyamanīcakravartī.* Ms. A reads *samayamanī-.* Ms. C reads *sayamanī-.* Ms. D reads *sayamanīna-.* The Tibetan (Shackleton Bailey 1951: 83) preserves *yang dag par sdom pa'i 'khor lo sgyur ba* —> Skt., <*saṃyamanika-*>. Edgerton (BHSD, s.v. *saṃyamanī*) queries "emperor of (residing in) Saṃyamanī (Yama's city)."

382 Divy 60.20–22, *sa imām eva samudraparyantāṃ pṛthivīm akhilām akaṇṭakām anutpīḍām adaṇḍenāśastreṇa dharmeṇa samayenābhinirjityādhyāvasiṣyati.* The more conventional and normative reading, however, would be as follows: "He will conquer the vast sea-bound earth, without punishment or weapons, justly and evenhandedly, and then rule there so that it will be entirely fertile, without enemies, and without oppression." Cp. *Dīgha-nikāya* i, 89 and ii, 17 (trans. in Walshe 1987: 112, 205), "He dwells having conquered this sea-girt land without stick or sword, by the law."

383 Divy 60.24, *maitreyāṃśena sphuritvā.* Cf. Divy 66.18, "suffusing this entire world with loving kindness" *(sarvam imaṃ lokaṃ maitreṇāṃśena sphuritvā).* Perhaps this should be emended to *maitreṇāṃśena,* replacing the *yā* with *ṇā.* The Tibetan (Shackleton Bailey 1951: 83–84) preserves "with immeasurable loving kindness" *(byams pa tshad med pa'i yan lag gis* —> Skt., *<maitryaprameyāṃśena>).* Shackleton Bailey thinks this is probably the correct reading here and at Divy 61.12 and 66.18.

384 Kalpana Upreti (1995: 25) suggests that each king had a respective treasure: turmeric *(piṅgala),* a type of rice *(pāṇḍuka),* cardamom *(elāpatra),* and conch *(śaṅkha).* In other sources, these "treasures" *(nidhi)* are guarded not by kings but by nāgas. In fact, J. Vogel (1926) has written convincingly that the origin of these "treasures" is to be found in the nāga cult. For a thorough account of these treasures and this passage in particular, see K. R. Norman 1983. In addition, see Edgerton (BHSD, s.v. *elapatra*).

385 Divy 61.20, *aśītibhikṣukoṭivāraḥ.* Vaidya (Divy-V 37.17) emends to *aśītibhikṣukoṭiparivāraḥ.* The Tibetan (Shackleton Bailey 1951: 84) reads 9.6 million monks *('khor dge slong 'bum phrag dgu bcu rtsa drug dang* —> Skt., *<ṣaṇṇavatibhikṣuśatasahasraparivāraḥ>).*

386 As Strong (2004: 220) notes, "The point [is] made, in virtually every version of this story, that since beings in Maitreya's time will be much bigger than they were at the time of Śākyamuni, Mahākāśyapa will seem tiny by comparison. In fact, in one text, Maitreya's disciples are contemptuous of Mahākāśyapa since his head seems to them no larger than that of an insect (T. 456, 14:433b)."

387 The Tibetan (Shackleton Bailey 1951: 84) reads "nine million six hundred thousand [beings] will devote themselves to the direct realization of arhatship and the virtues of the purified" *('bum phrag dgu bcu rtsa drug dgra bcom pa nyid dang sbyangs pa'i yon tan mngon du bya ba la brtson par 'gyur ro* —> Skt., *<ṣaṇṇavatiśatasahasrāṇy arhattvāya dhūtaguṇasākṣātkārāya ca yogam āpatsyante>).*

388 The Tibetan (Shackleton Bailey 1951: 84) omits this word.

389 The Tibetan (Shackleton Bailey 1951: 84) omits this phrase.

390 The Tibetan (Shackleton Bailey 1951: 84) reads "a son was born to King Vāsava's priest" *(rgyal po gos sbyin gyi mdun na 'don las* —> Skt., *<vāsavasya rājñaḥ purohitasya putraḥ>).*

391 Divy 64.10, *mahārāja balaśreṣṭho hi rājā no nipatitavyam.* However, following mss. AB (Divy 64n1) and Vaidya (Divy-V 39.4–5), read *balaśreṣṭhā hi rājāno,* and emend *nipatitavyam* to *nipatitavyāḥ.* Cowell and Neil (Divy 64n1) note that *no* is an interrogative. Perhaps, "Your majesty, this king is great because of his power. Shouldn't he be bowed down to?" The Tibetan (Shackleton Bailey 1951: 84) reads *rgyal po chen po rgyal po dpung chen po rnams la ni gtug pa bya dgos so* —> Skt., *<rājāno nipatitavyāḥ>.*

392 Adapted from Divy 65.30–66.3. Divy 64.25 (omitted).

393 Following Divy 64.12, etc., add *utthāyāsanāt.* Divy 66.2 (omitted).

394 The Tibetan (D kha 36b3–37a1) adds:

Then the Blessed One said to Ānanda, "Ānanda, let's go to the city called Vṛji."

"Bhadanta, I'll do as you say," the venerable Ānanda replied, consenting to the Blessed One's request.

Then the Blessed One, after wandering through the Vṛjika countryside, arrived in the city of Vṛji. He stayed in a *śiṃśapā* grove to the north of Vṛji. The Blessed One then said to the monks, "Monks, this is morality, this is concentration, and this is wisdom. Monks, if you practice morality, you can remain in concentration for a long time. If you practice concentration, wisdom will remain for a long time. And if you practice wisdom, the mind will become truly liberated from attachment, hate, and delusion. In this way a noble disciple whose mind is truly liberated will know—'My defilements are destroyed! I am devoted to the religious life! What is to be done has been done! I will know no existence other than this one.'"

When the Blessed One had said this, the monks rejoiced and praised his words.

395 Divy 67.8–9, *cakravartikulād rājyam apahāya*. Here the term *kulāt* is governed by *pravrajita*, but the reading is awkward. Cp. Divy 70.14, *cakravartirājyam apahāya*.

396 Divy 68.12, *devān gatvā*. Understand as *devanikāyān*.

397 This version omits "If he desired to predict a rebirth as a god, they would enter his navel."

398 Divy 69.13–14, *buddhā jagaty uttamahetubhūtāḥ*. Strong (1989: 203) translates this as "their causes are the highest in the world." More literally, one might translate this as "Buddhas are the greatest cause in the world," but I think the above rendering is more appropriate.

399 Following Divy-V 42.21 and Aśokāv 33.21, read *dhīra buddhyā*. Divy 69.17, *dhīrabuddhyā*. And following Divy-V 42.22 and Aśokāv 33.21, read *śramaṇa jinendra*. Divy 69.17–18, *śramaṇajinendra*.

400 Divy 70.18–19, *yathā te kṣamate tathainaṃ vyākuru*. However, following mss. AB (Divy 70n5), read *tathaivam*. The Tibetan (Shackleton Bailey 1950: 85) reads *de bzhin du lan thob cig* —> Skt., <*kṣamata evaṃ vyākuru*>. The expression in Pāli uses *kānti*, meaning "explain as you like."

401 Following the Tibetan (Shackleton Bailey 1950: 85), read *sa bon* —> Skt., <*bījam*>. Divy 70.26, "fruit" *(phalam)*.

402 Following Divy 71.18, read *no*. Divy 70.26, *kho*.

403 Following Divy 71.18, read *no*. Divy 70.28, *kho*.

404 Following the Tibetan (Shackleton Bailey 1950: 85), read *bdag gi* —> Skt., <*mam*>*aitat*. Divy 71.3, *naitat*.

405 Read *pradeśe*. The Tibetan concurs. Divy 71.4, *pradeśam* (mss., *pradeśaḥ*).

406 Divy 71.5, *sukhāropitam*. The manuscripts (Divy 71n2), however, read *sukhaṇapitam*. The Tibetan omits this.

407 Read *asyām utpattau*. Divy 71.6–7, *asmin utpanne*, though the manuscripts (Divy 71n4) preserve *asyām utpanne*. Cf. Divy 490.20–21, "Then at that time the Blessed One uttered a verse" *(bhagavān asyām utpattau gāthāṃ bhāshate)*. There the Tibetan (D nya 67a2) translates *asyām utpattau* as "on this occasion" *(byung ba 'di la)*.

408 Following Cowell and Neil's conjecture (Divy 71n5), read *bīje ca*. The Tibetan (Shackleton Bailey 1950: 85) concurs. Divy 71. 8, *bījena*.

409 Possessing a very long tongue is the twenty-seventh of the thirty-two marks of a great man. This list occurs in numerous texts. See, for example, the *Lakkhaṇa-sutta* in the

Dīgha-nikāya (iii, 142–79; trans. in Walshe 1987: 441–60). For more on these marks, see Lamotte 1944: i, 271–83.

410 Following the Tibetan (Shackleton Bailey 1950: 85), add *bcom ldan 'das kyis* —> Skt., <*bhagavān*>. Divy 71.19 (omitted).

411 Ms. H 26b3 reads *evam etad yathā hi brāhmaṇa*. Mss. ABD read *evam etad ya'thā*. Ms. C reads *evam eva tad yathā*. Cowell and Neil (Divy 71.21) emend the text to read *tad evam etan na yathā hi brāḥmaṇa*—perhaps, "This is certainly not the case, brahman." This is a reasonable conjecture, except that *na* is absent in both the Sanskrit and Tibetan. Considering this absence of a negative, one might conjecture *tad evam etad dhi yathā hi brāhmaṇa*—"This is just that, as it should be, brahman"—though the repetition of *hi* is problematic. The Tibetan (Shackleton Bailey 1950: 85–86; D kha 96b7) reads *bram ze nga yis ji skad bshad pa de bzhin pas | de bzhin gshegs pa yin zhes rtogs pa'i rigs*. Shackleton Bailey suggests a possible Sanskrit reading of *bhāṣe yathaivāsti tathā hi brāhmaṇa,* though I think a better reconstruction would be *mayā yathoktaṃ [ca] tathā hi brāhmaṇa.* Perhaps, "As I say, so it is, brahman." Shackleton Bailey's conjecture fits the meter of the verse, but it does take considerable liberties in reconstructing the Sanskrit. As the Tibetan suggests, the Sanskrit seems to be missing some form of the verb "to speak." Paul Harrison (personal communication) suggests that if the negative were not Cowell and Neil's conjecture, one might simply emend to *tad evam etan na yathāha brāhmaṇaḥ*: "Therefore this is the way it is, and not as the brahman says." My thanks to Shrikant Bahulkar for his thoughts on this passage.

412 Following Cowell and Neil's conjecture (Divy 72n4), add *adrākṣīt*. The Tibetan (Shackleton Bailey 1950: 86) concurs. Divy 72.8 (omitted).

413 Following Divy 67.17–69.8. Divy 72.16, "and so on as before" *(pūrvavat yāvat).*

414 Following Divy-V 42.21 and Aśokāv 33.21, read *dhīra buddhyā*. Divy 73.3, *dhīrabuddhyā*. And following Divy-V 42.22 and Aśokāv 33.21, read *śramaṇa jinendra*. Divy 73.4, *śramaṇajinendra.*

415 Divy 73.15, *kiṃtu*. Cp. Divy 70.1, which preserves in this same trope, "Then what?" *(kiṃ tarhi).*

416 Divy 73.15–16, *gatvā saṃsṛtya* (mss., *gatvā vyasamsṛtya*). The Tibetan (Shackleton Bailey 1950: 86) reads *lha dang mi rnams su nying mtshams sbyar cing 'khor nas* —> Skt., <*pratisaṃdhiṃ gṛhītvā saṃsṛtya*>. Cp. Divy 70.1–2, *saṃvācya saṃsṛtya.*

417 Following Divy 523.7, etc., add *api*. Divy 73.21 (omitted).

418 Divy 73.28–29, *kaścid anukūlaṃ bhāṣitaṃ kṛtvā*. The Tibetan (Shackleton Bailey 1950: 86) reads *rjes su mthun pa'i legs par smra ba 'ga' byas dang* —> Skt., <*kaccid anukūlaṃ subhāṣitaṃ kṛtvā*>.

419 Following the Tibetan (Shackleton Bailey 1950: 86), read *bkra shis rab tu bsngag* —> Skt., <*lakṣmīpraśastaḥ*>. Divy 74.7, "I mark you as praised" *(lakṣe prāśastaḥ).*

420 Following the manuscripts (Divy 74n2), read *surūparūpam iti*. Cowell and Neil (Divy 74.7) emend to the vocative *surūparūpa iti.*

421 Divy 74.8, *abhiprasannaḥ*. Though I generally translate *prasāda* as "faith," the term resists any single translation in English. *Prasāda* is more than "faith" or, as in this instance, "pleasure." In the *Divyāvadāna, prasāda* is implicated in a complex process that involves both seeing and giving. Cf. Rotman 2003b.

422 Following the Tibetan (Shackleton Bailey 1950: 86), read Skt., <*yo 'sau brāhmaṇo so 'yaṃ brāḥmaṇa eva tena kālena tena samayena*>. Divy 74.12 (omitted).

423 Following the Tibetan (Shackleton Bailey 1950: 86), read *gzugs dang lang tso dang thos*

pas rgyags par gyur nas —> Skt., <*rūpayauvanaśrutamadam anuprāptaḥ*>. Divy 74.18, *rūpayauvanaśrutam anuprāptaḥ*. The three objects of pride described in the Pāli sources (e.g., *Dīgha-nikāya* iii, 220, *Aṅguttara-nikāya* i, 14) are health *(ārogya)*, youth *(yobana)*, and life *(jīvita)*.

424 Read *tathāgatasya mūrdhānaṃ na avalokayasi*. Divy 75.10–11, *tathāgatasya mūrdhānam avalokayasi*.

425 Following the Tibetan (Shackleton Bailey 1951: 86), read *de yang ngo mtshar zhig* —> Skt, <*etad apy āścāryam*>. Divy 75.16–17, *etad asyāścaryam*.

426 Following Divy 71.25, read *yaṃ śrutvā*. Divy 75.25, "and so on" *(yathā)*.

427 Following Divy 72.3, read *abhiprasannam*. The Tibetan (Shakleton Bailey 1951: 87) concurs. Divy 76.1, *abhiprasannaḥ*.

428 Following Speyer's suggestion (1902: 110), read *anujñātaṃ prajñapayeti*. Divy 76.5, "you shall carry out what is permitted" *(anujñātaṃ prajñapayasi)*.

429 Following the Tibetan (Shackleton Bailey 1951: 87), read *rts[w?]a ku shas btags te* —> Skt., <*kuśā baddhā*>. Divy 76.8, *kulā baddhā*. Agrawala (1966: 71) suggests that "the Brāhmaṇas and the householders tied a strip of cloth to the Indrayaṣṭi [i.e., post] at the time of the Indramaha festival."

430 Divy 76.7–8, *anyair api brāhmaṇagṛhapatibhiḥ kuśalam adhiṣṭhānāya bhavatu iti viditvā*. Perhaps emend to *kuśalādhiṣṭhānāya*.

431 In the *Nātyaśāstra*, a similar Indra festival is described. In the name of Indra, a post is planted in the ground, at which time there is dancing and music, and then the post is uprooted and carried off to be immersed in water. For more on this festival, see Agrawala 1970: 49–66.

432 As Dutt notes in the *Gilgit Manuscripts* (iii 1, 73n1), the editors of the *Divyāvadāna* "should have separated this portion of the story from the preceding one and named it *Toyikāmahāvadānam* [The Story of the Toyikā Festival] instead of tagging it on to [the] *Indranāmabrāhmaṇāvadānam* [The Story of a Brahman Named Indra]." While this may be so, this would have led to confusion. The thirty-first avadāna in the *Divyāvadāna* is also entitled "The Story of the Toyikā Festival" (Divy 461–69), and though both avadānas contain a nearly identical portion that I mark with the subheading "Practices of Faith at Toyikā" (Divy 77.23–80.9, 466.19–469.18), each has a different frame story.

433 Divy 76.22–23, *pratodayaṣṭyā*. This image of the "goad-post" occurs in both "The Story of a Brahman Named Indra" and "The Story of the Toyikā Festival," but with different associations. Here the associated image is the Buddha-sized "post" *(yaṣṭi)* that in the preceding embedded story engendered a brahman's faith (Divy 75.14–19). In the latter, the associated image is the "goad" *(pratoda)* that in the narrative that precedes it was used to beat and bruise oxen (Divy 463.9–11).

434 Divy 76.25 (= ms. A), *bhavakṣayakaraḥ kṣaṇa eṣa brāhmaṇaḥ*. Ms. B reads *kṣubhavakṣayakaraḥ ṇa eṣa*. Ms. C reads *bhavakṣayakarakṣaṇa eṣa*. Ms. D reads *kṣūṇa eṣa*. In his "Critical Notes to the *Divyāvadāna*," Vaidya (Divy-V 545) explains that "*bhavakṣayakaraḥ kṣaṇaḥ* | *eṣa brāhmaṇaḥ* means that this is an auspicious moment which would put an end to the saṃsāra of this man, who is born a brahman."

435 Divy 76.25–26, *saced asyaivaṃ samyakpratyayajñānadarśanaṃ pravartate*. This clause may be corrupt. Although the expression *jñānadarśanaṃ pravartate*, which is preserved in the version of this passage in the *Gilgit Manuscripts* (iii 1, 74.11), is quite

common in the *Divyāvadāna* (e.g., Divy 83.7, 84.6–7, 147.26), to the best of my knowledge this configuration of the expression is unattested elsewhere in the text.

436 Following the GM iii 1, 75.7, read *dṛṣṭukāmāḥ iti*. Divy 77.19, *draṣṭukāma iti*. Cf. Divy 56.24.

437 What follows (Divy 77.23–80.9) is repeated almost verbatim in "The Story of the Toyikā Festival" (Divy 466.19–469.18).

438 Divy 78.6, *padāvihārāt*. This expression seems to be similar to the Pāli expression *jaṅghāvihāra*. Cf. Rhys Davids and Stede (PTSD, s.v. *jaṅghāvihāra*).

439 Divy 78.13, *bhagavatānyatra*. Cp. Divy 467.10, which preserves *bhagavatāsya tu*. Speyer (1902: 111) strongly favors this reading.

440 Divy 79.3, *pradīpamālā*. In Maharashtra, the term refers to a structure often located outside of Hindu temples that resembles a Christmas tree, with lamps at the end of each branch. Ratna Handurukande (1978: 77), however, translates *dīpamālā* as "rows of lamps."

441 Following GM iii 1, 77.17–78.8, add *cittaṃ cābhisaṃskṛtam | padāvihārasya mṛtpiṇḍadānasya muktapuṣpāṇāṃ mālāvihārasya pradīpadānasya gandhābhiṣekasya ceyat puṇyam uktaṃ bhagavatā | asmākaṃ chatradhvajapatākāropaṇe kiyat puṇyaṃ bhaviṣyatīti | atha bhagavāṃs teṣā[m api cetasā] cittam ājñāya bhāṣate |*

śataṃ sahasrāṇi suvarṇaparvatā meroḥ samā nāsya samā bhavanti |
yo buddhacaityeṣu prasannacitta āropayec chatradhvajāpatākāḥ ||
eṣā hi dakṣiṇā proktā aprameye tathāgate |
samudrakalpe saṃbodhau sārthavāhe anuttare || iti

teṣām etad abhavat | parinirvṛttasya tāvad bhagavataḥ kāraṇam iyat puṇya[m uktaṃ] bhagavatā | tiṣṭhataḥ kiyat puṇyaṃ bhaviṣyatīti | atha bhagavān. Divy 79.17, "and so on" *(evaṃ ca)*.

442 Divy 79.23, *apratihatadharmacakravartinām*. GM iii 1, 78.12 concurs. Divy 469.7, however, reads *apratihatadharmacakrapravartinām*. This latter reading is more grammatically correct, yet it breaks meter, suggesting that it may be a later hypercorrection.

443 Divy 79.28–80.1, *kaiścin mūrdhāgatāni* (mss. AC, *mūrdhnāgatāni*) *kaiścin murdhānaḥ* (mss., *mūrdhnānaḥ*). I understand the former expression to be a gloss of the latter.

444 GM iii 1, 78.17–18, "Some obtained the heat stages, some the summit stages, some those in accord with truth, and some the tolerance stages" *(kaiścid uṣmagatāni pratilabdhāni kaiścid mūrdhānaḥ kaiścid satyānuloma kaiścid kṣāntayaḥ)*. Cp. Divy 271.12, which reads "some produced roots of virtue for the heat stages..." *(kaiścit ūṣmagatāni kuśalamūlāny utpāditāni)*.

445 This incident is recounted in Ray 1994: 109–10.

446 Divy 82.11, *nagarāvalambikā*. This term seems to be the converse of *gocaragrāma*, which Edgerton (BHSD) translates as "sustenance-village, a village where food is supplied to monks."

447 Following GM iii 1, 80.18 and Divy 82.17, read *ācāmaḥ*. Divy 82.13, *āyāsaḥ*.

448 Following GM iii 1, 81.12, read *prāmodyam utpādayāmi*. Divy 82.28–29, "you should be happy" *(prāmodyam utpādayasi)*.

449 Elsewhere in the *Divyāvadāna* (Divy 61.28–29, 395.23 [= Aśokāv 90.6]) it is said that Mahākāśyapa is "foremost of those who preach the virtues of the purified" *(dhūtaguṇavādinām agraḥ)*. Among these virtues—which are, more accurately, a code of ascetic practices—is "eating in a single place" *(aikāsanika)*. If Mahākāśyapa observed

this ascetic code, he would eat only once a day and in only one place, and hence whatever the beggar woman offered him would have to suffice as his meal for the day (cf. Ray 1994: 145n39).

450 Divy 83.7, *tathā hy adhastād devānāṃ jñānadarśanaṃ pravartate no tūpariṣṭhāt.* Cf. Divy 147.26, 151.7, 194.26–27, etc. Elsewhere I read *jñānadarśanaṃ* as a *dvandva* and translate it as "knowledge and insight" (e.g., Divy 84.67). Here, however, it isn't just that "the knowledge and insight of gods operate below them and not above them," but that for the gods, "seeing" *(darśana)* does not always lead to "knowledge" *(jñāna).* While this relationship between seeing and knowledge may inform each instance of this expression, translating it as "knowledge and insight" often seems more appropriate. The Tibetan generally concurs (e.g., D nya 33a4, D nya 68a4), though the corresponding term in Pāli *(ñāṇadassana)* is glossed a number of ways in the commentaries (cf. *Saṃyutta-nikāya* v, 423 and *Visuddhimagga*, chaps. 21–22). James Ware (1928: 162) translates a very similar sentiment, *dharmatā khalv adhastād devānāṃ jñānadarśanaṃ pravartate nordhvam,* which occurs in "The Story of a Wretched Pig" (Divy 194.26–27), as "It is, of course, a law that sight by the intelligence exists for the gods downward by not upward."

451 Following GM iii 1, 82.5, read *tatra.* Divy 83.14, *yatra.*

452 GM iii 1, 83.6–7 reads only "merit" *(puṇyānām).* Divy 83.16, *puṇyāpuṇyānām.* This coincides with Śakra's statement in the next sentence.

453 Following GM iii 1, 83.7–8 and Divy 84.13 and 85.21, read *pratyakṣadarśyeva.* Divy 84.17, *pratyakṣadarśanena.*

454 Divy 84.6–7, *asamanvāhṛtyārhatāṃ jñānadarśanaṃ na pravartate.* Here I read *jñānadarśanam* as a *dvandva* and translate it as "knowledge and insight." Others, however, disagree. Kenneth Ch'en (1945–47: 289n184) translates this expression, which occurs in "The Story of Svāgata" (Divy 190.8), as "without concentration of mind, the insight of arhats does not go forth." He acknowledges, though, that the corresponding Tibetan (D nya 33a4, as well as P te 30a8, L nya 48a7, and N nya 51b1) treats *jñānadarśanam* as a *dvandva (shes pa dang mthong ba).* Bloomfield (1920: 337) translates the same sentence as "When Saints are careless they lose the sight of knowledge." In "The Miracle Sutra" (Divy 147.26), we find the similar expression *bhagavato jñānadarśanaṃ pravartate.* Burnouf (1844: 167) translates this as "Bhagavat possède la vue de la science."

455 Divy 84.10, *samūla ārūḍhaḥ.* GM iii 1, 83.9 reads *āvṛḍhaḥ.* This unattested term seems to be an incorrect Sanskritization of Pāli *abbuḷha.* The Tibetan (Shackleton Bailey 1951: 87) reads *rtsa nas phyung zin na* —> Skt., <*samūlo vyaparūḍhaḥ*>.

456 GM iii 1, 83.13 adds "or perform meritorious deeds" *(puṇyāni vā na karomi).*

457 Divy 84.15, *duḥkhā hy akṛtapuṇyatāḥ.* Vaidya (Divy-V 53.14) emends to *duḥkhā hy akṛtapuṇyatā.* GM iii 1, 83.14 reads *duḥkhaṃ hy akṛtapuṇyataḥ.*

458 Divy 84.16, *kṛtapuṇyāni.* GM iii 1, 83.15 reads *kṛtapuṇyā hi.*

459 Following Divy 84.25, read *devanikāye.* Divy 84.28, *deve.*

460 Following GM iii 1, 85.11, read *ṣaṣṭhe divase.* Divy 86.5, "on another day" *(anyadivase).*

461 According to GM iii 1, 85.18–20, "He ordered the workers: 'Tomorrow an abundance of even finer food is to be prepared and likewise distributed. Half should fall in the monks' bowls and half on the ground'" *(tena pauruṣeyāṇām ājñā dattā | śvo bhavadbhiḥ praṇītatara āhāraḥ kartavyaḥ prabhūtaś ca | evaṃ cārayitavyaḥ | upārdho bhikṣūṇāṃ pātre pataty ardho bhūmāv iti).*

462 Divy 87.13, *karpaṭaka* (generally, *karvaṭa* or *karvaṭaka*). Although the Tibetan of the *Mahāvyutpatti* (§9356) understands this to refer to a "mountain hamlet" *(ri 'or ba)*, in the *Divyāvadāna* the term seems to refer simply to a village, with no reference to its being in the mountains. I translate the term throughout as "market town." For more on the term, see Schopen 1996: 109n59.

463 Divy 87.17–18, *ṛṇahārako dhanahārakaś ca*. Contrary to brahmanical explanations that male children bring wealth to a family, here that understanding is reversed. As context makes clear (cf. BHSD, s.v. *ṛṇadhāra*), this doesn't mean "This son of ours will take away our debts and bring us wealth." The father isn't free from family burdens; rather, now he needs to go and earn money to provide for the new addition to his family.

464 Divy 87.23–24, *aham asya sukhaṃ* (mss. AB, *mukhaṃ*) *bhaktena yogodvahanaṃ kariṣyāmi*. GM iii 1, 87.10–11 reads "I'll provide him with food for you" *(ahaṃ tava bhaktena yogodvahanaṃ karomi)*.

465 GM iii 1, 87.13 reads "He provided him with food" *(so 'py asya bhaktena yogodvahanam)*.

466 Divy 88.2, *sānukālam*. For this otherwise unattested term, Edgerton (BHSD) postulates "at (some specified, but to me unknown) time." Considering that *sānu* means "peak," I've translated it literally, taking advantage of its metaphorical meaning in English.

467 As I understand this passage, the woman had intended to bring her son food that the householder's wife had prepared, but the wife was not preparing food on the holiday. The meager fare the woman had with her she had intended for her own consumption.

468 GM iii 1, 87.19–20 reads "I will bring [him] some of my own bland rice gruel" *(etām ātmīyām alavaṇikāṃ kulmāṣapiṇḍikāṃ nayāmiti)*. One could also read *ātmīyām* as "from me." Cp. Divy 88.19, *mama antikāt*.

Edgerton (BHSD) translates *piṇḍikā* as "(alms)food"—offering citations only to this story—but this translation isn't appropriate in every instance. In the present case, *piṇḍakā* seems to mean "some food" or "a little bit of food." As the text makes clear (Divy 88.7–8), a woman "has prepared some bland rice gruel for herself" *(tayātmano 'rthe 'lavaṇikā kulmāṣapiṇḍikā sampāditā)*, not "for herself [to give as an offering]." On Divy 89.1, however, *piṇḍikā* does refer to an "offering of alms."

469 Following GM iii 1, 87.20, add *kṣetram*. Divy 88.8 (omitted).

470 Following GM iii 1, 90.8, add *kapilavastu nagaram*. Divy 90.8 (omitted).

471 Following GM iii 1, 90.8–11, add *evaṃ mamāpi śāriputramaudgalyāyanāv agrayugaṃ bhadrayugaṃ syād ānando bhikṣur upasthāyikaḥ śuddhodanaḥ pitā mātā mahāmāyā kapilavastu nagaraṃ rāhulabhadraḥ kumāraḥ putraḥ*. Divy 90.9 (omitted).

472 In "The Story of Supriya" (Divy 105.25–27), it is explained that "in the great Vairambha Ocean blow [gale-force] winds called Vairambha that stir up the water" *(vairambhe mahāsamudre vairambhā nāma vāyavo vānti yais tad udakaṃ kṣobhyate)*.

473 Following GM iii 1, 91.4, read *upasthāyikaḥ*. Divy 90.30, "lay disciple" *(upāsakaḥ)*.

474 In the *Gilgit Manuscripts* (e.g., GM iii 2, 119.19–120.3), these are Śrāvastī, Sāketā, Vaiśālī, Vārāṇāsī, Rājagṛha, and Campā. In the Pāli tradition, Kosambī replaces Vaiśālī (e.g., *Dīgha-nikāya* ii, 146.13). For more on the function of these cities in Buddhist literature, see Schopen 1997.

475 Divy 93.2, *buddhacārikā*. Vaidya (Divy-V 58.32) emends to *buddhacandrikā*.

476 Following Divy 94.14, read *api tu sakalasya sārthasya mūlyaṃ parigaṇayya*. Divy 94.11–12, *api tu sakalasya sārthasya parigaṇayya*.

477 Following Divy 264.25–26, add *ajñātam adṛśyam aviditam avijñātam | dharmatā khalu buddhānāṃ bhagavatām*. Divy 95.12 (omitted). Cf. Vogel and Will 1984: 336–37.

478 Divy 95.18–19, *ṣaḍāyatanabhedakānām*. The text explains that buddhas "shatter the six sense bases," but since there are twelve sense bases, I have taken the referent to be the objects of the senses.

479 Following Divy 265.2, read *asaṃhatavihāriṇām*. Divy 95.19, *saṃghātavihāriṇām*.

480 Divy 95.23, *daśaśatavaśavartiprativiśiṣṭānām*. Edgerton (BHSD, s.v. *vaśavartin*) understands this to mean those "who are the (most) eminent among ten hundred dominant (all-powerful) persons."

481 Divy 96. 5–6,

> *apy evātikramed velāṃ sāgaro makarālayaḥ |*
> *na tu vaineyavatsānāṃ buddho velām atikramet ||*

This verse can also be understood in a slightly different way:

> Although the sea, the abode of creatures,
> may overflow its shores,
> the Buddha never goes beyond the limits
> of his beloved disciples under training.

Lamotte (1988: 646) offers this translation:

> The ocean, the abode of marine monsters, may forget the time of the tide;
> but never will the Buddha allow the hour for converting his dearly beloved sons to pass.

482 Following Divy 182.2–182.21. Divy 96.17, "and so on as before" *(pūrvavat yāvat)*.

483 Following Divy 177.28, 183.22, 310.20, etc. Divy 97.6–7 (omitted).

484 Usually (e.g., Divy 310.22–24), the following stereotyped passage occurs at this juncture: "when they had served and indulged them, with their own hands, with many courses of hard and soft foods, both fresh and fine, and were sure..."

485 Following Divy 282.1. Divy 97.25 (omitted). Elsewhere a long stereotyped passage occurs within this trope (e.g., Divy 281.24–282.1).

486 Divy 98.20, *udārapuṇyamaheśākhyaḥ*. I read this as a mis-Sanskritization of the Pāli expression, *mahesakkha*, "having great power." This alternate formation stemming from the root *śak* ("to be able") can also be seen later in this story (Divy 111.10) with *śakyāmi* occurring instead of *śaknomi* as the first person form of the present tense. Cf. Rotman 2003a: 106–9.

487 Divy 98.24, *yasyāḥ sakāśād garbho 'vakrāmati*, though Divy 2.6 and, correspondingly, GM iii 4, 160. 7 read *yasya sakāśād garbham avakrāmati*.

488 Read *anavatarantīm*. Divy 99.14–15, "treading on the ground below" *(avatarantīm adharimāṃ bhumim)*.

489 Divy 100.3, *vastra*. Cf. Divy 3.19, 26.12, and 58.17 (ms. D), which read "the science of building-sites" *(vastuparīkṣā)*.

490 Divy 100.5, *sarvagatigatijñaḥ*. Cowell and Neil (Divy 105n2) query *sarvagatiṅgitajñaḥ*.

491 Following Divy 3.19, add *aṣṭāsu parīkṣāsu*. Divy 100.5 (omitted).

492 Divy 102.23, *udāravīryaparākramatām anikṣiptotsāhatāṃ viditvā*. Cf. Divy 109.4, *dṛḍhavīryaparākramo 'nikṣiptotsāhaḥ*. Vaidya (Divy-V 64.24) emends to *parākramanām,* though *parākramasya* or *aparākramatām* are also possible emendations.

493 Following Divy 107.6, 107.8, 107.13 and 107.19. Divy 103.2, "the body of water [called] Dhūmanetra" *(dhūmanetram udakam).*

494 Divy 103.17, *gṛhītvā netre 'ñjayitvā śirasi baddhvā samālabhya.* This trope occurs frequently in this story (e.g., 104.14–15, 105.1–2, 105.19–20, 106.7–8). Cf. Divy 107.16, *tām auśadhīṃ gṛhītvā saśīrṣapādaṃ samālabhya.*

495 The text reads "in a second" (*dvitīye* | Divy 104.3–4), but since a second whirlpool has already been described, I omit this from my translation.

496 In the introductory summary of contents (Divy 102.28), the *rākṣasa* was referred to as Śaṅkhanābha.

497 Divy 104.21, *gambhīro 'yaṃ gambhīrāvabhāsaḥ.* Elsewhere this expression is used to descibed the dharma. In "The Story of a Good for Nothing" (Divy 492.18), the Buddha says, "My dharma is profound and it appears profound" *(gambhīro me dharmo gambhīrāvabhāsaḥ).* In the Pāli materials (e.g., *Dīgha-nikāya* ii, 55), the Buddha says the same about interdependent arising: "it is profound and it appears profound"—or, in the vernacular, "it is deep and it appears deep."

498 Divy 104.25, *guruguruḳāḥ.* This onomatopoetic expression for the sound of thunder has also continued in Indian vernaculars. For example, in his short story "Sandeep's Visit," Amit Chaudhuri (1997: 390) writes, "A moment's heavy silence, then the thunder spoke—guruguruguru." In Marathi, it represents a growling sound, like that of a tiger, or even the rumbling sound in one's stomach.

499 Read *mahāmakarī nāma auṣadhīm.* Divy 104.27–105.1, *mahāmakarīnāmauṣadhīm.*

500 Divy 105.11, *saṃvṛtaḥ.* In this story, the meanings at play for this semantically rich term include "closed up," "covered," "rounded," and "guarded." In what follows (Divy 106.26, 106.29, and 107.4), I translate the term differently according to context.

501 Nāgas with these poisonous attributes are also referred to in the Pāli canon. In "The Story of Saṅgharakṣita" (Divy 333.14–334.1), four nāgas are described, each with one of these poisonous characteristics.

502 Divy 106.13, *tāmrapaṭṭaiḥ.* This expression is unclear. It could mean also mean "pieces of *tāmra* wood" or "pieces of copper-colored cloth." In her translation of the *Supriyasārthavāhajātaka,* Handurukande (1988: 15) renders the term as "copper slabs."

503 Divy 106.29–30, *vetrapāśaṃ baddhvā.* In the *Supriyasārthavāhajātaka* (v. 168), one is instructed to cross the Aṣṭādaśavakrikā River by "binding one's feet with rattan cords" *(vetrapāśena pādau baddhvā).*

504 Divy 107.3, *tatrāyaskīlānāṃ koṭyātikramitavyam.* Presumably these "iron nails" *(ayaskīla)* are from Mount Ayaskīla or the Ayaskīlā River. These instructions also might mean that "he should make crampons for himself with iron nails and use them to cross over." In the *Supriyasārthavāhajātaka* (v. 170), a parallel passage occurs that reads *tatra mahadayaskīlān samākoṭyānataḥ kraman.* Handurukande (1988: 15) paraphrases this as "pierce it with iron pegs and go over it, bent low." The manuscripts (Handurukande 1988: 47n1), however, preserve many alternate readings: "*-koṭyānaro krama* A, *-koṭyātaro kraman* BCEG, *-koṭyātaro kramān* D, *-koṭyā tato kraman* F."

505 Divy 107.26, *saptāśīviṣam.* Though neither feminine nor plural, following Divy 107.22 understand as "Saptāśīviṣa Rivers."

506 In the *Supriyasārthavāhajātaka* (v. 186), the next mountain encountered is called Sudhāvarṇa (The Color of Lime).

507 Divy 109.10, *guṇavati phalake baddhvā.* This is an obscure expression, but it might

refer to the technique of ship building by which planks were stitched together with ropes (cf. Hourani 1963: 110, cited in Ray 1986: 117).

508 Divy 109.23, *ariṣṭādhyāyeṣu.* For more on such illnesses, see the section on the symptoms of imminent death in the *Carakasaṃhitā* (ii, 517–97/Indriyasthāna, chaps. 1–12).

509 Read *nānāśrutimanoramākhyāyikābhiḥ.* Divy 109.28, *nānāśrutimanorathākhyāyikābhiḥ.* What, if anything, differentiates a "story" *(ākhyāyikā)* from a "tale" *(kathā)* has been a longstanding debate in Sanskrit poetics. Bhāmaha (*Kāvyālaṅkāra,* chap. 1, vv. 25–29) regards the former as historical and the latter as fictional, but Daṇḍin (*Kāvyādarśa,* chap. 1, vv. 23–28) observes no fundamental distinction between the two. It is unclear whether such a distinction applies in avadāna literature. For more on this debate, see De 1959: 65–79 ("The Ākhyāyikā and the Kathā in Classical Sanskrit").

510 Divy 109.29–110.1, *upasthānakarmāṇi satputra iva pitaraṃ bhaktyā gauraveṇa śuśrūṣate.* Vaidya (Divy-V 68.29) emends to the locative *upasthānakarmaṇi.* Better, perhaps, would be the instrumental *upasthānakarmaṇā.*

511 Read *yātrayānam.* Divy 110.27, *yātrāyanam.*

512 Read *yat paktvā.* Divy 111.20, "heat up [part of that mountain?]" *(yaṃ paktvā).*

513 Divy 111.24, *śastravarṇa.* Cf. Ray 1986: 123.

514 Divy 112.26, *vetrapāśaṃ baddhvā.* Previously (Divy 106.29–30), I translated this as "tie up a rattan cord," though more literally it could be translated as "having bound up a piece of bamboo."

515 Divy 112.26–27, *mac charīre śarīrapūjāṃ kuruṣva.* More literally, one might translate this as "the worship of the body on my body." For more on this rite, see Schopen 1997: 101–11.

516 Divy 113.16, *tatra tvayā vetraśiṭāṃ baddhvā.* Edgerton (BHSD, s.v. *śitā*) translates this as "there you must gird yourself with staff and rope [for mountain-climbing] and pass over [them]." Cf. Divy 274.23 and 281.2. Perhaps *śiṭā* is akin to the Hindi "stairs" *(siḍhī).* It may even refer to a "rope ladder."

517 Divy 116.18, *dharmadeśanāvarjitāś caikaṃ saubhāsinikaṃ ratnam anuprayacchanti.* Though *saubhāsinikam* quite literally refers to something that is "exceptionally beautiful" or "resplendent," I understand the term to have the same sense as *subhāṣitasyārghamaṇi* ("a precious gem as a reward for your noble words"), which occurred previously in a parallel passage (Divy 115.11). The term appears to be a mistake for *saubhāṣanikam,* which is attested to in the *Avadānaśataka* (i, 219.2). A similar form, *saubhāsikī,* also occurs on Divy 502.12. The corresponding passage to this in the Tibetan (D nya 78a3) reads "brings one good fortune" *(skal ba can du 'gyur ba —> Skt., <subhāgyakarī>).* On Divy 229.12, in a parallel passage to Divy 502.12, *saubhāgyakarī* is likewise preserved. Clearly there is a confusion of terms. For more on these terms see Edgerton, though in an aside (BHSD, s.v. *saubhāṣanika*) he does provide the following odd reading for this passage: "being (previously) deprived of religious instruction, gave him a jewel as reward for his religious utterance."

518 Following Divy 116.3–116.17 (modified accordingly). Divy 117.7, "and so on as before" *(pūrvavat yāvat).*

519 Following Divy 116.21–28 (modified accordingly). Divy 117.19, "as before" *(pūrvavat).*

520 Divy 118.10, *vividhair dharmapadavyañjanaiḥ.* Cf. Divy 109.27, *citrākṣaravyañjanapadābhidhānaiḥ.*

521 Divy 118.20–21, *badaradvīpamahāpattane sarvasvabhūtam.* The sense here is that this treasure is, to be colloquial, the be all and end all of the great trading center

Badaradvīpa. This construction with *bhūta* also occurs frequently in what follows: Divy 118.24, *cinhabhūtam ālakṣyabhūtaṃ maṇḍanabhūtaṃ ca;* Divy 122.4, *jambudvīpaiśvaryabhūtena;* Divy 122.8, *sarvasvabhūtam.*

522 Following Divy 92.26, read *dvīpi.* Divy 119.8, *dvīpa.*

523 Incidents with this horse also occur in the *Mahāvastu-avadāna* (iii, 85–80; trans. in Jones 1949: ii, 88–92) and in the *Valāhassa Jātaka* (*Jātaka*, no.196, ii, 129; trans. in Cowell et al. 1990: ii, 90–91). Representations of this horse are found in sculptures at Mathura from the second or third century c.e., in paintings from Kyzil from the sixth century, in enameled brick panels in Pagan, Burma, from the eleventh century, and even in an illustrated Japanese handscroll from the thirteenth century (Meech-Pekarik 1982: 111–18).

524 For versions of the Meṇḍhaka story in Pāli, see the *Vinayapiṭaka* (i, 240–45; trans. in Rhys Davids and Oldenberg 1987: ii, 121–29; Horner 1938–66: iv, 329–36; and Warren 1984: 448–51) and the *Dhammapada-aṭṭhakathā* (iii, 363–75; trans. in Burlingame 1921: iii, 130–38).

525 Read *mrakṣati.* Divy 124.9, *rakṣati.* The Tibetan (Shackleton Bailey 1950: 90) reads *de gang gi tshe gang tsam drus pa de'i tshe | bdun tsam skyes par 'gyur te.* GM iii 1, 241.13 (omitted). While one might translate *mrakṣati* as "polished," *pratijāgarti,* which I translate as "looked after," is offered as an apparent synonym in what follows (Divy 124.9–10). For a comparison of the versions this story in the *Divyāvadāna, Gilgit Manuscripts,* and in the Tibetan, see Ch'en 1953: 400–403.

526 Divy 125.28, *daṃṣṭṛ.* Nevertheless, ms. A reads *draṣṭrigaṇa.* Ms. B reads *drastigaṇa.* Ms. C reads *draṣṭi.* Ms. D reads *uṣṭri.* In the *Divyāvadāna,* this term occurs with great variation (e.g., Divy 148.11, 182.5, 267.18–19). Cf. *Avadānaśataka* i, 108.4, *daṃṣṭri.*

527 Read *adhvagagaṇa.* Divy 126.2–3, *adhvagaṇa.* Though the same mistake occurs elsewhere (e.g., Divy 126.2, 148.14, 182.7–8), see *Avadānaśataka* i, 108.6, *adhvagagaṇa.*

528 Divy 126.10, *timita iva jalanidhiḥ sajala iva jalanidhiḥ.* Cp. Divy 148.21, 182.15, 267.28–29, *stimita iva jalanidhiḥ sajala iva jaladharaḥ.* These are apparently hyperbolic expressions: like X without its inherent uncertainties.

529 Following 182.17 and 268.1–2, add *samalaṃkṛtaḥ.* Divy 126.12 (omitted).

530 Following 182.21, add *samanvāgataḥ.* Divy 126.14 (omitted).

531 Divy 126.24, *dharmalābhaḥ.* This may constitute a parallel with an exclamation that Jain renunciants make during their almsrounds. For example, a mendicant from the Śvetāmbar Mūrtipūjaks, John Cort (1999: 95) explains, "comes to the door of the house, and announces his or her presence with the benediction, *dharm lābh* ('blessings to the religion')." As James Laidlaw (1995: 322–23) observes: "When food has been given the renouncer leaves the house and speaks for the first time other than to refuse food. She gives the blessing, *dharma labh.* This simple benediction is condensed and ambiguous. The word *dharma* is notoriously untranslatable, but 'religion' will serve in this context. *Labh* means increase, benefit or profit. The blessing can thus be glossed in two ways. First, as 'May your righteousness increase', that is, may you become more enlightened and detached from the world. Secondly, as 'May you profit from your good (religious) act', in which sense it echoes the popular expression *shubh labh*... *Dharma labh* wishes for householders both that they progressively withdraw from worldly attachments, and also that they receive all the worldly good fortune which is the reward of the generous donor."

532 This is said of the Buddha because he would cause fathers and sons to renounce and become monks in his order.

533 Divy 127.2, *kiṃ vayaṃ na tiṣṭhāmaḥ*. GM iii 1. 243.6 preserves the same. I translate this sentence without the negative, as does the Tibetan.

534 Following GM iii 1, 244.10, read *bhavanto dṛṣṭo vaḥ*. Divy 127.29–128.1, *bhavanto vo*.

535 Divy 128.1–128.2, *yas tāvad acetanāṃ bhāvān anvāvartayati sa yuṣmān nānvāvartayiṣyatīti*. This echoes the charge in the *Kevaddha-sutta* in *Dīgha-nikāya* (212–14; trans. in Walshe 1987: 175–76) that Buddhist monks convert nonbelievers by magic. Burnouf (1844: 191), however, offers this translation: "Seigneurs, celui qui change ainsi pour vous les objets matériels, changera bien aussi vos dispositions."

536 Divy 128.2, *kuta etat*. Perhaps, "How could this be true?" or "Where did you get this idea from?"

537 Divy 128.2–3, *sarvathāvalokitā bhavanto 'paścimaṃ vo darśanaṃ gacchāma iti*. GM iii 1, 244.12–13, *sarvathā avalokitā bhavantu bhavantaḥ | paścimaṃ vo darśanaṃ gacchāma iti*. Ch'en (1953: 377n6), however, offers this translation: "You are well taken care of here, sirs; we go, this is our final sight of you."

538 Divy 128.4–5, *so 'pi pravrajitaḥ yūyam api pravajitā bhikṣācarāḥ | kim asau yuṣmākaṃ bhikṣāṃ cariṣyatīti*. GM iii 1, 244.14–16 reads "He is a renunciant and you are renunciants as well. As one who survives on alms, will he prevent you from getting alms?" *(so 'pi pravrajitaḥ yūyam api pravajitāḥ | bhikṣopajīvitaḥ kim asau yuṣmākaṃ bhikṣāṃ vārayiṣyatīti)*.

539 Following GM iii 1, 245.1, add *bhagavān*. Divy 128.10 (omitted).

540 Following GM iii 1, 245.4, add *sthitaḥ*. Divy 128.13 (omitted).

541 GM iii 1, 245.5 (this sentence omitted).

542 Following Divy 71.25–72.2 (modified accordingly). Divy 128.22, "and so on as before" *(pūrvavat yāvat)*.

543 Following the Tibetan (Shackleton Bailey 1951: 91), add *bcom ldan 'das kyis ji ltar sus kyang mi tshor ba de ltar byin gyis brlabs nas* —> Skt., <*bhagavatādhiṣṭhitā tathā yathā...*>. Divy 129.3–4, *yathā aparijñātaiva kenacid eva meṇḍhakasya gṛpateḥ sakāśaṃ gatā*. GM iii 1, 244.21–22 (missing; text supplied from the *Divyāvadāna*).

544 Following Divy 71.25–6. Divy 129.22, "and so on" *(yāvat)*.

545 GM iii 1, 247.2, "who has transcended opposites, incomparable, pure, and with a golden complexion" *(nirdvandvam apratisamaṃ kanakāvadātam)*.

546 GM iii 1, 247.12–13, "Then, as the large crowd gathered, an assembly was formed that extended for a league around the Blessed One" *(tato mahājanakāyasaṃnipātād bhagavato yojanaṃ sāmantakena parṣat saṃnipatitā)*.

547 Divy 130.12–13, *tāṃ parṣadaṃ abhyavagāhya*. Edgerton (BHSD, s.v. *abhyavagāhya*), however, translates this passage as "perhaps 'having ripened, matured.'"

548 GM iii 1, 247.16 adds "[and so on] as before" *(pūrvavat)*.

549 At this point in the story, the *Gilgit Manuscripts* (iii 1, 248.7–248.17) includes a discussion of monastic regulations that links "The Chapter on the Great Fortune of the Householder Meṇḍhaka" and "The Story of Meṇḍhaka." For a translation of this passage, see appendix 1.

550 GM iii 1, 250.7–8 includes "There will be the great famine [called] Living-by-the-Stick" *(śalākāvṛtti mahādurbhikṣaṃ bhaviṣyatīti)*. Divy 131.20 (omitted).

551 Following Divy 132.1 and 132.4, add *kāle*. Divy 131.22 (omitted). It would be more

sensible to say, however, that people place seeds in a casket in times of plenty to prepare for times of hardship.

552 Divy 131.23–24, *mṛtānām anena te vījakāyaṃ kariṣyantīti.* GM iii 1, 250.11–12, "After we [have died], people will do what should be done with these seeds" *(asmākam anena bījena manuṣyāḥ kāryaṃ kariṣyantīti).* Ch'en (1953: 402) offers this translation: "The people, having thrown seeds into that box, keep them there out of consideration for future generations, and say thus to themselves, 'When we have died, the future generations will make seed-bodies with these seeds.'" My sense is that this famine is so-called because it prompts the opening up of seed boxes previously prepared by those now dead.

553 GM iii 1, 250.15–16, "Since this is connected with white bones, it is called White Bone" *(idaṃ śvetāsthisaṃbandhāt śvetāsthi ucyate).*

554 Divy 132. 4, *khalu vilebhyaḥ.* GM iii 1, 250.17, *khālabilebhyaḥ.* The Tibetan (L ga 46b2; cited in Ch'en 1953: 379) reads *gyul gyis ser gnas 'bru'i 'brum bu dag thur mas brus nas.* Ch'en translates this as "people would use sticks to dig up morsels of grain from the crevices of the threshing floor."

555 Emended accordingly. Divy 132.12, "they should return" *(upāgamiṣyanti).*

556 Following GM iii 1, 251.6, *me saparivārasya.* Divy 132.14, *me saparivārāṇām.* Bloomfield (1920: 348) also suggests this emendation.

557 Divy 132.17, *kośakoṣṭāgārāḥ.* Elsewhere (e.g., Divy 67.91, 23.20, 291.10, 319.5) I translate this as a *dvandva* meaning "treasuries and granaries." Tatelman (2000: 55, 59) translates this compound as "storerooms and warehouses" (Divy 32.37) and "treasuries and warehouses" (Divy 36.13). Here, however, it seems to be a reduplicative compound meaning only "granaries." This reading is further supported by the corresponding expression in the *Gilgit Manuscripts* (iii 1, 251.8), which unambiguously reads "granaries" *(koṣṭāgārāḥ).*

558 Divy 132.24–25, *sa ca gṛhapatir ātmanā ṣaṣṭo 'vasthito bhoktum.* GM iii 1, 251.16, "As for the householder, he sat ready to eat" *(sa ca gṛhapatiḥ sajjo 'vasthito bhoktum).*

559 Following GM iii 1, 251.19, read *paribhujya.* Divy 132.28, "even if I give up [this food]" *(parityajya).*

560 GM iii 1, 252.7 includes "as they desired" *(yatheṣṭam).* Divy 133.10 (omitted).

561 Divy 132.12, *evaṃvidhe sadbhūtadakṣiṇīye.* Cf. Divy 88.18, "such a righteous being so worthy of offerings" *(evaṃvidhe sadbhūte dakṣiṇīye).*

562 Following GM iii 1, 252.10, add *paśyāmi.* Divy 133.13 (omitted).

563 Divy 133.19, *yāvan mayā prayoga apratipraśrabdha iti.* GM iii 1, 252.15, *yan mayā prayogo na pratiprasrabdhaḥ.* The corresponding passage in the Tibetan is omitted.

564 Divy 133.23, *pañcaśatiko nakulakaḥ kaṭyām uparibaddhas tiṣṭhet.* GM iii 1, 252.19, *pañcaśataḥ kamarakaḥ kaṭyām upanibaddhas tiṣṭhet.* There are many such instances in this story when the *Divyāvadāna* and the *Gilgit Manuscripts* preserve the same narrative in different wording.

565 Divy 134.1–3, *yady ekasya gandhaṃ* (mss., *gandhān*) *yojayeyaṃ śataṃ vā sahasraṃ vā gandhaṃ ghrāsyati taṃ na ca parikṣayaṃ gaccheyuḥ.* Perhaps emend to *tan na ca parikṣayaṃ gacchet.* GM iii 1, 253.4–6, "If I prepare scents for one person, using them on a hundred or a thousand people, may they not diminish until I am finished" *(yady ekasyārthāya gandhān yojaye te śatasya vā sahasrasya vā upayujyeran na ca parikṣayaṃ gaccheyuḥ | yāvat prayogo na pratiprasrabdhaḥ).* The Tibetan (L ga 48a5; cited in Ch'en 1953: 402) reads *des brgya 'am stong byugs kyang.*

566 Divy 134.11, *yady ekāṃ mātrām ārabheyaṃ*. One might also translate this as "If I take hold of any household item." See, however, Divy 134.24. Cf. GM iii 1, 253.12–13, "[if] I take hold of one measure of grain" *([dhānyānām] ekāṃ mātrām ārabheyaṃ).*

567 Following GM iii 1, 254.15–16, *teṣām anukampāṃ kṛtvā*. Divy 134.15, "with compassion for them" *(teṣām anukampayā).*

568 Divy 134.20–21, *balabalī āśā*. GM iii 1, 253.20, *balavaty āśā*.

569 Following GM iii 1, 254.5, read *paribhuktā*. Divy 134. 25–26, *paribhuktam*.

570 Following GM iii 1, 253.6, read *paribhuktā*. Divy 134. 27, *paribhuktam*.

571 GM iii 1, 254.11–14, "The king said, 'After the whole world has died, then the householder opens up his granaries? Gentlemen, summon that householder.' They summoned him. Then the king said..." *(rājā kathayati | yāvat sarva eva lokaḥ kālagatas tadā tena gṛhapatinā koṣakoṣṭhāgārāṇy udghāṭitāni | āhūyatāṃ bhavantaḥ sa gṛhapatir iti | tair āhūtaḥ | tato rājñabhihitaḥ).* Divy 135.4 (omitted).

572 Divy 135.7, *phaladāyakam*. GM iii 1, 254.16, *phalitam*.

573 Divy 135.10, *abhiprasannaḥ*. The Tibetan (L ga 49b1; cited in Ch'en 1953: 403) concurs. GM iii 1, 254.19 (omitted).

574 Divy 138.24, *devān gatvā*. Understand as *devanikāyān gatvā*.

575 Following Divy-V 87.8 and Aśokāv 33.21, read *dhīra buddhyā*. Divy 139.27, *dhīrabuddhyā*. And following Divy-V 87.9 and Aśokāv 33.21, read *śramaṇa jinendra*. Divy 139.27–28, *śramaṇajinendra*.

576 Following Divy 35.8, add *ācchādya*. Divy 140.30 (omitted).

577 Divy 141.5, *divyaṃ mānuṣam*. Though elsewhere in the *Divyāvadāna* phenomena such as monastic requisites are described as having "divine and human natures" (*divyānāṃ manuṣyāṇāṃ ca* | Divy 143.7, 470.2–3; cf. 290.8–9), here there is no conjunction and none is implied as in the case of a *dvandva* (e.g., "I will satisfy gods and mortals" (*divyamānuṣyāṃs toṣayiṣyāmi* | Divy 159.25–26). The meaning of this expression seems to be "human yet of a divine nature." Cf. Divy 141.5, 262.20, 263.20, etc.

578 Divy 142.19, *vyākṛtaś ca bhave divye pratyekaś ca jino hy asau*.

579 For a Pāli version of this story, see the *Sarabhamiga Jātaka* (*Jātaka*, no. 483, iv, 263–67; trans. in Cowell et al. 1990: iv, 166–169). For quite different versions of this story, see the *Dhammapada-aṭṭhakathā* (iii, 199–228; trans. in Burlingame 1921: 35–55) and the Sinhalese version, which follows it closely (trans. in Hardy 1880: 300–313).

580 Divy 144.1–2, *ṛddhimantaḥ*. In this material, magical powers are thought to be acquired quite naturally through spiritual practice. They were not, as T. W. Rhys Davids (1899: i, 272) notes, "miracles in our Western sense. There was no interference by an outside power with the laws of nature. It was supposed that certain people by reason of special (but quite natural) powers could accomplish certain special acts beyond the power of ordinary men."

581 Divy 144.2, *jñānavādinaḥ*. I translate this term rather prosaically, though it may mean "argue logically" or "proponent of a path of knowledge" or even "teacher of gnosis."

582 Divy 144.3–4, *arhati jñānavādī jñānavādinā sārdham uttare manuṣyadharme ṛddhiprātihāryaṃ* (mss., *uttaraṃ manuṣyadharmaṛddhiprātihāryaṃ*) *vidarśayitum*.

More literally, one might translate this as "One who speaks knowledgeably should display, along with/in the presence of another who speaks knowledgeably, a miracle that arises from his magical powers and is beyond the capability of ordinary mortals."

There is, however, a miracle competition in what follows, so in my translation of this recurring trope I often add the verb "to compete." In addition, there is the problem of how to understand the compound *ṛddhiprātihārya*. I understand this to mean a "miracle" *(prātihārya)* that arises from one's "miraculous powers" *(ṛddhi)*, but it may simply mean "a display of miraculous powers" (cf. Gethin 1992: 100). Burnouf (1844: 164) translates this as "Il convient que celui qui sait discuter, lutte avec celui qui en sait autant que lui, en opérant, au moyen de sa puissance surnaturelle, des miracles supérieurs à ce que l'homme peut faire." Burnouf (1844: 164n1) also explains some of the technical aspects of these terms.

583 Divy 144.12–14, *tatrāsmākaṃ bhavatu śramaṇena gautamena sārdham uttare manuṣyadharme riddhiprātihāryam*. Again, one might translate this more literally as "And in that place, along with/in the presence of the ascetic Gautama, we shall make use of our magical powers and display a miracle that is beyond the capability of ordinary mortals." Burnouf (1844: 164–65) translates this as "Allons donc lutter avec le śramaṇa Gautama dans l'art d'opérer, au moyen d'une puissance surnaturelle, des miracles supérieurs à ce que l'homme peut faire." In what follows, I alternate between these two translations according to context.

584 Divy 146.10–11, *yūyam api śavā bhūtvā bhagavatā sārdhaṃ ṛddhiṃ prārdhadhve*. Vaidya (Divy-V 90.26) emends to *prārabhadhve*, for the final verb is peculiar (cf. BHSD, s.v. *prārdhate*). Following Vaidya's emendation, one might translate this as "You're as good as dead! Why begin [a competition of] magical powers with the Blessed One?" Edgerton (BHSD, s.v. *śava*) offers this translation: "Do you also, base as you are, aspire to (?) magic powers along with the Buddha." My thanks to Paul Harrison for his thoughts on this passage.

585 Following Divy 145.29–146.8. Divy 146.16, "and so on" *(yāvat)*.

586 Divy 146.25, *āhvayiṣyāmaḥ*. In what follows, I translate forms of *ā √hve* with forms of the verbs "to challenge" and "to call on." The former translation plays on the notion that what transpires between the heretics and the Buddha is a miracle competition. Yet, as I mentioned in a previous footnote, the text also downplays the idea that this is really a competition. In what follows, for example, the mendicant named Raktākṣa is "called on" (*āhūta* | Divy 151.26) by the heretics for his support because, as they explain, they have also "called on/challenged" (*āhūta* | Divy 151.28) Gautama to make use of his magical powers.

587 Read *adhvagagaṇa*. Divy 148.14, *adhvagaṇa*.

588 Divy 150.21, *sīmābandhaḥ kṛto bhavati*. Here I follow the recommendation of Edgerton (BHSD, s.v. *sīmābandha*), though this also might be rendered as "until he has marked out the bounds of propriety."

589 According to Malalasekera (DPPN, s.v. *saṅkassa*), Saṅkassa (= Sāṅkāśya) was thirty leagues from Śrāvastī, and it was there that the Buddha descended from Trāyastriṃśa heaven after preaching the Abhidhamma-piṭaka. The precise site of his descent was the city gate of Saṅkassa, and it is said that "all Buddhas descend at that spot to the world of men after preaching the Abhidhamma."

590 Divy 151.21–22, *atha vā pakṣaparyeṣaṇaṃ kartukāmaḥ*. Burnouf (1844: 172), "ou bien veut-il essayer de se faire un parti?"

591 Divy 152.3–4, *tvam api tāvat sabrahmacāriṇāṃ pakṣaparyeṣaṇaṃ kuruṣva*. Burnouf (1844: 172), "Toi, cependant, cherche aussi à nous faire des partisans parmi ceux qui suivent la même règle religieuse que nous."

592 Divy 152.11–12, *bhavadbhir api brahmacāriṇāṃ sāhāyyaṃ karaṇīyam.* Burnouf (1844: 172), "vous, cependant, vous devez aussi faire alliance avec ceux qui suivent la même règle religieuse que vous."

593 Add *niṣaṇṇasya.* Divy 153.11 (omitted). The expression "at a respectful distance" *(ekānte)*—more literally, "to one side"—is used very frequently in the *Divyāvadāna* in conjuction with forms of the verb "to sit" *(ni √ṣad).*

594 Read *upasaṃkrama.* Divy 154.18, *upasaṃkrāma.*

595 These are versions of the first, third, and fourth "principal trusts" *(agga-ppasāda)* that appear in the Pāli canon. For more, see Gethin 1992: 112–13.

596 Following Divy 154.20–21, *arūpiṇo vā rūpiṇo vā saṃjñino vā asaṃjñino vā.* Divy 155.2, "and so on" *(yāvat).*

597 Divy 155.11, *nirhṛtā.* This is a rarely attested meaning for this verb.

598 Read *śatasahasrahastaḥ caturṇāṃ pārṣadāṇāṃ maṇḍapo vitataḥ.* Divy 155.18–19 (following ms. C), *śatasahasrahastacaturṇāṃ maṇḍapo vitataḥ.* However, mss. ABD (Divy 155n2) read *śatasahasrahastaḥ caturṇāṃ maṇḍapo vitataḥ.*

599 Following Divy-V 96.10, *dhūpacūrṇāndhakāraḥ kṛtaḥ.* Divy 155.24, *dhūpaś cūrṇāndhakāraḥ kṛtaḥ.*

600 Divy 156.8, *yat khalu deva jānīyāḥ.* I usually translate this trope as "as you know" or "please be informed." Neither of these translations, however, is appropriate in this instance.

601 Gandhamādana is a mountain range that in Pāli materials is closely associated with solitary buddhas *(paccekabuddhas*; Skt., *pratyekabuddhas).* According to Malalasekera (DPPN), "when a new Pacceka Buddha arises in the world, he goes first to Gandhamādana and the other Pacceka Buddhas, who may be in the world, assemble there to greet him, and they all sit rapt in samādhi... These Buddhas will sometimes leave the mountain, and, having admonished those whom they wish to help, return again."

602 Following Cowell and Neil's conjecture (Divy 158n3). Cf. 479.12.

603 Divy 158.17, *cailavikṣepaṃ cākārṣuḥ.* This expression is obscure. Burnouf (1844: 178) translates this as "et firent tomber une pluie de vêtements." It could also mean that "they waved pieces of cloth."

604 Divy 158.21–22, *bhagavatā ekāyano mārgo 'dhiṣṭhitaḥ.* According to Edgerton (BHSD, s.v. *ekāyana*), the Buddha transformed the path so that it was "traversible only by one at a time."

605 Following Divy 48.23, 281.27, 342.1, read *sadyaḥ praśāntendriya.* Divy 159.12, *satyapraśāntendriyā.*

606 Following Divy-V 98.22, read *evaṃ sthitā.* Divy 159.12, *naiva sthitā.* Cf. Divy 48.24, which Vaidya (Divy-V 29.32) emends likewise, and Divy 342.2, *nopasthitā,* which Vaidya (Divy-V 211.23) also emends to *evaṃ sthitā.*

607 Read *devanikāyaiḥ.* Divy 159.15, *nikāyaiḥ.*

608 Divy 159.23–24, *ahaṃ tīrthyaiḥ sārdham uttare manuṣyadharme ṛddhiprātihāryaṃ vidarśayati.* Or, to follow my previous translation: "I will [compete] with the heretics in making use of my magical powers and performing a miracle that is beyond the capability of ordinary mortals."

609 Divy 160.20, *adhyeṣate.* Edgerton (BHSD) understands this to mean "requests."

610 Cowell and Neil (Divy 160.26) add *vidarśayatu.* Vaidya (Divy-V 99.16) does likewise.

611 Divy 161.4–5, *tejodhātum api saṃpadyate.*

612 For more on Nanda and Upananda, see Ch'en 1945–47: 278–79n133.

613 Divy 162.15–17, *evaṃ bhagavatā buddhapiṇḍī nirmitā yāvad akaniṣṭhabhavanam upādāya buddhā bhagavanto parṣannirmatam.* Cowell and Neil (Divy 162n2) query, "*'paryantaṃ nirmitam.*" Burnouf (1844: 184) translates this as "Et de même devant lui, derrière lui, autour de lui, apparurent des masses de bienheureux Buddhas, créés par lui, qui s'élevant jusqu'au ciel des Akaniṣṭhas, formèrent une assemblée de Buddhas, tous créés par le Bienheureux." Perhaps this passage should be understood as *buddhānāṃ bhagavatāṃ parṣannirmitā,* "such that there was an assembly, that is of lord buddhas, created [by the Blessed One]." However, Divy 163.1 reads *buddhapiṇḍyā nimittam.* Perhaps, then, a better reading is *parṣannimittam,* which could be rendered "so that these lord buddhas functioned as an object of meditation for the assembly."

614 Following Cowell and Neil's query, read *bhāṣante.* Divy 162.20, *bhāṣate.*

615 Divy 162.29–163.1, *pratigṛhṇīta bhikṣavo 'nupūrve sthitāyā buddhapiṇḍyā nimittam.* Speyer (1902: 116–17) suggests *buddhapiṇḍyā nirmittam.* That is, "Behold this miraculously created array of buddhas, standing in order, one on top of another." Cp. Divy 162.10, 15. See also Divy 57.1, *ārohapariṇāhaṃ nimittaṃ bhikṣavo yūpasya gṛhṇīta antardhāsyatīti.*

616 Divy 163.6, *vairavyārttaḥ.* Ms. B reads *railavyārttaḥ.* Mss. D and H 51a12 read *vailaravyārttaḥ.* This appears to be corrupt.

617 Vaidya (Divy-V 101.29) omits Divy 164.22–25.

618 On Pūraṇa's death, see Basham 1951: 84–90 and Rockhill 1972: 80.

619 Divy 165.1–2, *rathakārameṣa iva nikṛttaśṛṅgaḥ.* This is an obscure expression, and I am not sure of its significance. Burnouf (1844: 187) translates this as "semblable à un bélier noir, dont on aurait brisé la corne." Cowell and Neil (Divy 706) note that "much of this page is evidently in verse, but is too corrupt to be so arranged." I try to do so, nevertheless.

620 Divy 165.3–4, *dharmaṃ hy abhijñāya jinapraśastam āhiṇḍase* (mss., *māhiṇḍase*) *kolikagardabho yathā.* Both halves of this line are obscure. First, it might make more sense for the eunuch to tell Pūraṇa that he is ignorant of the Buddha's teaching. Hence, Burnouf (1844: 187) adds the negative to his translation: "ignorant la loi promulguée par le Djina, tu brais comme l' âne du Kôla (Kalinga?)." My sense, though, is that the eunuch is incredulous that Pūraṇa witnessed the Buddha's dharma and yet still couldn't grasp it. But what does this have to do with a weaver's donkey? Perhaps, unlike the potter's horse in "The Story of a Good for Nothing" (Divy 510.12–14), a weaver's donkey doesn't have to carry a heavy load and therefore moves faster. Maybe Pūraṇa is being compared to a senseless animal fleeing the scene. Rockhill (1972: 80) offers this translation of the Tibetan version of the text: "Whence comest thou, thus crestfallen, like a ram with broken horns? Ignorant though thou art of the truth (taught by) the Śakya, thou wanderest about without shame like an ass."

621 Burnouf (1844: 187) translates this as "J'ai connu les êtres; ils ont en partage le plaisir et la peine. La science des Arhats es [seule] en ce monde, sans voiles."

622 Divy 165.7–8, *dūrāpagato 'smi | paratimirāpanudaś ca tṛṣaṃ patati.* This passage, as Burnouf (1844: 187n1) acknowledges, is certainly corrupt. Vaidya (Divy-V 102.10) prints elipses after *'smi,* for something appears to be missing. Perhaps *me* should be added. Furthermore, *tṛṣaḥ patati* might be a better reading than *tṛṣaṃ patati,* though Burnouf follows the latter reading. Burnouf (1844: 187) translates this as "j'en suis bien éloigné. L'obscurité est profonde; celui qui la dissipe, tombe dans le désir."

623 In other words, he is naked.

624 Divy 165.22, *dharmaṃ saṃcarate*. Vaidya (Divy-V 102.31) suggests *dharmaṃ saṃśrayate*.

625 Divy 166.6–7, *yadi śrāvako bhāṣate nirmito 'pi bhāṣate*. One could also interpret this to mean that the two speak in unison—"when the disciple speaks, the magical image speaks as well." This ambiguity is also present in the upcoming verse (Divy 166.8–9).

626 Divy 166.10, *bhagavān vyākaroti*. According to the text, "the Blessed One himself gives the answer," but I follow Burnouf (1844: 188) and ascribe the answer to the magical image that the Blessed One has created.

627 Following Divy 22.8, add *udgṛhītāni*. Divy 166.15 (omitted).

628 Read *buddhakārakṛtāḥ*. Divy 166.25, *buddhakārakṛtau*.

629 According to B. C. Law (1976: 129), "The Śiśumāra hill was situated in the deer park at Bhesakalāvana in the Bharga country. It acquired its name because on the very first day of its construction a crocodile made a noise in a nearby lake. It could perhaps be present-day Chunar outside of Varanasi."

630 Read *anavatarantīm*. Divy 167.12, "treading on the ground below" *(avatarantī adharimāṃ bhumim)*. However, mss. BC (Divy 167n4) read *anavatarantī*.

631 Divy 168.25, *viyogasaṃjanitadaurmanasyaḥ*. More literally, one might translate this as "full of grief produced by separation." The Tibetan (D nya 19a5) does not contain this passage. Cf. Ch'en 1945–47: 250n10.

632 Following Speyer's suggestion (1902: 118), read *kiṃ tac chūnyaṃ bhaveta*. Cf. Bendall's manuscript fragments for this story (Divy 661.25). Divy 170.29, *kiṃ tad anyaṃ bhaveta*.

633 Following Divy 176.1, read *praviśanti*. Divy 171.17, *prativiśanti*.

634 Following Speyer (1902: 119) and Divy-V 107.11, add *paṇyam*. Divy 172.18 (omitted).

635 Here the merchants forget about Svāgata, and later in the story Ānanda also forgets about Svāgata. Such is the effect of his bad karma. Nevertheless, the Tibetan (D nya 21b3, P te 19b7, L nya 31a5, N nya 33a6; cited in Ch'en 1945–47: 253n17) reads *legs 'ongs khrid de 'phags pa*.

636 Divy 173.12 adds, "he was thrown out" *(sa niṣkāsitaḥ)*.

637 Following Speyer (1902: 119), read *sāsrakaṇṭhaḥ*. Divy 173.23, *sāsravakaṇṭhaḥ*.

638 Divy 173.22, *pūrvakarmāparādhaprabhāveṇa*. More literally, "under the influence of the faults of his previous actions." Speyer (1902: 119) suggests *prabhaveṇa*. Perhaps, "which originated from the faults of his previous actions."

639 Following Speyer (1902: 119), add *ca*. Divy 173.27 (omitted).

640 Divy 174.1–2, *asaṃprāpte viśeṣādhigame*. The Tibetan (D nya 22a2, P te 20a6, L nya 31b6, N nya 34a2; cited in Ch'en 1945–47: 254n17) reads "It is impossible and inconceivable for a being in his last state of existence to die and cut off the stream of life before he has obtained the destruction of the defilements" *(srid pa tha ma pa'i sems can zag pa zad pa ma thob par bar ma dor rgyun chad cing dus byed par 'gyur ba ni gnas ma yin skabs ma yin te)*.

641 Read *evaṃ māṃ bhaginījana saṃjānīta iti*. Divy 174.7–8, *evaṃ mā bhaginījana saṃjānīta iti*. Ms. H 55b7 concurs. Vaidya (Divy-V 108.9) emends to *evaṃ māṃ bhaginījanaḥ saṃjānīta iti*, which could be translated as "Sisters know me in this way." Cf. Divy 17.7–8, *syad āryaḥ śroṇa koṭikarṇa eva te bhaginījanaḥ saṃjānate*. Ch'en (1945–47: 254n18) proposes emending the text to *evaṃ māṃ bhāgini janaḥ saṃjānīta*. That is, "Sister, people know me as such." The Tibetan (D nya 22a4, P te 20a8, N nya 34a5, L nya 32a2) reads "Sister, I am" *(sring mo yin no)*.

642 Divy 175.6–7, *teṣām ekaikaśo vārtāṃ pratyavekṣate*. Ch'en (1945–47: 255n18) construes this differently. As he explains, "Svāgata reflected that since there were many people in Anāthapiṇḍada's household whose questions he would have to answer, and since there were many people in his father's household about whom his sister would ask, he surmised that his interview with his sister would take a long time."

643 Read *mamāpi*. Divy 175.27, *mayāpi*.

644 Following Speyer (1902: 120), read *mātrāsau*. Divy 177.4, *mātrāryā*. Cf. Divy 173.9, *māsau durāgato 'trāgataḥ syāt*. It seems unlikely here that these beggars would refer to Svāgata as a "noble one" *(ārya)*.

645 Divy 177.9–10, *sa nivartya vipralapitum ārabdhaḥ*. According to Speyer (1902: 113), this "cannot be understood and sins against grammar." He suggests emending *nivartya* to *nivartyamānaḥ*—hence, in Speyer's words, "When he, the poor *porte-malheur*, was thus being put outside, he began to weep aloud."

646 Cf. Divy 240.13, "Rejoice, Dharmaruci, in the different states of existence! Rejoice in the means that lead to these states of existence *(tṛpyasva dharmaruce bhavebhyas tṛpyasva bhavopakaraṇebhyaḥ)*!"

647 Vaidya (Divy-V 110.17) omits Divy 178.1–2.

648 This is especially ironic, since Ānanda is often characterized in scriptures as having an exceptional faculty of recollection.

649 Divy 178.8–9, *paśyati tatra pātraśeṣaṃ* <*ca*> *saṃsthāpitam*. Although the manuscripts (Divy 178n2) read *ca*, Cowell and Neil emend to *na*—that is, "he saw that in the bowl no food had been set aside."

650 Divy 178.9–10, *sa dharmatattvo* (ms. C, *saddharma-*) *vacasārtāroditum ārabdhaḥ*. Vaidya (Divy-V 110.21–22) emends to *sa dharmatattvo vacasā (?) atha roditum ārabdhaḥ*. Perhaps read *dharmatattvam*. This passage is corrupt and does not occur in the Tibetan. The Tibetan (N nya 37b7; cf. D nya 24a7) reads *sangs rgyas bcom ldan 'das rnams ni bsnyil ba mi mnga' ba'i chos nyid chan yin pas | bcom ldan 'das kyis legs 'ongs la lhung bzed kyi lhag ma bzhag pa mdzad do | de nas tshe dang ldan pa kun dga' bos bcom ldan 'das kyi lung bzed kyi pham phabs (?) blangs par brtsams pa dang | ji tsam tshe dang ldan pa kun dga' bos bcom ldan 'das kyis bdag la legs 'ongs la lhung bzed kyi lhag ma zhog shig ces bka' stsal pa | brjed pa dran nas des ngu bar brtsams pa dang.*

651 Following Divy 131.6–7, add *kṛtāni upacitāni*. Divy 178.14 (omitted).

652 This is a peculiar instance of "assigning the reward" *(dakṣiṇā + ā √diś)*. Though the Buddha offers food to Svāgata, it seems that Svāgata is the donor and the Buddha the recipient. It is the recipient of an offering who assigns the reward of that offering, and here it is the Buddha who assigns the reward from the offering to Svāgata. Still, why would the Buddha assign merit for an offering that he didn't receive?

653 For more on the gardener Gaṇḍaka, see Divy 155.

654 Divy 180.15–16, *cakṣuṣyaṃ karmāpanayo 'sya kartavya iti*. The precise meaning here is unclear. Vaidya (Divy-V 112.2) emends to *cakṣurbhyām*, "through his eyes." According to Ch'en (1945–47: 235), the Chinese reads "for these fragrant objects are beneficial to the eyes and there is no fault in smelling them." The Tibetan (D nya 25b6–26a1) reads "Svāgata began to distribute the blue lotuses to the monks, but the monks didn't take them. So the Blessed One said, 'Monks, all good smells are beneficial to the eyes, and they will bring about the purification of this one's karma. Take them.' Then the monks accepted those flowers" *(legs 'ongs kyis dge slong la utpala sngon po dag brim par brtsam pa dang | dge slong dag mi len nas bcom ldan 'das kyis bka' stsal pa | dge slong dag*

dri zhim po thams cad ni mig la phan zhing 'di'i las sbyang bar yang byas long[s?] shig | dge slong rnams kyis me tog de dag blangs so).

655 For more on this practice, see Ch'en 1945–47: 261–62.

656 According to Ch'en (1945–47: 235), the Chinese reads "Now, because I am established in the noble teachings of the Buddha, it is not wrong to call Svāgata again."

657 Divy 181.7–8, *sāṃpratam svāgato vyaktaṃ [saṃvṛtto na durāgataḥ] | sāṃpratam kāñcanaṃ dehaṃ dhārayāmi nirāśravam.* Cowell and Neil (Divy 181n1) explain that "for these two lines the MSS. read only *sāṃpratam svāgato vyaktaṃ dhārayāmi nirāśravam;* but B adds after *vyaktaṃ* and C in the margin *kāñcanaṃ dehaṃ vā pāṭha.* We conjecture a lost half line." Ms. H 68a13 reads only *sāṃpratam kāñcanaṃ dehaṃ dhārayāmi nirāśravam.*

658 Divy 181.9, *ratnāni pratilebhe hi.* This is probably corrupt. Perhaps it should be emended to *pratilabdhāni,* which scans. The Tibetan (D nya 26b1; citing Ch'en 1945–47: 266n94) reads, "In the case of those who desire to obtain the jewels, and who wish for heaven and release, it is good to associate with virtuous friends who desire the benefit of another." As Ch'en then notes, "In the light of the Tib. and Chinese, these two words [i.e., *pratilebhe hi*] should probably be emended so that the last two lines of the stanza would read, 'In the case of those who desire heaven and release and who desire to obtain the jewels, it is best to associate always with friends who wish well of others."

659 According to Ch'en (1945–47: 236–37), the Chinese reads "my renowned disciples have virtues as great as Mt. Sumeru, but they are often slighted by the ignorant crowds of the time. For no reason at all these ignorant people provoke wrong-doings and thus bring harm to their own beings. I must now make manifest the superior virtues of Svāgata."

660 Read *adhvagagaṇa.* Divy 182.7–8, *adhvagaṇa.*

661 For variations in this name, see Ch'en 1945–47: 279–80n135.

662 For a similar list of offerings raining down from heaven, see Divy 327.10–12.

663 Divy 187.2, *jarādharmā.* Cf. Divy 42.17.

664 Following Bloomfield's suggestion (1920: 336) and the Tibetan (D nya 31b3), read *hastimadyasya.* Divy 188.13, *hastimadhyasya.* For more Buddhist references to the practice of giving animals intoxicating drinks, see Bloomfield 1920: 336–39.

665 Divy 190.1–2, *ekāntaniṣaṇṇaḥ.* The standard trope reads "when he was sure that the venerable Svāgata was comfortably seated." Cf. Divy 65.4–5, 66.12–13, 81.19–20, etc.

666 Divy 190.7, *tena pānakaṃ sajjīkṛtya hastimadād aṅguliḥ prakṣiptā.* Perhaps, "After preparing a drink for the venerable Svāgata, the brahman Ahituṇḍika stuck his finger into some elephant's liquor and then into that drink." Bloomfield (1920: 336) suggests emending *prakṣiptā* to *prāk kṣiptā,* and offers this translation: "While preparing the drink, the brahman Ahituṇḍika's finger was thrust forth from the elephant's liquor." The Tibetan (D nya 33a3, P t 30a8, L nya 48a6, N nya 51a7; cited in Ch'en 1945–47: 289n183) reads "That brahman, having put his thumb in the elephant's liquor, stirred the drink with a grinding sound, and gave it to Svāgata" *(bram ze des glang po che'i chang gi nang du mdzub mo bcug ste skom gyi nang du krog krog dkrugs te | tshe dang ldan pa legs 'ongs la phul lo).* The corresponding passage in the Chinese (Ch'en 1945–47: 242) reads "Because the brahman wished to hasten the digestive process within Svāgata, he placed a small amount of elephant's liquor in his broth." As Ch'en (1945–47: 289n185) observes, "This episode of Svāgata's drinking liquor displays the widest diversity among the vinayas of the other Buddhist schools."

667 Read *ātapena spṛṣṭhaḥ*. Divy 190.10–11, *ātapena pṛṣṭhaḥ*.

668 For Tibetan and Chinese variants, see Ch'en 1945–47: 293n196.

669 Here the Chinese and Tibetan versions of the story detail the various grades of offense that result from drinking alcohol. However, as Ch'en (1945–47: 293n203) remarks, "it seems that the compiler of the *Divyāvadāna* omitted this portion and merely incorporated the interesting narrative account. One would suspect that the omitted part was in the original collection of stories, for in Divy 543–44, we do find such an account of the various offenses."

670 Divy 191.3, *śāstāram uddiśyadbhiḥ*. Bloomfield (1920: 337) suggests emending to *uddhiśyādbhiḥ,* and offers this translation—"With me, the Teacher, as authority, O ye Monks, liquor with water shall not be drunk or given (to drink), even with the tip of a blade of grass!" Speyer (1902:120) and Vaidya (Divy-V 118.8) suggest emending to *uddiśya bhavadbhiḥ*.

671 This is an example of how reified idiomatic language is in the *Divyāvadāna*. Here the idiom "like a tree cut down at the roots, he fell at his feet"—that is, he threw himself down in a full body prostration out of shame and veneration—is used even when the object of veneration is floating in the sky.

672 According to James Ware (1928: 159), the Tibetan can be found in mdo 29, 417a–430a, and the Chinese in Tripiṭaka, Tokyo xiv, 7.2 and in Taishō Issai-kyo, xv, 129.

673 This divine being, realizing that he will soon fall from his divine existence, cries out the names of various places in Indra's abode, Trāyastriṃśa heaven, to which he will no longer have access: the lotus pond at the base of Mount Meru and the Mandākinī River that springs from it; the various pleasure groves that populate this divine realm (i.e., Caitraratha, Pāruṣyaka, Nandanavana, Miśrakā, Pāriyātraka); the stone, resembling a white blanket, that is Indra's throne *(pāṇḍukambalaśilā);* the divine assembly; and Indra's city called Sudarśana. For more on these names and this cosmology, see Ware 1928: 160–61 and Kongtrul Lodrö Tayé 1995.

674 As Ware (1928: 162n9) notes, "According to the Skt. we are here confronted with a god who has fallen *upward*. Such, however, is not the case in the [Tibetan and Chinese versions of this story]." According to the Tibetan (cited in Ware 1928: 162n9), "after his death, he was later born among the gods of Tuṣita heaven" *('chi 'pho 'dus [dus?] byas nas dga' ldan phyi lha'i ris su skyes)*.

675 He was a "divine being" *(devaputra)* among the Trāyastriṃśa gods and now he is in the karmically superior position of being a "god" *(deva)* among the Tuṣita gods.

676 The Tibetan (cited in Ware 1928: 163n14) adds three verses:

> Those who day and night always
> call to mind the noble Buddha
> and come to the Buddha for refuge,
> they shall profit greatly.
>
> Those who day and night always
> call to mind the noble dharma
> and come to the dharma for refuge,
> they shall profit greatly.
>
> Those who day and night always
> call to mind the noble community

and come to the community for refuge,
they shall profit greatly.

gang dag nyin mtshan rtag par yang | sangs rgyas rje[s] su dran pa dang | gang dag sangs rgyas skyabs mchis pa | mi de dag ni rnyed pa che || gang dag nyin mtshan rtag par yang | chos ni rje[s] su dran pa dang | gang dag chos la skyabs mchis pa | mi de dag ni rnyed pa che gang dag nyin mtshan rtag par yang | dge 'dun rje[s] su dran pa dang | gang dag dge 'dun skyabs mchis pa | mi de dag ni rnyed pa che ||.

677 The Tibetan (cited in Ware 1928: 165) adds, "When the Blessed One had thus spoken, the monks rejoiced and delighted in the words of the Blessed One" *(bcom ldan 'das kyis de skad ces bka' stsal nas dge slong dag yi rangs te bcom ldan 'das kyis gsungs pa la mngon par bstod to).* Likewise Vaidya (Divy-V 121.24) adds, "This was said by the Blessed One. With their minds uplifted, the monks rejoiced" *(idam avocad bhagavān | āttamanas te bhikṣavo 'bhyanandan).*

678 For more on the connection between the practice of *buddhānusmṛti* and the *iti pi so* verse that contains this list, see *Visuddhimagga* 198–213/§7.2–67 (trans. in Buddhaghosa 1979: 206–30).

679 The version of this story in the *Śikṣāsamuccaya* (148.13–149.4; trans. in Śāntideva 1971: 147–48) begins here. It is introduced with the words: "This is recited by the noble Sarvāstivādins" *(āryasarvāstivādānāṃ ca paṭhayate).*

680 Vaidya (Divy-V 122.10–11) punctuates this as a question.

681 Divy 197.19 and 20, *iyatpuṇyaskandhaḥ*. The *Śikṣāsamuccaya* (148.17–18 and 18) reads "great roots of virtue" *(mahānti kuśalamūlāni)* instead of "such a mass of merit." In what follows in this story (Divy 197.23), the Buddha likewise refers to "great roots of virtue."

682 Following *Śikṣāsamuccaya* 149.1–2, add *duṣṭacittam utpādayati.* Divy 197.21–22, *nāham upālinn ito vahiḥ samanupaśyāmy eva kṣatiṃ copahatiṃ ca yathā sabrahmacārī sabrahmacāriṇo 'ntike.* Ms. H 64b3 omits *sabrahmacārī.* This passage appears to be corrupt. Hiraoka (1998: 431) interprets it differently, explaining "that the Buddha answers that if one gets angry, his merit disappears." The *Śikṣāsamuccaya* (148.18–149.2) reads "Upāli, I see no injury and harm worse than when one follower of the religious life entertains bad thoughts toward another follower of the religious life" *(nāham upale evaṃ kṣatiṃ copahatiṃ ca samanupaśyāmi yathā sabrahmacārī sabrahmacāriṇo 'ntike duṣṭacittam utpādayati).* Cf. Divy 338.34 for a similar sentiment.

683 Following *Śikṣāsamuccaya* 149.3 and Divy 534.24, read *dagdhasthūṇāyām.* Divy 197.25, *dagdhasthūṇāyā.* Bendall and Rouse (Śāntideva 1971: 148) translate this as "That even against the red-hot pillar we will not be angry, much less against a creature endowed with consciousness." In a footnote (Śāntideva 1971: 148n2), they explain that such a pillar was "used for torturing criminals to death by impalement or embracing." In Bendall's edition (Śāntideva 1897–1902: 149n1), however, he translates this as "even when [one is distraught] on the heated pillar, much less when the body has all its powers of perception."

684 Following Speyer's suggestion (1902: 120), read *bhavantāḥ*. Divy 198.13, *bhadantaḥ*.

685 Read *bhavantāḥ*. Divy 198.22, *bhadantaḥ*.

686 Following Divy 199.22–23. Divy 200.2, "and so on as before" *(pūrvavat yāvat).*

687 Divy 200.9–10, *ṣaṭsu kāmāvacareṣu deveṣu sattvā vyapasaṃsṛtya*. Cowell and Neil (Divy 200n2) query *sattvād*, but that would also be peculiar. I simply delete the term

in my translation (cf. Divy 140.18–19). This passage is further complicated by the term *vyapasaṃsṛtrya,* which Edgerton (BHSD) only attests in this instance. See glossary for definition of *six spheres of desire.*

688 Divy 200.16–17, *evaṃ śikṣitavyam yan no dharmaśravaṇābhiratā bhaviṣyāmaḥ.* This *yan no* is peculiar. I have taken it as *naḥ.* Cowell and Neil (Divy 220n2) query *nom.* Also possible is that it is a mistake for *yan nu,* though this form takes the optative not the future.

689 This section has close parallels with various accounts of the Buddha's final nirvāṇa—for example, the Pāli *Mahāparinibbāna-sutta* in the *Dīgha-nikāya* (ii, 102–23; trans. in Walshe 1987: 245–54). In Ernst Waldschmidt's (1951) comparative Sanskrit-Pāli-Tibetan-Chinese edition of the text, he notes those readings in the *Divyāvadāna* that differ from the Sanskrit recension, the *Mahāparinirvāṇa-sūtra* (MPS 202–28). Ernst Windisch's *Mara und Buddha* also contains an edition of this section of the *Divyāvadāna* printed in parallel with the corresponding version in Pāli (1895: 43–59).

690 Following Edgerton (BHSD, s.v. *bahuputra*), read *bahuputraka.* Divy 201.5, *bahupattrakam.*

691 Divy 201.8–9, *kalpaṃ vā tiṣṭhet kalpāvaśesaṃ vā.* For more on this much discussed and disputed passage, see Gethin 1992: 94–97 and Jaini 2001: 191–200.

692 Cowell and Neil (Divy 201n2) note that mss. BD, in the text, and ms. C, in the margin, insert a commentarial gloss on the four bases of success: *chandasamadhiprahāṇāya saṃskārasaṃskārasamāropaṇatā ṛddhipādaḥ cittarddhipādo vīryarddhipādo mīmāṃsāsamādhiprahāṇa-saṃskārasamanvāgata ṛddhipādaḥ.* For more on such formulaic explanations of the four bases of success, see Gethin 1992: 81–82, 92–94. Cf. Burnouf 1844: 625.

693 Read *bahuputrakam.* Divy 201.14, *bahupattrakam.*

694 Divy 202.6, *eko 'yaṃ bhadanta samayaḥ.* Speyer (1902: 121) suggests *ukto 'yaṃ bhadanta samayaḥ* and offers this translation: "'Yourself,' says Māra, 'have fixed that time.'" Cf. MPS 208/§16.5.

695 Following MPS 208/§16.8 and Divy 202.19, read *te.* Divy 202.14, *me.*

696 Following MPS 212/§16.14, read *samanantarotsṛṣṭāyuḥsaṃskāreṣu.* Divy 203.8–9, "as soon as the conditions for life were fully controlled" *(samanantarādhiṣṭhiteṣu jīvitasaṃskāreṣu).*

697 Divy 203.14, *vāditrabhāṇḍāni.* Cf. Divy 251.3–4. Cp. Divy 544.2. Perhaps *bheri* should be understood for *bhāṇḍa.*

698 Divy 203.16, *tulyam atulyaṃ ca saṃbhavam.* According to Buddhaghosa's commentary on the Pāli version of this verse (*Sumaṅgalavilāsinī* ii, 131–32/§3.169 Igatpuri Edition), *atulam* refers to "nirvāṇa" and *tulam* is a present participle referring to the process of evaluating phenomena in saṃsāra. Burnouf (1844: 80) translates this as "Le solitair a renouncé à l'existence, qui est semblable et différente, aux éléments dont se compose la vie."

699 Divy 203.18, *abhinat kośam ivāṇḍasaṃbhavaḥ.* Though one could translate this as "broke through becoming as though it were the shell of an egg" or "broke the egg of becoming as though it were a shell," I don't think this captures the intended meaning. The Pāli (cited on MPS 212; trans. in Walshe 1987: 247) reads *abhida kavacam iv' attasambhavan ti.* The Tibetan (cited on MPS 213) reads *srid pai 'adu ['du?] byed thub pas spangs | nang du dga zhing mnyam bzhag pas | brtson pa sgo nga mdsod [mdzod?] las*

byung ba bzhin. Cf. Bloomfield 1920: 340–41. My thanks to Paul Harrison for his thoughts on this passage.

700 Read *pratisaṃlayanād.* Divy 204.4, *atisaṃlayanād.*

701 Divy 204.24–25, *ābhayābhāṃ na pratyanubhavataḥ.* The idea here is that these places are so dark that even the sun and the moon cannot experience the light of their own light, i.e., their own luminosity. For a detailed account of this passage, see Edgerton (BHSD, s.v. *lokāntarikā*), who offers this translation: "And even those world-interstitial-spaces, (which are) miseries and covered over with miseries, darknesses, glooms of darkness,—in which the moon and sun here, which possess such great supernatural power and dignity (or capacity), are not capable of (producing) light by (their) light... even in them a great magnificent radiance appeared (at that time)."

702 Divy 205.21, *triparivartadvādaśākāram.* According to Speyer (1902: 121), "As the Wheel of Law has three revolutions *(parivartās)* [sic] and twelve spokes *(arās),* it is proper to read *triparivartadvādaśāraṃ* [sic] instead of *-dvādaśākāram.*" Edgerton (BHSD, s.v. *parivarta*) suggests no emendation, arguing instead that this formulation occurs "because each *parivarta* ['turning' of the wheel] refers to each of the four truths." More likely, however, is that this enumeration refers to the twelve links of interdependent arising. The calculation here may be that interdependent arising has three sections, each of which contains four components, or that interdependent arising has twelve links and that one cycles through them in the course of three lives.

703 Following Divy 201.8 and 201.17, read *sa.* Divy 207.1, *tathāgataḥ.*

704 Divy 207.7, *pratiśrāvayitum.* The *Mahāparinirvāṇa-sūtra* (MPS 220/§18.7) reads *prativeddhum,* and the corresponding Pāli (cited on MPS 220) reads *paṭivijjhitum.*

705 Divy 207.23–24, *yāvad alam eva bhikṣavaḥ sarvasaṃskārān saṃskaritum alam viramantu.* The manuscripts (Divy 207n5), however, read *virantu.* Burnouf (1844: 84) translates this as "...leur condition est le changement, tellement qu'il ne convient pas de concevoir rien de ce qui est un composé, qu'il ne convient pas de s'y plaire." The *Mahāparinirvāṇa-sūtra* (MPS 222/§19.6) reads *virantum*—hence, "And this, monks, is sufficient to condition [and] to lead to an end all conditioned things." Gethin (1992: 231) translates this as "In so far as this is so, one should condition all conditions, one should desist (from them)."

706 The *Mahāparinirvāṇa-sūtra* (MPS 224/§19.8) and the corresponding Pāli (cited on MPS 224) read "Which are these?" *(katame).*

707 Divy 208.9, *sapta bodhyaṅgāni.* Cowell and Neil (Divy 208n2) observe that ms. B offers the following gloss between *bodhyaṅgā* and the following *nyā—kāye kāyānupaści [anupaśyī?] smṛtyupasthānaṃ vedanācittadharma* || *utpannakuśalānāṃ saṃrakṣaṇam* | *anutpannānāṃ samutpādaḥ* | *utpannānām akuśalānāṃ prahāṇam anutpannānāṃ pāpānāṃ prala [pralayaḥ?] anutpādaḥ* || *prahāṇam* ||. This appears to be some sort of explanation of the four applications of mindfulness and four proper efforts. One might translate this as follows: "These are the applications of mindfulness. With regard to the body, one watches the body. With regard to feeling, one watches feeling. With regard to mind, one watches mind. With regard to dharmas, one watches dharma. Right effort is protecting virtuous dharmas that have arisen, arousing those that have not arisen, abandoning unvirtuous dharmas that have arisen, and destroying—not allowing to arise—sinful ones before they arise." Both this editorial gloss and the one that occurred previously in this story (i.e., in Divy 201n2) are rather loose—maybe shorthand reminders or perhaps just sloppy or hurried. Rupert Gethin (personal

communication) notes that these seem to be "quick reminders rather than careful commentarial explanations." For more on the four applications of mindfulness and their connection with the seven factors of awakening, see Gethin 1992: 29–68, especially 58. For more on the four proper efforts, see Allon and Glass 2001: 244–53.

708 Divy 208.25, *upavartanam*. This may, however, be a place name. See Edgerton (BHSD, s.v. *upavartana*).

709 Hereafter the text diverges from the *Mahāparinirvāṇa-sūtra* and the *Mahāparinibbāna-sutta* (MPS 228/§21.1).

710 Divy 209.8–9, *tā api devatā vaiśālyāṃ śabdo niścāritaḥ*. The term for "deities" occurs in a variety of forms in this passage. We find *devataiḥ* (Divy 209.5, 209.8) instead of the more standard *devatābhiḥ*, and here we find *devatā*, though this does not agree with the final verb.

711 Divy 210.10, *ṛṣayaḥ pravrajitvā*. Cf. Divy 224.26, *ṛṣīṇām antike pravajya;* Divy 224.27, *ṛṣibhiḥ pravrajitvā;* Divy 225.27–28, *ṛṣibhyaḥ pravrajitvā*. Such connections between renunciation and seers are rare in the rest of the *Divyāvadāna*.

712 Divy 210.11, *kalpavṛndaṃ prahāya*. Edgerton (BHSD, s.v. *kalpavṛnda*) suggests that what is being abandoned is "the whole mass of (brahmanical) ritual regulations." However, since *kalpavṛkṣa*s, or wish-fulfilling trees, occur throughout the story (Divy 217.28 ff.), I read *kalpa* here in the sense of "wish" or "aspiration." In a parallel passage (Divy 122.15), what is abandoned is sensual desire for objects of desire.

713 Burnouf's translation (1844: 89) of this story ends here.

714 For a well-known version of this story in the Pāli, see the *Māndhātu Jātaka* (*Jātaka*, no. 258, iii, 310–14; trans. in Cowell et al. 1990: ii, 216–18) and a reference to it in the *Dhammapada-aṭṭhakathā* (iii, 240; translated in Burlingame 1921: iii, 62).

715 Divy 210.14–15, *tad yathā tūlapicur vā karpāsapicur vā*. These two terms also appear together in the same way in Pāli materials (e.g., *Saṃyutta-nikāya* v, 284.1). As Edgerton (BHSD, s.v. *karpāsapicu*) notes, "there evidently was some difference between them, but what?" Perhaps one was *Gossypium herbaceum* and the other, *Gossypium arboreum*.

716 The lifespan of a Lord Śakra—what might be thought of as the term of office for being lord of the gods—is calculated later in the story (Divy 225.5–11).

717 Following Vaidya's emendation (Divy-V 130.23), read *devarājyaṃ pratīccha*. Divy 210.26, "My lord, accept the throne" *(deva rājyaṃ pratīccha)*. I also make the same emendation on Divy 210.28 and 211.2.

718 Divy 211.4–5, *ratnaśilayā*. Edgerton, citing Schiefner, offers "mosaic." Schiefner (1988: 2n2) translates the term as *edelstein-streu*, and Ralston translates this into English as "jewel-strewing." Cf. Divy 244.20.

719 These repetitions are present in the Sanskrit text.

720 Following Cowell and Neil's suggestion (Divy 212n1), read *mantrajñā mantrajñā*. Divy 212.11–12, *mantrajā mantrajā*.

721 Divy 212.20, *kasyaitāni puṇyāni*. More literally, this means "Whose meritorious deeds are these?"

722 Following Cowell and Neil's suggestion (Divy 706) and Edgerton (BHSD, s.v. *samanuviṣṭavān*), read *samanuśiṣṭavān*. Divy 214.21, *samanuviṣṭavān*.

723 Here the text (Divy 215.12–13) adds *āgato 'smi pūrvān*. As this passage is obscure, I leave it untranslated. It could mean "I have already come to these eastern islands," but I am not sure why the islands he has conquered would be referred to as "eastern

islands." Mss. AB (Divy 215n1) read *pūrvā,* which one could translate as "I have returned from there in the past," but this too is doubtful.

724 Divy 215.14–15, *yan nu devo gatvā svakaṃ bhaṭabalāgraṃ samanuśāset.* One might translate this more literally as "My lord should go there and govern his own army," but I think it makes more sense to read against the grammar. I also read this trope in the same way in what follows.

725 Divy 216.8–9, *etad deva uttarakauravakāṇāṃ manuṣyāṇām akṛṣṭoptaṃ taṇḍulaphalaśālim.* This place is reminiscent of the mountain on which the nāga named Agnimukha lives. In "The Story of Supriya" (Divy 120.1–3), it is said that there is a flat portion of land on that mountain that likewise is neither tilled nor sown yet produces rice that has perfect grains.

726 Following Vaidya's emendation (Divy-V 134.25), read *gacchatha.* Divy 217.21, *yacchata.*

727 The Tibetan contains an additional passage here. Following Schiefner's translation (1988: 11), "Thereupon their matted hair fell, and they themselves began to move on in front of him, their hands grasping bows and arrows. Then the treasure of the wife said to the king, 'O king, these Rishis are practising austerities; you ought to let them go free.' So the king let them go free; and when they had betaken themselves to their works of penance they became possessed of the five kinds of insights. But King Māndhātar ascended together with his hosts."

728 The text has miscalculated the overall height, so I have revised the figure accordingly. Divy 218.3, "its height was 6,000,000 leagues" *(ṣaṣṭiyojanaśatasahasram).*

729 The Karoṭapāṇi Gods, Māládhāra Gods, Sadāmatta Gods, and the four great kings are the four classes of gods who inhabit the heavens known as the Cāturmahārājika (Four Groups of the Great Kings).

730 Divy 219.21, *caturo vārṣikān māsān.* More commonly the text (e.g., Divy 202.23–24, 203.1) refers to "the three months of the rainy season."

731 Divy 220.20–21, *teṣu prākāreṣu caturvidhāḥ ṣoḍakā māpitāḥ.* Ms. C reads *ṣoḍakā* with *kramaśīrṣāṇi* written in the margin. Mss. AD reads *kramaśirṣāṇipitā.* Ms. B reads *pranīrṣāṇipitāḥ.* Cowell and Neil (Divy 220n2) observe that "*kramaśīrṣāṇi* is probably for *krayaśīrṣāṇi,* which may be a gloss on *śoḍaka.*" Cf. Edgerton (BHSD, s.v. *khoṭaka*).

732 Divy 220.22, *ūrdhvī ekā nibaddhā saṃkramaṇakā.* The manuscripts (Divy 220n2) read *urdhvi ekā nibaddhā saṃkramaṇakāḥ.* Edgerton (BHSD) explains that *saṃkramaṇaka* is "prob. pavilion for rest or private amusement, which might or might not be on a wall or roof." He also cites this passage and remarks that *ūrdhvī* here means "on a wall." Accordingly, one might translate this as "Built into one of the walls is a gallery." I don't follow Edgerton here, but I do translate *saṃkramaṇaka* as "gallery" in what follows (Divy 221.29).

733 Divy 221.6, *hemajāla.* Though this is a literal translation, the meaning of the term is unclear. Cf. Edgerton (BHSD).

734 Divy 221.8–10, *vedikāyāḥ sphaṭikamayā sūcī ālambanam adhiṣṭhānam | sphaṭikamayyā vaiḍūryamayī sūcī ālambanam adhiṣṭhānam.* The Tibetan contains a more detailed account of the construction of these pools. Following Schiefner's translation (1988: 15), "The steps of these basins were formed of four materials, of gold, silver, beryl, and crystal. The basins were surrounded by balustrades of four kinds, made of gold, silver, beryl, and crystal. The uprights, borders, and handles of the golden balustrades were made of silver; those of the silver balustrades were made of gold; those

of the beryl balustrades were made of crystal, and those of the crystal balustrades were made of beryl."

735 Divy 221.19, *tais tuṇḍicelaiś caturvidhāni kalpadūṣyāṇi*. It appears that *tuṇḍicela* is the "excellent material" from which is made "clothes from the tree that produces material as one desires" *(kalpaduṣya)*.

736 This is a list of three musical instruments, not four. In his translation from the Tibetan, Schiefner (1988: 15) lists "harps, pipes, guitars, and shells."

737 Divy 221.28, *pāripānam*. Citing only this instance, Edgerton notes that this is "a kind of drink."

738 Divy 221n9, *prāsādāmbāsanakā*. Cowell and Neil (Divy 221.29) emend to *prāsāda svāsanaka,* but Edgerton (BHSD, s.v. *ambāsanaka*) notes that this is "implausible." Edgerton suggests that *ambāsanaka* or *āmbāsanaka* is "some part, or accompaniment, of a palace," though perhaps it should be emended to read "resting rooms" *(āsvāsanaka)* or "recovery rooms" *(āśvāsanaka)*. The term could be understood to mean "benches under mango trees," but context suggests otherwise. I follow Agrawala (1966: 67–68), who thinks that *ambāsanaka* is the Sanskritized form of the Pāli *ambalāsana,* with *ambala* being a substitute for *ambara* or "sky." Hence, *prāsādāmbāsanakā* refers to an open-air platform in a palace. Cf. CPD, s.v.v. *ambalakoṭṭaka* and *ambalaṭṭhikā-pasāda*.

739 Read *annapānagṛham*. Divy 222.2, *annapānam*.

740 In Kālidāsa's *Raghuvaṃśa* (Canto 6, v. 73), King Kākutstha is likewise said to have shared an equal seat with Indra.

741 Divy 222.23–24, *tatra ca teṣāṃ devānāṃ devāsurasaṃgrāmaṃ bhavati*. More literally, "There among those [Trāyastriṃśa] gods, a war broke out between the gods and antigods."

742 Divy 224.4, *paścimā janapadāḥ*. One might translate this as "people in the west," but I am not sure what this would mean in this context. Perhaps this is an obscure corollary to the passage on Divy 215.12–13, which I discussed previously, that reads *āgato 'smi pūrvān*.

743 Divy 224.9, *catasṛbhiś ca mānuṣikābhir ṛddhibhiḥ*. According to Pāli sources (e.g., *Dīgha-nikāya* ii, 177, *Majjhima-nikāya* iii, 176), kings are said to have four "powers" *(iddhi)*: personal beauty, long life, good health, and popularity. More frequently, however, it is said that there are ten *iddhi*s. This list contains a variety of miraculous powers, including, as Rhys Davids and Stede (PTSD, s.v. *iddhi*) note, "most of those claimed for modern mediums." Here the intended meaning is probably the four bases of success.

744 The sentiment of this story is also expressed in the following popular verse (*Śāntiśataka* 2.6), which was taught to me by one of my teachers in India:

> A poor man wants one hundred.
> Having one hundred, he wants one thousand.
> Being lord of one thousand, he wants one hundred thousand.
> Having one hundred thousand, he wants to be guardian of the earth.
> Being master of the earth, he wants to be sovereign of the earth.
> Being sovereign of the earth, he wants sovereignty over the gods.
> Being master of the gods, he wants Brahmā's position.
> And Brahmā wants Viṣṇu's position, and Viṣṇu wants Śiva's position.
> Where does hope end?

niḥsvo vaṣṭi śataṃ śatī daśaśataṃ lakṣaṃ sahasrādhipaḥ |
lakṣasaḥ kṣitipālatāṃ kṣitipatiś cakreśatāṃ vāñchati |
cakreśaḥ surarājatāṃ surapatiḥ brahmaspadaṃ vāñchati |
brahmā viṣṇupadaṃ hariḥ śivapadaṃ āśāvadhiṃ ko gataḥ ||

745 According to Schiefner (1988: 19), the Tibetan includes the following: "King Māndhātar ordered irresistible sacrifices to be offered, and he said in ślokas—'If one knows the future lasts long but life is only brief, then ought one to acquire merits. If one does not acquire merits, then one has sorrow. Therefore must he who is acquiring merits offer sacrificial gifts, as is fitting. In this world and in the future he will, if he offers up gifts, obtain happiness.'"

746 Divy 225.10–11, *tisro varṣalakṣāḥ ṣaṣṭiś ca varśasahasrāṇi*. Schiefner (1988: 20n1) reads 36,000, but the text has been emended by Ralston, the translator, to read 3,600,000. Ralston also cites R. Spence Hardy's *Manual of Buddhism* (1880: 25), in which Śakra's lifespan is determined to be 36,000,000. For more on this calculation, see appendix 2.

747 Divy 226.21–23, *tatra viṣaye dharmatā yā acirodha dārikā bhartari pravahaṇekena pratipradīyate* (mss., *pratipādīyati*) *sā catūratnamayāni puṣpair avakīrya baddhakā svāmine pradīyate*. The form *pratipādīyati,* which occurs in the manuscripts (Divy 226n3), but which Cowell and Neil emend to *pratipradīyate,* is apparently a passive form of *pratipādayati*. Cf. Edgerton (BHSD, s.v. *pratipādayati*) and Speyer 1902: 122.

748 Divy 226.29–227.1, *tāni sarvābhibhuvā samyaksaṃbuddhenādhiṣṭhitāni tathā yathā sakaṭacakramātrāṇy abhinivṛttāni*. Vaidya (Divy-V 140.12) emends to *śakaṭa-*. The term *adhiṣṭhitāni* is often difficult to translate, and here is no exception. The idea is that as soon as those flowers "were accepted" by the perfectly awakened Sarvābhibhu, when they "were under his control" or "were under his power," then he manipulated them with his magical powers.

749 Divy 227.10, *ākāṅkṣatā vā* (mss., *vai*) *idam agrabodhim*.

750 Following Edgerton (BHSD, s.v. *utkarika*), read *cautkarikaḥ*. Divy 227.26, *cotkarikaḥ*. This obscure term, which occurs as a name here, also occurs as a descriptive epithet in what follows (Divy 228.5). Though Edgerton (BHSD, s.v. *okkarika*) doesn't associate either *okkarika* or *aukarika* with *utkarika* or *otkarika,* Agrawala (1966: 69) dissents and suggests that for all "the only derivative possible is from Skt., *utkara,* a heap." Edgerton suggests that *okkarika* (= *aukarika*) means something like "a dealer in agricultural products." Agrawala posits that it may refer to petty grain merchants, for they often display their goods in heaps. Elsewhere (Divy 485.7) the term *autkara* occurs as a subject in which brahmans were educated—perhaps it has to do with accumulating possessions.

751 Divy 227.29, *kaṇṭakam āhatya*. Though *kaṇṭaka* more often refers to a "thorn," or something "pointed" or "troublesome," I think here it refers to the rim of Lord Vipaśyin's begging bowl.

752 For more on this passage, see Ch'en 1953: 378–79, 401–2.

753 GM iii 1, 248.7–8, *pathyādinimittam*. I understand *pathya* to refer to substances that a doctor would prescribe to one who is convalescing. Dutt (GM iii 1, 33) and Ch'en (1953: 378), however, translate the term as "traveling expenses." This term could also refer to "tiffin meals" or "foods to be eaten on the road" *(pātheya)*.

754 GM iii 1, 248.10, *kalpakāraḥ*. The Pāli equivalent, *kappiyakāra,* refers to an official

who accepts or rejects accordingly, who decides what is to be taken and from whom. Upasak (1975: 66) defines *kappiyakāraka* as "A lay-devotee who makes the [sic] things 'formally acceptable' to the monks." Ch'en (1953: 378) translates the term as "one who made the gift allowable."

755 This is apparently a variant of the more common name Upāli.

756 GM iii 1, 248.12–13, *śrāmaṇerakasya jātarūparajatapratigrahaḥ*. Perhaps add *niṣiddaḥ*.

757 GM iii 1, 248.19, *āgārike*. Perhaps in this context "storekeeper" would be a better translation.

758 GM iii 1, 248.20, *sāptāhikam adhiṣṭhāya*. Ch'en (1953: 378) understands this to mean "having pronounced benediction over them for seven days." The gerund *adhiṣṭhāya* comes from the root *adhi √sthā,* which has a wide range of technical meanings in Buddhist Sanskrit, including "to control," "to exercise one's power over," and "to magically transform."

759 Read *samanvāharantu*. GM iii 1, 249.3, *samanvāharatā*.

760 GM iii 1, 249.8, *navakarmikena*. The Tibetan (cited in Ch'en 1953: 379n10; cf. *Mahāvyutpatti* §8735) reads *lag gi blas,* which Ch'en translates as "servants to monks." Edgerton (BHSD) discusses the term and its parallel in Pāli, *navakammika,* and tentatively suggests "perhaps lit. (one who performs) new initiate's work." Upasak (1975: 188) offers a different interpretation. He explains that the Pāli *navakammika* refers to "a monk who is in-charge of the repairs or the construction of a new *vihāra* [monastery] or any such building."

761 GM iii 1, 249.12, *na labhyaṃ bhikṣavas tenāmiṣeṇāmiṣakṛtyaṃ kartum*. Edgerton (BHSD, s.v. *āmiṣa*) offers this translation: "It is not allowable to pursue enjoyment with this worldly enjoyment (sugar added to food)."

762 The chart included here is a composite of the work of other scholars. See Collins 1998: 297–302; Gethin 1998: 112–32; Kloetzli 1997; and Kongtrul Lodrö Tayé 1995.

763 For more on this term, see Coomaraswamy 1939: 116–117.

764 The *Divyāvadāna* (225.10–11), however, determines that the lifespan of Śakra—the chief god of Trāyastriṃśa—is 360,000 years. See Collins 1998: 298 and Gethin 1998: 117.

765 The Pāli equivalents for the names of these first three cold hells all seem to refer to large numbers (cf. CPD, s.vv. *abbuda, aṭaṭa*). The idea here may be that the denizens of these hells suffer for a long time.

766 The Tibetan (Kongtrul Lodrö Tayé 1995: 247) has variant names for these last three hells. They are "Splitting Like a Blue Lotus" *(utpala ltar gas pa),* "Splitting Like a Lotus" *(padma ltar gas pa),* and "Splitting Like a Great Lotus" *(padma ltar cher gas pa).* Perhaps these names are meant to conjure an image of a lotus beaten down by the cold. This is an image not uncommon in Sanskrit literature. See, for example, Kālidāsa's *Meghadūta* (part 2, v. 23) and Bhāsa's *Svapnavāsavadatta* (book 5, v. 1).

Glossary

In compiling this glossary, I have relied heavily on the traditional numerical lists found in the *Mahāvyutpatti;* the commentaries on such lists in the *Visuddhimagga* and the *Abhidharmakośa;* and the glossaries found in the works of Luis Gomez (1996), John Strong (1989), and Robert Thurman (1983). Rupert Gethin's *The Buddhist Path to Awakening* (1992) was also particularly helpful.

Āgamas. See *four Āgamas.*

agaru. Agallochum, Amuris agaloccha. Closely connected to *aguru (Aquilaria agallocha),* the fragrant aloe tree.

aggregates (skandha). See *five aggregates.*

agniṣṭoma. A brahmanical ceremony that involves making offerings into a sacrificial fire.

agnihotra. An oblation to the fire god Agni, chiefly of milk, oil, and sour gruel.

analytic insights (pratisaṃvid). There are four: with regard to dharma, meaning *(artha),* languages and linguistic usage *(nirukti),* and eloquence *(pratibhāna).*

Ānanda. One of the Buddha's main disciples and a veritable treasurer of the dharma. He was the Buddha's cousin and, for the latter stage of the Buddha's life, his personal attendant.

Anāthapiṇḍada. The Buddha's chief patron. After purchasing a park from Prince Jeta, son of King Prasenajit, he had a monastery constructed there for the Buddha to pass the rainy season.

antigod (asura). One of a class of demigods whose home is beneath the waters at the base of Mount Meru. Positioned just below the lowest heavenly sphere, these "not [quite]" *(a)* "gods" *(sura)* often vie with the gods above them (cf. Divy 222.23ff.).

arhat. A "worthy one" who has destroyed all of his defilements and thereby attained awakening. Often an epithet of a buddha. According to Paul Griffiths (1994: 62), it is used as a title for a buddha "to indicate both Buddha's worthiness to receive the homage *(pūjārhattva)* and offerings of non-Buddhists, and, using a different etymology, Buddha's success in killing *(han-)* the enemies *(ari)* to awakening."

armed wheel-turning king (balacakravartin). A king who needs to use force or the threat of force to establish his dominion. For more, see Strong 1983: 49–56.

aśoka. Jonesia *Asoka roxb.* A tree that blossoms with red flowers when, according to poetic convention, kicked by beautiful women.

auspicious age (bhadrakalpa). An eon, such as the present one, in which five buddhas appear. In our present eon, the buddhas Krakucchanda, Kanakamuni, Kāśyapa, and Śākyamuni have already appeared, and Maitreya will be the fifth and last.

bakula. Mimusops elengi. A tree that is said by poets to bloom with fragrant flowers when young women sprinkle it with mouthfuls of wine.

Bhadanta. A respectful term used to address Buddhist monks.

blessed one (bhagavān). An epithet of a buddha. I translate *bhagavān* as "Blessed One" when it refers to Gautama Buddha, and as "lord" when it modifies a buddha (e.g., the lord Vipaśyin).

bodhisattva. One who has vowed to attain awakening as a buddha, and while on the path to becoming a buddha works compassionately for the welfare of all sentient beings.

Brahmā-like voice (brahmasvara). The twenty-eighth of the thirty-two marks of a great man. In the Pāli materials, such a voice is said to be "distinct, intelligible, charming, pleasant to hear, compact, concise, deep, and resonant" (*vissaṭṭo ca viññeyyo ca mañju ca savanīyo ca bindu ca avisārī ca gambhīro ca ninnādī ca* | *Dīgha-nikāya* ii, 211).

Brahmā World (brahmaloka). The world consisting of the four spheres in the formless realm *(ārūpyadhātu)* and the seventeen heavens in the form realm *(rūpadhātu)*. See appendix 2.

brahman. One of the four hereditary classes *(varṇa)* according to Brahmanical Hinduism (i.e., brahman, kṣatriya, vaiśya, śūdra) whose primary duties involve ritual activity.

buddha. One who has attained the highest possible awakening—who is, literally, an "awakened one." In the *Divyāvadāna*, "the Buddha" is often used as a title to refer to Śākyamuni.

buddha vision (buddhacakṣu). Buddhas are said to possess five faculties of vision: the physical eye *(māṃsacakṣu),* the divine eye *(divyacakṣu),* the wisdom eye *(prajñācakṣu),* the dharma eye *(dharmacakṣu),* and the buddha eye *(buddhacakṣu).* This last quality I translate as buddha vision.

celestial musician (gandharva). One of a class of beings who inhabit the lowest heaven, the realm of the Cāturmahārājika. Dhṛtarāṣṭra, one of the four great kings, is their lord. However, in the *Divyāvadāna* (Divy 202.29), Supriya is said to be their king.

community (saṅgha). The Buddhist order of monks *(bhikṣu)* and nuns *(bhikṣuṇī).* The text often speaks, however, of a community of monks *(bhikṣusaṅgha).*

coral tree (mandārava, māndārava, māndāraka). Erythrina indica. One of the five celestial trees. Flowers from this tree are sometimes said to rain down from heaven as a divine greeting of respect.

corruptions (āsrava). These negative karmic forces, which must be interrupted to escape from saṃsāra, are sometimes translated as "cankers" or "outflows." They are often equated with the *four floods.*

declaration of truth (satyavākya). A formal declaration of fact accompanied by a resolution that the desire of the speaker will be accomplished. This is frequently referred to as a "vow of truth."

desire realm (kāmadhātu). The world of desire and sense pleasure, which includes the realms of hell beings, animals, hungry ghosts, humans, and the first six divine realms. See appendix 2.

dharmic form (dharmakāya). The corpus of a buddha's teachings or, as it were, a buddha embodied in the dharma.

disciple (śrāvaka). A follower of the Buddha is known as a "hearer" *(śrāvaka),* signaling the importance in early Buddhism of listening to the Buddha's dharma. In the *Divyāvadāna,* however, devotees are enjoined to look, as much as to hear, for visual practices are represented as the primary means of cultivating faith.

divine sight (divyacakṣu). The quality of clairvoyance, the second of five superior qualities of vision. See *buddha vision.*

eight sciences (aṣṭavidyā). One list in the *Divyāvadāna* includes the sciences of elephants, horses, jewels, wood, cloth, men, women, and various commodities (Divy 100.1–3). Elsewhere, the sciences of young men and women occur instead of the sciences of men and women (Divy 58.19). In addition, there are instances in the text when some manuscripts attest to "the science of cloth" while others attest to "the science of building sites" (Divy 58.17, 100.3). The Tibetan (Shackleton Bailey 1950: 174) corresponding to Divy 26.12–14 lists the sciences of objects, cloth, jewels, wood, elephants, horses, young men, and young women.

eightfold path (āṣṭāṅgamārga). See *noble eightfold path.*

eighty minor marks (aśītyānuvyañjana). The secondary characteristics of a great man. Following Robert Thurman's enumeration (1983: 156–57), these are

> [1] fingernails the color of brass, [2] shiny [3] and long; [4] round fingers; [5] tapered fingers; [6] fingers wide-spreading; [7] veins not protruding, [8] and without tangles; [9] slender ankles; [10] feet not uneven; [11] lion's gait; [12] elephant's gait; [13] swan's gait; [14] bull's gait; [15] gait tending to the right; [16] graceful gait; [17]

steady gait; [18] his body is well covered, [19] clean, [20] well proportioned, [21] pure, [22] soft, and [23] perfect; [24] his sex organs are fully developed; [25] his thighs are broad and knees round; [26] his steps are even; [27] his complexion is youthful; [28] his posture is not stooped; [29] his bearing is expansive, [30] yet extremely poised; [31] his limbs and fingers and toes are well defined; [32] his vision is clear and unblurred; [33] his joints are not protruding; [34] his belly is relaxed, [35] symmetrical, [36] and not fat; [37] his navel is deep [38] and wound to the right; [39] he is completely handsome; [40] he is clean in all acts; [41] he is free of spots or discolorations of the skin; [42] his hands are soft as cotton; [43] the lines of his palms are clear, [44] deep, [45] and long; [46] his face is not overlong [47] and is bright as a mirror; [48] his tongue is soft, [49] long, [50] and red; [51] his voice is like an elephant's trumpet or like thunder, [52] yet sweet and gentle; [53] his teeth are rounded, [54] sharp, [55] white, [56] even, [57] and regularly arranged; [58] his nose is long [59] and straight; [60] his eyes are clear [61] and wide; [62] his eyelashes are thick; [63] the pupils and whites of his eyes are clearly defined, and the irises are like lotus petals; [64] his eyebrows are long, [65] soft, [66] evenly haired, [67] and gently curved; [68] his ears [69] are long-lobed and symmetrical; [70] his hearing is acute; [71] his forehead is high [72] and broad; [73] his head is very large; [74] his hair is as black as a bee, [75] thick, [76] soft, [77] untangled, [78] not unruly, [79] and fragrant; [80] and his feet and hands are marked with lucky signs [of the *śrīvatsa,* svastika, and *nandyāvarta*].

Thurman follows *Mahāvyutpatti* §269–348. Edgerton (BHSD, s.v. *anuvyañjana*) constructs a slightly different list. For alternate translations, see Jones 1976: ii, 40–41 and Mitra 1998: 130–31. For more on the lucky signs, see Bapat 1953.

elements (dhātu). "The psycho-physical constituent elements of the personality in relation to the outside world," to quote Franklin Edgerton (BHSD). There are eighteen: the six sense organs (i.e., eye, ear, nose, tongue, body, mind), the six objects of the sense organs (i.e., the visible, sound, odor, taste, tactile objects, mental objects), and the resultant six consciousnesses (i.e., eye consciousness, ear consciousness, nose consciousness, tongue consciousness, body consciousness, mind consciousness).

emptiness (śūnya). The Buddhist doctrine that all persons and things have no inherent existence.

eraka. A kind of grass used for making mats.

fervent aspiration (praṇidhāna, praṇidhi). A firm vow or resolution to attain some higher form of karmic development, usually in a future life.

field of merit (puṇyakṣetra). Entities, such as the Buddha or the community, who are great repositories of virtue, and as such make meritorious deeds directed toward them especially beneficial for the donor.

five aggregates (pañcaskandha). These constitute the physical and mental constituents of a person. They are matter *(rūpa),* feeling *(vedanā),* recognition *(saññā),* conditioning *(saṃskāra),* and consciousness *(vijñāna).*

five [bad] qualities (pañcāṅga). Equivalent to the five hindrances *(pañcanīvaraṇa).* These are sensual desire *(kāmacchanda),* ill will *(vyāpāda),* tiredness and sleepiness *(styānamiddha),* excitement and lethargy *(auddhatyakaukṛtya),* and doubt *(vicikitsā).*

five powers (pañcabala). Various powers to be developed by the Buddhist practitioner. These are essentially the same as the five spiritual faculties; perhaps thought of as their full development.

five realms of existence (pañcagati). The various categories of living beings. These are gods *(deva),* humans *(manuṣya),* animals *(tiryagyoni),* hungry ghosts *(preta),* and hell beings *(naraka).* Often the category of antigods *(asura)* is added between humans and hungry ghosts. See appendix 2.

five spiritual faculties (pañcendriya). These are virtues or capacities to be developed by the Buddhist practitioner. They are confidence *(śraddhā),* strength *(vīrya),* mindfulness *(smṛti),* concentration *(samādhi),* and wisdom *(prajñā).* See also *five powers.*

five subjects of knowledge (pañcavidyāsthāna). The sciences of grammar *(śabda),* logic *(hetu),* psychology *(adhyātma),* medicine *(cikitsā),* and crafts *(śilpa).*

five superhuman faculties (pañcābhijñā). See *superhuman faculties.*

four Āgamas. The fourfold division of the Buddha's discourses contained in the Sūtra Piṭaka. These collections are the *Longer Sayings (Dīrghāgama),* the *Middle-Length Sayings (Madhyamāgama),* the *Connected Sayings (Saṃyuktāgama),* and the *Gradual Sayings (Ekottarika).*

four applications of mindfulness (catvāri smṛtyupasthānani). A special awareness that is cultivated and focused on the body *(kāya),* feeling *(vedanā),* mind *(citta),* and dharma. See note 707, which offers a commentary on these practices.

four bases of success (caturṛddhipāda). The bases that lead one to acquire magical power and spiritual success. These are the desire to act *(chanda),* strength *(vīrya),* mind *(citta),* and investigation *(mīmāṃsā).* For more, see Gethin 1992: 81–103.

four Brahmā states (catvāro brahmavihārāḥ). Loving kindness *(maitrī),* compassion *(karuṇā),* joy *(muditā),* and equanimity *(upekṣā).* These are also known as the four immeasurables *(apramāṇa),* for one is to possess these desirable attitudes without limit toward all living beings.

four confidences (caturvaiśāradya). The confidence of being perfectly awakened to all dharmas *(sarvadharmābhisambodhivaiśāradya),* the confidence in the knowledge that all corruptions have been destroyed *(sarvāśravakṣayajñānavaiśāradya),* the confidence of having described precisely and correctly the obstructive conditions [to the religious life] *(antarāyikadharmānanyathātvaniścitavyākaraṇavaiśāradya),* and the confidence in the correctness of one's way of salvation for the realization of all good things *(sarvasampadadhigamāya nairyāṇikapratipattathātvavaiśāradya).*

four floods [of corruptions] (caturogha). These are desire *(kāma),* existence *(bhava),* ignorance *(avidyā),* and views *(dṛṣṭi).* One who has crossed these four negative flows of karma is an arhat.

four great kings (catvāro mahārājānaḥ). The guardians of the four directions who live in the divine realm known as Cāturmahārājika (Four Groups of the Great Kings). They are the gods Dhṛtarāṣṭra in the east, Virūḍhaka in the south, Virūpākṣa in the west, and Kubera (= Vaiśravaṇa, Dhanada) in the north. See appendix 2.

four islands (caturdvīpa). The four continents that humans inhabit. These are Jambudvīpa (Black Plum Island) to the south, Uttarakuru (Northern Kuru) to the north, Aparagodānīya (Western Godanīya) to the west, and Pūrvavideha (Eastern Videha) to the east.

four means of attracting beings [to the religious life] (catvāri saṅgrahavastūni). These are generosity *(dāna),* kind speech *(priyavacana),* beneficial conduct *(arthacaryā),* and exemplary behavior *(samānārthatā).*

four noble truths (caturāryasatya). The classic formulation of the Buddha's teaching. It is true that there is suffering *(duḥkha),* that it has a cause *(samudaya),* that it can end *(nirodha),* and that there is a path *(mārga)* that leads to its cessation.

four proper efforts (catvāri samyakprahāṇāni). The effort to prevent sinful states from arising, the effort to get rid of those sinful states that exist, the effort to produce good states, and the effort to maintain those good states already existing. Although *samyakprahāṇāni* is more literally "proper abandonings," the exegetical traditions in Buddhist Sanskrit, as in Pāli, understand these to be "proper efforts" *(samyakpradhānāni).*

four stages of penetrating insight (nirvedhabhāgīya). These are the four stages on the path of application *(prayogamārga).* They are heat *(uṣmagata),* tolerance *(kṣānti),* summit *(mūrdha),* and highest worldly dharma *(laukikāgradharma).* The first three of these four stages are themselves divided into three stages—weak, medium, and strong—hence there are ten stages in all.

gośīrṣa. A kind of valuable sandalwood. Its name literally means "cow's head," but the significance of this name is unclear. Perhaps it may be the sandalwood found on Gośīrṣa Mountain.

great king. See *four great kings.*

great man (mahāpuruṣa). One who has the thirty-two marks, and as such is destined to become either a wheel-turning king ruling the four quarters of the earth or a buddha.

great snake (mahoraga). One of a class of celestial beings that are said to have a human body with a serpent head.

great thousand third-order thousand world-system (trisāhasramahāsāhasralokadhātu). As one nineteenth-century Tibetan commentor explains,

> The area that includes the four continents, Mount Meru, and the outer rim of mountains... is referred to as a four-continent world-system. An identical world-system is located in space at a distance of one thousand times the magnitude of that world-system. A total of one thousand such world-systems [evenly distributed in space], encircled by a rim, is referred to as a first-order thousand world-system. This considered as a single unit, replicated one thousand times and surrounded by a perimeter, is referred to as a second-order thousand world-system. One thousand [second-order thousand world-systems] enclosed by a great rim is called a third-order thousand world-system. Thus, one billion four-continent world-systems is called one great thousand third-order thousand world-system. (Kongtrul Lodrö Tayé 1995: 102–3).

group of six monks (ṣaḍvargika, ṣaḍvargīya). These monks (i.e., Nanda, Upananda, Punarvasu, Chanda, Aśvaka, and Udayin) are unruly followers of the Buddha. In the *Divyāvadāna*, they seem to be close to heretics.

guhyaka. A kind of demigod. They are perhaps equivalent to yakṣas.

guide (vināyaka). An epithet of a buddha.

heat stages (uṣmagata). See *four stages of penetrating insight.*

heavenly bird (garuḍa). One of a class of bird-like supernatural beings. They are said to be an enemy of the snake-like nāgas.

highest worldly dharma stages (laukikāgradharma). See *four stages of penetrating insight.*

impermanence (anitya). The Buddhist doctrine that all conditioned things inevitably undergo change.

insight (vipaśyanā). A type of analytic meditation that promotes a direct understanding of the true nature of reality.

interdependent arising (pratītyasamutpāda). The Buddhist doctrine of causal interdependence, which describes the cycle of existence *(saṃsāra)*. By extension, the doctrine that all things are interdependent.

Jambudvīpa. The southern continent, usually identified with India. Though often translated as "Rose Apple Island," current research (Wujasyk 2004) suggests that a more accurate rendering is "Black Plum Island." See also *four islands.*

karma. Often translated as "deed" or "action," though left untranslated when it refers to the force exerted by the results of such deeds—for example, in determining the quality of one's rebirth, one's present experience, or inclinations.

karṇikāra. A tree from the island of Uttarakuru, where trees are said to bear perpetual fruit and foliage.

karpāsa. A kind of cotton.

kārṣāpaṇa. A kind of coin in ancient India, usually of copper or silver, though gold ones also circulated.

kaṭapūtana. A kind of ghost or demon. According to Monier-Williams (SED), "a form assumed by a deceased spirit of a *kṣatriya* who when alive neglected his duties."

Kauśika. An epithet of Śakra.

kinnara. A class of beings, often said to be half human and half animal, as indicated by their name—literally, "What *(kiṃ)* sort of man *(nara)*?" In the *Divyāvadāna*, we most often come across the beautiful and bewitching kinnara women *(kinnarī)* whose name might aptly be translated as "What a woman!"

kovidāra. An enormous flowering tree, or perhaps a grove, in Trāyastriṃśa heaven.

kṛtsna. A form of meditation practices whereby one focuses one's attention on one of ten external objects in order to form an imprint of that object in one's mind. These are blue *(nīla)*, yellow *(pīta)*, red *(lohita)*, white *(avadāta)*, earth *(pṛthvī)*, water *(ap)*, fire *(tejas)*, wind *(vāyu)*, sky *(ākāśa)*, and consciousness *(vijñāna)*.

kṣatriya. One of the four hereditary classes *(varṇa)* according to Brahmanical Hinduism (i.e., brahman, kṣatriya, vaiśya, śūdra) whose duties include maintaining order and inflicting punishment.

kulattha. Delichos biflous. A kind of black or grey-seeded lentil known in Hindi as *kulathī.* It is sometimes referred to as "horse gram."

kumbhāṇḍa. One of a class of evil spirits who, as their name would indicate, had "testicles" *(aṇḍa)* as big as "pots" *(kumbha).* Virūḍhaka, one of the four great kings, is their lord.

kuśa. A kind of grass used in ritual offerings.

lion throne (siṃhāsana). A seat of honor, often for a buddha, for he is likened to a lion.

lord (bhagavān). See *blessed one.*

lord of the world (lokanātha). An epithet of a buddha.

Mahākāśyapa. One of the Buddha's main disciples. He was present at the Buddha's death and was instrumental in leading the monastic community after the Buddha's demise.

Mahākātyāyana. One of the Buddha's main disciples and a master of doctrinal exposition.

Mahāmaudgalyāyana. The "great" *(mahā)* Maudgalyāyana. See *Maudgalyāyana.*

mahatī. A kind of lute.

Maitreya. A bodhisattva who lives in Tuṣita heaven, awaiting his final rebirth in the human realm when he will become a buddha.

mantra. A ritual formula that can function as a spell or charm.

Māra. An evil figure personifying death and temptation who assails Buddhist practitioners and tries to lead them astray. He is sometimes said to be king of the Paranirmitavaśavartin gods.

master (nātha). An epithet of a buddha.

mātṛkā. A list of significant points of doctrine.

Maudgalyāyana. One of the Buddha's chief disciples and regarded as foremost in the attainment of psychic powers.

Middle Country (madhyadeśa). One of five traditional divisions of India. These are Middle Country *(Madhyadeśa)*, North Country *(Uttarāpatha)*, Eastern India *(Prācya)*, South Country *(Dakṣiṇāpatha)*, and Western India *(Aparānta)*.

mindfulness of the body (kāyagatā smṛti). A special awareness with regard to the body. One of the *four applications of mindfulness*. For more, see the *Kāyagatāsati-sutta* in the *Majjhima-nikāya* (iii, 88–99; trans. in Ñāṇamoli and Bodhi 1995: 949–58).

moral code (śīlasamādāna). The observance of moral precepts. In the *Divyāvadāna*, equivalent to the five precepts traditionally observed by the Buddhist laity: not to take life, not to steal, not to be engaged in sexual misconduct, not to lie, and not to take intoxicants. See *precepts*.

most-treasured counselor. See *seven treasures*.

most-treasured elephant. See *seven treasures*.

most-treasured horse. See *seven treasures*.

most-treasured householder. See *seven treasures*.

most-treasured jewel. See *seven treasures*.

most-treasured wheel. See *seven treasures*.

most-treasured woman. See *seven treasures*.

Mount Meru. A sacred mountain located in Jambudvīpa, 80,000 leagues high, and considered to be the center of the world. On its terraces reside the gods of Cāturmahārājika, and on its summit the gods of Trāyastriṃśa. See Appendix 3.

Mount Sumeru. See *Mount Meru*.

Nanda. See *group of six monks*.

nandyāvarta. An auspicious symbol in which some lines of the svastika are repeated outside that figure, creating a kind of labyrinth. This is one of the lucky signs mentioned as the eightieth of the eighty minor marks.

nāga. A serpent, capable of taking on human form, who lives in the water and possesses miraculous powers. Though often dangerous to humans, these beings can be instructed in the dharma. Virūpākṣa, one of the four great kings, is their lord.

Nandana Grove (nandanavana). Quite literally "a grove of delight" in Trāyastriṃśa heaven, which is located atop Mount Meru and ruled by Śakra.

nine bonds to existence (navasaṃyojana). These are attachment *(anunaya)*, aversion *(pratigha)*, conceit *(māna)*, ignorance *(avidyā)*, views *(dṛṣṭi)*, clinging *(parāmarśa)*, doubt *(vicikitsā)*, envy *(īrṣyā)*, and avarice *(mātsarya)*. The term *saṃyojana* is usually translated as "fetter," but these nine do not correspond to the standard list of fetters (e.g, ten fetters, five lower fetters, three fetters).

nine successive states of quiescence meditation (navānupūrvavihāra). The four meditations or contemplations *(dhyāna)* of form; the four formless spheres—i.e., the sphere of infinite space *(ākāśānantyāyatana)*, the sphere of infinite consciousness *(vijñānānantyāyatana)*, the sphere of nothingness *(akiñcanyāyatana)*, the sphere of neither consciousness nor unconsciousness *(naivasaṃjñānāsaṃjñāyatana)*, and lastly, the cessation of conceptualization and sensation *(saṃjñāvedayitanirodha)*.

Nirgrantha. A monk who engages in practices of austerity in the hope of becoming, as the name indicates, "free from hindrances." In the *Divyāvadāna*, these monks are heretics who oppose the Buddha and his dharma. Mahāvīra, one of the founders of Jainism, originally belonged to this school.

noble eightfold path (āryāṣṭāṅgamārga). The proper path of conduct which has eight aspects: right view *(samyagdṛṣṭi)*, right intention *(samyaksaṅkalpa)*, right speech *(samyagvāc)*, right action *(samyakkarmānta)*, right livelihood *(samyagājīva)*, right effort *(samyagvyāyāma)*, right mindfulness *(samyaksmṛti)*, and right concentration *(samyaksamādhi)*.

noble path (āryamārga). See *noble eightfold path*.

nonreturner (anāgāmin). One who has attained the third of four stages of religious development that culminate in arhatship (e.g., stream-enterer, once-returner, nonreturner, arhat). Such a person will have no additional rebirths as a human; he will attain awakening after being reborn in one of the higher heavens.

North Country (uttarāpatha). One of five traditional divisions of India. These are Middle Country *(Madhyadeśa),* North Country *(Uttarāpatha),* Eastern India *(Prācya),* South Country *(Dakṣiṇāpatha),* and Western India *(Aparānta).*

no-self (anātman). The doctrine that individuals have no permanent or abiding self.

omniscient one (sarvajña). An epithet of a buddha.

once-returner (sakṛtāgāmin). One who has attained the second of four stages of religious development that culminate in arhatship (e.g., stream-enterer, once-returner, nonreturner, arhat). Such a person will attain awakening in his next rebirth.

palāśa. Butea frondosa. A kind of tree, also known as *kiṃśuka,* that bears beautiful blossoms.

path of application (prayogamārga). The second of the five paths of the religious practitioner—i.e., 1. the path of accumulation *(sambhāramārga),* 2. the path of application *(prayogamārga),* 3. the path of seeing *(darśanamārga),* 4. the path of cultivation *(bhāvanāmārga),* and 5. the path of no more learning *(aśaikṣamārga).*

perfectly awakened (samyaksambuddha). An epithet of a buddha. He is *perfectly* awakened, and hence his awakening is superior to the awakening of a disciple or solitary buddha.

perfumed chamber (gandhakuṭi). A special structure in a monastery for a buddha.

physical form (rūpakāya). The physical body of a buddha.

piśāca. A kind of demon. According to Monier-Williams (SED), "possibly so called either from their fondness for flesh *(piśa* for *piśita)* or from their yellowish appearance."

precepts (śikṣāpada). Quite literally the "rules of training" for monks, nuns, novices of both genders, etc. Generally this refers to the five precepts observed by lay Buddhists: not to take life, not to steal, not to be engaged in sexual misconduct, not to lie, and not to take intoxicants.

pūtana. A kind of spirit or demon.

quiescence (śamatha). See *tranquility.*

refuges (śaraṇagamana). See *three refuges.*

resolute one (dhīra). An epithet of a buddha.

root of virtue (kuśalamūla). A "virtuous deed" *(kuśala),* or the merit accrued from such a deed that functions as a "root" or "foundation" *(mūla)* for a request or aspiration.

Śakra. The chief of Trāyastriṃśa heaven, who is said to be the lord of the gods *(devendra).*

Śākyamuni. An epithet meaning "sage of the Śākya clan" used to designate Siddhārtha Gautama, the most recent buddha in our eon. See *auspicious age.*

śāla. Shorea robusta or *Vatica robusta.* The sal tree, though that name is not well known in English.

saṃsāra. The repeating cycle of life, death, and rebirth, which is characterized by suffering. In short, existence as we know it.

Śāriputra. One of the Buddha's chief disciples regarded as foremost in comprehending the dharma.

sense bases (āyatana). There are twelve: the six senses (i.e., eye, ear, nose, tongue, body, mind) and their corresponding objects (i.e., the visible, sound, odor, taste, tactile objects, mental objects).

sensual desire (kāmacchanda). This is the first of the five bad qualities, also known as the five hindrances.

seven factors of awakening (saptabodhyaṅga). The factors that lead one to awakening. These are the awakening factors of mindfulness *(smṛti),* dharma analysis *(dharmapravicaya),* strength *(vīrya),* joy *(prīti),* serenity *(praśrabdhi),* concentration *(samādhi),* and equanimity *(upekṣā).*

seven meditative concentrations (saptasamādhi). Buddhas bestow the means for becoming a stream-enterer, a once-returner, a nonreturner, an arhat, a solitary buddha, a bodhisattva, and an omniscient tathāgata.

seven treasures (saptaratnāni). The special possessions of a wheel-turning king. They are the most-treasured wheel *(cakraratna),* the most-treasured elephant *(hastiratna),* the most-treasured horse *(aśvaratna),* the most-treasured jewel *(maṇiratna),* the most-treasured woman *(strīratna),* the most-treasured householder *(gṛhapatiratna),* and the most-treasured counselor *(pariṇāyakaratna).*

śiṃśapā. Dalbergia sissoo. A kind of tree, perhaps the same as the *aśoka* tree.

single guardian [which is mindfulness] (ekārakṣa). According to Pāli sources, the third of ten noble dispositions *(ariyavāsa).* The *Dīgha-nikāya* (iii, 269) explains that the single guardian is, in fact, mindfulness.

six [good] qualities (ṣaḍaṅga). According to Pāli sources, the second of ten noble dispositions *(ariyavāsa).* The *Dīgha-nikāya* (iii, 269) explains that one who is endowed with these qualities remains equanimous and mindful in six instances: upon seeing a sight, hearing a sound, smelling a smell, tasting a flavor, touching an tactile object, and cognizing a mental object with the mind.

six perfections (ṣaṭpāramitā). These are virtues that are to be practiced and perfected by the bodhisattva. They are the perfection of generosity *(dānapāramitā),* the perfection of morality *(śīlapāramitā),* the perfection of tolerance *(kṣāntipāramitā),* the perfection of strength *(vīryapāramitā),* the perfection of meditation *(dhyānapāramitā),* and the perfection of wisdom *(prajñāpāramitā).*

six spheres of desire (ṣaṭkāmāvacara). The worlds of desire and sense pleasure inhabited by the gods of the first six divine realms. See appendix 2.

six superhuman faculties (ṣaḍābhijñā). See *superhuman faculties.*

solitary buddha (pratyekabuddha). One who attains awakening on his own, as would a buddha, but who does not found a community.

special knowledges (vidyā). There are three: the knowledge of remembering past lives *(pūrvanivāsānusmṛtijñāna),* the knowledge of the passing away and arising [of beings] *(cyutyupapādajñāna),* and knowledge of the destruction of the corruptions *(āsravakṣayajñāna).* Following *Saṅghabhedavastu* ii, 249–50. See also *Dīgha-nikāya* i, 81–85.

sphere of desire (kāmāvacara). See *six spheres of desire.*

stratum of the golden wheel (kāñcanacakra). The golden disk upon which Mount Meru and the four continents rest. For more, see *Abhidharmakośa* 451–55.

stream-enterer (srotāpanna). One who has attained the first of four stages of religious development that culminate in arhatship (e.g., stream-enterer, once-returner, nonreturner, arhat). Such a person will attain awakening within seven rebirths.

stūpa. A mound-like monument that generally contains relics, such as a buddha's hair and nails.

suffering (duḥkha). The Buddhist diagnosis that existence in saṃsāra is fundamentally unsatisfactory.

sugata. An epithet of a buddha. Often said to mean "one who has attained bliss" or "one who is fully realized."

sughoṣaka. A kind of musical instrument.

summit stages (mūrdhan). See *four stages of penetrating insight.*

superhuman faculties (abhijñā). Powers and abilities possessed by arhats. These are clairvoyance *(divyacakṣu),* clairaudience *(divyaśrotra),* telepathy *(paracittajñāna),* remembering past lives *(pūrvanivāsānusmṛti),* and magical powers *(ṛddhi)*—for example, levitation, passing through solid objects, and appearing in multiple bodies. Sometimes included as a sixth faculty is the knowledge of the destruction of the corruptions *(āsravakṣayajñāna).*

supreme knowledge (anuttarajñāna). See *unsurpassed perfect awakening.*

sūtra. A discourse attributed to a buddha. It is also one of the three main divisions of the ancient Buddhist canon (i.e., *sūtra, vinaya, abhidharma*).

svastika. An auspicious symbol that, as its name indicates (*su* = good; *asti* = being; *ka* = making), is meant to be beneficent.

tagara. Tabernaemontana coronaria. A fragrant plant.

tamāla. Xanthocymus pictorius. A tree with dark bark and white blossoms.

tathāgata. An epithet of a buddha. This term has a variety of interpretations (e.g., "Thus come," "Thus gone," "Thus not gone") but is used only in reference to a buddha. Often it is used by Śākyamuni Buddha to refer to himself. For a more complete exegesis of the term, see Bodhi 1978: 331–44.

tenfold path of evil actions (daśākuśalakarmapatha). Taking life *(prāṇātipāta),* taking what is not given *(adattādāna),* sexual misconduct *(kāmamithyācāra),* lying speech *(mṛṣāvāda),* harsh speech *(pāruṣyavacana),* malicious speech *(paiśunyavacana),* idle chatter *(sambhinnapralāpa),* covetousness *(abhidhyā),* ill will *(vyāpāda),* and wrong views *(mithyādṛṣṭi).*

tenfold path of virtuous actions (daśakuśalakarmapatha). To abstain from the tenfold path of evil actions.

ten powers (daśabala). Powers by which a buddha exercizes his influence. They are the power from knowing what is possible and impossible *(sthānāsthānajñānabalam),* the power from knowing the results of actions *(karmavipākajñānabalam),* the power from knowing various inclinations [of living beings] *(nānādhimuktijñānabalam),* the power from knowing [the world with its] various elements *(nānādhātujñānabalam),* the power from knowing the superiority and inferiority of the faculties [of living beings] *(indriyavarāvarajñānabalam),* the power from knowing courses of conduct that lead to all destinations *(sarvatragāmanīpratipattijñānabalam),* the power from knowing the defilement, cleansing, and emergence of contemplations, liberations, meditative concentrations, and attainments *(sarvadhyānavimokṣasamādhisamāpattisaṅkleśavyavadānavyutthānajñānabalam),* the power from remembering past lives *(pūrvanivāsānusmṛtijñānabalam),* the power from knowing the passing away and rebirth [of living beings] *(cyutyutpattijñānabalam),* the power of the destruction of the corruptions *(āśravakṣayabalam)*. For a slightly different list, with helpful glosses, see *Majjhima-nikāya* i, 69–70; trans. in Ñāṇamoli and Bodhi 1995: 166.

thirty-two marks of a great man (dvātriṃśat mahāpuruṣalakṣaṇa). The primary characteristics of a great man. According to the *Lakkaṇa-sutta* in the *Dīgha-nikāya* (iii, 143–45; following trans. in Walshe 1987: 441–42), these are—

> [1] He has feet with level tread. This is one of the marks of a great man. [2] On the soles of his feet are wheels with a thousand spokes, complete with felloe and hub. [3] He has projecting heels. [4] He has long fingers and toes. [5] He has soft and tender hands and feet. [6] His hands and feet are net-like. [7] He has high-raised ankles. [8] His legs are like an antelope's. [9] Standing and without bending, he can touch and rub his knees with either hand. [10] His male organ is enclosed in a sheath. [11] His complexion is bright, the colour of gold. [12] His skin is delicate and so smooth that no dust can adhere to his body. [13] His body-hairs are separate, one to each pore. [14] His body-hairs grow upwards, each one bluish-black like collyrium, curling in rings to the right. [15] His body is divinely straight. [16] He has the seven convex surfaces. [17] The front part of his body is like a lion's. [18] There is no hollow between his shoulders. [19] He is proportioned like a banyan-tree: the height of his body is the same as the span of his outstretched arms, and conversely. [20] His bust is evenly rounded. [21] He has a perfect sense of taste. [22] He has jaws like a lion's. [23] He has forty teeth. [24] His teeth are even. [25] There are no spaces between his teeth. [26] His canine teeth are very bright. [27] His tongue is very long. [28] He has a Brahmā-like voice, like that of the *karavīka*-bird. [29] His eyes are deep blue. [30] He has eyelashes like a cow's. [31] The hair between his eyes is white and soft like cotton-down. [32] His head is like a royal turban.

three jewels (triratna). The Buddha, the dharma, and the monastic community.

three kinds of objects for self-control (trividhadamathavastu). See *three objects for self-control*.

three objects for self-control (tridamathavastu). Presumably these are body, speech, and mind.

three realms (traidhātuka). See *three worlds.*

three refuges (triśaraṇa). According to the Buddhist formula for ordination, one takes refuge in the Buddha, the dharma, and the community.

three special applications of mindfulness (trīṇyāveṇikāni smṛtyupasthānāni). The establishing of one's attention in three ways. Being equanimous when others are being attentive *(śuśrūṣamāṇeṣu samacittatā),* being equanimous when others are being inattentive *(aśuśrūṣamāṇeṣu samacittatā),* being equanimous when others are being attentive and inattentive *(śuśrūṣamāṇāśuśrūṣamāṇeṣu samacittatā).*

three worlds (triloka). The three levels of existence in a world-system such as our own. These are the realms of desire *(kāma),* form *(rūpa),* and formlessness *(ārūpya).* The Buddha is said to be the teacher of the three worlds.

tolerance stages (kṣānti). See *four stages of penetrating insight.*

tranquility (śamatha). A type of meditation that aims at the development of concentration and leads to the attainment of magical powers.

truth. See *four noble truths.*

tūla. A kind of cotton.

udumbara. Ficus glomerata. This form of fig tree is said to bloom very rarely, and hence its blossoming is a metaphor for the rarity of the arising of a buddha. In fact, the tree doesn't produce flowers at all; its sprouts turn directly into fruit.

unsurpassed perfect awakening (anuttarasamyaksambuddha). The complete awakening of a buddha.

Upananda. See *group of six monks.*

upoṣadha. Fortnightly periods of observance, on the days of the new and full moon. Lay people are enjoined to observe additional precepts, further restricting sexual and sensual activities. Monastic communities convene to recite the disciplinary code, confess any offenses that may have been committed, and expound the dharma.

uṣṇīṣa. A protuberance on top of a buddha's head that makes it appear to be turbanned. This is the last of the thirty-two marks of a great man. It may also be taken to mean "turban" more literally, as it is one of the five royal insignia that King Bimbisāra removes before approaching the Buddha (Divy 147.11–14).

vallaka. A kind of aquatic animal or monster.

vallikī. A kind of lute.

victor (jina). An epithet of a buddha.

view of individuality (satkāyadṛṣṭi). The false belief that an individual really exists. For more, see Collins 1982: 93–94, 132–33.

vīṇā. A kind of lute.

virtues of the purified (dhūtaguṇa). A code of twelve ascetic practices. They are wearing dirty rags *(pāṃśukūlika)*, wearing the three monastic robes *(traicīvarika)*, wearing garments of felt (or wool) *(nāmantika)*, living on almsfood *(paiṇḍapātika)*, eating in a single place *(aikāsanika)*, not eating after the appropriate time *(khalu-paścād-bhaktika)*, living in the forest *(āraṇyaka)*, living at the foot of a tree *(vṛkṣamūlika)*, living in the open air *(ābhyavakāśika)*, living in cremation grounds *(śmāśānika)*, always sitting and not lying down *(naiṣadika)*, and accepting any seat that is offered *(yāthāsaṃstarika)*. For more, see Ray 1994: 293–323.

Viśvakarman. The chief architect, designer, and decorator of the gods who lives in Trāyastriṃśa heaven.

wheel turner. See *wheel-turning king*.

wheel-turning king (cakravartin). One who uses the seven treasures to conquer the four corners of the earth and rule an entire world-system.

yakṣa. Minor deities who possess magical powers and are associated with forests. Often depicted in the *Divyāvadāna* as helping Buddhist practitioners. Kubera (= Vaiśravaṇa, Dhanada), one of the four great kings, is their lord.

Bibliography

Abhidharmakośa and *Abhidharmakośabhāṣya* of Vasubandhu.
Edition. See Dwarikadas Sastri 1987.
Translations. See La Vallée Poussin 1971 and 1988–90.

Agniveśa. See *Carakasaṃhita.*

Agrawala, Vasudeva S. 1964. "Brief Communication: A Note on the Word cārikā in the Divyāvadāna." *Journal of the American Oriental Society* 84 (1): 55–56.

______. 1965. *Indian Art: A History of Indian Art from the Earliest Times up to the Third Century A. D.* Varanasi: Prithivi Prakashan.

______. 1966. "Some Obscure Words in the Divyāvadāna." *Journal of the American Oriental Society* 86 (2): 67–75.

______. 1970. *Ancient Indian Folk Cults.* Varanasi: Prithivi Prakashan.

Ali, Agha Shahid. 1997. *The Country without a Post Office.* New York: Norton.

Allon, Mark, with a contribution by Andrew Glass. 2001. *Three Gāndhārī Ekottarikāgama-Type Sūtras.* British Library Kharoṣṭhī Fragments 12 and 14. Seattle and London: University of Washington Press.

Alter, Robert. 1981. *The Art of Biblical Narrative.* New York: Basic Books.

Andersen, Dines, and Helmer Smith, eds. 1965. *Suttanipāta.* London: Pali Text Society.

Aṅguttara-nikāya.
Edition. See Morris and Hardy 1885–1900.
Translation. See Woodward and Hare 1932–36.

Apte, Vaman Shivaram. 1986. *The Practical Sanskrit-English Dictionary, Revised and Enlarged Edition.* Kyoto: Rinzen Book Company.

Arthaśāstra of Kauṭilya.
Edition. See T. Gaṇapati Sastri 1990.
Translation. See Kangle 1972.
Aśokāvadāna.
Edition. See Mukhopadhaya 1963.
Translation. See Strong 1989.
Avadānakalpalatā of Kṣemendra.
Edition. See Das and Vidyabhushana 1888.
Edition. See Vaidya 1959b.
Avadānaśataka.
Edition. See Speyer 1992.
Edition. See Vaidya 1958.
Translation. See Feer 1891.

Banerjee, Anukul Chandra. 1979 (1957). *Sarvāstivāda Literature.* Calcutta: The World Press Private Limited.

______. 1994. "The Sarvāstivāda School of Buddhist Thought." In Sanghasen Singh, ed. *Sarvāstivāda and Its Tradition*, pp. 1–14. Delhi: Department of Buddhist Studies, Delhi University.

Bapat, P. V. 1949. "Another Valuable Collection of Buddhist Sanskrit Manuscripts." *Annals of the Bhandarkar Oriental Research Institute* 30: 241–45.

______. 1953. "Four Auspicious Things of the Buddhists: śrīvatsā, svastika, nandyāvarta and vardhamāna." In B. G. Gokhale, ed. *Indica: The Indian Historical Research Institute Silver Jubilee Commemoration Volume*, pp. 38–46. Bombay: Examiner Press.

Bareau, André. 1962. "La construction et le culte des stūpa d'après les Vinayapiṭaka." *Bulletin de l'ecole Française d'Extrême-Orient* 50: 229–74.

Basham, A. L. 1951. *History and Doctrine of the Ājīvakas: A Vanished Indian Religion*. London: Luzac.

Baums, Stephan. 2002. "Jyotiṣkāvadāna." In Jens Braarvig, ed. *Buddhist Manuscripts, vol. 2*, pp. 287–302. Manuscripts in the Schøyen Collection, III. Oslo: Hermes Publishing.

Bendall, Cecil. ed. 1897–1902. *Śikṣāsamuccaya.* Biblioteca Buddhica, 1. St. Petersburg: Académie impériale des sciences.

Bendall, Cecil and W. H. D Rouse, trans. 1971 (1922) *Śikṣāsamuccaya: A Compendium of Buddhist Doctrine.* Delhi: Motilal Banarsidass.

Bloomfield, Maurice. 1920. "Notes on the Divyāvadāna." *Journal of the American Oriental Society* 40: 336–52.

Bodhi, Bhikkhu, trans. 1978. *The Discourse on the All-Embracing Net of View: The Brahmajāla Sutta and Its Commentarial Exegesis*. Kandy, Sri Lanka: Buddhist Publication Society.

______, trans. 2000. *The Connected Discourses of the Buddha: A Translation of the Saṃyutta Nikāya*. 2 volumes. Boston: Wisdom Publications.

Bongard-Levin, G. M. 1971. "The Historicity of the Ancient Indian Avadānas: A Legend about Aśoka's Deposition and the Queen's Edict." In *Studies in Ancient India and Central Asia*, pp. 123–41. Soviet Indology Series, no. 7. Calcutta: Indian Studies Past and Present.

Bongard-Levin, G. M., and O. F. Volkova. 1965. *The Kunāla Legend and an Unpublished Aśokāvadānamālā Manuscript*. Calcutta: Indian Studies Past and Present.

Borromeo, Alberto. 1992. "Il Prabhāsa-Avadāna a Kizil." *Rivista Degli Studi Orientali* 66 (1–2): 59–78.

Brown, Norman, trans. 1921. *Buddhist Legends Translated from the Original Pali Text of the Dhammapada Commentary (Dhammapada-aṭṭhakathā)*. 3 volumes. Harvard Oriental Series, vols. 28–30. Cambridge: Harvard University Press.

Buddhaghosa. See *Visuddhimagga*.

Burlingame, Eugene Watson, trans. 1921. *Buddhist Legends Translated from the Original Pali Text of the Dhammapada Commentary (Dhammapada-aṭṭhakathā)*. 3 volumes. Harvard Oriental Series, vols. 28–30. Cambridge: Harvard University Press.

Burnouf, Eugène. 1844. *Introduction a l'histoire du buddhisme indien*, vol. 1. Paris: Imprimerie Royale.

Carakasaṃhita of Agniveśa.

Edition and translation. See Sharma and Dash 1977.

Carter, James Ross, and Mahinda Palihawadana, eds. and trans. 1987. *The Dhammapada*. Oxford: Oxford University Press.

Chakravarti, Uma. 1987. *The Social Dimensions of Early Buddhism*. Delhi: Oxford University Press.

Chāndogya Upaniṣad.

Edition and translation. See Gambhirananda 1992.

Translation. See Olivelle 1998.

Chandra, Lokesh. 2001. *Tibetan-Sanskrit Dictionary*. New Delhi: International Academy of Indian Culture and Aditya Prakashan.

Chaudhuri, Amit. 1997. "Sandeep's Visit." In Salman Rushdie and Elizabeth West, eds. *The Vintage Book of Indian Writing, 1947–1997*, pp. 379–408. London: Vintage.

Chavannes, Édouard, trans. 1910–34. *Cinq cents contes et apologues du Tripiṭaka chinois*. 4 volumes. Paris: E. Leroux.

Ch'en, Kenneth K. S. 1945–47. "A Study of the Svāgata Story in the *Divyāvadāna* in Its Sanskrit, Pali, Tibetan and Chinese Versions." *Harvard Journal of Asiatic Studies* 9: 207–314.

______. 1953. "Apropos the Meṇḍhaka Story." *Harvard Journal of Asiatic Studies* 16: 374–403.

Clarke, Shayne. 2006. "Miscellaneous Musings on Mūlasarvāstivāda Monks: The *Mūlasarvāstivāda Vinaya* Revival in Tokugawa Japan." *Japanese Journal of Religious Studies* 33 (1): 1–49.

Collins, Steven. 1982. *Selfless Persons: Imagery and Thought in Therāvāda Buddhism*. Cambridge: Cambridge University Press.

______. 1998. *Nirvana and Other Buddhist Felicities*. Cambridge: Cambridge University Press.

Coomaraswamy, Ananda. 1928. "Indian Architectural Terms." *Journal of the American Oriental Society* 48: 250–75.

______. 1939. "Some Pali Words." *Harvard Journal of Asiatic Studies* 4 (2): 116–90.

______. 1995. *Essays in Architectural Theory*. Edited with an introduction by Michael W. Meister. New Delhi: Indira Gandhi National Centre for the Arts. Delhi: Oxford University Press.

Cort, John E. 1999. "The Gift of Food to a Wandering Cow: Lay-Mendicant Interaction among the Jains." *Journal of the Association of Asian Studies* 34 (1): 89–110.

Cowell, E. B., and R. A. Neil, eds. 1886. *Divyāvadāna*. Cambridge: The University Press.

Cowell, E. B., Robert Chalmers, W. H. D. Rouse, Henry Thomas Francis, and Robert Alexander Neil, trans. 1990 (1895). *The Jātaka*. Delhi: Motilal Banarsidass.

Cunningham, Alexander. 1879. *The Stupa of Bharhut*. London: W. H. Allen and Company.

Das, Sarat Chandra, and Hari Mohan Vidyabhushana, eds. 1888. *Avadānakalpalatā*. Calcutta: Bibliotheca Indica, New Series.

Davidson, Ronald. 1990. "An Introduction of the Standards of Scriptural Authority in Indian Buddhism." In R. E. Buswell, ed. *Chinese Buddhist Apocrypha*, pp. 291–325. Honolulu: University of Hawai'i Press.

De, S. K. 1959. *Some Problems of Sanskrit Poetics*. Calcutta: Firma K. L. Mukhopadhyay.

Dehejia, Vidya. 1972. *Early Buddhist Rock Temples: A Chronological Study*. London: Thames and Hudson.

Dhadphale, M. G. 1980. *Synonymic Collocations in the Tipiṭaka: A Study*. Poona: Bhandarkar Oriental Research Institute.

Dhammapada.

Edition and Translation. See Carter and Palihawadana 1987.

Dhammapada-aṭṭhakathā.

Edition. See H. C. Norman 1906–14.

Translation. See Burlingame 1921.

Dīghanikāya.

Edition. See Rhys Davids and Carpenter 1890–1911.

Translation. See Rhys Davids 1899 and Walshe 1987.

Dimitrov, Dragomir. 2007. "Some Remarks on the *Rūpyāvatyavadāna* of the *Divyāvadāna(mālā)*." In Dragomir Dimitrov, Michael Hahn, and Roland Steiner, eds. *Bauddhasāhityastabakāvalī: Essays and Studies on Buddhist Sanskrit Literature*. Indica et Tibetica, 36. Marburg: Indica et Tibetica Verlag.

Divyāvadāna.

Edition. See Cowell and Neil 1886.

Edition. See Vaidya 1959a.

Edition and translation of stories 1, 2, etc. See Tatelman 2005.

Translation and study of story 2. See Tatelman 2000.

Translation of all or parts of stories 2, 10, 12, 17, etc. See Burnouf 1844.

Study of stories 9 and 10. See Ch'en 1953.

Translation (from the Chinese) and study of story 13. See Ch'en 1945–47.

Translation of story 14. See Ware 1928.

Translation of part of story 17. See Schiefner 1988.

Doniger, Wendy. 1998. *The Implied Spider: Politics and Theology in Myth.* New York: Columbia University Press.

Dreyfus, Georges B. J. 2003. *The Sound of Two Hands Clapping: The Education of a Tibetan Buddhist Monk.* Berkeley and Los Angeles: University of California Press.

Dutt, Nalinaksha. 1930. *Aspects of Mahāyāna Buddhism and Its Relation to Hīnayāna.* London: Luzac & Company.

______. 1940. "The Place of Faith in Buddhism." *Indian Historical Quarterly* 16: 639–49.

______, ed. 1984 (1950). *Gilgit Manuscripts.* 4 volumes. Delhi: Sri Satguru Publications.

______. 1987 (1970). *Buddhist Sects in India.* Delhi: Motilal Banarsidass.

Edgerton, Franklin. 1993 (1953). *Buddhist Hybrid Sanskrit Grammar and Dictionary.* 2 volumes. Delhi: Motilal Banarsidass.

Ellis, William Ashton, trans. 1966 (1813–83). *Richard Wagner's Prose Works.* 8 volumes. New York: Broude Brothers.

Fausbøll, V., ed. 1877–96. *The Jātaka Together with Its Commentary.* 6 volumes. London: Trübner and Co.

Feer, Léon, ed. 1884–98. *Saṃyutta-nikāya.* 5 volumes. London: Pali Text Society.

______, trans. 1891. *Avadana-Çataka: cent légends (bouddhiques).* Annales du Musée Guimet, vol. 18. Paris: E. Leroux.

Frauwallner, Erich 1956. *The Earliest Vinaya and the Beginnings of Buddhist Literature.* L. Petech, trans. Roma: Istituto Italiano per il Medio ed Estremo Oriente.

Gambhirananda, Swami, ed. and trans. 1992. *Chāndogya Upaniṣad, with the Commentary of Śri Śaṅkarācārya.* Calcutta: Advaita Ashrama.

Gernet, Jacques. 1995. *Buddhism and Chinese Society: An Economic History from the Fifth to the Tenth Centuries.* Franciscus Verellen, trans. New York: Columbia University Press.

Gethin, Rupert. 1992. *The Buddhist Path to Awakening: A Study of the Bodhi-Pakkhiyā Dhammā.* Leiden, The Netherlands: E. J. Brill.

______. 1998. *The Foundations of Buddhism.* Oxford and New York: Oxford University Press.

Giest, William E. 1987. "You Can Call It Ray's, but Expect a Lawsuit to Go: A Journey into the Heart of a Pizza Success Turns Up No Real Ray." *New York Times,* 2 May 1987.

Ginzburg, Carlo. 1980. "Clues: Morelli, Freud and Sherlock Holmes: Clues and Scientific Method." *History Workshop* (9): 5–36.

Gnoli, Raniero, ed. 1977–78. *The Gilgit Manuscript of the Saṅghabhedavastu*. 2 volumes. Roma: Istituto Italiano per il Medio ed Estremo Oriente.

Gombrich, Richard F. 1996. *How Buddhism Began: The Conditioned Genesis of the Early Teachings*. School of Oriental and African Studies: Jordan Lectures in Comparative Religion XVII. London and Atlantic Highlands, NJ: Athlone Press.

Gomez, Luis. O. 1996. *Land of Bliss: The Paradise of the Buddha of Measureless Light (Sanskrit and Chinese Version of the Sukhāvatīvyūha Sutras)*. Honolulu: University of Hawai'i Press; Kyoto, Japan: Higashi Honganji Shinshū Ōtani-ha.

Grey, Leslie. 2000. *A Concordance of Buddhist Birth Stories*. Third edition. Oxford: Pali Text Society.

Griffiths, Paul J. 1981. "Buddhist Hybrid English: Some Notes on Philology and Hermeneutics for Buddhologists." *Journal of the International Association of Buddhist Studies* 4 (2): 7–32.

______. 1994. *On Being Buddha: The Classical Doctrine of Buddhahood*. Delhi: Sri Satguru Publications.

Gyani, R. G. 1951. "Identification of the So-Called Sūrya and Indra Figures in Cave no. 20 of the Bhājā Group." *Bulletin of the Prince of Wales Museum of Western India* 1: 15–21.

Hahn, Michael. 1992. *Haribhaṭṭa and Gopadatta. Two Authors in the Succession of Āryaśūra. On the Rediscovery of Parts of their Jātakamālās*. Studia Philologica Buddhica. Occasional Papers Series I. Second edition. Tokyo: The Reiyukai Library.

Handurukande, Ratna, ed. 1967. *Maṇicūḍāvadāna* and *Lokānanda*. Sacred Books of the Buddhists, vol. 24. London: Luzac and Co.

______. 1970. "The Story of the Shell Maidens." In J. Tilakasiri. ed. *Añjali: A Felicitation Volume Presented to Oliver Hector DeAlwis Wijesekera*, pp. 46–49. Peradeniya: University of Ceylon.

______. 1976. "A Propos Kṛkin's Daughters." In Oliver Hector DeAlwis Wijesekera, ed. *Malalasekera Commemoration Volume*, pp. 116–27. Colombo: Malalasekera Commemoration.

______. 1978. "The Benefit of Caitya Worship." In Leelananda Prematilleke, Karthigesu Indrapala, and J. E. Van Lohuizen-De Leeuw, eds. *Senarat Paranavitana Commemoration Volume*, pp. 75–77. Leiden: E. J. Brill.

______, ed. 1988. *The Supriyasārthavāhajātaka*. Indica et Tibetica, 15. Bonn.

Hardy, R. Spence. 1880. *Manual of Buddhism*. London: Williams and Norgate.

Hartmann, Jens-Uwe. 1980. "Notes on the Gilgit Manuscript of the *Candraprabhāvadāna*." *Journal of the Nepal Research Centre* 4: 251–66.

______. 1985. "Zur Frage der Schulzugehörigkeit des Avadānaśataka." In Heinz Bechert, ed. *Zur Schulzugehörigkeit von Werken der Hīnayāna Literatur*, pp. 219–26. Göttingen: Vandenhoeck & Ruprecht.

Hirakawa, Akira. 1990. *A History of Indian Buddhism: From Śākyamuni to Early Mahāyāna*. Paul Groner, trans. and ed. Asian Studies at Hawai'i, no. 36. Honolulu: University of Hawai'i Press.

Hiraoka, Satoshi. 1998. "The Relation between the *Divyāvadāna* and the *Mūlasarvāstivāda Vinaya*." *Journal of Indian Philosophy* 26: 1–16.

Hofinger, Marcel, ed. and trans. 1982 (1954). *Le Congres du lac Anavatapta (Vies de Saintes Bouddhiques): Extrait du Vinaya des Mūlasarvāstivāda Bhaiṣajyavastu*, vol. 1: *Légendes des Anciens (Sthavirāvadāna)*. Louvain-la-Neuve: Institut orientaliste.

Horner, I. B., trans. 1938–66. *The Book of Discipline (Vinaya-piṭaka)*. 6 volumes. London: Pali Text Society.

______, trans. 1969 (1963). *Milinda's Questions (Milindapañha)*. 2 volumes. London: Pali Text Society.

Huber, Edouard 1904. "Études de Littérature Bouddhique." *Bulletin de l'Ecole Française d'Extrême-Orient* 4: 698–726.

______. 1906. "Les sources du Divyāvadāna." *Bulletin de l'Ecole Française d'Extrême-Orient* 6: 1–43, 335–40.

Hult, David. 1991. "Reading it Right: The Ideology of Text Editing." In Marina S. Brownlee, Kevin Brownlee, and Stephen G. Nichols, eds. *The New Medievalism*, pp. 113–30. Baltimore and London: The Johns Hopkins University Press.

Ishihama, Yumiko and Yoichi Fukuda, eds. 1989. *A New Critical Edition of the Mahavyutpatti: Sanskrit-Tibetan-Mongolian Dictionary of Buddhist Terminology*. Tokyo: Toyo Bunko.

Iwamoto, Yutaka, ed. and trans. 1968. *Sumāgadhāvadāna*. Kyoto: Hozokan-Verlag.

______. 1978. *Bukkyō setsuwa kenyū josetsu [An Introduction to the Study of Buddhist Legends]*. Tokyo: Kaimei Shoin.

Jaini, Padmanabh S. 1989. "Political and Cultural Data in References to Mathurā in the Buddhist Literature." In Doris Meth Srinivasan, ed. *Mathurā: The Cultural Heritage*, pp. 214–22. New Delhi: Manohar Publications.

______. 2001. *Collected Papers on Buddhist Studies*. Delhi: Motilal Banarsidass.

Jäschke, H. A. 1987 (1881). *A Tibetan-English Dictionary*. Delhi: Motilal Banarsidass.

Jātaka.

Edition. See Fausbøll 1877–96.

Translation. See Cowell et al. 1990.

Jones, J. J., trans. 1976 (1949–1956). *Mahāvastu Avadāna*. 3 volumes. London: Luzac and Company, Ltd.

Jorgensen, Hans, ed. and trans. 1931. *Vicitrakarṇikāvadānoddhṛta: A Collection of Buddhistic Legends*. London: Royal Asiatic Society.

Kangle, R. P. 1972 (1963). *The Kauṭilīya Arthaśāstra*. 3 volumes. Bombay: University of Bombay.

Kauṭilya. See *Arthaśāstra*.

Khoroche, Peter, trans. 1989. *Once the Buddha Was a Monkey: Ārya Śūra's* Jātakamālā. University of Chicago Press.

Klaus, Konrad, ed. and trans. 1983. *Das Maitrakanyakāvadāna (Divyāvadāna 38): Sanskrittext und deutsche Übersetzung*. Bonn: Indica et Tibetica Verlag.

Kloetzli, W. Randolph. 1997 (1983). *Buddhist Cosmology: Science and Theology in the Images of Motion and Light*. Delhi: Motilal Banarsidass.

Kongtrul Lodrö Tayé (Kong sprul Blo gros mtha' yas). 1995. *Myriad Worlds: Buddhist Cosmology in Abhidharma, Kālacakra, and Dzog-chen* [Selections from *Shes bya mtha' yas pa'i rgya mtsho*]. Ithaca, NY: Snow Lion Publications.

Kṣemendra. See *Avadānakalpalatā*.

Laidlaw, James. 1995. *Riches and Renunciation: Religion, Economy, and Society among the Jains*. New York: Oxford University Press.

Lamotte, Étienne, trans. and ed. 1944. *Le traité de la grande vertu de sagesse de Nāgārjuna (Mahāprajñāpāramitāśāstra)*, vol. 1. Louvain: Bureaux du Muséon.

______. 1988. *History of Indian Buddhism from the Origins to the Śaka Era*. Sara Webb-Boin, trans. Louvain-la-Neuve: Institut Orientaliste. Original French edition published in Louvain, 1958.

La Vallée Poussin, Louis de. 1989. "A Summary Note on the Path." In La Vallée Poussin 1988–90, vol. 3, pp. xiv–xxii.

______, trans. 1988–90. *Abhidharmakośabhāṣyam*. Translated from the French by Leo M. Pruden. 4 volumes. Berkeley, CA: Asian Humanities Press.

______, trans. 1971 (1923–31). *L'Abhidharmakośa de Vasubandhu: traduction et annotations*. 6 volumes. Brussells: Institut Belge des Hautes Études Chinoises.

Law, Bimala Churn. 1976. *Historical Geography of Ancient India*. Delhi: Ess Ess Publications.

Law, Narendra Nath. 1925. *Studies in Indian History and Culture*. London: Luzac and Company.

Lenz, Timothy. 2003. *A New Version of the Gāndhārī Dharmapada and a Collection of Previous-Birth Stories: British Library Kharoṣṭhī Fragments 16 + 25*. Contributions by Andrew Glass and Bhikshu Dharmamitra. Gandhāran Buddhist Texts Series, vol. 3. Seattle and London: University of Washington Press.

Lévi, Sylvain. 1907. "Les éléments de formation du Divyāvadāna." *T'oung Pao* 8: 105–22.

______. 1915. "Sur la récitation primitive des textes bouddhiques." *Journal Asiatique* 5: 401–47.

______. 1932. "Note sur des manuscrits Sanscrits provenant de Bamiyan (Afghanistan), et de Gilgit (Cachemire)." *Journal Asiatique* 220: 1–45.

Lewis, Todd. 2000. *Popular Buddhist Texts from Nepal: Narratives and Rituals of Newar Buddhism*. Translations in collaboration with Subarna Man Tuladhar and Labh Ratna Tuladhar. Albany: State University of New York Press.

Lienhard, Siegfried, ed. 1963. *Maṇicūḍāvadānoddhṛta: A Buddhist Rebirth Story in the Nevārī Language*. Stockholm: Almqvist & Wiksell.

Lüders, Heinrich, ed. 1926. *Bruchstücke der Kalpanāmaṇḍitikā des Kumāralāta*. Kleinere Sanskrit-texte aus den Turfanfunden, no. 2. Leipzig: Deutsche Morganelandische Gesellschaft.

Mahāparinirvāṇasūtra.

Edition and Translation. See Waldschmidt 1951.

Mahāvastu Avadāna.

Edition. See Senart 1977.

Translation. See Jones 1949.

Mahāvyutpatti.
Edition. See Ishihama and Fukuda 1989.
Majjhima-nikāya.
Edition. See Trenckner and Chalmers 1888–89.
Translation. See Ñāṇamoli and Bodhi 1995.
Malalasekera, G. P. 1995 (1938). *Dictionary of Pali Proper Names.* 2 volumes. New Delhi: Munshiram Manoharlal Publishers.
Malamoud, Charles. 2003. "Remarks on Dissuasion in Ancient India." In Denis Vidal, Gilles Tarabout, and Āric Meyer, eds. *Violence/Non-Violence: Some Hindu Perspectives*, pp. 209–18. First published in French in 1994. Delhi: Manohar Publications.
Manorathapūraṇī.
Edition. See Walleser and Kopp 1924–57.
Masefield, Peter, trans. 1994. *The Udāna.* 2 volumes. Oxford: Pali Text Society.
______, trans. 1994a. *The Udāna-aṭṭhakathā.* Oxford: Pali Text Society.
Meech-Pekarik, Julia. 1982. "The Flying White Horse: Transmission of the *Valahassa Jataka* Imagery from India to Japan." *Artibus Artisae* 43 (1–2): 111–28.
Meister, Michael W. 1988–89. "Prāsāda as Palace: Kūṭina Origins of the Nāgara Temple." *Artibus Asiae* 49 (3/4): 254–80.
Milindapañha.
Edition. See Trenckner 1880.
Translation. See Horner 1969.
Mirashi, Vasudev Vishnu. 1981. *The History and Inscriptions of the Sātavāhanas and the Western Kshatrapas.* Bombay: Maharashtra State Board for Literature and Culture.
Mitra, Rajendralal. 1981 (1882). *The Sanskrit Buddhist Literature of Nepal.* New Delhi: Cosmo Publications.
______. 1998 (1853–81). *The Lalita-Vistara: Memoirs of the Early Life of Sakya Sinha (Chs. 1–15).* Delhi: Sri Satguru Publications.
Monier-Williams, Monier. 1990 (1899). *A Sanskrit-English Dictionary.* Delhi: Motilal Banarsidass.
Moore, Lorrie. 1998. *Birds of America.* New York: Alfred Knopf.
Morris, R., and E. Hardy, eds. 1885–1900. *Aṅguttara-nikāya.* 5 volumes. London: Pali Text Society.
Mosley, Walter. 1998. *Blue Light.* Boston: Little, Brown, and Co.

Mrozik, Susanne Petra. 2006. "Materializations of Virtue: Buddhist Discourses on Bodies." In Ellen T. Armour and Susan M. St. Ville, eds. *Bodily Citations: Religion and Judith Butler*, pp. 15–47. New York: Columbia University Press.

Mukherjee, Biswadeb. 1984. "On the Relationship between the Sarvāstivāda Vinaya and the Mūlasarvāstivāda Vinaya." *Journal of Asian Studies (Madras)* 2 (1): 131–65.

Mukhopadhyaya, Sujitkumar. 1954. *Śārdūlakarṇāvadāna*. Edition. Santiniketan: Visvabharati.

______, ed. 1963. *The Aśokāvadāna: Sanskrit Text Compared with Chinese Versions*. New Delhi: Sahitya Akademi.

Ñāṇamoli, Bhikku, trans. 1979 (1956). *The Path of Purification (Visuddhimagga)*. Kandy: Buddhist Publication Society.

Ñāṇamoli, Bhikku, and Bhikkhu Bodhi, trans. 1995. *The Middle Length Discourses of the Buddha: A New Translation of the Majjhima Nikāya*. Boston: Wisdom Publications.

Nariman, G. K. 1923. *Literary History of Sanskrit Buddhism*. Bombay: Indian Book Depot.

Negi, J. S. 1993–. *Tibetan-Sanskrit Dictionary*. Sarnath, Varanasi: Dictionary Unit, Central Institute of Higher Tibetan Studies.

Nikam, N. A. and Richard McKeon, ed. and trans. 1959. *The Edicts of Aśoka*. Chicago: University of Chicago Press.

Norman, H. C., ed. 1906–14. *Dhammapada-aṭṭhakathā*. London: Pali Text Society.

Norman, K. R., trans. 1971. *The Elders' Verses II: Therīgāthā*. London: Pali Text Society.

______, trans. 1984. *The Group of Discourses (Sutta-nipāta)*. With alternative translations by I. B. Horner and Walpola Rahula. London: Pali Text Society.

______. 1983. "The Nine Treasures of a Cakravartin." *Indologica Taurinensia* 11: 183–93.

Ohnuma, Reiko. 1997. "Dehadāna: The 'Gift of the Body' in Indian Buddhist Narrative Literature." Ph.D. dissertation, University of Michigan at Ann Arbor.

______. 2007. *Head, Eyes, Flesh, and Blood: Giving Away the Body in Indian Buddhist Literature*. New York: Columbia University Press.

Oldenberg, H., ed. 1879–83. *Vinayapiṭaka*. London: Pali Text Society.

Olivelle, Patrick, ed. and trans. 1998. *The Early Upaniṣads: Annotated Text and Translation*. New York: Oxford University Press.

Osthoff, Wolfgang. 1996. *Richard Wagner's Buddha-Project "Die Sieger" ("The Victors"): Its Traces in the Ideas and Structures of "The Ring" and "Parsifal."* William Buchanan, trans. Zurich: Museum Rietberg. Original German edition published in 1983.

Panglung, Jampa Losang. 1981. *Die Erzählstoffe des Mūlasarvāstivāda-Vinaya Analysiert auf Grund der Tibetischen Übersetzung*. Tokyo: The Reiyukai Library.

Perera, H. R. 1966. "Apadāna." In G. P. Malalalasekera, ed. *Encyclopaedia of Buddhism*, vol. 2, pp. 2–3. Colombo: Govt. of Ceylon.

Pollock, Sheldon. 1985. "The Theory of Practice and the Practice of Theory in Indian Intellectual History." *Journal of the American Oriental Society* 105 (3): 499–519.

Prakash, Shyam. 1970. *Divyāvadān meṃ saṃskṛti ka svarūp [The Formation of Culture in the Divyāvadāna]*. Agra: Pragati Prakashan.

Prebish, Charles. 1975. *Buddhist Monastic Discipline: The Sanskrit Prātimokṣa Sūtras of the Mahāsaṃghikas and Mūlasarvāstivādins*. Delhi: Motilal Banarsidass.

Przyluski, J. 1914. "Le Nord-ouest de l'Inde dans le Vinaya des Mūlasarvāstivādin et les textes apparentés." *Journal Asiatique* 4: 493–568.

______. 1923. *La légende de l'empereur Aśoka (Aśoka-avadāna) dans les textes indiens et chinois*. Paris: P. Geuthner.

______. 1929. "Fables in the Vinaya-Piṭaka of the Sarvāstivādin School." *Indian Historical Quarterly* 5: 1–5.

Ramanujan, A. K. 1999. *The Collected Essays of A. K. Ramanujan*. Oxford: Oxford University Press.

Ratnamālāvadāna.
Edition. See Takahata 1954.

Ray, Himanshu Prabha. 1986. *Monastery and Guild: Commerce Under the Sātavāhanas*. Delhi: Oxford University Press.

Ray, Reginald. A. 1994. *Buddhist Saints in India: A Study in Buddhist Values and Orientations*. New York: Oxford University Press.

Rhi, Ju-hyung. 1991. "Gandharan Images of the 'Sravasti Miracle': An Iconographic Reassessment." Ph.D. dissertation, University of California–Berkeley.

Rhys Davids, T. W., trans. 1899. *Dialogues of the Buddha (Dīgha-nikāya)*, volume 1. London: Pali Text Society.

Rhys Davids, T. W. and J. E. Carpenter, eds. 1890–1911. *Dīgha-nikāya*. London: Pali Text Society.

Rhys Davids, T. W., J. E. Carpenter, and W. Stede, eds. 1886–1932. *Sumaṅgalavilāsinī*. London: Pali Text Society.

Rhys Davids, T. W., and H. Oldenberg, trans. 1987 (1882–85). *Vinaya Texts (Vinayapiṭaka)*. 3 volumes. Delhi: AVF Books.

Rhys Davids, T. W., and William Stede. 1986 (1921–25). *The Pali Text Society's Pali-English Dictionary*. London: Pali Text Society.

Rockhill, W. Woodville. 1972 (1884). *The Life of the Buddha and the Early History of His Order*. India: Orientalia Indica.

Rosenberg, Joel. 1975. "Meanings, Morals, and Mysteries: Literary Approaches to the Torah." *Response* 9 (2): 67–94.

Rotman, Andy. 2003a. "Monks, Merchants, and a Moral Economy: Visual Culture and the Practice of Faith in the *Divyāvadāna*." Ph.D. dissertation, University of Chicago.

______. 2003b. "The Erotics of Practice: Objects and Agency in Buddhist Avadāna Literature." *Journal of the American Academy of Religion* 71 (3): 555–78.

______. 2008. *Thus Have I Seen: Visualizing Faith in Early Indian Buddhism*. New York: Oxford University Press.

Roy, Sitaram, ed. and trans. 1971. *Suvarṇavarṇāvadāna*. Historical Research Series, vol. 7. Patna: K. P. Jayaswal Research Institute.

Rushdie, Salman. 1990. *Haroun and the Sea of Stories*. New York: Granta.

Salomon, Richard. 1999. *Ancient Buddhist Scrolls from Gandhāra: The British Library Kharoṣṭhī Fragments*. Seattle: University of Washington Press.

______. 2006. "Recent Discoveries of Early Buddhist Manuscripts and Their Implications for the History of Buddhist Texts and Canons." In Patrick Olivelle, ed. *Between the Empires: Society in India 300 B.C.E to 400 C.E.*, pp. 349–82. New York: Oxford University Press.

Saṃyutta-nikāya.

Edition. See Feer 1884–98.

Translation. See Bodhi 2000.

Sander, Lore. 1991. "The Earliest Manuscripts from Central Asia and the Sarvāstivāda Mission." In Ronald E. Emmerick and Dieter Weber, eds. *Corolla Iranica: Papers in Honour of Prof. Dr. David Neil MacKenzie on the Occasion of his 65th Birthday...*, pp. 135–50. Frankfurt am Main: Peter Lang.

Sangharakshita, Bhikṣu. 1967. *The Three Jewels*. London: Rider.

Śāntideva. See *Śikṣāsamuccaya*.

Śāntiśataka of Śilhaṇa Miśra.
Edition and translation. See Schönfeld 1910.

Sarkar, Sadhanchandra. 1981. *A Study on the Jātakas and the Avadānas: Critical and Comparative*, part 1. Calcutta: Sarkar and Sucharita Sengupta.

______. 1990. *Studies in the Common Jātaka and Avadāna Tales*. Calcutta: Sanskrit College.

Sastri, Nilakantha. 1945. *Gleanings on Social Life from the Avadānas*. Calcutta: Indian Research Institute Publication.

Sastri, Dwarikadas, ed. 1987. *Abhidharmakośa and Bhāṣya of Ācārya Vasubandhu with Sphuṭārthā Commentary of Ācārya Yaśomitra*. 2 volumes. Bauddha Bharati Series, nos. 5–8. Varanasi: Bauddha Bharati.

Sastri, T. Gaṇapati. 1990 (1924). *The Arthaśāstra of Kauṭalya*. Delhi: Bharatiya Vidya Prakashan.

Schiefner, F. Anton von. 1988 (1893). *Tibetan Tales*. Translated from the German by W. R. S. Ralston. Delhi: Sri Satguru Publications.

Schlingloff, Dieter. 1989. "Die Pūrṇa-Erzählung in Einer Kizil-Malerei." *Zentralasiatische Studien* 21: 180–95.

______. 1991. "Traditions of Indian Narrative Painting in Central Asia." In Gouriswar Bhattacharya, ed. *Akṣayanīvī: Essays Presented to Dr. Debala Mitra in Admiration of Her Scholarly Contributions*, pp. 163–69. Bibliotheca Indo-Buddhica, no. 88. Delhi: Sri Satguru Publications.

Schmithausen, Lambert. 1987. "Beiträge zur Schulzugehörigkeit und Textgexchichte kanonischer und postkanonischer buddhistischer Materialien." In Heinz Bechert, ed. *Zur Schulzugehörigkeit von Werken der Hīnayāna-Literature*, vol. 2, pp. 305–406. Gottingen: Vendenhoeck and Ruprecht.

Schönfeld, Karl, ed. and trans. 1910. *Das Śāntiśataka: mit einleitung, kritischem apparat, übersetzung und anmerkungen*. Leipzig: O. Harrassowitz.

Schopen, Gregory. 1994a. "Doing Business for the Lord: Lending on Interest and Written Loan Contracts in the Mūlasarvāstivāda-vinaya." *Journal of the American Oriental Society* 114 (4): 527–54.

______. 1994b. "Ritual Rights and Bones of Contention: More on Monastic Funerals and Relics in the Mūlasarvāstivāda-vinaya." *Journal of Indian Philosophy* 22: 31–80.

______. 1995. "Monastic Law Meets the Real World: A Monk's Continuing Right to Inherit Property in Classical India." *History of Religions* 35 (2): 101–23.

______. 1996. "The Lay Ownership of Monasteries and the Role of the Monk in Mūlasārvāstivādin Monasticism." *Journal of the International Association of Buddhist Studies* 19 (1): 81–126.

______. 1997. *Bones, Stones, and Buddhist Monks: Collected Papers on the Archaeology, Epigraphy, and Texts of Monastic Buddhism in India*. Honolulu: University of Hawai'i Press.

______. 2000. "Hierarchy and Housing in a Buddhist Monastic Code: A Translation of the Sanskrit Text of the Sayanāsanavastu of the Mulasarvastivāda-vinaya. Part One." *Buddhist Literature* 2: 96–196.

______. 2004. *Buddhist Monks and Business Matters: Still More Papers on Monastic Buddhism in India*. Honolulu: University of Hawai'i Press.

Senart, Emile, ed. 1977 (1882–97). *Le Mahāvastu: texte sanscrit publié, pour la première fois et accompagné d'introductions et d'un commentaire*. 3 volumes. Tokyo: Meicho-Fukyu-Kai.

Shackleton Bailey, D. R. 1950. "Notes on the *Divyāvadāna*, part 1." *Journal of the Royal Asiatic Society:* 161–84.

______. 1951. "Notes on the *Divyāvadāna*, part 2." *Journal of the Royal Asiatic Society:* 82–102.

Sharma, Ram Karan, and Bhagwan Dash, trans. 1977. *Agniveśa's Carakasaṃhita: Text with English Translation and Critical Exposition Based on Cakrapāṇi Datta's Āyurveda Dīpikā*. 2 volumes. Varanasi: Chowkhamba Sanskrit Series Office.

Sharma, Sharmistha. 1975. "Meaning, Origin and the Development of the Avadānas." *Buddhist Studies* (Journal of the Department of Buddhist Studies, University of Delhi) 2: 28–33.

______. 1985. *Buddhist Avadanas: Socio-Political Economic and Cultural Study*. Delhi: Eastern Book Linkers.

______. 1992. *Astrological Lore in the Buddhist Śārdūlakarṇāvadāna*. Delhi: Eastern Book Linkers.

Śikṣāsamuccaya of Śāntideva.

Edition. See Bendall 1897–1902.

Translation. See Bendall and Rouse 1971.

Śilhaṇa Miśra. See *Śāntiśataka*.

Sivaramamurti, C. 1942. *Amaravati Sculptures in the Madras Government Museum*. Madras: Government Press.

Skilling, Peter. 1994. *Mahāsūtras: Great Discourses of the Buddha: Critical Editions of the Tibetan Mahāsūtras with Pali and Sanskrit Counterparts as Available*. Oxford: Pali Text Society.

Speyer, J. S. 1902. "Critical Remarks on the Text Divyāvadāna." *Wiener Zeitschrift fuhr die Kunde des Morgänlandes* 16: 103–30, 340–61.

______ . 1992 (1902–6). *Avadānaśataka: A Century of Edifying Tales Belonging to the Hīnayāna*. 2 volumes. Bibliotheca Buddhica, vol. 3. Delhi: Motilal Banarsidass.

Steinthal, P., ed. 1885. *Udāna*. London: Pali Text Society.

Strong, John. 1985. "The Buddhist Avadānists and the Elder Upagupta." In Michel Strickmann, ed. *Tantric and Taoist Studies in Honour of R. A. Stein. Mélanges chinois et bouddhiques* 22 (3): 862–81. Brussels.

______ , trans. 1989 (1983). *The Legend of King Aśoka (Aśokāvadāna)*. Princeton: Princeton University Press.

______ . 1992. *The Legend and Cult of Upagupta: Sanskrit Buddhism in North India and Southeast Asia*. Princeton: Princeton University Press.

______ . 1999. "Relics of Previous Buddhas: The Case of the Stūpa of Kāśyapa at Toyikā." Presented at the 12th Conference of the International Association of Buddhist Studies in Lausanne, Switzerland.

______ . 2004. *Relics of the Buddha*. Princeton and Oxford: Princeton University Press.

Suttanipāta.

Edition. See Andersen and Smith 1965.

Translation. See K. R. Norman 1984.

Sumaṅgalavilāsinī.

Edition. See Rhys Davids, Carpenter, and Stede 1886–1932.

Sykes, Marjorie, trans. 1950. *Rabindranath Tagore: Three Plays—Muktadhara, Natir Puja, Chandalika*. Bombay, New York: Oxford University Press.

Takahata, Kanga, ed. 1954. *Ratnamālāvadāna*. Oriental Library Series D, vol. 3. Tokyo: Toyo Bunko.

Tatelman, Joel. 2000. *The Glorious Deeds of Pūrṇa: A Translation and Study of the Pūrṇāvadāna*. Critical Studies in Buddhism, no. 9. Richmond: Curzon Press.

______, ed. and trans. 2005. *The Heavenly Exploits: Buddhist Biographies from the Divyāvadāna, vol. 1.* New York: New York University Press and JJC Foundation.

Thomas, E. J. 1933. "Avadāna and Apadāna." *Indian Historical Quarterly* 9: 32–36.

______. 1950. *The Quest of Enlightenment: A Selection of Buddhist Scriptures Translated from the Sanskrit.* London: John Murray.

Tierney, John. 1991. "In a Pizza War, It's 3 Rays Against the Rest." *New York Times*, 25 March 1991.

Thurman, Robert, trans. 1983 (1976). *The Holy Teaching of Vimalakīrti: A Mahāyāna Scripture.* University Park and London: The Pennsylvania State University Press.

Todorov, Tzvetan. 1990. *Genres in Discourse.* Catherine Porter, trans. Cambridge: Cambridge University Press.

Trenckner, Vilhelm, ed. 1880. *The Milindapañho: Being Dialogues between King Milinda and the Buddhist Sage Nāgasena.* London: Williams and Norgate.

______, et al. 1924–. *A Critical Pali Dictionary.* Copenhagen, Commissioner: Munksgaard.

Trenckner, Vilhelm, and Robert Chalmers, eds. 1888–89. *The Majjhima Nikāya.* London: Pali Text Society.

Tucci, G. 1971. "Note et Appunti sul *Divyāvadāna.*" *Opera Minora: Parte 1.* Rome: Dott. Giovanni Bardi, pp. 27–48. Reprinted from *Atti del Reale Instituto di Science, Letterera et Arti*, 1921–22, vol. 81 (part 2), pp. 499ff.

Udāna.
Edition. See Steinthal 1885.
Translation. See Masefield 1994.

Udāna-aṭṭhakathā [= *Paramatthadīpanī*, vol. 1].
Edition. See Woodward 1977.
Translation. See Masefield 1994a.

Upasak, C. S. 1975. *Dictionary of Early Buddhist Monastic Terms.* Varanasi: Bharati Prakashan.

Upreti, Kalpana. 1995. *India as Reflected in the Divyāvadāna.* Delhi: Munshiram Manoharlal Publishers Pvt. Ltd.

Vaidya, P. L., ed. 1958. *Avadānaśataka.* Buddhist Sanskrit Text, no. 19. Darbhanga: The Mithila Institute of Post-Graduate Studies and Research in Sanskrit Learning.

______, ed. 1959a. *Divyāvadāna*. Buddhist Sanskrit Text, no. 20. Darbhanga: The Mithila Institute of Post-Graduate Studies and Research in Sanskrit Learning.

______, ed. 1959b. *Avadānakalpalatā*. Buddhist Sanskrit Text, nos. 22–23. Darbhanga: The Mithila Institute of Post-Graduate Studies and Research in Sanskrit Learning.

Vasant, Suresh. 1991. "Dipaṅkara Buddha at Ajanta." In Gouriswar Bhattacharya, ed. *Akṣayanīvī: Essays Presented to Dr. Debala Mitra in Admiration of Her Scholarly Contributions*, pp. 171–76. Bibliotheca Indo-Buddhica, no. 88. Delhi, India: Sri Satguru Publications.

Vasubandhu. See *Abhidharmakośa*.

Vinayapiṭaka.
Edition. See Oldenberg 1879–83.
Translation. See Rhys Davids and Oldenberg 1987.
Translation. See Horner 1938–66.

Vira, Raghu, and Lokesh Chandra. 1995. *Gilgit Buddhist Manuscripts*. Revised and enlarged compact facsmile edition. Biblica Indo-Buddhica Series, nos. 150–52. Delhi: Sri Satguru Publications.

Visuddhimagga of Buddhaghosa.
Edition. See Warren 1950.
Translation. See Ñāṇamoli 1979.

Vogel, Claus, and Klaus Wille. 1984. "Some Hitherto Unidentified Fragments of the Pravrajyāvastu Portion of the Vinayavastu Manuscript Found Near Gilgit." *Nachrichten der Akademie der Wissenschaften Göttingen, Philologisch-Historische Klasse*, pp. 299–337. Göttingen: Vandenhoeck und Ruprecht.

Vogel, J. P. 1910. *Archaeological Museum at Mathura*. Allahabad: F. Luker.

______. 1926. *Indian Serpent-Lore*. London.

Vorobyova-Desyatovskaya, M. 2000. "A Sanskrit Manuscript on Birch-Bark from Bairam-Ali: II. Avadānas and Jātakas." *Manuscripta Orientalia* 6 (3): 23–32.

Waldschmidt, Ernst, ed. and trans. 1951. *Das Mahāparinirvāṇasūtra*. Abhandlungen der Deutschen Akademie der Wissenschaften zu Berlin. 3 volumes. Berlin: Akademie Verlag.

Walleser, M. and H. Kopp, eds. 1924–57. *Manorathapūraṇī*. 5 volumes. London: Pali Text Society.

Walshe, Maurice, trans. 1987. *Thus Have I Heard: The Long Discourses of the Buddha (Digha-nikāya).* London: Wisdom Publications.

Ware, James R. 1928. "Studies in the Divyāvadāna: I. *Sūkarikāvadāna.*" *Journal of the American Oriental Society* 48: 159–65.

Warren, Henry Clarke, ed. 1950. *Visuddhimagga.* Revised by D. Kosambi. Cambridge: Harvard University Press.

Warren, Henry Clarke. 1984. *Buddhism in Translations.* New York: Atheneum.

Weeraratne, W. G. 1966. "Avadāna." In G. P. Malalasekera, ed. *Encyclopedia of Buddhism,* vol. 2, pp. 395–98. Colombo: Government of Ceylon.

Welbon, Guy Richard. 1968. *The Buddhist Nirvana and Its Western Interpreters.* Chicago: University of Chicago Press.

Wille, Klaus. 2000. "Fragments of the Aśoka Legend." In Jens Braarvig, Jens-Uwe Hartmann, Kazunobu Matsuda, and Lore Sander, eds. *Buddhist Manuscripts in the Schøyen Collection, vol. 1,* pp. 219–32. Oslo: Hermes Publishers.

Wilson, Liz. 1996. *Charming Cadavers: Horrific Figurations of the Feminine in Indian Buddhist Hagiographic Literature.* Chicago: University of Chicago Press.

Winder, Marianne. 1987. "Vaiḍūrya." In G. Jan Meulenbeld and Dominik Wujastyk, eds. *Studies on Indian Medical History,* pp. 91–101. Groningen: Egbert Forsten.

Windisch, E. 1895. *Mara und Buddha.* Leipzig: S. Hirzel.

Winternitz, Moriz. 1993. *History of Indian Literature, vol. 2, part 1.* Translated and revised by Bhaskara Jha. India: Bharatiya Vidya Prakasha. Original German edition published in Leipzig, 1913.

Woodward, F. L., ed. 1977. *Paramatthadīpanī.* 5 volumes. London: Pali Text Society.

Woodward, F. L., and E. M. Hare, trans. 1932–36. *The Book of Gradual Sayings (Aṅguttara-nikāya).* 5 volumes. London: Pali Text Society.

Wujastyk, Dominik. 2004. "Apples or Plums? Jambudvīpa: The Continent of the Jamun Tree." In Charles Burnett, Jan P. Hogendijk, Kim Plofker, and Michio Yano, eds. *Ketuprakāśa: Studies in the History of the Exact Sciences in Honour of David Pingree,* pp. 287–301. Leiden: Brill Publications.

Index

About the Translator

ANDY ROTMAN is an associate professor in the Religion Department at Smith College in Northampton, Massachusetts, where he has taught since 2000. He received his Ph.D. in South Asian languages and civilizations from the University of Chicago in 2003 and his B.A. in religion from Columbia University in 1988. His research concerns the ways in which narratives and images in South Asia function as a part of social history and material culture. He is also the author of *Thus Have I Seen: Visualizing Faith in Early Indian Buddhism* (Oxford University Press, 2008), which considers the construction of faith as a visual practice in Indian Buddhist literature.

About Wisdom Publications

WISDOM PUBLICATIONS, a nonprofit publisher, is dedicated to making available books about Buddhism for the benefit of all. We publish works by ancient and modern masters across Buddhist traditions, translations of important texts, and original scholarship. We also offer books that explore East-West themes, which continue to emerge as traditional Buddhism encounters modern culture in all its complexity. Our titles are published with an appreciation of Buddhism as a living philosophy, and with a commitment to preserve and transmit important works from Buddhism's many traditions.

You can contact us, request a catalog, or browse our books online at our website. You can also write to us at the address below.

Wisdom Publications
199 Elm Street
Somerville, Massachusetts 02144 USA
Telephone: (617) 776-7416
Fax: (617) 776-7841
Email: info@wisdompubs.org
www.wisdompubs.org

Supporting the *Classics of Indian Buddhism* Series

The volumes in the *Classics of Indian Buddhism* series adhere to the highest standards of accuracy and readability, making them works that will stand the test of time both as scholarship and as literature. The care and attention necessary to bring such works to press demand a level of investment beyond the normal costs associated with publishing. If you would like to partner with Wisdom to help make the series a success, either by supporting the meticulous work of translators and editors or by sponsoring the publication costs of a forthcoming volume, please send us an email at cib@wisdompubs.org or write to us at the address above. We appreciate your support.

Wisdom is a nonprofit, charitable 501(c)(3) organization affiliated with the Foundation for the Preservation of the Mahayana Tradition (FPMT).